Lady Blomfield

Lady Blomfield

Her Life and Times

by

Robert Weinberg

George Ronald
Oxford

George Ronald, *Publisher*
Oxford
www.grbooks.com

*A catalogue record for this book is available
from the British Library*

ISBN 978–0–85398–550–1

Cover design: Steiner Graphics

CONTENTS

ILLUSTRATIONS

'At home' for the New Constitutional Society for Women's Suffrage, circa 1913

Newspaper cutting regarding Mary Blomfield's plea to the King and Queen for the suffragettes

Wellesley Tudor Pole

Eglantyne Jebb on a boat, possibly on Lake Geneva

The investiture of 'Abdu'l-Bahá, Haifa, 27 April 1920

Shoghi Effendi during his stay in England

Between pages 242 and 243

Lady Blomfield and women of 'Abdu'l-Bahá's household in Haifa, shortly after Lady Blomfield's arrival in the Holy Land with Shoghi Effendi following the Master's passing

Lady Blomfield with members of 'Abdu'l-Bahá's household in Haifa, following the Master's passing

Lady Blomfield and Bahíyyih <u>Kh</u>ánum, the Greatest Holy Leaf, in Haifa after Lady Blomfield's arrival in the Holy Land with Shoghi Effendi following the Master's passing

Lady Blomfield in the garden of the original Western Pilgrim House at 4 Haparsim Street, Haifa, in 1922

Bahá'ís from around the world called by Shoghi Effendi to Haifa to consult about the future of the Bahá'í Cause

Lady Blomfield at the citadel in 'Akká, 1922

Lady Blomfield, with 'Abdu'l-Bahá's daughter Rúḥá <u>Kh</u>ánum

A group of Bahá'ís in London, April 1923

Between pages 306 and 307

London Bahá'í Community, 1931

Conference on 'Some Living Religions within the Empire', 22 September – 3 October 1924, held at the Imperial Institute, South Kensington, London

Lady Blomfield with Masíḥ Ágáh, Jamshid Munajjim and Abbas Dehkan in the Western Pilgrim House, Haifa, 1930

Lady Blomfield on the balcony of the Western Pilgrim House at 4 Haparsim Street, Haifa

Lady Blomfield and friends, late 1930s

Lady Blomfield with George Townshend and members of his family, 1935

Lady Blomfield and friends at Sowberry Court

The new headstone at the grave of Lady Blomfield, Hampstead Municipal Cemetery, London

For Beverley, Aidan and Noah,
shining stars all,
whose friendship I treasure beyond words

ACKNOWLEDGEMENTS

As in all projects of this scale and duration, there are many to be thanked: first and foremost, the Universal House of Justice for sharing Lady Blomfield's correspondence with both 'Abdu'l-Bahá and Shoghi Effendi, approving the use of provisional translations of 'Abdu'l-Bahá's letters, and granting permission to publish numerous priceless photographs; the National Spiritual Assembly of the Bahá'ís of the United Kingdom for access to its archives and for its efforts to refurbish Lady Blomfield's grave, ably executed by Michele Wilburn, the late David Lewis and Ron Batchelor; the U.S. National Bahá'í Archives, Wilmette, for useful documents; Nell Golden and the literary executors of the estate of Amatu'l-Bahá Rúḥíyyíh Khánum for providing letters between Lady Blomfield and May Maxwell; the descendants of Bishop Charles James Blomfield for their kindness and interest – the late Brigadier Denis Blomfield-Smith and his wife Moyra, David Blomfield, as well as Alex, Hugo, Paul, Robin, Barbara, and Elizabeth Blomfield; Lil Abdo, for sharing her doctoral thesis on early British Bahá'í history; Janet Sono for important archival documents relating to the Blomfield family which she collected while preparing her play, *Lady Blomfield – An Experiment in Bilingual Theatre*; Jean-Paul Vader for material related to Lady Blomfield's sojourns in Switzerland; Amy Sahba for her assistance in researching the local history of Kensington; staff at the British Library Newspaper Collection; Anne P. Moloney of the Tipperary Heritage Unit and Mary Darmody of the Tipperary Joint County Library; Jonathan Makepiece and the staff at the Royal Institute of British Architects in London for access to its biographical files on Sir Arthur Blomfield; Peter Grimwood, Local Studies Assistant to the Head of Libraries and Arts for the Royal Borough of Kensington and Chelsea; Dr Richard Palmer of Lambeth Palace Library; Douglas Sulley, Archives Assistant for the Royal Archives; Maureen Webb of the Church Commission; and Anne Rodda, for her genealogical detective work on Lady Blomfield's sister Cecilia Gilmore and her daughter Ruth. I am grateful to Fleur Missaghian for her assistance in typing up pages of handwritten documents and to Neda Juzgado Sokout for speedily transferring into electronic format all the material contained in the Appendixes.

For his singular contribution to this project, my enduring thanks must go to the late David Hofman. His distinctive voice, hearty laughter and theatrical facial expressions lingered in my mind as I incorporated his recollections in these pages and my heart overflowed again with admiration for his inestimable services to the Cause of Bahá'u'lláh, with affection for his spirit and enthusiasm, and with gratitude for the encouragement he gave me to write this book. I am only sorry that I did not complete it soon enough for him to see it published by the company he founded, George Ronald. The contribution he made to this book has reinforced my conviction that the memories kept by those senior citizens amongst us must be drawn out of them and recorded, before it is too late to do so.

For the 15 years of this book's gestation, the names of the scores of others friends who have encouraged and inspired me, shared in the excitement of discoveries and reminded me of its importance are too numerous to mention. Of them all, I am most grateful to May Hofman, Erica Leith and Wendi Momen of George Ronald, who prompted me into renewed action on many occasions. To them, and to all who urged me to complete this endeavour, especially my parents, I express my heartfelt gratitude.

PREFACE

When Sara Louisa, Lady Blomfield passed away on 31 December 1939 at the age of 80, the nascent worldwide Baháʼí community lost not only a dedicated believer but one of its most socially distinguished adherents. Posterity remembers her primarily as the gracious and generous hostess to ʻAbduʼl-Bahá on His historic visits to London and as a chronicler of Baháʼí history in her book *The Chosen Highway*. Yet beyond this, she was a tireless advocate of the Baháʼí Faith's spiritual and social teachings within the circles she frequented; a defender of her persecuted co-religionists in Iran; a champion of the rights of women, children, prisoners and animals; and an ardent promoter of peace and interreligious understanding. In more contemporary Baháʼí terminology, it might be said that her speciality was 'external affairs' work. In this, she was – without equal – a pioneer.

In the seminal document *Century of Light* published in 2001 by the Universal House of Justice to mark the turn of the millennium, Lady Blomfield is numbered among the 'galaxy of unforgettable women' who 'became the principal exponents of the Baháʼí message on both sides of the Atlantic'.[1] Her acceptance of the Baháʼí teachings in 1907 was an outstanding milestone in her lifelong search for spiritual truth, a process set in motion by her childhood experiences of religious conflict in Ireland. Her quest took her, as it did so many of her contemporaries, through a study of Theosophy, eastern spiritual traditions and some of the more radical interpretations of Christianity that emerged during the closing years of the 19th century. Yet her acceptance of Baháʼuʼlláh as the Manifestation of God to the age of human maturity was by no means the completion of the journey. Her recognition of the pertinence of His teachings to the needs of the age in which she lived reinforced in her the desire to see justice and equality established in the world, a concern expressed in her selfless involvement in all manner of philanthropic causes as well as in direct service to those in need. The Bahá'í teachings offered spirit and form to her hopes and convictions. *Century of Light* hails Lady Blomfield as one whose social position 'lent added force to the ardour with which she championed the teachings'.[2]

Shortly after the death of Lady Blomfield, her devoted daughter Mary, who had been commissioned to write an obituary article for *The Bahá'í World*, volume 3, 1938–1940, wrote that it seemed 'trivial to record worldly episodes and circumstances', for her mother 'lived greatly in spiritual spheres above ordinary existence. And yet she was so near the heart of Humanity, that she felt keenly the world's suffering, and never relaxed in her efforts for its alleviation.'[3]

Such an outstanding figure in the early history of the Bahá'í Faith in the West has long deserved a biography chronicling her life and times. This offering is a first attempt to convey to Lady Blomfield's spiritual descendants, those who follow in her footsteps as ambassadors for the Cause of Bahá'u'lláh, something of the character and activities of a devoted, conscientious soul whose life spanned the first, dawning moments of a new era in the world's religious experience.

INTRODUCTION

Bright star, would I were steadfast as thou art . . .[4]
John Keats

Throughout the ages, stars have served as guiding lights to travellers who have lost their way in the darkness of the night. With the assistance of stars, seafarers and explorers have charted their position and set their course. While remaining far out of reach, the light of a star can be observed by all who choose to cast their eyes heavenward, towards that irresistible point of attraction in the darkness.

In the metaphorical language of religion, night can represent more than just physical darkness. It can symbolize a period of spiritual slumber on the part of humanity, when vision is diminished and shadows prevail, when man finds himself lost and alone, unable to plot his course. In such moments of hopelessness, certain individuals can emerge as stars, as illuminated beacons, sources of direction for the lost and the desperate. Sara Louisa, Lady Blomfield was just such a light. Perhaps for this reason 'Abdu'l-Bahá, the son of Bahá'u'lláh, the Manifestation of God for this day, gave to Lady Blomfield the Persian name Sitárih, meaning 'star'.

But the life of a star begins shrouded in obscurity, its particles of gas and dust pulled together by gravitational attraction. The impact generates enormous thermal energy and the star begins to shine. Sara Louisa Ryan's life likewise began in obscurity, unknown to the world outside a small, rural village in Ireland. It would be several decades before this luminous star came to be noticed. And it would take an attraction to a phenomenal source of power for it to shine so brightly.

CHAPTER ONE

BECOMING LADY BLOMFIELD

*If poverty overtake thee, be not sad; for in time the Lord of wealth shall
visit thee. Fear not abasement, for glory shall one day rest on thee.*[1]
Bahá'u'lláh

Thursday 21 April 1887. The citizens of London awoke to a bright, clement
day. Readers of the morning's edition of *The Times* learned that Her Majesty
Queen Victoria, holidaying in Aix-les-Bains, had been walking in the
gardens of the Villa Mottet. In Cairo, the death of Sherif Pasha had caused
'the liveliest regret among all classes' since he was 'genial, warm-hearted
and above all, an honourable gentleman, who secured firm friends, fascinated acquaintances, and made no enemy'.[2] The two finest British actors
of the age – Mr Henry Irving and Miss Ellen Terry – were treading the
boards at Irving's own Lyceum Theatre in Goethe's *Faust* while Wilkie Collins's drama in four acts, *Man and Wife*, was packing out the Haymarket.
The Duke of Teck, President of the Royal Botanic Society, accompanied
by his wife and daughters, had been visiting the brilliant flower show at
Regent's Park. 'The exhibition was worthy of the fine weather,'[3] enthused
The Times reporter.

Across the rooftops of Kensington the distinctive peal of the ten bells of
St Mary Abbots rang out, tolling a joyful occasion. The renowned architect
Arthur William Blomfield – a son of the late Bishop of London and five
years a widower – was marrying for the second time. The imposing church
in which he awaited the arrival of his bride had only been completed some
eight years before. Bishop Blomfield had once described the previous
building on the same site as the ugliest in his diocese. In 1866 it had been
demolished, its fate sealed by bulging walls and dry rot. The new edifice
raised in its place was 'on a scale', according to its then vicar, Archdeacon
Sinclair, 'proportionate to the opulence and importance of a great Metropolitan parish'.[4] The final stone in its spire, said to be the highest in the

capital, had been put in place with a silver trowel by the Reverend Edward Carr Glyn, who precariously conducted a dedication service from the scaffolding, swaying in blustery winds, some 250 feet above an enthralled and somewhat nervous congregation.

On this day in 1887, however, Reverend Carr Glyn – back on *terra firma* and glowing from the recent Easter services for which the ladies of the parish had transformed the interior of the church into an ocean of seasonal blooms – had stepped aside for the Bishop of Colchester, the groom's brother, who had been invited to preside over the wedding ceremony. Arthur Blomfield was marrying Miss Sara Louisa Ryan, a young Irish-born woman, 30 years his junior. Joining in the festivities were her mother Emily and younger sister Cecilia, as well as Blomfield's three children from his first marriage – Charles, who was but three years younger than his father's new bride, Arthur and Adele, who had been just nine years old when her mother died.

As she stepped forward beneath the soaring gothic arches towards the altar and marriage into one of England's most celebrated clerical families, what emotions might have been surging in the heart of Sara Louisa Ryan? It was all a far cry from rural Ireland where her life had begun 28 years earlier in an atmosphere of sectarian conflict.

Ryan is one of the most common surnames in Ireland. With its family crest showing the heads of three griffins facing proudly to the left, its origins lie with the family of Ó Maoilriagháin, meaning a descendant of a devotee of St Riaghan. The surname is first found during the 14th century in the barony of Owney on the borders of counties Limerick and Tipperary, where the Ó Maoilriagháin clan displaced the Ó Heffernans. By 1890 Ryan was the seventh most common surname in Ireland. To this day there is a high concentration of Ryans living in the area and more than 28,000 in the whole country.

Until the end of the 19th century civil parishes – originally initiated by Ireland's medieval church – were the main units of administration for local and central government. Knockanevin in county Tipperary where Sara Louisa Ryan was born in 1859 came under the civil parish of Glenkeen. The nearest large town to Knockanevin is Borrisoleigh, which derives its name from the ancient territory Ui Luighdheach in which it was situated. Best known as the home of Tipperary Natural Mineral Water, today it is a bustling market town with a few attractive traditional shop fronts and a 15th century tower house.

It was in Borrisoleigh on 17 November 1816 that the baptism was recorded of Sara Louisa's father, Mathias. Mathias was the second of ten children born to Michael 'Mick' Ryan and his wife, Ellen, née Crowe, known as 'Nelly'. Their first child, Bridget, had been born one year earlier in 1815, their third – two years after Mathias – was another boy, Denis. Seven siblings followed: Michael, Patrick, Catherine, Honora, William, John and another William, so named as the first William died young – that is, one child roughly every two years or so up until Mathias, by that time known as Matthew, was 20 years old.

Existence was far from easy for the Ryans and their neighbours. Sporadic violent confrontation was a characteristic of rural life in Ireland in the first half of the 19th century. Smouldering age-old tensions with Britain were fanned by news of the French Revolution, inspiring the uprising of the United Irishmen in 1798, which was duly crushed. In 1800 the Dublin parliament was abolished. Anti-English feeling was rife but only a small minority dared take action. The limited Irish administration was powerless in the face of the presence of British troops who were firmly established in imposing barracks in most towns. A more professional police force was emerging and Anglo-Protestants monopolized jobs in the legal profession, the civil service and local government. Resentment among the Irish sporadically flared up into violent resistance to the collection of church tithes. Most significantly, there was an evident – though often denied – political dimension to Roman Catholicism in Ireland, born of the church's influence on the masses, the strength of its links with Rome and the power of the clergy. A popular mass movement orchestrated by the Catholic Association arose to challenge the lack of civil rights for Catholics. The movement was not without success, resulting in Catholics being allowed to sit in the Westminster parliament and hold most high offices in 1829.

Despite some promising developments, however, the problems spawned from rural poverty remained. The 'Great Hunger', caused by a fungus which totally ravaged the potato crop in the late 1840s and exacerbated by the indifference of the British government, reduced the Irish population by two million over four years. Around half of these died of starvation and associated diseases such as cholera and typhus. The other half emigrated. A total of two million Irish left for North America between 1847 and 1861. The limited nature of land reform measures further stimulated Irish nationalism, led by the Young Ireland movement until its suppression in 1848.

It is small wonder, then, that an atmosphere of religious and nationalistic tension prevailed throughout Mathias Ryan's marriage to his Anglo-Protestant wife, Emily. Ryan – a staunch Roman Catholic – held the strong conviction that his eldest daughter, Sara, born in 1859, would one day join a convent. The possibility of losing her in such a manner was intolerable to Emily. The Ryans' marriage over, the young Sara was taken from her homeland by her mother, who at this point may have been pregnant with her second daughter, Cecilia, to live in England. It was in this initial experience of the clash of loyalties during her most formative years that a seed was planted in Sara Louisa to search constantly for religious truth. She spoke little of this childhood pain to her own children but it evidently left lasting scars. 'The tragedy of religious intolerance', her own daughter Mary wrote many years later, 'had burnt deeply into her soul, and had inspired her quest for the path of truth, which she found at last when she came into touch with the Bahá'í Revelation . . . The misery of that childhood can easily be imagined.'[5]

For Sara's future husband, Arthur William Blomfield, childhood and family life could not have been more of a contrast. He was born on 6 March 1829 in Fulham Palace, London – the official residence of the Bishop of London – shortly after his father, Charles James Blomfield, had been ordained in the position.

The Blomfield family had a long and chequered history, tracing their roots as far back as the 17th century to a Suffolk family predominately composed of non-conformist Puritans. One exception was William Blomfield of Wattisham, who was nominated for the order of the Royal Oak after the Restoration. In 1794 a town in New Jersey was named Blomfield after one General Joseph Blomfield in recognition of his services in the War of Independence. In 1803 he enjoyed the position of governor of the state of New Jersey and an Elizabeth Blomfield, in a letter to her poet brother Robert, described her meeting with the old man at Philadelphia, during which he told her that his great-grandfather had fled from England at the time of Oliver Cromwell. By the 19th century, however, the Blomfield family back home could not have been more 'establishment'.

Arthur Blomfield was the fourth son of the Bishop and his second wife, Dorothy. Born in 1786, Charles Blomfield was a brilliant man. He had gained a Bachelors degree at Trinity College, Cambridge where he was made a Fellow, and after being presented to St Botolph's, Bishopsgate, was ordained Bishop of Chester in 1824, transferring to the See of London four years later. From his earliest years he achieved renown as a classical scholar, editing five plays of Aeschylus with notes and glossaries, as well as three Greek lyric poets for Gaisford's *Poetae Minores Graeci* in 1823. He was a regular contributor on classical subjects to journals. Family legends told of Charles spending between 16 and 18 hours a day over his books, a worker of 'stupendous energy and great ability'.[6] *The Gentleman's Magazine* in 1816 confirmed that 'Mr Blomfield's academical career was distinguished by every honour that could adorn the brow of youth and give an earnest of future excellence'.[7]

Charles's brother Edward Valentine Blomfield, born in 1788, was also an outstanding scholar, lecturing from a young age in classics at Emmanuel College. Edward won five gold medals for Greek and Latin verse between 1808 and 1811. His *magnum opus*, a translation of Matthiae's *Greek Grammar*, appeared posthumously, edited by his brother. A glimpse of the kind of life the Blomfields were accustomed to can be found in the memoirs of the acclaimed architect Sir Reginald Blomfield, one of Charles's grandsons. Just three years before his death Edward travelled to Stockholm with two of his Cambridge associates. 'He was profoundly impressed by the beauties of the place,' wrote Sir Reginald, 'but formed a low opinion of its people . . . Although they began their dinners with brandy and drank wines of sorts at dinner, they left the table as soon as it was over, and Edward Valentine deplored the absence of the after-dinner port to which he had been used in the combination rooms of Cambridge.'[8] Edward's untimely death at the age of 28 was said by Charles, at the end of his own life, to be the 'greatest grief he had ever known'.[9]

The union of Charles Blomfield and his first wife, Anna Heath, who had come from Norfolk to marry him in 1810, brought six children into the world. Only one daughter survived. Anna died after giving birth in 1818 and one year later Charles married the widowed Dorothy Kent, née Cox. She had no doubt once been an attractive girl, depicted in George Henry Harlow's popular painting *The Proposal*. But Sir Reginald remembered her as 'a shrewd and rather hard old lady'.[10] Together Charles and Dorothy had eleven children, ten of whom survived. The oldest was Frederick, who became the Rector of St Andrew Undershaft in Aldgate, London. Mary, next in line, married Charles Dalton, Rector of Highgate. Then came Charles who emigrated to Canada; Henry who commanded a ship in the Mediterranean and became a full admiral; Isabella, Lucy, then

Arthur; Frank – who drowned at sea whilst saving a life; Dora, wife of Canon Routledge of Canterbury; and the youngest, Alfred, who became Bishop of Colchester.

Bishop Blomfield's arduous clerical duties extended to his being a tutor to the royal family. In March 1830 the then Duchess of Kent, mother of the future Queen Victoria, called upon Blomfield and his colleague, the Bishop of Lincoln, to examine her daughter to see if her education was proceeding successfully. Both clergymen were 'completely satisfied'[11] with the princess's answers to their examination. Thus began Blomfield's role in the education of the future Queen, and later the Queen's children.

Despite his onerous professional life, the Bishop gave great importance to devoting time to his numerous children. 'Their education was watched by him with an unfailing interest,' recalled his son Alfred. 'As was natural, his own tastes gave a colouring to his children's studies; next to scripture and theology, music and the classical languages taking the most prominent place, the elements of the last entering even into the course of education prescribed by him for his daughters.'[12] According to one of the girls, the half to one hour before breakfast each day was the happiest time, when Charles would patiently teach his children 'without any angry words'.[13] The Bishop had a natural fondness for the young. 'During his holidays, or when he had more leisure than usual,' wrote Alfred, 'he would take part in his children's recreations, and sometimes entertain them by composing amusing or descriptive verses, either about the incidents of a tour, or any circumstance of the hour.'[14] Blomfield was a firm believer in gathering the family together for prayers and, in an expressed spirit of equality and fellowship, insisted that their servants were also present. The evenings were spent in making music and cheerful conversation.

However, as in most large families, at times there were disagreements and, later, an inevitable parting of the ways. Sir Reginald, who was a Blomfield through both his mother and father, wrote that it 'has also been an unfortunate tradition of our family for each branch of it to go off on its own at the earliest opportunity. It was said of us in the old days at Fulham, that if as a family we could have stuck together, we might have gone far, but like the bundle of sticks in Aesop's fable, we preferred to remain disunited. It is the defect of a fine quality of independence derived from Puritan ancestors, and as a family we have paid for it in the past.'[15]

Most of the time, however, growing up at Fulham Palace seems to have been quite idyllic for Arthur Blomfield and his brothers and sisters:

'The house, so spacious, yet so thoroughly comfortable and domestic, the garden half hidden on the margin of the Thames, with its spreading lawn of soft and level turf shadowed with choice shrubs and goodly trees, the avenue of ancient elms, the circling moat, guarding the whole from intrusion – all these, within a few miles of the metropolis, give to the Palace at Fulham a charm peculiarly its own; so close upon the restless world, yet itself "a haunt of ancient peace".'[16]

With his reputation as a scholar and wit surviving into the early years of the 20th century, Bishop Blomfield was a man with a strong sense of mission, tirelessly running the London diocese for nearly three decades. Diagnosing the city as being in a state of spiritual impoverishment, he endeavoured to improve it by prescribing a hugely ambitious programme of church construction. In 1836, when Arthur Blomfield was eight years old, his father instituted a fund for building and endowing churches, which eventually, 18 years later, was merged into the London Diocesan Church Building Society. Consequently, as a practising architect, Arthur found himself with many church building projects on his drawing board. In total, some 200 churches were consecrated in London during Bishop Blomfield's episcopate.

Arthur Blomfield was educated at Rugby during the headship of Dr Archibald Campbell Tait, a vigorous evangelizer with broad-minded views, who later became Archbishop of Canterbury – 'No archbishop probably since the reformation had so much weight in parliament or in the country generally.'[17] Coming from a family that valued classical training so highly, Arthur Blomfield found Cambridge the natural place to carry on his studies. His years at Trinity College saw him achieving a Bachelor's degree in 1851 and a Master's in 1854, an education to which he 'owed . . . much of that equipment of the true English gentleman which was characteristic of him'.[18] Arthur and his brother Frank were known as 'Thunder and Lightning' at Cambridge, on account of the 'pace they went, as I never heard of either of them having done any reading at all',[19] wrote Sir Reginald Blomfield.

Being so entrenched in Christian life, it might have seemed an obvious path for Arthur to follow his father and several of his brothers into the church. His choice to become an architect, however, was an equally respectable one. The great era of church-building was underway and his father's passion for raising up places of worship throughout the capital was a sure guarantee of a good livelihood for an architect. More than this, though, Arthur was a dedicated and discriminating lover of architecture. He became articled – for the usual term of three years – to the office of Philip Charles Hardwick, architect to the Bank of England, a post that later Arthur also took on.

Overseas excursions were a common activity for young architects of the time and in 1855 Arthur travelled to Rome, Florence and other European cities with a colleague, Frederick Pepys Cockerell, son of Charles Cockerell, professor of architecture at the Royal Academy. Frederick was a charming character and the two men relished their adventures abroad. Blomfield was captivated by the then fashionable Gothic style with its elements of medieval design and made it his own right up until his death, despite the changing tastes around him. He quickly established his own offices and moved to new premises in Adelphi Terrace in 1856. The practice would continue until the 1930s under the direction of his two eldest sons, Charles James Blomfield (1862–1932) and Arthur Conran Blomfield (1863–1935).

In 1857 Bishop Blomfield passed away at the age of 71. Thanks to his father's legacy and his connections with the clergy, a steady flow of commissions continued to come to Arthur Blomfield's office. He was in the unique position of being able to bring his intimate knowledge of Anglican liturgical requirements to his work but nevertheless brought some radical innovations to church architecture. He advocated the installation of galleries and the use of iron columns and screens to divide the aisles from the nave because he had noted that in aisled churches there was always a large proportion of the congregation cut off from the altar, the pulpit or the reading desk. At the time, one of the objections against the use of iron was that there was no mention of iron architecture in the Bible – an objection that was no less applicable to stained glass. It was the purpose rather than the appearance of a church that gained precedence in Blomfield's mind. He paid attention to lighting, heating and acoustics and, unusually, the actual comfort of the congregation. His concern for assisting the worshippers to have the most uplifting experience even extended to the design of St Saviour's Church for the Deaf and Dumb on London's Oxford Street in 1874 where his main intention was to provide as much light and visibility as possible.

Life in the Blomfield practice was relaxed and cheerful. There was no formal instruction and the amount of work was not overwhelming. In his *Memoirs of an Architect*, Sir Reginald Blomfield writes of his early experiences working for his uncle:

I entered his office full of enthusiasm, thinking that I should find myself in an atmosphere of high ideals, a modern version of the schools or studios of the Italian Renaissance. Instead of this I found myself in the company of a somewhat depressed managing clerk, two or three assistants and half a dozen cheerful young fellows who were serving their articles as pupils, and most of whom were much more interested in the latest news, sporting or otherwise, than in the latest experiment in Architecture. The usual remark of one of the pupils every morning was, 'Any spice in the papers?' One pupil, an old Etonian, took a genuine interest in his work; the principal interests of another, also an Etonian, a rowing man and a very good fellow, were shooting and drawing wild ducks, and looking after a lot of boys, the forerunners of the Boy Scouts . . . My uncle was very good to me, and so far as his time allowed took unusual trouble to instruct me . . .[20]

Whatever the passions or pastimes of his apprentices, Arthur Blomfield remained a man dedicated to nurturing the talents of others. In 1862 a promising young architect from Dorset joined the practice after six years of working in Dorchester. Blomfield had been looking for a specialist in ecclesiastical drawing and on 5 May took the apprentice on at a salary of £110 per annum. Despite winning two architectural prizes the following year, this young man increasingly devoted more time to his passion for writing. His name was Thomas Hardy and within ten years of joining the Blomfield office he was beginning to enjoy literary acclaim with his novel *Under the Greenwood Tree*.

Hardy described Arthur Blomfield as 'a lithe, brisk man'.[21] They shared a passion for music, with Blomfield himself in possession of a strong bass voice and encouraging his staff to sing part songs with him. Hardy reportedly enjoyed his role in the office choir. Arthur also took his young assistant out on site visits and a firm friendship was forged. Hardy even wrote a tribute to Arthur Blomfield in the poem, 'Heiress and Architect', dedicated 'For AWB':

She sought the Studios, beckoning to her side
An arch-designer, for she planned to build.
He was of wise contrivance, deeply skilled
In every intervolve of high and wide –
Well fit to be her guide.

'Whatever it be,'
Responded he,
With cold, clear voice, and cold, clear view,
'In true accord with prudent fashionings
For such vicissitudes as living brings,
And thwarting not the law of stable things,
That will I do.'

'Shape me,' she said, 'high walls with tracery
And open ogive-work, that scent and hue
Of buds, and travelling bees, may come in through,
The note of birds, and singings of the sea,
For these are much to me.'

'An idle whim!'
Broke forth from him
Whom nought could warm to gallantries:
'Cede all these buds and birds, the zephyr's call,
And scents, and hues, and things that falter all,
And choose as best the close and surly wall,
For winter's freeze.'

'Then frame,' she cried, 'wide fronts of crystal glass,
That I may show my laughter and my light –
Light like the sun's by day, the stars' by night –
Till rival heart-queens, envying, wail, "Alas,
Her glory!" as they pass.'

'O maid misled!'
He sternly said,
Whose facile foresight pierced her dire;
'Where shall abide the soul when, sick of glee,
It shrinks, and hides, and prays no eye may see?
Those house them best who house for secrecy,
For you will tire.'

'A little chamber, then, with swan and dove
Ranged thickly, and engrailed with rare device

Of reds and purples, for a Paradise
Wherein my Love may greet me, I my Love,
When he shall know thereof?'

'This, too, is ill,'
He answered still,
The man who swayed her like a shade.
'An hour will come when sight of such sweet nook
Would bring a bitterness too sharp to brook,
When brighter eyes have won away his look;
For you will fade.'

Then said she faintly: 'O, contrive some way –
Some narrow winding turret, quite mine own,
To reach a loft where I may grieve alone!
It is a slight thing; hence do not, I pray,
This last dear fancy slay!'

'Such winding ways
Fit not your days,'
Said he, the man of measuring eye;
'I must even fashion as my rule declares,
To wit: Give space (since life ends unawares)
To hale a coffined corpse adown the stairs;
For you will die.'[22]

One of Arthur Blomfield's most admired characteristics was his humility. In spite of his outstanding professional achievements, he remained modest and even retiring, with a dislike of publicity. His colleague Professor Cockerell once told him while they stood together at Ludgate Hill, looking at St Paul's Cathedral, that he felt the old architects were giants while modern architects were only pygmies. Blomfield often applied the words to himself. He said that few of his buildings were worth mentioning, although there remain many excellent churches that bear his name. One of his finest is the parish church at Privett in Hampshire, built as a memorial by a gin-maker from London, George Nicholson, whose son and three of his workers had died when overcome by gin fumes. Among the other buildings with which Blomfield felt least dissatisfied were a private chapel at Tyntesfield,

St Mary's church in Portsea, Queen's School and Lower Chapel at Eton, the Fleet Street Branch of the Bank of England – now a pub – and Sion College Library on the Thames Embankment. He worked on the erection of London's Law Courts in 1881, the scheme for Church House at Deans Yard Westminster and St Alban's Church – the English Church – in Copenhagen. He also carried out projects for the Prince of Wales – the future King Edward VII - at Sandringham and made important restorations to the cathedrals of Salisbury, Canterbury, Lincoln, Chichester and to the nave of St Saviour's in Southwark. Overseas commissions included St George's Cathedral in Georgetown and Christ Church Cathedral in Port Stanley. 'Perhaps,' wrote Reginald Blomfield, 'it was unfortunate that he was so much in demand by the clergy of the Church of England for churches, schools and 'restorations'. He did a great deal of work, in some cases for quite inadequate remuneration, for he was a most generous man, and the incessant repetition of the same sort of problem, and much too much of it, checked the development of the promise of his younger days.'[23]

Shortly after being made a fellow of the Royal Institute of British Architects, Blomfield designed and built a grand family home in Fife Road, Sheen. Blomfield had married Caroline Case Smith from Bury St Edmunds in Suffolk and they had two sons – Charles and Arthur – and a daughter, Adele. Life could not have been more satisfactory. Around this same time a young girl was being brought to England by her mother from Ireland to escape the tensions of religious intolerance at home. A quarter of a century later the paths of Sir Arthur Blomfield and Sara Louisa Ryan would cross and their lives become intimately linked.

Blomfield was immensely popular among his clients and his peers. He was, according to an article in *The Builder*, 'a most pleasant companion in social life; he had a cultivated taste for various forms of intellectual recreation; he was very fond of society and social meetings, and was particularly liked by young men for his genial and companionable manner to them. In fact he was himself, in spirit, a young man all his life; one who enjoyed life . . .'[24] 'He was the most delightful of men,' wrote Reginald Blomfield. '. . . witty, cheerful, a first-rate amateur actor and a skilful painter in water-colours.'[25] Arthur had inherited his father's wit and humour and, as one contemporary appreciation put it, 'nature had endowed him with qualities which under other circumstances would have made him a most successful comedian'.[26] Blomfield was a happy and prosperous man, knowing little of hardship.

Then, in 1882, at the age of 42, his wife Caroline died, leaving him with two adult sons and a nine year old daughter.

Five years followed where Arthur Blomfield's career continued apace. In 1883 he was appointed architect to the Bank of England. Three years later he became the vice president of the Royal Institute of British Architects. 'No man had a firmer hold on his clients,' wrote Arthur Edmund Street in the Institute's *Journal*, 'not only because his work consistently reached a certain level which the world had come to expect of him . . . but also because he made friends of them. No one who came into touch with Blomfield could be insensible to the winning kindliness and courtesy of his manner, or miss the truth that the manner was an exact index of the man.'[27]

Such benign humanity would not go unnoticed by a young woman who had been raised in an atmosphere of conflict. How the 28 year old Sara Louisa Ryan came to meet the distinguished architect is regrettably lost to history. If she did ever speak of it and the years between leaving Ireland as a girl and becoming Mrs Arthur Blomfield, then their daughter Mary chose not to record it for posterity in the only surviving written memoir about her mother.

All that it is now possible to do is to speculate about the meeting that resulted in Arthur Blomfield's second marriage. By this time Blomfield and his young daughter had moved into a tall, opulent Victorian terraced house at 28 Montagu Square, Marylebone. Sara's address on their marriage certificate, however, is given as 'Number 1 Campden Houses'.

Campden Houses, situated on Peel Street, Kensington, was a 'model dwelling', a tenement block built by the National Dwelling Society to provide cheap and sanitary accommodation for the poor, particularly labourers. What circumstances might have brought Sara to live in such a location? Among the occupations of Campden Houses' occupants, the 1881 census lists a housemaid, a garden boy, a navy pensioner, two scholars, an engine fitter, a plumber, an art student, an artist, a footman, a cook and a lady's maid. There is no mention of Sara Louisa Ryan at the address in that census. There was quite a large Irish community in West London at this time, particularly in Hammersmith and North Kensington where the laundry industry used Irish workers, and there were numerous Irish domestic servants in employment. Indeed in the 1881 census, there are several Sarah Ryans listed as servants in the Kensington area. Could Sara Louisa have been a maid in Sir Arthur's home? If so, she surely might have appeared on the census as living there, although she may have joined the household between census surveys. Might she have been working as a governess or tutor to his, by now, teenage daughter? She does not appear in records at Windsor Castle of those serving in the royal household. Might she have been in service to one of London's distinguished churchmen, or working as a clerk in Sir Arthur's offices? Or had she been a model for one of the many Royal Academicians in Arthur's circle? An elegant portrait of her as a young woman is held in the Bahá'í archives at 27 Rutland Gate in London to this day.

Sara's younger sister, Cecilia, had a career as a stage actress in London and in New York. The family loved the theatre and both Sara's daughters with Arthur became actresses. He was known to be keen on amateur dramatics and loved to sing and perform himself. Had he encountered or seen the young Sara playing in a theatre or music hall somewhere?

Recalling his meetings with Lady Blomfield six decades after her passing, a friend of hers, David Hofman, dismissed the possibility of her having a working class background. He mentioned her deep, affected voice, still tinged with an Irish accent, and said she gave the impression of being 'every inch nobility', born and bred. Admittedly he had known her some 50 years after her marriage to Arthur Blomfield, surely time enough to reinvent herself and live and speak in a manner to which she had become accustomed.

More than this, alas, it is difficult to discover and perhaps that is how Lady Blomfield wished it to be. What is known, however, is that on 21 April 1887 Arthur William Blomfield processed down the aisle for a second time – with Sara Louisa Ryan. The marriage was reported on the front page of *The Times* on Saturday 23 April:

> On the 21st inst., at St Mary Abbot's, Kensington, by the Bishop of Colchester, brother of the bridegroom, ARTHUR WILLIAM BLOMFIELD to SARA LOUISA, elder daughter of MATTHEW JOHN RYAN.[28]

Life for Sara was now far removed from the basic accommodation of Campden Houses and, indeed, the poverty afflicting thousands of Londoners just a few miles east of her marital home in Montagu Square. However much her personal circumstances had changed, a concern for justice and the rights of the underprivileged remained strong in her. During her early married life Sara took a close interest in politics. Arthur was described by his daughter Mary as a 'light-hearted Conservative' while Sara identified herself as a Liberal up until the time of the women's suffrage campaign, when she was so appalled by the government's treatment of the suffragettes that she left the party and never joined another. She came to deplore labels and, in her opinion, party politics were a dilatory expedient for holding up necessary reforms. While 1887 saw Queen Victoria celebrating her Golden Jubilee and a great groundswell of affection for the monarchy, the issue of Irish independence was never far from the public mind. It had been the greatest single source of violence and upheaval in English politics for the entire century and would continue to dominate discussions in the British parliament until the outbreak of the Great War. Sara Blomfield watched events unfold with evident distress but chose to speak little of it to her family.

Honours continued to be bestowed on Arthur Blomfield as he settled into married life again. He was elected an Honorary Member of the Royal Academy of Arts of Copenhagen, of which he was the architect, and was presented with the Order of the Dannebrog by the King of Denmark. In 1888 he was made an associate of the Royal Academy in Britain and on the 4 June 1889 he was knighted by Queen Victoria at Windsor Castle. Sara Louisa was now Lady Blomfield, at the very heart of the British establishment. She was also, more importantly for her, a devoted mother to three children of her own – Mary Esther, born in 1888; Frank, born the following year; and Rose Ellinor Cecilia, who arrived in 1890.

The 1891 census gives a glimpse of the kind of life that the Blomfields were leading. It is recorded that the household consisted of Sir Arthur, 62, and Sara, 32, and their children – Mary Esther aged 3, Frank aged 2 and Rose Ellinor Cecilia aged 9 months. In addition, there lived at their home Mary Lupton, a 26 year old nurse; Elizabeth Addle, 27, their cook; Hannah Wood, 34, parlour maid; Frances Dickinson, 26, housemaid; Emily Granger, 21, under-nurse; and Mary Sullivan, 20, under-housemaid. The Blomfields' close neighbours were military people, among them Captain Horace Barnet of the Royal Engineers and Captain Francis Baring of the 3rd batallion of the Hertfordshire Regiment.

The Blomfields enjoyed the conventional but glittering life of London society, with Sara, the devoted and dutiful wife, delighting in the wit and brilliance of eminent Victorians. Before the countless functions she attended, adorned in her finest jewellery, Sara climbed the stairs to the nursery to hear her children say their prayers and to wish them goodnight. The young Mary recalled that she thought that no queen could have looked more lovely. Such was the nature of Lady Blomfield's conscience, however, that the jewels would later be sold for the benefit of some philanthropic cause.

At this time Mary wrote that her father was 'ever youthful at heart, in spite of his grey curls, dignified appearance and monocle'.[29] Sir Arthur frequently took part in amateur theatricals at St George's Hall or in drawing room entertainments of his own composition at home. His acting, wrote one colleague, 'was something quite unlike that of the ordinary amateur, and the rounded completeness of his "Daddy Hardacre" [in John Palgrave Simpson's play] is an abiding memory with those who were privileged to see it'.[30] The Blomfields' love for the theatre was inherited by their daughters.

Acting, though, had to take second place to Sir Arthur's many professional and social commitments. On 2 March 1891, the Royal Institute of British Architects unanimously resolved that, subject to the Queen's approval, Sir Arthur should be the recipient of the Royal Gold Medal for the Promotion of Architecture. The award had been instituted in 1848 when its first recipient was Charles Cockerell, father of Frederick Cockerell with whom Sir Arthur had travelled through Europe as a young man. On the 22 June at 8 p.m. a ceremony was held at the Royal Institute presided over by its president, J. Macvicar Anderson. In his address Anderson highlighted the privileged position enjoyed by an architect:

> . . . for while following his bent and indulging his fancy, he can – and if his taste be rightly inspired he should – contribute to the comfort and happiness of society by the fitness and the elegance of his creations, and further, by integrity, independence, and honourable dealing in his practice, he can raise the tone of his profession, and establish it in the good opinion of men; for his is much more than an ordinary avocation or means of subsistence, it is the pursuit of the beautiful and the useful, and in proportion as he aspires to such attainments, so, and in the same proportion, will he be likely to reach celebrity and to leave his mark on his age . . .
>
> . . . Many centuries have passed since the wise man declared 'How much better is it to get wisdom than to get gold' and although the undoubted truth of this aphorism may at first sight appear to detract from the value of the Gold Medal which Sir Arthur Blomfield will tonight add to his other well-earned honours, it really enhances it, for this Medal is but the recognition of that wisdom which is the result of

years of study and labour, and is manifested in the numberless works which have so surely established his fame as an accomplished architect.[31]

Sir Arthur accepted the award with his typical modesty, saying,

> . . . however worthy the recipient of this honour may at any time be, and however conscious of his own merits, I think he would be a still more exceptional character if on an occasion of this kind, and before such an assembly as I see here tonight, he did not find those sentiments of pride and gratification mingled in a large degree with diffidence and embarrassment . . .
>
> . . . it now becomes at once my privilege and my pain to ask you to bear with me, and listen for a very short time while I say a few words about myself – and they shall be very few; I can at least promise you that my dose of egotism shall be homeopathic in quantity.[32]

Sir Arthur retold his favourite story about modern architects being 'pygmies' in relation to the giants of earlier centuries. 'Perhaps on an occasion of this sort, and with so indulgent an audience, I might be excused if I were to fall back upon the apologetic platitude of saying that, however little I have done, I have at least done my best.'[33]

As she raised her three children, Sara, Lady Blomfield was ever mindful of the conflicts that had tainted her own childhood. She tried to remain loyal to what both her parents had believed, teaching her children the beauties of both the Roman Catholic and Protestant forms of Christianity, endeavouring to hide the bigotry which divided them. As an evidence of her inborn sense of justice, Sara said she could understand the views of a sincere Catholic and a fearless Protestant who both lived piously up to the light that was in their respective faiths. But religious intolerance had left its mark deep on her soul and inspired in her a quest for truth.

With Mary and Rose at her side, Sara rejoiced in the sacred images of virgin and child, the fragrant incense and the chanting at the occasional Roman Catholic services they attended. Equally uplifting were the rollicking hymns of the Salvation Army they heard around London's parks. When her daughters were old enough to discover for themselves the bitter prejudices that cleft the church, they began to ask their mother questions. She endeavoured to answer them wisely and truthfully. Fearing that she had over-emphasized the errors of Catholic ecclesiasticism, she sent her daughters to a French convent school where she hoped they would learn to appreciate all that was beautiful in the Catholic faith while improving their French. The former accomplishment, in Mary's case, outstripped the latter to such a degree that after a year Sara was horrified to read that Mary was to be received as a 'Child of Mary', who had the right to wear the distinctive blue cape of the Virgin until her wedding day. Lady Blomfield hurriedly removed the girls from the school mid-term.

There were other incidents in Lady Blomfield's early married life that illustrate her courage. One day, as the family walked near their country home at Broadway in the Cotswolds, a runaway pony came headlong down the hill towards them with a little girl, screaming in terror, clinging to its mane. Lady Blomfield, who was not at ease with horses, having had two bad accidents herself, forgot her own safety, rushed to meet the pony, seized the bridle, and although she was dragged off her feet, managed to stop the animal just before it reached a rough stone wall, collision with which would surely have seriously injured the child.

Another instance of her physical bravery occurred while the family holidayed in Switzerland. Out walking once again, they heard a man crying out in pain. His leg was trapped between two heavy tree logs that had rolled off a cart. His workmate was trying to pull one of them away but did not have sufficient strength to do so. It took Lady Blomfield, her two daughters and their governess, Beatrice Platt, to free the injured fellow's leg, which Lady Blomfield bound with their handkerchiefs, sending the second man for a doctor.

During this period of her marriage Lady Blomfield's quest for religious truth was just beginning. Among those she called 'friends of the mind', who influenced her outlook, was Sir Edwin Arnold. Born in 1832, Arnold was a poet, journalist, translator and traveller who had made an extensive study of Persian, Turkish and a variety of Indian languages. Following his studies at University College, Oxford, he was appointed principal of the Deccan College in Poona. Returning to London at the age of 29, he became leader writer for the *Daily Telegraph* and in 1873 its Chief Editor. Arnold was an excellent journalist but it was as a poet that he yearned for recognition. His best-known work, *The Light of Asia* – published in 1879 – is an epic poem on the life of the Buddha. The average reader would have known very little of Buddhism at the time of its publication, as most of the accounts of the Buddha's life were limited to oriental journals and travel writers of the day conveyed little of Buddhism's Indian origins. Arnold utilized his knowledge of Sanskrit to use Indian names and terms accurately and dedicated the last section of his poem to the Buddha's teachings, attempting to convey the meaning of the Four Noble Truths, the Eightfold Path and Nirvana. Lady Blomfield considered *The Light of Asia* to have revealed to her the truth at the heart of Buddhism.

Another friend was Sir William Crookes whose scientific approach to psychic research shed a new light on the mysterious phenomena taken so much for granted in Lady Blomfield's homeland. Crookes' long life was one of persistent scientific study. His interests – ranging across pure and applied science, physics and chemistry as well as economic issues – made him a well-known personality. His greatest discoveries were the element thallium and the properties of cathode rays but the experiments he carried out were always more valuable to the research of other scientists than for the conclusions he himself made about his findings. Crookes' research into psychic happenings was strongly criticized but it at least demonstrated that he considered all phenomena worthy of investigation and that he refused to be bound by tradition and convention.

British society's taste for spiritualism was at its height in the late 19th century. The belief that the dead communicate with those still living began around the middle of the century with Emanuel Swedenborg's writings on the spirit world. His ideas were reinforced by Anton Mesmer's research into hypnotism which he claimed involved the influence of celestial bodies on the terrestrial. Many Victorians – among them the writer Elizabeth Barrett Browning – were strong in their conviction about its truth. Seances became commonplace and mysterious characters such as Daniel Dunglas Home – apparently able to float in the air and levitate heavy items without touching them – were the talk of London. Prominent figures such as the writer Sir Arthur Conan Doyle – creator of Sherlock Holmes and spiritualism's most famous adherent – were impressed that Crookes had personally tested and endorsed a number of mediums on the circuit. Indeed, Sir William said that he had witnessed Dunglas Home – parodied by Robert Browning as 'Mr Sludge, the Medium' – float out of an upper storey window, travel over the street below and reenter the building by another window on the same floor. By 1869 there were four monthly spiritualist journals in London and the city was packed with mediums, conjuring up spirit voices and apparitions to willing customers.

Although she respected Crookes, Lady Blomfield never became absorbed by practical spiritualism, believing that to seek communication with the other world disturbed the peace or activities of the departed. Science, to her mind, however, was another matter. If the barrier between the natural and the so-called supernatural could have been broken down she would have accepted the truth that matter and spirit, in the Spiritualist sense, were continuous, divided only by human beings' limited perception, and that, in the words of Alexander Pope whose 'Essay on Man' she knew by heart, 'All are but parts of one stupendous whole, Whose body nature is, and God, the Soul.'

Lady Blomfield was not scared of causing consternation among others by sticking to her principles. At a time when religious customs and observances were considered sacrosanct, she would often turn heads by refusing to stand with the congregation whenever the Athanasian Creed was being read in church. The creed sets forth the orthodox doctrine of the trinity and deals with the incarnation of Jesus Christ. Lady Blomfield took particular offence to the closing statement of the Creed that says that those who have done good will enter eternal life, while those who have done evil will enter eternal fire. She told her daughters that although hell fire might be everlasting, it was blasphemy to say that God would punish a man forever for a sin he had committed in a moment of depravity, or even for a lifetime of sin which, however long it lasted, was only temporary. There was ultimate salvation she believed, even for the most dire of sinners.

Late in October 1899 Sir Arthur Blomfield was attending a meeting of the Westminster Abbey Glee Club of which he was president. There was, as was commonplace, an 'In Memoriam' chorus sung in memory of a recently deceased member. Little did those who listened to it suspect that they would have to hear it sung again at the next meeting to the memory of their genial and popular president. On Monday 30 October 1899 Sir Arthur Blomfield collapsed suddenly from a heart attack while at the Royal Society's Arts Club at 40 Dover Street, London. His death came as a devastating shock to his wife, his children and his professional colleagues. *The Architect and Contract Reporter* journal reported that just before his death he 'looked to be vigorous as well as happy'.[34]

At a time when most of its pages were taken up with the latest reports of the Boer War which had been declared early that same month, *The Times* on Wednesday 1 November published a full obituary of Sir Arthur:

We regret to record the death of Sir Arthur Blomfield, the distinguished architect, which took place quite suddenly on Monday night. He was seized with syncope from heart disease while at his club, and died before medical aid reached him . . .

Blomfield was a man of untiring energy and power of work. Probably no architect has built or restored so many churches, and there are few countries where his work may not be seen . . .

But up to the day of his death he remained hard at work constantly travelling on business to different parts of the country, his holidays being generally spent at his country house at Broadway, near Stratford-on-Avon . . .

Sir Arthur Blomfield inherited in a great degree the ready wit which was characteristic of his father, the Bishop of London. He was a conversationalist of great charm and was universally popular both in society and his profession.[35]

The Builder on 4 November 1899 also published an obituary praising not only his achievements as an architect but his humanity. *The Journal of the Royal Institute of British Architects* wrote:

He was a charming companion, intelligent and sympathetic, seasoning his conversation with something of the wit and humour of his father. Among his fellow-workers he was universally liked and esteemed, and the larger world of society rated him no less highly, for no man was less of a recluse . . .[36]

Sir Arthur's funeral took place in Broadway, Worcestershire, on 3 December 1899. 'No fitter resting-place', wrote the architect Arthur E. Street, 'could be found for a man who had no liking for the pomps of the world than the charming village of Broadway, where he had made his country home.'[37] The funeral was officiated by the Reverend H. Russell Wakefield, the rector of St Mary's Bryanston Square, London, assisted by the rector of the parish. Lady Blomfield led the mourners followed by her two daughters, Mary and Rose, and stepdaughter Adele. Then came her two stepsons, Charles and Arthur, and son Frank, Sir Arthur's nephew Reginald and his niece, the poetess Dorothy Frances Gurney. There was also a large gathering of the clergy and people of the neighbourhood. Simultaneously with the interment, a memorial service was being held at St Mary's, close to the

Blomfields' Montagu Square home. The Archdeacon of London and the Reverend R. Dixon officiated. Archdeacon Sinclair delivered an address in which he sketched out the life and work of Sir Arthur. Among the distinguished guests were Kenneth Grahame, then Secretary of the Bank of England and author of *The Wind in the Willows*, and the playwright Sir Arthur Wing Pinero.

The passing of this well-loved pillar of both the architectural and religious establishments caused sadness in London and beyond. Sir Arthur Blomfield was a decent, Christian man. He was 'the stamp of a man produced by the old schools of architecture, now fast dying out; and apart from his professional status, his modest and genial nature, his conversational powers, his kind and generous friendship, always willing to aid younger members of the profession with the fruits of his experience, endeared him to all who knew him. And, further, he was staunch upholder of the necessity for honour, high principles and morality amongst English gentlemen.'[38] Soon after Sir Arthur's passing a small memorial brass was fixed in the Bryanston Square church, a building that had been reseated and redecorated under his guidance 25 years previously. The brass reads:

In Memory of Arthur William Blomfield, Knight, MA and ARA, Architect for many years resident in this parish and an earnest worker for its welfare. Under his direction this church was improved and adorned An:Dom: 1875.

Barely 40 years old and the mother of three young children, Lady Blomfield was embarking on the next chapter of her life, during which her passionate search for spiritual meaning would continue unabated.

CHAPTER TWO

THE SEARCH FOR TRUTH

. . . we must exert ourselves to the utmost in investigating and turning toward the Sun of Reality, no matter from what dayspring or dawning point it may appear.[1]
'Abdu'l-Bahá

Sir Arthur Blomfield left Sara a wealthy woman. With an estate valued at almost £29,000 – the equivalent of more than £2,000,000 today – she was bequeathed the household contents and an income for life. His second son from his first marriage, Arthur Conran Blomfield, and Henry Russell Wakefield, the rector of St Mary's Church in Bryanston Square, were appointed the guardians of Mary, Frank and Rose in the event of their mother's untimely passing. The residue of Sir Arthur's wealth was set up as a trust with his two eldest sons and Joseph Watson Overbury, a stockbroker, as trustees. Lady Blomfield now found herself with three children to raise alone and two large homes to manage – in London's Montagu Square and at Broadway in Worcestershire.

A studio photograph from around this time, taken in Eastbourne, depicts a proud-looking woman comfortable with her status in society. Smartly dressed in a fancifully embroidered jacket, lace blouse, twin rows of pearls and a small, feathered velvet hat, Lady Blomfield is the picture of late Victorian elegance. Yet there is something bohemian about her appearance reminiscent of studio portraits of the actresses of the time and the heavy-lidded eyes denote a compassionate nature. This period must have been one of the unhappiest of her life yet, as her daughter Mary wrote, 'I can remember, from the earliest days, her valiant spirit meeting sadness and difficulties with radiant acquiescence and invincible faith.'[2]

With the passing of Sir Arthur, Lady Blomfield decided that it was timely to leave behind the whirl of their social life in the city and retreat to their country home, Springfield House in Broadway. Her husband's remains had been laid to rest there in a secluded corner of the graveyard of St Eadburgha church, in the shadow of its 12th century red sandstone tower. A slender granite gravestone – a decorative Celtic cross – remains there to this day, its inscription barely legible. Their residence, along a hedgerow-lined track heading out of Broadway, was a spacious, Cotswold stone country house in the English vernacular style, homely and comfortable, but a far cry from the elegance of Montagu Square.

While Broadway, nestling at the foot of the Cotswold Hills at the southernmost tip of Worcestershire, offered the kind of natural peace and tranquillity rarely found in London, Lady Blomfield was never far away from stimulating company. The village's reputation as a retreat for the cultured elite boomed in the last decades of the 19th century. The great socialist visionary, designer and writer William Morris had discovered its charms while staying at Broadway Tower, a striking 18th century folly, then home to an Oxford tutor, Carmel Price. Price played host to many celebrated people of the day in his home from whose turrets spectacular 360 degree views extend as far as the Welsh mountains and the Severn Valley, encompassing as many as 12 counties. While on a visit to the tower, the author Leonard Hutton with the botanist and landscape painter Sir Alfred Parsons had been encouraged by Morris to take a walk down the valley to visit the village with its attractive stone farm houses and charming cottages. Hutton was enchanted by the place and, returning to London, informed two American artists – the graphic illustrator Edwin Austin Abbey and Francis Millet – of his discovery. The two men had been on a quest to find the perfect English village and subsequently rented Farnham House on Broadway Green. The cream of the arts world followed – the writer Henry James, the distinguished actor and theatre manager Sir John Hare, the painter John Singer Sargent along with many others arrived to set up home in Broadway, making it arguably the most famous village in England of the period. One American magazine reported, 'Nowhere can the ideal of old England be found in such a perfect state of preservation or so untouched by modern improvements as Broadway. There is scarcely a house which hasn't been painted by a famous artist, there isn't a chimney or doorway which hasn't been sketched.'[3] The ravishing Sargent masterpiece *Carnation, Lily, Lily, Rose* of 1885–6, one of the most popular paintings in the collection at London's Tate Britain, depicts an atmospheric Broadway evening scene as two children, clad in white, light oriental lanterns in a luxurious, lily-festooned garden.

Access to Broadway had improved in the mid-19th century with the opening of the London–Oxford–Worcester railway line. The nearest stop was Evesham until 1904 when Broadway received its own railway station. Despite the inevitable increase in visitors for whom exploring the Cotswolds had become a popular pastime, the town still managed to maintain the idyllic charm and picturesque quality that remains to this day.

With Sara's son Frank now away studying at Eton, Broadway was the perfect place for her to come to terms with the loss of her husband and to raise her daughters away from the pressures of life in London without isolating herself from the stimulating company of England's cultural elite. The 1901 census records that Sara, by then aged 42, was 'living on own means' at Springfield House with Mary aged 13, Rose aged 10, the girls' 23 year old governess Beatrice Platt, and two local women who lived with them – their cook Amy Keen, aged 33, and 39 year old Harriet Spinner, listed as the Blomfields' 'parlour maid/domestic'. During this period, Sara's sister Cecilia married divorcee William Gilmore from Pennsylvania, who enjoyed some acclaim as a Broadway stage director, and settled in New York.

Lady Blomfield felt at home among the artistic luminaries who had gathered in Broadway. Pleasant evenings were passed at the home of Frank Millet, who had converted his barn into a large drawing room and studio. Millet was a fascinating, well-travelled man who had served as a drummer boy to a Massachusetts regiment during the American Civil War. Excelling at Harvard University, he became a reporter and then city editor of the *Boston Courier*. His artistic career began as a pastime of making lithographs and portraits of friends. An excellent decorative artist and painter whose work can be found at the Metropolitan Museum of Art in New York and at the Tate in London, Millet was among the 1,523 victims of the *Titanic* disaster in 1912, famously finishing a game of cards with friends in the first-class smoking room as the ship sank in the icy waters of the north Atlantic.

Also among Lady Blomfield's close friends in Broadway was the first American superstar actress Mary Anderson, who had retired from the stage in 1890 when she married Count Antonio Fernando de Navarro, a fellow American working in London. They had two children, a son José and a daughter Elena, and settled at Court Farm in Broadway where Mary became a noted hostess, welcoming guests from her circle of musical and literary friends as well as ecclesiastical acquaintances of the Count. From time to time she staged evenings of dramatic readings or performances in which the Blomfield girls eagerly participated. Mary Anderson remained in Broadway, rarely venturing back into the public eye, until her death in 1940 at the age of 80.

Other visitors Sara enjoyed meeting in Broadway and occasionally entertained in her own home included the Boer War veteran Lord Elcho and his wife; the French-born Maude Valérie White, one of the most successful composers of English song of the Victorian era; Lady Maud Bowes-Lyon, an aunt of the future Queen Elizabeth the Queen Mother; the legendary actress Mrs Patrick Campbell, for whom George Bernard Shaw created the role of Eliza Doolittle in *Pygmalion*; and the *Punch* caricaturist Phil May. Relatives were also close by – Sir Arthur Blomfield's niece Dorothy Frances Gurney was the poet who penned the wedding hymn 'O Perfect Love', as well as 'God's Garden', which is so often seen quoted on sundials and garden benches:

> The kiss of the sun for pardon,
> The song of the birds for mirth –
> One is nearer God's heart in a garden
> Than anywhere else on earth.

Lady Blomfield found Dorothy a delightful companion and they enjoyed a long and devoted friendship. Gurney's obituary published in *The Times* in 1932 stated that a 'wide circle of friends of every creed and class knew that they could take to her all their troubles, great or small, and come away with the burden of them lightened or removed'.

Lady Blomfield had been immersed since the age of 28 in the British establishment. Now facing life as a young widow, the next major stage in her spiritual search was under way. Deriving pleasure from the rural yet bohemian world she inhabited, she was beginning to find even greater contentment and satisfaction in her exploration of the sphere of spiritual contemplation and thought. From this time onward, her society life as it had been previously gave way to associations with those who were working for some philanthropic cause or shared her interests in spiritual matters. Within a few years, as Broadway became connected by rail to major cities such as Birmingham, Cheltenham, Worcester and Oxford, tourism to the peaceful village began to boom. Perhaps for this reason and the desire to be closer to those who shared her esoteric interests, Lady Blomfield decided to return to London with her daughters to live there permanently.

In 1904, by which time her son Frank had finished his schooling and had joined the Royal Navy, Lady Blomfield and her two daughters moved back to London and into new accommodation at 10 Welbeck Mansions, 97 Cadogan Gardens just off fashionable Sloane Square. The Cadogan estate, covering around 90 acres in the Knightsbridge and Chelsea areas of London, dated back to the early years of the 18th century when Sir Hans Sloane bought the Manor of Chelsea. Immediately he began to develop the land, building houses along Cheyne Walk. On Sir Hans's death, the estate was further developed by Lord Cadogan who was married to one of Sloane's daughters. The grand red-brick mansion blocks of Cadogan Gardens with their elaborate ironwork railings, where Lady Blomfield set up home, were built at the end of the 19th century and remain one of London's most sought-after addresses, each apartment now fetching seven figure sums. A wide range of spiritual teachers now became part of Lady Blomfield's circle of acquaintances and made a profound impact on her thinking. In 1911, 97 Cadogan Gardens would become the setting for the most significant event of all their lives.

The fascination of London society with alternative approaches to religion and spirituality had grown during the closing decades of the 19th century. Despite Bishop Blomfield's best efforts, the church was fighting a losing battle against the scientific logic of Darwinists, the growth of atheism and widespread improvements in material wealth. Within the church itself, there were ongoing struggles between traditionalists and reformers. Increased access to knowledge about mysticism, eastern religions or occultism allowed people the freedom to develop personal spirituality, away from the dogma and corruption of religious institutions. Women, in particular, sought out forms of worship that, both figuratively and literally, cut out the middleman. Some historians have noted that the mid- to late-19th century preoccupation with spiritualism was largely a female one. It has been suggested that, finding most religious organizations male-dominated, the woman medium – having been barred from accepted institutions of power – established for herself an alternative, higher source of authority. Society women were also the main benefactors of new spiritual movements. Around 1899 two women in London quietly began to share among their friends and acquaintances a new religious teaching from Persia they had discovered. They were a divorcee, Mary Virginia Thornburgh-Cropper

– formerly the wife of an English army officer – and a portrait miniaturist from the city of Bath, Ethel Jenner Rosenberg. Within a few years Lady Blomfield's encounter with Rosenberg would irrevocably change her life.

Sara's inspirational acquaintances of this period included the Austrian Roman Catholic theologian Friedrich von Hügel, Baron of the Holy Roman Empire. Born in Florence, von Hügel had moved to England with his family in 1867 when he was 15. Having studied natural science, philosophy and religious history, he adopted critical views of the Old Testament and later went on to found the London Society for the Study of Religion. He was a profound Christian who passionately desired communion with God and sympathized with all genuine religion. This broad approach to Christianity appealed greatly to Lady Blomfield, remembering a childhood riven by sectarian antagonism. But her spiritual interests did not stop at Christianity.

Her friendships with Sir William Crookes and Sir Edwin Arnold led her to a thorough study of Theosophy which taught that a universal wisdom lay at the heart of all genuine religious and occult traditions. The Theosophical Society had been founded in 1875 by Helena Blavatsky, a Russian occultist, and Colonel Henry Olcott, an American freemason. It is thought that Blavatsky was born in 1831, the daughter of a Russian aristocrat, and her early years were spent living a bohemian life, including a period as a spirit medium. She claimed she had been contacted by a Tibetan sage who taught her about a divine hierarchy that rules the cosmos. It was claimed that this sage – Morya, who was visible only to initiates – was a member of a Great White Brotherhood of Masters, who were immortal and invisible. Among the members of the Brotherhood were Buddha, Moses, Plato and various other enlightened teachers. An important element of their message for that particular period in history was that Darwin was mistaken in thinking man had descended from apes, rather the human race had come from spirit beings who had arrived on Earth via other planets.

When the Theosophical Society was founded, its aims were threefold: to form a nucleus for the universal brotherhood of mankind irrespective of race, religion, gender, cast or skin colour; to promote the study of comparative religion, philosophy and science; and to investigate the unexplained laws of nature as well as the hidden potential of man. The Society aimed to be free from religious dogma and adopted the slogan, 'There is no religion higher than truth'. After Blavatsky's death in 1891, her successor in Theosophy's Esoteric Section was Annie Besant, who, like Lady Blomfield, was half-Irish, half-English. Besant had originally proclaimed herself an atheist after walking out of an early marriage to an unpleasant churchman. She later became a notorious birth control campaigner, losing custody of her children along the way. After discovering Theosophy at the age of 42, she flung herself into its work. The appeal of Theosophy for its adherents lay in the abandonment of clergy and theology, the mystery of reincarnation and the anticipation of the imminent appearance of a World Teacher. Besant was convinced that the Maitreya or World Teacher who had previously revealed himself in the person of Jesus Christ was about to make himself known to humanity again.

Lady Blomfield avidly read the works of Besant and another prominent Theosophist, Alfred P. Sinnett, and often attended meetings to hear the authors. Besant, clothed in billowing white robes, was an inspirational speaker, lecturing in a beautiful, mesmerizing voice. Her ambition was to make Theosophy the world's leading ecumenical religion and social move-ment and she succeeded in moving it onto a social level, founding several schools and becoming president of the Indian National Congress. She was also heavily involved in the Boy Scout movement and in Co-Masonry, a version of Freemasonry that admitted women. But the Society was riven with internal wrangling and disagreements. Sinnett was a journalist who had worked in London, Hong Kong and Allahabad. He and his wife, both keen spiritualists, had met Helena Blavatsky in India. Sinnett was dismissed from his newspaper in India for allowing Blavatsky too much space in it to proclaim her ideas. Sinnett and Besant were bitter enemies, he being resentful of her rise to prominence in the Society above him.

Sinnett would often call on the Blomfields to recount the latest devel-opments in the Society. Young Mary Blomfield later remembered being thrilled by his talk of astral conflicts between the 'White and Black forces'. Her mother listened attentively and asked pertinent questions, challeng-ing the fallibility of Sinnett's notions. Mary noted how a wise inward calm would show in Lady Blomfield's smile 'as Mr Sinnett in his matter-of-fact way would tell these wonders, taking them for granted as soberly as the multiplication table'.[4]

If she was aware of the internal conflicts in the Theosophical Society, Lady Blomfield seems not to have let them interfere with her interest in its teachings. She confidently told her daughters that a great world teacher was awaited by the enlightened of all faiths and she believed that she herself would see him. Whenever a new guru or spiritual master arrived in London, she would attend his lectures, hoping to find him to be the Promised One.

Among those she sought out was Swami Vivekananda, an Indian monk whose fame spread after he represented Hinduism at the first World Parliament of Religions held in Chicago in 1893. Vivekananda was a handsome and colourful personality who had a vast knowledge of eastern and western culture, coupled with deep spiritual insight. He pleaded eloquently for the West and the East, for science and religion to come together. Lady Blomfield clearly found much to agree with in Swami Vivekananda's teaching but ultimately she was not convinced he was the great teacher she sought. By 1910 the Theosophists had fixed their attention on the young Indian boy Krishnamurti, whom they claimed, and trained, to be the incarnation of the World Teacher, a role he later came to strongly despise, shunning his followers and resigning from the Theosophical Society in 1930.

The Theosophical doctrine of reincarnation fascinated Lady Blomfield, and her romantic nature and Irish love of myth found appeal in hearing their version of human evolution with its forgotten races, moon ancestors, shape-shifting water-creatures known as Hyperboreans and the lost inhabitants of Atlantis who passed on their wisdom to humanity's forebears. Ultimately, though, Lady Blomfield was disenchanted by the manner in which Theosophy divided up the spiritual world. She preferred 'the many mansions of infinity'. In the long run, her gradual dissatisfaction with Theosophy came about from a critical doubt about the validity of its spiritualistic sources. She felt that the communications from beyond were very open to fraudulent abuse, either by charlatans on this plane or the so-called 'astral'. Lady Blomfield's mind instinctively turned towards the ethical aspects of religion and their practical effect on human behaviour.

The truths inherent in Christianity were never far from her thinking. Among her papers is a poem in her own handwriting, reflecting a profound belief in Christ's redeeming mission:

Oh Love for Man, Oh perfect thought
Which from the heart of Christ arose
When all his work on earth was wrought
'Conquered is death and all man's foes.'

In the eternal, long past ages
Thou foresawst the Easter morn
Which should dawn to glad the Sages
Who rejoiced when Christ was born.

Oh Angel of Easter Morning
Oh Herald of Life to be
Breathe from God on the sinful man
And his soul is free.
Slave of Satan and serf of sin, the bondsman of death and time
Loaded with ills of his fathers and his body crushed down by his crime
Heard, received the great tidings of Easter and came to God with his plea

It was life that spake from the darkness
It was light that sprang to the Blind
When the Lord had rent asunder the chains
that had bound the Mind.
Souls held down and enchained
By Satan to death and the grave
Enthralled and entrammelled with fetters of flesh
and dead to all that was brave
Rose up swiftly when Jesus spake
And they knew there was life to find.[5]

Over and above her Theosophist friends, Lady Blomfield found most inspiration in the missions of two prominent and outspoken churchmen from whom she derived immense inspiration – the Reverend R.J. Campbell and Basil Wilberforce, Archdeacon of Westminster.

Reginald John Campbell was a non-conformist Congregational Minister who had made quite a stir when, as a young preacher, he took over as pastor at perhaps the most prestigious church in England – the City Temple in London's Holborn. Campbell made for an extraordinary presence in the pulpit with his shock of prematurely white hair and apparent vulnerability. On his first Sunday at the City Temple seven thousand people attended its morning and evening services. For the first two years of his ministry Campbell was judged to be a successful and exciting minister and the immediate publication of his sermons spread his fame internationally. In 1907 Campbell began preaching his controversial new theology which was compared by one theologian to a bad photograph: underdeveloped and overexposed. Campbell critiqued both the utter transcendence of God – God above and beyond His creation – and pantheism – God identified with creation. His position of panentheism veered towards the notion that God can be readily seen and known through creation but is not limited to or contained by it. The new theology stated that man knows nothing and can know nothing of the Infinite Cause from which all things proceed, except as He is read in His universe and in human souls. Campbell believed Jesus to be divine but also stressed the divinity of all human beings who should strive for oneness with God and live the life Jesus lived.

From this position, Campbell preached a thoroughly revised version of Christianity. While not claiming direct influence from Hinduism, Buddhism or Taoism to which his ideas bore some similarity, Campbell stated his intention was to recapture the purity of early Christianity. There are certainly, and not surprisingly for the period, elements of Theosophy in his views. Campbell came under fire from orthodox theologians who suggested that he had never been trained in theology. Undeterred, he sought to apply his thinking to social causes, joined the Independent Labour Party and the Fabian Society – with its progressive socialist tenets of social justice – and supported divorce and votes for women. He visited the Western Front at the beginning of the Great War and Lloyd George made his first public statement on the conflict at the City Temple. In 1915, as Campbell's campaigning and the criticism it attracted took its toll on his fragile health, his congregation asked him to go – unhappy with his new theology, socialist convictions and other views they deemed unacceptable. He joined the Church of England and espoused more conventional theology from then on. 'When he had gone,' one observer wrote, 'those who had sat under his spell must have wondered if it had not all been a dream. They had had the sense of riding the crest of a new reformation into a reformed society. The Kingdom of Heaven was attainable – perhaps almost at hand. Then the angelic man who had brought them to these heights became confused, confessed his error, and left them, as the War came upon them and swept away the old Europe. When the great let-downs of the world are recounted, a special word will need to be said for the pre-War congregation at London's City Temple.'6 Campbell's departure from the City Temple, however, was preceded by a singular service he rendered to the Bahá'í Movement which his admirer Lady Blomfield was soon to embrace.

Sara considered Campbell a fearless thinker but she held an even greater and deeper respect for the interpretation of Christianity given by Basil Wilberforce, the then Archdeacon of Westminster. Every Sunday she would take her daughters to St John's, Smith Square to hear him preach. St John's was built in 1728 and is one of the masterpieces of English Baroque architecture. The church was dubbed 'Queen Anne's Footstool' after a supposed incident when the architect, Thomas Archer, consulted the monarch on what the new church should look like. In reply, the queen petulantly kicked over her footstool and said, 'Like that!' The church's distinctive four towers are thus said to resemble an upturned footstool. St John's superb acoustic has today made it a world class classical music venue.

Basil Wilberforce, who was made Archdeacon of Westminster in 1900 after 23 years' service at St Mary's in Southampton and then later as Chaplain to the House of Commons, was regarded as a spiritual teacher of the highest order. As the son of the Bishop of Winchester and the great-grandson of William Wilberforce, the great anti-slavery campaigner, he was a staunch Liberal, although he had no sympathy with party politics. In his position as Archdeacon he was regarded as having brought a new light to the church, transforming the old doctrines into living realities, something which must have clearly appealed to Lady Blomfield in her quest for a religion of ethics and action.

Like Campbell, Wilberforce was a well-loved, charismatic preacher whose congregations flocked in huge numbers to hear him. While making a great moral appeal or rallying his troops to some act of national duty, he was second to none. But his sermons were not simplistic – one report recounts that Wilberforce 'seemed to believe in the virtue of long words to make difficult things easy. After all "the mysterious power behind phenomena" only says in many syllables what "God" says in one; but the congregation of St John's drank in this eloquence with open mouths and ears, and firmly believed that it helped them to understand what would otherwise have been unintelligible.'[7]

During Archdeacon Wilberforce's tenure, one notable feature of the 800-strong congregation at St John's was that women outnumbered men by ten to one. Wilberforce's manner with women was gentle, respectful and sympathetic. Women, it was observed, 'felt safe with Wilberforce, pouring out their troubles into his patient ears, secure not only of genuine sympathy, but also of sensible advice'.[8] He was an eager advocate of women's right to vote and was even magnanimous when suffragettes tried to destroy St John's. More controversially, he backed the remarriage of divorced people and celebrated the legalization of marriage with a wife's sister.

As a churchman in the post-Darwin age, Wilberforce understood the intellectual difficulties and honest doubts of many of his contemporaries and attempted to demonstrate the spiritual significance of such doctrines as the Atonement, the Trinity and the Resurrection which he believed had been lost in academic interpretations which failed to satisfy the mind or touch the soul. He also decried the materialism that had crept into the life of the church and chose to mix freely with a wide range of people – poets, statesmen, scientists and actors. His wife Charlotte had a reputation as a skilled hostess who had mastered the art of blending various widely differing personalities into sociable and harmonious company.

The number of Wilberforce's admirers was equalled by the number of his critics. When he administered the sacrament of anointing the sick with oil, there was an outcry among traditionalists in the Church of England. He was also a dedicated participant in spiritualist seances and a regular visitor to the Broadlands Centre in Hampshire where Quakers would rub shoulders with Spiritualists, Swedenborgians and members of other religious groups. He was rigorous and conservative in some matters and hugely flexible and liberal in others. For example, along with large numbers of clergymen of his day, he was a staunch lobbyist for the temperance movement that advocated abstention from alcohol. He even tried to introduce grape juice as a replacement for communion wine. He had little respect for the medical profession and totally opposed vivisection.

Lady Blomfield also felt deeply concerned about the rights of animals. Anti-vivisection became a potent issue during 1907 when police, feminists, medical students and trade unionists fought in Battersea Park over the statue of a brown dog. Two women, Louise Lind-af-Hageby and Liesa Schartau, had enrolled in the London School of Medicine for Women to learn physiology with the intention of using that knowledge to expose the practice of vivisection. They witnessed the suffering of a brown terrier dog for more than two months and were inspired to put up a statue of the dog in the park with an inscription stating that the dog had been done to death by the students of University College as part of their experiments. Protest meetings to have the inscription removed came to nothing so medical students vandalized the statue, leading to rioting. The statue was eventually removed in 1910. Lady Blomfield became a close friend of Louise Lind-af-Hageby. She was introduced to her by A. P. Sinnett who called the girl a 'Divine Being, a spiritual descendant of St Francis of Assisi'.[9] Their friendship lasted for decades and, many years later, they worked alongside each other in Geneva.

Above all others, Archdeacon Wilberforce was the central focus of Lady Blomfield's spiritual life, a much loved and revered mentor. Sorting through her mother's papers after her passing, Mary found many letters from him which Lady Blomfield had treasured along with correspondence from Sir Edwin Arnold, her other great spiritual guide. In the spring of 1907 Wilberforce gave a series of lectures on the relationship of eastern religions to Christianity. His universalist point of view and the quality of his inspiration greatly impressed his audience. These lectures, precisely at that moment, set the stage for Lady Blomfield to attain her heart's desire within a matter of weeks. She was about to discover that the great World Teacher she was anticipating from God had indeed come.

CHAPTER THREE

THE HIGHWAY CHOSEN

Thou art but one step away from the glorious heights above
and from the celestial tree of love.[1]
Bahá'u'lláh

During the Easter period of 1907 Lady Blomfield and her elder daughter Mary were holidaying in Paris. The French capital in the early years of the 20th century was experiencing its *belle époque*, a period of prodigious artistic activity. Avant-garde artists and musicians were the recipients of generous patronage and liberal attitudes prevailed. A pioneering black American writer Jessie Fauset wrote of that time, 'I like Paris because I find something here, something of integrity, which I seem to have strangely lost in my own country. It is simplest of all to say that I like to live among people and surroundings where I am not always conscious of "thou shall not".'[2] This was a city where anything was possible and diversity flourished. Even so, Parisians could still be shocked. In March 1907, breaking all the rules of composition and perspective, Pablo Picasso exhibited *Les Demoiselles d'Avignon*, causing an unlikely stir with its grouping of five nude female figures, their bodies distorted into geometric shapes, their faces reminiscent of tribal sculpture. Some recognized the influence of an exhibition of African masks shown in Paris earlier in the year. The city had become an effervescent centre for the meeting of diverse cultures and ideas.

Most significantly in the unfoldment of Lady Blomfield's spiritual quest, Paris was also home to Europe's first community of Bahá'ís – many of them expatriate North Americans resident in the city as artists or students of the arts. Since a young American woman, May Ellis Bolles, had encountered the Movement at the end of the 19th century, a number of the outstanding figures of early western Bahá'í history had learned of its principles from her in the French capital. Among the first to be drawn through her teaching to the magnetic personality of the then head of the

Bahá'ís, 'Abdu'l-Bahá, were the scholar Hippolyte Dreyfus; an architecture student, Charles Mason Remey; the Englishman Thomas Breakwell and the heiress Laura Clifford Barney. The group was reinforced by an admired American Impressionist painter, Edwin Scott; artists Juliet Thompson and Marion Jack; and Edith Sanderson, whose sister Sybil was a celebrated opera singer of her time – a muse of the composer Massenet, feted by Toulouse Lautrec and the first love of American newspaper magnate William Randolph Hearst, whose philanthropist mother was one of the most prominent American followers of 'Abdu'l-Bahá. Another associate of the Bahá'ís at this time was Raymond Duncan, brother of the avant-garde dancer Isadora Duncan. Thus the circles that the Bahá'ís moved in were culturally sophisticated and open-minded.

'All that the [early believers in Paris] knew of the Bahai Cause', wrote Remey,

> was what someone had heard from someone else, and thus the word was passed on . . . we had very little real information about the Teachings. We depended mostly upon our faith and on our feelings rather than on actual information. It was a time, however, of great spiritual romance and adventure. The great religious fire of the Cause was uppermost in our minds. We all sang, as it were, a lyric Spiritual Song, and like all youth the adventure and the new outlook created a tremendous enthusiasm in our hearts . . . having so little [written literature] we were obliged to dwell largely on the emotional plane. Dreams and visions frequently made up to us our lack of actual knowledge.'[3]

The early followers of what is now known as the Bahá'í Faith did not consider themselves to be members of a new world religion nor did they deem it a necessary step to renounce or stop practising their own inherited religions. Generally speaking, their belief consisted of being in agreement with the few teachings they knew about and a devotion to 'Abdu'l-Bahá based upon the stories they had heard of His exceptional personality. 'When I first heard of the Cause in Paris,' recalled Marion Jack, 'I heard of it as something "queer". This thought made me curious & fortunately I was led to someone, Mr. Charles Remey, who explained things so beautifully & reverently, that I found the "queer" was something great & precious.'[4]

The 'Bahá'í Movement', as it was then called, had begun to spread to the West under the leadership of 'Abdu'l-Bahá shortly after the passing of His father Bahá'u'lláh, its Prophet-Founder. Coincidentally, for Lady Blomfield, Bahá'u'lláh's teachings had been given prominent mention by a Christian speaker at the 1893 World Parliament of Religions in Chicago where Swami Vivekananda, whom she had admired, had made such an impact.

The story of the Bahá'í Movement, as its early members would have heard it, began in Persia in 1844 when a young merchant – a descendant of the Prophet Muḥammad – named Siyyid 'Alí-Muḥammad adopted the title 'Báb' – meaning 'Gate' – and taught His followers that He had been sent to prepare the way for 'Him Whom God shall make manifest' – a Messenger from God whom the followers of all religions anticipated would be sent to establish His Kingdom on earth. The Báb's teachings attracted a widespread following and caused a great commotion in Persia. The country's religious leaders launched a campaign of bitter persecution against the Bábís and after six years of fierce opposition, the Báb Himself was publicly executed. Thousands of Bábís were subsequently tortured and killed.

The romance of the story of the Báb was a powerfully attractive one to artists in the West. The poet Matthew Arnold wrote of the Báb in *A Persian Passion Play*, Sarah Bernhardt commissioned a work, apparently never performed, about the Báb's first female follower – the poetess Ṭáhirih – and the Russian writer Izabella Grinevskaya turned the Báb's life into a play that was staged in Paris in 1912. The Báb's status, however, in the minds of early western Bahá'ís was primarily a minor prophetic figure, akin to John the Baptist, whose sole mission was to announce the coming of a teacher far greater than Himself.

Among the surviving followers of the Báb, one personality began to win over the hearts of the dispirited and sorely oppressed community. He was Mírzá Ḥusayn 'Alí or Bahá'u'lláh (meaning 'the Glory of God') – a Persian nobleman, renowned for His acts of charity and great learning. He had renounced His wealth and the offer of a position in the court of the Shah to devote His energies to defending the Cause of the Báb. Imprisoned in a foul, subterranean dungeon where He experienced an extraordinary vision of His forthcoming mission, and then banished to Baghdad for His open allegiance to the new religion, Bahá'u'lláh continued to guide the group of exiles in Iraq. In 1863, after a decade of rebuilding the shattered Bábí community while demonstrating extraordinary perception and producing profoundly mystical and inspirational writings containing spiritual and social guidance, Bahá'u'lláh announced publicly that He was in fact 'Him

Whom God shall make manifest' and the Promised One foretold by the Báb and the Messengers of the past. He explained that the covenant which God had made with humankind to always protect and guide His creation had been renewed and that He was the latest 'Manifestation of God', sent to give the newest instalment of divine revelation from the Creator to His creation, set forth in previous centuries by Abraham, Krishna, Moses, Jesus Christ, Muḥammad, Zoroaster and countless others. Thus Bahá'u'lláh's Revelation – which took the form of some one hundred volumes of writings – was essentially unveiling and updating eternal spiritual truth, tailored to suit the new conditions of humanity, at a time when the outmoded institutions of the past were no longer able to deal effectively with the challenge of a scientifically and intellectually advanced world.

Bahá'u'lláh's Revelation took the theme of unity as its cornerstone. The day was approaching, He taught, when the human race would, either through an act of collective will or out of dire necessity, put aside war and conflict once and for all and establish a world brotherhood and civilization. For this message, which He proclaimed to the unheeding ears of the kings and rulers of His time, He endured 40 years of imprisonment and exile at the hands of the Persian authorities and then the Turkish Ottoman Empire.

Shortly before He passed away in the Holy Land in 1892, Bahá'u'lláh received a visit from the distinguished Cambridge orientalist Professor Edward Granville Browne. Browne had taken a keen interest in the origins and growth of the Bábí community and had devoted a large part of his early life to studying it. He had presented and published academic papers on it to the dismay of his contemporaries, who wondered why he was spending so much of his time studying what they considered to be an insignificant sect of Shi'i Islam. However, Professor Browne saw in the history of the new religion similarities to the phenomenon of the birth of other great religious systems and chose to record for posterity the heroism that the followers of the Báb had displayed. The effect of the personality of Bahá'u'lláh on Professor Browne was recorded in one of the few pen portraits of the Manifestation. Browne described Him as a 'wondrous and venerable figure' whose 'piercing eyes seemed to read one's very soul; power and authority sat on that ample brow . . . No need to ask in whose presence I stood, as I bowed myself before one who is the object of a devotion and love which kings might envy and emperors sigh for in vain!'[5]

On the same night in 1844 that the Báb had declared His mission in the Persian city of Shiraz, Bahá'u'lláh's wife had given birth to a baby boy named 'Abbás, who would become known as 'Abdu'l-Bahá – 'the Servant of Bahá'. From the age of nine 'Abdu'l-Bahá shared in the sufferings of His father and spent 55 years as a prisoner and an exile. Bahá'u'lláh Himself gave 'Abdu'l-Bahá the title of the 'Master', along with the task of protecting the new Faith – which was now identified as 'Bahá'í' rather than 'Bábí' – from its enemies and helping its growth. The Master's special qualities were also recorded by Edward Granville Browne, who said of Him:

> Seldom have I seen one whose appearance impressed me more. A tall strongly-built man holding himself straight as an arrow, with white turban and raiment, long black locks reaching almost to the shoulder, broad powerful forehead indicating a strong intellect combined with an unswerving will, eyes keen as a hawk's, and strongly-marked but pleasing features . . . One more eloquent of speech, more ready of argument, more apt of illustration, more intimately acquainted with the sacred books of the Jews, the Christians, and the Muhammadans, could, I should think, scarcely be found even amongst the eloquent, ready, and subtle race to which he belongs . . . About the greatness of this man and his power no one who had seen him could entertain a doubt.[6]

'Abdu'l-Bahá was recognized as the model of how to live a Bahá'í life. Despite His exhibiting extraordinary spiritual perception, He did not have the station of a prophet or divine Messenger, rather He was understood to be the perfect human exemplar of Bahá'u'lláh's teachings. In His Will Bahá'u'lláh established 'Abdu'l-Bahá as the 'Centre of the Covenant' to whom all the Bahá'ís must turn for guidance. Those among Bahá'u'lláh's followers who rejected 'Abdu'l-Bahá's authority and actively worked to undermine it were expelled from the community as 'covenant-breakers'. 'Abdu'l-Bahá's pronouncements, interpretations and writings were given the same authority as Bahá'u'lláh's own. His exemplary moral character, His gentle and kindly 'Christ-like' manner, and His spiritual authority were of immense importance to the followers of the Movement as it emerged from the Middle East and established its roots further afield.

The American millionairess Phoebe Hearst, mother of William Randolph Hearst, had been moved deeply by what she had heard of the Bahá'í teachings and in 1898 decided to visit 'Abdu'l-Bahá, who was still a captive in the Ottoman prison-city of 'Akká. In a spirit of generosity she invited others to accompany her and put together a travelling party which included her devoted friend Mrs Thornburgh-Cropper from London and May Ellis Bolles, who returned, spiritually elevated by the journey, to establish the first European Bahá'í centre in Paris where her brother was studying architecture at the École des Beaux Arts.

Lady Blomfield herself has left a vivid description of the life-changing moment when in Paris she encountered her first Bahá'ís. She and her daughter Mary were attending a reception at the home of Madame Lucien Monod. Born in Milwaukee, Wisconsin, of Scottish origins, Charlotte Todd MacGregor was the second wife of Monod, a celebrated painter of landscapes and portraits who also specialized in lithography. He was a regular exhibitor at the Salon and at the National Society of Fine Arts. Madame Monod is listed in some Bahá'í sources as a member of the Paris Bahá'í community of that time. Her eldest son, Jacques, born in 1910, grew up to be a Nobel Prize winning molecular biologist.

Among the guests attending the reception at the Monod's was Bertha Herbert, an interior designer and follower of Bahá'u'lláh, later the first wife of the distinguished American believer Horace Holley, who managed the progressive Ashnur Gallery in Paris from 1912 to 1914.

Miss Herbert, according to Sara's description was 'a tall, graceful girl with shining dark eyes',[7] who caught the Blomfields' attention with the ebullient statement, 'If I *look* happy, it is because I *am* happy. I have found the desire of my heart!'[8] Bertha Herbert crossed the room and seated herself between Mary and Sara, who later described their conversation:

'I should like to tell you why I am so happy. May I?'

'Yes,' we answered.

'It is true! True!'

We fixed questioning eyes upon her glowing face.

'We have been taught to believe that a great Messenger would again be sent to the world: He would set forth to gather together all the peoples of good will in every race, nation, and religion on the earth. Now is the appointed time! He has come! He has come!'[9]

Lady Blomfield wrote that these words struck a chord to which her 'inner consciousness instantly responded'.[10] Having spent years hearing from Theosophists of the imminent appearance of the great World Teacher, she felt convinced that she was about to learn the truth that she had sought for so long. In the introduction to her book, *The Chosen Highway*, she explains:

> Great awe and intense exaltation possessed me with an overpowering force as I listened.
>
> Miss Herbert continued:
>
> 'The Bearer of the Message suffered much persecution, and left an uncomprehending world in 1892. But His Son is still a captive in the fortress prison of 'Akká in Palestine . . . You *are* interested?' she asked.
>
> 'Indeed, yes, how could we fail to be interested?'
>
> The news of the momentous event, long prayed for, steadfastly awaited in the 'Faith, which is the substance of things hoped for,' had come.
>
> How should we not be *interested*?'[11]

Bertha Herbert informed the Blomfields that there was a woman visiting Paris who had just returned from a pilgrimage to 'Akká where she had had the privilege of meeting 'Abdu'l-Bahá, the son of Bahá'u'lláh, the 'Bearer of the Message'. Bertha offered to make an appointment for them all to meet up and hear more of His teachings. As she rose to go, she realized that, in her excitement, she did not know how to get in contact with the Blomfields – or even their names. The appointment was made and Lady Blomfield and Mary were subsequently introduced to the first French Bahá'í, Hippolyte Dreyfus, and his English guest, Ethel Jenner Rosenberg.

Hippolyte Dreyfus, who at the time of meeting Lady Blomfield was 34 years old, was a brilliant lawyer and scholar and the first westerner of Jewish origins to embrace the Bahá'í teachings. He had taught himself Persian and Arabic to enable him to translate the writings of Bahá'u'lláh and 'Abdu'l-Bahá from their original languages. He was a warm-natured, cultured man, widely admired for his openness of spirit, lack of prejudice and inquisitive nature. May Bolles wrote of her first encounter with him:

> He was at the time an agnostic who believed that life and character are above dogma and creed. Although he had never believed in any force transcending nature, nor had he received intimations of the possible existence of a Supreme Being, yet after hearing of the advent of Bahá'u'lláh his inner susceptibilities became unfolded and in his subsequent study of the teachings and his visit to 'Abdu'l-Bahá in the prison

of 'Akká, he attained a supreme realization of the significance and importance of this message to the world.[12]

Dreyfus's parents, sister and brother-in-law all joined him in espousing the Bahá'í teachings.

Ethel Jenner Rosenberg enjoyed a close friendship with Dreyfus and his future wife, the American heiress Laura Clifford Barney. They were counterparts of each other, pioneer workers engaged in the same important task of spreading the Bahá'í teachings in their respective countries. Rosenberg, a painter of portrait miniatures, was descended from a distinguished family of artists from the city of Bath. She had also been taught – by her mother – to expect the coming of a great teacher from God and had learned of the Bahá'í teachings from Mary Virginia Thornburgh-Cropper, immediately responding to its message and endeavouring to teach herself Persian so as to gain a better understanding of the Bahá'í writings. Rosenberg's efficient nature and precise mind ensured her a pivotal role in the building of the first Bahá'í community in London and the British Isles. At the time of Lady Blomfield's arrival in Paris, Rosenberg had just returned from meeting 'Abdu'l-Bahá in the Holy Land and was assisting Laura Barney with the manuscript of her book *Some Answered Questions*, compiled from talks they had heard 'Abdu'l-Bahá give at His dinner table in 'Akká.

Lady Blomfield wrote in *The Chosen Highway* that Ethel Rosenberg and Hippolyte Dreyfus told her 'much concerning the sacred task of the Great One, Bahá'u'lláh'.[13] There could not have been two more suitable people to convey this message to her. Dreyfus was a brilliant intellectual who tempered his intelligence with gentle, compassionate humour and infinite patience. His grasp of the Bahá'í teachings among Europeans was second to none. Ethel Rosenberg, while perhaps not so personable as Dreyfus, shared with Lady Blomfield a strong foundation in the New Testament, was a stickler for accuracy, devoted to the Movement and more than at home with the British upper classes. Laura Barney also made a profound impact on Lady Blomfield, who would come to love and greatly admire her as an outstanding Bahá'í.

Sara and Mary Blomfield were deeply impressed by what they learned of the teachings of Bahá'u'lláh and the life of His son and successor. One can only imagine the extent of Lady Blomfield's joy at the recognition of the advent of the world-redeeming Messenger she had been so ardently seeking and the knowledge that 'Abdu'l-Bahá was alive in the world, fulfilling all the qualities she sought in a spiritual teacher. After so many years of search, her response was immediate and wholehearted.

Returning to London, Lady Blomfield took her daughters to meetings that the Bahá'ís arranged at the Higher Thought Centre in Kensington. It was situated at 10 Cheniston Gardens, off Wrights Lane, not far from the church where Lady Blomfield had been married some two decades before. The Centre promoted a set of metaphysical teachings based on spiritual healing. Mary Baker Eddy, who was healed by Higher Thought's founder Phineas P. Quimby, later drew inspiration from his system for her Christian Science Movement. One of Higher Thought's most prominent members was Judge Thomas Troward, a close friend of Archdeacon Wilberforce.

The Blomfields were impressed to see the eagerness with which Miss Rosenberg and Mrs Thornburgh-Cropper welcomed to their meetings anyone who was interested to investigate everything connected with what Lady Blomfield called 'the Event'. 'Under the guidance of these two devoted ladies,' she wrote, 'we met to make plans for spreading the glad tidings . . . Ever since these days, when this call to awakening was heard in Britain, it gradually became the foremost desire of my heart to spread the message which I had myself received . . .'[14]

Britain had begun to undergo profound changes in the eight years since Lady Blomfield had become a widow in 1899. The Victorian era and its preoccupations had come to an end with the deaths of the three most influential figures of the time – Gladstone in 1898, Queen Victoria in 1901 and Lord Salisbury in 1903. In its wake the Edwardian period, covering the reign of King Edward VII from 1901 to1910, was a turbulent time for politics. On one hand, the British Empire was at the peak of its powers, covering nearly a quarter of the earth's land surface. For the privileged such as the Blomfields, electric light was becoming easily available along with the use of telephones, typewriters, gramophones and automobiles. Yet poverty was still widespread and the Liberal governments of 1905 to 1915 sought to make profound changes. Free school meals were introduced along with old age pensions. Winston Churchill saw through the introduction of labour exchanges while the National Insurance Bill of 1911 made sure that compulsory insurance was paid to certain workers in times of illness and unemployment. The modern welfare state was being born yet arguments raged over who would foot the bill, with the burden falling on the incomes of the very rich. Lloyd George's 'People's Budget' met with strong opposition. The Liberals were attempting to face up to many issues that had long been delayed. Their political rivals, the Liberal Unionists, were frustrated as they regarded themselves as the natural rulers of the nation. Lady Blomfield's inborn sense of justice and innate compassion were stirred by such changes in society, especially in the case of increasing demands for women's suffrage, which now resonated even more for her with her knowledge of the Bahá'í teachings' stance on the equality of women and men.

The movement to give women the vote had enjoyed some progress since attempts had been made to amend the 1867 Reform Act. Women could now vote in local elections and for the synod of the Church of England. They stood as candidates for local councils, school boards and the poor law board. But, for many, it was not enough. The National Union of Women's Suffrage Societies, which in 1897 united a number of well-established organizations, made considerable headway in allowing women to vote for the national parliament. Its efforts, however, were soon overshadowed by the Pankhursts' Women's Social and Political Union, which increasingly advocated violence against property and politicians.

On 13 February 1907 a crowd of suffragettes stormed the Houses of Parliament. Dozens were arrested and many were injured in struggles with police. News reached London the following month of Finnish women becoming the first in the world to win seats in a national parliament. Early in 1908 Emmeline Pankhurst was sentenced to six weeks in Holloway prison for obstructing police around the Houses of Parliament. On 21 June several hundred thousand people marched on Hyde Park to call for the vote to be given to British women. Christabel Pankhurst spoke from the platform, along with Annie Kenney from Manchester, who drew attention to the number of men in the crowd who had come to voice support for their cause.

For many previously indisposed to the issue of universal suffrage, there was undeniably something inspiring about the passion with which the WSPU went about its work. 'I confess there was something in this society which, from the beginning, appealed to me,' wrote Charlotte Despard, the erstwhile romantic novelist who became one of England's most outspoken women's rights campaigners.

The youth of many of the members; the fact that they had come together in womanly frankness and love, not for political ends, not to further the candidature of party men for public place and power, but for social and political ends which would affect themselves and the world; the dashing courage of the little band, their selflessness, their quiet endurance of the results of their lawless action – these things attracted me. Sometimes I asked myself, 'Can this be the beginning? Is this indeed a part of that revolutionary movement for which all my life long I have been waiting?'[15]

Lady Blomfield was always a great sympathizer with the campaign for women's right to vote. In the early days she admired the self-sacrificing behaviour of suffragettes and even gave over a cottage on her Broadway estate for the use of those who were in desperate need to escape victimization in the capital.

'I am proud to remember that my mother did all in her power to help the women to escape from this injustice,' wrote Mary. 'They would arrive, exhausted, under assumed names and disguises. The village policeman would prowl round the house suspecting . . . but whether it was from a secret sympathy with them, or from a respectful affection for my mother, he never reported their refuge to the authorities.'[16]

Alongside their interest in the profound political changes that resonated with the principles they espoused, the members of the Bahá'í Movement endeavoured to build bonds of friendship and a sense of community. They were assisted in their efforts by a number of visitors from Persia who brought with them greater knowledge of Bahá'u'lláh's teachings and their practical application. Luṭfu'lláh Ḥakím, whose grandfather had been the first Jew to become a follower of Bahá'u'lláh, arrived in England in 1910 to study physiotherapy. Another young Persian studying in London, Yúḥanná Dávúd, whose marriage ceremony would be conducted in the city by 'Abdu'l-Bahá in 1911, also helped the Bahá'ís to increase their understanding of the teachings. Dávúd devoted much energy to a translation of 'Abdu'l-Bahá's treatise, now known as *The Secret of Divine Civilization*, which under the title *The Mysterious Forces of Civilization* was published in London in 1910. The amount of literature available to the Bahá'ís was increasing all the time. The growth of the American Bahá'í community to more than a thousand believers resulted in an upsurge in publications in English that the British Bahá'ís could purchase to educate themselves further. The Kitáb-i-Íqán – the seminal text in which Bahá'u'lláh explains

Bahá'í concepts of God and His Manifestations as well as the basic teaching of progressive revelation – had been available since 1904 in a translation by Ali Kuli Khan. In the same year a translation of the Hidden Words was made available. Other important works such as Ṭarázát, Tajallíyát and I<u>sh</u>ráqát were also published in English.

In 1908 the London publisher Kegan, Paul, Trench, Trubner and Company printed the eagerly-awaited volume *Some Answered Questions* – the only example of 'pilgrims' notes' of that period to become part of the canon of Bahá'í sacred literature. Laura Barney's notes were given particular weight since 'Abdu'l-Bahá Himself had read and modified them and given her permission to publish them. The 300-page book addressed 84 questions ranging from biblical prophecy to a diverse range of subjects such as healing, industrial strikes and astrology.

Lady Blomfield and her daughters, who all enjoyed the dramatic arts, must also have enjoyed receiving Laura Barney's publication *God's Heroes*, a poetic drama about the early history of the Báb and His followers. The sumptuously produced boxed volume sold for twelve shillings and sixpence and was the most expensive Bahá'í book available at that time.

One significant breakthrough for the British Bahá'ís was the publication in 1909 of *The Splendour of God*, an anthology of Bahá'í sacred writings in the popular 'Wisdom of the East' series, published by The Orient Library. The aim of these books was, in the words of its editors L. Cranmer-Byng and S.A. Kapadia, to 'be the ambassadors of good-will and understanding between East and West – the old world of Thought and the new of Action'.[17] Among the Advisory Committee of the Orient Library were Professor E.G. Browne of Cambridge University and Dr J. Estlin Carpenter of Oxford University, who would welcome 'Abdu'l-Bahá to his college within a few years of the publication. The book was compiled by British Bahá'í Eric Hammond, who in his introduction stated,

> Wherever Bahá'ís meet they meet on common ground. Throwing aside all the accumulated antagonisms of the past, they rejoice unreservedly in the glad communion of the present; of the day of their Lord . . . The spiritual unification of the race is the great aim of Bahaism. It does not propose the wholesale disintegration of creeds and cults, but, looking through these, discerns the shining of the light, behind, beyond. It recognizes the truth in each religious phase, but decries any attempt of any phase to pose as sole interpretation of the truth.[18]

Lady Blomfield and her daughters certainly continued, like most other Bahá'ís of that period, to attend church. The strength of Sara's connections with Archdeacon Wilberforce and the Reverend R.J. Campbell does not seem to have been in the least threatened by her recognition of Bahá'u'lláh. In fact, quite to the contrary, both churchmen would be of immeasurable assistance in efforts to promote the Bahá'í Movement in the months ahead. The regularity of Lady Blomfield's churchgoing was now enhanced by an increasing number of Bahá'í meetings. As a result of the extensive correspondence that Ethel Rosenberg maintained with believers in the United States, the London Bahá'ís tried whenever it was feasible to host their gatherings on the same dates as their American counterparts. Meetings would usually consist of the reading of prayers and scriptures and then sharing in refreshments. If a believer or visitor had recently been able to visit the Holy Land then a talk might be included, with the latest news of, or guidance from, 'Abdu'l-Bahá.

By mid-1908 the thoughts of the Bahá'ís turned often to the safety of their Master as the Ottoman Empire, under which He was still being held a prisoner, seethed with unrest. The Sultan of Turkey – Abdul Hamid II – was forced to call for parliamentary elections after widespread upheavals. The Young Turk revolutionary movement was demanding freedom of religion, education and the press. An uprising began within the Turkish army in Macedonia and the Young Turks aligned themselves immediately with Major Ahmed Niyazi and the revolt spread. In July 1908 the Sultan was forced to reintroduce a constitution for the Turkish Empire devised in 1876 when Sultan Abdul Hamid I had succumbed to liberal demands. As a result, all the Sultan's political and religious prisoners were freed. After 40 years in the fetid atmosphere of the penal colony of 'Akká, 'Abdu'l-Bahá and His family were released from captivity, giving the Bahá'ís enormous cause for celebration and relief.

'The Beloved Prisoner was free!' wrote Lady Blomfield. 'Free to obey the charge laid upon Him by Bahá'u'lláh to go forth into all the world to carry the message of the Renewal of Peace and Unity, of Joy and Service, and to call mankind to immediate action for averting the "Great Woe".'[19]

The unexpected release of 'Abdu'l-Bahá coincided with a major proclamation of the Bahá'í teachings in London at the Seventeenth Universal Peace Congress held in London at the Caxton Hall where Ethel Rosenberg was invited to present a paper on 'Bahaism: Its Ethical and Social Teachings'. Her address was published in the *London Post* and the Congress's *Transactions*.

A number of other capable women joined Lady Blomfield and her daughters in the Bahá'í Movement as the first decade of the 20th century drew to a close, although the extent to which these individuals met with each other and operated together as a 'community' is unclear. Alice Buckton, eight years younger than Lady Blomfield, shared with her a passionate desire to improve the lot of the poor in London and increase the provision of education for women. With this in mind, she visited the Pestalozzi-Fröebel-Haus in Berlin where she made a lasting friendship with its principal, Annet Schepel. Buckton persuaded Schepel to come to London to manage a similar house. This 'Sesame House for Home Life Training' at 43 Acacia Road, Highgate, was part of a network that spread advanced educational methods from Europe into Britain. Buckton was also a keen poet and playwright. In 1904 her nativity play *Eager Heart* had caught the nation's imagination and brought Buckton some degree of fame. *Eager Heart* was followed by *Kings of Babylon*, which was given a performance at the Haymarket Theatre in London with music by Gustav Holst, celebrated composer of *The Planets* orchestral suite.

Alice Buckton also shared an acquaintance with Lady Blomfield in Archdeacon Wilberforce. On 20 July 1907 Wilberforce had arranged a meeting with some of London's more open-minded thinkers – including Buckton and R.J. Campbell – to hear a presentation from a 23 year old Welshman, Wellesley Tudor Pole, about a sapphire blue bowl that his sister had discovered hidden in a well in Glastonbury the previous year. Katharine Tudor Pole and a group of young women friends had taken the bowl to Bristol where they set up a shrine to it at 16 Royal York Crescent, Clifton. They made the object the centrepiece of mystical services, open only to women, combining Christianity and Celtic rites. Because of Glastonbury's associations with the legends of Joseph of Arimathea, there was a suggestion that this bowl might be the Holy Grail used by Christ during the Last Supper, a notion that even Archdeacon Wilberforce was keen to support. During his research into the bowl, Tudor Pole was informed by a psychic that there were documents concerning its history buried beneath the ruins of Justinian's Palace in Constantinople. The quest would periodically occupy Tudor Pole with little result for the rest of his life. What he experienced in Constantinople in 1908, however, was his first encounter with Bahá'ís from which he brought home interesting stories and information that he began to circulate among his esoterically-minded friends in London and Bristol.

In 1910, following 'Abdu'l-Bahá's release, Alice Buckton and Annet Schepel made the journey to the Holy Land to meet Him. 'Our hearts have been made glad with the supremest joy', wrote a London correspondent to the *Bahai News* (later *Star of the West*), 'in hearing the verbal messages brought us by Miss Buckton and Miss Schepel who have spent a few weeks at Acca. Miss Buckton is a strong club woman here and her return has been the means of spreading the 'Glad-tidings' among many who otherwise would have waited long for this Message.'[20]

Another woman who first encountered the Bahá'í Movement in 1908 was Elizabeth Herrick. Herrick, who lodged above the Higher Thought Centre, was born near Birmingham in 1864. She had left school at 13 to earn a living when her father's business failed. She was both intellectually gifted and a good craftswoman and entered a milliner's shop as an apprentice. Within a few years she was running her own prosperous wholesale business in Aldersgate Street in the city of London. Despite her success, Herrick, along with so many women of her time, saw her first aim in life to seek out religious truth. Initially a dedicated Sunday School teacher in the Church of England, she transferred her allegiance to a Baptist Chapel to which she devoted an enormous amount of time. She also made many influential friends, including the suffragette Christabel Pankhurst. When Herrick's Baptist minister and his family left England to settle in America, she wound up her business and joined them, thinking it was the Will of God for her to serve Him in this way. But in America she discovered a new avenue of interest in the Christian Scientist teachings, which she felt brought her even closer to the truth she sought. A rift opened between Herrick and her Baptist companions and she returned to England to begin her career again, this time as an assistant in a London shop. Once again her enterprising talents saw her rise to managing her own millinery salon in one of the big department stores in Kensington High Street, under the name of Madame Corelli.

At the time of Herrick's first encounter with the Bahá'ís she was 44 years old, an attractive woman with a fair complexion and large blue eyes. On Sundays she packed away her millinery and gave over a large room to Bahá'í meetings. Here many of the believers met Tudor Pole for the first time and a succession of believers from the East passing through London. 'The Assembly is splendidly harmonious and growing healthily,'[21] wrote the London correspondent to *Bahai News* in 1910. Indeed it seemed that the Bahá'í Movement in London was in a very healthy state.

Hippolyte Dreyfus, en route for America, gave an inspiring talk at the regular Friday night meeting held at the Higher Thought Centre. Afternoon feasts enabled believers to attend from as far afield as Eastbourne on the Sussex coast, Surrey and Essex. A dental practitioner, Dr Edwin Fischer – later a pioneering Bahá'í in Germany – gave a series of lectures on Bahá'u'lláh's mystical masterpiece, the Seven Valleys. Prominent American Bahá'ís Isabella Brittingham and Roy Wilhelm sent literature and personal letters that kept the London believers informed of developments across the Atlantic. A Burmese Bahá'í, Khosroe Bohman, visited the city and shared his insights as well as stories of the growth of the movement throughout Asia.

For Britain as a whole, the Edwardian era was drawing to a close – the last age in British history to bear the name and hallmark of its monarch. King Edward VII enjoyed grand state occasions and pageantry more than had his mother Queen Victoria and did everything within his power to put the monarchy more in the public eye than it had been. In contrast to his reclusive predecessor, he was a constantly visible monarch, frequently pictured in the newspapers at race meetings and shooting parties. The King made pleasure the fashion of the day, his charm and social exploits resonating with a nation keen to break free of the stuffiness of the Victorian age.

Despite her growing preference for matters of the spirit, Lady Blomfield maintained her position in London's social circles. On Friday 4 March 1910 she and her daughters attended Court at Buckingham Palace at 10 o'clock in the evening. The invitation card called for 'Full Dress. Ladies with Feathers and Trains', thus emphasizing the King's obsession for court protocol, while exercising the most dubious double standards in his personal life. The King's sudden death at the age of 68 on 6 May 1910 was a genuine blow to the mood of the nation. *The Times* generously eulogized him as 'sagacious, popular, cautious, courageous and tactful'. The historian Sir Robert Ensor has written of the Edwardian period as 'one of calm and contentment, of pomp and luxury, of assured wealth and unchallenged order. Court splendours apart, it was none of those things. It was an era of growth and strain, of idealism and reaction, of swelling changes and of seething unrest. At home, politics had never been so bitter; and abroad the clouds were massing for Armageddon.'[22]

The death of the King did not go unnoticed by 'Abdu'l-Bahá who, speaking in Haifa on 10 May, referred to his passing.

The English king, with his pomp and grandeur, used to address the sun and say: 'Thou dost never disappear from my lands' . . .; but now he is buried under the earth. Some time ago the flags at the top of the masts proclaimed the day of his ascension to the throne; but today the flags are at half-mast, for he is dead. The flags and banners of the Beloved are ever waving at the top of the masts; they are never inverted; nay, rather they go on higher day by day; in fact, theirs is the sovereignty. Without fighting forces they conquer the cities; and without taking any tribute they bestow and give freely. The kings gain their victory through bloodshed and the taking of life; whereas the Beloved of God confer life and are victorious. The sovereignty of the friends is an eternal one.[23]

Since 1907, despite His continued confinement, 'Abdu'l-Bahá had been gradually transferring His family and their affairs to Haifa, across the bay from 'Akká, at the foot of Mount Carmel. Among the first acts He completed after His release was to lay to rest the remains of His father's forerunner, the Báb, in their permanent mausoleum on the slopes of the mountain, some 60 years after they had been rescued from a moat outside Tabríz where they had been unceremoniously discarded. Then, in October 1910, news reached the believers that 'Abdu'l-Bahá had left the Holy Land for the first time in 42 years and journeyed to Egypt. He had informed very few people of His departure. It was the first leg of a historic journey that would take Him to the great cities of Europe and North America on an unprecedented peace mission that had, up to that point, been prevented by His lifelong incarceration. The decade just beginning would bring with it the worst carnage the world had yet seen and few were aware of what lay ahead.

'Would His strength be sufficient for these journeys?' wrote Lady Blomfield. 'Our hearts sank as we thought of His captivity in the pestilential air of 'Akká. Entering it as a young man of twenty-four; leaving that death-dealing atmosphere at the age of sixty-four . . .'[24]

Lady Blomfield throughout this period lent her support to the Bahá'í meetings and activities. In her own personal teaching endeavours she managed to engage the sympathetic interest of her daughters' former governess, Beatrice Marion Platt, known as Patsy. Around the time that 'Abdu'l-Bahá was beginning His sojourn in Alexandria, a meeting was organized in collaboration with the Reverend R.J. Campbell at the City Temple at which a Persian student named Tammaddun'ul-Mulk, visiting

London from Paris, gave an address on the Bahá'í Movement. After the young man's address, the meeting was thrown open for questions. Considerable interest was expressed about the persecution of Persian Bahá'ís and Reverend Campbell asked a question about the future Houses of Justice ordained by Bahá'u'lláh, which Ethel Rosenberg duly answered. Campbell also remarked that he had received a very gracious message from 'Abdu'l-Bahá who took great interest in his work in London. Campbell added that there were many gaps in the recorded Christian teachings that needed to be filled. Such comments must have generated great excitement among the Bahá'ís gathered at the City Temple.

A month after the Master's arrival in Egypt, Wellesley Tudor Pole visited 'Abdu'l-Bahá at Ramleh, near Alexandria. He found 'Abdu'l-Bahá in good health. 'He spoke much of the work in America,' reported Tudor Pole, 'to which he undoubtedly is giving considerable thought. He also spoke a good deal about the work that is going forward in different European centres as well as in London, and he expects great things from England during the coming year.'[25]

On 28 December 1910, *The Christian Commonwealth* newspaper – on whose editorial board Reverend Campbell sat – published an article by Tudor Pole, entitled 'A Wonderful Movement in the East' along with a message from 'Abdu'l-Bahá. 'Not one Englishman in a thousand has heard of this religious and social uprising in the East, yet its adherents are estimated to number millions, and its power and influence are growing week by week!' reported the newspaper.[26] *The Christian Commonwealth* was first published in 1881 as an organ of the Baptist Spurgeon Movement but by the turn of the century was describing itself as the 'Organ of the Progressive Movement in Religion and Social Ethics'. Albert Dawson, a member of the City Temple, became its editor in 1901 and the newspaper did much to spread Reverend Campbell's thinking throughout the country and beyond. 'Abdu'l-Bahá had sent a letter and a selection of quotations from the writings of Bahá'u'lláh to the newspaper which it published. It later gave extraordinary publicity to His journeys to London in 1911 and 1913.

'Let me try to give you a word-picture of him,' wrote Tudor Pole of 'Abdu'l-Bahá in his article. 'He is sixty-five years of age, of medium height and of commanding presence; he has long silver-gray [*sic*] beard and hair, blue-grey eyes, a fine forehead, a wonderful carriage, and a sweet but powerful voice. He was dressed when I saw him, in cream white robes and a white Persian headdress. You feel at once that here is a master of men and a marvellous spiritual personality. He seemed to me to focus in a truly divine manner the spiritual ideal of the coming age. When one has come in contact with Abdu'l-Baha's power, or rather the power behind him, one has no doubt that this movement will vitally affect the religious and social evolution of the whole world.'[27]

Tudor Pole reported that the Bahá'í Movement was 'beginning to take a more serious hold on public attention . . . and that during the next few weeks a number of meetings are to be held in London, Bristol and in the North, which are likely to produce far-reaching results. A Bahai paper is to be read at the Universal Races Congress in London next July.'[28] His comments were not an exaggeration. Activities and interest were both increasing. One of the Movement's most distinguished teachers, Marion Jack, arrived in London, lodged with Elizabeth Herrick and participated in weekend meetings for inquirers. Interest in the teachings was beginning in the northwest of England as Edward T. Hall responded positively to Tudor Pole's article in *The Christian Commonwealth* and began to involve his own friends and family in Manchester.

On 31 December 1910 at the Higher Thought Centre, a meeting was called for Tudor Pole to speak of His visit to 'Abdu'l-Bahá. With some 80 people present, it was the largest Bahá'í meeting yet held in London and may have been the first time that many of the London Bahá'ís had properly encountered Tudor Pole, whose discovery and espousal of the Movement had largely been carried out in isolation from any developing Bahá'í community activities. The crowd heard how 1911 would be a year of very great importance and that London would be the focal point for great events. It was time, said Tudor Pole, for the establishment of an international residential and social club open to all comers without distinction of race, creed or gender. He urged his hearers to do all in their power to work together in harmony and joy for the great ideal of universal unity and peace. Lady Blomfield remarked that Tudor Pole 'explained to us the deeper significance of what afterwards became known as the Great Event of the Bahá'í Cause'.[29]

On 25 February Tudor Pole again met with the London believers and spoke to them of his visit to the Master. He expressed a view that was largely shared by the Bahá'ís of this time that they should remain in existing organizations and churches as far as possible, endeavouring to spiritualize them and to communicate the Bahá'í spirit to others within those groups. In addition, there was a flurry of excitement over the possibility that

'Abdu'l-Bahá Himself might come to London to address the First Races Congress to be held at the University of London in July. Lady Blomfield wrote:

> News came of His sojourn in Alexandria from one who said of Him: 'Seeing 'Abdu'l-Bahá and His most holy life has made me believe in Christ. Never before did I think His existence possible. Now I can understand.'
>
> As we thought upon all these marvels, we waited and wondered whether it was to be our privilege to see Him. Would it be given to us to hear the teaching of Bahá'u'lláh from 'Abdu'l-Bahá Himself?[30]

Tudor Pole was a great advocate of the power of thought and urged the Bahá'ís to mentally prepare themselves and others for a visit from the Master. 'The Bahais are uniting in prayer and concentration each evening at 9 o'clock, upon love and unity,' wrote Arthur Cuthbert to *Star of the West*, 'and that we may be fittingly prepared as a fertile soil to receive the seed which Abdul-Baha will sow in our midst; also other Societies of those who desire Abdul-Baha to come are joining us in this 9 o'clock concentration.'[31] Lady Blomfield acknowledged Tudor Pole's assistance in helping the believers to understand the realm of thought and it is likely that she too was engaging her spiritual friends and acquaintances in this preparation. Many of them would become key players in His imminent visit.

On Sunday 1 March 1911 Archdeacon Wilberforce spoke at St John's Westminster about the Bahá'í teachings and the next week answered many questions which he had received by post. Following on from Wilberforce's presentation, a Unitarian minister from Highgate asked for a Bahá'í to speak from his pulpit about the Movement. In August Tudor Pole spoke at a Theosophical Society summer school on 'Bahaism'. Also present was the campaigner Charlotte Despard, who spoke on 'Some Aspects of the Women's Movement'. By September the Women's Freedom League newspaper *The Vote* ran a three-part article by Mrs Despard entitled 'A Woman Apostle in Persia', recounting the life of the Bábí poetess Ṭáhirih.

'The believers in London are indeed steadfast and true,' wrote 'Abdu'l-Bahá at this time,

> they are resolute, they are constant in service; when put to the test, they do not falter, nor doth their fire abate with the passage of time; rather,

they are Bahá'ís. They are of heaven, they are filled with light, they are of God. Without any doubt they will become the cause of raising high the Word of God, and advancing the oneness of the world of man; of promoting the teachings of God, and spreading far and near the equality of every member of the human race.

It is easy to approach the Kingdom of Heaven, but hard to stand firm and staunch within it, for the tests are rigorous, and heavy to bear. But the English remain steadfast under all conditions, neither at the first sign of trouble do their footsteps slip. They are not changeable, playing fast and loose with some project and soon giving it up. They do not, for some trivial reason, fail in enthusiasm and zeal, their interest gone. No, in all they do, they are stable, rock-solid and staunch.

Although ye dwell in western lands, still, praise be to God, ye did hear His call from out the east and, even as Moses, did warm your hands at the fire kindled in the Asian Tree. Ye did find the true path, were lit like unto lamps, and have come into the Kingdom of God. And now have ye arisen, out of gratitude for these blessings, and ye are asking God's help for all the peoples of the earth, that their eyes as well may behold the splendours of the Abhá Realm, and their hearts, even as mirrors, reflect the bright rays of the Sun of Truth.

It is my hope that the breaths of the Holy Spirit will so be breathed into your hearts that your tongues will disclose the mysteries, and set forth and expound the inner meanings of the Holy Books; that the friends will become physicians, and will, through the potent medicine of the heavenly Teachings, heal the long-standing diseases that afflict the body of this world; that they will make the blind to see, the deaf to hear, the dead to come alive; that they will awaken those who are sound asleep.

Rest ye assured that the confirmations of the Holy Spirit will descend upon you, and that the armies of the Abhá Kingdom will grant you the victory.[32]

The First Races Congress, an initiative of the Union of Ethical Societies of America and England, was given support from more than 50 countries by, among others, some 30 presidents of parliaments and 40 colonial bishops. The Congress aimed to cultivate mutual knowledge and respect between the peoples of East and West. To complement the sessions of the Congress, which also attracted a number of Bahá'ís from the United States, the London believers held unity meetings and evening lectures – commencing on 18 July with 'Awakening of the East' by Mrs Jean Stannard, 'Personal Experiences of Bahá'ís' the following night by Sydney Sprague, 'Arab Life and Religion' by Mr S.H. Leeder on the 20 July, and finally, Alice Buckton speaking on 'The Relation of the Bahai Work and Teaching to Christianity' on 21 July. On 9 August *The Christian Commonwealth* reported that a well-attended public meeting hosted by the Bahá'í community was held at Caxton Hall, Westminster, to explain how the Bahá'í teachings related to other religious and social movements. The speakers included Hippolyte Dreyfus, Louise Waite, Tudor Pole and Jean Stannard. Their contributions, as quoted in the newspaper, give a fascinating insight into how the members of the Bahá'í Movement viewed themselves and their new-found Cause in relation to other religious congregations.

'Miss Alice Buckton dealt with the fear of disloyalty that many members of orthodox churches feel in regard to the movement,' wrote the article's author, Jessie Phillips. 'She herself was a member of an orthodox church, and she re-assured the audience that Bahaism did not mean the refusal of anything that had gone before. It was a pure and unadulterated universalism, such as had been the prophetic spirit of all religions.'[33]

'But although Baha Ulla was a spiritual focal point,' commented Tudor Pole, 'the light was radiating through us all. We were not to come out of our societies but to reillumine them.'[34]

Much to the disappointment of the Bahá'ís, 'Abdu'l-Bahá did not attend the Congress, announcing instead that he would not leave Egypt until the following month. It has been suggested that He may not have attended owing to the appearance there of Mírzá Yaḥyáy-i-Dawlatábádí, a follower of Bahá'u'lláh's treacherous half-brother Ṣubḥ-i-Azal. Later, 'Abdu'l-Bahá wrote that a 'Persian took the substance of the Epistles of His Holiness Bahá'u'lláh, entered that Congress, gave them forth in his own name and published them, whereas the wording was exactly that of His Holiness Bahá'u'lláh.'[35]

Tudor Pole and many other Bahá'ís deemed the Congress to be a great success, not least because it generated a lot of interest in their Movement. 'Ten years ago', he wrote, 'the holding of such a gathering would have been impracticable, and it has created a foundation from which to work for future congresses. The immediate tangible results of the discussions may not be very evident; the press reports have been inadequate; and many of the speakers could not be heard beyond the platform. Also it must be admitted that the stifling heat of the hall did not conduce toward clear thinking or debate. Nevertheless, this congress has triumphantly demonstrated the possibility of bringing together in friendly intercourse representatives of nearly every race and religion under the sun, and the spiritual and moral effects of this fact alone can never be undone.'[36]

Lady Blomfield, though, was disappointed that 'Abdu'l-Bahá had not managed to travel to the Congress as her overriding desire was now to meet Him in person.

'Should we travel to Egypt, or would He come to Europe?' she wondered:

If He were to come to London, where would be the roof to shelter Him? We who had quietly prepared our home in the hope that He might deign to sojourn there awhile, sent the invitation. Soon a telegram came:

"Abdu'l-Bahá arriving in London 8th September. Can Lady Blomfield receive Him?'

And now at last 'Abdu'l-Baha was coming into the western world, even to us in London![37]

Two weeks after the close of the First Races Congress, 'Abdu'l-Bahá set sail from Egypt for Europe. 'Forty years in captivity!' wrote Lady Blomfield.

Entering the prison city of 'Akká a young man of twenty-four years. Released at sixty-four!

Was ever so great a victory over material conditions? The opposing forces utterly routed!

The radiant spirit of 'Abdu'l-Bahá, undaunted and eager!

He began to make plans for journeying to the western world in accordance with His Father's sacred charge to bring to mankind the knowledge of the Divine Plan for establishing the 'Kingdom of God, where His Will shall be done on earth as it is in Heaven.' He was ready to go forth with that vital transforming spirit which would change a World, now wet with tears, into the delectable Paradise of Love and Justice.

Oh, the marvel of such a preparation for such a Mission! Was ever such unfaltering, unswerving determination?[38]

Within a month, the Blomfields' home at Cadogan Gardens would be overflowing with visitors from all over the world come to pay their respects to the Master.

CHAPTER FOUR

THE MASTER'S HOSTESS

Heaven has blessed this day.[1]
'Abdu'l-Bahá

'He arrived, and who shall picture Him?' wrote Lady Blomfield of 'Abdu'l-Bahá's arrival by steamer in the port of London.

> A silence as of love and awe overcame us, as we looked at Him; the gracious figure, clothed in a simple white garment, over which was a light-coloured Persian *'abá*; on His head He wore a low-crowned *táj* round which was folded a small, fine-linen turban of purest white; His hair and short beard were of that snowy whiteness which had once been black; His eyes were large, blue-grey with long, black lashes and well-marked eyebrows; His face was a beautiful oval with warm, ivory-coloured skin, a straight, finely-modelled nose, and firm, kind mouth. These are merely outside details by which an attempt is made to convey an idea of His arresting personality.[2]

Thus Sara Louisa, Lady Blomfield described her impressions of the man she had waited four years to meet. Now, the living exemplar of the teachings she had first encountered in Paris had arrived in London to proclaim His father's message after a lifetime of imprisonment.

'His figure was of such perfect symmetry,' she observed, 'and so full of dignity and grace, that the first impression was that of considerable height.'

> He seemed an incarnation of loving understanding, of compassion and power, of wisdom and authority, of strength, and of a buoyant youthfulness, which somehow defied the burden of His years; and such years!
>
> One saw, as in a clear vision, that He had so wrought all good and mercy that the inner grace of Him had grown greater than all outer

sign, and the radiance of this inner glory shone in every glance, and word, and movement as He came with hands outstretched.[3]

'Abdu'l-Bahá had left Egypt on 11 August 1911 bound for Marseilles in France. 'He arose,' wrote His grandson Shoghi Effendi on the centenary of the births of both his religion and his grandfather, 'with sublime courage, confidence and resolution to consecrate what little strength remained to Him, in the evening of His life, to a service of such heroic proportions that no parallel to it is to be found in the annals of the first Bahá'í century . . .'

> He, Who in His own words, had entered prison as a youth and left it an old man, Who never in His life had faced a public audience, had attended no school, had never moved in Western circles, and was unfamiliar with Western customs and language, had arisen not only to proclaim from pulpit and platform, in some of the chief capitals of Europe and in the leading cities of the North American continent, the distinctive verities enshrined in His Father's Faith, but to demonstrate as well the Divine origin of the Prophets gone before Him, and to disclose the nature of the tie binding them to that Faith.[4]

Having rested for a few days at Thonon-les-Bains on the shores of Lake Geneva in France, 'Abdu'l-Bahá continued His route across Europe to London, 'capital city of the largest and most cosmopolitan empire the world has ever known'.[5] Awaiting Him on His arrival at Victoria station, an automobile put at His disposal for His entire stay by Mrs Thornburgh-Cropper, who had visited 'Abdu'l-Bahá for the first time 13 years previously among the pioneering group of western pilgrims to 'Akká. How new and different the views through the window must have been to 'Abdu'l-Bahá as the car took Him through the streets of London, possibly around Sir Charles Barry's Houses of Parliament with their stately clock tower by Augustus Pugin, past elegant terraced houses, mansion blocks and well-stocked shop windows, through wide thoroughfares lined by tall, leafy plane trees, to aristocratic Belgravia and Lady Blomfield's home at Cadogan Gardens where a sizeable group of His followers had gathered to greet Him.

'Heaven has blessed this Day,' 'Abdu'l-Bahá told them. 'It was said that London should be a place for a great proclamation of the Faith. I was tired when I went on board the steamer, but when I reached London and beheld the faces of the friends my fatigue left me. Your great love refreshes me. I am very pleased with the English friends.'[6]

'Are you pleased to receive such a guest?' 'Abdu'l Bahá asked them.

'I think', wrote Lady Blomfield, 'our souls must have answered, for I am not conscious that anyone uttered an audible word.'[7]

For the 29 days of 'Abdu'l-Bahá's first visit to London the Blomfields gave up their apartment and stayed at the home of friends nearby. Each day they returned to Cadogan Gardens for meals and to help marshal the long procession of guests and callers.

'Oh, these pilgrims, these guests, these visitors!' Lady Blomfield exclaimed. 'Remembering those days, our ears are filled with the sound of their footsteps – as they came from every country in the world! Every day, all day long, a constant stream. An interminable procession!'[8]

Despite the, at times, exasperating task, nothing could have made Lady Blomfield happier as she hung upon the Master's every word, committed to heart every teaching and watched, enthralled, every action, every gesture. 'The intense elation and ecstasy of that time have somehow blurred the outward circumstances in my memory,' recalled Mary.

> I can see my beloved mother, eager, vital, full of sublime enthusiasm, never losing a word or a movement of the Master's, fully realizing that this visit was an event which belonged to the world . . . At this time she had the beauty of a mature soul. The moulding of her face was lovely and she remained beautiful to the last. Her facial expressions, ever changing, reflected the spiritual harmony within. Her dress, not fashionable in the ordinary sense, was distinctive and individual without being strange. She wore garments with long flowing lines which made her seem taller than her natural height, and she was as upright always in her outward stature as she was in her soul . . . I can see her, her eyes shining, welcoming the pilgrim guests to the presence of the Master.[9]

'Isn't it wonderful? Isn't it wonderful?' Lady Blomfield would exclaim, her hands emphasizing her words with an emphatic movement. Not only was 'Abdu'l-Bahá in their midst but believers and devoted friends had arrived from all over the world to bask in the warmth of His presence and to lend their assistance to His work. Lady Blomfield was particularly delighted that Hippolyte and Laura Dreyfus-Barney were on hand to assist in translation 'and were altogether helpful, courteous, and charming'.[10]

The day after 'Abdu'l-Bahá's arrival, Albert Dawson, the editor of *The Christian Commonwealth* newspaper, arrived to conduct an interview. Lady Blomfield was also pleased to introduce the Reverend R.J. Campbell, who was eager to meet the Master. 'It was interesting to find Abdul Bahá well acquainted with *The Christian Commonwealth*,' wrote Dawson. '"He is very pleased with what you write in your paper," were the first words, after a cordial welcome that came through the interpreter. "Some of the papers write things that he does not like and are not correct, but you write about what you know." The production of an early copy of our last issue caused some merriment. The fact that it was printed a day before the date it bore amused him, and when the paragraph, "A meeting between Abdul Baha and the editor of *The Christian Commonwealth* took place yesterday (Tuesday) afternoon. Some particulars will probably appear in our next issue," was translated to him, he said, with twinkling eye, he was very pleased with our "prophetic writing". Of the preceding passage, referring to the fundamental unity of all religious faith, Abdul Baha said, "You have written all that I can say to you. That shows that we are one in spirit."'[11]

As Reverend Campbell arrived, 'Abdu'l-Bahá rose from His chair to greet him with His arms extended. 'Standing face to face,' observed Dawson, 'linked hand in hand, in the centre of the room, these two spiritual leaders of world-wide fame – Eastern and Western, but essentially one in their outlook on life – formed an impressive picture that is stamped indelibly on the mind's eye of all who were privileged to be present.'[12]

'Here are two men,' 'Abdu'l-Bahá told Campbell, 'one living in the East and one in London, whose hearts were coming to meet one another long ago. Although in the material world we were far apart, we have always been near in the spiritual world. The real nearness is the nearness of the heart, not of the body . . . I have read your sermons and speeches,' said 'Abdu'l-Bahá.

'And I have read yours,' replied Campbell.

'That is a proof of unity,' laughed the Master. 'As I have read your sermons, you have to read mine!'

Reverend Campbell invited 'Abdu'l-Bahá to visit his church. 'I should like to come,' replied 'Abdu'l-Bahá. 'I know that the City Temple is a centre of progress in the religious world, and seeks to promote universal understanding.'[13] Lady Blomfield must have rejoiced that one of her dearest spiritual guides would now play host to the Master in a building in which she had spent many hours contemplating the nature of truth and the reality of religion.

Every day that 'Abdu'l-Bahá spent in London was filled with extraordinary events and encounters. Lady Blomfield listed the callers:

> Ministers and missionaries, Oriental scholars and occult students, practical men of affairs and mystics, Anglican-Catholics and Nonconformists, Theosophists and Hindus, Christian Scientists and doctors of medicine, Muslims, Buddhists, and Zoroastrians. There also called: politicians, Salvation Army soldiers, and other workers for human good, women suffragists, journalists, writers, poets, and healers, dressmakers and great ladies, artists and artisans, poor workless people and prosperous merchants, members of the dramatic and musical world, these all came; and none were too lowly, nor too great, to receive the sympathetic consideration of this holy Messenger, who was ever giving His life for others' good.[14]

Foremost among the visitors were 'Abdu'l-Bahá's own followers from London, among them Mary Virginia Thornburgh-Cropper, Ethel Rosenberg, Annie Gamble and Elizabeth Herrick. Other pilgrims who had sailed especially from North America included the lawyer Mountfort Mills, Charles Mason Remey, Claudia Coles, Julia Culver and the composer Louise Waite. In addition, a number of believers travelled from Persia. Several, descended from martyred heroes of the Cause, were given a very special, loving welcome from the Master. 'We were all overcome by the poignant emotions of such meetings,' wrote Lady Blomfield.[15]

Soon after His arrival in London, 'Abdu'l-Bahá also received a visit from Lady Blomfield's great mentor, Archdeacon Wilberforce.

'This was a remarkable interview,' she enthused. 'Our dear friend, the Archdeacon, sat on a low chair by the Master. 'Abdu'l-Bahá spoke to him in His beautiful Persian. He placed His hand on the head of the Archdeacon, talked long to him, and answered many questions. Evidently His words penetrated further than the outer ears, for both were deeply moved.'[16]

As the days passed, the apartment filled up with gifts of flowers and fruit brought by the visitors. 'Abdu'l-Bahá would stand at the dinner table, picking off bunches of grapes from their stems and offering them to the guests.

'He talked to us of the joy of freedom,' recalled Lady Blomfield, 'of how grateful we should be for the privilege of dwelling in safety, under just laws, in a healthy city, with a temperate climate, and brilliant light – "there was much darkness in the prison fortress of 'Akká!"'

After His first dinner with us He said: 'The food was delicious and the fruit and flowers were lovely, but would that we could share some of the courses with those poor and hungry people who have not even one.'

What a lesson to the guests present!

We at once agreed that one substantial, plentiful dish, with salad, cheese, biscuits, sweetmeats, fruits, and flowers on the table, preceded by soup and followed by coffee or tea, should be quite sufficient for any dinner. This arrangement would greatly simplify life, both as to cookery and service, and would undeniably be more in accordance with the ideals of Christianity than numerous dishes unnecessary and costly.[17]

'Abdu'l-Bahá's days at 97 Cadogan Gardens took on a routine. He rose early, chanted prayers, took tea, wrote or dictated letters. He then began to receive visitors, some of whom arrived just after dawn and waited on the doorstep. Early in His visit Lady Blomfield received a telegram from the Bahá'í Assembly in Tehran: 'That the holy feet of 'Abdu'l-Bahá have crossed your threshold receive our felicitations. Blessed are ye.'[18]

Lady Blomfield enlisted the assistance of her daughters, their former governess Beatrice Platt, Ethel Rosenberg and Dr Luṭfu'lláh Ḥakím to coordinate all the activity and make appointments as well as to take notes of His addresses. Every moment spent in the presence of 'Abdu'l-Bahá was for Lady Blomfield a lesson in how to live.

'This station of Servitude – how great! How marvellous!' she enthused.

We very gradually began to have a tiny glimmer of comprehension of what Service could mean, as the life of this Servant unfolded itself daily before our eyes.

The Master's custom was to receive the visitors by twos or by threes, or individually, during the early hours of the morning. Then, about nine o'clock, He would come into the dining-room whilst we were at breakfast to greet us. 'Are you well? Did you sleep well?'

We tried to prevail upon Him to take some breakfast with us (we were always concerned that He ate so very little). At last one day He said He would like a little soup – then we had it brought in every morning. He smiled and said: 'To please you I will take it. Thank you, you are very kind.' Then to the servitor who offered it to Him: 'I give too great trouble,' He said.

In a few minutes He would go to His room, where He would resume the chanting of prayers and dictating of Tablets in reply to the vast number of letters which incessantly arrived.

Visitors having gradually gathered in the drawing-room (about ten o'clock), 'Abdu'l-Bahá would come to us, pausing just inside the door, smiling round at the guests with a look of joyous sympathy which seemed to enfold each and all who were present; they rose simultaneously, as though the kingship of this Messenger were recognized by an inner perception.

'How are you? My hope is that you are well. Are you happy?'

Speaking so to us, He would pass through our midst to His usual chair. Then He would talk rather *with* us than *to* us; so did He reply to unspoken questions, causing wonderment in those who were waiting to ask them – weaving the whole into a beautiful address, in the atmosphere of which all problems and pain and care and doubt and sorrow would melt away, leaving only happiness and peace.

The power of Divine Love we felt to be incarnated in Him, Whom we called 'the Master'.

Now came the hour when He would receive those who had asked for appointments for private audiences. Careful timetables were made and strictly adhered to, for very numerous were these applicants for so unique an experience, how unique, only those knew when in the presence of the Master, and we could partly divine, as we saw the look on their faces as they emerged – a look as though blended of awe, of marvelling, and of a certain calm joy. Sometimes we were conscious of reluctance in them to come forth into the outer world, as though they would hold fast to their beatitude, lest the return to things of earth should wrest it from them.[19]

One such caller was the writer Constance Elizabeth Maud, who was deeply impressed by the Master. In her book *Sparks among the Stubble*, Maud recalled how a

look of wonderful love, joy, and understanding came into his profoundly far-seeing old eyes, when he recognised in his visitor a pure heart, a soul of light; and it was as though he had found a brother or sister, someone near of kin. But when he spoke of the discord, misery, and sorrow of the world, his eyes took on an expression of unfathomable sadness, and pictures rose up before one of the ghastly scenes of death and torture those same eyes must have been forced to witness.[20]

On Wednesday 6 September, around 50 or 60 people gathered at the home of Mrs Thornburgh-Cropper. One of her friends, a Mrs Drakoules, who had founded the Humanitarian League more than 20 years before, presented 'Abdu'l-Bahá with a leaflet about its work. When He discovered its aims were kindness, He made this the theme of His talk.

'You are all one family,' He said, 'you have grown out of one root.'

Each of you is like a branch, a flower, a fruit. You must look on no one as a stranger. You should try to show the greatest love to all men and to every creature. I have come to you as to my own people – brothers and sisters, sons and daughters. My bond is with all mankind; so should yours be. Try to follow the teachings of Baha'o'llah, then each one will shine like a star. Since the time of Adam there has been no other teaching; until the end of time there will be no other.[21]

Two days later Lady Blomfield hosted a morning meeting at her home. Hippolyte Dreyfus presented one Madame Olga de Nèvosky, who had been actively promoting the Bahá'í teachings in Paris. Mrs Drakoules then showed 'Abdu'l-Bahá a photograph of her husband, a leading Greek reformer. While he objected to the word 'leader', 'Abdu'l-Bahá told Mrs Drakoules that He could discern the goodness and spirituality of her husband from the photograph.

'I can see Him', wrote Mary Blomfield, '. . . pacing the room where He received the pilgrims at home. I can repicture His kingly walk which swung the folds of His garments gently from side to side. I can see the descriptive gestures of His hands – so eloquent that the meaning of His words often reached His audience before the translation was given.'[22]

Later that day 'Abdu'l-Bahá visited the Passmore Edwards Settlement Centre in Tavistock Place which was the site for a number of interesting educational developments and innovations. It housed the first fully equipped classrooms for children with disabilities living in the community. The school, which had opened in 1898, provided course work, physical therapy and meals. The second crucial innovation was the development of a play centre for children. By 1902 more than 1,200 children were attending sessions. The Centre provided a place of warmth and safety and the opportunity for children to develop their play and comradeship in a situation where bullying could be contained. Alice Buckton was intimately involved with the work of the Centre and the following day she invited 'Abdu'l-Bahá to visit her and Annet Schepel at their home in Byfleet, Surrey, some 20 miles from London, where a number of working women of the Passmore Edwards Settlement were spending a holiday.

'We gathered round him in a circle, and he made us sit beside him in the window seat,' wrote one of the women.

> One of the members, who was ill, had a specially beautiful greeting from him. 'Abdu'l-Bahá began by saying, as he seated himself: 'Are you happy?' and our faces must have shown him that we were. He then said: 'I love you all, you are the children of the Kingdom, and you are accepted of God. Though you may be poor here, you are rich in the treasures of the Kingdom. I am the Servant of the poor. Remember how His Holiness Jesus said: "Blessed are the poor!" If all the queens of the earth were gathered here, I could not be more glad!'[23]

Later He walked through the village where He talked with children, mothers whose babies were unwell and unemployed men. Returning to the house, He remarked how the garden reminded Him of a Persian garden. He presented everyone with a purple heartsease from the garden as He left for London.

Sunday 10 September was a historic day in the history of the Bahá'í Faith and opened a new chapter in the ministry of 'Abdu'l-Bahá. Accepting Reverend Campbell's invitation, 'Abdu'l-Bahá attended the evening service at the City Temple at Holborn Circus. The visit had been kept secret as attendance at the service was usually very large, numbering around two thousand. The service proceeded as usual until the hymn that immediately preceded the sermon. While this was being sung, to the surprise of the congregation 'Abdu'l-Bahá, in full Persian robes and turban, arrived and ascended the stairs to the pulpit. When the hymn was finished, Reverend Campbell sat the Master in his own chair and then said to the congregation, 'I propose to shorten my sermon this evening, because we have a visitor in the pulpit whose presence is somewhat significant of the spiritual drawing-together of East and West, as well as of the material drawing-together which has long been going on, and I think you would like to hear his voice, if only for a few moments.'[24]

Campbell proceeded to deliver his sermon on 'The Use of the Will in Prayer'. He then said:

This evening we have in the pulpit of the City Temple the leader of one of the most remarkable religious movements of this or any age, a movement which includes, I understand, at least three million souls. The Bahai movement, as it is called, in Hither Asia rose on that soil just as spontaneously as Christianity rose in the middle territories adjoining, and that faith – which, by the way, is very closely akin to, I think I might say identical with, the spiritual purpose of Christianity – that movement stands for the spiritual unity of mankind; it stands for universal peace among the nations. These are good things, and the man who teaches them and commends them to three millions of followers must be a good man as well as a great. Abdul Baha is on a visit to this country – a private visit – but he wished to see the City Temple; and I think I am right in saying for the first time in his life he has consented to lift up his voice in public. He does not address public meetings, he does not preach sermons; he is just a religious teacher. He spent forty years in prison for his faith, and from his prison directed the efforts of his followers. There is not much in the way of organization, but simple trust in the Spirit of God. We, as followers of the Lord Jesus Christ, who is to us and always will be the Light of the World, view with sympathy and respect every movement of the Spirit of God in the experience of mankind, and therefore we give greeting to Abdul Baha – I do not know whether I could say in the name of the whole Christian community – that may be too much – but I think in the name of all who share the spirit of our Master, and are trying to live their lives in that spirit. Abdul Baha, I think, intends to say a word of two in response to this greeting that I address to him in your name.[25]

'Abdu'l-Bahá moved to the front of the pulpit in full view of thousands of people. For the first time in His life He was to address a public gathering.

'At first the people were attentive,' observed Charles Mason Remey, 'then just a bit restless before all seemed to catch the spirit of what he was saying. Hardly any understood Persian. Then a stillness and a quietness fell over the assemblage and as Abdul-Baha raised his hands in prayer and benediction, we were all conscious of the Omnipresent spirit of God, for every soul seemed to vibrate in unison with the soul of Abdul-Baha, who is God's servant here upon earth today.'[26]

'. . . the tense thrill vibrating throughout the whole building was most strongly marked,' reported Wellesley Tudor Pole.[27] For eight minutes 'Abdu'l-Bahá spoke in Persian, His voice rising and falling, His hands animated. At the end, He put His hands together as if in prayer while Tudor Pole read the translation:

O noble friends; seekers after God! Praise be to God! Today the light of Truth is shining upon the world in its abundance; the breezes of the heavenly garden are blowing throughout all regions; the call of the Kingdom is heard in all lands, and the breath of the Holy Spirit is felt in all hearts that are faithful. The Spirit of God is giving eternal life. In this wonderful age the East is enlightened, the West is fragrant, and everywhere the soul inhales the holy perfume. The sea of the unity of mankind is lifting up its waves with joy, for there is real communication between the hearts and minds of men. The banner of the Holy Spirit is uplifted, and men see it, and are assured with the knowledge that this is a new day.

This is a new cycle of human power. All the horizons of the world are luminous, and the world will become indeed as a garden and a paradise. It is the hour of unity of the sons of men and of the drawing together of all races and all classes. You are loosed from ancient superstitions which have kept men ignorant, destroying the foundation of true humanity.

The gift of God to this enlightened age is the knowledge of the oneness of mankind and of the fundamental oneness of religion. War shall cease between nations, and by the will of God the Most Great Peace shall come; the world will be seen as a new world, and all men will live as brothers.

In the days of old an instinct for warfare was developed in the struggle with wild animals; this is no longer necessary; nay, rather, co-operation and mutual understanding are seen to produce the greatest welfare of mankind. Enmity is now the result of prejudice only.

In the *Hidden Words* Bahá'u'lláh says, 'Justice is to be loved above all.' Praise be to God, in this country the standard of justice has been raised; a great effort is being made to give all souls an equal and a true place. This is the desire of all noble natures; this is today the teaching for the East and for the West; therefore the East and the West will understand each other and reverence each other, and embrace like long-parted lovers who have found each other.

There is one God; mankind is one; the foundations of religion are one. Let us worship Him, and give praise for all His great Prophets and Messengers who have manifested His brightness and glory.

The blessing of the Eternal One be with you in all its richness, that each soul according to his measure may take freely of Him. Amen.[28]

The Reverend R.J. Campbell then arose to speak again.

I think you will probably agree with me that this is an interesting as well as a unique occasion, and that what we have been listening to, in that brief message uttered by a spiritual teacher from the East, is in spirit the same message that you are listening to on the authority of Jesus week by week. It is a great time, a time of the drawing-together of all people. East and West join hands in the City Temple to-night.[29]

'It seemed to us', recalled Tudor Pole, 'as if a new page in history was being turned over and as if a new religious and spiritual epoch was being outwardly launched upon an expectant world before our very eyes.'[30]

After the service, in the vestry, Campbell invited 'Abdu'l-Bahá to inscribe a few sentences in the pulpit Bible. 'Abdu'l-Bahá expressed his delight at the reverent spirit of the gathering and wrote, 'This book is the Holy Book of God, of celestial inspiration. It is the Bible of Salvation, the noble Gospel. It is the mystery of the Kingdom and its light. It is the Divine Bounty, the sign of the guidance of God.' As He left the City Temple, 'Abdu'l-Bahá said in English, 'I am very happy!'[31] A crowd gathered about the door, extending their hands towards Him. 'Abdu'l-Bahá remarked that Bahá'u'lláh had told Him many years before that He would proclaim the Bahá'í Cause in this part of the world.

'With that discourse', writes the distinguished Bahá'í historian Hasan M. Balyuzi, "Abdu'l-Bahá opened a phase of His ministry which must, in every aspect, remain unrivalled. In His sixty-eighth year, in precarious health, He stepped into a crowded, demanding arena to proclaim to the Christian West the essential verities of the Faith of His Father.'[32]

The following Sunday, after another full week of visits and visitors, 'Abdu'l-Bahá offered His message to a large public audience once again in the church of St John the Divine, Smith Square, Westminster. The long cherished hope of Lady Blomfield to hear the Master speak in her own favoured church, led with such fearless independence by her friend Archdeacon Wilberforce, was at last to become a reality. Eighteen months previously Wilberforce had sent a message to 'Abdu'l-Bahá saying, 'We are all one there, behind the veil.' 'Abdu'l-Bahá replied, 'Tell him the veil is very thin, and it will vanish quite.'[33]

'All who were present', reported *The Christian Commonwealth*, '. . . could not fail to realise that the veil was vanishing. Archdeacon Wilberforce's beautiful intercessory service was a means to that end . . . Then Dr. Wilberforce told of the teacher – "Master" he called him – who had come to London to emphasise unity, and who was present that evening at St. John's to proclaim the meaning of it. "Whatever our views," the Archdeacon said, "we shall, I am sure, unite in welcoming a man who has been for forty years a prisoner for the cause of brotherhood and love."'[34]

The congregation waited expectantly while the Archdeacon left the church. He returned a brief moment later, having removed his white surplice, with 'Abdu'l-Bahá, the two distinguished figures walking down the aisle. Lady Blomfield observed, 'The beloved Messenger from the East passed through the midst of the crowded church, hand in hand with Archdeacon Wilberforce, up to the chancel, where they stood together, two men of God, one from the East and one from the West, united in their loving service to the "Ruler of the throne and of the dust".'[35]

Controversially, the Archdeacon sat 'Abdu'l-Bahá in the Bishop's chair on the chancel steps in front of the altar. He then introduced his guest to the congregation, talking of His imprisonment, His suffering and His faith.

'Rudyard Kipling has said, "East is East and West is West and they twain never shall meet",' reflected Wilberforce, 'but I say they can and do meet on the common ground of Love and here is the proof.'[36]

Then 'Abdu'l-Bahá rose for the second time in one week to address a Christian congregation. Once again the singing intonation of His voice and His decisive hand movements gave many the impression that they had understood His talk, despite it being in Persian.

"Abdu'l-Bahá's beautiful voice filled the church with its powerful vibrations,' wrote Lady Blomfield. '. . . This was indeed a soul-stirring event, far-reaching in its influence!'[37] Having finished His address, 'Abdu'l-Bahá sat again as the Archdeacon, standing beside Him, read the translation of 'Abdu'l-Bahá's talk himself, saying 'I would I could reproduce the musical inflections of the Master's voice':[38]

O noble Friends! O Seekers for the Kingdom of God! Man all over the world is seeking for God. All that exists is God; but the Reality of Divinity is holy above all understanding.

The pictures of Divinity that come to our mind are the product of our fancy; they exist in the realm of our imagination. They are not adequate to the Truth; truth in its essence cannot be put into words.

Divinity cannot be comprehend*ed* because it is comprehend*ing*.

Man, who has also a real existence, is comprehended by God; therefore, the Divinity which man can understand is partial; it is not complete. Divinity is actual Truth and real existence, and not any representation of it. Divinity itself contains All, and is not contained.

Although the mineral, vegetable, animal and man all have actual being, yet the mineral has no knowledge of the vegetable. It cannot apprehend it. It cannot imagine nor understand it.

It is the same with the vegetable. Any progress it may make, however highly it may become developed, it will never apprehend the animal, nor understand it. It is, so to speak, without news of it. It has no ears, no sight, no understanding.

It is the same with the animal. However much it may progress in its *own* kingdom, however refined its feelings may become, it will have no real notion of the world of man or of his special intellectual faculties.

The animal cannot understand the roundness of the earth, nor its motion in space, nor the central position of the sun, nor can it imagine such a thing as the all-pervading ether.

Although the mineral, vegetable, animal and man himself are actual beings, the difference between their kingdoms prevents members of the lower degree from comprehending the essence and nature of those of the superior degree. This being so, how can the temporal and phenomenal comprehend the Lord of Hosts?

It is clear that this is impossible!

But the Essence of Divinity, the Sun of Truth, shines forth upon all horizons and is spreading its rays upon all things. Each creature is the recipient of some portion of that power, and man, who contains the perfection of the mineral, the vegetable and animal, as well as his own distinctive qualities, has become the noblest of created beings. It stands written that he is made in the Image of God. Mysteries that were hidden he discovers; and secrets that were concealed he brings into the light. By Science and by Art he brings hidden powers into the region of the visible world. Man perceives the hidden law in created things and co-operates with it.

Lastly the perfect man, the Prophet, is one who is transfigured, one who has the purity and clearness of a perfect mirror – one who reflects the Sun of Truth. Of such a one – of such a Prophet and Messenger – we can say that the Light of Divinity with the heavenly Perfections dwells in him.

If we claim that the sun is seen in the mirror, we do not mean that the sun itself has descended from the holy heights of his heaven and entered into the mirror! This is impossible. The Divine Nature is seen in the Manifestations and its Light and Splendour are visible in extreme glory.

Therefore, men have always been taught and led by the Prophets of God. The Prophets of God are the Mediators of God. All the Prophets and Messengers have come from One Holy Spirit and bear the Message of God, fitted to the age in which they appear. The One Light is in them and they are One with each other. But the Eternal does not become phenomenal; neither can the phenomenal become Eternal.

Saint Paul, the great Apostle, said: 'We all, with open face beholding as in a mirror the glory of God, are changed into the same image from glory to glory, as by the Spirit of the Lord.'

O God the Forgiver! O Heavenly Educator! This assembly is adorned with the mention of thy holy Name. Thy children turn their face towards thy Kingdom, hearts are made happy and souls are comforted.

Merciful God! Cause us to repent of our shortcomings! Accept us in thy heavenly Kingdom and give unto us an abode where there shall be no error. Give us peace; give us knowledge, and open unto us the gates of thy heaven.

Thou art the Giver of all! Thou art the Forgiver! Thou art the Merciful! Amen.[39]

The congregation was profoundly moved. Archdeacon Wilberforce invited 'Abdu'l-Bahá to pronounce the blessing, and following the minister's example, the congregation knelt to receive the benediction while the Master stood with extended arms, His voice rising and falling. Mary Blomfield recalled how it was 'wonderful to see Him standing on the chancel steps of a Christian Church, and to hear Him interpret the living eternal Christ to a Christian congregation. His white head-dress crowned His silver hair,

His long sand-coloured robe falling in long folds accentuated His majestic bearing. He seemed to combine the hierarchy of the Prophets as He called men to worship the everlasting Dynasty of God's Messengers to Man, and to open their eyes to the Sun of Truth shining resplendent for those who had vision, in this chaotic age.'[40]

As 'Abdu'l-Bahá and the Archdeacon processed down the aisle to the vestry, hand in hand, the hymn 'O God our help in ages past' was sung by the standing congregation. 'We do not speak his language,' Wilberforce was heard to say, 'nor he ours, but for the angels of God there is no Babel.'[41] Outside St John's, as they left, 'Abdu'l-Bahá caught sight of members of the Salvation Army holding their meeting. He was deeply impressed at the gathering of men, women and children praying and singing on the street corner.

Earlier in the day of Sunday 17 September 'Abdu'l-Bahá had visited the Indian Religious Centre of Keshun Niketon in Hampstead. Lady Blomfield recalled that the Master seemed always pleased to be with Indian friends. A deputation from the Bramo-Somaj Society arrived, inviting the Master to address them. The Society traced its origins back to the start of the 19th century and a Bengali Hindu by the name of Raja Ram Mohan Roy who had challenged the idolatry of Hinduism and pronounced that throughout history, saints and prophets had appeared in every land and that to claim finality and exclusivity of any revelation was misguided. Roy studied the Bible in Hebrew and, in his mid-30s, wrote a book called *Precepts of Jesus: The Guide to Happiness and Peace in Life*. He also studied the Qur'án in Arabic as well as his own Hindu scriptures and in 1828 founded the first theistic church in India. 'Abdu'l-Bahá was pleased with the enlightened spirit of the Bramo-Somaj movement and His other Indian visitors.

> He would speak to them of the 'Spiritual Sun of Truth, which has always shown from the eastern horizon, and again of the great Spiritual Teachers, who have all arisen in the East'. The Message of Krishna was a Message of Love; every true Prophet of God has given the same message, that of Love. We must all strive to spread this Love among the sons of mankind.
>
> 'It would be well for the Western peoples to turn to the East for illumination,' He would say again and again.
>
> 'The East and the West should unite to give to each other what is lacking in each. This exchange of gifts would form a true civilization,

where spiritual ideals would be translated into action in the material world.'[42]

'The picture of the Persian pilgrims rises in my memory,' wrote Mary Blomfield, 'so many and so patient that they would wait for hours for a glimpse of the Master, some of them sitting on the stairs, humbly, with folded hands, and heads bent reverently in meditation, sons of martyrs, or themselves martyrs to be, men who had travelled from the distant East to see 'Abdu'l-Bahá directly the glad news of His freedom had reached them.'[43] In addition to the Persian believers who had travelled so far to be with 'Abdu'l-Bahá, others from His homeland sought His company. One, Jalálu'd-Dawlih, who was responsible for the torture and murder of two Bahá'ís in Persia, begged to be received by 'Abdu'l-Bahá, imploring His forgiveness for his crimes. Members of the Persian Legation also arrived along with a Persian nobleman, Dúst-Muḥammad Khán (Mu'ayyiru'l-Mamálik) who was a constant visitor and sometimes accompanied the Master to meetings.

'Certain of those who thronged to see the Master, having travelled from far countries,' wrote Lady Blomfield, 'were naturally anxious to spend every possible moment with Him, Whose deeds and words appealed to them as ever-filled with grace and love. Therefore it came about that day after day, whilst the Master was teaching, the luncheon gong would sound, and those who remained would be invited to sit at food with Him. We grew to expect that there would be nineteen guests at table, so often did this number recur.'[44] The chaos in the kitchen can be imagined as Beatrice Platt coordinated the meals, attempting to manage 'Abdu'l-Bahá's own cook Khusraw alongside Lady Blomfield's overwhelmed staff.

'Like all popular prophets and preachers,' observed Constance Maud, 'he suffered not a little from his disciples; the incense-burners and daily adorers bored and wearied him to the core. I have often noted the happy smile of frank relief from strain with which he would turn to welcome some young thing, a wide-eyed child with fixed gaze of curiosity upon his white turban, or one of the hostess' young daughters who, sitting at his feet, would mischievously imitate some of the "yearners" till he laughed like a schoolboy.'[45] At times, 'Abdu'l-Bahá became annoyed by extravagant worship and strongly reproved individuals who acclaimed Him as a reincarnation of Christ. One woman would sit at his feet and gaze up with adoration while He was speaking. One day, He glanced casually at her during His address. At the end she asked Him what He had been saying at that particular moment, to which He replied that He had been describing how the vegetable world arose out of the mineral. She, expecting a more flattering remark, received the gentle rebuke humbly and modified her ostentatious piety. Lady Blomfield was greatly amused by this incident although she kept it between herself and her daughters.

'Abdu'l-Bahá's affection for the Blomfields grew with every passing day of His sojourn in their home. Once, while they were out driving, Mrs Thornburgh-Cropper asked Him if He was not missing His wife and children. 'Abdu'l-Bahá told the ladies that they were as beloved by Him as His own daughters. 'Our hearts thrilled with joy and awe as He spoke,' wrote Lady Blomfield. 'How can we serve to be even a little worthy of so high an honour?'[46]

Each of them was given a Persian name by the Master: Sitárih, meaning 'star' for Lady Blomfield, a name she from then on used, sometimes in its more common form, Esther; Maryam for Mrs Thornburgh-Cropper; Parvine for Mary; and Nouri for Rose Ellinor. Lady Blomfield's neighbour Gabrielle Enthoven was known to the Master as Hamsá'ih, meaning precisely 'neighbour'. Lady Blomfield's son Frank was also given a Persian name, now lost to us.

Another incident demonstrating 'Abdu'l-Bahá's consideration for all also touched Sitárih. A workman who had left his bag of tools in the hallway of the block was welcomed with immense kindness by 'Abdu'l-Bahá. Sadly the man said: 'I don't know much about religious things, as I have no time for anything but my work.'

'That is well. Very well,' replied the Master. 'A day's work done in the spirit of service is in itself an act of worship. Such work is a prayer unto God.'

Sitárih described how 'the man's face cleared from its shadow of doubt and hesitation, and he went out from the Master's presence happy and strengthened, as though a weighty burden had been taken away'.[47]

Early on during His first visit, many attempts were made to photograph 'Abdu'l-Bahá. Press photographers camped out in Cadogan Gardens, waiting for an opportunity to get a picture. Sitárih was disturbed by their presence and protested to one of them.

'Do you think it very courteous to insist on photographing a guest from a distant country against His will?'

'No, Madam,' the photographer replied, 'but if others succeed and I fail, my chief will think me a fool.'

'When I told this to 'Abdu'l-Bahá,' Sitárih reported,

He laughed heartily and said: 'If the photographs must be, it would be better to have good ones. Those in that paper are very bad indeed.'

Thereupon he consented with His unfailing, smiling grace, to be photographed. 'To please the friends,' he said. 'But to have a picture of oneself is to emphasize the personality, which is merely the lamp, and is quite unimportant. The light burning within the lamp has the only real significance.'

He signed a photograph, writing His name on the white part of his turban. 'My name is my crown,' said 'Abdu'l-Bahá – 'Servant of God, the Most Glorious.'[48]

'Those who have sought interviews with him have been of all ranks and classes,' wrote Ethel Rosenberg to Albert Windust, editor of *Star of the West*,

amongst them many clergy of the Anglican church and other denominations. It is indeed a most marvellous privilege to have him in our midst and I hope that blessing may be yours next year. He has said many kind things about the firmness and steadfastness of the English believers. Many have brought their young children to see him to be blessed and it is very beautiful to see him with the little ones, folding them in his arms, kissing and blessing them.

. . . It is a matter of extreme difficulty for us to find time for the interviews of the many hundreds of people who desire to see Him. There have been notices of his visit in nearly all the daily papers, most of them extremely sympathetic, notably so the interviews in the Daily News of Sept. 14th, of which I will enclose a cutting; also that of the Daily Mail.[49]

Despite the long years of imprisonment and His advanced age, 'Abdu'l-Bahá's ability to summon up new reserves of energy impressed His hostess. After a whole day of visiting and meeting people, Lady Blomfield noted how tired the Master seemed and bewailed the fact that He would have so many stairs to climb to her apartment. To her amazement, on reaching the staircase, 'Abdu'l-Bahá bolted up the steps to the top without stopping for breath. With a bright smile, He turned to the rest of the party slowly ascending the stairs and said, 'You are all very old! I am very young! . . . Through the power of Bahá'u'lláh all things can be done. I have just used that power.'[50]

'That was the only time we had ever seen Him use that power *for Himself*,' wrote Sitárih, 'and I feel that He did so then to cheer and comfort us, as we were really sad concerning His fatigue.

'Might it not also have been to show us an example of the great Reserve of Divine Force always available for those of us who are working in various ways in the "Path of the Love of God and of Mankind". A celestial strength which reinforces us when our human strength fails.'[51]

The Master's enthusiasm for the evolving powers of material civilization was also keenly noted by His hosts. 'I can see 'Abdu'l-Bahá watching aeroplanes ascend at Brooklands,' wrote Mary Blomfield, recalling many years later their visit to one of Britain's first airfields near Weybridge in Surrey. 'He would speed them into the sky laughing with pleasure, and making a sweeping upward movement of His arms. The progress of material civilization gave him intense satisfaction, as long as its inventions were not used for the prosecution of war.'[52]

On His penultimate weekend in England 'Abdu'l-Bahá accepted an invitation from Wellesley Tudor Pole and his wife to visit them at their home at 17 Royal York Crescent, Clifton, Bristol. Sitárih was among the other guests who joined Him on the journey, setting out from London's Paddington station and arriving around midday on the Saturday at Bristol Temple Meads station, where Tudor Pole met them.

Every detail for the Master's comfort had been lovingly considered as it was known that He needed some well-earned rest after the exacting weeks of His sojourn in London. The bedroom prepared for 'Abdu'l-Bahá was filled with white lilies. On the wall was hung a verse from the Psalms, translated into Persian: 'O send out thy light and thy truth; let them lead me; let them bring me unto thy holy hill and to thy tabernacles.'[53]

After partaking of coffee on His arrival, 'Abdu'l-Bahá walked joyously on the broad paved terrace in front of the house, accompanied by His interpreter Tammaddunu'l-Mulk and a few of the ladies. The Master was quite taken with the spectacular sea views from the Guest House and the fresh air. Tudor Pole, who had also received a cable from the Tehran Bahá'ís congratulating him on the Master's visit to his home, laid on carriages to take 'Abdu'l-Bahá and His entourage to see many of the local beauty spots.

The believers were impressed by 'Abdu'l-Bahá's freshness and the spontaneous interest and delight which He took in all He saw. He was very impressed by the vivid greens of the countryside. At one point a young woman galloped past on horseback followed by several more riding bicycles on their own.

'This is the age of woman,' remarked 'Abdu'l-Bahá.

She should receive the same education as her brother and enjoy the same privilege; for all souls are equal before God. Sex, in its relation to the exigencies of the physical plane, has no connection with the Spirit. In this age of spiritual awakening, the world has entered upon the path of progress into the arena of development, where the power of the spirit surpasses that of the body. Soon the spirit will have dominion over the world of humanity.[54]

That night, a long table was laid out for a company of 19 visitors and guests. Sitting down to dinner, 'Abdu'l-Bahá told the assembled company that this supper was a great and holy occasion and would be recorded in history. 'The meal itself,' wrote Tudor Pole, 'partaken of in love and harmony, was indeed a sacrament and a mark of unity and fellowship that would bring the blessing of Bahá' Ulláh upon all gathered round the board.'[55]

'What struck some of those present was his extremely natural and simple behaviour,' wrote one observer, 'and the pleasant sense of humour, which his long imprisonment and awful trials had not succeeded in destroying.'[56]

'Those of us who were included in the kind invitation of Mr. and Mrs. Tudor-Pole to accompany 'Abdu'l-Bahá on His visit to the Clifton Guest House, Clifton, will forever remember the wonderful three days under that hospitable roof,' wrote Lady Blomfield.[57]

After dinner a meeting had been arranged for some 90 people who had arrived to meet the Master. The meeting began with a duet for violin and piano followed by Tudor Pole offering a few words about the Bahá'í Movement, reminding the guests of the long imprisonment and suffering of Bahá'u'lláh, 'Abdu'l-Bahá and their followers in Persia.

'Abdu'l-Bahá then entered the room, at which point everyone rose out of respect. He seated Himself with His interpreter and, though fatigued, spoke clearly and with great vigour about the new age which was dawning in the world, challenged His audience to look upon all races as members of one organism, and blessed the whole gathering.

'The time of youth has come again to the earth,' He told the audience. 'May those here be watered by those holy springs that are renewing life in the world. Just as day follows night and after sunset is passed, dawn is at hand; just as the sun sets to rise, and sets again; so, in the time of darkness a new light came to illumine the sons of men.'[58]

Following the meeting 'Abdu'l-Bahá bade goodnight to the visitors at the doorway, taking the hand of each with a warm and loving grasp. He then went up onto the balcony and looked out across the city of Bristol, 'a fairy-like scene lit up by thousands of lamps'.[59]

The next morning Sitárih and the rest of the party welcomed 'Abdu'l-Bahá to breakfast. Now and then He spoke, remarking on the contrast between the simple meal before Him and the costly banquets of the wealthy. His gaze scanned the room and rested momentarily on each guest's face with a love that embraced them all. The party then went out driving and walking on the downs. Afterwards He gathered all the servants of the house together and gave them a small address full of practical advice about the blessedness of work. He asked them to serve Tudor Pole faithfully, and to each of them He gave a token of His appreciation for their services. He then went into every room in the house, blessing and dedicating it to the service of Bahá'u'lláh and promising that the house would become a centre of peace and rest for pilgrims from East and West. It is reported that He also inspected the famous blue bowl from Glastonbury that had become the focus of a women's cult. A prayer for 'Abdu'l-Bahá was subsequently added to one of the shrine's service books.

'Abdu'l-Bahá seemed to be energized by the air at Clifton and slept well in the Tudor Poles' home. Towards the end of the stay He consented to be photographed with His devotees on the terrace outside of the Guest House. Around midday on the Monday He wrote a beautiful prayer and blessing in the visitors' book before leaving on the train back to London.

'. . . we shall always be grateful that we were privileged to share in the sunshine of those days,' wrote Sitárih of their visit to Bristol.[60]

Just one week was remaining of 'Abdu'l-Bahá's historic first stay in London and still the visitors continued to arrive at the door of 97 Cadogan Gardens. Sir Richard and Lady Stapley were frequent visitors. Sir Richard, a co-founder and director of the prosperous London clothing business of

Stapley and Smith, was a member of the Corporation of London for more than 30 years. He had a lifelong concern with education and philanthropic causes. Regretting that he had never been to university, he set up a trust to give promising but impoverished young people the chance to continue their education at universities, colleges and beyond. Sir Richard also served on the editorial board of *The Christian Commonwealth*.

The Stapleys gave a reception in honour of 'Abdu'l-Bahá at which they brought out a large iced cake with a flock of snow-white doves radiating from it. The Master gave an iced dove to each guest as a souvenir. On that occasion, there being no room for one of 'Abdu'l-Bahá's entourage, Mírzá Asadu'lláh, in the car, Sitárih believed he had been left behind. However when they arrived at their destination they discovered the old man scrambling down from the roof of the limousine where he had leapt at the last moment. Until the end of her days Lady Blomfield loved to tell this story over and over. One can only imagine the extraordinary sight as the car proceeded through London's more salubrious suburbs with an oriental man in full robes and turban clinging to the roof.

Mary also recalled 'Abdu'l-Bahá's sense of humour, something which Sitárih has not recorded in too much detail in her book *The Chosen Highway*. 'My mother,' Mary remembered, 'like all great souls had a strong, but always kindly, sense of humour, and I often heard laughter during those wonderful days with 'Abdu'l-Bahá.'[61] On one occasion, the Master gave Mary a 'cat's-eye' stone. As He was handing it to her, He said laughing, 'Pussy Eye!' Mary had it set in a ring which she wore for the rest of her life.

The influential newspaper man and spiritualist W.T. Stead, editor of the *Review of Reviews*, had a great sympathy towards the Bahá'í teachings, having run a feature on the Movement in 1907. He arrived to challenge 'Abdu'l-Bahá on the issue of communication with the departed. Constance Elizabeth Maud was a witness to their conversation and recorded it in *Sparks among the Stubble*:

> 'I have preached Bahai doctrine, but I have added to it a truth which Bahá Ullah failed to give to the world,' said W.T. Stead eagerly, and blissfully regardless of the somewhat delicate ground on which he was venturing in his walking boots.
>
> 'What truth is that?' inquired Abdul Baha, alert, and it must be admitted, somewhat surprised.

'The truth of actual present communication between dwellers on earth and our loved ones who have passed on to the other side.'

Abdul Baha replied that he taught and believed absolutely and literally in the communion of saints, but to teach the expediency of seeking communication in séances he regarded as unwise.

'You make no provision, then, for the poor doubting Thomases,' rejoined Mr. Stead, 'those longing for evidence, for proof, for consolation. Julia's Bureau, dedicated to St. Thomas, opens a way for this sad and numerous company to belief in God, the soul and immortality.'

Abdul Baha, with infinite gentleness, explained that in his opinion the average man needed all his energies concentrated on an actively holy life, and a danger lay in emphasizing too much the unseen world around him, though he himself was vividly conscious of the reality of the Unseen, and knew as an experienced fact that 'all religions are based on inspiration from the Unseen'.

'You have this personal experience,' W.T. Stead took him up quickly, 'but see how, like the priest of all ages, you would keep the pearl of great price in your own hands, instead of giving it freely to all the people. To the poor you allow no access to truth except through certain prescribed channels.'

'Meat is for strong men, not babes,' replied Abdul Baha. 'Christ said there were many things He could tell, "but you cannot bear them now".'

The wise old eyes regarded his accuser with sympathy and affection. There were things, perhaps, aspects of truth he had attained, which few of his hearers could have borne. You cannot pour more wine into a goblet than it will hold. But it was not for himself that W.T. Stead had taken up the cudgels, and this Abdul Baha felt instinctively, recognizing in his visitor one whose very reason of being was love for his fellow men.[62]

For Lady Blomfield a key concern was clarified by 'Abdu'l-Bahá during His visit. Dating back to the days of her study of Theosophy, she had been fascinated by the concept of reincarnation, despite rejecting most everything else the Theosophists had taught her. One day while walking with Lady Blomfield in Battersea Park, 'Abdu'l-Bahá set her mind at rest by saying, 'The Theosophists are mistaken in their concept of reincarnation. Why should the soul return to this world, when there are so many worlds?'[63]

The Theosophist leader Annie Besant visited the Master, as did Lady Blomfield's old friend A. P. Sinnett, who came several times. 'Abdu'l-Bahá

Sir Arthur William Blomfield

A photograph of Lady
Blomfield taken in Eastbourne,
possibly soon after the passing
of Sir Arthur Blomfield

Springfield Cottage at Broadway, Worcestershire

Right, the slender granite gravestone of Sir Arthur Blomfield in a secluded corner of the St Eadburgha churchyard, Broadway, *below*

A studio portrait of the young Lady Blomfield, signed later by her as Sitárih <u>Kh</u>ánum in April 1919

Sitárah Khánoum

April 1919

The Lord Chamberlain is commanded by Their Majesties to summon

Lady Blomfield

+ 2 Misses Blomfield

to a Court, to be held at Buckingham Palace on Friday the 4th March, 1910 at 10 o'clock p.m.

Full Dress.
Ladies with Feathers <u>and</u> Trains.

The Doors of the Palace will be opened at 9.30 o'clock p.m.

An invitation to Lady Blomfield and her daughters to attend a royal court, 4 March 1910

Three professional photographs of 'Abdu'l-Bahá taken during His first visit to London

'Abdu'l-Bahá at Clifton Guest House, Bristol, September 1911

'Abdu'l-Bahá on the platform of Passmore Edwards Settlement Hall, 29 September 1911

The Reverend Reginald John Campbell

Lady Blomfield, *second from left*, seated outside with her daughters – Mary Esther, *far left*, and Rose Ellinor Cecilia, *second from right* – and Beatrice 'Patsy' Platt, *far right*, their governess. The four of them together compiled their notes into the book which became known as *Paris Talks*, following 'Abdu'l-Bahá's first visit to London and Paris in 1911.

'Abdu'l-Bahá and entourage at the Clifton Guest House, Bristol, during the Master's second visit to the city, 16–17 January 1913. *Left to right*: Mu'ayyiru'l-Mamálik, Ahmad Sohrab (?), Luṭfu'lláh Ḥakím, 'Abdu'l-Bahá, Mírzá Maḥmúd-i-Zarqání, Mírzá Asadu'lláh.

'Abdu'l-Bahá taking a walk on the promenade of Clifton Terrace, Bristol

'Abdu'l-Bahá looks from the balcony of the Clifton Guest House to see who is calling on Him

accepted their invitations to speak at the Theosophical Society's new head-quarters in Tavistock Square on 30 September.

After Sinnett conveyed a general history of the Bahá'í Movement and offered sympathetic words of welcome, 'Abdu'l-Bahá delivered to the packed room an address upon the distinctive characteristics of Bahá'í teaching while commending the eagerness of the Theosophy Society in its search for truth.

A number of Sitárih's friends from spiritualist or Theosophist circles claimed they saw manifestations of 'Abdu'l-Bahá's power at the level of the aura. 'Many were the "Signs" spoken of by those friends gifted with the clairvoyant sense,' she wrote.

'I have just seen a great light, as a halo shining round the Master's head! Wonderful! Wonderful!'

'Have you not seen it yourself?' said one of these friends.

I replied, 'In the sense you mean, no. I am not gifted with a constant clairvoyance, but to me He is always clothed in a sacred light.'

'But,' she persisted, 'there must be miracles. Many miracles, are there not?'

'Yes, of course. But 'Abdu'l-Bahá says:

'"Miracles have frequently obscured the Teaching which the Divine Messenger has brought. The Message is the real miracle. The phenomenal miracles are unimportant, and prove nothing to anybody but the witnesses thereof, and even they will very often explain them away! Therefore miracles have no value in the teaching of religion."'

'Yes, I understand,' she answered, 'but when a dear friend was being carried to the operating room to undergo a serious operation, 'Abdu'l-Bahá seemed to walk before her, smiling encouragement, and stayed whilst the doctors did their work. The dreaded ordeal was overpast, and she who had been despaired of, even by the doctors, recovered most unexpectedly. Are you not surprised?'

'No, for this reason; on the day she left London, to join her mother, that lady's daughter came to implore 'Abdu'l-Bahá to "bear in mind the critical hour of the operation, and to come to her mother's help". I am of course not surprised that He granted her request.'

Another friend said: 'At that gathering which I attended, the radiant light emanating from 'Abdu'l-Bahá spread over the whole hall. It looked like showers of golden drops, which fell upon every person in the assemblage.'

We who observed and pondered these things grew to take the unprecedented happenings as a part of the whole, not with surprise, but rather with thankfulness that such things could be.[64]

One other visitor of note among those who thronged to the apartment during the Master's visit was the poet Ezra Pound, who thought 'Abdu'l-Bahá 'a dear old man'[65] but later treated Him flippantly in one of his works.

On another occasion, while several people were talking with 'Abdu'l-Bahá, a man's voice was heard at the hall door. Sitárih takes up the story:

'Is the lady of this house within?' The servitor answered 'Yes, but – '
'Oh please, I must see her!' he interrupted with despairing insistence. I, overhearing, had gone into the hall.
'Are you the hostess of 'Abdu'l-Bahá?' he asked.
'Yes. Do you wish to see me?'
'I have walked thirty miles for that purpose.'
'Come in and rest. After some refreshment you will tell me?'
He came in and sat down in the dining-room. In appearance he might have been an ordinary tramp, but as he spoke, from out the core of squalor and suffering, something else seemed faintly to breathe.
After a while the poor fellow began his pitiful story:
'I was not always as you see me now, a disreputable, hopeless object. My father is a country rector, and I had the advantage of being at a public school. Of the various causes which led to my arrival at the Thames embankment as my only home, I need not speak to you.'
'Last evening I had decided to put an end to my futile, hateful life, useless to God and man!'
'Whilst taking what I had intended should be my last walk, I saw "a Face" in the window of a newspaper shop. I stood looking at the face as if rooted to the spot. He seemed to speak to me, and call me to him!'
'"Let me see that paper, please," I asked. It was the face of 'Abdu'l-Bahá.
'I read that he is here, in this house. I said to myself, "If there is in existence on earth that personage, I shall take up again the burden of my life."'
'I set off on my quest. I have come here to find him. Tell me, is he here? Will he see me? Even me?'

'Of course he will see you. Come to Him.'

In answer to the knock, 'Abdu'l-Bahá Himself opened the door, extending His hands, as though to a dear friend, *whom He was expecting.*

'Welcome! Most welcome! I am very much pleased that thou hast come. Be seated.'

The pathetic man trembled and sank on to a low chair by the Master's feet, as though unable to utter a word.

The other guests, meanwhile, looked on wonderingly to see the attention transferred to the strange-looking new arrival, who seemed to be so overburdened with hopeless misery.

'Be happy! Be happy!' said 'Abdu'l-Bahá, holding one of the poor hands, stroking tenderly the dishevelled, bowed head.

Smiling that wonderful smile of loving compassion, the Master continued:

'Do not be filled with grief when humiliation overtaketh thee.

'The bounty and power of God is without limit for each and every soul in the world.

'Seek for spiritual joy and knowledge, then, though thou walk upon this earth, thou wilt be dwelling within the divine realm.

'Though thou be poor, thou mayest be rich in the Kingdom of God.'

These and other words of comfort, of strength, and of healing were spoken to the man, whose cloud of misery seemed to melt away in the warmth of the Master's loving presence.

As the strange visitor rose to leave Him Whom he had sought and found, a new look was upon his face, a new erectness in his carriage, a firm purpose in his steps.

'Please write down for me His words. I have attained all I expected, and even more.'

'And now what are you going to do?' I asked.

'I'm going to work in the fields. I can earn what I need for my simple wants. When I have saved enough I shall take a little bit of land, build a tiny hut upon it in which to live, then I shall grow violets for the market. As He says "Poverty is unimportant, *work is worship.*" I need not say "thank you", need I? Farewell.' The man had gone.[66]

Another famous story related by Lady Blomfield reiterates 'Abdu'l-Bahá's loving concern for the happiness of all:

Every detail of one evening remains in the memory of those who were present.

Two ladies had written from Scotland asking if it were possible that 'Abdu'l-Bahá would spare them one evening.

They accepted my invitation to dinner. Having come straight from the train, and being about to return the same night, every moment was precious.

The Master received them with His warm, simple welcome, and they spontaneously, rather than consciously, made more reverent curtsies than if in the presence of the ordinary great personages of the earth.

Everybody was feeling elated at the prospect of a wonderful evening, unmarred by the presence of any but the most intimate and the most comprehending of the friends.

Not more than half an hour had passed, when, to our consternation, a persistent person pushed past the servitors, and strode into our midst. Seating himself, and lighting a cigarette without invitation, he proceeded to say that he intended writing an article for some paper about 'Abdu'l-Bahá, superciliously asking for 'Some telling points, don't you know.' He talked without a pause in a far from polite manner.

We were speechless and aghast at the intrusion of this insufferable and altogether unpleasant bore, spoiling our golden hour!

Presently 'Abdu'l-Bahá rose and, making a sign to the man to follow Him, went to His own private room.

We looked at one another. The bore had gone, yes, but alas! so also had the Master!

'Can nothing be done?' Being the hostess, I was perturbed and perplexed. Then I went to the door of the audience room, and said to the secretary: 'Will you kindly say to 'Abdu'l-Bahá that the ladies with whom the appointment had been made are awaiting His pleasure.'

I returned to the guests and we awaited the result.

Almost immediately we heard steps approaching along the corridor. They came across the hall to the door. The sound of kind farewell words reached us. Then the closing of the door, and the Beloved came back.

'Oh, Master!' we said.

Pausing near the door, He looked at us each in turn, with a look of deep, grave meaning.

'You were making that poor man uncomfortable, so strongly desiring his absence; I took him away to make him feel happy.'

Truly 'Abdu'l-Bahá's thoughts and ways were far removed from ours![67]

On the evening of 29 September Mrs Thornburgh-Cropper arranged a large farewell reception for 'Abdu'l-Bahá in the hall of the Passmore Edwards Settlement. The room was filled to capacity with almost 500 guests from all walks of life. The meeting began with the Lord's Prayer spoken in unison by all present, followed by a prayer of Bahá'u'lláh for unity and a 5th century prayer attributed to Pope Gelasius. The chair for the evening, Professor Michael Sadler, then welcomed the guests and introduced the evening's speakers: Sir Richard Stapley, Eric Hammond, Mr Claude Montefiore – a progressive-thinking and highly influential member of the Jewish community – Mrs Stannard from Egypt, Alice Buckton and others.

'We have met together to bid farewell to 'Abdu'l-Bahá,' said Professor Sadler, 'and to thank God for his example and teaching, and for the power of his prayers to bring Light into confused thought, Hope into the place of dread, Faith where doubt was, and into troubled hearts, the Love which overmasters self-seeking and fear.'

> Though we all, among ourselves, in our devotional allegiance have our own individual loyalties, to all of us 'Abdu'l-Bahá brings, and has brought, a message of Unity, of sympathy and of Peace. He bids us all be real and true in what we profess to believe; and to treasure above everything the Spirit behind the form. With him we bow before the Hidden Name, before that which is of every life the Inner Life! He bids us worship in fearless loyalty to our own faith, but with ever stronger yearning after Union, Brotherhood, and Love; so turning ourselves in Spirit, and with our whole heart, that we may enter more into the mind of God, which is above class, above race, and beyond time.[68]

After a sequence of talks, each building on the theme of unity, 'Abdu'l-Bahá stood to give His farewell address, taking His audience to a new vision of a united world:

> As the East and the West are illumined by one sun, so all races, nations, and creeds shall be seen as the servants of the One God. The whole earth is one home, and all peoples, did they but know it, are bathed

in the oneness of God's mercy. God created all. He gives sustenance to all. He guides and trains all under the shadow of his bounty. We must follow the example God Himself gives us, and do away with all disputations and quarrels.

Praise be to God! the signs of friendship are appearing, and as a proof of this I, today, coming from the East, have met in this London of the West with extreme kindness, regard and love, and I am deeply thankful and happy. I shall never forget this time I am spending with you . . .

I leave you with prayer that all the beauty of the Kingdom may be yours. In deep regret at our separation, I bid you good-bye.[69]

The morning before He left London 'Abdu'l-Bahá answered an invitation from the Lord Mayor, Sir Thomas Strong, to visit him. Sir Thomas was a self-made businessman who dealt in paper, and an advocate of temperance – a teetotaller. 'Abdu'l-Bahá duly went to the Mansion House and told Lady Blomfield He was greatly pleased with the interview, which covered many subjects including the efforts being made to improve social conditions, prisons and prisoners – a cause close to Lady Blomfield's heart.

'When the Lord Mayor told Him how people were working to improve the treatment of these poor creatures in prison,' she wrote, 'and to secure help for them when they were released, the Master said:

'It is well with a country when the magistrates are as fathers to the people.

'There is a great spiritual light in London, and the ideal of justice is strong in the hearts of the people.

'I am always pleased to remember an instance of this sense of justice, which so amazed the Eastern people of the place.

'A certain Páshá, having most unjustly and cruelly beaten one of his servants, was arrested and brought before that just man who represented Britain. To the intense surprise of the Páshá, he himself was sentenced to a term of imprisonment, and told that he richly deserved the punishment. He could not think it possible that so great a person as himself could be sent to prison, and offered a large bribe for his release. This was sternly refused. A much larger sum was offered with the same result, and the unjust lord was compelled to accept the punishment awarded him for his cruelty to his servant.

'The news of this incident, being noised abroad, did much to show the Eastern people that British justice is in reality the same for the rich and for the poor, and therefore worthy of all respect.'

The Lord Mayor remarked that he was delighted to hear so pleasing a story of British administration in the East. 'Sometimes, alas! there are adverse criticisms,' he added.[70]

'For us,' remembered Sitárih as the visit drew to an end, 'every day was filled with joyous interest and marvelling, where simple happenings became spiritual events.'

One day we were invited to accompany the Master to East Sheen, where a number of friends were gathered, invited by Mr. and Mrs. [John Henry] Jenner [relatives of Ethel Rosenberg who later moved to Tasmania]. Their three small children clambered on to His knee, clung round His neck, and remained as quiet as wee mice whilst the Master spoke, He meanwhile stroking the hair of the tiny ones and saying:

'Blessed are the children, of whom His Holiness Christ said: "Of such are the Kingdom of Heaven." Children have no worldly ambitions. Their hearts are pure. We must become like children, crowning our heads with the crown of severance (from all material things of the earth); purifying our hearts, that we may see God in His Great Manifestations, and obey the laws brought to us by those, His Messengers.'

After we had enjoyed the hospitality of the parents of those sweet children, the Master, always loving trees and pastures, went into Richmond Park, where He watched a race on ponies between some boys and a girl. When the latter won, He clapped His hands, crying out 'Bravo! Bravo!'

On the way back the evening light was waning as we crossed the Serpentine bridge. Rows of shining lamps beneath the trees, stretching as far as our eyes could see into the distance, made that part of London into a glowing fairyland.

'I am very much pleased with this scene. Light is good, most good. There was much darkness in the prison at 'Akká,' said the Master.

Our hearts were sad as we thought on those sombre years within that dismal fortress, where the only light was in the indomitable spirit of the Master Himself! When we said 'We are glad, oh! so full of gladness that you are free,' He said: 'Freedom is not a matter of place, but of condition. I was happy in that prison, for those days were passed in the path of service.

'To me prison was freedom.

'Troubles are a rest to me.

'Death is life.

'To be despised is honour.

'Therefore was I full of happiness all through that prison time.

'When one is released from the prison of self, that is indeed freedom! For self is the greatest prison.

'When this release takes place, one can never be imprisoned. Unless one accepts dire vicissitudes, not with dull resignation, but with radiant acquiescence, one cannot attain this freedom.'[71]

The extraordinary first episode in 'Abdu'l-Bahá's travels to Britain was drawing to a close. Looking back, Mary Blomfield recalled how careful her mother was to insist that the humble and diffident were admitted to the Master's presence as well as the great and important.

'How wise she was in this', wrote Mary, 'is evident in the fact that many of the humble remained faithful to the Cause, while, with a few exceptions, the great were so impressed by their own importance, that they came to air their own views and went away, missing the significance of the divine Messenger they had come to see.'[72]

One person who regretted being unable to find time to meet with the Master during His first sojourn in London was Professor Edward Granville Browne. They had first met at the Mansion of Bahjí some two decades earlier when Browne was privileged to attain the presence of Bahá'u'lláh. Knowing of their long acquaintanceship, Lady Blomfield took the trouble to invite Professor Browne to a supper on the eve of the Master's departure from British shores. On Sunday 1 October, Browne wrote to Lady Blomfield saying he would very much have liked to have joined them but was not able to since he had a prior engagement in Cambridge which could not be cancelled.

'I am very sorry indeed that 'Abdu'l-Bahá is leaving on Tuesday morning early,' wrote Browne, 'so that I shall just miss him. If by any chance he should delay his departure, I should be so grateful if you would let me know . . .'[73]

'The last morning came,' wrote Lady Blomfield. 'The secretaries and several friends were ready to start for the train.'

'Abdu'l‑Bahá sat calmly writing. We reminded Him that the hour to leave for the train was at hand. He looked up, saying: 'There are things of more importance than trains,' and He continued to write.

Suddenly in breathless haste a man came in, carrying in his hand a beautiful garland of fragrant white flowers. Bowing low before the Master, he said:

'In the name of the disciples of Zoroaster, The Pure One, I hail Thee as the "Promised Sháh Bahrám"!'

Then the man, for a sign, garlanded 'Abdu'l‑Bahá, and proceeded to anoint each and all of the amazed friends who were present with precious oil, which had the odour of fresh roses.

This brief but impressive ceremony concluded, 'Abdu'l‑Bahá, having carefully divested Himself of the garland, departed for the train. [74]

Almost one full month had passed since 'Abdu'l‑Bahá first landed in Great Britain. On 3 October 1911 He and His entourage boarded a train at London's Victoria station bound for the coast and an English Channel crossing to France. The final glimpse that His friends had of Him was seeing His tender face, gazing out of the train window with a look of wonderful benevolence towards those He was leaving behind.

'O daughter of the Kingdom!' wrote 'Abdu'l‑Bahá to the newly‑named Sitárih Khánum on His arrival in the French capital.

Praise be to God, we reached Paris safely and in a state of utmost happiness and contentment with thee. The services thou didst render and the troubles thou didst endure during our stay in London were indeed considerable and worthy of praise. Nor shall I ever forget them. I cherish the hope that, through divine bestowals, thy family may be blessed with everlasting honour, and that thy home may ever remain the gathering place of the sons and daughters of the Kingdom. May thou receive at every moment a heavenly confirmation, arise with sacrificial devotion in the path of Bahá'u'lláh, guide the souls to the kingdom of glory, and, through the aid of the Holy Spirit, speak with an eloquent tongue and shine as a brilliant candle.

Upon thee be the Glory of the Most Glorious.

[Signed] 'Ayn 'Ayn[75]

In a postscript the Master added, 'According to thy promise, I anticipate thine arrival.'[76]

Within days, Lady Blomfield, her daughters and Beatrice Platt left London for a nine-week stay in Paris, a remarkable sojourn that inspired them to make a significant contribution to the burgeoning literature of the Bahá'í Movement.

CHAPTER FIVE

THE DIADEM OF THE MOST GREAT GUIDANCE

. . . this Lady Blomfield is dearer to me than all the queens of the world.[1]
'Abdu'l-Bahá

France at the time of 'Abdu'l-Bahá's first visit to the city was embroiled in a diplomatic crisis with Germany which almost brought the two nations to war with each other. For many years the aim of French foreign policy had been *revanche* – return match – with the aim of recapturing the provinces of Alsace and Lorraine that had been taken by Germany in 1871. The two decades from 1890 until 'Abdu'l-Bahá's arrival saw France building alliances so that it could take on Germany. France was also eager to maintain her influence in Morocco. To resolve the crisis of 1911, France met Germany's demands for a part of the French Congo in exchange for recognizing France's control over Morocco. As a result, there was intense public indignation and hostility towards Germany brewing among the French. Against this backdrop of national tension, 'Abdu'l-Bahá arrived in Paris to proclaim His message of brotherhood and unity.

'The city of Paris is very beautiful,' 'Abdu'l-Bahá told His followers on the evening of Friday 20 October 1911.

> . . . a more civilized and well-appointed town in all material development it would be impossible to find in the present world. But the spiritual light has not shone upon her for a long time: her spiritual progress is far behind that of her material civilization. A supreme power is needed to awaken her to the reality of spiritual truth, to breathe the breath of life into her dormant soul.'[2]

It was 'Abdu'l-Bahá's mission to summon His followers to reanimate the peoples of Paris.

He took up residence at 4 Avenue de Camoens in the Quai de Passy, an apartment found for him by Hippolyte and Laura Dreyfus-Barney, whom Lady Blomfield particularly loved. 'It was charmingly furnished, sunny, spacious,' recalled Sitárih. A flight of steps from the Avenue led directly into the Trocadéro Gardens where the Master could often be seen walking and quietly admiring the view, across the park and over the Seine towards the Eiffel Tower that dominated every vista. 'Sheltered in this modern, comfortable, Paris flat, He Whom we revered, with a secretary, servitors, and a few close friends, sojourned for an unforgettable nine weeks,'[3] Sitárih reminisced.

The Master's stay in the French capital saw Him once again expounding the fundamental teachings of His father's Cause. Whether He was addressing the friends in His private rooms, meeting with large groups of spiritual seekers or simply strolling in the Trocadéro Gardens, 'Abdu'l-Bahá managed to entrance most of the people who came into contact with Him.

'The French people would gaze at Him in awe,' wrote Mary Blomfield, 'and one day I saw a young man with more than ordinary perception, cross himself instinctively. He had recognized one of the Great Ones of God.'[4]

Freed from the responsibilities of being the Master's hostess, Lady Blomfield seems to have relished all the more the act of observing His interactions with people:

> Who is this, with a branch of roses in His hand, coming down the steps? A picturesque group of friends (some Persians, wearing the *kuláh*, and a few Europeans), who are following Him, see little children coming up to Him. They hold on to His *'abá* (cloak), confiding and fearless. He gives the roses to them, caressingly lifting one after another in His arms, smiling the while that glorious smile which wins all hearts.
>
> Again, we saw a cabman stop his fiacre, take off his cap and hold it in his hand, gazing amazed, with an air of reverence, whilst the majestic figure, courteously acknowledging his salutation, passed by with that walk which a friend had described as 'that of a king or of a shepherd'.
>
> Another scene. A very poor quarter in Paris – Sunday morning – groups of men and women inclined to be rowdy. Foremost amongst them a big man brandishing a long loaf of bread in his hand, shouting, gesticulating, dancing.

Into this throng walked 'Abdu'l-Bahá, on His way from a mission hall, where He had been addressing a very poor congregation at the invitation of their pastor. The boisterous man with the loaf, suddenly seeing Him, stood still. He then proceeded to lay about him lustily with his staff of life, crying 'Make way, make way! He is my Father, make way!' The Master passed through the midst of the crowd, now become silent and respectfully saluting Him. 'Thank you, my dear friends, thank you,' He said, smiling round upon them. The poor were always His especially beloved friends. He was never happier than when surrounded by them, the lowly of heart.[5]

Lady Blomfield was always delighted to notice the effect the presence of 'Abdu'l-Bahá had upon children. One little girl was heard to whisper, 'Look, that is Jesus when He was old.'

'Perhaps their unstained nature sensed the breath of holiness which was always with Him,' Sitárih mused, 'and caused these little ones to liken Him to the most Holy One of Whom they were conscious.'[6]

As it had been in London, 'Abdu'l-Bahá's daily routine revolved around meetings with individuals and groups of visitors. To each He gave a special lesson or insight to assist them in their lives. Among the multitudes of guests Sitárih noted

all nationalities and creeds, from the East and from the West, including Theosophists, agnostics, materialists, spiritualists, Christian Scientists, social reformers, Hindus, Súfís, Muslims, Buddhists, Zoroastrians, and many others. Often came workers in various humanitarian societies, who were striving to reduce the miseries of the poor. These received special sympathy and blessing.[7]

'Abdu'l-Bahá gave His addresses in Persian, which Hippolyte Dreyfus-Barney translated into French and Laura into English. Lady Blomfield, her two daughters and Beatrice Platt took copious notes of the talks each day. 'The words of 'Abdu'l-Bahá can be put on to paper,' wrote Lady Blomfield, 'but how to describe the smile, the earnest pleading, the loving-kindness, the radiant vitality, and at times the awe-inspiring authority of His spoken words?'

The vibrations of His voice seemed to enfold the listeners in an atmosphere of the Spirit, and to penetrate to the very core of being. We were experiencing the transforming radiance of the Sun of Truth; henceforth, material aims and unworthy ambitions shrank away into their trivial, obscure retreats.

'Abdu'l-Bahá would often answer our questions before we asked them.[8]

Ever sensitive to religious intolerance, Lady Blomfield particularly noted the visit of a group of bigoted churchmen who proceeded to bitterly condemn anyone who did not accept their view of religion. 'The new revelation was too great for their narrowed souls and fettered minds,' she observed.

The heart of 'Abdu'l-Bahá was saddened by this interview, which had tired Him exceedingly. When He referred to this visit there was a look in His eyes as if loving pity were blended with profound disapproval, as though He would cleanse the defiled temple of Humanity from the suffocating diseases of the soul. Then He uttered these words in a voice of awe-inspiring authority:

'Jesus Christ is the Lord of Compassion, and these men call themselves by His Name! *Jesus is ashamed of them!*

He shivered as with cold, drawing His *'abá* closely about Him, with a gesture as if sternly repudiating their misguided outlook.[9]

'Abdu'l-Bahá's sadness at the condition of humanity was becoming increasingly apparent in the words of warning He addressed to His Paris audiences. Events taking place in the world were evidently causing Him great distress. Italy was at war with Ottoman Turkey over Libya.

'The news of the Battle of Benghazi grieves my heart,' mourned 'Abdu'l-Bahá. 'I wonder at the human savagery that still exists in the world! How is it possible for men to fight from morning until evening, killing each other, shedding the blood of their fellow-men: And for what object? To gain possession of a part of the earth!'[10] He charged His listeners to concentrate all their thoughts on love and unity: 'When a thought of war comes, oppose it by a stronger thought of peace.'[11]

Even though the pernicious influence of the covenant-breakers was not widespread in the West and 'Abdu'l-Bahá had clearly established His ascendancy over His faithless family members, certain individuals emerged during His western visits who tried to cause trouble and undermine His authority. One person in particular began to whisper slanderous lies about the Master and came daily to distort the teachings amongst the pilgrims. According to her daughter Mary, Sitárih dreaded this woman's appearance. One morning Lady Blomfield withdrew into a quiet room and repeated the prayer of the Báb known as the Remover of Difficulties. The individual did not appear that day nor did she ever come again.

Lady Blomfield spoke to the Master about those, even among His own entourage, who tried to damage His reputation. One day, she received a disquieting letter from someone whose sincerity she did not doubt. The letter asked her to warn the Master not to visit a certain country in the near future as it might be dangerous for Him. She rushed to inform 'Abdu'l-Bahá of her concerns.

'To my amazement,' she wrote, 'He smiled and said impressively: "My daughter, have you not yet realized that never, in my life, have I been for one day out of danger, and that I should rejoice to leave this world and go to my Father?"

> 'Oh, Master! We do not wish that you should go from us in that manner.' I was overcome with sorrow and terror.
>
> 'Be not troubled,' said 'Abdu'l-Bahá. 'These enemies have no power over my life, but that which is given them from on High. If my Beloved God so willed that my life-blood should be sacrificed in His path, it would be a glorious day, devoutly wished for by me.'
>
> Therefore the friends surrounding the much-loved Master were comforted, and their faith so strengthened, that when a sinister-looking man came up to a group who were walking in the gardens and threateningly said: 'Are you not yet sufficiently warned? Not only is there danger for 'Abdu'l-Bahá, but also for you who are with Him,' the friends were unperturbed, one of them replying calmly: 'The Power that protects the Master protects also His other servants. Therefore we have no fear.'[12]

Two days before the end of 'Abdu'l-Bahá's visit a woman rushed into the gathering at His apartment. Lady Blomfield recounts her words:

> Oh, how glad I am to be in time! I must tell you the amazing reason of

my hurried journey from America. One day, my little girl astonished me by saying: 'Mummy, if dear Lord Jesus was in the world now, what would you do?' 'Darling baby, I would feel like getting on to the first train and going to Him as fast as I could.' 'Well, Mummy, He *is* in the world.' I felt a sudden great awe come over me as my tiny one spoke. 'What do you mean, my precious? How do you know?' I said. 'He told me Himself, so [of] course He *is* in the world.' Full of wonder, I thought: Is this a sacred message which is being given to me out of the mouth of my babe? And I prayed that it might be made clear to me.

The next day she said, insistently and as though she could not understand: 'Mummy, darlin', why isn't you gone to see Lord Jesus? He's told me two times that He is really here, in the world.' 'Tiny love, Mummy doesn't know where He is, how could she find Him?' 'We see, Mummy, we see.'

I was naturally perturbed. The same afternoon, being out for a walk with my child, she suddenly stood still and cried out, 'There He is! There He is!' She was trembling with excitement and pointing at the windows of a magazine store where there was a picture of 'Abdu'l-Bahá. I bought the paper, found this address, caught a boat that same night, and here I am.'[13]

Another interested caller that Sitárih was able to introduce to 'Abdu'l-Bahá while in Paris was an English-born friend of hers, now an Italian princess. She was the daughter of a bishop and had been brought up in an ecclesiastical circle. On reading the Bible by herself, she told Lady Blomfield, that she used to feel a glow of spiritual life, but when she listened to church services, she said she felt quite cold and uninspired. Her husband was a sceptic in religious matters and in his home she felt that she seemed to be in utter darkness, so much so that she felt at times as if she could not bear it. Meeting 'Abdu'l-Bahá, she said, had been the happiest day in all her life. In His presence she felt the same sort of glow that she used to feel in reading the Bible, only far more powerful. She said she had felt the hunger of her soul satisfied as never before.[14]

During the days in Paris, 'Abdu'l-Bahá took the opportunity to outline for the first time His plans for the administrative development of the Bahá'í community in Britain. The Master spoke with Lady Blomfield about His hope that a small committee be established in London which would be responsible for the collection of funds and the publication of the transcripts taken of His talks in England. 'Abdu'l-Bahá personally requested that the committee be made up of Ethel Rosenberg, Mrs Thornburgh-Cropper, Mrs Alexander Whyte of Edinburgh, Alice Buckton, Lady Blomfield, Tudor Pole and the Blomfields' neighbour Gabrielle Enthoven. Lady Blomfield passed on this guidance in correspondence to Ethel Rosenberg who, when she arrived in Paris, questioned 'Abdu'l-Bahá further on practical arrangements. His first response to her thanks for the guidance was to pay high compliment to Lady Blomfield, saying that He found her entirely sincere and pure-hearted. He urged Ethel Rosenberg to value Lady Blomfield's friendship.

'Abdu'l-Bahá spoke at considerable length with Rosenberg about the procedures He wished the committee to follow in regard to general expenses, funds and collections. He said, first of all, that they had to make it very clearly understood that all offerings were to be entirely voluntary. There was to be no obligation in this matter and if a believer felt unable to afford to contribute then giving nothing was acceptable. Those who wished to give, however, should choose a sum within their means and contribute this regularly. He told Rosenberg that it would be a good plan to have the amount decided upon paid into the fund each month and entered into a book so at the end of a year the amounts could be balanced. Thus the committee would know how much it had at its disposal after general expenditure. Rosenberg noted that 'Abdu'l-Bahá was very interested in all the details of the fund and spoke very fully and enthusiastically about it. He told her the meetings in London would grow in numbers and would improve in every way. He particularly wished that the Bahá'ís whom He had named should consult together and arrange matters as they thought wisest and best on the general basis He had suggested.

'How are the believers in London?' 'Abdu'l-Bahá asked in a message sent from Paris, 'Are they happy? Are they spreading the call of the Kingdom? Are their tongues engaged in the commemoration of God? Are they full of zeal? Do they comfort the unhappy? Do they raise the fallen? Are they kind to all the people of the world? Do they serve the Cause of Universal Peace and Goodwill amongst the nations? Do they sympathise with the unfortunate? Are they the stars of the Heaven of Bahá? Are they the waves of the most great sea? Are they the illuminating path of the travellers? Are they the bright torches of reality? . . .

'The friends of God must become fully informed of the Teachings. It is well to be thoroughly versed in the sciences and arts and literature, and one must be established in the Kingdom of God on a like basis. The results of physical science are limited. His holiness Christ said, "Leave thy nets. Come and I will make thee fishers of men."

'The results of the Divine sciences, the guidance of God, the spiritual arts, are unlimited, and train the real man. My spirit communicates with you. It annihilates time and space. God willing, the confirmation of the Supreme Concourse shall descend upon you uninterruptedly.'[15]

As the historic meetings in Paris drew to a close, Sitárih noted that 'we who witnessed them seemed to be in a higher dimension, where [there] were natural indications of the presence of the Light which in all men is latent and in 'Abdu'l-Bahá transcendent.'

> The constant awareness of an exhilaration, which carried us out of our everyday selves, and gave us the sense of being 'one with the Life Pulse, which beats through the Universe' is an experience to be treasured rather than an emotion to be described.[16]

In His farewell talk to the friends gathered at 15 rue Greuze on 1 December, 'Abdu'l-Bahá noted that receptivity had increased during His sojourn in the city.

'When I arrived in Paris some time ago for the first time,' He told His followers, 'I looked around me with much interest, and in my mind I likened this beautiful city to a large garden.'

> With loving care and much thought I examined the soil, and found it to be very good and full of possibility for steadfast faith and firm belief, for a seed of God's love has been cast into the ground . . .
>
> Since my arrival a few weeks ago, I can see the growth of spirituality. At the beginning only a few souls came to me for Light, but during my short sojourn among you the numbers have increased and doubled. This is a promise for the future![17]

Nevertheless, in a talk later given in New York on 15 April 1912, 'Abdu'l-Bahá was once again mourning the materialism of Paris.

'Paris is most beautiful in outward appearance,' He told visitors to the home of Mountfort Mills.

The evidences of material civilization there are very great, but the spiritual civilization is far behind. I found the people of that city submerged and drowning in a sea of materialism. Their conversations and discussions were limited to natural and physical phenomena, without mention of God. I was greatly astonished. Most of the scholars, professors and learned men proved to be materialists. I said to them, 'I am surprised and astonished that men of such perceptive caliber and evident knowledge should still be captives of nature, not recognizing the self-evident Reality.'[18]

'Now I say "Goodbye",' were 'Abdu'l-Bahá's farewell words to His followers in Paris. 'This I say only to your outer selves; I do not say it to your souls, for our souls are always together.'[19]

Bereft at the thought of a prolonged separation from Him, Lady Blomfield had already conversed with the Master about the possibility of her visiting Him in Egypt within a few months of His departure from Paris, followed by a pilgrimage that she had long desired to the Shrines of the Báb and Bahá'u'lláh.

As 'Abdu'l-Bahá departed Europe to winter in Alexandria, Sitárih intended to head for Switzerland with her daughters and their former governess, Beatrice Platt – 'Patsy' – with an important task in hand. The Master had encouraged them to arrange for the publication of His talks in Paris. Yet, despite her intention to get swiftly to work, 'Abdu'l-Bahá had other plans for Lady Blomfield.

In the southern German city of Stuttgart, a series of misunderstandings amongst the Bahá'ís was having unfortunate repercussions. Germany had been opened to the Bahá'í Faith when the American dentist Dr Edwin Karl Fischer moved to Stuttgart in 1905. However, more significant for the long-term development of the community was the arrival two years later of Alma Knobloch, of German-American parentage, who had built on the small nucleus of believers that Dr Fischer had confirmed and raised the largest Bahá'í community in Europe by the end of the first decade of the 20th century. Knobloch travelled extensively throughout Germany and later helped establish the Faith in Austria and Switzerland.

The disunity in Stuttgart emerged from some of the conflicting ideas held by those Bahá'ís who had previously been schooled in Theosophy or Christian Science, as well as relying upon their own spiritual or mystical interpretations of the New Testament. Others were convinced they had received spiritual messages through automatic writing and psychic phenomena. Furthermore, the enthusiastic method that Dr Fischer used to promote the Bahá'í teachings was causing agitation to some of his fellow believers. Unfortunately, the disagreements had given rise to two groups, and some enquirers, attracted to the beauty of the teachings but confronted with signs of disunity, refused to investigate further and were never seen again. To help restore unity, 'Abdu'l-Bahá had penned a specific message to His followers in Stuttgart. Lady Blomfield was tasked with delivering it, in person.

On the evening of Saturday 2 December 1911 she arrived in Stuttgart, along with her German translator Mrs Earle, Mírzá Asadu'lláh and Mirza Ahmad Sohrab. They were met at the station by Miss Knobloch and Dr Fischer, along with other Bahá'ís – Messrs Eckstein and Braun, and Mr and Mrs Wilhelm Herrigel – all of whom extended a very warm welcome to their visitors. Lady Blomfield and Mrs Earle went to stay with the Herrigels while the Ecksteins entertained the Persians.

At 11 o'clock the following morning, Lady Blomfield invited Alma Knobloch to meet her in private. This friend, who had herself suggested – and then been encouraged by 'Abdu'l-Bahá – to leave Stuttgart and begin teaching work in Leipzig, was overwhelmed with anxiety about what the Stuttgart believers might do were she to leave. 'She seemed to think that everything would be likely to go wrong in the way of erroneous teaching,' Lady Blomfield later reported to 'Abdu'l-Bahá.[20] During a frank discussion, Sitárih encouraged Miss Knobloch to inform the believers that same afternoon that she would now go and begin anew in Leipzig. This course of action, she assured her, had the Master's blessing.

At luncheon the German friends were thrilled to hear of the Master's achievements in London and Paris. Lady Blomfield made no mention of any knowledge of the challenges being faced by the Stuttgart community, thinking it wiser to offer the teachings of 'Abdu'l-Bahá from a wider, impersonal standpoint which, she hoped, 'from its very grandeur, would cause all personal likes and dislikes to melt away, as too trivial to obtrude themselves'.[21]

Their meal over, the Herrigels and Dr Fischer shared with Lady Blomfield details of what had happened to cause the unfortunate split in the community. Some of them told her about the psychic messages they claimed to have received. With her long experience and knowledge of esoteric matters, Lady Blomfield later reported that she felt there was some authenticity in the guidance that somehow had been channelled to the Stuttgart believers.

'Through these Counsels, several devout seekers after Truth have been led into the Kingdom of Bahá, and there confirmed and established,' she wrote to 'Abdu'l-Bahá. 'Through these messages also, some of these souls have been led to work with all their might in the Cause of Unity and have translated into German much of the Bahá'í literature.'[22]

Lady Blomfield was impressed that these devoted believers had been responsible for much of the teaching of the Faith in Stuttgart. However, she learned that Dr Fischer had perhaps been 'more enthusiastic than wise'[23] in his attempts to teach his patients as they reclined in his dentist's chair.

'For instance, officers of the Army would surely need the introduction of the Cause of Peace to be presented to them gradually!' she reported. 'But, when given to them in a Dentist's chair, with the mouth gagged, probably in pain, and certainly not in the best of tempers – they, unable to reply at the moment, became furious in their antagonism to Dr Fisher and the Teaching he advocated!'[24]

Dr Fischer also spoke of some of the psychic messages he felt he had been receiving and how some of the friends were accusing him and others of spiritualism and anything else that occurred to them as a possible explanation of things that had transpired.

'However, I understood,' Lady Blomfield told the Master, 'how these mischievous reports were spread abroad with an opposing force, born of lack of knowledge rather than of desire to persecute!'[25]

Dr Fischer had lost many of his patients as a result of the reports against him being circulated.

'He, persecuted, suspected and misunderstood is now reduced to a miserable state,' reported Lady Blomfield. 'His money gone, his heart sore, his health broken down by a sense of failure and unmerited suffering; the only prospect before him that of absolute starvation! Most pathetic!!'[26]

Lady Blomfield appealed to 'Abdu'l-Bahá to consider giving Dr Fischer a fresh start in London or elsewhere. She sought advice on whether she could raise some £50 or £60 among the believers to assist him. She contributed 100 francs herself to a subscription list in the hope that it could help Dr Fischer leave Stuttgart and start anew.

On the Sunday afternoon Lady Blomfield addressed a large gathering of enthusiastic believers at the Bürger Museum. She noted the presence of Miss Knobloch who was at the meeting with some of her circle of friends, as well as several who had refrained from joining either group. All exchanged friendly greetings as if no discord had ever marred the community. Then, after a hearty welcome, Lady Blomfield rose to deliver the stirring message from 'Abdu'l-Bahá:

> Rejoice! Rejoice! Because of the Glad-tidings! You have attained to the light of the Kingdom. The glory of the Sun of Truth penetrates all regions.
>
> Rejoice! Rejoice! Glad-tidings I send unto you. The doors of the Kingdom are open. The heavenly manna has descended upon you.
>
> Rejoice! Rejoice! There were many holy messengers sent into the world; they came one after another, and all diffused the breath of the Holy Spirit.
>
> Praise God! Praise God! That you have turned your faces toward the Kingdom. The rays of the sun of truth are illuminating you.
>
> Strive with heart and soul that the Heavenly Light may descend upon all people and that through it every heart may be enlightened and that the spirit of the human race may partake of Its glory. Work and strive until all regions of the world are bathed in this Light. Fear not when trouble overtakes you. You will be criticized; you will be persecuted; you will be cursed and reviled. Recall in those days what I tell you now: Your triumph will be sure; your hearts will be filled with the Glory of God, for the heavenly power will sustain you, and God will be with you. This is my message to you.[27]

All present were moved and stirred by the Master's message. At the end of the meeting Lady Blomfield stood at the door and gave a warm handshake on behalf of 'Abdu'l-Bahá to each of those attending as they left the room.

'Many of the people had tears in their eyes and asked that their love and gratitude, and heartfelt thanks might be conveyed to the Master, with their strong faith and hope that it was really a precursor of a touch of His own beloved Hand, when He should come in person to gladden their eyes!!'[28]

As the children were brought, Lady Blomfield took them in her arms and kissed each one of them from the Master. Their mothers conveyed special greetings to be sent to 'Abdu'l-Bahá. One little boy of about two and a half years old named Wolfgang Sturm, whose mother had passed away, clung tightly to Lady Blomfield's neck and kissed her again and again, as if he understood from whom the embrace had been sent.

'How near some little ones are to the Kingdom!' Lady Blomfield observed.[29]

That evening, Lady Blomfield delivered the Master's message again, this time to a unity gathering where she felt it had an even greater effect than in the afternoon.

'Something was felt by several at this Assembly of a Grand Spirit of Harmony! Some great signs were seen! They were growing nearer to an understanding! A beautiful Peace seemed to brood over the friends!' she reported.[30]

She also delighted in being able to hold a three month old baby called Noor, who stayed in her arms during the tea, looked up and smiled, perhaps also understanding – Lady Blomfield thought – that progress was being made.

The following evening, Monday 4 December, another meeting was held which also had a big impact on the Stuttgart believers.

'The flowers on the tables were not more sweet and gentle than the dear people, who between the speeches, drank tea, ate cakes, listened to the singing of Bahá'í songs, and conversed in the utmost kindness with each other.'[31]

Mr Herrigel called a meeting of his friends the next night. Lady Blomfield's reading of 'Abdu'l-Bahá's message was again met with great enthusiasm. The audience rose to its feet at the message's end and cried out, 'Alláh-u-Abhá'.

After reading the letter, Lady Blomfield delivered several talks of the Master from her notes. When she no longer had another one left to share, the gathering requested she speak more which she did, telling 'Abdu'l-Bahá later, 'I spoke of Unity, how that all societies who worked for the uplifting of Humanity were blessed by the Master, and that all found a place in the service of the Bahá'í Cause. I went on to the effect that adverse criticism on the methods of other Bahá'í brothers, even if we did not understand them, was surely not good! That there are many different ways of serving the Cause! Many gardeners could find work in the garden of the Kingdom! That souls in differing stages of development did not all need the same kind of food! About that there could be no hard and fast rule! Various groups must be permitted to study in their own way – the way that most helps them! Whether Theosophy! Christian Science, Mysticism or Spiritual Interpretation of Holy Scriptures, or all of these subjects! No disapproval should be expressed by those who do not agree, neither understand! Nothing! Nothing!! must be allowed to break down the bond of "unity" amongst the Bahai brothers! We tarnish the Cause in the eyes of the world when we show that we are not careful to live the "Unity" we teach! (and much more to the same effect),' she reported to the Master.[32]

In her remarks Lady Blomfield urged the Stuttgart Bahá'ís to spread the bond of unity not only in their city but throughout all of Europe, which would catch ablaze from its divine flame. 'Abdu'l-Bahá would only come to visit them when the unity was strong in Stuttgart, she told them.

One afternoon Lady Blomfield and Mrs Earle joined Alma Knobloch on an excursion out to Esslingen to visit relatives of the Herrigels who had been estranged from the community for some time. A delightful afternoon was spent at which Lady Blomfield told the story of Ṭáhirih to her hosts, conveying the Persian poetess's courage, firmness and love for women's rights.

'The dear tender-hearted German people, man and woman, with tears in their eyes, pondering on her sufferings for the Cause, seemed to be gathering to themselves an echo of her spirit, her strength!' she reported. 'There was no sign of dis-union! But a beautiful atmosphere of friendship seemed to encircle all!'[33]

Lady Blomfield believed that the battle was over, that the lesson of unity had been learned in Stuttgart. She praised the spirit and devotion of the Herrigels, 'the most saint-like people it has ever been my privilege to meet'.[34]

On 7 December 1911 Lady Blomfield returned to Switzerland to be reunited with her daughters.

'I returned late on Thursday night and met the girls here,' she wrote to 'Abdu'l-Bahá the following Monday. 'I have prepared a report of the Battle for the King, at whose command I went forth!'[35]

'The Master speaks of having given trouble when staying at our house!' she added, referring to a letter He had sent her. 'In reality we were so grateful to be permitted the privilege of ministering to Him for that short space of His daily life – making those arrangements was a true joy! I shall never cease to praise God that to my humble home came that delight! How could it be otherwise when God's Messenger deigned to honour my roof by staying under it whilst He gave His Holy Message to my dearly loved country? In this I shall remain grateful to the end of my earth life and after, in the Heavenly Kingdom, the thankful memory will continue with me.'[36]

'Abdu'l-Bahá had previously teased Lady Blomfield, saying that she wrote few letters to Him.

'If such long letters were to arrive often He would be so tired of them that He would surely be glad that they should come seldom!' she joked in return.[37]

'O thou who art attracted to the Kingdom of God!' replied 'Abdu'l-Bahá. 'During the days I spent in thy home I was the recipient of thine utmost kindness. I shall never forget it, and I cherish the hope that, through the grace of Bahá'u'lláh, thou shalt be so enkindled in London with the heat of the love of God as to set aflame all who meet thee.'[38]

'O thou candle of the Love of God!' He wrote again on 4 January.

During my sojourn in London I witnessed thine utmost kindness and I am most pleased with thee. Praise be to God that thou wert confirmed, even as I had hoped, in thy service to the Kingdom of God during thy journey to Stuttgart, and didst become the means of spreading the word of God. In the assemblage of the friends thou didst shine forth as a bright candle with the light of God's love, and thou wert aided by the breaths of the Holy Spirit. With the utmost courage, thou didst unloose thine eloquent tongue and deliver a persuasive speech.

It behoveth thee to render a thousand thanks at every moment for the bounty of being thus crowned with the diadem of the most great guidance, and it befitteth thee to pride thyself above all the queens of the world. For thousands of worldly queens shall come and go, leaving behind neither name nor trace, neither sign nor fruit; but through the light of God's love thou wilt shine forth above the horizon of eternity and thy remembrance will bring solace to the hearts of men and women in ages and centuries to come.[39]

Her mission to Stuttgart accomplished, Lady Blomfield, her daughters and Beatrice Platt settled down to examine their transcriptions and notes of 'Abdu'l-Bahá's talks in Paris with the goal of preparing them for publication. Their base in Switzerland was the Hotel Belvedere, close to the holiday villa 'Daro's-Salam' built by Hippolyte Dreyfus at Mont Pèlerin, a mountain village above Vevey with spectacular panoramic views over Lake Geneva.

In compiling the talks for publication, the four women said they tried to maintain the quality of spontaneous simplicity that was ably given by the Master's French translators, the Dreyfus-Barneys. '. . . my two daughters, my friend and I took notes,' wrote Lady Blomfield in the book's Preface. 'Many friends asked us to publish these notes in English, but we hesitated. At length when 'Abdu'l-Bahá Himself asked us to do so, we, of course, consented – in spite of our feeling that our pen is "too weak for such high message".'[40]

'Abdu'l-Bahá's lessons, collected in *Talks by 'Abdu'l-Bahá Given in Paris* – later retitled *Paris Talks* – range over a broad collection of spiritual and social themes including, among numerous other subjects, the nature of man and the soul, the Prophets of God and the establishment of world peace. The second section, as conceived by Lady Blomfield and her daughters, is an attempt to present the fundamental teachings of the Bahá'í Faith as 11 principles, defined by them as: The Search after Truth; the Unity of Mankind; Religion ought to be the Cause of Love and Affection; the Unity of Religion and Science; Abolition of Prejudices; Equalization of Means of Existence; Equality of Men before the Law; Universal Peace; Non-Interference of Religion and Politics; Equality of Sex – Education of Women; and the Power of the Holy Spirit.

Paris Talks is a presentation of deeply profound concepts conveyed with a clarity and simplicity that has ensured that the book has remained a popular and accessible exposition of the Bahá'í teachings, reprinted many times since the original 1912 edition. A third section was added to subsequent editions, including an address given by the Master at the Friends' Meeting House in London in January 1913; His discourses on love, prayer and evil – also given during His second visit to London; and a Tablet dated 28 August 1913 concerning the equality of men and women.

With regard to the preparation of the book, it was felt important to expedite its publication so that it would be available when 'Abdu'l-Bahá next left Egypt and embarked on His mission to the United States of America.

'The presence of Abdu'l-Baha in Europe and His approaching visit to America will be sufficient advertising for the book,' Mirza Ahmad Sohrab wrote to Lady Blomfield, 'and no publisher – no matter how important he is – can give us more publicity than we already have.'[41]

'If the addresses of Abdu'l-Bahá in London are sufficient for a volume, well and good,' wrote Sohrab. 'If they are not, his Paris addresses could be added to them and both put together in one volume.'[42] In the event, *Talks by 'Abdu'l-Bahá Given in Paris* and *'Abdu'l-Bahá in London* appeared as separate publications, the latter edited by Eric Hammond.

'My talks in Paris and London were recently corrected,' 'Abdu'l-Bahá wrote to Lady Blomfield, having reviewed transcriptions of His talks. 'Whenever they are translated I will send thee a copy for publication and distribution . . .'[43]

'Abdu'l-Bahá was deeply touched by Lady Blomfield's efforts to make His talks in both London and Paris available to a wider audience. Speaking on His return to London in December 1912, the Master said that He would like to see all of the talks that He gave in the United States of America – which at that point were uncollected – compiled into one or two volumes.

'He called attention to how quickly the Paris and London addresses delivered last year were printed; and this was done through one woman, Lady Blomfield,' Mirza Ahmad Sohrab wrote to *Star of the West*.

'. . . just now this Lady Blomfield is dearer to me than all the queens of the world,' said 'Abdu'l-Bahá.[44]

Longing to see the Master again and willing to travel to Egypt should she be granted permission to do so, Lady Blomfield wrote to Him on 12 January 1912 seeking His guidance.

'As to thy coming to Egypt,' He replied, 'it will bring happiness both to thy heart and to ours.'

> I suggested this to thee two months ago, that we proceed to Egypt together, and that thou then makest a journey to Haifa. But upon arriving in Egypt I found that the East was in a state of turmoil and agitation. Secondly, in the months of January and February the sea is very stormy. My sister, the Greatest Holy Leaf, is presently in quarantine on rough seas, and it is not known when she will be released. Thirdly, I will not remain in Egypt more than two months. I will probably leave at the end of March, but will not proceed directly to Haifa. As it is my wish to meet thee both in Egypt and in Haifa, it is better that thou shouldst come next year at the end of November or the beginning of December, that thy journey to Egypt may conclude with a visit to the sacred Dust. Thus it will be made complete and bring about great joy and happiness.[45]

With the wider diffusion of the Bahá'í teachings always at the forefront of her mind, Lady Blomfield asked the Master whether it was wise for her to attend and address meetings of the Theosophists. He encouraged her to continue, saying that the confirmations of the Holy Spirit would assist her. But He warned her against arguing with the Theosophists over the question of reincarnation, saying that, at this stage, 'their ideas must be treated with forbearance'.

'"Return"', He wrote, 'is a reality, but reincarnation is not.'[46]

'Abdu'l-Bahá clearly recognized Lady Blomfield's capacity to faithfully present His father's teachings to others, and in His wisdom saw that her presence in Switzerland might be a key to attracting many souls to His Cause, particularly those of the progressive internationalist thinkers gathering around Geneva. On 12 February 1912 He encouraged her to help establish a Bahá'í centre on the shores of Lake Geneva. She should, He said, collaborate with a Miss Gibbs whom He described as a 'revered lady'.

'She is highly capable and ready to acquire the teachings of Bahá'u'lláh,' wrote 'Abdu'l-Bahá. 'She is endowed with great intelligence and hath the capacity and potential to become wholly attached to the divine Kingdom.'[47]

Geneva by the end of the 19th century had emerged as an international city. In October 1863 it had hosted the conference of 16 nations which adopted various resolutions – and an emblem, the red cross – to improve assistance to the sick and wounded during wartime. Aspiring to see the Red Cross principles become accepted into international law, the following year saw a diplomatic meeting held in the city at the invitation of the Swiss government. This assembly formulated the Geneva Convention for 'The Amelioration of the Condition of the Wounded and Sick in Armed Forces in the Field', signed by 12 states and later accepted by virtually all. A second Geneva Convention addressing members of the armed forces at sea was first adopted in 1906. In time, building upon this reputation as a centre for reconciliation and arbitration, Geneva became the seat of the League of Nations in 1920.

A first step was for Lady Blomfield and Miss Gibbs was to establish a regular Wednesday night meeting in the historic town of Villeneuve, situated where the Rhone river runs into Lake Geneva at the opposite end of the lake from Geneva city. Villeneuve had become an attractive and popular destination for countless visitors over the decades including the composer Richard Wagner, the author Victor Hugo and the Nobel Prize winning novelist Romain Rolland.

'I first learned of Baha'ism at Geneva,' Rolland wrote six years later.

. . . It is above all a religious ethic, which does not conceive of religion without putting it into practice, and which seeks to remain in accord with science and reason, without cult or priests. The first duty is that each has a profession: work is holy, it is divine benediction.

I have noticed an analogy with Christian Science. In my spirit, I prefer Baha'ism. I find it more flexible and subtle. And it offers the poetic imagination a rich feast. Its roots are sunk in the great meta-physical dreams of the Orient. There are some luminous pages in the discourses of St Jean d'Acre [i.e. *Some Answered Questions*] of 'Abdu'l-Bahá. Bahá'u'lláh, a prisoner, succeeded in writing and answer-ing some 'tablets' of an admirable and moral beauty, under the name 'the Oppressed One' . . .[48]

Rolland referred to the Bahá'í Faith in his book *La Vie de Tolstoi* and later quoted from *Some Answered Questions* in his novel *Clerambault*.

'Thou hast taken in hand a shining lamp and art dispelling and casting away the darkness of waywardness from the hearts,' 'Abdu'l-Bahá wrote to Lady Blomfield. 'In whatever city thou dost enter, be it Paris, London, or the cities of Switzerland, turn to the Abhá Beauty, seek confirmation from the Holy Spirit, and then unloose thy tongue. Know thou of a certainty that wondrous meanings will flow from thy lips! To whatever hostel thou art invited, betake thyself, and attend whatever gathering where thou art summoned. The Blessed Beauty is with thee; rest assured.'[49]

Anxious about the future of the Geneva meetings should she return for a while to her home in London, Lady Blomfield was reassured by the Master that 'undoubtedly the maid-servant of God Miss Gibbs will con-tinue; indeed she is most kind and hospitable. I hope that through the bounteous favours of the Blessed Beauty she may burn as a bright candle in the Kingdom of God and shine as a brilliant star in the realm of glory.'[50]

In the meantime, as Lady Blomfield continued to render service at the request of the Master in Switzerland, He was preparing for His gruelling eight-month journey across North America.

'I had been waiting to answer your letter,' Lady Blomfield wrote from Mont Pèlerin on 10 March to Mirza Ahmad Sohrab, who would serve as the Master's interpreter throughout His next visit to the West, 'expecting daily that the "Paris Notes" were published and that I could send off a large number of copies to you as my contribution to the work of "Preparation" for 'Abdu'l-Bahá's visit; the money for which your Committee would have sold them, to be used for the benefit of the Preparation Fund, thus as I thought and intended, helping doubly in the "Work".'[51]

'Now to my great surprise and grief, a letter has just come, telling me that the "Paris Notes" sent off at the end of January, after being looked through, and approved by Madame Dreyfus, are not yet published!! It is a terrible blow!'[52]

Back in London, Ethel Rosenberg had been struggling valiantly to get the book published but setbacks in collecting the funds had delayed progress. Concerned that the book would not be ready for another three months, Lady Blomfield sent a telegram to the printers instructing them to send the whole packet of *Talks by 'Abdu'l-Bahá Given in Paris* to the Bahá'í Publishing Society in Chicago so that they were there in time for the Master's arrival, as He had wished.

'Lady Blomfield seems to be under the impression that her book will be ready within a week!' an exasperated Ethel Rosenberg wrote to Ahmad Sohrab. 'I fear it cannot be ready for at least another 3 weeks – or maybe a few days longer – but we are doing our very best to hurry matters forward.'[53]

On the other hand, preparations for *'Abdu'l-Bahá in London* were progressing well.

'We are hoping to sell this at 1/- [one shilling] per copy – and as Lady Blomfield's *Talks of 'Abdu'l-Bahá in Paris* is quite twice as large – I fear that cannot sell at less than 2/- per copy,' Rosenberg informed Sohrab. 'We are binding the Paris book in stiff paper to make it lighter weight for transport.'[54]

'I only wish for the spread of the beautiful "Talks" and for nothing else,' wrote Lady Blomfield. 'Our names have not been mentioned in the matter, only our initials for identification . . .'[55]

'In regard to the name of the compilers,' wrote Sohrab, 'it is my conviction that it should bear the full names of yourself, your daughters and Miss Platt. Please write me on this matter directly because I feel that your full name should appear on the title. It will give to the book an authority and a personal touch which are lacking in anonymous compilations and works.'[56]

Lady Blomfield evidently won the argument. *Talks by 'Abdu'l-Bahá Given in Paris* went to press with only the initials of its compilers added to the end of the Preface.

On 25 March 1912 'Abdu'l-Bahá left Egyptian shores aboard the SS *Cedric* and sailed for Italy on the first leg of His journey. With Him were His eldest grandson Shoghi Effendi, His personal attendants Siyyid Asadu'lláh and Áqá Khosrow, His secretary Maḥmúd, Mírzá Munír, and His translator Dr Faríd. The American believers urged the Master to leave the *Cedric* in Italy and sent funds for Him to travel by rail and boat to England there to join the maiden voyage of the *Titanic*. Fortunately, 'Abdu'l-Bahá declined the offer, returning the money for charity.

At Naples, Italian doctors who boarded the *Cedric* insisted that Shoghi Effendi, Munír and Khosrow must disembark and return to Egypt, diagnosing an eye infection that meant all three of them were unable to enter the United States. Six western believers including Louisa Mathew of London, who had also joined the *Cedric* at Naples, rallied behind the Master in trying to persuade the Italian physicians to reconsider. But the doctors were adamant. This painful episode at the very start of the journey greatly saddened the Master.

Lady Blomfield had also hoped to make a trip to Naples to see 'Abdu'l-Bahá but instead decided to donate what she would have spent on the journey to the poor.

'Thy decision not to travel to Italy was in full accord with my good pleasure,' wrote the Master, 'for it became the means of contribution to the poor.'[57]

Across the Atlantic there was mounting excitement at the Master's imminent arrival.

'All kinds of preparations are being made – there is much interest everywhere,' Mirza Ahmad Sohrab wrote to Lady Blomfield. 'So many invitations from churches, societies and clubs have been extended to Abdul-Bahá to address them that He will be kept fully busy for the next five or six months addressing them, day and night.'[58]

Sitárih's thoughts at this time were also turning frequently to the friends she had met in Stuttgart. Despite her best efforts, the believers were still struggling to achieve unity.

'I hope that egotism may be entirely dispelled, that the lights of divine bestowals may shine forth as they should,' 'Abdu'l-Bahá wrote to her. 'Were this odour not to be found in Stuttgart, that city would by now have become wholly illumined. In brief, I pray that the hearts may attain such purity as to harbour naught save the love and the knowledge of God.'[59]

Another source of anxiety that preoccupied Lady Blomfield's mind was the well-being of her sister, the actress Cecilia Gilmore, who lived in New York. On 16 May, Cecilia brought a legal suit for separation and alimony against her husband, the Broadway director William H. Gilmore. The couple had already separated in 1907 with the agreement that 'Billy' would pay $60 a month to Cecilia and their then one year old daughter, Ruth. Gilmore, however, returned to live in the family apartment in June 1911, but claimed he was only a lodger in the house. By November 1912 the case had become something of a public scandal generating a good deal of salacious press coverage. Cecilia charged Gilmore with desertion and cruelty, claiming that at the end of July 1911 he had declared he was tired of living with her and wanted a divorce. When she refused, Gilmore threatened her with physical violence. The following month Gilmore had told Cecilia that he had been having a liaison with a 'noted woman'. Cecilia told the court that she had fainted for the first time in her life when Billy made his confession. She argued that he broke the previous separation agreement when he returned to live with her in June 1911. She claimed that Gilmore earned $75 a week and had an annual income of almost $1000 from his grandmother's trust fund.

Lady Blomfield shared some of her concern for her sister in correspondence with 'Abdu'l-Bahá who, anticipating His forthcoming journey to New York, assured her, 'I will surely meet thy sister in New York and will console her.'[60] By May the following year Cecilia had won her case as well as an appeal that Gilmore had made against a previous decision, thus requiring him to pay her $1200 a year. Gilmore died at the age of 49 in 1929 at his Madison Avenue home, from acute heart problems.

At 11:40 p.m. on 14 April 1912 the ship on which the American believers had hoped 'Abdu'l-Bahá would cross the Atlantic – the *Titanic* – collided with an iceberg four days into her maiden voyage. More than 1,500 passengers and crew died, among them Lady Blomfield's good friend from her days as a young widow in Broadway, the painter Frank Millet. Millet's death was also a cause for sadness for another believer, Agnes Parsons, who raised Millet's fate with 'Abdu'l-Bahá a few days after the disaster.

'Where one has been devoted to his work in life – art, or whatever it may be,' the Master replied, 'it is regarded as worship and he is undoubtedly surrounded by the mercy of God.'[61]

The journalist and spiritualist W.T. Stead – with whom the Master had conversed while in London - also perished in the *Titanic*. Presciently, in 1892 Stead had penned a novel, *From the Old World to the New*, which told the story of a ship sinking after hitting an iceberg in the North Atlantic. In Stead's book a number of passengers were picked up by a passing ship, the *Majestic*, captained by one E.J. Smith, whom Stead wrote into a number of his stories. Two decades later, Smith was the captain of the *Titanic* and Stead was among his ill-fated passengers.

Nine days after the sinking, 'Abdu'l-Bahá reflected upon the disaster. 'Although such an event is indeed regrettable,' He told an audience gathered in Washington DC, 'we must realize that everything which happens is due to some wisdom and that nothing happens without a reason.'

> Therein is a mystery; but whatever the reason and mystery it was a very sad occurrence, one which brought tears to many eyes and distress to many souls. I was greatly affected by this disaster. Some of those who were lost voyaged on the *Cedric* with us as far as Naples and afterward sailed upon the other ship. When I think of them, I am very sad indeed. But when I consider this calamity in another aspect, I am consoled by the realization that the worlds of God are infinite; that though they were deprived of this existence, they have other opportunities in the life beyond . . .

'Therefore, the souls of those who have passed away from earth and completed their span of mortal pilgrimage in the *Titanic* disaster have hastened to a world superior to this,' He said.[62]

In a letter to the American Bahá'í composer Louise Waite, more than a year later, Lady Blomfield wrote that she was extremely distressed to learn that two letters she had written to Waite had never been received.

'One was to thank you for your delightful Bahá'í music which we so greatly appreciate,' she wrote, 'this I sent you from Switzerland, and I can only suppose that it went down in the *Titanic*, with several registered packets, of which I received notice. These of course were only valuable to myself and the friends who did not receive them. Some were letters to the Master, when he should arrive in America!'[63]

Returning to London in the early summer of 1912, Lady Blomfield was relieved finally to receive the first edition of *Talks by 'Abdu'l-Bahá Given in Paris*. She immediately dispatched a copy to the Master and 25 copies to *Star of the West* magazine in Chicago.

'We loved our work of putting the "Talks in Paris" into English, for the edification of those who had not the blessed privilege of hearing the Beloved one,' she wrote to 'Abdu'l-Bahá.[64] After receiving a telegram from Him which contained news of three meetings in Chicago attended by thousands of people, she wrote back that she was there 'in heart and spirit', wishing she had been present 'at this blessed time'.[65]

After being absent from London for some nine months, Lady Blomfield enjoyed reuniting with her fellow Bahá'ís whose activities had continued since the Master's departure from their midst. Lady Blomfield cherished the hope that 'Abdu'l-Bahá would return to the city and wrote to Him from the apartment in Cadogan Gardens where He had stayed ten months earlier that His 'London home is awaiting Him, whenever His glorious work may bring Him here. He knows well how we all have welcoming hearts, and even the house is waiting with an expectant smile for His presence.'[66]

In anticipation of the Master's possible return, Mary and Ellinor had started taking Persian lessons from Dr Luṭfu'lláh Ḥakím and were working hard to make progress.

'We ardently wish Him to rest here after His arduous American work – in the house of his devoted daughter in the Holy Service,' wrote Lady Blomfield.[67]

'Undoubtedly, by the time of my arrival in London they will be fluent in Persian,' 'Abdu'l-Bahá replied.[68]

'O thou revered lady!' the Master told Sitárih. 'Thou must raise aloft the banner of Bahá'u'lláh in London and become so aflame with the fire of the love of God as to rouse and stir every listless soul and confer a new life upon the dead . . .'[69]

'Abdu'l-Bahá encouraged Lady Blomfield to give eloquent speeches and gather friends together once a week to commemorate God. He also warned her about the presence in the city of Azalís, followers of Bahá'u'lláh's disloyal half-brother Mírzá Yaḥyá.

'Moreover, the bearers of the "Golden Key" are in reality Azalís. They have been stealthily seduced and instructed to be duplicitous and dissembling, and they are indeed dissemblers. Admit them not into your circle and avoid their company, for they are hypocrites . . .' wrote the Master, warning her also that Professor E.G. Browne was 'in perfect league with the enemies of Bahá'u'lláh and hath become an instrument in their hands.' 'In the heart of every soul he doth meet he instilleth doubt and suspicion, and whatever lies and calumnies the enemies teach him, he imparteth unto others. You should know this. Erelong, however, he will find himself in the utmost remorse.'[70]

Lady Blomfield was saddened to hear the news of Professor Browne's coming under the influence of covenant-breakers and hoped that he might return to the appreciation of the truth.

'Be not grieved at this . . .' wrote 'Abdu'l-Bahá. 'We showed the utmost kindness to Professor Browne. He was most grateful, and in his first book . . . he expressed the highest praise. Later, however, the enemies in Persia surrounded him and flattered him to such a degree as exceedeth all description . . . but erelong he will understand that this is naught but manifest loss, and will regret his actions.'[71]

Lady Blomfield asked 'Abdu'l-Bahá if she should convey the warning to shun the Azalís to all the Bahá'í friends. He advised her to warn only those in whom she could confide and who would not spread it further.

Contemplating spreading the true message of Bahá'u'lláh to those with whom she had once had intimate contact through her husband's family, Lady Blomfield decided in July 1912 to deliver some articles she had written, based on 'Abdu'l-Bahá's talks, to the Archbishop of Canterbury, the principal leader of the Church of England. The Archbishop at that time was a Scotsman, Randall Thomas Davidson, who served in the post from 1903 until 1928, and was married to the daughter of a previous Archbishop of Canterbury, Archibald Campbell Tait, who had been Sir Arthur Blomfield's headmaster at Rugby.

The Archbishop's response to Lady Blomfield's proclamation of the Bahá'í message was civil but not to Sitárih's hopeful expectation. He returned the papers soon afterwards with a letter stating, 'I have heard and read a good deal about this particular matter. At present I am not prepared to assign to this teacher whom you commend the position of religious leadership which he somewhat solemnly claims. But I am very glad to have the facts before me in the compendious form in which you have put them.'[72]

Amongst Lady Blomfield's surviving papers is a draft in pencil of a letter that clearly shows she was agonizing on how to answer the Archbishop's response.

'I thank you for returning my short paper on the work of Abdul-Bahá,' she wrote. 'If it appears to your Grace that he makes claim to any honours for himself, it must be entirely due to my failure in accentuating the fact that he discourages emphatically any attachment to personality. I have never seen a truer humility; his only claim is one which we all, if we are Christians, make, and some are able to substantiate i.e.: to be a Servant of God, working in the Divine Cause of the Grand Unity of the whole Human Race. His special mission is to call upon all God's servants in every tribe and nation, to unite in working for this Universal Brotherhood, and to emphasise the truth that all children must be taught Religion, for without it there can be no lasting civilization!'[73]

At the end of July, still struggling with how to respond to the Archbishop, Sitárih wrote to 'Abdu'l-Bahá, informing Him that a 'high Ecclesiastical Dignitary' did not refer to her article in an 'appreciative manner' and asking the Master whether she should write again or just let the matter drop.[74] Evidently she persevered. A copy of *Talks in Paris* was sent to the Archbishop with the suggestion that they might meet. Lady Blomfield heard nothing. Undeterred, she wrote again enclosing a copy of *The Hidden Words of Bahá'u'lláh*. On 30 November 1912 Archbishop Davidson thanked her for the 'pamphlet' and expressed his distress that Sitárih did not receive his gratitude for the edition of *Talks in Paris*.

'I thought it had been acknowledged, but possibly I was mistaken,' he wrote. 'I am not myself resident in London at present, and I am afraid that such an interview as you suggest would be practically impossible.'[75]

The summer of 1912 saw Lady Blomfield occupied with numerous Bahá'í activities in London. In addition to holding a weekly gathering in her home on Friday evenings, she made a presentation to workers of the Church Army, hosted an afternoon meeting at which she spoke on the history and message of the Bahá'í Cause, and made a similar presentation to some Theosophists. A friends of hers, a Mrs Rooper, organized a meeting for 20 of her friends in her own home at which Lady Blomfield spoke and read some of the Master's talks. The response, she reported, was very positive and many of those in attendance expressed an interest in attending the Friday evening meetings. She informed 'Abdu'l-Bahá that after the talk she served tea, coffee and sweets, since this encouraged the guests to stay and ask questions.

'Holding receptions in thy house on Friday evenings where tea, coffee and sweets are served is most agreeable,' commented the Master.[76]

Lady Blomfield also supported a meeting hosted by the elderly believer Annie Gamble in Putney where there were several people interested in the Faith. She attended a gathering hosted by Ethel Rosenberg at which some of the friends from Stuttgart were present. There was an invitation too from another friend, a Mrs Gordon, who invited Sitárih to speak on the Cause at a reception in her home to be held the following October.

Lady Blomfield was also delighted to report to the Master that a Miss Franckel was working on a Swedish translation of *Talks in Paris*.

'Rest assured', 'Abdu'l-Bahá told her, 'that in heart and spirit I am with thee, and that at every moment I seek for thee divine confirmations.'[77]

'Perchance on my return I will pass through London and upon reaching it I will find it luminous,' wrote the Master from New York City.[78]

During this period the British Bahá'ís learned that the acclaimed Oxford theologian and biblical critic Professor Thomas Kelly Cheyne was showing a profound interest in the Bahá'í message. An ordained Anglican priest, Cheyne was on the editorial board of *The Christian Commonwealth*, which had extensively covered 'Abdu'l-Bahá's first visit to London. For 23 years, after lecturing in Hebrew and divinity, Cheyne served as Oxford University's prestigious 'Oriel Professor of the Interpretation of Holy Scripture', specializing in the field of Old Testament Studies. In July 1912 Ethel Rosenberg encountered Cheyne, now in his seventies and almost entirely an invalid, on his way through London.

'He is a reverent and deeply convinced Bahá'í,' Lady Blomfield reported to 'Abdu'l-Bahá. 'He wishes to read up a good deal on the Sacred Cause, as he intends, when in better health, to write a book in its favour.' The book, she added, 'will surely be an antidote to anything that the enemy's book can say!'[79]

'Abdu'l-Bahá instructed Lady Blomfield to 'Write in particular to Professor Cheyne at Oxford University, give him my deepest love and highest regards, and tell him that I have the utmost desire and longing to meet him. I beseech God that he may shine even as a star above the horizon of true knowledge.'[80]

Lady Blomfield duly conveyed the Master's greetings to Cheyne.

'. . . your Message of our loved and venerated Head is a heavenly surprise,' wrote the professor on 11 September, adding that he and his wife were both eagerly anticipating a second visit of 'Abdu'l-Bahá to Britain. 'I want so much to make Bahai views of "love" a reality for me. But I cannot move about . . . Now, would this Great One confer on me the favour of a visit? I live close by to Manchester College, the Head of which [Dr Estlin Carpenter] would readily grant the use of lecture-hall. I long for it.

'In any case, some day will you not arrange for a Bahai meeting? We will try to get those who sympathise to come . . .'[81]

The thought of welcoming the Master to Oxford took hold of Cheyne's imagination and in the following month he wrote again to Lady Blomfield assuring her that should He pay them a visit, 'Abdu'l-Bahá would see at once that Oxford 'is a first-rate place for "sowing the seed".'[82]

'. . . it is important that we should endeavour to make the word of the kingdom known here,' wrote Cheyne, urging Lady Blomfield also to contemplate visiting the city to speak on the Bahá'í Cause. 'Would you introduce the subject to our audience? I understand that you have often spoken at such meetings . . . A long lecture room, often used by professors, is offered for our use by Dr Carpenter, the Principal at Manchester College. We think any Wednesday would be the best day, there are plenty of trains. 3 pm would be the best time . . . Mrs Cheyne and I would be so glad if you would join us at lunch with any other friend who may accompany you.'[83]

Sitárih took up Cheyne's invitation and spoke at Manchester College on 30 October. The Cheynes sent out the invitation which read:

WHAT IS THE BAHAI RELIGION?
You are invited to a meeting to be held in Manchester College (Oxford) on Wednesday October 30th at 3 pm. There will be an address by Lady Blomfield preparatory to the second English visit of Abdul Baha, the Persian Prophet. T.K. Cheyne Emeritus Professor of Interpretation, etc.[84]

'Dear Lady Blomfield,' wrote Dr Estlin Carpenter on 7 November, the week after Lady Blomfield's talk at his college. 'Thank you very much for sending the little volume of talks by 'Abdu'l-Bahá in Paris. They breathe exactly that lofty air of character and devotion which you so aptly described to us.'[85]

By the end of the year the Master would be joining Lady Blomfield and Estlin Carpenter at Manchester College, preceded by an encounter at Cheyne's Oxford home, in her words, 'fraught with pathos'.[86]

'Indeed thou art my daughter and the dear maidservant of Bahá'u'lláh,' wrote 'Abdu'l-Bahá to Lady Blomfield on 17 September 1912, a day on which He was newly arrived in Minneapolis.

Therefore I beseech the Kingdom of Bahá'u'lláh that the confirmations of the Holy Spirit may descend upon thee unceasingly, that thou mayest progress in this Cause day by day, that thou mayest so shine in faith and certitude, in constancy and steadfastness as to astonish every soul, that thou mayest become the cause of guidance of a great multitude, and that all London may become a glass globe and thou its lamp. Marvel not if the gracious favours and bestowals of Bahá'u'lláh were to cause a mere star (*sitárih*) to shine as brightly as the moon wherewith to illumine the horizon of London.[87]

For Sitárih, the day when the Master would return to London was a bright prospect indeed.

CHAPTER SIX

✳ THE BRILLIANT LIGHT

I beseech God to grant thee His divine confirmation and assistance,
that thou mayest become the luminous candle of that city
and summon all the people to the Kingdom of God.[1]
'Abdu'l-Bahá

On 5 December 1912 'Abdu'l-Bahá sailed away from New York City after
239 days tirelessly proclaiming Bahá'u'lláh's message of universal peace to
the people of North America. His historic journeys to the West – and in
particular this eight-month tour of the United States of America – wrote
Shoghi Effendi some three decades later, 'may be said to have marked the
culmination of His ministry, a ministry whose untold blessings and stupendous achievements only future generations can adequately estimate'.[2]
Just as the 'day-star of Bahá'u'lláh's Revelation had shone forth in its merid-
ian splendour' when the Manifestation of God had addressed the kings
and rulers of the earth from Adrianople, observed the Guardian, so too
did 'the Orb of His Covenant mount its zenith and shed its brightest rays
when He Who was its appointed Centre ('Abdu'l-Bahá) arose to blazon the
glory and greatness of His Father's Faith among the peoples of the West'.[3]

'Abdu'l-Bahá's second visit to Great Britain came at the end of an eight-
day crossing of the Atlantic Ocean aboard the SS *Celtic*. The 20,000 ton
ship had been making the regular return journey between England and
America since 1901. The Master's voyage aboard the *Celtic* was on seas
which were, for the first four days, as 'calm as a mirror'.[4] 'Abdu'l-Bahá sent
two boxes of roses to the Captain and lavished sweets and fruit on the
stewards. The Captain made a courtesy call to 'Abdu'l-Bahá on 7 December and expressed his pleasure at having Him on board.

As the smooth crossing continued, the Master remarked that He would
like to see a big storm. The heavens complied and by five o'clock in the
evening on 9 December, three days of relentlessly turbulent weather were

unleashed upon the *Celtic* and its storm-tossed passengers. Up on the deck, 'Abdu'l-Bahá delighted in the elements.

'Look at that imperial wave, how it mounts high and devours the smaller waves!' He enthused. 'It is a wonderful sight. This is the best day. I am enjoying it.'[5]

Not wishing to miss any opportunity to spread His father's message, 'Abdu'l-Bahá addressed more than 60 first class passengers on the last night of the voyage, recounting stories of His eight months in America.

'They were all greatly impressed and came and expressed their pleasure,' wrote Mirza Ahmad Sohrab,[6] 'Abdu'l-Bahá's interpreter who took copious notes every day of the Master's journey to North America and His second visit to Europe.

The *Celtic* forged ahead through the unabating storm, around the southernmost tip of Lady Blomfield's homeland Ireland and, as the waters calmed, arrived in a dank and rainy Liverpool on the northwest coast of England. It was Liverpool's port, and in particular its alliance with the slave trade, that had been responsible for the city's expansion in the 18th century. By the early years of the following century, 40 per cent of the world's trade passed through the city. On Friday 13 December 1912 the majority of the city's inhabitants were unaware, however, of the historic events unfolding at their port. As the *Celtic* docked, a dozen Bahá'ís gathered, waving handkerchiefs to welcome the Centre of Bahá'u'lláh's covenant back to British shores.

Lady Blomfield did not join her fellow believers in Liverpool as the Master stepped for the second time onto English soil. It had been left to Elizabeth Herrick to make the journey from London and arrange a small programme of talks for the Master in the city. Hippolyte Dreyfus, from Paris, was also present, along with a small band of Bahá'ís from the north of England.

'Suddenly we caught sight of Abdul-Baha in the ship's bow,' wrote one of them, Isabel Fraser, 'and as she hove to he walked slowly down the long deck till he stood quite alone, in the very centre of the centre deck. All eyes on the landing stage were at once rivetted upon him as he peered over the ship's side into the rain and gloom of Liverpool. The huge modern boat made a fitting frame for the Master-symbol, as it is of this outpouring of power, designed as it is to bring brothers into closer touch, and Abdul-Baha, the Centre of this dispensation, appeared standing in command.'[7]

'It was but for an hour or so that we were in contact with that great soul,' recalled Edward Hall from Manchester, who had journeyed to Liverpool for a glimpse of the Master, 'yet from that time began a real and enduring assurance of the truth in my life . . . I did not go for romantic reasons nor to witness anything sentimental. I went to welcome a mighty figure of the coming Kingdom.' Hall described his encounter with the Master as a 'brief but very beautiful incident in my life – one worth many years of a person's existence.'[8]

'Abdu'l-Bahá spent two days in Liverpool, staying at the Midland Adelphi Hotel, 'the most beautiful hotel in the city'.[9] During His stay, He addressed two public meetings – the first at the Theosophical Society and the following day at Pembroke Chapel, a Baptist church where Elizabeth Herrick had once worshipped. In both presentations He delivered His talk in Persian with Hippolyte Dreyfus translating into English.

'The Theosophists are very dear to me, for they have abandoned all prejudice,' the Master said at the first gathering. 'We both (Theosophists and Bahais) have abandoned all dogmas in our earnest search for truth. But look at the tribes and nations of the world – why are they seething with contention? Because they are not seeking truth. Truth is one.'[10]

The following night, Reverend Donald Fraser welcomed the Master to the Pembroke Chapel expressing his deep appreciation at having Him in his church. 'Abdu'l-Bahá hesitated to climb up to the pulpit saying He did not like to be above the audience. When someone pointed out to Him that those in the gallery would be above Him and would hear all the better were He to do so, He consented to speak from the pulpit. The Master spoke about the oneness of humanity after which the hymn 'All People That on Earth Do Dwell' was sung. Later, in the vestry, 'Abdu'l-Bahá wrote a blessing for Reverend Fraser in the church book, 'O Thou Kind Almighty, confirm Thou this servant of Thine, Mr. Fraser, in the service of Thy Kingdom. Make him illumined; make him heavenly; make him spiritual; make him divine! Thou art the Generous, the King!'[11]

On the morning of Monday 16 December, 'Abdu'l-Bahá departed Liverpool for London by train, in the company of Hippolyte Dreyfus-Barney, Ahmad Yazdi, Elizabeth Herrick and Isabel Fraser.

'I am most pleased with you,' the Master informed the two women. 'You are the real servants of the Covenant.'[12]

'You must become like a burning torch,' He said, 'so that you may be able to melt mountains of snow. Europe is filled with mountains which are snowcapped all the year around. May you attain to such a degree of heat that you may melt the snow. Europe is submerged in materialism. People are not thinking of God. All their attention is turned toward matter and nature. Like unto cows they graze in the meadows which are overgrown with grass. They can see nothing beyond their noses. America is much better. People in that country are investigating the Reality. They are more susceptible to spiritual life.'[13]

Shortly before two o'clock in the afternoon, the train carrying the Master and His entourage reached London's Euston station where some 50 of His admirers had gathered to welcome Him. Lady Blomfield was there with a car, ready to transport Him back to her home at 97 Cadogan Gardens. He joined her and her daughters in the automobile without His interpreter. Much to their surprise, Sitárih's daughters – now young women in their twenties – discovered that 'Abdu'l-Bahá's proficiency in the English language had much improved since they had last welcomed Him to their home. They later recounted that He conversed with them quite fluently in their mother tongue during that journey across London.

Once again the Blomfields vacated their apartment and moved in with friends nearby to give the Master and His entourage the necessary space for their stay. That afternoon 'Abdu'l-Bahá chose to rest and then, after a short walk in the garden, a group of reporters arrived to interview Him. Questions ranged across the teachings of Bahá'u'lláh and 'Abdu'l-Bahá's thoughts on the visit to America, a nation of which He could not speak highly enough. On many occasions during this second stay in Britain the Master shared His unbounded enthusiasm for the reception He had received across the Atlantic.

On the evening of 'Abdu'l-Bahá's arrival Lady Blomfield hosted a dinner, inviting a Christian minister whom she had met in Switzerland, the Reverend Daniel Cooper-Hunt. When Sitárih had been in Geneva earlier that year, 'Abdu'l-Bahá had addressed a message to the clergyman.

'Convey my utmost love and respect to Reverend Daniel Cooper-Hunt', the Master had written, 'and say: Praise be to God, the doors of the Kingdom have been opened wide, the angels of confirmation are unceasingly descending, the breath of the Holy Spirit conferreth a new life at every moment, and the hosts of heaven vouchsafe their assistance. I beseech God that thou mayest become the Paul of the Bahá'í Dispensation, may rend asunder the veils that blind the people, open their eyes, and make deaf ears to hear.'[14] The Master spoke in great detail with the clergyman, telling him of an opulent religious procession He had witnessed in Denver and how it contrasted with the simple life of Christ.

The following day, a believer from Belfast – most likely one Joan Waring – arrived to pay her respects to the Master. 'Abdu'l-Bahá welcomed her and told her, 'You must become the cause of the illumination of Ireland.'[15] Recounting the story of a believer from Persia who had attracted some 40 souls to the Bahá'í teachings in one year, the Master urged this follower to ignite 'four thousand lamps'[16] in the same period of time. She responded that many that she spoke to were afraid of a new religion, saying the religion of their ancestors remained good enough for them.

'They are like unto those souls who say: "We don't like fresh flowers but we are satisfied with withered and decayed flowers",' replied 'Abdu'l-Bahá. 'Decayed flowers do not have sweet fragrance; their odour is not good; they have no freshness and charm . . . Every new year needs a new flower, new fruits are necessary, fresh and gentle breezes are needed. Every new day requires new food, you cannot partake of the decayed food of yesterday.'[17]

On the afternoon of 17 December a large reception was held for the Master at Caxton Hall, at that time used as the Town Hall for the City of Westminster and much in demand as a concert hall and a venue for public meetings, including those of the suffragettes. A large gathering of friends and sympathizers heard 'Abdu'l-Bahá pay tribute once again to the American people and emphasize the unity between the United States of America and Britain. After the meeting He walked back to Cadogan Gardens where, no sooner had He arrived, than more people began to gather.

'Abdu'l-Bahá's second sojourn in London took on a similar character to the first. There were private audiences and gatherings – day in and day out – at Lady Blomfield's apartment, as well as other meetings and receptions at the homes of His followers and admirers in the city. Believers from abroad arrived to pay their respects and bask in the warmth of His presence. In the case of Laura Dreyfus-Barney, newly arrived from Paris, conversation with the Master focused on a proposed return visit for Him to the French capital. 'My mother much loved and admired Madame Dreyfus-Barney,' wrote Mary Blomfield.[18]

The elderly Hand of the Cause of God Ḥájí Amín, an Apostle of Bahá'u'lláh and the trusted courier of His mail and finances, arrived from Iran via Paris with three young Persians. When 'Abdu'l-Bahá received them, they threw themselves at His feet and wept.

'It was a touching scene,' observed Ahmad Sohrab. 'He took them up, kissed their cheeks and showed them much love.'[19]

One morning Ḥájí Amín, soon after His arrival, presented his cotton handkerchief to the Master who unwrapped it to find a piece of dry black bread and a shrivelled apple. Lady Blomfield reported:

> The friend exclaimed: 'A poor Bahá'í workman came to me: 'I hear thou goest into the presence of our Beloved. Nothing have I to send, but this my dinner. I pray thee offer it to Him with my loving devotion.'
>
> 'Abdu'l-Bahá spread the poor handkerchief before Him, leaving His own luncheon untasted. He ate of the workman's dinner, broke pieces off the bread, and handed them to the assembled guests, saying, 'Eat with me of this gift of humble love.'[20]

Among the countless callers who arrived at 97 Cadogan Gardens to hear 'Abdu'l-Bahá on the morning of 18 December was Professor Edward G. Browne. No mention was made of his recent contact with individuals who were inimical to 'Abdu'l-Bahá's leadership of the Bahá'í community, although the Master did call Browne to His room for a private conversation after His public talk was ended.

'The last time I met you,' He told the distinguished Orientalist, 'was twenty-two years ago in Acca under different environment, but now I have the pleasure of seeing you in London.'[21]

The two men then conversed in Persian together, reportedly ranging over subjects as diverse as Persia, inventions, the history of the Bahá'í Movement, and the education of women.

The memory of His extraordinary experiences in the United States did not diminish as 'Abdu'l-Bahá's stay in London continued. One rainy day, having intended to take a walk, He hailed a taxi and rode through Hyde Park and Regent's Park, noticing that the streets were not very clean. He talked to His companions about the cleanliness of Broadway, New York, and its night-time illuminations – 'the Ben Hur horses, the advertisement of Spring Water, the advertisement of pepsin, the advertisement of automobiles; and many others which are lighted at night; he told about the electric office in Denver which is a tall and magnificent building, how at night the whole structure is lighted from top to bottom.'[22] 'Abdu'l-Bahá even spoke about His high opinion of America to the ambassador and consul from the Persian embassy who called to meet Him on consecutive days. He praised the system of government in the United States, its federal system, its educational opportunities and the resources. He also spoke about Persia and Turkey and His concerns over the war that had been rocking the Balkan region of Europe.

For months the situation in the Balkans had been growing more volatile. Fear of Austro-Hungarian expansion combined with the instability caused by a vulnerable Ottoman Empire weakened by its war with Italy over Libya since 1911, prompted the formation of the Balkan League. This was an alliance of Bulgaria, Greece, Montenegro and Serbia formed under Russian auspices in the spring of 1912 with the purpose of taking Macedonia away from the Ottomans. Bulgaria was also disturbed by the growing concentration of Turkish troops on her borders in Adrianople, the town where 'Abdu'l-Bahá had been exiled with Bahá'u'lláh and His followers almost 50 years previously. War was officially declared at the beginning of October in a move to repatriate large parts of Balkan ethnic populations who were living under the Ottoman Empire. The swift campaign ended five centuries of Ottoman rule in the Balkans. Hostilities officially ceased on 2 December as the victorious allies set conditions for negotiations over the status of various territories they had taken. Peace talks were underway in London, as 'Abdu'l-Bahá commenced His visit.

Equally alert and deeply sensitive to the injustices and perilous conditions of society, Lady Blomfield was meanwhile watching with mounting anxiety the cause of women's suffrage, which she supported despite deploring their resorting to extreme tactics to promote their cause. A famous story has been passed down of the Master's conversation with a suffragette, possibly Emmeline Pankhurst, which tells how, when the visitor referred to 'Abdu'l-Bahá as a 'prophet', He replied 'Oh, no! I am a man, like you.'[23]

Mrs Pankhurst certainly met the Master during this visit to London. He advised her and the other suffragettes He encountered that they should not resort to violent measures such as window smashing, wrecking trains and letter boxes, 'nay, rather they should demand their rights with the power of intelligence, with scientific accomplishments, with artistic attainments,' He said. 'Unseemly deeds would rather retard the realization of their cherished hope. In this age a weak person resorts to frightful measures, but an intelligent person uses the superior power of intelligence and wisdom.'[24]

Lady Drower, better known as the author Ethel Stefana Stevens, was also among the callers, journeying all the way from Southampton to meet the Master. She had travelled extensively in the Middle East from where she drew the inspiration for her books. Three years previously she had stayed for several months in the Holy Land where she had been inspired to use the Bahá'í community of Haifa and 'Akká as the setting for her romantic novel, *The Mountain of God*, published by Mills and Boon in

1911. 'Abdu'l-Bahá expressed His happiness at seeing her again and they enjoyed an extended conversation. She informed Him that she was writing a novel about the second coming of Christ. 'Abdu'l-Bahá told her how all the nations and religions had circumscribed limits for His coming and how when He came, many rejected Him.[25]

A remarkable cosmopolitan gathering filled the large hall at the Westminster Palace Hotel five days before Christmas, where the Master spoke on the subject of peace. The room was packed to capacity, with some attendees forced to sit on the floor or squeeze into the doorways. Writers, thinkers, scientists, diplomats, and distinguished guests from East and West were in the audience which was 'set aglow', wrote Ahmad Sohrab.

'All the faces were shining, and all the people were responsive. Indeed to have such a well attended meeting in London at this time of the year is nothing short of a miracle.'[26]

The Liberal politician and former head of the British Chamber of Commerce Sir Thomas Barclay chaired the meeting. He introduced the Bahá'í teachings as a 'system of thought and conduct'.

'I wonder if I have understood the Revelation of Baha'o'llah,' he said. 'If I have, it has a singularly good Christian ring and I should interpret its meaning as "Be a real Christian and you will be a good Bahai".'

'But I am merely presiding and not proselytising,' he hurriedly added as he introduced the Master to the crowd.[27]

'Abdu'l-Bahá spoke earnestly, reported Isabel Fraser, 'gesticulating freely and one could almost follow his thoughts as the light and fire played over his countenance.'

Once again the conflict in the Balkans was very much at the forefront of the Master's mind:

' . . . blood is being freely and copiously shed,' He mourned, 'lives are being destroyed, houses are pillaged, cities are razed to the ground, and all this through religious prejudice; while in reality, the foundation of the religion of God is love.'[28]

'As the English government is a just government,' the Master concluded, 'and as the British nation is a noble nation and accomplishes whatever it undertakes, it is my hope that in this matter it will manifest the utmost wisdom and sagacity, so that the sun of peace may dawn on the horizon of the Balkans, so that eternal fellowship may be realized among them, and whenever in the future there is any difficult problem a conference may be called for its settlement, so that through these various conferences all the troubles of humanity may be solved.'[29]

'Abdu'l-Bahá's words were met with a deep silence. Sir Thomas Barclay introduced Charlotte Despard, President of the Women's Freedom League, who expressed the deep privilege she felt at 'Abdu'l-Bahá's presence amongst them.

'There is unrest everywhere,' she told the meeting,

> . . . unrest in industry, unrest among the women of the country, unrest intellectually and unrest religiously, and some are frightened as they look out, and wonder if these days mean the disintegration of which we have been hearing, which is the very fruit of this. But some of us think that this unrest at the present moment is actually a healthy symptom. That it is on account of the unreality of things that people generally are troubled and anxious and longing for some settled thing.
>
> We have the mighty movements – the women's movement, the religious movement, the spiritual movement. At the basis of all the great religions that have moved the world there are the same great truths. This unrest at the moment, and of ancient times though in different words and different form are still the same. God is one. There is nothing but God anywhere. He is the one eternal life; because we are in Him therefore we are eternal; death is but the dropping of a garment.
>
> This is the principle of unity and we are thankful beyond measure that it has been brought to us today.[30]

'Abdu'l-Bahá closed the meeting with a blessing, hands outstretched, palms turned upward.

> O Thou Kind Almighty, we supplicate at the Throne of Grace for mercy for the blood that has been shed in the Balkans; the children that are being made orphans; the mothers losing their dear sons; the sons who have become fatherless; the cities that have been destroyed; the many hearts that have been filled with sorrow; the many tears that are being shed and the many spirits that are in a state of agitation!
>
> . . . O Lord! confirm this just government in the establishment of peace, so that it may hold aloft the banner of reconciliation in the Balkans. May the light of love shine and flame forth undefiled. O Lord! Thou art Almighty; Thou art Merciful; Thou art Clement; Thou art Kind![31]

Many of the guests who attended the Westminster Palace Hotel meeting went to Cadogan Gardens the following morning to greet 'Abdu'l-Bahá. Among them was a woman who had travelled 40 miles the previous day to hear Him. She told the Master of a friend of hers who had lost the power of speech and the use of his hands in an accident but who wrote by manoeuvring a pen in his mouth. This young man sorely wished to have a signed photograph of the Master. 'Abdu'l-Bahá gave her a message for the young man. She was to tell him that although he was speechless yet he had the language of the heart and spoke with the tongue of the intellect. The Master hoped that he would acquire the language of the Kingdom, which was not in need of any outward means to convey thoughts.

The Blomfields' daughters had inherited their parents' keen love of the theatre and both were budding actresses. It being Christmas, Mary was performing in the nativity play *Eager Heart* at Church House, Westminster. Dedicated to 'all who see and worship the One in the many', *Eager Heart* was the first major stage work written by Alice Buckton, one of 'Abdu'l-Bahá's devotees, and with which she enjoyed a huge success for the entire first half of the 20th century. It had become a perennial feature of the Christmas season since it was first produced in 1904.

The play tells the story of a young girl called Eager Heart – played in this production by Mary Blomfield – who on Christmas Eve is preparing a humble meal in the hope that a 'royal' guest the whole city is talking about will stop by her door and rest. In the best tradition of English Christmas entertainments, Eager Heart has two unpleasant sisters, Eager Fame and Eager Sense, the first being strong-willed and domineering, the second glamorous and gluttonous. Both sisters are also keen to meet the special visitor and believe he will be attracted by their ostentation. While her two siblings venture into the streets to join the waiting crowds, Eager Heart receives an unexpected visit from a travel-weary couple, carrying a small baby and seeking food and shelter. They ask her if they can rest there. Initially torn between her hope of hosting the expected royal visitor and helping the needy arrivals, Eager Heart allows them in and feeds them before going outside to see if the anticipated one has arrived. On the way, she encounters shepherds, kings and travellers, all seeking him. She is amazed to see them gravitating towards her home where they bow in adoration before the weary family, and in particular the small child. Eager Heart realizes exactly who it is she has in her house, and her sisters, returning home, also recognize the folly of their ways.

At 3:30 on the afternoon of Saturday 21 December, 'Abdu'l Bahá left Cadogan Gardens in Mrs Thornburgh-Cropper's car for a performance of the play, one of the first dramatic performances He had ever witnessed in His life.

'This was a memorable occasion,' wrote Lady Blomfield.[32] Some 1200 people packed the hall as Mary Blomfield opened with the lines,

> To-night the weary world is husht and still!
> Out on the plains the shepherds watch! And we,
> Dwelling in cities, keep our doors ajar,
> Lest He should come this way, the royal Child,
> Two thousand years our King! Alas, to think
> How many highways He must tread to-night,
> Will know Him not, nor see Him as He comes!

'Abdu'l-Bahá was rapt throughout the entire performance. Lady Blomfield observed how the Master was keenly interested in the story unfolding on stage and 'wept during the scene in which the Holy Child and His parents, overcome with fatigue, and suffering from hunger, were met by the hesitation of Eager Heart to admit them to the haven of rest which she had prepared, she, of course, failing to recognize the sacred visitors'.[33]

Mary Blomfield interpreted the character of Eager Heart, according to another spectator, with a 'delicacy and artistic appreciation that was wonderful. There was such longing, such unutterable desire in every movement and word for the King.'[34]

Following the performance 'Abdu'l-Bahá went up onto the stage to speak with the actors who circled around Him.

'It was an arresting scene,' reported Lady Blomfield. 'In the Eastern setting the Messenger, in His Eastern robes, speaking to them in the beautiful Eastern words of the Divine significance of the events which had been portrayed.'[35]

After complimenting them on their performance, 'Abdu'l-Bahá spoke of the coming of Christ and how those who had eagerly awaited the appearance of the Promised One rejected Him on the grounds that He did not fulfil their interpretations of the signs that were meant to accompany the Messiah's coming.

'All these people thought they were waiting for Christ and that they were His intimate friends, but later on it was shown that He was quite foreign to them,' said 'Abdu'l-Bahá,

> . . . for when He came they knew Him not. Some used to pray day and night, saying when will that day come, when He will manifest himself? O God! Hasten that day when He shall be on earth. But when He came they did not know Him; they denied Him and were offended at Him. Every trouble befell Him; they crowned Him with thorns, and finally killed Him. Imagine how ignorant they were. Some of them shouted out, 'Crucify Him for he is not the true Messiah, whose coming is to be under special conditions, which must take place according to the facts mentioned in the Bible: but this man is from Nazareth, and we know where He lives, how does He claim to have come from Heaven while we know He is the son of Mary . . .'[36]

Christ's birthday, 'Abdu'l-Bahá told the cast, was a glorious day.

> I hope that this Christmas may be a blessed one for this noble nation and this just government. This nation can be blessed through being an instrumentality in establishing the Balkans Peace.
> Then these fighting nations shall become friendly and these dark clouds of enmity that have encircled the horizon of Balkans shall be removed. The light of Peace shall shine forth, darkness and enmity shall vanish . . .[37]

The Master commended everyone on their performances.

'It was very effective,' He said. 'I wept when I saw Christ in His mother's bosom coming homeless and lonely in the world. I hope you will succeed in portraying many illumined scenes in the future.'[38] To those who had played angels, He recommended that they all 'be angels as long as they live'.[39]

The following morning the Master spoke again to friends assembled at Lady Blomfield's apartment about the performance, which evidently left a marked impression on Him. After praising the actors once more, He reflected on the expectations of people who, when the Promised One appears, are unwilling to offer Him shelter.

'They prepare palaces for Him, they decorate the streets, they arrange downy couches,' the Master said, 'but He, the Son of Man, cometh when no one knoweth. Through the highways and byways He walks, people unconscious of His divine presence, pursuing their own pleasure and yet expecting His arrival as a king and ruler.'[40]

Later that same day an actress arrived to meet 'Abdu'l-Bahá.

'We also have a theatre,' the Master told her. The visitor immediately became interested and enthusiastic.

'Where is it?' she asked. 'I should love to see it. Can I play in it?'

'Our theatre,' the Master answered, 'is built in a country where there is eternal springtime, the streets of that city are as clean as the surface of a mirror, the lights of that playhouse are the rays of the Sun of Reality, the actors of our drama are the Holy Manifestations of God, the audience is composed of pure and sanctified souls. They play their parts with the most delicate art, they deliver their words with power and potency.

'The stage of our theatre is the arena upon which is played the sublimest tragedy, the most terrible dramas, the most thrilling and heart throbbing events of life. Come and join our company. You have acted all your life in the material stage, now come and act on this celestial stage. Your fellow actors will assist you, will coach you in your part and step by step you will become a star shining in the galaxy of these heavenly inspired dramatists.'[41]

Every day of the Master's visit Lady Blomfield brought to Him those who had travelled from near and far, curious to meet Him. It must have been a particular delight for her to introduce to Him on Sunday 22 December three of her late husband's grandchildren with their mother, the wife of Lady Blomfield's stepson, Charles. One of the children, a small girl, went straight to the Master. He embraced her, gave her some candy and held her in His arms.

'My dear baby, my sweet, my very sweet baby,' He said to her. 'I have not seen a child for a day or two,' He told Lady Blomfield, hugging the girl closer. The child sang 'Abdu'l-Bahá a Christmas carol before telling Him about her doll and horses and cars and elephants. The Master told her how He would like to take her to the land where Christ was born, where orange trees blossom, where the sun always shines, where the stars always glow and the weather is always clear.[42]

'This girl will progress very much,' He informed her mother. 'She is intelligent and keen. Educate her properly. Give her Bahá'í instruction, so that her thoughts may become luminous, her susceptibilities become keen, she may become absolute good in the world of humanity. God willing, she will study in the school of God, she will acquire ideal and heavenly knowledge and she will be informed with the mysteries of phenomena.'[43]

On 22 December Lady Blomfield received a letter from Francis Henry Skrine, a retired member of the Indian civil service and friend of the author Mark Twain. Skrine had written a book entitled *Bahaism: The Religion of Brotherhood and Its Place in the Evolution of Creeds* which had been published earlier that year by Longmans, Green and Co. His conclusion about the ideals promoted by the Master was that 'Bahaism may come with a rush that nothing can resist'.[44] Skrine was on his way to Scotland for Christmas as his father-in-law, the 'Venerable Laird of Ardvorlich' was ailing.

'Hence, to my greatest grief,' wrote Skrine, 'I cannot pay our personal respects to the Master.

'But a charming and enlightened Indian Prince, who has read my "Bahaism" is most anxious to call upon Abdul Baha. If he can be converted, what a blessing it will be for India – and he is in principle a Bahaist already,' wrote Skrine.[45] He asked Lady Blomfield to arrange an invitation to be delivered to the Maharajah of Jhalawar – a small state in what is now Rajasthan – who was then residing in South Kensington.

Lady Blomfield, describing the Maharajah as an 'enlightened and cultured prince',[46] related how he subsequently paid many visits to 'Abdu'l-Bahá:

> He gave an elaborate dinner and reception in His honour, to which we also were invited. The Maharajah and members of his suite sometimes dined at our house with the Master, who delighted all the guests with His beautiful courtesy, recounting interesting stories, often full of humour; He always loved to see happy laughing faces. And what grace He possessed – as of a king – this serene and dignified Personage Who had spent a lifetime in prison![47]

The Master also loved to see nature and particularly enjoyed one excursion to Richmond Park. Unusually for a December day in London, the sun had come out. 'Abdu'l-Bahá took off His coat for the hour-long walk, during which He talked and answered questions, occasionally making witty remarks about the horsemen and women riding by.

'In brief, it was a heavenly hour,' wrote Ahmad Sohrab.[48] Another enjoyable drive in Mrs Thornburgh-Cropper's car took the Master to Battersea Park, just south of the River Thames. On His return 'Abdu'l-Bahá met several workmen who had come some distance to see Him.

'Although I am not a Bahá'í,' said one of them, 'I like [*sic*] to tell you what I think of you. You are the Napoleon of Peace.'[49]

To another, who worked on roads, the Master said, 'Thou art paving the material roads, may thou become able to straighten the pathway of heaven. That is more important. Straighten the path for the Kingdom of God is nigh. Be thou a heavenly lineman.'[50]

Christmas Eve was a comparatively quiet day at the Blomfield's apartment. After receiving a few visitors, 'Abdu'l-Bahá reflected on the life of Jesus Christ, beginning with the trials of the Virgin Mary and the poverty and hardships of the Holy Family, and concluding with the crucifixion.

'But today, they worship His name,' the Master told the small gathering,

. . . they commemorate His birth in thousands of churches, they celebrate His virtues and they spread sumptuous feasts. Kings glory in His name. Emperors are proud to wear the golden crowns of Christendom, royalties in their luxurious palaces sing the hymns of praise and glorification because the Son of Man was born. But the King of Kings was born in a stable, He did not have a place to lay His head, He was shunned, persecuted, a crown of thorns adorned His heavenly brow. This has ever been the custom of the people, to worship those who are dead, to martyr those who are living.[51]

Sitting down to dinner that evening, the Master told His companions that He was not hungry, but that He had agreed to come to the table because Lady Blomfield had insisted. Two despotic monarchs of the East had not been able to command Him and bend His will, He laughed, but the ladies of America and Europe, because they were free, gave Him orders.[52]

'To be with the Master is a never failing joy,' wrote Mirza Ahmad Sohrab on Christmas Day, 'to listen to His words is a heavenly boon, to bask under the sunshine of His Love is eternal honour, to follow in His footsteps is the greatest happiness, to serve Him is to serve humanity, to receive His advice is the source of spiritual beatitude and to spread His Teachings and His instructions is the supreme privilege.'[53]

Throughout Christmas morning guests arrived to wish 'Abdu'l-Bahá the season's greetings. One gift brought Him much pleasure. He had previously informed Isabel Fraser on the train journey from Liverpool to London that He had learned to sew in case of emergency. She brought Him the smallest sewing kit she could find, consisting of needles, scissors, thimble and thread, all in a leather box, prompting much laughter from the Master and the promise that He would use it. To another friend who asked Him a particularly abstruse ethical question, the Master laughed, 'I will answer that some other time. Today we sing carols.'[54]

Sitárih and her daughters brought in gifts for the Master and His Persian entourage.

'They were really so kind that it made me quite ashamed,' reported Ahmad Sohrab.[55] 'Lady Blomfield is a very remarkable woman, a most sincere Bahai, an active worker, and an enthusiastic speaker; really a wonderful woman.'[56]

After holding one particularly expensive gift lovingly for a moment, 'Abdu'l-Bahá said to the gentleman who had brought it, 'You see, I have accepted your beautiful present, and it has made me very happy. I thank you for it. And now I am going to give it back to you. Sell it and give the money to the poor. The rich in England are too rich, and the poor are too poor.'[57]

'To each who came to Him on that Christmas Day,' observed Elizabeth Herrick, 'He gave a spiritual present – compatible with the capacity of each; for Abdul Baha's method of teaching the people so that they become moved with conviction, is through the heart.'[58]

At noon 'Abdu'l-Bahá spoke to those gathered about the marvels of the 20th century, linking the great stirring that occurs in the world with the birth of every Manifestation of God. Later He was taken to Mrs Thornburgh-Cropper's home to meet Lord and Lady Lamington. Lamington, born Charles Cochrane Baillie, and his wife Mary Houghton Hozier, were close friends of a number of the early Bahá'ís in Britain. Lamington had been a colonial administrator for the British government, serving as Governor of Queensland, Australia, from 1896 to 1901 and Bombay, India, from 1903 to 1907. He had a strong interest in the Middle East and spoke frequently on the subject in the House of Lords. He had been entertained by the Master in Alexandria the previous year and on this Christmas day they talked about many subjects, the Lamingtons listening attentively and referring to 'Abdu'l-Bahá as 'our Beloved Master'.

Lady Blomfield's afternoon was concluded by accompanying 'Abdu'l-Bahá to the Salvation Army shelter in Westminster where several hundred, perhaps as many as a thousand, poor men were being fed. As the Master entered, all the men rose to greet Him. Lady Blomfield was introduced by Captain Spencer of the Salvation Army. She spoke to those gathered about who 'Abdu'l-Bahá was, His sympathy for the poor, His love for those upon whom fortune has not smiled. The Master then rose and spoke of His pleasure at being present at such a gathering, how all the Prophets had been poor and of humble origin, how Christ Himself had been born in a manger. Many of the men were so taken by His presence that they forgot to eat the food in front of them, allowing it to grow cold as they listened attentively.

'My lot has ever been with those who have not the goods of this world,' the Master told them. 'When we look at the poor of humanity, we behold a world of brothers. All are the sheep of God; God is the real shepherd. The poor have ever been the cause of the freedom of the world of humanity; the poor have ever been the cause of the upbuilding of the country; the poor have ever laboured for the world's production; the morals of the poor have ever been above those of the rich; the poor are ever nearer to the threshold of God; the humanitarianism of the poor has ever been more acceptable in the threshold of God.'[59]

'You are elected by God,' said the Master. 'Christ was the associate and helper of the poor. Bahá'u'lláh was poor. He was called Darveesh. He gave up all He had in order to help the poor ones on earth. Therefore be ye happy. Always thank God.'[60]

Before entering the hall the Master had changed many pounds into shillings. He had 20 gold sovereigns and some five hundred shillings to divide among the poor men gathered. The Salvation Army captain had another idea however. He suggested using the money to host another dinner for all those present on New Year's Eve in the name of 'Abdu'l-Bahá. The Master consented.

'Our honoured guest has just given me the money for a New Year's dinner,' the Captain told the gathering, 'and all of you at this occasion will be His guests.'[61]

The men broke out into spontaneous applause, rising from their seats, cheering and waving their cutlery for many minutes. Then the Captain took 'Abdu'l-Bahá, Lady Blomfield and the retinue through the buildings to see the large clean halls furnished with good beds. Here the poor could sleep, wash clothes and get a breakfast for three pence a night. The Master was very impressed. As He was leaving, the Master said to Captain

Spencer, 'May God prosper you. May you all be under the protection of the Almighty!'[62]

'This was a notable day in the history of the Cause in England,' wrote Ahmad Sohrab that night. 'It was not only the Christmas of two thousand years ago, but to us it had a double significance, for before our eyes we could see how Christ lived in that far off period, how He taught the people, how He conversed with them and how He associated with the lowly and downtrodden.'[63]

Throughout the four days following Christmas Lady Blomfield's routine of joyfully bringing guests and visitors to the Master in her home, as well as accompanying Him to meetings with other believers, continued. There was a talk at the studio flat shared by Elizabeth Herrick and the Canadian believer Marion Jack, who was much admired by 'Abdu'l-Bahá. The Master also ventured as far as East Putney to the home of His devoted follower Annie Gamble.

'Should Prayer take the form of action?' someone asked the Master at Lady Blomfield's home on 26 December.

'Yes,' He replied.

In the Bahá'í Cause arts, sciences and all crafts are (counted as) worship. The man who makes a piece of notepaper to the best of his ability, conscientiously, concentrating all his forces on perfecting it, is giving praise to God. Briefly, all effort and exertion put forth by man from the fullness of his heart is worship, if it is prompted by the highest motives and the will to do service to humanity. This is worship: to serve mankind and to minister to the needs of the people. Service is prayer. A physician ministering to the sick, gently, tenderly, free from prejudice and believing in the solidarity of the human race, he is giving praise.

'What is the purpose of our lives?' someone else asked.

To acquire virtues. We come from the earth; why were we transferred from the mineral to the vegetable kingdom – from the plant to the animal kingdom? So that we may attain perfection in each of these kingdoms, that we may possess the best qualities of the mineral, that we may acquire the power of growing as in the plant, that we may be adorned with the instincts of the animal and possess the faculties of

sight, hearing, smell, touch and taste, until from the animal kingdom
we step into the world of humanity and are gifted with reason, the
power of invention, and the forces of the spirit.[64]

'To have seen the world's greatest prisoner amid these surroundings was a
never-to-be-forgotten picture, but one hard to repeat in words,' recalled
Elizabeth Herrick. 'Many beautiful and touching incidents could be
related of that Christmas had we the records of the hundreds that thronged
to see Him.'[65]

Eager to ensure that the wish of Reverend T. K. Cheyne to host 'Abdu'l-Bahá
in Oxford was granted, Lady Blomfield kept the Professor apprised of the
Master's movements prior to the Christmas holiday, as well as arranging to
journey with Him by train to the university city on New Year's Eve.

'I am so delighted to hear of the welfare of the beloved Master,' Cheyne
replied to her on 23 December, 'and of the spiritual impression which he
seems to have made; so delighted, too, that he can come to Oxford. Christmas and the New Year are bad times for getting up meetings; we can only
hope to get a few sympathetic hearers.'[66]

The party left London's Paddington station at 20 past ten in the morning
of 31 December and arrived in Oxford some 90 minutes later. Professor
Cheyne had invited the Master and His entourage to lunch with him and
his wife at their home close to Manchester College, where a platform had
been arranged for the Master to speak later in the afternoon.

'The meeting will begin with a short passage from the Bible and prayer,'
Cheyne informed Lady Blomfield, 'as there are hindrances to having it in
a church or chapel.'[67]

'The visit to Oxford was one of notable interest,' Sitárih remembered.
'The meeting between 'Abdu'l-Bahá and the dear, revered higher critic, Dr
T. K. Cheyne, was fraught with pathos. It seemed almost too intimate to
describe, and our very hearts were touched, as we looked on, and realized
something of the sacred emotions of that day.'[68]

When 'Abdu'l-Bahá arrived at the Cheynes' home, he embraced the
elderly professor and praised Him for 'his courageous steadfastness in
his life's work, always striving against increasing weakness, and lessening
bodily health. Through those veiling clouds the light of the mind and
spirit shone with a radiant persistence,' wrote Lady Blomfield.[69]

Cheyne showed the Master preliminary drafts of his writings about the Bahá'í teachings, expressing his faith with great fervour. His belief so moved 'Abdu'l-Bahá that He kissed Cheyne several times on the head and face and stroked his head as he spoke. 'Abdu'l-Bahá also paid much attention to Cheyne's wife, Elizabeth Gibson, a poet who cared for her husband with a devotion that also greatly touched the Master.

Surpassing Cheyne's expectations of a small turnout on New Year's Eve, a large audience gathered to hear 'Abdu'l-Bahá speak at Manchester College. The meeting was presided over by its Principal, Dr J. Estlin Carpenter, a prominent Unitarian minister and authority on comparative religion. Dr Carpenter paid an eloquent tribute to 'Abdu'l-Bahá and His work in his introductory remarks, saying that what He promoted 'was a movement not to inspire another religion, but to create peace and goodwill amongst the people'.[70]

'Abdu'l-Bahá's theme for the talk was the importance of science, which distinguishes man from the animal.

'All the sciences and crafts were once the mysteries of nature,' the *Oxford Times* reported the Master as saying, 'but man had discovered them, and out of the plain of invisibility he had brought them into visibility. This showed that he had power to break the mysteries of nature.'[71] Religious knowledge and understanding now needed to catch up with science, the Master said. The fundamental basis of religion was love, but this had been forgotten.

Concluding His speech, 'Abdu'l-Bahá commented how the great universities were carrying on the work of peace and reconciliation, and He expressed the hope that each member of the audience would become a voice of opposition to warfare.

'He was very hopeful of the future,' reported the *Oxford Times*. 'He was a great optimist and he hoped that the bounties of God would descend upon them.'[72] After 'Abdu'l-Bahá concluded His remarks, there being no questions from the floor, some of the academics returned with Him to the home of the Cheynes.

'Abdu'l-Bahá's brief visit to Oxford left a profound impression on those who heard Him, notably Cheyne and Carpenter.

'Why I am a Baha'i is a large question,' Cheyne wrote later, 'but the perfection of the character of Baha'u'llah and Abdu'l-Baha is perhaps the chief reason.'[73] 'Abdu'l-Bahá gave Cheyne a Persian name, Ruhani, meaning 'spiritual'.

'Evidently he thought my work was not entirely done and would have me be ever looking for help to the Spirit,' wrote Cheyne in 1914, in the preface to his book *The Reconciliation of Races and Religions*.[74]

J. Estlin Carpenter in his volume entitled *Comparative Religion*, published in 1913, wrote that the Bahá'í Faith 'claims to be a universal teaching; it has already its noble army of martyrs and its holy books; has Persia, in the midst of her miseries, given birth to a religion which will go round the world?'[75]

On the train back to London, with tears in His eyes, 'Abdu'l-Bahá spoke particularly of Mrs Cheyne to Lady Blomfield and Mrs Thornburgh-Cropper: 'She is an angelic woman,' He said, 'an example to all in her unselfish love. Yes, she is a perfect woman. An angel.'[76]

1913 got under way with 'Abdu'l-Bahá talking to the friends gathered at 97 Cadogan Gardens about the changing character of civilization.

'Civilization is like unto a moving hill of sands,' He said.

> Today it is here, tomorrow it's many thousand miles away. It is subject to constant transference . . . Who knows what course of nobler and higher civilization is not made ready for the East – the cradle of spiritual civilization, the foundation of the moral life of man, the mainspring of divine effulgences and the horizon from which the Day-Star of hope is arising with resplendent beauty? When the material civilization joins hands with divine civilization, then the world will have reached the goal of a new order of things. There there will be no poverty, no squalor, no crime, no shame. There will be no night and no winter. Eternal day and perennial spring will gladden all hearts.[77]

A doctor arrived and told the Master that he was attending to the physical ailments of humanity.

'May you be able to heal the spiritual sicknesses of the hearts,' 'Abdu'l-Bahá told him. 'This is more important. God will assist you in this work and I will pray that you may become confirmed in this great service.'[78]

'This being New Year's Day, Lady Blomfield and her two daughters came in,' wrote Ahmad Sohrab, 'and a constant flow of New Year's greetings was kept on. She received the wonderful blessing of the Master.'[79]

Violets, roses, carnations and sweets were presented to 'Abdu'l-Bahá as signs of love from His devoted followers in London.

The Master joined Lady Blomfield and her daughters for a luncheon at Mrs Thornburgh-Cropper's apartment. Nineteen guests were present for a sumptuous meal of many courses, including pigeon and chicken. 'Abdu'l-Bahá told Mrs Thornburgh-Cropper that Hájí Amín was going to file a suit against her. When she asked Him why, He replied that because she was giving Hájí Amín such delicious foods, he would become so fat as to lose his stylish waist and would be unable to return to Persia to face the believers.

An itinerary for 'Abdu'l-Bahá's upcoming visit to Edinburgh was presented to Him. He laughingly told the friends that He had not reached that city yet and they had already planned what He must do during every hour. Then He joked about the rigid customs, date fixing and programme-making of the westerners.

'Abdu'l-Bahá left the table to rest, returning later to say in English, 'Good sleep. I good sleep today.'[80]

A further appointment followed at the centre of an organization interested in psychic and spiritual matters called the Cosmos Society. More than three hundred people gathered to hear Lady Blomfield introduce 'Abdu'l-Bahá, who spoke about the visible and invisible realities of man and the rising and setting of the suns of truth.

The activities of New Year's Day concluded at a popular vegetarian restaurant, in the company of Sir Richard Stapley and the veteran painter Felix Moscheles. Moscheles was the son of a famous pianist, Ignaz Moscheles, and was named for his godfather, the composer Felix Mendelssohn. Moscheles was a keen Esperantist and a pacifist, and President of the International Arbitration and Peace Association. Moscheles, like all others who met 'Abdu'l-Bahá, was greatly impressed by Him. At the end of the meal, the gathering of 16 rose to drink the health of the Master. Towards the end of His visit 'Abdu'l-Bahá would dine again with the Stapleys and attend an 'At Home' at the Moscheles residence in Elm Park, Chelsea. The Master also agreed to sit for a portrait by Moscheles.

Two of Lady Blomfield's 'friends of the mind', as she called them, were among the visitors to Cadogan Gardens on Thursday 2 January. John Lewis, a journalist who had met 'Abdu'l-Bahá in Egypt, was prominent in the International Psychical Research club, while C. W. Child was a celebrated practitioner of palmistry. Lewis told the Master of his intention to publish a number of Bahá'í articles in the club magazine of which he was editor, starting that month with an introductory article by Arthur Cuthbert, followed by a transcript of the Master's address to the Cosmos Society the day before. Child, meanwhile, asked 'Abdu'l-Bahá if He would permit him to take an impression of His hands, to which the Master agreed. Child brought out four sheets of paper which he blackened with charcoal and obtained four prints of the Master's palms. They were later reproduced in the magazine with Child's analysis and published as a separate pamphlet.

J. Murray Macdonald, then Liberal Member of Parliament for Falkirk Burghs, called on the Master to discuss matters to do with Persia. Macdonald was a member of the Persia Committee with which Professor Browne was also deeply involved. Macdonald discussed developments in the country with 'Abdu'l-Bahá, who took the opportunity to talk about the Bahá'í ideals of peace and brotherhood.

An excursion to Battersea Park in Mrs Thornburgh-Cropper's automobile later that same day saw 'Abdu'l-Bahá enter a playground where some three hundred children were entertaining themselves. As He entered, many of the boys and girls left their play and gathered around Him. For a few minutes, He tenderly greeted the children and, reaching into His pockets, brought out handfuls of half-shillings which He scattered over their heads.

'There you see a mass of future generation, going down to grab the money, happy noises, amiable scramble and delightful confusion!' wrote Ahmad Sohrab, who then accompanied the Master back to the car, followed by a crowd of children, vigorously waving their handkerchiefs and hats, calling 'Good day, Sir!', 'God keep you, Sir' and 'Happy New Year!'[81]

The Reverend R. J. Campbell, Pastor of the City Temple where 'Abdu'l-Bahá had given His first ever public talk more than a year previously, arrived to pay a return visit to the Master, who rose from His seat and advanced towards him, showing great joy and pleasure at seeing him. 'Abdu'l-Bahá told Campbell that He had yearned to see him since He had returned to Britain and had many times inquired after him. Campbell had been suffering from nervous tension from overwork in the intervening period since they had last met and had moved to a quieter house outside of London to live with his parents. Campbell told the Master that wherever he gave an address during his own recent visit to the United States, the Bahá'ís came to hear him and expressed their gratitude and pleasure. 'Abdu'l-Bahá invited Campbell to visit Him in the Holy Land for a few months and also encouraged him to visit Persia. In the meantime, however, a date was arranged for 'Abdu'l-Bahá to have dinner with him, his parents and other invited ministers on 19 January.

Lady Blomfield and her daughters then joined the Master for afternoon tea with one of their neighbours, who lived in the same block. 'Abdu'l-Bahá's attention was taken by a picture of Napoleon Bonaparte on the neighbour's wall and He spoke in detail of the story of Napoleon's defeat in 'Akká and his subsequent travels to Egypt. Then the conversation turned to drama and the Master talked about the religious plays of Persia that sometimes took ten days to perform. The plays were so intense, so dramatic and so realistic, He said, that often the spectators forgot that they were at a play. Once an unfortunate actor was even killed by one of the audience members who thought that his friend in the performance was actually being murdered on the stage.

Charlotte Despard, the prominent suffragette, welcomed 'Abdu'l-Bahá to the Cedar Club House, maintained by the Women's Service League which provided food to needy mothers and assisted their young children with nutrition. The Master and His entourage entered a large assembly room, still draped with the green and red decorations of the Christmas season. At two long tables, some 60 women and more than a hundred children sat, enjoying an afternoon tea. 'Abdu'l-Bahá was invited to speak from a podium but as was His wont, He walked straight to the impoverished women and spoke as He mingled with them, pacing up and down the aisle between the two tables, His face beaming.

'I am very glad', He said, 'to be among you, who are blessed in God's name with children. They are the true signs of His spiritual love. The most divine gifts of God. These little ones will grow to be fruitful trees. We must look to them for the founders of many beautiful families. Let their education be directed in the ways of purity and useful service. Here are the seeds of the future race and upon them may be granted God's blessing.'[82]

At the end of one table the Master patted the head of a small child in his mother's arms. The child stretched out his tiny hand and the Master gently closed it over with a bright new shilling. Down the long rows He passed, pausing with each child for a moment and bestowing coins.

'The absence of tears from the many wee souls,' wrote one of the party,

. . . who are not given to complacently accepting strange faces, singularly illustrates the infinite sincerity of the very young, who respond to the same quality that is ever present in matured spiritual character. One noticed, too, the thoughtful gaze of the women as they watched the distinguished visitor in white turban and brown burnous, moving in their midst. It is often too true that the very poor are keenly suspicious of foreigners, especially if their mission is a religious one, but Abdu'l Baha brings into every environment a profound truth and sympathy that seems to crush the barriers, raised by isolated imaginations.[83]

That night the Master was invited to speak at Essex Hall to the Women's Freedom League, of which Mrs Despard was the President. The League's professed aim was:

> To secure for Women the Parliamentary Vote as it is or may be granted to men; to use the power thus obtained to establish equality of rights and opportunities between the sexes, and thereby to promote the social and industrial well-being of the community.[84]

While the policy of the Pankhursts' Women's Social and Political Union was generally open warfare on the government, the WFL held its militant options in reserve. Mrs Despard merged all her interests, including the right to vote, Theosophy and vegetarianism, into one concept for spiritual evolution, all preparations – as she saw it – for 'the divine event toward which the whole creation moves'.[85]

As they arrived at the door, 'Abdu'l-Bahá discovered hundreds of people clamouring to get in, and no seats vacant inside the hall or gallery. More than a thousand suffragettes were present. After Mrs Despard's stirring introduction, the Master began to speak on the subject of the equality of men and women, His remarks, often witty, eliciting laughter and a shower of approval. After every few sentences the crowd burst into applause. At the end of the address, Lady Blomfield made some closing remarks and many people surged forward to shake hands with the Master.

'It was considered the best meeting ever held in London,' reported Ahmad Sohrab. 'There was a constant flow of enthusiasm and interest. The faces were illumined and the hearts were rejoiced.'[86]

A few days later Lady Blomfield received a letter from Florence A. Underwood of the League, which asked her to 'kindly convey to His Excellency Abdul Baha our warmest and most grateful thanks for coming to our meeting and for speaking so splendidly on behalf of women. We are proud of the fact that he has so honoured us, and I am sure that his powerful advocacy of our cause will do an incalculable amount of good.'[87]

One afternoon Lady Blomfield's younger daughter Ellinor went out with 'Abdu'l-Bahá to Regent's Park without His interpreter. On the way, in Mrs Thornburgh-Cropper's car, and as they walked in the park, He taught them Persian words.

'They had a most enjoyable time with Him,' wrote Ahmad Sohrab.[88]

Ellinor was happy to bring her elocution teacher, a celebrated actress, to meet the Master. Lady Blomfield was also present as the visitor emphatically declared that she was an 'anti-suffragist'. She said she did not believe in women getting votes and that she was working against the realization of such a dreadful thing. The Master was amused and told her that she had found a foe worthy of her steel.

'What is your reason for working against suffrage?' He asked her.

'Oh! I feel that women must attend to the duties of the house and child rearing,' she answered.

'Abdu'l-Bahá replied that this was not a question of feeling, that He required the reason for her opposition.

'Suppose a judge is sitting in the chair and you and a suffragist are going to decide your case,' He said. 'The suffragist would say that the plant and animal life already enjoy suffrage. There are male and female, their rights are equal and they never fight over who is superior or who is inferior because they receive the same kind of natural education. But in the human kingdom there is this fight. In the vegetable kingdom, only the female is productive; the male is barren. A female palm tree yields dates; a female fig tree produces figs; a female mulberry tree gives fruits etc; while the male trees are good for nothing. What would she say to this? Besides, a lioness is more valorous than the lion. The hunters are not as much afraid of him as the lioness. The lion may flee at the sight of a hundred hunters with their rifles aimed at him but the lioness will stand her own ground . . .'[89]

The actress laughed and admitted that 'Abdu'l-Bahá's arguments were unanswerable.

On the evening of 4 January Lady Blomfield hosted a meeting in her drawing room. The Master entered at half past eight and expounded upon love. Sitárih later decided to include His words as an additional chapter in *Paris Talks*.

'What a power is love!' said the Master. 'It is the most wonderful, the greatest of all living powers.'

Love gives life to the lifeless. Love lights a flame in the heart that is cold. Love brings hope to the hopeless and gladdens the hearts of the sorrowful.

In the world of existence there is indeed no greater power than the power of love. When the heart of man is aglow with the flame of love, he is ready to sacrifice all – even his life. In the Gospel it is said God is love.

There are four kinds of love. The first is the love that flows from God to man; it consists of the inexhaustible graces, the Divine effulgence and heavenly illumination. Through this love the world of being receives life. Through this love man is endowed with physical existence, until, through the breath of the Holy Spirit – this same love – he receives eternal life and becomes the image of the Living God. This love is the origin of all the love in the world of creation.

The second is the love that flows from man to God. This is faith, attraction to the Divine, enkindlement, progress, entrance into the Kingdom of God, receiving the Bounties of God, illumination with the lights of the Kingdom. This love is the origin of all philanthropy; this love causes the hearts of men to reflect the rays of the Sun of Reality.

The third is the love of God towards the Self or Identity of God. This is the transfiguration of His Beauty, the reflection of Himself in the mirror of His Creation. This is the reality of love, the Ancient Love, the Eternal Love. Through one ray of this Love all other love exists.

The fourth is the love of man for man. The love which exists between the hearts of believers is prompted by the ideal of the unity of spirits. This love is attained through the knowledge of God, so that men see the Divine Love reflected in the heart. Each sees in the other the Beauty of God reflected in the soul, and finding this point of similarity, they are attracted to one another in love. This love will make all men the waves of one sea, this love will make them all the stars of one heaven and the fruits of one tree. This love will bring the realization of true accord, the foundation of real unity.

But the love which sometimes exists between friends is not (true) love, because it is subject to transmutation; this is merely fascination. As the breeze blows, the slender trees yield. If the wind is in the East the tree leans to the West, and if the wind turns to the West the tree leans to the East. This kind of love is originated by the accidental conditions of life. This is not love, it is merely acquaintanceship; it is subject to change.

Today you will see two souls apparently in close friendship; tomorrow all this may be changed. Yesterday they were ready to die for one another, today they shun one another's society! This is not love; it is the yielding of the hearts to the accidents of life. When that which has caused this 'love' to exist passes, the love passes also; this is not in reality love.

Love is only of the four kinds that I have explained. (a) The love of God towards the identity of God. Christ has said God is Love. (b) The love of God for His children – for His servants. (c) The love of man for God and (d) the love of man for man. These four kinds of love originate from God. These are rays from the Sun of Reality; these are the Breathings of the Holy Spirit; these are the Signs of the Reality.[90]

Early in the morning of Monday 6 January Lady Blomfield and her daughters collected the Master from the apartment and travelled with Him to Euston railway station. After saying their farewells, the Blomfields departed for a few days' rest at the coast, while the Master commenced His mission to Scotland. He had been invited by Mrs Jane Elizabeth Whyte, 'one of the noblest and kindliest women that I have ever met,' wrote Ahmad Sohrab.[91] A friend of Mrs Thornburgh-Cropper, Mrs Whyte had travelled with her on a visit to the Master in 'Akká in 1906. Mrs Whyte's husband, Alexander, was a leading figure in the United Free Church of Scotland and a former Moderator of its General Assembly. Their expansive manse at 7 Charlotte Square in Edinburgh's New Town district was a fine Georgian house, attached to St George's United Free Church.

Edinburgh at the time of the Master's visit enjoyed a reputation for being a cosmopolitan city, with a population of 375,000, whose university – and in particular its medical department – attracted students from as far afield as Burma, Russia, Egypt, India and Persia, some of whom 'Abdu'l-Bahá would meet during His stay in the city.

On the train journey to the Scottish capital, the Master told His company that the work of teaching the Bahá'í Faith was only just beginning in the city and that they should associate with the people with exemplary devotion. 'Abdu'l-Bahá stayed at the Whytes' home with Ahmad Sohrab while the rest of His entourage stayed in a hotel. The Whytes had prepared for the Master a room on the third floor with its own fireplace, which gave it 'an air of comfort and a glow of peace'.[92]

The manse in Charlotte Square quickly took on the appearance of Lady Blomfield's home at 97 Cadogan Gardens. Eminent citizens, Esperantists,

Theosophists, suffragettes, churchmen as well as students from the East packed into its elegant, high-ceilinged drawing room to pay their respects to one about whom they had heard much. Mrs Whyte had organized a full programme for the Master, inviting the Outlook Tower Society, the Edinburgh Esperanto Society and the Scottish Theosophical Society each to host one of His public meetings. Her personal friend, the educational and social reformer Sir Patrick Geddes, was the founder of the Outlook Tower Society and played a major role in the Master's visit to the city.

For the native Scots, the weather for 'Abdu'l-Bahá's sojourn in their capital was considered to be mild and sunny. The Master however found the cold very trying and, one morning, He was taken around the city's clothing shops to buy more appropriate attire, much to the interest and admiration of several shopkeepers unused to seeing a visitor from the East.

But this visit to Edinburgh stirred up more controversy than any other aspect of the Master's stay in Britain. There were a number of hostile letters in the newspapers, and once He had left the city, a correspondence in the press ensued denouncing His teachings as damaging to the missionary achievements and unique message of Christianity. The Master, though, considered His visit to Edinburgh had been a great success. Many people accepted the teachings, according to Ahmad Sohrab, 'to the extent that they came to Him and asked how they should join the Bahai Cause. I believe from now on there will be Bahais in Scotland and, of course, many people who will be always interested and many societies will be glad to have Bahais speak from their platform.'[93]

One of the Master's first acts on leaving Edinburgh was to consider how the teaching work could be continued there. Alice Buckton was on His mind as a suitable teacher for the Scottish people.

'The people are greatly interested,' He told her the following day. 'Edinburgh has a great capability. There are many souls who are attracted.'[94]

Sitárih, Mary and Ellinor, along with Beatrice Platt, eagerly awaited the Master's return from Edinburgh on 10 January. Shortly after He arrived at 97 Cadogan Gardens, 'Abdu'l-Bahá said that He felt He had troubled them too much and expressed His desire to go to a hotel and have only the meetings in the apartment.

'Lady Blomfield, her daughters and Miss Platt moaned and lamented and pleaded, the latter on her knees,' wrote Ahmad Sohrab, 'that the Master consented to stay.'[95]

The cold and rain of London, following straight on from the chill weather of Edinburgh, was hardly endearing 'Abdu'l-Bahá to the British climate.

'I not like dark. I like light,' He said sadly in English.[96]

'Abdu'l-Bahá had not been fully well before leaving for Scotland and He certainly was finding that the prevailing temperatures did not suit Him. He nevertheless maintained His gruelling schedule of meetings and talks with happiness and determination.

'One very definite impression . . .' wrote Lady Blomfield after 'Abdu'l-Bahá's visit to Edinburgh, 'was of His power to refresh Himself from some spiritual source when His strength had been overtaxed.'[97]

On the afternoon of 11 January Mrs Thornburgh-Cropper had organized another large farewell meeting for the Master at Caxton Hall. As the entourage arrived, they found the hall was filled to overflowing, with many of the audience standing. 'Abdu'l-Bahá's speech on the life of Bahá'u'lláh, which included stories of the early martyrs of the Faith including Ṭáhírih, made a profound impression. After His address 'Abdu'l-Bahá went into a large adjoining room where cakes and fruits were arranged on long tables. Mrs Thornburgh-Cropper introduced an array of clergymen, parliamentarians, ministers, writers and thinkers who were pleased to shake 'Abdu'l-Bahá's hand. While 'Abdu'l-Bahá was receiving the distinguished guests, the talks were continuing in the main hall. Lady Blomfield spoke, along with a Roman Catholic bishop, Alice Buckton and Eric Hammond.

That evening Sir Richard Stapley organized a dinner for the Master at his home in Bloomsbury Square. Several professors were present, along with more churchmen, philanthropists and other prominent men and women. 'Abdu'l-Bahá was intrigued to see the ladies and gentlemen lead each other arm in arm into the dining room. He asked Ahmad Sohrab if this was the custom, to which His interpreter replied that he supposed it was. Without waiting for an introduction, the Master went forward and took hold of the arm of an older woman and proceeded into the dining room with her. Lady Stapley was somewhat put out, since the custom would have been for the lady of the house to conduct the guest of honour.

The dining room was decorated most lavishly with flowers on the table. In front of the Master a large cake was placed with the word 'Unity' on it. On each of the four corners of the cake were beautiful white doves and in the centre two hands clasped together as a symbol of the unity of East and West.

'I heard Lady Blomfield quoting last night a few lines from Longfellow,' wrote Ahmad Sohrab the following day as 'Abdu'l-Bahá was preparing to speak at the New Congregational Church in Woolwich, southeast of the River Thames, an arsenal district, where 'cannon, powder and rifles are made to kill our brothers'.[98]

With 'all the fire and enthusiasm of a lover of peace',[99] Lady Blomfield recited from Longfellow's 1845 poem, 'The Arsenal at Springfield':

> Were half the power, that fills the world with terror,
> Were half the wealth, bestowed on camps and courts,
> Given to redeem the human mind from error,
> There were no need of arsenals or forts . . .

The church at Woolwich was full when the Master arrived at half past six in the evening. The congregation rose as He stepped in. The minister, the Reverend J. J. Pool, gave a brief account of the history of the Cause with the greatest enthusiasm.

"Abdu'l-Bahá calls Himself the Servant of God,' said the minister, 'but I prefer to call him my Master and myself His Servant . . .'[100]

'Abdu'l-Bahá gave such a penetrating address,' wrote Ahmad Sohrab, 'that even Lady Blomfield and Mrs Cropper who have heard Him often thought it the most wonderful of all. It stirred the souls and created a holy atmosphere of love and good fellowship.'[101]

'The congregation seemed spell-bound by the power which spread like an atmosphere from another, higher world,' Lady Blomfield said later.[102]

After the address the Master gave.£5 to Reverend Pool as His contribution for the poor of the church. The minister was astonished but 'Abdu'l-Bahá told him it was His custom to contribute something to every church He went to. On leaving the church, the congregation had formed two lines through which the Master passed and then gathered around Mrs Thornburgh-Cropper's car to bid farewell to their visitor from the Orient.

A little over a week remained of 'Abdu'l-Bahá's visit to London yet many unique encounters and meetings were still in store, including two excursions out of the capital. On Wednesday 15 January the Master returned to Bristol to stay one night at the Clifton Guest House. Wellesley Tudor Pole met 'Abdu'l-Bahá once more at the railway station and took Him for a drive before a gathering with many of the guests and neighbours He had previously met more than a year previously. In the evening, some 150 guests – including a group of students from the East – gathered to hear the Master speak. 'Abdu'l-Bahá gave the eastern greeting of raising the palms of His hands to His forehead, after which He told the gathering that since last seeing them, He had been half over the world. 'In fact,' He said, 'I have come to Clifton this time via Los Angeles and Chicago.'[103]

In a persuasive speech, 'Abdu'l-Bahá shared with His audience ten major principles of the teachings of Bahá'u'lláh and concluded, 'The divine table is spread, the heavenly illumination is all-encircling; eternal life is provided for all; divine food is prepared for all! Therefore let us practise the divine essence of love and love each other from our very hearts and souls so that the East and West shall embrace each other and realize that all are the sheep of God. God is the good shepherd – then will we gather under the tabernacle of His mercy!'[104]

After the meeting, the guests met with the Master in the library. Among them were five Egyptian students, replete with the red fez. 'Abdu'l-Bahá spoke to them in Arabic and emphasized the necessity for a universal language. He said that in the future many such groups would gather from the four corners of the earth for the purpose of mutual understanding.

On His return to London the following day, Lady Blomfield presented 'Abdu'l-Bahá with a statement she had prepared which she wished to send to King George V, suggesting a meeting might be arranged. 'Abdu'l-Bahá thanked her for preparing it but advised against her contacting the King, saying He had come to the West to meet the poor, not monarchs and noblemen. He would meet any seeker with affection but had no particular wish to meet the rulers. Such a move could be misunderstood and misconstrued, He said, and might create alarm.[105]

'The Cause has become very great,' 'Abdu'l-Bahá told a gathering at 97 Cadogan Gardens later that day.

Many souls are entering it – souls with different mentalities and range of understanding. Complex difficulties constantly rise before us. The administration of the Cause has become most difficult. Conflicting thoughts and theories attack the Cause from every side. Now consider to what extent the believers of God must become firm and soul-sacrificing. Every one of the friends must become the essence of essences; each one must become a brilliant lamp. People all around the world are entering the Cause, people of various tribes and nations and

ns and sects. It is most difficult to administer to such heterogene-
... elements. Wisdom and Divine insight are necessary. Firmness and
steadfastness are needed at such a crucial period of the Cause.

All the meetings must be for teaching the Cause and spreading the Message, and suffering the souls to enter into the Kingdom
of Bahá'u'lláh. Look at me. All my thoughts are centred around the
proclamation of the Kingdom. I have a lamp in my hand searching
throughout the lands and seas to find souls who can become heralds of
the Cause. Day and night I am engaged in this work. Any other deliberations in the meetings are futile and fruitless. Convey the Message!
Attract the hearts! Sow the seeds! Teach the Cause to those who do not
know. It is now six months that Siyyid Asadu'lláh implored that I write
a few lines to my sister, my daughters. I have not done this because I
find I must teach. I enter all meetings, all churches, so that the Cause
may be spread. When the 'Most Important' work is before our sight,
we must let go the 'Important' one. If the meeting or spiritual assembly
has any other occupations the time is spent in futility. All the deliberations, all consultations, all the talks and addresses must revolve around
one focal centre, and that is: Teach the Cause. Teach. Teach. Convey
the Message. Awaken the souls. Now is the time of laying the foundation. Now must we gather brick, stone, wood, iron, and other building
materials. Now is not the time of decoration. We must strive day and
night and think and work; what can I say that may become effective?
What can I do that may bring results? What can I write that may bring
forth fruits? Nothing else will be useful today. The interests of such a
Glorious Cause will not advance without such undivided attention.
While we are carrying this load we cannot carry any other load![106]

On the eve of 17 January, 'Abdu'l-Bahá bestowed a unique gift upon
Gabrielle Enthoven, a neighbour of the Blomfields, to whom the Master
gave the name 'Hamsá'ih', meaning neighbour. Enthoven was a passionate
lover of the theatre whose collection of stage memorabilia later formed the
basis of the Theatre Museum in London's Covent Garden. 'Abdu'l-Bahá
informed her that He would give her the scenario for a play. 'The circle of
friends, who were gathered round Him that evening, held a tense silence,
while, in His deep sonorous voice, He unfolded the pageant of His sublime
imagination,' wrote Mary Blomfield.[107] With the exception of pauses for
translation, the Master recited the lengthy scenario without referring to

any notes. As it happened, Enthoven did not write the play but Mary did, two decades later. It was entitled *The Drama of the Kingdom*.

The next day, Friday, 'Abdu'l-Bahá was driven by Sir Richard and Lady Stapley to the small market town of Woking for perhaps the most unusual visit of His second stay in England. In the 1870s, a Hungarian-born linguist and editor of the *Asiatic Review*, Dr Gottlieb Wilhelm Leitner, had set up an Oriental University in Woking. He hoped that it would develop a curriculum for Asians living in Europe and provide them with a familiar living environment, while also allowing Europeans who wished to travel the opportunity to learn about the eastern way of life. Leitner had died in 1899 and the institute he founded closed along with the mosque he had built in its grounds ten years earlier, the first purpose-built mosque in Europe outside of Moorish Spain. It was periodically reopened for use on special occasions, most notably for a memorial service for the Persian king Muzaffari'd-Dín Shah who had died in 1907. Five years later a missionary for the Ahmadiyya religious movement, Kwaja Kamel ud Din, arrived in Britain and re-opened the mosque.

'Abdu'l-Bahá's visit was at the request of a number of Muslims who had previously visited Him at Cadogan Gardens. Under the auspices of the *Asiatic Review*, they invited Him to give a talk at the mosque on the theme of world unity. Lady Blomfield described those who congregated to meet Him at Woking as 'an important gathering of their friends' who 'gave an enthusiastic welcome to Him Who, albeit the bearer of the new Message to all the religions of the world, was descended from the ancient line of nobles in Islám'.[108]

On His arrival 'Abdu'l-Bahá was welcomed by Henry Leitner, son of the founder, who spoke to the Master of his father's lifelong devotion to orientalism. After lunching with various Muslim and Christian notables, 'Abdu'l-Bahá walked to the steps of the mosque and addressed the gathering of British, Turkish, Indian and Egyptian friends in the courtyard outside the small, white-domed building.

'During my sojourn among many lands and peoples,' He told them, 'I have been desired to speak in Christian churches, in Jewish synagogues, and in every kind of religious gathering.'

> In all of them I summoned the people to work for the unity of the human race, and for the peace of the whole world. I told them the

principles of the religion of God, saying unto them 'The foundation of the religion of God is one.' That 'one' is absolute truth and reality, which is indivisible, and not able to be multiplied or separated.

The religion of God is the means of the education of man, and leads him to become a manifestation of the highest virtues of humanity. It encourages the people to uphold the principle of peace. The great underlying truth of the religion of God is love . . .'[109]

Following the Master's brief address, Dr John Pollen, representing the East India Association, remarked that 'Abdu'l-Bahá was hastening that 'diviner day' when all men would work together 'in noble brotherhood'.[110] On behalf of Leitner, Dr Pollen announced that from that day onward the building would be open for Muslims to worship at any time they pleased.

Before leaving the mosque the Master wrote in its visitors' book, 'O God, illumine this "Review", and ignite this Society like unto a lamp, so that it may spread the Light in all directions.'[111]

On His final Sunday in London 'Abdu'l-Bahá honoured His arrangement with the Reverend R.J. Campbell and had lunch with the clergyman's parents as well as some other divines. The Master spoke to them about the opening verses of the Gospel of St John. The luncheon was followed by a visit to the artist Felix Moscheles who had an 'At home' meeting with a number of guests.

'We had witnessed a solemn act in the Mysterious Sacred Drama of the World,' wrote Sitárih, who had played such a significant role in that drama as it unfolded in London.[112]

'Abdu'l-Bahá's historic visits to Britain were ended. 'We stood bereft of His presence,' said Lady Blomfield.

Of the friends who gathered round Him at the train, one had been a constant visitor, a charming Eastern potentate [the Maharajah of Jhalawar], dignified and picturesque in his jewelled turban. He was an example of earthly kingship, one of the many other great personages of the world, all of whom, absent and present, were so small, so insignificant, when compared with the Ambassador of the Most High, as He stood, clad in a simple garment, speaking courteous words of farewell, smiling that love-laden smile which comforted all hearts.

Discarding preconceived ideas, a new consciousness seemed to awaken when in His presence.

Some of the minds, though as yet so finite, reached out to a recognition of the Light of the great Manifestation, now being diffused by 'Abdu'l-Bahá on all Humanity. To us He was impregnated with that Light, 'as a vesture wrapped about him, like a garment round him thrown'.

Small wonder that we mortals were overwhelmed with awe, as we drew near to the heavenly Messenger of that immortal Spirit of Truth and Light, which had come to save the children of men from chaotic destruction.

Would Humanity awaken? Or would they continue to sleep 'unaware'?[113]

On Tuesday 21 January 1913, more than five weeks since returning to Britain, the Master left London for the final time, on a train bound from London's Victoria station to the coast from where He would sail to France.

'O my beloved daughter! Thy letter was received,' responded 'Abdu'l-Bahá to a letter from Lady Blomfield on His arrival in Paris. '. . . As to thy statement that thy house is now empty: wheresoever thou art, know that that place is not empty but abundantly filled. For I am with thee wherever thou dwellest; that place is overflowing with spiritual susceptibilities, and the light of the Kingdom casteth its effulgence upon it.'[114]

A historic episode in the Heroic Age of the Bahá'í Faith – indeed in the history of London and the British Isles – had ended. But for Sara Louisa, Lady Blomfield, named Sitárih Khánum by the Centre of the Covenant – those sublime days would remain vividly in her mind until her last breath. They would inspire, in the three decades of life left to her, services of exceptional scope and significance.

'. . . the star (sitárih) is shining,' 'Abdu'l-Bahá observed, '. . . she speaketh forth and summoneth the people to the Kingdom of God. It is certain that her brilliance shall increase as day followeth day.'[115]

CHAPTER SEVEN

PURE AND GOODLY DEEDS

The betterment of the world can be accomplished through pure and goodly deeds,
through commendable and seemly conduct.[1]
Bahá'u'lláh

With the Master departed from British shores, it might be thought that life for His followers in London would have returned to some semblance of normality. Normality for them, however, was seldom without intense activity and for Lady Blomfield, settled back into her home at 97 Cadogan Gardens, exertion for the Bahá'í Cause showed no sign of abating.

The early months of 1913 saw Sitárih widening her circle of friends, especially those who were eager to learn more of the Bahá'í teachings. She also began to visit once again some of her older acquaintances whom she felt she had neglected before and during the weeks of the Master's stay. She was pleased to discover that one such friend, a Lady Nicholson – who may have been the wife of Sir Charles Nicholson, like Sir Arthur Blomfield an architect of churches – had been curious about the teachings as far back as 1896 from which time she had collected newspaper cuttings about the Bahá'í Movement. Lady Nicholson was fascinated to hear of the work of 'Abdu'l-Bahá, and Lady Blomfield felt that it appeared likely she would assist in spreading the message.

'Convey my respects to Lady Nicholson', wrote 'Abdu'l-Bahá, 'and deliver this message to her on my behalf: This century is the century of God and the dawning place of the Sun of Truth. Endeavour as far as thou canst to receive thy share of its radiance.'[2]

Lady Blomfield was told by another interested acquaintance, Baroness Drückman, that she planned to contact her relatives in Germany and encourage them to visit the Master during His forthcoming stay in Stuttgart. 'Abdu'l-Bahá's message to the Baroness was, 'The fountain of eternal life is gushing forth. Wert thou to drink but a draught thereof, thou wouldst see this world to be another world and wouldst find the East and the West illumined with the rays of the Sun of Truth.'³

Lady Blomfield also maintained a regular correspondence at this time with Maude Holbach, a travel writer whose works included *Bosnia and Herzegovina: Some Wayside Wanderings* and *Bible Ways in Bible Lands: An Impression of Palestine*. Maude, her husband Otto – who took the photographs for her books – and daughter Dorothy lived in Oxford, were well acquainted with Professor Cheyne, and attended Christian Science as well as Anglican meetings, in addition to their interest in the Bahá'í message.

With Bahá'í activities maintaining their momentum in London in the wake of the Master's second visit, Sitárih contemplated selling Springfield House, the country home in Broadway, Worcestershire, to which she had retreated in the early days of her widowhood. Being free from the business of keeping the property in order, she believed, would allow her more time to concentrate her efforts on the Bahá'í work. She wrote to 'Abdu'l-Bahá in Paris, seeking His blessing for her idea to sell the home and purchase another in London which she might put to good use to serve the Cause. 'Abdu'l-Bahá responded through Luṭfu'lláh Ḥakím, who was with the Master in the French capital, that she should be careful not to lose money on it – if there was someone who was willing to offer a good price, then she should sell the house and buy a new one.

'If not,' conveyed Ḥakím, 'let it, and then hire one in London instead.'⁴

While the property was still in her hands, however, Sitárih extended an invitation to one of 'Abdu'l-Bahá's daughters, Rúḥá – who had just undergone surgery in Paris – to consider making the journey across the English Channel to recuperate in the fresh Cotswolds air.

'It would make me extremely happy to be in your home,' Rúḥá responded, in the first letter that her doctor had allowed her to write since she had left Haifa. 'I am sure I will feel quite at home there. I have heard so much of you from the Master that I would like very much to meet you and your dear daughters before I leave Europe but I am not quite sure yet if I will be able to take the trip to England . . . It would be a great disappointment for me to come to France and be so near England where my friends are and not be able to just cross the channel and go to see them. I am sure I will regret it always.'⁵

Rúḥá's doctor was well enough satisfied with her recuperation following the operation that she did manage to make the journey and spend some precious days convalescing with the Blomfields, who showed her the quality of welcome that her father had so much appreciated.

'I cannot find a word to thank you enough for all your kindness and hospitality,' she wrote to Lady Blomfield after her stay. 'Indeed I enjoyed very much my visit with you and can never forget those happy days I spent in your dear home. I have learned so much from you and you have done much for me, that really I do not know what to say or how to thank you.'[6]

Another Bahá'í friend whom Lady Blomfield took under her motherly wing was a Persian man in his thirties named Mírzá 'Alí-Akbar Rafsan-jání. Mírzá 'Alí-Akbar, who had become a believer a decade before Lady Blomfield, in 1897, had been forced to leave his home and business as a paper merchant after a wave of persecution against the Bahá'ís in Iran erupted in 1903. From Rafsanján, he moved to Tehran where he attended a class for Bahá'í teachers that was being held by the esteemed teacher Ṣadr al-Ṣudúr. Mírzá 'Alí-Akbar became an outstanding promoter of the Bahá'í Cause, demonstrating great skill at memorizing the sacred scriptures which he chanted in a beautiful voice. In 1911 the Master summoned Mírzá 'Alí-Akbar to Paris, after which he was sent by Him on a teaching tour through Germany and England with Luṭfu'lláh Ḥakím as his translator.

Mírzá 'Alí-Akbar visited 97 Cadogan Gardens on a number of occasions and proved to be of some assistance to Lady Blomfield, clarifying for her aspects of the Bahá'í teachings about which she still lacked clarity. One such matter was the question of capital punishment, which she and Mírzá 'Alí-Akbar discussed at length.

'Last night when I came at home,' 'Alí-Akbar wrote to her in his fractured English after one such conversation, 'immediately I looked in the little book which I have it for my pocket and I saw that I have said true about it but when I read the verse after I saw Bhaollah has commanded for this punishment an eternal prison. I became so happy that I am not able to express my happiness. I asked Lotfulla to translate these two verse for you and I sent them to you my dear mother . . .'[7]

On 13 May 1913 when Mírzá 'Alí-Akbár was in London and Lady Blomfield was out of town, he wrote to her, 'Sometimes think at myself that this City without dear Lady is really like a body without spirit or an eye without light. Every one know that body without spirit it is no thing . . .'[8]

Mírzá 'Alí-Akbár provided invaluable assistance to Professor Cheyne, researching texts for him in the British Museum as the venerable theologian prepared his book about the Bahá'í teachings, *The Reconciliation of Races and Religions*. When the possibility of Mírzá 'Alí-Akbár leaving London for Stuttgart was mooted, Lady Blomfield was most insistent he should stay.

'The work he is doing . . . is needed by Dr Cheyne for the scholarly book he is writing in the service of the Holy Bahái Cause, and is of the greatest importance,' she wrote to Maude Holbach. 'It is also imperative that there should be as little delay as possible – the health of dear Dr Cheyne being in so precarious a condition!! Seeing the importance of time in this work, it is to my mind not wise for Ali Akbar to go to Stuttgart until the museum work for Dr Cheyne is finished – that he may have all possible data at hand in the compilation of his book, so that he may not be hampered by having to wait. It is for the future welfare of the Kingdom!!! I know you will quite understand. I feel that (in fact I know) the Master wishes this to be assisted by Ali Akbar with all his power.'⁹

The well-being of Cheyne and his wife was very much in the mind of the Master, who urged Lady Blomfield to show them the 'utmost of consideration and kindness'.

'He is a very good and noble person . . .' wrote Luṭfu'lláh Ḥakím on 'Abdu'l-Bahá's behalf. 'She is a very chaste, honourable and kind lady. Again He said to tell Lady, Mrs Cropper and Miss Rosenberg, "Have consideration for him".'¹⁰

The Master Himself wrote to Cheyne,

O thou my spiritual philosopher! Many professors are living in this world but the majority of them are deprived of the reality of the Kingdom; but praise be to God that thou hast become the candle of all the Professors, hast found the way to the Universe of the Kingdom, thou art not travelling on the earth but hast soaring in thy wings.

There were many Doctors amongst the Jews but they were all earthly but St Paul became heavenly, because he could fly upwards. In his own time no one duly recognized him nay rather he spent his days amidst difficulties and contempt. Afterward it became known that he was not an earthly bird, he was a celestial one; he was not a natural philosopher but a divine philosopher . . .

It is similarly my hope that thou mayest become filled with Bahá Ullah and become a first herald in that country and region – so that thou mayest shine from the horizon of reality like unto a star for ever and ever.¹¹

'When Professor and Mrs Cheyne pay thee a visit at thy summer home,' 'Abdu'l-Bahá told Lady Blomfield, 'make thou an effort, that they may become wholly spiritual and illumined, and that, in the latter days of his life, he may light a candle whose radiance may endure for all eternity.'[12]

Cheyne would live until 16 February 1915, one year after his book on the Bahá'í Cause was published.

Friday 21 March 1913 – the new year of the Bahá'í calendar – coincided with the Good Friday holiday of the Easter period. As 'Abdu'l-Bahá celebrated the Naw-Rúz festival with guests at a special luncheon in His hotel in Rue Lauriston, near the Place de l'Étoile in Paris, Lady Blomfield wrote to Him from Cadogan Gardens, expressing her appreciation of the prayers He was continually offering on behalf of her family.

'I prize with heartfelt delight and gratitude the assurance that you are praying for us,' she wrote, 'and that you will ever ask Blessings and Confirmations of the Spirit for my girls, my son and for myself.'[13]

Lady Blomfield's son, Frank, may have been an ongoing source of worry for her. He is mentioned rarely in any of her letters and was bequeathed nothing in her will. Some years after her passing, a young Bahá'í actor living in London – David Hofman – was instructed by Sitárih's daughter Mary to take a five pound note on her behalf to her brother. Hofman found a dishevelled Frank living in a rundown bedsit in Camden Town. How this Eton-educated son of aristocracy, who had once served in the Royal Navy, who had been blessed with a Persian name from the Master – had fallen upon such sorry times is lost to history.

The final leg of 'Abdu'l-Bahá's sojourn in Europe was about to begin, as He prepared to travel onward from Paris to Germany, Hungary and Austria, and then make one last return to the French capital before departing for Egypt. His gratitude to Lady Blomfield and her daughters, along with Beatrice Platt, for compiling His talks in Paris was evident from a message in which He wrote, 'O Thou kind Lord! This daughter of the Kingdom hath made a great exertion and hath written down the addresses of 'Abdu'l-Bahá. O Lord! Assist her and her daughters to spread abroad the splendours of the Kingdom.'[14]

'I like the Lady very much,' the Master told Ḥakím. 'She is very dear to me. I always remember her. She is indeed very dear and her whole aim is for serving the Cause.'[15]

On Thursday 12 June 'Abdu'l-Bahá departed from His Paris hotel and took a 12-hour train journey to Marseilles, where He rested for the night. The following morning He boarded a steamship, the *Himalaya*, and returned to Egypt.

'A most significant scene in a century-old drama had been enacted,' reflected Shoghi Effendi on the conclusion of his grandfather's historic travels to the West.

> A glorious chapter in the history of the first Bahá'í century had been written. Seeds of undreamt-of potentialities had, with the hand of the Centre of the Covenant Himself, been sown in some of the fertile fields of the Western world. Never in the entire range of religious history had any Figure of comparable stature arisen to perform a labour of such magnitude and imperishable worth. Forces were unleashed through those fateful journeys which even now, at a distance of well nigh thirty-five years, we are unable to measure or comprehend.'[16]

'Abdu'l-Bahá would never fail to remember Lady Blomfield's unique contribution to that glorious chapter of history.

'O my heavenly daughter! From the day I departed London until now, I have not forgotten thee for a moment. Thou hast ever been and remain in my thoughts,' wrote the Master from Egypt on 15 September 1913.

> I cherish the hope that, through the blessings and confirmations of God, thou mayest day by day become more illumined and draw nearer to Him, that the confirmations of the Holy Spirit may reach thee, that thy words may touch the hearts and become the cause of the guidance of the souls, and that, through the protection and help vouchsafed by Bahá'u'lláh, thou mayest raise aloft in London a blazing torch that may endure eternally and cause that land to become illumined.[17]

Lady Blomfield did her utmost to ensure that the work promoting the Bahá'í teachings in London was progressing well, particularly a public meeting which was held weekly at King's Weigh House, a Congregational church off Oxford Street in central London, today known as the Ukrainian Catholic Cathedral of the Holy Family in Exile.

Charles Mason Remey was one among many believers from other countries who passed through London and were impressed by the activities in the city.

'There were meetings practically every day in the week in various parts of the city and it was most encouraging and hopeful to mingle with the people and to see and to feel their devotion to the cause of humanity. We were quite touched by the kindness and the hospitality of the friends,' he wrote in his 1915 account, *Through Warring Countries to the Mountain of God*.

> I will describe one meeting, never to be forgotten. It was a so-called feast, an institution which has been enjoined by each of the three great Bahai teachers of this day, a coming together of people in order to partake of both material and spiritual food in the form of refreshments and food, together with reading, speaking and conversation about the Divine Cause and its realities.
>
> This particular feast to which I refer was held in the King's Weigh House, where the regular weekly Bahai meetings had for some time been held. It was quite typical of the work of our friends in London.
>
> Over one hundred persons assembled, people of different nationalities, races, and religions, and representing many varied movements and interests. There were Moslems and Hindus from the East, and Jews and Orthodox Christians, Theosophists, New Thought people, and others of the new modern movements from the West, each attracted to the Bahai light and enthusiastic over its broad principles.[18]

Sitárih believed the public meetings to be very useful, 'for all sorts of enquirers attend and ask questions; and strangers are easier to manage there than in Private Meetings, where sometimes undesirable people make things difficult for the young in the Cause, whom they entice away! In a Public Meeting, this is not so much attempted.'[19]

The Christmas and New Year period of 1913–14 witnessed another staging of Alice Buckton's nativity play *Eager Heart*, which had so moved the Master the previous year.

'We are gradually getting back into normal days after the Eager Heart time,' wrote Lady Blomfield, who astonishingly entertained more than 700 people over the seasonal festivities. 'Several people said "only for our day at Springfield, seeing Eager Heart, and having our Christmas Tea, we should have had no Christmas at all".'[20]

Among the Blomfields' visitors over the Christmas holidays were Mírzá

'Alí-Akbar and Dorothy Holbach, whose parents were travelling in the Holy Land. Lady Blomfield decided to invite 'Dot' back to spend the Easter holidays with her daughters, one of whom – Ellinor – was preparing to perform in Shakespeare's *Twelfth Night*.

'Well your dear little Dot looks well and is happy in her studies at her school,' Sitárih wrote to Maude on 28 January 1914. 'We read your letters together, and felt that we touched hands across the space which divides us; we simply gloated over the descriptions, and felt one with all the glorious holy time and spiritual influence of the "Holy Land" . . .'²¹

Lady Blomfield had long cherished the hope to visit Haifa, a journey she had come close to making on a number of occasions only to find her plans thwarted by various practical considerations. She had sent 'Abdu'l-Bahá a scarf as a Christmas gift, along with other presents for His daughters, and she yearned to see the Master again and meet His family. She was interested to learn that the Holbachs were staying in a convent in Haifa.

'It might be just the place for us, when we shall be able to go to the desired land. I think we should love to stay there,' she wrote, as she continued to try to let or sell the house in Broadway before she could free herself to make the journey eastwards.²²

'I expect thine arrival and that of thy respected daughters during this or the following spring,' 'Abdu'l-Bahá wrote to her on 24 February 1914. 'Undoubtedly ye will come. If possible, pass through Stuttgart on your way to the Holy Land. Ye will indeed bring great joy to the hearts in this household, for all are longing to see you.'²³

Having returned to the Holy Land in early December 1913, in addition to His manifold duties attending to the needs of the Bahá'í community who had been deprived of His presence during His western journeys, the Master welcomed a continuous stream of pilgrims and maintained an extensive correspondence with His followers around the world, offering unceasing guidance, encouragement and advice with a care, consistency and attention to personal detail that was nothing less than superhuman. Lady Blomfield was the recipient of many such letters.

'During my sojourn in London,' He wrote to her, 'although my physical health was precarious, yet the confirmations of the heavenly spirit were unceasing.'

How many days and nights did we converse together with perfect joy and radiance, speaking of the eternal outpourings of God's grace and

imparting the glad-tidings of the advent of His Kingdom! No doubt
thou dost recall all those memories.

Wherefore, O my heavenly daughter, strive with heart and soul that
day by day the light of guidance may shine forth more brightly in that
land, that thou mayest become like unto a candle that giveth light to
its inhabitants.[24]

Sitárih delivered one of the public talks at King's Weigh House on 27
February 1914, using 'Abdu'l-Bahá's guidance to the believers in Stuttgart
as the basis of her address. The Master told her that the talk would have 'a
far-reaching effect', saying that 'undoubtedly thou wilt speak at the next
meeting with still greater eloquence and fluency. Convey to that gathering
the following message on my behalf':

Praise be to God, this century is an illumined century. It is the century
of the divine spirit. It is the century of truth, in which the sun of truth
will shine with such intensity as to obliterate the darkness of blind
imitation and to entirely banish contention and conflict, hatred and
hostility from amongst mankind. For all are God's flock, and God is
their true Shepherd, and His compassion embraceth them all. Therefore, all mankind must, under the sheltering protection of the true
Shepherd, embrace each other, roam in the utmost love and harmony
in the meadow of divine mercy, grow and develop therein, and attain
infinite joy and happiness.[25]

As the militancy of the suffragette movement reached its zenith, each day's
news announced yet more violent struggles and acts of vandalism committed by women. Emmeline Pankhurst had been sentenced to three years in
prison in April 1913 for inciting destruction of the home of the Chancellor of the Exchequer: a group of militant campaigners stormed Manchester
Art Gallery where they mutilated more than a dozen paintings; corro-
sive acid was regularly poured into letter boxes destroying the contents;
in February 1914 women campaigners broke the windows of the Home
Secretary's London office and in May 1914 an attempt was made to set fire
to the building of the New Castle Lawn Tennis Club, Nottingham Park.

Lady Blomfield found such actions profoundly shocking. Even a fellow
Bahá'í, Elizabeth Herrick, felt compelled to join in the campaign of shop
window smashing, believing that by breaking a small window in a back

street post office she might get no more than three days in prison. Unfortunately for her, she was sentenced to six weeks. Untroubled by the verdict, she casually asked in court if she might have her hammer back. It was a family heirloom, she said.

The fortress-like Holloway women's prison, situated in northeast London, was no laughing matter, however. Herrick described how the walls of her cell were covered with obscenities – phrases so vile and disgusting that she spent her days and nights attempting to cleanse the atmosphere by reciting prayers and repeating the Greatest Name – Alláh-u-Abhá – over and over. Regulations allowed the prisoner to demand an interview with the governor, the doctor or the chaplain. While most of the detained women did not know this, Herrick exercised her rights and demanded an interview with each of them every day. She insisted that the chaplain recognize her right to be identified as a Bahá'í rather than an Anglican. From the doctor she secured a daily ration of fruit, not just for herself but the other prisoners.

Despite her distaste for militant action, Lady Blomfield was appalled by the government's treatment of the suffragettes. Under the so-called 'Cat and Mouse Act', hunger striking prisoners who had earlier been forcibly fed were allowed not to eat but when they fell ill, were released for recovery, then rearrested. While Mrs Pankhurst was let out of prison after her hunger strike, her accomplice, Mary Richardson, who had also stopped eating to secure her own release, was kept in and subjected instead to force-feeding.

Aware of the passion that Lady Blomfield's daughters had for the matter of gender equality, 'Abdu'l-Bahá expressed His hope that they might one day go to Persia to promote the idea.

'The emancipation of women is one of the pillars of the Cause of God . . .' the Master wrote to Sitárih.

In Persia, owing to the extreme fanaticism of the inhabitants, women have not yet attained full emancipation – indeed, were a woman to be fully emancipated, they would immediately tear her to pieces – yet in spite of this the believers of God are day by day advancing on this path. I hope that erelong the full emancipation of women will be achieved.[26]

Yet the Master urged Mary and Ellinor to keep their passion for women's rights within the boundaries of the law.

'For the present . . . thy daughters must speak with moderation concerning the emancipation of women in Europe,' He told Lady Blomfield.

They must not appear strident, for stridency bringeth about other harms. One's speech must be mild. In the Bible God instructed Moses and Aaron to speak mildly to Pharaoh. Thy revered daughters must engage in teaching the Cause of God: That Cause compriseth all that is good, among which is the emancipation of women and their equality with men.[27]

The Blomfield girls' stance on suffrage soon became well known, however, and in a very public way.

King George V had instituted a series of evening receptions with the intention of allowing closer contact with his people, albeit those who were deemed worthy by name, title or achievement to attend. On Thursday 3 June 1914 Lady Blomfield travelled by car with a young married woman she intended to present to the Court, unaware that her daughters had hatched a plan that same evening to appeal to the King to intervene over the treatment of imprisoned suffragettes. Mary and Ellinor arrived at Court after their mother, and without her knowledge. Following presentations to the King and Queen of a Lady Townsend and her sister, Mrs Walrond, Mary appeared before their majesties, suddenly dropped down onto one knee, flung out her hands, and cried out, 'For God's sake, Your Majesty, put a stop to forcible feeding!'

The Queen, it was reported, turned pale and made no effort to conceal her displeasure. Brigadier General Sir Douglas Dawson, a Comptroller in the Lord Chamberlain's office who was standing at the right of the King with the Lord Chamberlain, swiftly summoned officials and half led, half carried Mary out of the King's presence who, as the *Daily Mirror* phrased it, had remained serene.[28] Most of those in the Throne Room simply thought that a debutante had fainted. Lady Blomfield had to intimate to the press her repudiation of what her daughter had done, claiming she saw nothing of the incident. In a letter to the *Daily Mail* she stated that she was 'in no way connected with the militant suffragists'.[29] Sylvia Pankhurst later wrote, in somewhat of an exaggeration, 'Lady Blomfield had been enthusiastic for militancy of the most extreme kind, so long as it was committed by other people's daughters.'[30]

'A member of the Blomfield family' was quoted in the *New York Times* as saying, 'I should like it as widely known as possible that we dissociate ourselves entirely from this girl's misguided act. We are sick and disgusted to a degree. I know the head of the family shares my views, and I can speak safely for all the rest of us, with the exception of this small contingent.'[31]

'I cannot imagine what has come over my half sisters,' Charles Blomfield told another newspaper. 'Mary would have made a capital doctor. Elinor is a born lawyer . . . Every relative the girls have is highly indignant at their outrageous action. We have taken both of them to the country. I do not intend to let them return to town.'[32]

When the incident had blown over, the Queen was said to have remarked, 'If this had been the worst thing the women had done, they might perhaps be forgiven.'[33] Mary's outburst, however, resulted in precautions being taken at later such Courts, with officials vigorously examining the guest lists and withdrawing invitations to groups of women whom they suspected of having suffragette tendencies.

Perhaps to Lady Blomfield's discomfort, news of the event reached the ears of Bahá'ís around the world. However they were nothing less than in awe of Mary's act, spurred on by 'Abdu'l-Bahá's own enthusiasm at her courage. The distinguished Bahá'í teacher and Disciple of 'Abdu'l-Bahá Joseph Hannen – who himself visited prisoners and consoled the distressed – wrote to Lady Blomfield from Washington DC and likened Mary's act to the calls for women's liberation voiced by the first woman follower of the Báb, Ṭáhirih, almost 70 years before:

> . . . when I read in our daily papers of the brave deed of your noble daughter, both Mrs Hannen and I were filled with admiration. We conduct a Sunday School Class for the Bahá'í children here, and it was with much pride and pleasure that I told them the following Sunday of the heroic deed of this Western Qurat-El-Ayn. Later, one of the dear believers intimated that the act might not have been wise, and that you were probably inimical to its spirit. I therefore forbore sending a letter which I had framed mentally, praising Miss Mary's courageous act and congratulating you on the possession of such a splendid Bahai daughter. And now I know the inward meaning of the scriptural utterance 'Quench not the Spirit!' For that letter should have been written! At this late date I read the Master's Praise, and in sending it to you, it is with regret that mine was not sent sooner. Nevertheless it is not meet for the servant to speak before his Master, and so perhaps it is just as well that I have kept silent until now.[34]

Indeed, it was in a letter which Hannen had received from Mirza Ahmad Sohrab that the western believers learned of 'Abdu'l-Bahá's reaction to the event.

'The Daily Sketch, of London, Saturday June 6,' wrote Sohrab, 'contains a long article concerning the attendance of Misses Mary and Ellinor Blomfield at the Court of England, and the speech of the former in behalf of the Suffrage Cause.'

The paper publishes the photographs of Lady Blomfield and her two daughters. Above the photograph of Miss Mary (Parveen) Blomfield, on the first page, is written: 'The Suffragette in the Throne Room: Lady Blomfield's daughter, who caused the sensation at Court'. Below the photo, the following is written, 'Your Majesty, for God's sake stop forcible feeding.' Here is Miss Mary Blomfield, the Society Suffragist, who made the impassioned appeal to the King in the Throne Room, and created the Court sensation that everyone in England was talking about yesterday. It was the first time in history that so dramatic a speech had been made by a girl at the Throne of England.' The paper was given to me by the mail-man in the morning, and I read the article on page 7 with much interest. In half an hour, every Bahai knew about it, the Pilgrims were talking about it and admiring the supreme courage and fearlessness of Parveen Khanum. As everybody knows, Lady Blomfield and her daughters were the Master's hostesses on the occasion of his two visits to England; therefore our interest in this matter resolves itself into a more particular form. 'What matchless resolution! What an heroic deed!' were the words uttered by every lip as soon as they heard the story and looked at the picture. I had the hardest time to keep the paper in my possession, because everyone wanted to have it for himself. At last the afternoon came around and the Beloved sent for me. I took the paper with me to show it to Him. I knew He would be interested to hear the news. As soon as I entered the room, He said, 'What is in thy hand?' I gave the paper to him. At first glance he recognized Lady Blomfield and her daughters, 'Oh! What is this?' Then I gave him an outline of this most dramatic event. He listened most attentively, and then laughed heartily. 'What courage!' he said 'Come! Take the paper and read the article to me,' which I did with equal ardour and spirits. He was especially pleased with the remark in the Christian Commonwealth of June 10th, in an Editorial on 'King and People', in answer to the criticism of the Press. It says: 'The original idea of these Royal receptions was to afford an opportunity for the Sovereign to become personally acquainted with his subjects and to receive any communication they might wish to make to him.'

After this, he dictated eleven Tablets for the believers in America and Persia, and just as he was going to continue his dictation they brought the news that the Commander, accompanied by the General of the forces in Damascus, would call on him in a few minutes. After a while, they came and the Master welcomed them at the doorway . . . After a few minutes' conversation, the Blessed One said: 'Today we have received a newspaper from London containing the photograph of a Baha'i girl who has given a most dramatic speech before the King and Queen of England in favour of the Suffrage Cause. Will you look at her photograph, as well as that of her mother and sister? When I was in England, I met many leaders of the Suffrage Movement, amongst them Mrs Pankhurst. Day by day they are getting nearer to their goal. In fact, according to the report of this last paper, one of their lecturers felt that "such an action as that which took place on Thursday night must enormously help the Cause because the King and Queen know now, if they did not know before, that the women mean business". Again she says, "Whether we are militants or whether we are not, I do not think it matters. We must all take our hats off to the woman who showed such terrific courage." The question of the equality of right between male and female is one of the fundamental laws of nature, and it will be realized sooner or later. It is bound to come. However the leaders of the Suffrage Movement in England must not retard the realization of their aspirations through incendiary and militant methods. Such rash and unseemly deeds are not worthy of the noble station of womanhood. They must hold fast to pacific methods, like their American sisters across the Atlantic, who have secured the right of universal suffrage in nine states, with others on the list. If the English women desire to keep their traditional dignity and natural self-respect, they must avoid all revolutionary and lawless methods. They should demand their rights through the acquirement of sciences, arts, belles-lettres and literature, and not through window smashing, derailing of trains, putting bombs in the churches, burning the houses of public officials and destroying the letters in the post-boxes.' He continued to speak along this line and admired the pluck and energy of Miss Mary Blomfield.[35]

In her book *The Suffragette Movement*, Sylvia Pankhurst recalled how she had received a visit from Lady Blomfield, expressing her delight that 'Abdu'l-Bahá 'of whom she was proud to call herself a follower', had spoken with sympathy of the Suffragettes.

'He had suffered forty years' imprisonment, she told me ecstatically, for preaching the unity of religions and the brotherhood of man. Under his teaching she had lost all regard for the pomps and vanities of earthly existence.'[36]

Sitárih became so ashamed of the way the Government was dealing with the issue of votes for women that she relinquished her membership of the Liberal Party and never joined another one. Nevertheless, she would never bring herself to approve of incendiary devices going off in London churches or Velázquez's masterpiece, the *Rokeby Venus* being badly slashed at the National Gallery.

The outbreak of the First World War saved many suffragettes from facing prosecution. 'Even the suffragettes had the sense to realize that while men fought and died in France,' one commentator has written, 'the British people would have little patience with women who smashed shop windows.'[37] Unbowed, Christabel Pankhurst would announce, 'This great war . . . is God's vengeance upon people who held women in subjection.'[38]

In addition to women's right to vote, the other great political concern of the day with which Lady Blomfield sympathized was that of home rule for Ireland, the land of her birth. The third Home Rule bill, allowing self-government for Ireland within a United Kingdom of Great Britain and Ireland, was, when passed, the first law ever enacted by the British parliament that sought to establish devolved government in a part of the United Kingdom. The Ulster Unionists were indignant, adopting the slogan 'Ulster will fight and Ulster will be right'. With the country hovering on the precipice of a civil war, thirty thousand service rifles each with a hundred rounds of ammunition were shipped illegally into Northern Ireland from Germany.

Any kind of violence deeply pained Sitárih and she preferred not to speak about the events transpiring on the other side of the Irish Sea. As was the case with the campaign of the suffragettes, however, Britain's declaration of war with Germany intervened. Hundreds of thousands of Irishmen then found themselves joining the conflict, fighting on the side of an Empire from which they had campaigned so long to rid themselves. The third Home Rule act never took effect.

The gunning down in Sarajevo on 28 June 1914 of Archduke Franz Ferdinand, heir to the Austro-Hungarian Empire, sent shock waves throughout the world. 'The assassination comes like a clap of thunder to Europe,' wrote *The Daily Chronicle*. Within a month, countries were arming themselves for what would become the most devastating war the world had yet witnessed. The cordiality that had once been characteristic of relations between Russia and Germany collapsed, with Germany declaring war on 1 August and Russia marching over Kaiser Wilhelm's borders the following day. German troops began their push into France, Luxemburg, Switzerland and Belgium. By the second week of August, Britain had entered the war – a conflict, as the then Chancellor of the Exchequer David Lloyd George put it, 'on behalf of liberal principles, a crusade on behalf of the "little five-foot-five nations" like Belgium, flagrantly invaded by the Germans, or Serbia and Montenegro, now threatened by Austria-Hungary'.[39] Seventeen million men from eight nations were mobilized into action.

During His travels in the West, 'Abdu'l-Bahá had predicted on numerous occasions the inevitability of war on the European continent, which He described as 'like an arsenal, a storehouse of explosives ready for ignition,' one spark of which would 'set the whole of Europe aflame'.[40] Throughout Britain there was broad agreement as to the rightness and justice of the conflict, which even became talked about as a holy cause, supported by the leaders of the church.

'These warring nations believe that the object of the religion of God is war and strife!' 'Abdu'l-Bahá told a gathering of believers on Mount Carmel on Monday 3 August. 'This is the most preposterous idea that any man could let enter into his mind! . . . It is as though there is not a single iota of love in the hearts of men, as though they have never heard the name of love, as though their hearts are the sepulchres of hatred and envy! Man is the *most ferocious animal*, yet does he accuse the wild beasts of this quality! The ferocious beasts kill other beasts, but not one belonging to their own species.'[41]

Until its end – despite the devastation and the slaughter of some 16 million military personnel and civilians – the majority of the population maintained that the war was just and necessary. The Master entertained no such illusion that the ends justified such horrifying means.

'No sane person can at this time deny the fact that war is the most dreadful calamity in the world of humanity,' He wrote to one of the English believers, Beatrice Irwin, 'that war destroys the divine foundation, that war is the cause of eternal death, that war is conducive to the destruction of populous, progressive cities, that war is the world-consuming fire, and that war is the most ruinous catastrophe and the most deplorable adversity.'[42]

As the fighting commenced, Lady Blomfield and her daughters were staying in Geneva, the outbreak of hostilities putting paid to hopes of their long-anticipated pilgrimage to the Holy Land. A letter from the Master on 14 October must come as a bitter disappointment: 'O thou noble Lady!' 'Abdu'l-Bahá wrote.

> It was our hope that this winter thou wouldst travel to Haifa, stay for a while in this blessed and luminous Spot in the Holy Land, receive an abundant portion of the outpourings of divine grace, and that we couldst meet together every day. But the present war and upheaval have rendered this impossible. I hope that in the coming year this great aim may yet be realized and that thou and thy noble daughters may be able to visit the Holy Land and acquire a share of God's infinite grace.
>
> Thou art ever in my thoughts, and I beg for thee from the source of divine providence unfailing aid and protection, that thou mayest spend thy days in acquiring that which is conducive to eternal glory – for material honour and prominence endureth not and are as fleeting as an image traced upon the water. Whereas I have desired for thee and for thy noble daughters the illumination of the world of the Kingdom and the splendour of the dominion of the Most High, that ye may draw nigh unto God and forget aught else save Him, that your faces may become radiant and that your hearts may shine as brightly as the expanse of heaven. It is my ardent hope that ye may attain unto this exalted station and sow seeds that will flourish forevermore and continually produce a bountiful harvest.[43]

During His visit to Paris 'Abdu'l-Bahá had described to Lady Blomfield His wish to see a group of British believers working collectively as an administrative committee, responsible for collecting funds and publishing literature. The Master had chosen the membership of the committee to include Lady Blomfield herself and her neighbour Gabrielle Enthoven, Ethel Rosenberg, Mrs Thornburgh-Cropper, Mrs Whyte, Alice Buckton and Tudor Pole. The Bahá'í 'Consultation Committee' which met at the home of Miss Rosenberg on 16 November 1914 had a somewhat different membership. Lady Blomfield was by then devoting her energies to the war effort. Tudor Pole, initially engaged in government work producing biscuits, felt that he was failing in service to his country and had volunteered as a Royal Marine. Of the original recommended membership set out by the Master, only Rosenberg and Thornburgh-Cropper were present. The other members were Eric Hammond, who was elected chairman, Annie Gamble, Luṭfu'lláh Ḥakím, Mrs Crosby and Florence 'Mother' George.

Mother George had embraced the Bahá'í teachings in France where she had studied painting under the American artist and believer Frank Edwin Scott. During the Master's sojourn in Paris she had seen Him every day and felt impelled to return to England with His blessing. She provided invaluable help to the London believers, serving on the committee, booking public meetings, managing a lending library and offering a Sunday school class every week in her own home.

But 'everything stopped during the war,' Mother George later remembered. 'Lady Blomfield and her daughters went to Paris to work in the hospitals. No one kept the Bahá'í meetings except myself; and I felt this was the most useful 'war work' I could do. Of course Zeppelins prevented going out after dark. Before the war there had been five meetings a week at the houses of different Bahá'ís!'[44]

The early months of 1915 saw a serious threat to continued communication with the Master in Haifa. The Commander of the 4th Army Corps, Jamal Pasha, took up his mission to overrun the Suez Canal and drive the British out of Egypt. Turkish leaders persuaded the Islamic clergy to designate their campaign as a 'holy war'. A reign of terror came to Syria.

Jamal Pasha was a ruthless character known instantly to kill anyone he believed to have a prominent reputation. Gallows were set up in every town and large numbers of noteworthy citizens were eliminated. Arab nationalists were particularly victimized, facing almost certain execution. Taking advantage of the situation, the disloyal members of 'Abdu'l-Bahá's own family saw a fresh opportunity to plot against the Master and invent ways to provoke Jamal Pasha against Him, depicting Him as a political mischief-maker. Representing themselves to the authorities as ones who had been wronged and victimized by 'Abdu'l-Bahá, they proffered extravagant gifts, including precious mementos that had belonged to Bahá'u'lláh, and accused the Master of having designs to inaugurate a new monarchy. On one occasion they presented Jamal Pasha with a painted flag of the Greatest Name symbol, saying it was 'Abdu'l-Bahá's new 'Standard of the Monarchy'.

'A number of followers of self and passion,' wrote the Master to Lady Blomfield,

> . . . even as Judas Iscariot, have strayed from the Cause of God and arisen to instil doubt in the hearts, that they may tear down the foundations of the Covenant and strike at the root of the Tree of the Cause. They have no aim but sedition and mischief. Wolves are they, though outwardly they may claim to be shepherds. They are even as those souls who, in the days of the former Manifestations, sought through all manner of machinations to foster doubt within the Cause of God. But the sanctified souls who were firm and steadfast avoided them and protected the flock of God from the clutches of such wolves. It is my hope that thou wilt be one of those holy souls, who even as a glass unto the flame of the Cause of God, guard it from contrary winds.[45]

In the event of guidance from the Holy Land being completely cut off, the administrative committee in London decided that those believers specifically named by 'Abdu'l-Bahá to serve on it would be authorized to resolve any difficult questions that might arise.

The contribution of Lady Blomfield and her daughters to the war effort began with correspondence with Bernard Harrison of the British Red Cross Society in Paris. He wrote to Sitárih, informing her of the formalities needed for work in a French hospital. All requirements duly observed, they arrived soon afterwards to lend their support.

Baron Leslie Haden Guest – possibly already known to Lady Blomfield as a keen Theosophist – was a doctor by training and founder of the Anglo-French committee of the Red Cross. He was managing a hospital unit set up at the Hôtel Majestic in Paris. The Blomfields moved into the nearby Hôtel d'Jena from where they could easily walk to the Majestic, where they had signed up to serve as Voluntary Aid Detachments (VADs). VADs, largely middle class women eager to 'do their bit' for the war effort, worked under the instruction of fully trained nurses. On arrival, their list of tasks included cleaning tables, sinks, patients' lockers and crockery, sorting linen and sweeping. The reality was much more harrowing. Nothing could have prepared Lady Blomfield and her daughters for what they now encountered – scenes that could not have been further removed from the tranquillity of Cadogan Gardens and the atmosphere of loving calm which the Master's presence had brought to their home.

'On the face of it no one could have been less equipped for the job than these gently nurtured girls who walked straight out of Edwardian drawing-rooms into the manifold horrors of the First World War,' wrote Lyn MacDonald in *The Roses of No Man's Land*, the story of the women volunteers who arose to serve in a medical capacity during the war.

> It was all a far cry from the old myth of the 'ministering angel'. These girls had to be tough . . . They nursed men with terrible wounds and saw them off to convalescent camp, or laid them out when they died. They nursed in wards where the stench of gas-gangrenous wounds was almost overpowering. They nursed men choked to death as the fluid rose in their gassed lungs, men whose faces were mutilated beyond recognition, whose bodies were mangled beyond repair, whose nerves were shattered beyond redemption.[46]

The Blomfields were shocked by what they found on their first morning in the wards.

'Any kind of suffering touched my mother profoundly,' wrote Mary, 'but the sight of young men maimed for life, and the new and horrible experiences she had to endure during the dressing of their wounds, her mental agony reflecting their pain, tortured her beyond words. After that first heart-rending morning in the wards, we were silent as we walked back to the Hotel d'Jena for luncheon. We imagined ourselves unable to touch any food. But my mother's courage and strength of mind prevailed. She said quietly: "We must eat, or we shall be ill ourselves. Then we shall not be able to help."'[47]

On the other side of the border, many of the Bahá'ís that Lady Blomfield had met in Stuttgart were also engaged in nursing, taking care of wounded German soldiers who, according to Alma Knobloch, were 'well remembered with flowers, cigars, chocolates and cakes'. Prisoners of war were also receiving the same care, 'yet a good many of them are mistrustful and believe they will be killed yet. What astonishes me the most is that so little hatred is shown by the Germans, though the German soldiers are almost always brought back in a terrible condition,' wrote Alma.[48]

With the imminent spread of the war to the Haifa and 'Akká regions, 'Abdu'l-Bahá became concerned to protect the Bahá'í community and alleviate their anxiety. All who were merchants lost their wares as the government seized everything they possessed, leaving them without the most basic provisions. If anyone protested, hanging was the immediate response.

'Those Bahá'í friends who were merchants suffered great losses,' Lady Blomfield later wrote, 'for all their stores of tea, sugar, etc., were commandeered by the Government, without payment.'[49]

Rumours of an allied bombardment of Haifa stirred panic amongst its citizens including the believers.

'The friends, in spite of the reassurances of the Master that no guns would be turned on Haifa, were living in constant fear, and the children, having heard terrible stories which were being told everywhere, grew quite ill, always looking round and about with frightened eyes,' wrote Sitárih.[50]

'Abdu'l-Bahá arranged to remove the remaining Bahá'í community to Abú-Sinán, a peaceful Druze town to the east of 'Akká, away from any possible bombardment. Some 140 adults and an equal number of children were taken in, sustained by supplies of wheat, vegetables and corn that had been grown and stored at 'Abdu'l-Bahá's instruction. 'Their food was of the simplest: lentils, dried beans, delicious olives and their oil, and sometimes milk, eggs, and even some goat's meat,' wrote Lady Blomfield, who would eventually herself pay a visit to Abú-Sinán in the spring of 1922. 'The fresh pure air was, of course, wonderfully good for their health, and they quickly recovered calm nerves and strength of body.'[51]

The village head Shaykh Sálih had enormous respect for the Master and personally housed His sister, wife, daughters and their families, as well as Edith Sanderson and Lua Getsinger who were then staying in the Holy Land. From the Shaykh's balcony the family would watch for the Master's return on the days when He was expected back from Haifa or 'Akká.

Star of the West reported that the Master was in excellent spirits. 'He is happier than at any time since the war began.'[52]

'In spite of all the difficulties which surrounded them, the sojourn at Abú-Sinán village was a time of great happiness,' wrote Lady Blomfield. 'Was not the Beloved One more with them than ever before? It was many years since His family had seen so much of their Father.'[53]

When their hospital unit moved from Paris, the Blomfields returned to London but continued to do whatever they could to support the war effort. Lady Blomfield volunteered in various hospitals, served on committees and kept open house at Cadogan Gardens for soldiers of the Australian

To meet Abdul Baha (H. E. Abbas Effendi)

The Mosque, Woking, Surrey,

Friday, January 17th, 1913,

at 3.15 o'clock.

THE ASIATIC QUARTERLY

TRAIN LEAVES WATERLOO AT 2.20 P.M. FOR WOKING.
RETURN TRAINS LEAVE WOKING AT 4.59 P.M. AND 5.8 P.M.

An invitation to the Woking Mosque to hear 'Abdu'l-Bahá speak

'Abdu'l-Bahá at Woking Mosque, 17 January 1913

and Friends.

The New Constitutional Society for Women's Suffrage.

PRESIDENT - - MRS. CECIL CHAPMAN.

AT HOME,

EVERY TUESDAY.

SPEECHES 3 p.m.   TEA 4-30 p.m.

8, PARK MANSIONS ARCADE, KNIGHTSBRIDGE.

January 7th—"The Financial Status of Wives."

Mr. REGINALD POTT.

HOSTESS—Mrs. BULL.

January 14th—"The Boarding out of Children."

Miss M. MASON.

HOSTESS—Mrs. FORSYTH.

January 21st—"Bahaism."

LADY BLOMFIELD.

HOSTESS—Mrs. CECIL CHAPMAN.

TEA, 6d.

January 28th—No meeting will be held at the Office. All members are invited to the Annual Meeting at Mrs. Cecil Chapman's, 24, Buckingham Gate, S.W. at 8 30 p.m.

'At home' for the New Constitutional Society
for Women's Suffrage, circa 1913

Wellesley Tudor Pole

Eglantyne Jebb on a boat,
possibly on Lake Geneva

The investiture of 'Abdu'l-Bahá, Haifa, 27 April 1920

Shoghi Effendi during his stay in England

and New Zealand Army Corps – the so-called Anzacs – who were recovering from their wounds.

Among her papers is a handwritten poem entitled 'Anzac!' by her husband's niece – the poetess Dorothy Frances Gurney – that Lady Blomfield must have admired:

> Anzac, Anzac, you came to help and save
> Our little old, old country from a shameful grave;
> Rapscallion, saint or martyr,
> You did not stop to barter,
> Anzac, Anzac, bravest of the brave!
>
> Anzac, Anzac, Mother Nature smiled
> And gave you a hunter's body and the heart of a little child,
> Eyes clear for long distance,
> Mouth set for resistance –
> Anzac, Anzac, wildest of the wild!
>
> Anzac, Anzac, from your mountains blue,
> The bush and the wide pasture, the white sheep wander through
> You came – you heard us call you –
> Little recked what might befall you –
> Anzac, Anzac, truest of the true.
>
> Anzac, Anzac, one with the strength of ten
> To tell your deeds of valiance would take an angel's pen
> You who flinched for no men
> Won praise from niggard foemen –
> 'God! If I could lead them, glorious fighting men!'
>
> Anzac, Anzac, while the Earth shall spin
> Her many coloured web and throw the shuttle out and in
> The shimmer of your glory
> Shall be woven in its story –
> Anzac, Anzac, who did but die to win!

On 25 April 1915, Sitárih received a telegram from the Bahá'í Spiritual Assembly in Tehran, dated ten days previously, stating that 'Venerable

Behai martyred Meshed. Preparing uprising against Behais. Help us, ask justice from Persian Government, parliament. Telegraph your Legation here. Advertise Paris others.'[54]

<u>Sh</u>ay<u>kh</u> 'Alí-Akbar-i-Qu<u>ch</u>ání, one of the best-known and most distinguished Bahá'ís of <u>Kh</u>urásán, had been shot in the back on 14 March in the bazaar in Ma<u>shh</u>ad on the instruction of one of that city's most prominent clerics, who was one of his former pupils. <u>Sh</u>ay<u>kh</u> 'Alí-Akbar's body lay where it fell in the bazaar for some days. The animosity to the Bahá'ís had reached a point where no one dared move it for fear of triggering a purge on the Bahá'í community. A photograph of 50 believers was posted in the bazaars and they were shunned in all the shops.

The British Consul-General in Ma<u>shh</u>ad, Colonel Haig, reported the murder of <u>Sh</u>ay<u>kh</u> 'Alí-Akbar and added that the 'people, suspecting an intention of burying the body in a Muhammadan burying ground and resenting the arrest of those suspected of the murder, raised a disturbance in the Shrine. The body was at last removed secretly by night from the place where it lay and carried off to Kuchan.'[55] Colonel Haig recorded in his diaries that the Bahá'ís in <u>Kh</u>urásán, under threat of a general massacre, felt increasingly vulnerable in the weeks that followed.

The London Bahá'í committee meeting at Ethel Rosenberg's home discussed the situation at length. The members decided that Sir Richard Stapley, who had been such a strong supporter of the Master during His London visits, might be approached with a view to a question being raised in Parliament. Sir Richard, however, was reluctant to do so, saying that, in the war climate, tabling such a question would not be wise. Letters were also officially sent to Lord Lamington, Lady Morell – the wife of a Member of Parliament who had interested herself in the matter – and to the British Admiral in the Persian Gulf.

Lady Blomfield, for her part, immediately wrote to Mary, Countess of Wemyss – formerly Lady Elcho, an old acquaintance from her days in Broadway – whom she had introduced to 'Abdu'l-Bahá when He was in London. The Wemyss's daughter was married to the son of Prime Minister Asquith, whose brother-in-law was Jack Tennant, the Under Secretary of State for War. 'One thing of great use which occurs to me, (*can* you do this?) to write to Mr J. Tennant,' Lady Blomfield asked Mary Wemyss. '*Could* he have a telegram sent to the British Legation at Teheran, or to the British Consulate at Meshed, to stop the persecution of the Baha̤ïs, the dear harmless people! Meshed is a sacred city of the Shia Mahommedans, and the people are very fanatical there, for this reason comes the danger to the Baháís. *Some way* of helping will, I know, occur to you, it is *very urgent!*'[56]

Countess Wemyss appears to have been extremely embarrassed to have to forward Lady Blomfield's request. Yet she did write to Tennant – in a manner that veered between the apologetic and the sympathetic – perhaps because the memory of the Master's personality had left an indelible mark on her mind:

> You will I fear think me *quite mad*, and very bad too to trouble you when such a load of care and responsibility which already rests upon your shoulders. I feel I ought not to take the few seconds it may take you to read this letter but you will please believe me when I say that you certainly must not answer.
>
> I received yesterday a rather mad letter from Lady Blomfield (Theosophist!!! of a sort). She used to put up the venerable Beháï from Persia (who is or was quite a genuine old saint, I believe and who with his followers are really harmless (preaching *peace*! and harmony! and *love*) and *non*-political). But I imagine these sort of people are particularly *maddening* to fanatics and are bound to fare badly in troublous times – still they are really I believe most innocent and really put their non-aggressive and non-political principles into practice – and the Engl. Gov. [English Government] is supposed to protect the weak – I gather that if harm (a rising) was really meant them it is all over by now, but I felt I must send on the telegram, with some sentences from Lady B's letter ommitting [*sic*] the Balderdash – as much as I can – if there is or has been trouble you will of course have heard of it – through the proper, recognized channels, which makes my writing seem doubly futile and intrusive. The *Christian Commonwealth* recognizes the Beháï and his followers and I visited him in London and used to talk about him to Lord Hugh Cecil. I am curious to know what has happened to him – it's an ill world for peaceful souls![57]

Lady Blomfield also told Countess Wemyss that she had written to the wife of Colonel Percy Sykes, formerly the British Consul General at Mashhad.

'Now please forgive me! for obeying this wild and worried lady's bequest [*sic*],' wrote Wemyss in a note appended to her letter,

– my sister Pamela knows the old Bahaï too as he came to her house – If the Behaïs are in danger - can *Sir E. Grey* reach out a paw of protection?

Of course I can't help feeling that if there is an innocent population in danger of persecution – that they have *some means* of communicating through the recognized channels to the *proper* source.[58]

Jack Tennant forwarded the letter to the Foreign Office. Once received, a memorandum dated 29 April was drafted, saying:

Lady Blomfield has written to various personages urging enquiry at Teheran regarding a reported massacre of that unorthodox sect in Meshed – the Bahaïs.

I submit, however, that our most able Consul General at Meshed – Col. Haig - and Mr Marling at Teheran are well able to take any action locally that may be necessary. Moreover, while numerous, the sect is *anathema* to the orthodox Persian and while there is still some faint sign of agitation for a *jehad* it would not be politic to champion for the cause of the Behaï.[59]

George Clerk, a Foreign Office official, added a note to Tennant's memorandum, saying, 'I think we might enquire whether Colonel Haig has reported any violence against the Bahaïs. They are an inoffensive people, with sympathizers in this country, and we might find out what is happening to them.'[60]

The enquiry to Charles Marling, British minister at Tehran, resulted in a curt telegram which read, 'No truth in reports of massacres. One Bahai was murdered March 14th.'[61]

The anticipated purge against the believers in Mashhad did not occur, but the high level of activity generated by Lady Blomfield and her friends in order to respond to the request of their co-religionists in Persia served once again to remind the prominent people of British society of the presence in London of the Bahá'ís, whose existence had been largely ignored since the departure of 'Abdu'l-Bahá from their shores. The incident also signalled the first occasion when the Bahá'ís of Britain arose to defend their persecuted brethren in Iran, calling upon the leaders of their country to exert their influence, thus launching a pattern of action that has continued into the opening years of the 21st century.

Reflecting on the murder of Shaykh 'Alí-Akbár, 'Abdu'l-Bahá at Abú-Sinán is reported to have said,

Thousands upon thousands of people are presently being killed on the battlefield, though their deaths will bear no fruit or benefit whatsoever. But one sanctified soul is martyred in the path of God and thousands of others are given life. They water the tree of God with their blood . . . How cruel are the Iranians! They have not eased their oppression. So many calamities and adversities have befallen them and yet they continue with their former persecutions. But they must pay some day. It is revealed, 'God gives them time but does not overlook them.'[62]

In addition to London and Manchester, a third local community of British Bahá'ís emerged during the war years – in Bournemouth. At the centre of this development, which cheered the hearts of 'Abdu'l-Bahá's devotees, was Dr John Ebenezer Esslemont, a Scotsman who first heard of the Bahá'í Movement from the wife of a colleague, Kathleen Parker. Her meeting with the Master in London had immediately sparked Esslemont's interest. By March 1915 he was enthusiastically following the 19 day Bahá'í fast and addressing the Bournemouth Lodge of the Theosophical Society about the teachings.

'In this time of strife and bloodshed,' Esslemont wrote to Luṭfu'lláh Ḥakím, 'it is a great comfort to have Bahá'u'lláh's promise of the Most Great Peace and to feel that a spiritual power is at work which by-and-by will turn the swords into plough shares and the spears into pruning hooks.'[63]

In Britain, the war also gave rise to a measure of persecution of anyone who appeared to be voicing opinions against the conflict. The Bahá'ís in London struggled to decide how best to continue meetings and to present the message, which was not getting a sympathetic hearing in the prevailing climate. Mother George believed the war could represent a time of great spiritual awakening, when many who would not listen before might now begin to do so. The challenge was actually to get people together, she averred, while a public meeting with few in attendance would convey the wrong impression.

At a time when Britain had no effective air defences, raids by German Zeppelin airships brought all kinds of evening activities in London to a halt. On 1 June 1915, the East End was bombarded with 90 incendiaries and explosive bombs. By 1917 the Zeppelins were replaced by Gotha heavy bomber aeroplanes and the raids increased. More than 20 German planes reached London on 7 July and badly damaged properties around St Pancras railway station. A 50 kilogram bomb was dropped outside the Bedford Hotel, Bloomsbury, on 24 September, killing 13.

'The air raids have been of course very terrible and trying,' wrote Ethel Rosenberg to her friend Helen Goodall in California. 'The noise of the firing is tremendous. Our chief danger in these parts is from unexploded shells – some of which have fallen very near. What anxiety we feel about our dear friends in Palestine – God keep them safe and protected . . . These air raids have brought us really into the war now.'[64]

Despite the difficulties of gathering together, the London Bahá'ís did manage to meet at Lady Blomfield's home on 17 November 1917 to celebrate the centenary of the birth of Bahá'u'lláh, five days after the anniversary.

'We had a delightful Unity Meeting at Lady Blomfield's on the 17th,' Ethel Rosenberg wrote. 'Unfortunately she could not hold it on the 12th but we all enjoyed it very much. She spoke, then I did so and after that Mrs George and Mrs Howard.'[65]

Lady Blomfield and the London believers were profoundly relieved and 'rejoiced beyond words' to receive news of 'Abdu'l-Bahá's health and safety.

'We think of him, walking in the garden of his home, and great is our longing for the day when we may be in the light of his presence,' Sitárih wrote to Mirza Ahmad Sohrab. 'We all unite in our gratitude at hearing news of our beloved one, for his Salutation, and for his benediction. We ask his continued prayers for our Protection and Grace that we may consecrate our lives anew to the Glory of God and to the service of humanity.'[66]

Lady Blomfield wrote how she had been able to help in nursing injured servicemen and being of some comfort to the wounded.

'Some of those who come to us, afflicted with the loss of their sight, are pleased to talk of Holy things – which gives them solace in their darkened world. Will the kind and benevolent one pray for them and for Miss Helen Grand who has brought them to us, and whose life is spent in their welfare and whose heart is set on bringing them into the Kingdom of Glory? . . . Indeed, the sure and certain hope of the coming of the 'Most Great Peace of God' is our support and comfort in this terrible time of the Most Great War!'[67]

The close connections nurtured by 'Abdu'l-Bahá between believers across the world led them to call upon each other for small favours during wartime. Corinne True, one of 'Abdu'l-Bahá's most distinguished followers in the United States and later a Hand of the Cause of God, wrote to Lady Blomfield about a nephew of hers, stationed with the Aviation Corps in

London. She asked Sitárih if she might get in touch with the young man, Duncan Knight, and befriend him.

Reports of the Master rarely made it out of the Holy Land during the war years, but when they did the British Bahá'ís derived great strength and encouragement from them. However, when news arrived that the Master's own life may once again be in danger, it came as a tremendous shock to the believers. It was through their efforts, mobilized by Wellesley Tudor Pole, that a calamity was averted.

Tudor Pole had arrived in Egypt on 23 November 1917 and had been sent up to the Palestine front immediately as a member of the Egyptian Expeditionary Force. Just ten days later near Jerusalem, he was wounded in his left arm and shoulder by a sniper's bullet, fired from an olive tree. He was then posted as an intelligence officer to the general headquarters of General Allenby in the Second Echelon of the Occupied Enemy Territory Administration.

'I was able to drive down and hobble into the Bahai gathering . . . and I presented the greetings of the London friends,' Tudor Pole wrote to Ethel Rosenberg from Egypt on 22 December.

> They have some method of getting through information concerning A.B. quite ingenious, but one cannot mention it in writing. Up to the end of November he was well & the family in safety. The problem will arise when our advance commences in that direction. I hope to be on that portion of the Front next month & trust to get through in due course. The authorities here have promised me they will do their best to afford protection when the time comes & I feel my efforts may not prove wasted in the end. The Intelligence people here owned up to have quite forgotten the presence of A.B. and His party at 'H', and promised me they would give the matter consideration . . . I need all possible support in the form of Cables urging protection and help for A.B. when the opportunity arises.'[68]

The Master was certainly facing danger. Jamal Pasha had stated his definite intention to take the lives of 'Abdu'l-Bahá and those around Him should the Turkish Army be compelled to evacuate Haifa and retreat north. The British were preparing to move towards Haifa but for a number of reasons the advance had to be delayed until the summer.

'Abdu'l-Bahá's position was not understood by the British authorities, as Tudor Pole explained in a letter to Sir Mark Sykes MP, written two days after Tudor Pole's letter to Ethel Rosenberg.

> It is not even realized that he controls a remarkable religious movement, wholly devoid of political and military associations; which can number many millions of adherents through the Near and Middle East. Jews, Moslems of various Sects, Christians, Parsis, Hindoos, Kurds unite under the Bahai banner of Spiritual Fellowship. May not these people contribute much, later, to the harmonising of Sectarian and Oriental Religious feuds? Is it too much to ask the Authorities at home to request the Authorities here to afford Abdul Baha every protection and consideration? . . . A word from Whitehall works wonders.[69]

Tudor Pole's letter to Sykes did not reach the Foreign Office until 6 February. He tried without success to arouse interest in 'Abdu'l-Bahá's plight among those who were responsible for intelligence activities, including General Gilbert Clayton, Sir Wyndham Deedes, Sir Ronald Storrs – the recently-appointed Governor of Jerusalem – and Major-General Sir Arthur Money, the Chief Administrator of Occupied Enemy Territory, Tudor Pole's own chief. None of them knew anything about the Master, nor could Tudor Pole rouse them to realize the urgent need to ensure His safety.

Tudor Pole then set out on an extremely dangerous course of action. Risking a court martial, he decided to evade the very strict censorship, bypass his military superiors and the War Office in London and find a way to approach directly the British Cabinet. Major David Ormsby Gore was in Egypt as an attaché for the Foreign Office to the Zionist Commission. Tudor Pole met Gore at the Sporting Club in Alexandria and enlisted his services. As a serving officer he too was subject to King's Regulations and censorship control but he agreed to carry an uncensored letter from Tudor Pole to London addressed to the elderly Walburga, Lady Paget, a writer who had once been an intimate friend of Queen Victoria. She passed the letter to her son-in-law, Lord Plymouth, who took it directly to the Foreign Secretary, Lord Balfour. Balfour arranged for its contents to be placed on the agenda of a meeting of the War Cabinet at which he, the Prime Minister Lloyd George and the Leader of the House of Lords, Lord Curzon, were present.

At the same time Lady Blomfield and some other believers also launched themselves into action, pleading for 'Abdu'l-Bahá's protection. Sitárih reported that she was 'much startled and deeply disturbed by a telephone message: "Abdu'l-Bahá in serious danger. Take immediate action.'[70]

'Do you know anyone of influence whom you could interest in the matter?' she wrote straight away to Ethel Rosenberg.

Any one in touch with 'Intelligence' or W.O. [War Office] here? I do think it so very important, don't you? The author of the Persian History, is he in England now? Would Lord Glenconner do anything do you think? Or Lord Wemyss? I have sent a copy to Mrs. T.C. who might get into touch with Lord Lamington at any rate I asked her to try. It seems too dreadful that our W.O. people (Central certainly) – in Egypt – should practically know nothing about Abdul Baha and have forgotten his whereabouts. What a mercy that WTP is out there. I dare say you will be able to think of someone who might help?[71]

The next day Lady Blomfield drafted a note:

Abdul Baha – sometimes called Abbas Effendi – is now, with his wife and family, either at Haifa or on Mount Carmel. Abdul Baha is the leader of the Bahai Movement which has, for its object, the establishment of true peace in the world, individual and international. He has suffered much persecution at the hands of various fanatical bodies. Abdul Baha's friends in Great Britain and in America are anxious that He and his family should not suffer any unpleasantness when our Army arrives because of his identity not being known. These friends would be very grateful if a cable may be sent without delay commending him to consideration and protection at the hands of our command in Palestine.[72]

The meeting with Lord Lamington quickly transpired. His 'sympathetic regard for 'Abdu'l-Bahá, his understanding of the ramifications and "red tape" necessary for "immediate action" were of priceless value,' wrote Lady Blomfield.[73] Lamington, who treasured memories of the Master's London visit, enjoyed considerable influence and wrote immediately to Lord Balfour explaining 'Abdu'l-Bahá's position and the urgent need to protect Him.

'In the past he has undergone much persecution at the hands of fanatics and anxiety is felt by his many friends in Gt. Britain and America lest he, his wife and family should not receive adequate protection during the British advance owing to his identity not being known to our authorities,' wrote Lamington.[74]

'Through the influence of Lord Lamington, and his prompt help,' wrote Lady Blomfield, 'the letter, with its alarming news, was at once put into the hands of Lord Balfour.'[75]

Mrs Whyte, who had hosted the Master on His visit to Edinburgh, also joined the campaign, writing to her son Frederick, who was a Member of Parliament. He informed Sir Mark Sykes in a letter dated 25 January:

> ... I presume I need not waste your time in giving an account of Abdul Baha himself, whose personality and work must be well known to you. But as you are aware, he has a good many followers, if one may so call them, in this country; and in general there is a number of people who, like myself, are much interested in his work and will be prepared to do something to make sure that the Military Authorities in Palestine are aware of his presence. I know that at one time Lord Curzon was very deeply impressed with the Bahai Movement in Persia itself and he may be willing to interest himself in the matter now.[76]

'I am very glad to hear of the wonderful work you have been doing lately with regard to the safeguarding of the Beloved,' wrote Luṭfu'lláh Ḥakím to Lady Blomfield. 'I trust and hope that successful results have been obtained.'[77]

This sudden activity on behalf of 'Abdu'l-Bahá succeeded in alerting the British authorities to His existence. Lamington received a letter from the Foreign Office within a week which informed him that Secretary Balfour 'has requested His Majesty's High Commissioner for Egypt to call the attention of the British Military Authorities to the presence of Abdul Baha at Haiffa [sic], and to request them to treat him and his family with all possible consideration in the event of a further advance by the British forces in Palestine'.[78]

A cable was sent to the British High Commissioner in Egypt asking that he warn the General Officer that 'Abdu'l-Bahá and His family should be treated with special consideration in the event of their occupying Haifa. The despatch passed through Tudor Pole's hands in Cairo on its way to the British Army Headquarters at Ludd, and was duly delivered to be dealt with by the Headquarters Staff there. No one at HQ had heard of 'Abdu'l-Bahá or the

Bahá'í movement, and Intelligence was requested to make urgent enquiry. In due course the demand for information reached the Headquarters of Intelligence at Cairo's Savoy Hotel and was ultimately passed to Tudor Pole for action. As a result, General Allenby was provided with full particulars in regard to 'Abdu'l-Bahá's record and the history of the Movement.

Allenby at once issued orders to the General Commanding Officer in command of the Haifa operations to the effect that immediately the town was entered, a British guard was to be posted at once around 'Abdu'l-Bahá's house and a further guard was to be placed at the disposal of His family and followers. Means were found for making it known within the enemy lines that stern retribution would follow any attempt to cause death or injury to the Master or any of His household.

When the British finally took Haifa in September 1918, information about 'Abdu'l-Bahá's safety was swiftly transmitted to London, to the great relief of his friends and followers.

'My dear Lamington,' wrote Lord Balfour on 30 September. 'You will remember that you wrote to me in January last, regarding the safety of Abdul Behar [*sic*] and the Bahais at Haifa. I have now received a telegram from the Chief Political Officer in Palestine, reporting that on the occupation of Haifa, Abdul Behar was found to be still in the town and in good health, and that he is being well cared for.'[79]

'Abdul Baha is extraordinarily well and has suffered very little during the past year or nine months,' wrote Tudor Pole to Ethel Rosenberg on 4 November 1918.

> I should like you and all those who took the trouble to act on my suggestion last February to know that the result of that work has proved invaluable. As a consequence of the Foreign Office intervention and of my personal interview with the Chief Administrator and the Chief Political Officer, everything was made easy for Abdul Baha and his family when we occupied Haifa and his house property was protected and he was given facilities to receive and send letters through this department. A large number of cables were sent over and the letters that accumulated at Port Said are gradually being delivered in Haifa.[80]

At 11 o'clock in the morning of the 11th day of the 11th month of 1918 the Great War ended. An entire generation, more than ten million people, had been wiped out, six million of them civilians.

'Praise be to God that the swords have been sheathed, the awful carnage has stopped, the battle-flags have been unfurled and the "Parliament of Man, the Federation of the world" is well nigh to be established,' wrote 'Abdu'l-Bahá's grandson Shoghi Effendi, full of the optimism of the hour, to Dr Esslemont.[81]

'When the glad news became known in London scenes of remarkable enthusiasm were witnessed,' reported the *Daily Mirror*.

> Flags appeared on all sides with amazing rapidity. They floated proudly over all public buildings, they appeared like magic from private houses, they were waved in the streets, worn (in miniature) on hats, pinned on coats, waved frantically on bus tops, lorries, charabancs, taxi-cabs, costers' carts and on every description of vehicle that could pass through the surging joyous multitudes that thronged the main arteries of London's traffic.[82]

For the believers in London, it was a moment not only for celebration but rededication to the cause of universal peace. Mother George longed to see Bahá'í meetings happening once again in the city. With the blessing of Ethel Rosenberg and others, she visited a number of possible venues and settled on the Lindsay Hall in Notting Hill Gate where weekly meetings could be held on Wednesday evenings. The believers were most relieved, however, that the Master and His family were safe and looking toward the future.

'This world-war has come to an end,' 'Abdu'l-Bahá wrote to the Bahá'ís of the British Isles. 'We trust that at least it will lead to the preliminaries of universal peace, just as it is plainly foretold in the blessed Tablets.'[83]

The news of the Armistice reached Tudor Pole sitting in his office in Cairo, where the atmosphere was entirely different. He gave a small dinner for his staff and, having toasted them, said,

> Many of you do not at present realize that we stand at perhaps the most remarkable point in the history of the world. One era has closed before our eyes; it is closed in the midst of carnage and tumult. We are now actually witnessing the birth of a New Day, a Day during which the human race will be enlightened, transformed, regenerated. Do not let this hour pass lightly; enjoy the outward triumph of the Armistice but let your thoughts run deep as well . . .

Those of us who have looked death in the face during the past few years, and who realize something of the tragedy that war brings in its wake, have determined to carry out two resolutions: We will bring home to our children and to those around us some idea of what war really means . . . We will create in the minds of the next generation such a detestation of human warfare, its horror, its uselessness, that the tradition of peace universal shall grow up firmly implanted in the human consciousness of the future, and war will become inconceivable. Secondly, we have determined that the world of our own generation shall be lifted out of gloom and sorrow towards peace and steadfast happiness.

. . . After destruction, Reconstruction! We can each in our humble sphere help forward the building of a new and better world upon the basis of a sure foundation. Let us be very sure of our own foundations before we begin to build, either within or without, and all will be well.[84]

By the end of November, Tudor Pole was himself able to pay an unannounced visit to the Master.

'Captain Tudor Pole, the beloved of Abdul Baha, arrived today at Acca all of a sudden, and how deep our pleasure and surprise has been,' Shoghi Effendi wrote.[85]

The Master greeted His unexpected visitor 'with that sweet smile and cheery welcome for which he is famous,' reported Tudor Pole. 'For 74 long years Abdul Baha has lived in the midst of tragedy and hardship, yet nothing has robbed or can rob him of his cheery optimism, spiritual insight and keen sense of humour.'[86]

Tudor Pole found 'Abdu'l-Bahá looking a little older than he had remembered Him from the unforgettable visit to his Bristol home seven years earlier. How much they had both endured since those memorable days. Yet, Tudor Pole noted, 'Abdu'l-Bahá seemed to be much more vigorous than He had been after His exhausting American journey. His voice was 'as strong as ever, his eyes clear, his step virile . . .'[87]

'I have made all the necessary arrangements, military and governmental, for the comfort and security of the Master and his household,' Tudor Pole wrote to Ethel Rosenberg, 'and you can advise all concerned, both in England and America, that there is no danger of the Persian Colony in Palestine running short of provisions this winter, or of receiving adequate protection. I am arranging for Abdul Baha to visit Jerusalem as the military Governor's guest, and hope to see him again before the year is out.'[88]

Sir Herbert Samuel, the first High Commissioner for Palestine under the British Mandate, took an early opportunity of paying a visit to 'Abdu'l-Bahá at His home in Haifa. Sir Herbert 'felt privileged' to make the acquaintance of the Master, telling Lady Blomfield that he 'was impressed, as was every visitor, by 'Abdu'l-Bahá's dignity, grace, and charm. Of moderate stature, his strong features and lofty expression lent to his personality an appearance of majesty. In our conversation he readily explained and discussed the principal tenets of Bahá'ism, answered my inquiries and listened to my comments.'[89]

Indeed, calling upon the Master was becoming a regular feature of life for the occupying British forces in Palestine.

'English officers of all ranks, Major General, Brigadier General, Colonels, Majors, Lieutenants, Captains and non-commissioned men and privates have called on him and drank tea with him and listened reverently to his words of wisdom,' Mirza Ahmad Sohrab told *Star of the West*.

> The military Governors of Acca and Haifa have often met him; the former being his guest at dinner. Once about eight members of the Australian Flying Corps, who have their aerodrome at the foot of Mount Carmel, were his guests all day in Bahje, near Acca. They visited the tomb of Baha'o'llah, listened to the lecture of Abdul-Baha on the history of this Cause and its principles, and left in the evening in their large auto with glad hearts and beaming faces.[90]

Tudor Pole encouraged the friends in London to convey their gratitude for the consideration shown to 'Abdu'l-Bahá since the British occupation to both General Allenby and General Sir Arthur Money. At the same time, he urged that a memorandum should also be sent to the Foreign Secretary who was responsible for instructing the Military Authorities to safeguard 'Abdu'l-Bahá and to give Him full protection. To Allenby, the letter read:

> We, the friends of Abdul Bahá Abbas Effendi in Great Britain wish to convey our thankful appreciation of your most kind and prompt action undertaken for the protection and help of him and his family since the British advance on Haifa. We recognise how much we owe to you and we desire you to accept our unbounded gratitude.[91]

The Bahá'ís thought it best to have the letter signed by a few of 'Abdu'l-Bahá's 'leading' followers on behalf of the entire Bahá'í community. The letter was sent out over the names of Mrs Whyte, Mrs Thornburgh-Cropper, Miss Rosenberg and Lady Blomfield.

'From all that Major WTP has told us we feel that we can hardly be sufficiently grateful to the personages named in his Memorandum for all they have done for our beloved Abdul Bahá, his friends and his family,' Ethel Rosenberg wrote to Bahá'ís in North America.[92]

To Sir Arthur Money, the letter read, 'We recognize how greatly indebted we are to you for this splendid service and we desire you to accept our unbounded gratitude.'[93] To Balfour: 'That this result has taken place we abundantly recognize is due to your great kindness and promptitude, and we therefore desire you to accept our heartfelt unbounded gratitude.'[94]

'How grand a privilege for Britain, who was able to do this service to the "Servant of God" through the chosen instruments of "The Protector, The Supreme",' enthused Lady Blomfield.[95]

'I hope that you and yours are well and recovering from the strain of the war and of the splendid war work that you have undertaken both in France and in England,' Tudor Pole wrote to Lady Blomfield.[96] Certainly Sitárih had witnessed more than she might ever have imagined. But the days following the joy and relief of the Armistice were not without personal sorrow either. In the early months of 1919 Lady Blomfield lost her mother, Emily Ryan.

'Grieve not over of the death of thy revered mother,' wrote 'Abdu'l-Bahá on 16 May, 'for she hastened from a world of darkness to a realm of light and soared from a narrow prison to the loftiest of mansions.'[97]

On 29 July the Master once again urged Sitárih not to be grieved over the death of her mother. 'Tearfully and with utmost lowliness I will implore forgiveness and pardon for her at the divine threshold, that she may be submerged in the sea of lights and immersed in the realm of mysteries.'[98]

In addition, Lady Blomfield's concern for the well-being of her son Frank was ongoing.

'I will also pray and supplicate on behalf of thy dear son,' 'Abdu'l-Bahá assured her, 'that his may be a luminous heart and a heavenly spirit, and that he may be aided by the boundless effusions of celestial grace.'[99]

When the Great War came to an end, few nations had any plans in hand as to what should transpire once the hostilities had ceased. It was America's President Woodrow Wilson whose ideas, by default, laid the foundation for the peace that was established. His 'Fourteen Points', presented to the American Congress on 8 January 1918, ten months before the Armistice, provided the only coherent framework considering how the peace might be negotiated and consolidated. Opposition to the points came from Britain and France. Britain rejected Wilson's second point concerning freedom of navigation of the seas, while France demanded war reparations. President Wilson was forced to compromise a number of his ideals in order that his most important concept, the establishment of the League of Nations, was accepted. The Treaty of Versailles, signed on 28 June 1919, which ended the war between Germany and the Allied Powers, went against many of Wilson's points. His own Senate refused to consent to the ratification of the Treaty and the United States of America never joined the League of Nations, hampering its credibility as a mediator for conflicts.

'Although the representatives of various governments are assembled in Paris in order to lay the foundations of Universal Peace', observed the Master, 'and thus bestow rest and comfort upon the world of humanity, yet misunderstanding among some individuals is still predominant and self-interest still prevails. In such an atmosphere, Universal Peace will not be practicable, nay rather, fresh difficulties will arise. This is because interests are conflicting and aims are at variance . . .'[100]

Nevertheless, despite the protestations of politicians, 'Abdu'l-Bahá believed that President Wilson was 'indeed serving the Kingdom of God for he is restless and strives day and night that the rights of all men may be preserved safe and secure, that even small nations, like greater ones, may dwell in peace and comfort under the protection of Righteousness and Justice. This purpose is indeed a lofty one. I trust that the incomparable Providence will assist and confirm such souls under all conditions.'[101]

The primary goals of the League of Nations included preventing war through collective security, disarmament and settling international disputes through negotiation and arbitration. Other goals included regulating labour conditions, the just treatment of native inhabitants, the arms trade, global health and the protection of minorities in Europe. Little wonder, then, that the Bahá'ís of East and West observed the League's establishment with a joyous optimism, interpreting its formation as a sign of the Lesser Peace which, as prophesied by Bahá'u'lláh, was certain to follow calamitous events that would, out of necessity, unite the nations. An editorial in *Star of the West* read, 'Now is the time, to use the words of President Wilson, for humanity to "rise to the clear heights of (God's) own justice and mercy".'[102]

'There will be much unrest and fermentation in Europe for years yet, I expect,' Dr Esslemont wrote to *Star of the West*, 'but unrest is better than the placid acquiescence with vile conditions – with slums, drunkenness, prostitution, sweated labour and profligate extravagance; and it seems to me that on the whole, things are moving towards a better state of affairs – towards the Most Great Peace. There must be destruction before reconstruction, and the old structure of society in Europe had to be thrown on the scrapheap.'[103]

To Woodrow Wilson must be ascribed, Shoghi Effendi later wrote, 'the unique honour, among the statesmen of any nation, whether of the East or of the West, of having voiced sentiments so akin to the principles animating the Cause of Bahá'u'lláh, and of having more than any other world leader, contributed to the creation of the League of Nations – achievements which the pen of the Centre of God's Covenant acclaimed as signalizing the dawn of the Most Great Peace . . .'[104]

'For the first time in the history of humanity', Shoghi Effendi reflected, 'the system of collective security, foreshadowed by Bahá'u'lláh and explained by 'Abdu'l-Bahá, has been seriously envisaged, discussed and tested . . . For the first time in human history tentative efforts have been exerted by the nations of the world to assume collective responsibility, and to supplement their verbal pledges by actual preparation for collective action.'[105]

However promising the signs were that humanity stood on the threshold of a new era of global security, 'Abdu'l-Bahá knew that the League of Nations was incapable of establishing universal peace. 'But the Supreme Tribunal which Bahá'u'lláh has described', He wrote to the Executive Committee of the Central Organization for a Durable Peace in the Hague, 'will fulfil this sacred task with the utmost might and power.'[106]

The League was 'doomed to failure from the outset,' wrote Mary Blomfield. 'To begin with the refusal of the United States to become a State Member rendered the League incomplete. Bahá'u'lláh had enjoined a League including ALL nations.'[107]

Nevertheless, having witnessed first hand the devastation of the war, Lady Blomfield determined to return to Switzerland to proclaim the Bahá'í message and influence the thinking of the global community gathering around the League of Nations. In Geneva, she 'attempted to inculcate the principles of the Bahá'í Faith in a way which showed her discrimination and wisdom perhaps more markedly than in any other work she had done for the Cause,' wrote Mary.[108]

It was in Geneva also that Sitárih would form a close bond with the Englishwoman with whom she would collaborate for the well-being of the children of Europe, whose very survival hung in the balance in the aftermath of the carnage of the Great War.

CHAPTER EIGHT

THE FIRST OBLIGATION

To contribute towards the cause of these pitiful children, and to protect and care
for them is the highest expression of altruism and worship, and is
well-pleasing to the Most High, the Almighty, the Divine Provider.[1]
'Abdu'l-Bahá

Lady Blomfield, her daughter said, had always keenly felt the world's suffering. Among her mother's papers, Mary found one of Sitárih's thoughts, penned in her own handwriting, which Mary believed illustrated the theme of Lady Blomfield's life:

'It would seem that in one day,' it read, '*s'en dégager et éclairer la vie* [to free oneself and clarify life] – there is a rebirth of spiritual life which is the reaction against the doctrines of those who have attempted to destroy the ideal which has ever existed in the heart of Man. In order to acquire the power to serve Mankind, it is worthwhile greatly to renounce earthly joys. The end of Renunciation is accomplished only in acquiring thereby power to succour humanity.'[2]

Since her earliest days as a follower of Bahá'u'lláh, and more particularly since 'Abdu'l-Bahá's visits to London during which He had become well-acquainted with her natural gift for communicating, the Master had urged Lady Blomfield to develop her talent for speaking, encouraging her to give talks that were lucid and eloquent.

He wrote to her on 29 July 1919, after learning of two such presentations about the Bahá'í Cause she had made – to a ladies' gathering and a philosophical meeting. 'I pray God that thou mayest deliver in numerous meetings such discourses on the divine teachings, which are the spirit of this age and the light of this century, for this twentieth century of the Christian Era is as the body and the teachings of Bahá'u'lláh are as the spirit.'

'Strive as far as thou canst to diffuse these teachings, that those who are asleep may awaken, the blind may see, and the dead be quickened to life,' the Master told her.[3]

One month before this letter was written, the Covenant of the League of Nations was signed by 44 states and the Master had hopes that Lady Blomfield would play a part in the promising processes that were underway.
'This is but the beginning of the dawn of peace,' He told her,

> . . . and only a faint ray thereof hath shone forth. But we cherish the hope that the day-star of universal peace will shine with such intensity that all beings, that is, the entire world of creation, will attain perfect tranquillity. This can in no wise be realized save through the penetrating power of the Word of God. Political measures can have great influence, but only on condition that they be associated with the power of the Word of God and assisted by the aid of the Holy Spirit. For otherwise the foundations of this mighty edifice cannot stand secure but will be shaken every day for a different reason. Now, praise be to God, this is the beginning of the establishment of its foundations. It is our hope that, supported by a celestial might, a heavenly power and an everlasting grace, this edifice may become firmly established and may rise up to the highest heaven.[4]

Entering the seventh decade of her life, Sitárih, Lady Blomfield – 'Abdu'l-Bahá's star – was brightly shining. Her enthusiasm was contagious, and 'the intense light of her faith and the captivating charm of her presence . . . made her loved and revered by all,' wrote Hasan Balyuzi.[5] The moment had now arrived for her to make a more concerted commitment to the promotion of the Cause in the Swiss city where, seven years earlier, she had been instructed by the Master to establish a Bahá'í centre. The seat in Geneva of the League of Nations made the reasons for her presence there all the more urgent. 'Abdu'l-Bahá prayed that her efforts would 'free the souls from the darkness of the world of nature, and lead them to the splendorous light of the Kingdom'.[6]
'This world of dust is fraught with peril,' He wrote,

> . . . and surrounded on all sides with trials and afflictions. Hapless humanity is plunged in this vortex. A divine power is needed to rescue and guide it to the shore of safety. I pray God that thou mayest become

the captain of the ark of existence, deliver it, and all who dwell within it, from this whirlpool, and guide it safely to the harbour of the Kingdom of mercy.[7]

By the end of January 1920, Lady Blomfield had arrived in Geneva and had settled into a room at the prestigious Hôtel d'Angleterre. Designed in 1872 by a celebrated Swiss architect, Anthony Krafft, the Hôtel offered spectacular vistas across Lake Geneva towards Mont Blanc. But Sitárih's interests did not lie with taking in the views. Encouraged by the Master, she was determined to assist the efforts of those gathered in the city by influencing their deliberations with the teachings of Bahá'u'lláh. Soon, in the person of Eglantyne Jebb – an Englishwoman of immense energy and determination – Lady Blomfield discovered a kindred spirit.

Eglantyne Jebb was born in 1876 into a wealthy Shropshire family. The Jebbs were by no means conventional Victorian landowners. The women were passionately interested in acquiring knowledge of new things, and their delight in reading gave them a broad and enlightened world view. Despite their affluence, Eglantyne grew up admiring the simplicity of life in the country. She despised the class system, believing that respect accorded to people 'should not depend upon the way they spend their working hours. In a social sense there should only be one class – the great class of humanity'.[8]

Eglantyne's inquisitive mind benefited further from the burgeoning of educational opportunities for women. In 1895 she went up to Lady Margaret Hall in Oxford to study history. There she took a vigorous interest in world issues and enjoyed debating them with other young women. After Oxford, despite a range of opportunities open to young women from privileged backgrounds, Eglantyne felt the need to do something useful for society. She trained to be an elementary teacher in the impoverished south London suburb of Stockwell. The following year she was appointed to a post at a school in Marlborough where she quickly won her pupils' affection but, after just 18 months, ill health forced her to resign. Depression set in and Eglantyne agonized over what she could offer that was of value. She privately gave lessons to a niece and nephew, travelled with her mother in Europe, attempted to write a novel and became involved with the Charity Organization Society, where she began studying how the issue of poverty was being dealt with in Cambridge and developed a good understanding of how charitable organizations worked.

In 1913 Eglantyne received a request from the Macedonian Relief Fund in London, inviting her to deliver relief money after the Balkan Wars. It was practically unheard of for an English woman to venture alone around her own country without a male escort, let alone in a war zone. In Macedonia she witnessed for herself the aftermath of the conflict and was especially incensed by the suffering of thousands of starving, displaced refugees, uprooted from their homes. Returning to England, she urged the Fund to act more constructively, settling refugees on the land rather than carrying out short-term relief. Her pleas were ignored.

By the time the Great War broke out, Eglantyne was working with the Agricultural Organization Society. Her sister, Dorothy Buxton, concerned that the British press was doing nothing to highlight the realities of the suffering in Europe, began to publish a newsletter carrying translations of reports from the continent. Eglantyne joined her in this enterprise.

As the war was coming to an end, people on mainland Europe were suffering not only from the devastation wreaked by the war but also from the Allied blockade which continued, after the fighting ceased, in an attempt to force the defeated powers to agree to a peace treaty. The reports which the Jebb sisters received were horrifying – people were starving and newly born children were being wrapped in newspapers because linen was unavailable.

'Our minds are appalled at the magnitude of this catastrophe, however sluggish our imagination may be!' wrote Lady Blomfield of the dire torture being suffered by Europe's children. 'Their cries reached the inner ears of two heroic women, who with breadth of vision, and hearts awakened to universal conceptions, having faith in the spiritual potency, arose and set about their Father's business.'[9]

Eglantyne and Dorothy participated in a campaign called the Fight the Famine Council but it soon transpired that while the Council campaigned, there was a very real need to provide immediate help to the thousands in distress. Thus their Save the Children Fund was born and, on 19 May 1919, Eglantyne and her sister addressed a large crowd on the Fund's aims. The public arrived supplied with rotten apples to throw at the heads of these women who wanted to raise money for 'enemy children'. But the Jebbs were unperturbed and Eglantyne's passionate conviction won over the crowd. The public launch of Save the Children was an unqualified success. Support for relief work swelled and soon after the launch money began pouring in. The Archbishop of Canterbury was appealed to, then the Free Churches and the Patriarch of the Greek Church. The cooperation secured was remarkable.

Eglantyne believed that there was a great need to get the widest possible publicity to ease the suffering. In an unprecedented move for that time, the Save the Children Fund employed a professional publicist and, on his advice, took out full-page advertisements in the national press. The tactic worked and while they were criticized for 'wasting money', the first advertisement, which cost some £5,000, brought donations in of £120,000. Save the Children raised almost £400,000 in its first year – a sum equal to about £8 million in today's money.

Local branches of the Fund started up. The first was opened in Fife, Scotland, in 1919. Within two years there were three hundred groups across the United Kingdom and one million pounds had been collected. Committees were also set up in Ireland, Canada, Australia and New Zealand. In December 1919 Eglantyne had a crucial audience with Pope Benedict XV in Rome, during which he unequivocally supported Save the Children, to the extent of donating £25,000 of his own money and declaring Innocents Day – 28 December – a day to collect funds via the Church. The Pope insisted that his contributions were not to be limited only to the relief of children from Roman Catholic backgrounds but were to be used wherever the need was greatest. Lady Blomfield wrote,

> The widespread collections in all the Churches of Christendom on Holy Innocents Day 1919 and 1920 were one of the first great results of this beginning of the translation into action of the continually talked of Brotherhood of Mankind . . . Had it not been, however, that Pope Benedict XV was stirred to pity by the sufferings of the children and their mothers in the famine-stricken lands, and had he not translated the holy compassion of his into practical action by coming to their rescue, it could not have been possible to establish at Geneva the International Union of the Save the Children Fund.[10]

Eglantyne Jebb believed that every country should do its best to help its own people, and not just rely on aid. So as Save the Children spread, the focus was not just on relief for war victims but also for the disadvantaged children of each country. On 6 January 1920 she launched the Save the Children International Union, in Geneva. The International Committee of the Red Cross offered its patronage, recognizing in the movement the same ideals of universal charity expressed in practical service to humanity which had inspired its own founders. The Red Cross placed its own representatives in war-stricken countries at the service of the Union and instructed them to act as International Commissioners for Save the Children, coordinating and supervising the work at different centres.

Ever ready to champion any cause to protect the innocent from injustice, Lady Blomfield was swift to lend her support to the work of Save the Children after her arrival in Switzerland.

'It is my hope that thou mayest be confirmed in that important cause, which is of greatest service to the world of humanity,' 'Abdu'l-Bahá encouraged her, 'for those poor children are dying of hunger and their condition is truly heart-rending. This is but one of the many evils of war.'[11]

The Master was in no doubt that the work of the Fund's founders would receive blessings from God.

'The English lady who hath established this society will assuredly become the recipient of the confirmations of the Abhá Kingdom,' He wrote. 'I hope that this lady, Eglantyne Jebb, and her sister, Mrs Buxton, may both become attracted to the teachings of Bahá'u'lláh, for in reality they are serving His teachings.'

> To these two esteemed ladies convey my respectful greetings and say: 'Ye are serving both the world of humanity and the Sacred Threshold of God. Ye are praised by Bahá'u'lláh, for ye are acting in accordance with His teachings. My hope is that ye may shine as two bright candles upon the world of humanity, serve the cause of divine civilization, be aided to obtain everlasting life, and attain honour in the Kingdom of God.'[12]

Eglantyne responded warmly to 'Abdu'l-Bahá's encouragement. She was a spiritually sensitive woman who had had a number of transcendental – some might say, psychic – experiences and was inclined to a more mystical interpretation of Christianity. Like so many women of her generation, she favoured a more direct relationship with the Creator than offered by the traditional church and had made a personal study of the scriptures of Hinduism as well as other schools of thought. She had independently arrived at the notion of the spiritual unity of all people and, along with most of the other people who gathered in Geneva, longed to do something of moral and social value for humanity. Lady Blomfield felt sure that the Master would have been pleased to witness 'how a great number of "Waiting

Servants" have arisen to do the Behests of the Lord of Compassion, and moreover combining in the most Wonderful Unity of all Branches of the Christian Churches . . .

> Would it not be glorious if the Eastern Brothers would join? And if the Bahá'í Friends 'as a whole' would be part of this Unity it would be so splendid, for it is of course essentially Bahá'í Work, though not as yet called by the Name. Some Jewish Society in America have joined and I am writing to approach some influential Jews in London with a view to extending Unity in that direction. It may be that this Work of Compassion in the Cause of Holy Charity may do much to consolidate a real 'League of people of the World'!! That is our hope![13]

'Abdu'l-Bahá replied,

> . . . God be praised, such an association for the education of impoverished children and the relief of orphans hath been formed in which almost every faith and nation is represented. My hope is that, through the special favours of God, this association may be confirmed; that it may day by day progress both spiritually and materially; that, entering at last beneath the one-coloured pavilion of the Kingdom and reposing within the ark of true existence, it may be preserved from every danger; and that the oneness of the world of humanity may raise its banner in the midmost heart of the world.[14]

Sitárih discovered that many of the people involved in humanitarian work were genuinely interested in the Bahá'í teachings. She sent the Master a list of their names so that He might pray for them. One of them, Clara Guthrie d'Arcis – originally from New Orleans – had established the World Union of Women for International Concord in 1915 with 36 women from various countries. Another, a close Swiss colleague of Eglantyne Jebb – Suzanne Ferrière – was the niece of Dr Frédéric Ferrière, a public health expert who had worked with the Red Cross for four decades and had spent the war working for civilian relief and protection. Sitárih told the Master that the two ladies were both attracted to the Bahá'í Cause. 'Abdu'l-Bahá asked Lady Blomfield to convey His 'greetings to the revered Suzanne Ferrière'.

It is my hope that the material services of that honoured soul to the world of humanity will be joined with spiritual service to the Kingdom of God.

Convey also my highest regards to Madame d'Arcis.[15]

A Dutchman living in Geneva, Mr Reelfs, was also attracted to the message, as was his Finnish wife. Lady Blomfield also made the acquaintance of the Indian-born Sufi teacher Hazrat Inayat Khan, who was in Geneva promoting the unity of religion. Lady Blomfield was naturally very sympathetic to his ideas.

Sitárih returned to London in August 1920 for a few months to attend to personal matters. The necessity to sell her country home became pressing and Beatrice Platt, her daughters' former governess who had assisted in the compilation of *Paris Talks*, had recently lost her sister.

'The death of a sister is in truth exceedingly hard to bear,' 'Abdu'l-Bahá wrote to Sitárih. 'But tell her not to be overwhelmed with grief, nor to wail and lament, for she will find her kind sister in the everlasting world and will behold her in a state of utmost joy.'[16]

But the Master was not keen for Lady Blomfield to stay in London any longer than she needed to. He wished her to return to Switzerland and continue the work with Eglantyne Jebb and her sister.

'Praise be to God that thou hast been confirmed in serving impoverished children and showing kindness to the poor, and hast been assisted in spreading abroad the teachings,' He wrote to Sitárih. 'God willing, thou wilt become in Switzerland the cause of the illumination of the world of humanity and wilt expound the divine teachings.'[17]

'Abdu'l-Bahá also urged Lady Blomfield not to neglect the work of sharing the teachings of Bahá'u'lláh in a direct way with souls she found to be receptive to His message.

'In public gatherings expound the heavenly teachings, but avoid speaking of religious doctrines, for the teachings of Bahá'u'lláh are a universal grace and will establish the oneness of the world of humanity,' He wrote.[18]

The Master took an unusually close interest in the work of Save the Children and encouraged its efforts. He also offered guidance on its development in a series of letters to Lady Blomfield.

Convey my greetings and affection to those two sisters and tell them that although they are enduring many troubles, they have, praise be to God, become helpers of the helpless and affectionate mothers unto the orphans. In the divine Kingdom this service is pleasing in the sight of God. Would that other souls could also arise to serve with such pure intentions . . .'[19]

'As time goes on the essentially spiritual character of the work for the children impresses me more and more,' Eglantyne Jebb responded to Lady Blomfield. 'It would be of incalculable help to us if we had friends all over the world who . . . prayed with a true understanding of the great issues involved.'[20]

'Convey my greetings and regards to Miss Eglantyne', the Master instructed Sitárih on another occasion, 'and say: "Thou art serving, not only the people, but God Himself; thou art caring, not only for the orphans, but for the children of God. Thou hast no desire but to see the banner of universal peace unfurled. This is the first of the teachings of Bahá'u'lláh. I commend thee for this lofty aspiration."'[21]

Eglantyne was greatly encouraged and strengthened by 'Abdu'l-Bahá's support.

'Words quite fail me . . .' she wrote. 'How grateful I am for the encouragement – and oh! Much more than encouragement – real direct help, the incalculable spiritual help we so much need.'[22]

Although Eglantyne was 'completely in tune with the basic Bahá'í principle of the "oneness of humankind"', her biographer has written, 'she never joined the movement. Her own faith was enough to sustain and, she believed, guide her.'[23]

By August 1921, conditions in Central Europe were slowly getting better. However, at that time a devastating famine struck the 'bread basket' Volga region of Russia. Eglantyne and Save the Children needed to go to work with renewed vigour. It was this catastrophic event that also forced Eglantyne and her sister Dorothy to realize that Save the Children needed to be a permanent organization and could not simply be disbanded once the job of repairing war damage in Europe was done. So, from 1921 to 1923, despite many protests against helping the closed and communist state of Russia, Save the Children swung into action. Press campaigns and motion pictures were made and feeding centres set up. More than 157 million meals for 300,000 children were provided during the Russian famine. Save the Children demonstrated its efficiency by proving it could feed a child for a shilling a week.

As they studied together one of the Master's communications in which He urged that the children be educated as well as fed, Lady Blomfield and Eglantyne Jebb decided it best if Sitárih concentrate her efforts on instituting workrooms in collaboration with children's establishments where orphans would be taught manual work and useful trades by which they would be enabled to earn their own living. In return for their work, the children would receive food and a small wage.

'We feel that to prolong the charity of giving food alone would be an endless work,' Sitárih wrote to 'Abdu'l-Bahá, 'whilst to let the children be taught to earn their food would give self-respect, and after a time would not require to be helped by Charity but would arrive at being self-supporting. Thus, an important bit of the re-constructive work of the world would be started amongst the children, upon whom, with the help of God, depends the future of much of the civilization of the unhappy and devastated regions of Europe.'[24]

Soon Save the Children was supporting initiatives that included training in trades for girls and Eglantyne was promoting a range of constructive programmes looking at education and housing in addition to health and nutrition. Lady Blomfield particularly admired the work of a Hungarian friend of Eglantyne, Julie Eve Vadjkai, who had already successfully started workrooms in Budapest 'for the poor children, who would without them, be wandering the streets in summer's heat or winter's cold, with nobody to care whether they lived or died'.[25] Captain A. G. Pedlow, who for two years was the Commissioner to Hungary for the American Red Cross, commended Vadjkai's workrooms to Lady Blomfield.

'Any action', he wrote, 'which equips the young people, physically or mentally, so that they can earn their own living, is the best means of providing a lasting benefit for the Community.'[26]

Sitárih created a special account, the 'Blomfield Fund', to finance the workrooms for children, which she saw constituting an increasingly important part of the activities of the Save the Children Fund. She appealed for contributions to be made to her, via the Save the Children offices at 4 Rue Massot in Geneva, or to the President of Save the Children, Lord Weardale – formerly the Liberal MP Philip Stanhope – in London.

Furthermore, Lady Blomfield was keen for the Bahá'ís around the world to be mobilized into supporting the work of Save the Children – 'this great Crusade', as she described it, 'to rescue the poor children from the grave danger of being left to themselves and the terrible vices, which are ever ready to assail neglected youth, and from the worst of all misfortunes, that of growing up into ignorant men and women – materialists, like animals!'[27]

To convey the message to 'Abdu'l-Bahá's supporters around the world, Sitárih began work on a small booklet, entitled *The First Obligation*.

'This servant feels that the joining of the Bahá'í friends in this grand International work of Charity to all children, who are unhappy, whether of friends or former enemies, of all nationalities, and of all religions, and of all sects of religion – would give to the world a practical demonstration of the Teaching of the Bahá'í Revelation on this important matter of child rescue and training,' Lady Blomfield wrote to the Master. 'Will the beloved and compassionate 'Abdu'l-Bahá give His Blessing to this effort for Unity in Charitable Work, and supplicate for success, great success! Until all the children, now languishing in misery may have a happy chance in life?'[28]

In response, 'Abdu'l-Bahá described the war that had recently ended as a 'great calamity to the world of humanity'.

It was like unto a mighty torrent rushing down from the summit of the mountains with utmost force and laying waste every city and town in its wake. But forty years ago Bahá'u'lláh had already, in His epistles, clearly warned of this momentous event. Addressing all the rulers and nations of the world, He summoned them to hold back this torrent, but none responded. 'Abdu'l-Bahá also cried out repeatedly, in Europe and in America, 'O ye who are endued with insight! The continent of Europe hath become even as an arsenal, in whose basement is heaped up every manner of explosives. Soon a single spark will ignite a conflagration. Make ye an effort, that this fierce blaze may be averted.' But none gave heed. This volcano erupted – cities were turned upside down, villages were devastated, properties were plundered, millions were killed, households were obliterated, millions of fathers lost their sons, millions of children became fatherless, and millions of women were left destitute. Such nakedness, hunger and abandonment befell the innocent children – with no father and no mother, with no clothing on their backs, no place to sleep, no food to eat, no one to care for them – that they became mere skin and bones. How evident, then, to what an extent benevolence towards these children will be conducive to the good pleasure of the Almighty![29]

The Master approved the idea of Lady Blomfield's pamphlet and requested that she print His words as a Foreword:

> To contribute towards the cause of these pitiful children, and to protect and care for them is the highest expression of altruism and worship, and is well-pleasing to the Most High, the Almighty, the Divine Provider. For these little ones have no protecting father and mother, no kind nurse, no home, no clothing, no food, no comfort, no place of rest.
>
> In all these things, they call for our kindness, they merit our help, they are deserving of mercy and of our utmost pity.
>
> The eyes of all who love Justice are filled with tears, and every understanding heart burneth with pity!
>
> Oh ye peoples of the World, show compassion!
>
> Oh ye Concourse of the Wise, hold out your hands to help!
>
> Oh ye Nobles, show Loving Kindness. Be Bountiful!
>
> Oh ye Wealthy of the Earth, shower Contributions!
>
> Oh ye Men, strong and brave of heart, manifest your Benevolence![30]

In the opening pages of *The First Obligation* Lady Blomfield carefully compiled extracts from the *Hidden Words of Bahá'u'lláh* which appealed to humanity to show forth good deeds, to care for the poor and to disregard racial differences.

'The First Obligation is to strive by all means', she quotes Bahá'u'lláh as saying, 'to instruct the children. Endeavour with all your souls to train and educate all children, boys and girls alike; instruction and education are not optional, they are definitely commanded. On this point no excuses can be accepted. He who educates his own child or any other child, it is as though he educated a Child of God.'[31] A collection of 'Abdu'l-Bahá's words follows, starting with His instruction to 'Give to the children a manual profession, something whereby they may be able to support themselves and others.'[32]

In the second part of the pamphlet Lady Blomfield reproduced a number of 'Abdu'l-Bahá's letters in which He gave special blessing to Eglantyne Jebb and her co-workers in the Save the Children Fund.

'The foregoing extracts from Tablets of Abdul Baha show how very near to his heart is this work for the children,' wrote Lady Blomfield. 'And would it not be well if the Bahais of the world were to arise and take their part in this Holy Crusade of Rescue?'[33]

And surely there can be no greater purpose in this day of the world's sorrow than the Rescue of these pitiful little ones. If we are apathetic, or negligent, or asleep to their danger, the hosts of evil are ever alert and watchful to seize upon those whom we, in our slothful acquiescence in all that ought not to be in this dark world, abandon to misery and death of body and of soul.

Do not forget, you who read this appeal, that these children, for whom we plead, are the sons and daughters of God. Will you not therefore without delay enlist in the army of Light by joining in this Crusade?[34]

In terms of organizing the work of the Fund, Lady Blomfield wrote that it was suggested that there should be in every country of the world a committee which would gather together representative men and women of all shades of thought in the service of the children and who would undertake the practical task of collecting funds for them. The committees had a dual duty of collecting funds for the children of their own country as well as for the poorest children of whatever nationality.

From the point of view of the Bahá'ís, Lady Blomfield stated that this duty should consist not merely in giving children food to eat but in training them to earn food for themselves in later years by their own works.

'Wherever there is impoverishment,' she wrote, 'there is a menace to child-life, and the Save the Children Fund, reinforced by the Bahá'ís of the world, should be the Ark to carry the children safely through this time of stress and strain.'[35]

In her pamphlet Sitárih then devotes a section to the work of the British Save the Children Fund and its support of workrooms 'where the older children are given food and a small wage in return for work'.

The interest, the occupation, the discipline, the warm cheerful rooms, where they work under good conditions, all tend to restore their happiness and self-respect, so cruelly undermined by constant privation, enforced idleness, and the terrible temptations to which these give rise. Moreover, the training given in the workroom helps to fit them for a useful, self-supporting life in the future, and it is touching to note that, great as is their gratitude for the food they so urgently need, they often express still greater gratitude for being given an interest and a chance in life. The writer has herself investigated this system at Budapest and can vouch for the excellence of its results.[36]

'We are embarking on a colossal undertaking. To save myriads of little ones!' wrote Lady Blomfield. 'But our spirits dare not quail before our bounden duty of service, whilst we can ask for and receive in great measure that Spiritual Potency, that Grace which is sufficient for us; if we use this Power, the Fire of the Love of God, all the frozen depths of misery will melt away from the lives of the dear children in the merciful warmth of its shining.'[37]

The First Obligation ends as it began, with a quotation from the Master:

If tremendous progress in a short time be desired by a people in any Social Reform, any undertaking for the good of Humanity, they must lay hold of this Spiritual Potency. Then will their advancement appear phenomenal, their success magical. This spiritual Potency will enable the worker to keep before the eye of the mind the picture of the Divine Civilization, that Kingdom, for the coming of which we have been praying for nigh 2,000 years.[38]

The international travel teacher Charles Mason Remey promised Lady Blomfield that he would widely distribute the pamphlets to large numbers of Bahá'ís in America, while a friend in Geneva who was attracted to the teachings offered to translate it into French. Lady Blomfield firmly believed that joining the Bahá'ís with the work of the Fund would give to the world a practical demonstration of the Bahá'í teachings on child education.

The response of the followers of 'Abdu'l-Bahá around the world is not clearly ascertainable. While the Bahá'í community was not yet strong enough to provide widespread institutional support, some individuals were no doubt moved by Lady Blomfield's appeal. Although Eglantyne Jebb passed away in 1928 and Sitárih's international activities became more limited as old age set in, she remained active in the work of the Save the Children Fund until shortly before her death. In her last years she served on the Council of the Save the Children Fund in Britain and was for a time its vice president. Just two months before her passing, Sitárih attended a Council meeting, having offered earlier in the year to give up her seat to make way for a younger candidate. The other Council members pressed her to remain a member until after the Second World War.

The British friends of 'Abdu'l-Bahá were delighted when news reached them that the Master was to be invested with the insignia of the Knight-hood of the British Empire. The knighthood was conferred upon Him in recognition of His humanitarian work during the Great War for the relief of distress and famine.

'When the British arrived in Haifa,' wrote Lady Blomfield,

> . . . where the blockade had caused a perilous condition for the inhab-itants, it was discovered that 'Abdu'l-Bahá had saved the civilian population from starvation. Provisions which He had grown, buried in under-ground pits, and otherwise stored, had been given out to the civilians of every nation living in Haifa. 'Abdu'l-Bahá did this in a mili-tary way as an army would give rations, and deep was the gratitude of those women and children who had been saved by His power to see into the future of tragedy and woe as early as 1912, when He began the preparations for the catastrophe which was to overtake that land in 1917 and 1918. When Haifa was finally occupied by the British, reserve provisions had not yet come for the army, and someone in authority approached the Master . . .[39]

'Abdu'l-Bahá was not interested in the slightest in titles and honours but accepted the knighthood as a courteous gift 'from a just king'.[40]

'As a token of good will and kindly feeling this warmed his heart as a basket of peaches from the Royal gardens would have probably equally done,' mused the author Constance Maud, one of Lady Blomfield's friends who had met the Master in London. 'One cannot help feeling, however, there is something strangely incongruous in knighting a prophet, who is already Master of such an order as "Servants of the Glory", the only star that meant anything to his old eyes of wisdom being that followed by Gaspar, Melchior, and Balthazar.'[41]

The knighting ceremony was specifically held for 'Abdu'l-Bahá at the residence of the British Governor in Haifa on 27 April 1920.

'The dignitaries of the British crown from Jerusalem were gathered in Haifa, eager to do honour to the Master, Whom every one had come to love and reverence for His life of unselfish service,' wrote Lady Blomfield.

> An imposing motor-car had been sent to bring 'Abdu'l-Bahá to the ceremony. The Master, however, could not be found. People were sent in every direction to look for Him, when suddenly from an unexpected

side He appeared, alone, walking His kingly walk, with that simplicity of greatness which always enfolded Him.

The faithful servant, Isfandíyár, whose joy it had been for many years to drive the Master on errands of mercy, stood sadly looking on at the elegant motor-car which awaited the honoured guest.

'No longer am I needed.'

At a sign from Him, Who knew the sorrow, old Isfandíyár rushed off to harness the horse, and brought the carriage out at the lower gate, whence 'Abdu'l-Bahá was driven to a side entrance of the garden of the Governorate of Phoenicia.

So Isfandíyár was needed and happy.[42]

In the summer of 1920 'Abdu'l-Bahá called upon Lady Blomfield to render another singular service to a member of His family. His beloved grandson Shoghi Effendi was taking up his studies in England and the Master wished for Sitárih to keep a maternal eye on him.

Shoghi Effendi was becoming an increasingly prominent figure on the international Bahá'í scene through his communications to *Star of the West* and his excellent translations of the Master's letters. His hope, in studying in England, was to perfect his English to such an extent that he could act as his grandfather's secretary and adequately translate the scriptures of the Faith.

'Shoghi Effendi is proceeding to those regions,' 'Abdu'l-Bahá wrote to Lady Blomfield. 'Thou wilt undoubtedly consider and treat him as thine own son and wilt fulfil all the requirements of motherly affection.'[43]

Shoghi Effendi arrived in London carrying Tablets from the Master to Lady Blomfield, Lord Lamington and Major Tudor Pole expressing His wishes for the education of His grandson. Within days he had secured interviews with a number of prominent academics from Oxford and London including Sir E. Denison Ross and Professor William Ker.

During his brief sojourn in England, Shoghi Effendi became intimate friends with the English Bahá'ís and did much to cheer their hearts during his stay amongst them. His experience studying at Oxford, according to his widow Rúhíyyih Rabbaní, 'shaped and sharpened his already clear and logical mind, heightened his critical faculties, reinforced his strong sense of justice and reasoning powers, and added to the oriental nobility which characterized Bahá'u'lláh's family those touches of the culture we associate with the finest type of English gentleman'.[44]

Lady Blomfield met Shoghi Effendi and enjoyed a long conversation with him about his translation work on Thursday 29 September 1921. He expressed the hope that she might assist him in rendering the Bahá'í writings into a style of English that would somehow reflect the poetic quality of the original verses in Persian or Arabic. The next day he wrote to Sitárih from his lodgings in Bloomsbury Square expressing his pleasure at seeing her and thanking her for her encouragement.

'Your interest in my work of translation has encouraged me a great deal & my hope is that I shall in the near future realize my aspiration of rendering adequately & forcibly the words of Baha'u'llah & the Master into English,' he wrote.

> I am enclosing a copy of one of the earliest of Baha'u'llah's prayers revealed in the early days of his stay in Baghdad. The prayer in Arabic is simply exquisite & I am not sure whether my rendering it into English has any merit whatever & whether it conveys anything of the charm of the original. You may keep it, if you think it worth your while, as I have duplicates of it.
>
> I shall very gladly submit to your kind consideration & criticism my translations of the Epistles to Nap. III & Queen Victoria, of the Book of the Covenant & of other miscellaneous writings & prayers of Baha'u'llah & the Master, after I reach Oxford & hope to forward later my version of the Arabic Hidden Words . . .[45]

Shoghi Effendi evidently valued Lady Blomfield's considerable literary sensibility and skill. He would collaborate with her and continue to call upon her to review his translations in the years to come.

More than two decades had now passed since Lady Blomfield, at the age of just 40, had lost her husband. It would have been impossible for the young widow in 1899 to imagine how her life would change beyond recognition after the death of Sir Arthur Blomfield. The years since then had been filled with ceaseless activity, serving humanity through a divine Cause which, in those days, she could only have dreamed might exist. During those years, it is unlikely that there had been much time or opportunity to contemplate the possibility of a second marriage. But now as both her daughters were themselves wed – Mary to a Royal Navy captain, Basil Hall, and Rose Ellinor to one Harold Maule – it seems that Lady Blomfield did meet someone whose intentions in that direction were quite serious. As in all other matters, Sitárih's first thought was to seek the guidance of the Master. His response came via His daughter Rúhá who wrote, appropriately on St Valentine's Day, 14 February 1921.

> Now about the question you wish me to ask the Master which I did. He said if you think you will be happy with this man and you be more free in life and can serve the Cause in a better way and he is not against the Bahaie Teachings marry him. He hopes you will both be very happy together living in perfect unity and love and after you marry him you will be able to do much more for this Great Cause. Is the man interested in Bahaie Teachings? I hope you will be able to convert him and soon make him a beautiful Bahá'í. Now my dear friend I ask you one thing as you are very dear to me and I hope you will do it, that is before you decide to marry this man, study him well and be sure of his character. Find out how he feels about Bahaism, then you give your consent, you deserve a good man who will appreciate you.[46]

It can only be assumed that Sitárih heeded the advice and proceeded exactly as she was told. There was to be no marriage. Presumably she felt that this gentleman – whose name she chose not to divulge in her letters – would not be able to support her in her services to the Cause that had become the enduring and dominating passion of her life.

In the spring of 1921 Lady Blomfield was finally successful in selling her country house in Broadway, Worcestershire. One of the financial contributions she was able to make from the proceeds was a sum of 19 guineas – valued at around £130 in today's money – to the fund for building the first Bahá'í House of Worship in the West on the shores of Lake Michigan. A receipt note from Corinne True in Chicago also mentions that Lady Blomfield was contemplating a visit to the United States of America.

'The American Bahais will be so glad to see you face to face,' wrote True. 'We heard so much of your devoted service to Abdul Bahá . . . and we know your presence will help fill our hearts with the spirit of service to the Great Cause of Baha'o'llah . . . Be sure to advise us when your plans are definite – for your American trip.'[47]

But before any visit to her American friends could be seriously considered, Lady Blomfield still had her long awaited journey to the Holy Land to make. The Master had informed her that she had His permission to make an extended stay, for which she was truly grateful.

'You asked about what time is good to visit Haifa, because of the weather,' Luṭfu'lláh Ḥakím wrote to her.

> I think if you have the intention of visiting the Master in this year the best time would be sometime in October or November. At that time the weather would not be so warm . . . I assure you that you will have a most wonderful welcome here and in addition to that you will have a most wonderful experience in this wonderful spot. It is on Mt Carmel that His Holiness Christ, Elijah and most of the Prophets have passed some of their time in meditation and prayer. Walking on the places that have so much to tell one of the time of the Divine Messengers will give one an extraordinary happiness and peace that it is beyond any description. I hope that you will be able to make your visit soon. And I hope that I shall have the pleasure of seeing you in His Holy Presence. And if you can not come so late as Oct. why not come earlier than that? Everything will be done for your comfort and I am sure you will not suffer much for the heat.[48]

'I hope you will soon start for your trip to Palestine,' wrote the Master's daughter, Rúḥá. 'We all be so happy to meet you. We have beautiful climate in March. Please try the best you can to come. How I wish you could bring Parvin and Noori with you when you come out to us. I feel so homesick for them.'[49]

Lady Blomfield settled on a date in October to make the journey, telling the Master, 'I am so grateful for the blessed invitation to stay a long time; oh how I long to do this!!'[50]

The journey would indeed be made at the end of 1921 but in circumstances woefully different from those she had long anticipated.

CHAPTER NINE

DAWN OF THE GUARDIANSHIP

O ye the faithful loved ones of 'Abdu'l-Bahá!
It is incumbent upon you to take the greatest care of Shoghi Effendi . . .[1]
'Abdu'l-Bahá

In the 14 years since she had first encountered the Bahá'í message in Paris, Lady Blomfield had been a witness to – and an active participant in – some of the most significant events of the opening years of the 20th century. Her unflinching courage and sense of moral responsibility had both motivated and sustained her service to the wounded during the most horrific conflict the world had yet seen. Those same qualities had inspired her to lend her support to the campaign for women's suffrage. The tenderness of her heart and indefatigable energy had moved her to throw in her lot with a handful of visionary women who devoted themselves to protecting the rights of children whose prospects had been devastated by war. And the generosity of her spirit had greatly eased the ordeal of the gruelling journey undertaken by 'Abdu'l-Bahá to proclaim His father's Cause in the West. Those momentous visits in which she had played such an integral part would, until the very end of her life, remain her most precious memory. But now, as the British Bahá'ís had just begun to put behind them the long war years during which interest in the Cause had been severely diminished, their faith and certitude was once again about to be tested. At half past nine in the morning of 29 November 1921, news reached London that would bring them the deepest possible sorrow. 'Abdu'l-Bahá had passed away. His 'great work was now ended,' His grandson Shoghi Effendi later wrote.[2] His spirit had 'winged its flight to its eternal abode, to be gathered, at long last, to the glory of His beloved Father, and taste the joy of everlasting reunion with Him'.[3]

Once again, Lady Blomfield was to find herself at the centre of events of profound historic significance. Major Tudor Pole was at his offices at 61 St

James's Street when he received the cablegram announcing 'Abdu'l-Bahá's passing. It had been dispatched from Haifa at three o'clock the previous afternoon and read: 'His Holiness 'Abdu'l-Bahá ascended Abhá Kingdom. Inform friends. [Signed] Greatest Holy Leaf.'[4]

Tudor Pole notified the believers in London by telephone, letter and wire, and immediately called Shoghi Effendi, requesting him to travel down from Oxford without revealing the reason for his summons. The Master's devoted grandson arrived around noon. Returning to his private office to meet his young visitor, Tudor Pole found Shoghi Effendi in a state of collapse, bewildered by the catastrophic news conveyed by the cable that he had spotted lying open on a desk.

Lady Blomfield was among those immediately called upon to care for the distraught young man as he spent a number of days bedridden in the home of a Canadian believer, Helen Grand. Two days after learning of the Master's passing, Dr Esslemont also arrived from Bournemouth to be of service to Shoghi Effendi, with whom he had established a close friendship.

'I went up on Thurs. morning and found poor Shoghi in bed, absolutely prostrate with grief,' wrote Esslemont. 'At first he seemed absolutely overwhelmed by the loss, unable to eat, to sleep, to think.'[5]

During the day, however, Shoghi Effendi rallied enough to drink some tea and join Lady Blomfield, Dr Esslemont, Helen Grand and two Persian friends resident in London – Mírzá Yúḥanná Dávúd and Ḍiyá'u'lláh Asgharzádih – in the drawing room. Shoghi Effendi chanted a prayer, and read and translated to the small gathering the last letter he had received from the Master. His sister Rúḥangíz who was studying in London also did whatever she could to comfort her heartbroken brother.

The following day, gathered again at Helen Grand's home, the group decided that Lady Blomfield would accompany Shoghi Effendi and his sister to Haifa as soon as the journey could be arranged. What added sadness must Sitárih have felt as she realized her long anticipated visit to the Holy Land would now finally be going ahead but without the warmth of the Master's loving welcome to look forward to on her arrival. Perhaps she took some comfort in the fact that she was responding to 'Abdu'l-Bahá's wish for her to fulfil for Shoghi Effendi 'all the requirements of a motherly affection'.[6]

Asgharzádih also offered to go and to bear all the expenses of the journey.

'Shoughi Rabbani and his sister will be returning to Haifa towards the end of the present month, and they will be accompanied by Lady Blom-field, and by Ziaoullah Asgarzade,' Tudor Pole wrote to *Star of the West*. '. . . The pressure here is so great that at the moment we cannot enter into further details, much as we should like to do so . . .'[7]

Obituary notices about the Master were penned for the major news-papers, with Tudor Pole making every effort to ensure that inaccuracies or misstatements did not appear. 'Abdu'l-Bahá's passing was reported in, among others, *The Times*, *The Morning Post* and the *Daily Mail*.

'We are of course, not satisfied with the references that have been made,' wrote a disappointed Tudor Pole, '. . . but we have done the best we could.'[8]

The Times printed an appreciation of some seven column inches under the unfortunate heading, 'DEATH OF THE BAHAI – CHIEF OF THE BABIST CULT'. 'Abdu'l-Bahá, *The Times* reported, was nevertheless 'a man of great spiritual power and commanding presence, and his name was held in rev-erence throughout the Middle East . . . The British Authorities recognized his position of influence, and it was at Lord Allenby's suggestion that he was knighted last year.'[9] *The Morning Post* described how 'Abdu'l-Bahá's 'persistent messages as to the divine origin and unity of mankind were as impressive as the Messenger himself. He possessed singular courtesy. At his table Buddhist and Mohammedan, Hindu and Zoroastrian, Jew and Christian sat in amity.'[10] Lord Lamington conveyed the news of the Mas-ter's passing to Winston Churchill, then the British government's Secretary of State for the Colonies. 'I have just heard of the death of Abdul Baha;' wrote Lamington, 'as leader of the Bahais his influence is widespread and beneficent . . . in his death I lose a cherished friend.'[11] Churchill telegraphed the High Commissioner for Palestine, Sir Herbert Samuel, requesting him to convey to the Bahá'í community, a 'suitable expression of condolence'.[12]

Shoghi Effendi travelled with Dr Esslemont to Bournemouth for a few days of much needed convalescence after the devastating shock of his grand-father's death. Shoghi Effendi was at times, according to his friend, 'very sad and overcome with grief, but on the whole he kept up very bravely, and gradually, the conviction that although the bodily presence was removed, the Spirit of the Beloved was as near, as powerful and as accessible to us as ever, seemed to revive his strength and hope'.[13]

Writing to a Bahá'í student in London, Shoghi Effendi described how the 'terrible news' had for some days 'so overwhelmed my body, my mind and my soul that I was laid for a couple of days in bed almost senseless, absent-minded and greatly agitated. Gradually His power revived me and breathed in me a confidence that I hope will henceforth guide me and inspire me in my humble work of service. The day had to come, but how sudden and unexpected. The fact however that His Cause has created so many and such beautiful souls all over the world is a sure guarantee that it will live and prosper and ere long will compass the world!'[14]

Shoghi Effendi wrote that he was returning to Haifa to receive instructions that the Master had left and that he had made a 'supreme determination' to dedicate his life to 'Abdu'l-Bahá's service. Although he was not yet aware of his appointment in the Master's Will as Guardian of the Bahá'í Faith, he was already beginning to demonstrate the spiritual intuition that came to characterize his approach to his duties in the decades to come.

> The Holy Land will remain the focal centre of the Bahá'í world; a new era will now come upon it. The Master in His great vision has consolidated His work and His spirit assures me that its results will soon be made manifest.

'I am starting with Lady Blomfield for Haifa . . .', wrote Shoghi Effendi.[15]

Owing to passport difficulties, Shoghi Effendi was not able to leave Britain until the middle of December. Word reached the Bahá'ís in the Holy Land that he, Lady Blomfield and Rúhangíz would leave on 16 December. They set sail for Port Said on the P&O steamship *Kaiser-i-Hind*, 'Empress of India', that had been first launched in October 1914 for the record-breaking 18-day London to Bombay route. The ship had also seen service during the First World War but until Shoghi Effendi stepped onto its gangplank it had surely never transported any man as significant to the long-term peace of the world as the future Guardian of the Bahá'í Faith. Lady Blomfield and her precious ward sailed via Marseilles to Port Said in Egypt from where they took the train to Haifa.

Almost two full weeks later, on the afternoon of 29 December 1921, Sitárih – gazing out from the window of their carriage – finally saw Mount Carmel for the first time. A number of believers had gathered to meet the train as it pulled into Haifa's railway station at twenty past five. The trauma of 'Abdu'l-Bahá's passing was still apparent in the appearance of Shoghi Effendi who, newly overcome with grief, had to be physically helped up the steps of the Master's house and to a no doubt emotionally-charged reception from his beloved great-aunt, Bahíyyih Khánum, the daughter of Bahá'u'lláh, known as the Greatest Holy Leaf.

For Lady Blomfield, there was a reunion with her fellow believer from London, Ethel Rosenberg, who had arrived at the beginning of the month, unaware of the Master's passing until a passport inspector on the train from Port Said had informed her during the overnight journey to Haifa. Among other friends also gathered in grief beneath the shadow of Mount Carmel were Lady Blomfield's old friend from London Lutfu'lláh Hakím, Florian Krug and his wife Grace from New York, Johanna Hauf – whom Sitárih knew from Stuttgart – and a young American, Curtis Kelsey, who had installed on 'Abdu'l-Bahá's instruction electric light at the Shrines of the Báb and Bahá'u'lláh. Lady Blomfield also made the acquaintance of Jean Stannard, an American Bahá'í who had spent time in India at the Master's request and with whom Sitárih would later collaborate in Geneva. Among the many hours they spent together in fellowship, service to the Holy Family and mourning, Lady Blomfield and some of the American and German friends paid a visit on New Year's day, 1922, to Saint Luke's Mission Church and its gardens in the Arab quarter at the foot of Mount Carmel.

On her first visit to the Shrine of the Báb Lady Blomfield was profoundly impressed by the building, every stone of which had been 'raised and placed in position' by the Master, 'with infinite tears and at tremendous cost'.[16] On entering the simple Shrine, where 'Abdu'l-Bahá's remains were now also laid to rest, Lady Blomfield was struck by its peacefulness and lack of ostentation.

'I wish you could see the Tomb of the Bab,' she wrote to her daughter Mary,

> . . . it is a large beautiful room with precious Persian rugs on the floor – lovely branched candlesticks give a subdued light with their wax candles: on either side of this room there is an arch, leading into a room for men and another for women. Lovely Persian rugs cover these floors also – the spiritual atmosphere cannot be described, it can only be felt. Prayers are chanted as we kneel or stand. There is nothing tawdry or forced or insincere – only the Majesty of a sacred simplicity! In which the worship of hearts seems to vibrate and ascend.
>
> There is no touch of our idea of a Tomb. The casket is beneath the

floor, covered by the centre rug, with the branched candlestick at either end. Our Beloved One's Tomb is exactly like that of the Bab – another set of 3 rooms being under the same roof – there are lovely gardens round . . .[17]

Sitárih sent both her daughters a rose each from the gardens.

'You must feel the Beloved One near you,' she wrote to Mary on her birthday. 'I shall feel very near you . . . praying for every blessing to be with you throughout the year, and always. Thousands of loving wishes will fly to you all the day!'[18]

During the days immediately following her arrival, Lady Blomfield would hear many stories recounted by the women of 'Abdu'l-Bahá's household of the last moments of His earthly life. Their days were now spent receiving endless visits of condolence from guests 'who sit all day long and every day, according to the custom of the East,' wrote Ethel Rosenberg, ' – a most truly trying custom I call it!'[19]

'Today, Wednesday, is the Ladies' At Home day,' Lady Blomfield wrote to Mary on 4 January. 'Crowds of Eastern ladies arrive looking like black ghosts, no face showing. When inside the Reception room they put back their veils and show often very lovely intelligent faces.'[20]

Despite the predominating sadness of such meetings, in lighter moments the oriental ladies were eager to learn from Sitárih about the nature of western marriages.

'They were delighted to hear that I was on the side of woman's freedom,' wrote Lady Blomfield, whose remarks to the women were translated by 'Abdu'l-Bahá's daughters.

They wanted to hear what British husbands' manners and customs were. When I told them, they said 'Do write it all down and let us have it translated into Arabic, to show to our husbands!! or better still would you write to our men and talk to them.' I replied that it would give me great pleasure but that I should not be able to re-educate them with one or two talks and I should certainly rather antagonize them!! However I have many invitations to stay here and help them to some hope in their lives! The dear women! They are so pretty and witty!'[21]

On one occasion, 'Abdu'l-Bahá's widow Munírih <u>Kh</u>ánum, the Holy Mother, informed Sitárih that Bahá'u'lláh was very fond of beautiful things and did not approve at all of the example set by past religions in their severity and the sacrifice of all beauty in their surroundings. He said, Lady Blomfield learned, that the believers must, as they can afford, have beautiful works of art around them.

At another time, the Holy Mother told Lady Blomfield of the importance that the Master placed in the believers finding ways of interesting intellectual and cultured people in the principles of the Faith. In this respect, she told Lady Blomfield that, shortly before His passing, 'Abdu'l-Bahá had said that He wished to speak with Sitárih about a very important matter. He was most disappointed, she learned, that her travel to the Holy Land had been delayed.

'It is heartbreaking!!' wrote Sitárih. 'I cannot reconcile myself to the fact that I was not here to receive His directions – but the dear ladies are going to write down for me all they know of what He wished to say to me – they are very sweet and try to console me by saying that His Spirit will direct me, so that I shall be informed of His wishes.'[22]

When Lady Blomfield asked Munírih Khánum to speak about her illustrious husband, the Holy Mother replied,

> For fifty years my Beloved and I were together. Never were we separated, save during His visits to Egypt, Europe and America.
>
> O my Beloved husband and my Lord! How shall I speak of Him?
>
> You who have known Him, can imagine what my fifty years have been – how they fled by in an atmosphere of love and joy and the perfection of that Peace which passeth all understanding, in the radiant light of which I await the day when I shall be called to join Him, in the celestial garden of transfiguration.[23]

A few days after their return to the Holy Land, Shoghi Effendi received yet another devastating blow. His great-aunt, the Greatest Holy Leaf, shared with him the contents of 'Abdu'l-Bahá's Will and Testament. The document had been addressed to Shoghi Effendi but had already been scanned by the Greatest Holy Leaf to see if the Master had left any instructions as to where His remains should be interred. What Shoghi Effendi now learned was that he had been appointed the Guardian of the Bahá'í Faith, a sacred institution about which neither he nor the Bahá'ís had any previous knowledge. All the descendants of the Báb and Bahá'u'lláh, the Hands of the Cause of God and the believers were instructed to turn to Shoghi

Effendi for guidance, advice and authorized interpretation of the sacred writings. The Guardian was to be the permanent head of the Universal House of Justice and both it and the Guardianship were under the care and protection of Bahá'u'lláh and the shelter and unerring guidance of the Báb. On Tuesday 3 January, in the home of 'Abdu'l-Bahá's daughter Rúḥá, the Master's Will and Testament was read aloud to nine men, most of them members of 'Abdu'l-Bahá's family, and its seals, signatures and His handwriting throughout were clearly shown to them.

Lady Blomfield's first concern was for the well-being of the new Guardian. The day after the Will was read, she reported that Shoghi Effendi was 'a little better, but still very far from well. The doctor says that the shock hurt his heart, and great care is necessary! I feel that the Master's spirit will guide him to a wonderful strength of soul to still further establish the Cause, for which our Lord Christ and these three Holy Ones, lived and suffered and died.'[24]

Forty days after the Master's passing, on Friday 6 January, a great memorial feast was held at Rúḥá's home, in which the whole of the ground floor had been cleared of its furniture to make way for the tables for the two hundred guests that were expected. The previous evening 'Abdu'l-Bahá's daughter had given Sitárih and Ethel Rosenberg an early viewing of the arrangements. The places were set out either side of the tables, while every plate had a linen table napkin at its centre arranged into a mitre shape. Down the centre of the tables were alternately placed dishes of olives and cut radishes.

'The long tables were decorated with trailing branches of Bougainvilliers [*sic*],' observed Lady Blomfield. 'Its lovely purple blooms mingled with the white narcissus, and with the large dishes of golden oranges out of the beloved Master's garden made a picture of loveliness in these spacious lofty rooms, whose only other decoration was the gorgeous yet subdued colouring of rare Persian rugs. No useless trivial ornaments marred the extreme dignity of simplicity.'[25]

After the visit Lady Blomfield took tea with the members of the Holy Family.

'I never imagined that any beings out of heaven could be so holy,' she reflected.

We in the Western World have never even begun to realize the Divine-ness of Him, and its reflection in them: the absolute selflessness!

Of his whole life. How near to our Lord Christ, in Spirit and in Truth they seem to be one in some mystic way which can be felt but is not to be explained. All sorts and conditions of individuals recognize it. Christians, Jews, Moslems, Greek Orthodox and Druses! About 400 of these are coming to the Feast tomorrow. Eleven of them are going to make speeches.[26]

The following day at one o'clock the great gathering of believers and dignitaries from Haifa, 'Akká and the surrounding parts of Palestine and Syria, headed by the Governor of Phoenicia, commenced. A magnificent dinner was served, prepared entirely by the members of 'Abdu'l-Bahá's household, who had worked for the entire week from morning until evening. As the meal got underway within the house, some 150 of Haifa's less privileged residents were also gathered in a place prepared especially for them where they were fed and entertained. As was always the custom when the Master was alive, every single guest, regardless of creed, class or rank, received the same loving welcome.

Lady Blomfield was asked to assist in offering the tea and sweets, which she considered a great honour. The serving of the food went like clockwork, so impressing the English governor that he enquired who had organized and arranged everything so well. When he was informed that it had been prepared in its entirety by the women of the household without outside assistance, he was astonished.

Having eaten, the guests then walked the small distance to the adjacent house where 'Abdu'l-Bahá had resided, and into the large central hall, sparsely decorated except for a portrait of the Master and some antique Persian tapestries hanging on one wall. A platform had been set out from which speeches were to be made in His honour. The name of each speaker was announced as he mounted the rostrum.

'Many a time have we assembled in this home, which was the place of pilgrimage for scholars and the fountainhead of virtues,' said Abdullah Effendi Mukhlis, Secretary of the National Mohammedan Society.

Then we used to find it budding and blossoming, the fragrances of its flowers pervading everywhere, the birds singing on its tall tress, the Water of Life overflowing and beauty of happiness on the faces of those who lived herein.

But today, why do we see its pillars fallen in ruins, everything sad and sorrowful, its face beclouded, its flowers wilted, its leaves fallen and scattered, its birds silent, everything completely submerged with grief and anxiety – the mineral, vegetable and human sharing alike in this desolation?

We have more than once partaken of the food from this Hatimic table. (Hatim Tai was known to be the most generous man according to Arabian history.) We used to partake of its food with the utmost ease and drink its water copiously; today – why are we so choked with every mouthful and strangle with every drop?

This roof has covered us at many scientific and educational meetings – gatherings that were full of happiness and joy, wherein voices sounded, and argument and discussion continued – today, why do we not utter even a word? It is as if birds were perched upon our heads (so silent are we). That happiness has changed to sorrow, that joy into grief and those discussions to quietness and silence. Is it because this home was confronted by circumstances and overpowered by the hosts of torture, or surrounded by calamities from all sides? No. It is neither this or that; nay rather, it is because the Lord of this home, its departed mystery, its spirit and its joy, Abdul-Baha Abbas, has ascended from this mortal world.

Therefore, it has become lifeless and its appearance changed. We have lived in his time, and we have associated with him for tens of years without any fatigue or weariness; nay rather, we could hardly pass a moment without receiving a portion of his guidance. We know not how the years have passed! Why is it that our days have become long, our patience deficient, our sorrow increased, our endurance decreased? – and it is only forty days since his departure!

During this sad period we have found only degradation for the world because of his departure, and glory for the spiritual realm because of his presence. He was the standard-bearer of knowledge, the proclaimer of the verses of unity, the herald of the knowledge of God, the exhorter of good, the prohibitor of evil, the confirmer of the pillars of peace, and the promoter of harmony instead of strife.

The Prophet (Mohammed) – upon him be peace – said: 'If knowledge were to be found in the stars, Persian men would reach it.' Verily, he spoke the truth. Islam and all it includes of ordinances, traditions, even language and ethics were classified and systematized by men of Persia. Unquestionably, our departed one was the seal thereof.

Today, the Arab, the Persian, the Oriental, the Occidental, the Mohammedan, the Christian, and the Jew have equal share in this memorial service. Since his departure is a calamity for the whole world, therefore the people of the East and the West weep for him. Even though our calamity be most great, yet, praise be to God, his family has been spared for us. This is our great recompense.[27]

As the speeches continued, the Governor of Phoenicia took the platform, representing the High Commissioner of Palestine who was temporarily away, and the Civil Secretary Sir W. H. Deedes, who was detained by work in Jerusalem. Both sent their greetings to the gathering and their deep sympathy to the family of the Master.

'Most of us here have a clear picture of Sir Abdul-Baha Abbas,' said the governor,

. . . of his dignified figure walking thoughtfully in our streets, of his courtesy and gracious manner, of his kindness, of his love for the little children and for the flowers and of his generosity and care for the poor and suffering. So gentle was he, and so simple, that in his presence one almost forgot that he was also a great teacher, and that his writings and his conversations have been a solace and an inspiration to hundreds and thousands of people in the East and West.

It is possible to regard his teaching in many lights. Some may say that it did merely reassert truths which form the basis of all religious teachings. Some may declare that it was premature and impractical, but everybody can appreciate the beauty of his ideals and agree that if the doctrine of universal brotherhood was carried out this world would be a better and a happier place.

To us who have just passed through the throes of one of the fiercest wars in the history of mankind, and whose minds and lives are still disturbed – words of peace and goodwill sound almost strange upon our ears. We find it difficult to credit them, but everywhere men of many nations and of diverse creeds proclaim the imperative needs of peace. The conscience and imagination of mankind have been stirred and there is a widespread hope that one by one the conflicting interests and misunderstandings that promote strife and hatred will be removed, and that better and more friendly relations will prevail between the nations, between communities and between individuals. Whenever these better times come we may be sure that the name of Abdul-Baha who lived among us here in Haifa, will be remembered with gratitude and affectionate esteem.[28]

The solemn gathering was also informed of the provisions of the Master's Will and was anxious to have the new Guardian address a few words to them, but Shoghi Effendi felt unable to join the meeting, 'too distressed and overcome'[29] to meet the assembled guests. From the room of the Greatest Holy Leaf who was comforting her great-nephew, he quickly composed a short message to be read to the meeting: 'The shock has been too sudden and grievous for my youthful age to enable me to be present at this gathering of the loved ones of beloved 'Abdu'l-Bahá.' He thanked the Governor and the guests for their tributes to the Master, saying they had 'revived His sacred memory in our hearts . . . I venture to hope that we his kindred and his family may by our deeds and words, prove worthy of the glorious example he has set before us and thereby earn your esteem and your affection. May His everlasting spirit be with us all and knit us together for evermore.'[30]

The following day 'Abdu'l-Bahá's Will and Testament was once again read in full, on this occasion to an assembled gathering attended by the British Bahá'ís along with fellow believers from Persia, India, Egypt, Italy, Germany, America and Japan. The entire document was chanted in Persian, taking a full 90 minutes. Whenever Shoghi Effendi's name was mentioned during the recitation, the entire congregation rose to its feet as a mark of its respect for the chosen appointee of 'Abdu'l-Bahá. On that same day the Greatest Holy Leaf sent two cables to Persia. One informed the believers that in His Will and Testament, the Master had left instructions on how the Bahá'í community should continue to function. The other announced, 'Will and Testament forwarded Shoghi Effendi Centre Cause.'[31]

Amidst the sadness of those days Lady Blomfield appears to have welcomed the companionship of the believers who were serving at the Sacred Threshold, and those who, increasingly, were gathering in the Holy Land to lend their support to Shoghi Effendi and the Holy Family in their hour of distress.

'Lotfullah is here in the Pilgrim House, doing kind services for everybody, as when the Beloved One was with us in Cadogan Gardens,' Sitárih wrote to Mary.

... The only other attendant living in the House is Fujita, a nice intellectual Japanese man with hair *en brosse* and long mustache, just like an old Japanese print. He cooks such things as do not come from the Master's house and serves the meals with the help of Lotfullah. A chubby little Arab maid, Fatimeh, comes in every morning but I make my own bed and tidy my room as do the other Pilgrims. Dear Mrs Hoagg, Dr and Mrs Florian Krug from New York, Mr and Mrs Boche from California – all dear devoted people . . .[32]

Isabel Fraser was also present from Britain, 'and a lady Doctor Ebbs, and a dear old Irish gentleman,' wrote Sitárih, 'as clever and scholarly as he can be, full of inborn wit and the most complete crowd of Paddy stories you ever heard – if they go through London on their way back to the States you must see them'.

A few days ago 14 Persian Pilgrims arrived, such wonderful devotion. Poor darlings! A man and his wife gave their house, garden and all the furniture as a nucleus of a Mashrak al Azkar in their village. Then they started off on their pilgrimage here – travelling on donkeys, mules, camels, then 3rd class on ships and trains!! Starting early in November with the hope in their hearts of seeing our Beloved Master! Only a few days before their arrival here did they hear the sad news! Their grief is terribly pathetic. Ah! They said to me, our master has been to your country, your house – but not to our country, only in the Celestial Realm, shall we see our Adored one face to face'! It is too pitiful! To think of the thousands of people who saw Him in the West and were too blind to perceive! No wonder He loved His Persians, the families of the martyrs![33]

Ethel Rosenberg, however, tested Lady Blomfield's patience somewhat. Sitárih told her daughter that Rosenberg was busy 'ferreting in and out! She is a dear, and if her suggestions are apt to be tiring. I just say a firm, unvarnished "No".'[34]

Lady Blomfield was particularly moved by the lives of the women of 'Abdu'l-Bahá's household.

'Oh! The stories I could write, if I had time!' she told Mary. 'I want to write the lives of the women of the Holy families. The wife of the Bab, of Baha'u'llah and of Abdul Baha, also of Khanum – the Greatest Holy Leaf and of the daughters – but letters to people, coordinating, matters of the Cause takes up much time.'

> They all send their love to you, and told me to say that they always pray for you and Nouri and that they are glad to have your Mother with them . . . They said that the Master wanted us all to come. When he was told I was coming alone, he said 'Lady is a jewel, we must take great care of her'! Rouha Khanoum read my letter to Him the week before He passed away. 'Is Lady coming soon?' When she could not give the date, He just sighed and said 'Send for Shoghi at once, at once, or he will be too late for the funeral.'
> 'Don't cable, it will be a shock, too great for him.' Then a letter from Laura, 'Is she coming at once?' Another sigh!!! It is all too pathetic!![35]

As Shoghi Effendi and the women sorted through the Master's papers, Lady Blomfield was touched to learn that some of the letters she had written to 'Abdu'l-Bahá had been kept and re-discovered.

> Some of the boxes of documents had been buried under the earth for years, in hiding not only from avowed enemies, but from 'His own kindred, His own Father's house.' There are a number of Tablets from Bahá'u'lláh in His wonderful handwriting! There is an old trunk which came through their wanderings, and a saddle bag thing off a mule! The pathos of it all is beyond my description![36]

Sitárih was also moved when Shoghi Effendi gave her a rendering of the 'Greatest Name' in the calligraphy of the great Persian penman Mishkín-Qalam to give to Mary.

In the first week of February as the mourning activities became less intense, Lady Blomfield was free to make an excursion, spending nine days in Jerusalem visiting the holy sites of Christianity, Judaism and Islam. She relished walking through the city's streets which had witnessed centuries of religious history. She enthused about her visit to Mary:

> It all seems a glorious dream! I must remember things to tell you which I cannot write – a wedding, at which I found myself an unexpected guest, the mosque of Omar, the Tomb of David will figure in the story.

Also the High Priest of the Samaritans. Surely, never was a nine days so full!!![37]

On one of the days in Jerusalem, Sitárih – escorted by one of the eastern believers – stopped near the entrance to the tomb of King David that was being guarded by a doorkeeper wearing a turban. As Lady Blomfield approached, the doorkeeper gestured for her to step back, speaking rapidly in Arabic.

'What is he saying?' Sitárih asked her companion.

'He says you are not permitted to enter.'

'Why should I not?' retorted Lady Blomfield.

'No Christians can go in.'

'Are only Jews privileged to do so?'

'Neither Jews nor Christians may enter this Holy Place of Islam.'

The guardian of the tomb began to speak more volubly than before. When she asked her translator what he was saying, he replied, 'He says 'that lady must not come near, for she despises Muhammad, the Prophet of Allah.'

Firmly, Sitárih responded, 'Now please say to this guardian that he is not a good man, for he is talking a falsehood.'

'Oh Lady, I cannot say that to him!'

'Yes, you must, please! I will make it right afterwards.'

The doorkeeper looked amazed at Lady Blomfield's bold statement. Sitárih said to her companion, 'Now say to him, "the Lady reverences Moses; she loves and reverences Jesus Christ; she believes that Muhammad is the Prophet of Allah, and so reverences him as you reverence Christ."'

The translation complete, the guardian of the tomb held out both his hands and said, 'Then we are friends.'

'Yes,' responded Sitárih, 'we are friends.'

The gatekeeper opened the door to let Lady Blomfield into the tomb. However there was a problem. Lady Blomfield would have difficulty proceeding if she removed her shoes and high garters.

'Wait, wait!' said the doorman who hurried off, returning with two cloths, one pink and the other grey which he began wrapping around her feet. Thus equipped, one foot pink and one foot grey, he led her into the tower and left her to pray at the tomb of King David.

'Hewn in the rock, made smooth by the centuries of devoted pilgrims who had knelt there,' wrote Sitárih later. 'No other ornamentation to mar its dignity, I felt an overwhelming sense of the sanctity of that Holy Place and how easy it was to make friends with Islam, who shared our reverences, and to them religion was so great a reality. When I emerged I found my friend and the doorkeeper in evident disagreement. The Muslim saying: No! I do not wish to accept coins for showing the lady into the tower of David, for she revered Muhammad, the prophet of Allah, and so is our friend.'[38]

More importantly than sightseeing, though, was the opportunity Lady Blomfield had to appeal to the British authorities in Jerusalem to secure protection for the Shrine of Bahá'u'lláh. Shortly after the Master's passing, His scheming half-brother Mírzá Muhammad-'Alí had called upon the civil authorities to give him the custodianship of Bahá'u'lláh's Shrine, claiming that he was 'Abdu'l-Bahá's lawful successor. The British refused on the grounds that it appeared to be a religious issue. On Tuesday 30 January, Muhammad-'Alí's younger brother Badí'u'lláh, with some of his supporters, visited the Shrine and forcibly seized the keys from the Bahá'í caretaker, Abu'l-Qásim-i-Khurásání, and demanded that Muhammad-'Alí be recognized by the authorities as the Shrine's legal custodian. The Governor of 'Akká then ordered the keys to be given to the authorities and posted guards at the Shrine, refusing to hand the keys to either party. Lady Blomfield's intervention seems to have gone some way towards easing the restrictions, and although the keys to the inner tomb were still held by the authorities, access to the other rooms of the Shrine was now granted to the Bahá'ís and, unfortunately, to the covenant-breakers also.

Despite suffering an appalling series of shocks – his grandfather's passing, the behaviour of his family members, followed closely by the news that he was now Guardian of the Cause – Shoghi Effendi's ability to rise to the challenge of his new appointment deeply impressed Sitárih. The situation facing the Bahá'í Cause, coupled with the Guardian's apparent youthfulness and inexperience, led some of his family and other members of the community to believe it was an opportune moment for the Universal House of Justice to be formed. There was a belief that the young Guardian, who refused to dress like his grandfather or to follow the customs and traditions that 'Abdu'l-Bahá had kept, needed more experienced believers to guide his actions and direction. Under such intense pressure, Shoghi Effendi took the decision to call to Haifa a number of the most capable and experienced Bahá'ís from East and West to consult upon the future of the Cause.

'Shoghi is taking up his charge with a deep sincerity and dignity, in one so young it is very touching,' wrote Lady Blomfield.

One sees more and more the wisdom of the Beloved Master's choice. If he were not so entirely selfless, pure-minded and humble, the tremendous power and influence might mislead him. His mentality is great, his vision so universal, and his wisdom so astonishing as to seem miraculous. Of course, he is informed with the Spirit of the Master, and all the people needed for his helpers are being drawn here from the uttermost ends of the earth.[39]

Despite being laid up in bed with a cold for a number of days, Sitárih was pleased to learn that her dear friends Hippolyte and Laura Dreyfus-Barney were arriving in the Holy Land by way of Indo-China, Burma and Bombay. Also arriving were Mason Remey, Roy Wilhelm, Mountfort Mills, Corinne True and her daughter Katherine, and some prominent Persian believers. Consul and Alice Schwarz from Germany were also joining the deliberations, along with Siyyid Muṣṭafá Rúmí from Burma. Tudor Pole was expected, though he had suffered a bad attack of influenza in Cairo.

'So the principal Bahais from all over the world will be here,' wrote Sitárih, 'when the chief Persian and Indian brothers arrive! Oh! What a unique and thrilling part of the world's history is being enacted here and now!'[40]

'The master said "Before long, after I am gone, Men will arise who will change the face of the earth",' wrote Lady Blomfield. 'Indeed signs of the fulfilment of this prophecy are many! From Lausanne a distinguished University Professor writes in *Aujourd Hui*, "This is the only religion which should be taught in every school in the world to all classes and all races."'[41]

The professor in question was the renowned Swiss entomologist and psychiatrist Dr August Forel, who had become a believer in Bahá'u'lláh shortly before the passing of the Master. Lady Blomfield immediately wrote to Dr Forel, encouraging him to make the acquaintance of her friends in Geneva and the staff of the League of Nations who were attracted to the Bahá'í teachings.

Lady Blomfield was not the only western believer to marvel at the young Guardian's exceptional strength during those difficult days. The American lawyer Mountfort Mills later told the believers in the United States,

We met Shoghi Effendi, dressed entirely in black, a touching figure. Think of what he stands for today! All the complex problems of the great statesmen of the world are as child's play in comparison with the great problems of this youth, before whom are the problems of the entire world.

. . . The Master is not gone. His Spirit is present with greater intensity and power, freed from his bodily limitations. We can take it into our own hearts and reflect it in greater degrees. In the centre of this radiation stands this youth, Shoghi Effendi. The Spirit streams forth from this young man. He is indeed young in face, form and manner, yet his heart is the centre of the world today.[42]

'Shoghi is showing each and every day, an increase of the beloved Master's spirit,' Lady Blomfield told Mary,

. . . it is so wonderful as to be miraculous. These men here, experienced in the world as they are, are amazed at the wisdom he shows in the administration of the cause. Such tasks!! And he is only 24. Such a sweet simple-pure-minded boy, trained all his life by the Master who says in His Testament, 'Oh Friends take care of Shoghi Effendi. Let not the dust of despondency shadow his radiant nature!!' It is really a sacred trust.[43]

Lady Blomfield felt responsible for protecting the young Guardian from those believers who would add to his burden. 'Of course, as you can imagine,' she wrote to Mary,

. . . I am alert to keep away depressing, whining apes. I say, 'Oh don't pay any attention to that donkey. I will write to him.' 'But Ladyee, perhaps he isn't yet quite a donkey.' I always try to make him laugh, but it is too pathetic! His only recreation is translating some Tablet or prayer written in wonderful classic, mystic Arabic – enough to weary the brain of a well-fed savant with nothing else to do! If the care of all those churches (so few comparatively) overwhelmed St Paul, what would the dear saint do with the task of our wonderful Shoghi?[44]

A diary kept by one of the American believers reports that

Shoghi Effendi was occupied much of the time in consultation with Mountfort Mills, Roy Wilhelm, the Dreyfus-Barneys, Lady Blomfield, and Major Tudor Pole, and then later when they came the Schwarzes, about the foundation of the Universal House of Justice. I heard in a general way of the matters they discussed. It seems that before the Universal House can be established the Local and National Houses must be functioning in those countries where there are Bahá'ís.[45]

The outcome of these discussions shows the determination of the young Guardian to begin to lay the foundations for the Bahá'í Administrative Order. He knew well that if the Bahá'í Movement were to survive the upheaval of losing its irreplaceable Master and for it to take its rightful place among the recognized, independent, divinely-inspired religious systems of the world, he had to speedily evolve its world-encompassing Administrative Order, designed by Bahá'u'lláh, elaborated upon by 'Abdu'l-Bahá, and destined to provide the embryonic agencies for a new world civilization. Without any question of negating or undermining the believers' devotion to the Central Figures, the Guardian was faced with the task of teaching them to transfer their allegiance from prominent teachers and personalities to institutions ordained by the Manifestation Himself. Roy Wilhelm and Mountfort Mills were sent to tell the American believers that their Executive Board was now to take on a legislative function. The Schwarzes returned to Germany to try to establish local bodies and a national one. The British friends were similarly instructed. Ethel Rosenberg was told by Shoghi Effendi to call, on her return to London, an election for a spiritual assembly.

On 26 February Shoghi Effendi joined the believers for a memorial meeting for Helen Goodall, one of the pioneer members of the American Bahá'í community, who had opened her home in Oakland, California, for seekers. Many gatherings had been held there over the years and those who knew Mrs Goodall spoke of her sweetness and dignity, her modesty and graciousness. Shoghi Effendi chanted a Tablet of 'Abdu'l-Bahá, revealed to Mrs Goodall's daughter Ella Cooper, in which He mentions the passing of Phoebe Hearst and speaks of the great work done by the Disciples of Christ after His crucifixion. For the memorial meeting the women prepared a great quantity of flat, sweet biscuits, piled high in three dishes. The table around them was heaped with red and pink roses. Lady Blomfield joined Luṭfu'lláh Ḥakím and Emogene Hoagg in offering the refreshments. The meeting lasted a long time and Sitárih left early with Ethel Rosenberg and Laura Dreyfus-Barney as they wanted to hasten back to their lodgings before it got dark. It was an unusually gloomy evening as a heavy thunderstorm brewed over the Mediterranean. The women were anxious during their entire walk down the mountain that they would be caught in the storm but they were safe inside just before the rain started to pour down.

At the end of such precious days spent in the company of the Holy Family, Lady Blomfield wrote frequently to her daughter Mary, keeping her informed of all their activities and news that was reaching the Holy Land from Bahá'ís around the world. Some of it may not have been very reliable but, nevertheless, it appealed to Sitárih's profound sense of the moment.

'A piece of interesting news came from Ishkhabad,' she wrote on one occasion.

> Lenin sent word to the Bahai Assembly: 'Inform me of what your religion consists! If I find it false, I will destroy your Temple – the Mashrak-el-Askar – will level it with the ground.' When he read the principles of Baha'u'llah, he said, 'This is from God', He then wrote a courteous letter to the Assembly, accepting the Teaching, so that wonderful fulfilment of prophecy that the building of the Mashrak el Askar would bring illumination to Russia! Great events are daily being born.[46]

'The dear ladies send their hearts' love to you,' Sitárih wrote to Mary, 'and are so happy that you spend your time helping forward things for the bettering of poor humanity! They always pray for confirmations for you in all your doings!! and they long to see you. I gave your letter to the Greatest Holy Leaf. She was so pleased with it, the angel. Oh! how like our Beloved she looks, when she smiles and sends messages to Parvine!'[47]

In her inimitable manner, Lady Blomfield began taking notes of the conversations she enjoyed with the women of the Holy Household, particularly the Greatest Holy Leaf and 'Abdu'l-Bahá's widow Munírih Khánum.

'Only they can tell certain things, and if not collected now, it would be lost to the world of the future. Shoghi considers this a matter of the greatest importance. So I shall stay and work hard at this most congenial at the same time very difficult undertaking.'[48]

In Lady Blomfield's mind, an idea was beginning to emerge of writing a history of the Bahá'í Cause based on the accounts of some of its surviving protagonists. This idea would come to full fruition in the last few years of her life with the composition of her book *The Chosen Highway*.

Observing the Greatest Holy Leaf on a daily basis, Lady Blomfield longed to take her away for a rest.

'She needs a change so badly but never never thinks of herself for a moment, the Angel,' Sitárih told Mary. 'She looked so like the Master today! She sends her best love to you, also the dear Holy Mother and the 4 dear daughters – they are only little more than girls. Tooba Khanoum, so pretty with such bright eyes, and merry laugh is only 16 years older than her big manly son of 21. I could write for hours about them . . .'[49]

In the meantime, and with Shoghi Effendi's encouragement, Sitárih also set about gathering various stories of the last moments of 'Abdu'l-Bahá's earthly life and preparing an account in collaboration with the Guardian which was later published under the title *The Passing of 'Abdu'l-Bahá*. It was one of the first acts of Shoghi Effendi after his return to Haifa, well aware as he was that the Master's loved ones around the world were anxiously waiting to receive some details of the closing events of His unique and wonderful life.

'We have now come to realize,' they wrote,

. . . that the Master knew the day and hour when, his mission on earth being finished, he would return to the shelter of heaven. He was, however, careful that his family should not have any premonition of the coming sorrow. It seemed as though their eyes were veiled by him, with his ever-loving consideration for his dear ones, that they should not see the significance of certain dreams and other signs of the culminating event. This they now realize was his thought for them, in order that their strength might be preserved to face the great ordeal when it should arrive, that they should not be devitalized by anguish of mind in its anticipation.[50]

In her diary of those days, an American pilgrim, Ruth Randall, reported how Lady Blomfield, 'a delightful Irish woman' stopped by her room for a few minutes when Ruth, who had sprained her ankle, was being visited by the Guardian. 'She has been getting together with Shoghi Effendi the little pamphlet to be called *The Passing of 'Abdu'l-Bahá 'Abbás*,' wrote Ruth. 'She was wondering if she had left out anything of importance and said one thing had been told her which had impressed her greatly, which she could not seem to fit in. When the Master's funeral procession was passing up Mt. Carmel and during the service, there was not a sound, not a cock crowed nor a dog barked. The most intense silence was over everything and only the weeping of the people and the chanting could be heard.'[51]

On 4 March, Lady Blomfield joined Ruth Randall along with Shoghi Effendi, members of his family and the other pilgrims for a treasured visit to the Shrine of Bahá'u'lláh.

'The sun shone down through the glass roof, and the garden was green and lovely,' wrote Ruth.

> The American friends stood together in the little alcove, and so we could see Shoghi Effendi as he approached the Threshold. One could never forget his face. The expression of adoration and humbleness, combined with a great majesty, cannot be put into words.
>
> Then he chanted and of course, his voice is heavenly, but there, it was surely the voice of an angel singing.[52]

Shoghi Effendi had requested that some of the western friends sing the hymn *Nearer, My God, to Thee* in the Tomb of Bahá'u'lláh. But as he motioned to Ruth to begin the singing, the sound of the women of the Holy Family sobbing and weeping in a side room brought forth tears from all who heard them.

'Then Lady Blomfield, Mrs. Hoagg, and Mrs. True were sobbing, and you know what I do under such conditions,' wrote Ruth. 'How to sing! Well, I controlled my emotions and when I started my voice was very unsteady, but when everyone joined in, I found courage, and Shoghi Effendi was very pleased. It was a very impressive few minutes . . .'[53]

Throughout the months she remained in the Holy Land, Lady Blomfield was always pleased to receive news of her daughters and their husbands, communicated in regular letters from Mary, which were filled with amusing gossip about their family and friends. Sitárih was particularly delighted to learn in March 1922 that her younger daughter Rose Ellinor Cecilia – who she referred to as 'Baby' or 'Babs' in her letters – had been offered a part in the popular play *Trilby*, based on George du Maurier's novel about a young diva in Paris and her mentor Svengali. Rose was also to understudy the lead role. Her husband Harold had also been offered a part in the play, as Taffy Wynn, a good-natured English cavalryman-turned-painter.

'How glorious that Baby has the part – bless her!' wrote Sitárih. 'My loving wishes for all good luck to her and to Harold. He will be a very good Taffy and if Babs once gets the opportunity to play Trilby – well she will have arrived!!! I feel the Master's blessing is with you all – he is so near.'[54]

Lady Blomfield was always deeply touched to meet the offspring of the heroic believers of Persia who had readily laid down their lives for the Cause. On 24 March 1922, she, along with the Dreyfus-Barneys, the Schwarzes, Mason Remey and Mountfort Mills, organized a tea for some 70 of the Persian friends, including 12 pilgrims from Khurasan where some of the most brutal murders of Bábís had taken place in 1852.

'These people are unbelievably like the early Christian Saints and, so far from thinking a Martyr's end terrible, they long for that exalted station!' Sitárih wrote to Mary.

> They sent beautiful messages to England. I thought their minds must have been quite awake to the ease with which we receive the holy Teaching – no hardship or persecution being our lot! Neither imprisonment, torture nor death! Perhaps its very ease is one of the causes of our lukewarmness, as a nation I mean! . . .
>
> We pushed the tables up to the wall, opened the double doors into the three bedrooms, put rugs into the doorways, the rest the rugs we spread on the floor, about 3 dozen chairs, the others sat on the floor on their heels – the dears, they all wrote their names in my book. They enjoyed their delicious tea and cakes and candies. Laura is worthy to be Earl Marshal so amazingly well did she manage it all.[55]

An expedition to Beirut and Damascus with the Dreyfus-Barneys was another memorable moment of Lady Blomfield's first sojourn in the Middle East. The intrepid group set off north from Haifa in a Buick, driven by Hippolyte, crossing the border into French-occupied Lebanon, passing through fragrant orange groves to the ancient Phoenician city of Tyre and the port of Sidon. All was going well, with the ladies revelling in the passing landscape, until the Buick ground to a halt in desert sands.

'Laura and I walked on,' Lady Blomfield wrote to her daughters.

> Some Bedouin women came up and talked very cheerily to us inviting

us to their homes! Though in Arabic, so descriptive were their gestures that we understood a good deal of what they said. We did not accept. They were tall, slender and handsome after one got used to the tattoo marks covering their chins and continued up their jaw bones. Brilliant eyes and gleaming teeth.

We were casting eyes at the sand-hill behind which Hippolyte was grappling with the motor – and wondering what he had called to his help, a brace of little black oxen, or a string of camels led by a donkey on which an Arab resplendent in a pure satin petticoat, a purple coat and voluminous orange striped head-gear. All of which we had met and watched disappear behind the sandhill where we had abandoned the car to Hippolyte. The Chauffeur and a picturesque Arab guide who rode on the step and was most decorative, handsome rather like our friend Ali Akbar – in blue voluminous trousers, beautiful purple jacket and wonderful head gear of purple and blue green striped silk. The car at length appeared, after we had an anxious glimpse of it nearly disappearing into the brook Kishon, now quite a formidable rapid stream, with booby trap holes in it – they say that YWD lorries had disappeared into it!! At one moment we quite expected to see all our own belongings engulfed, 3 of the wheels were in the stream. However all was well and we went on gaily.[56]

The landscape of the Lebanon made a profound impact on Sitárih.

Oh! the orange groves, the purple, pink, yellow, blue, scarlet and orange flowers in the grass – living Persian carpets all the way along the road, till we began to climb the slopes of the rocky wilderness where we sat on rocks and ate our lunch – close to the French frontier between Palestine and Syria – henceforth the Tricolor gave itself to the breeze instead of the Union Jack. Blue important air-wireless boys cropped up every here and there and chattered French. So glad to see us – their lives must be very monotonous when the romance of the situation had worn off, or perhaps never disturbed their dreams. To me everything was a marvel. Laura and Hippolyte are ideal travellers, capable, calm, restful, no fuss whatever transpires.[57]

Arriving in Beirut, the travellers rested two nights at the graceful Grand Hôtel d'Orient, built on the seafront in the late 19th century to accommodate the growing stream of foreign travellers to the city. Lady Blomfield observed how many of the streets were 'demolished by the Turkish Government (before the French) in order to build up imposing western houses and widen the streets giving the effect of bombardments – as the French are leaving them as they are, at any rate until the Mandates are signed'.[58] In the city, Sitárih and the Dreyfus-Barneys met up with young Bahá'í men who were studying at the Jesuit and American colleges and enjoyed eating local pastries with them.

'Sohail, son of Touba Khanum . . . and a fascinating dear boy about 17, pupil at the American College, fell upon our necks, came out lunched with us and escorted us over Bayrouth. A delightful lady doctor who is a Baha'i came to see us there. They all know Laura and Hippolyte and positively adore them, small wonder! I know of none to equal them!'[59]

On Tuesday 28 March the party set off to lunch at Baalbek, some 53 miles northeast of Beirut, renowned for its monumental temple ruins from the Roman period, when the town, then known as Heliopolis, was one of the largest sanctuaries in the Empire. All was going well until the car's magneto began to play up, delaying their reaching Baalbek until some 12 hours later.

'But it was worth every minute of it – over the Lebanons and Anti Lebanons, through Caravans of Arabs,' enthused Sitárih.

> All quite friendly. Oh! those glorious snow topped mountains and the Persian carpet-like fields, the snow tops, the purple slopes, the vivid green grass, the red earth all of an indescribable beauty. Then Baalbek, marvellous – the Phoenician under all, then the Roman Temples to Jupiter and to Bacchus, the Pantheon, the Christian basilica. Then the Arabs with their Mosque and fortifications then earthquakes – in spite of all – glorious red granite columns with the Acanthus decoration still stand, the carving clear cut as though only just done! The gigantic stones – 64 feet long, 13 feet high, 10 feet thick!!! How could they have been raised up on to 23 feet high wall? But these are only details! It is the 4th dimension atmosphere of it which counts! And cannot be described only felt. I am so glad we went.[60]

Sitárih thought how much her late husband's son Charles would have been amused by the characters they met on their travels.

'I wish Charley could have seen a fat German mechanic who came out from Bayrouth to make the car go! He had to sit in the car – what splendid mimicking Charley could have got from his appearance etc.'[61]

The following day, Sitárih and the Dreyfus-Barneys motored south some 47 miles to Damascus, having passed the river Barada as it flowed through the mountains.

> We found the Persian consul general awaiting us in his motor – looking very dignified with his blue cloth garments, tan coloured Aba, black Kola with a gold sort of plaque in front but the chauffeur in sky blue livery with silver cords and grey chinchilla kola and the attendant in brighter sky blue high boots and black kola were even more imposing. The Persian flag flew on the car – ah most gorgeous.[62]

One of the Bahá'ís – Aine-ul-Mulk – tried to persuade the travellers to stay with him but Laura stood firm and refused 'with great courtesy and even greater determination'.[63] They were, however, swept off to dinner at his home, where Lady Blomfield appreciated the kindness of his mother, sister and wife.

> The next day the Car [of the Persian consul] was placed at our disposal, we went about in all its gorgeousity. I felt that we ought at least to have had 'mantles with rich ermine lined' on and tiaras and veils if not crowns!! No wonder the people in the bazaars asked us ridiculous prices for things! All yelling together! I just fled out of their shops – the only things I bought were two tasbihs [prayer beads], and a cord for leading a donkey. We never know when it may come in useful!![64]

Lady Blomfield found Damascus to be most wonderful and was overwhelmed by its great mosque, 'its glorious simple dignity, its vastness and its solemn silence, only broken by a venerable sheikh chanting verses from the Quran were most impressive! In comparison, our Christian churches seem overloaded with ornament, even when not tawdry.'

> The head of John the Baptist was there in a wonderful casket. The well stone from which our lady used to draw water reverently cared for. Then the place dedicated to the prophet Hud! I felt in a dream. The charming venerable old Mulla, who took us round explaining things to us – with beautiful calm face and manners 'gnawed his sandal strings'

when we said goodbye. Hippolyte gave him a pound and he demanded two! We walked on, nose in air, disgusted with his greed, whereupon he hurled abuse after us!! As bad in its way as hanging up a menu tariff of the Holy Sacraments, Marriage, Baptism in the porch of a Church – indeed indeed. Religion needs restating and rescue from the slanders of religionists! We went to a Bahai gathering in the evening at the home of Sheikh Sayed *docteur endroit* [doctor of law] – a charming learned man – delighted to get from us the latest news from the centre of the administration of the Cause – Arabs, Persians, French and English also two Indians were there. The dears sat in rows at our hotel giving up their whole day so as to see as much as possible. The veiled ladies of the families also came to visit us. All unique experience.[65]

One encounter particularly impressed itself on Sitárih's memory – a meeting with Count Eustache de Lorey, who was the director of the French Institute of Archaeology and Muslim Art. He had travelled widely in the Orient and had spent two years in Persia as a member of the French legation to the Court. Sitárih was particularly thrilled to hear that Count de Lorey believed he had discovered the house on Straight Street in Damascus where the blinded Saul of Tarsus – later Saint Paul – had had his sight restored by Ananias, a momentous incident in Christian history mentioned in chapter nine of Acts of the Apostles.

The travellers enquired about taking an excursion from Damascus to the ancient Aramaic city of Palmyra some 130 miles northeast but they were warned that it was too dangerous.

'We could only have gone with a Government Escort and our late experience with a car did not encourage me to risk being stranded in the desert 50 miles from anywhere!!' wrote Lady Blomfield, who was jubilant when the Dreyfus-Barneys gave up the idea of an expedition.[66]

On Friday 31 March the travellers took the car back on the train from Damascus to Haifa. Aine-ul-Mulk and the other Bahá'ís met them on the platform and presented them with a gigantic basket of fruit before waving them off.

'We passed through glorious country and stopped about an hour beside the Lake of Galilee,' recounted Sitárih, 'where was a British camp of soldiers, mostly Indians, a very talkative Indian officer, splendid to look upon, got into our train! He was going on leave, he was interesting about the situation in India. We also heard during our journey much about French

Lady Blomfield and women of 'Abdu'l-Bahá's household in Haifa, shortly after Lady Blomfield's arrival in the Holy Land with Shoghi Effendi following the Master's passing. Pictured are: (*back row*) Lady Blomfield, Bahíyyih <u>Kh</u>ánum, Munírih <u>Kh</u>ánum; (*front row*) unknown, Rúḥá <u>Kh</u>ánum.

Lady Blomfield with members of 'Abdu'l-Bahá's household in Haifa, following the Master's passing. Pictured are: (*standing left to right*) Ṭúbá Khánum, Rúḥá Khánum, unknown; (*seated left to right*) Lady Blomfield, Bahíyyih Khánum, surrounded by some of the grandchildren of 'Abdu'l-Bahá.

Lady Blomfield and Bahíyyih Khánum, the Greatest Holy Leaf, in Haifa after Lady Blomfield's arrival in the Holy Land with Shoghi Effendi following the Master's passing

Lady Blomfield in the garden of the original Western Pilgrim House
at 4 Haparsim Street, Haifa, in 1922

In February 1922, Shoghi Effendi called to Haifa a number of the most capable and experienced Bahá'ís from around the world to consult about the future of the Bahá'í Cause. *From left to right:* Curtis Kelsey, Emogene Hoagg, Mountfort Mills, unknown, Shoghi Effendi, unknown, Laura Dreyfus-Barney (?), unknown, Ethel Rosenberg, behind her (?), Lady Blomfield, behind her Roy Wilhelm, Saichiro Fujita, behind him Ruth Randall

Lady Blomfield at the citadel in 'Akká, 1922. 'The Ammunition you see has not been tidied away since Napoleon's time,' she wrote on the back of the photograph which she sent to her daughters. 'I have some of the little square flints they used for the guns.'

Lady Blomfield, with 'Abdu'l-Bahá's daughter Rúḥá Khánum

A group of Bahá'ís in London, April 1923. Lady Blomfield is seated holding the portrait of 'Abdu'l-Bahá. Immediately left of Lady Blomfield is Mrs Thornburgh-Cropper and, left of her, Elizabeth Herrick. Seated in the front row, far left, is Luṭfu'lláh Ḥakím who in 1963 was elected to the first Universal House of Justice. The bald gentleman with a moustache in the centre of the front row is Ḍiyá'u'lláh Aṣgharzádih, later named by Shoghi Effendi as a Knight of Bahá'u'lláh for the Channel Islands.

and Syrians, British and Palestinians and Jews. Most complicated and bewildering. Both British and French seem to be doing very good work.'[67]

The experience of venturing through such an historical land, with its connections to the stories from the Bible which were so close to her heart, and with such wonderful companions as the Dreyfus Barneys, was one of the high points of Lady Blomfield's travels, despite the intermittent automobile problems. Sitárih relished the company of Laura and Hippolyte and was saddened by the prospect of their imminent departure from the Holy Land.

'They are darlings – and the best Baha'is in the world I think from the mental as well as the spiritual plane,' Sitárih wrote to Mary. 'I could tell you reams of their adventures in Indochina – always working for the Divine Cause of Peace and Unity without the narrow sectarianism which is likely to be a danger in the future – a real pitfall to be avoided . . . The Dreyfuses' adventures also broadened out to Jungles and Tigers and things.'[68]

Returning to Haifa, Sitárih began to think about what next to do in her service to the Cause. Among her considerations was returning to Cadogan Gardens for a little while to lend her assistance to organizing the elections for the London Spiritual Assembly and first National Spiritual Assembly.

'Upon us devolves much of the carrying on of the work to which our Master has given his life and his English Family will not fail!' she wrote to her daughter.[69]

She was relieved to learn that Shoghi Effendi had clarified that membership of the Bahá'í assemblies was open to women.

'Shoghi was grand but some others, well! My heart was in my boots for a few days. I needn't have been troubled! Shoghi had no intention of agreeing to put that consideration off, as some wished, for a future date when Eastern conditions should have made it possible for such a plan in their lands.'[70]

Thinking about what services she could usefully render in London, Sitárih suggested to Mary that they 'might do much amongst people who already think along universal lines – these are capable of receiving still broader and higher views, and these only! Those who live in grooves, busily scrambling up and down them, wear deeper and deeper ruts, and simply forget that there really is a world, which they might see if they could reach up to look over the edge of their particular rut – are hopeless. It is waste of time to mention universal things to them! They must just even wait until another incarnation, or whatever we choose to call the condition of renewed opportunity . . .'[71]

However, Shoghi Effendi had other plans in the short term for Lady Blomfield. He asked her to stay longer in Haifa to gather more stories about the Master's life during the Great War as well as to continue collecting the reminiscences of the ladies of the household.

'They have lived a life of such utter self-effacement but there are many amazing episodes,' Sitárih told Mary.

> Their dreams are extraordinary. Some of these I have, and a description of the trousseau of Asiah Khanum [the wife of Bahá'u'lláh]. There were jewellers working in her father's house for 6 months before her marriage making jewellery – jewelled buttons etc. for her clothes. It was some of these later which she cut off and sold for bread on their terrible journey to Baghdad! If only I could get enough material, the events were these!![72]

After four full months of grappling with the burden that had so suddenly and unexpectedly been placed upon his shoulders, and suffering under the strain created by renewed machinations on the part of the faithless members of 'Abdu'l-Bahá's family, Shoghi Effendi left the Holy Land on 5 April 1922, seeking to restore his health in the mountains of Switzerland.

'This servant, after that grievous event and great calamity – the ascension of His Holiness Abdul-Baha to the Abhá Kingdom,' Shoghi Effendi wrote,

> . . . has been so stricken with grief and pain and so entangled in the troubles (created) by the enemies of the Cause of God, that I consider my presence here, at such a time and in such an atmosphere, is not in accordance with the fulfilment of my important and sacred duties.
>
> For this reason, unable to do otherwise, I have left for a time the affairs of the Cause, both at home and abroad, under the supervision of the Holy Family and the headship of the Greatest Holy Leaf – may my soul be a sacrifice to her – until, by the Grace of God, having gained health, strength, self-confidence and spiritual energy, and having taken into my hands, in accordance with my aim and desire, entirely and regularly the work of service, I shall attain to my utmost spiritual hope and aspiration.[73]

'God will, of course, frustrate the intrigues of all opposers!' Lady Blomfield wrote to Yúḥanná Dávúd in London.

> But that the enemies should be of 'the Master's kindred, and his own Father's house' – is naturally a bitter sorrow to the dear Guardian, as well as to the other members of the beloved family. The unprecedented work, and this sorrow combined with the shock he had sustained, proved so great a burden that he at length yielded to appeals from us all, to go right away out of it all – to go into a kind of Retreat, where he would have time and opportunity to rest, meditate, pray, and concentrate upon the stupendous task which lies before him, gaining at the same time the physical strength necessary for so important a work. Until this period is ended he replies to no letters. Many of these, naturally, can be dealt with by the various local Assemblies, and it is well that these bodies should now grow accustomed to take upon themselves the burden of deciding such questions . . .[74]

As Shoghi Effendi sought to recover his strength in the mountains of Switzerland, Lady Blomfield, accompanied by three of 'Abdu'l-Bahá's daughters and three of His young grandsons, took the train from Haifa to 'Akká on 1 May. Shortly after their arrival, Sitárih and Rúḥá visited the barracks, known as the Most Great Prison, where they met a very courteous British officer who offered to later show them over all the parts of the fortress including the prison cell of Bahá'u'lláh. Shoghi Effendi's younger sister Mehrangíz then arrived in the company of the son of an early believer, Áqá Ridáy-i Qannad. He took them to see the caravanserai where Bahá'í pilgrims used to stay, having made the arduous journey on foot from Persia, hoping to see Bahá'u'lláh.

'Here we came to the long, stone-floored room, where the friends used to spread out their bedding and rest, also the rows of little rooms where families encamped,' described Lady Blomfield.

> There was a room where a school for little children was afterwards arranged – poor little scholars – from early morning till sunset in an airless room, with dull studies, nothing interesting, nothing amusing; no breaks now and then for play! Such scanty, tasteless scraps called dinner!
>
> After the Ascension of Bahá'u'lláh there was also a room set apart for the little girls, who were, if possible, in a worse case than even the boys.

The Khán is a wonderfully picturesque building, built round a large court-yard, with rows of rounded arches and columns on three sides.

Here the Master's custom was to assemble all the poor, especially the children, of 'Akká, on Feast Days, both Christian and Muslim, also on the anniversary of the Sultán's coronation. Here He regaled them with sweets, cakes, fruit, and tea. He had the middle fountain filled with _sharbat_, which was a great treat. After this, we went through the narrow, winding streets of this unique historic town to the great mosque. There we met a polite Shaykh, who had become a devoted friend of 'Abbás Effendi; he turned back with us, and showed us the little room where the Master used to retreat, when He wished to meditate in peace and quiet.

. . . Then the Shaykh took us into the mosque – impressive in its silent and reverent atmosphere. He pointed out a small alcove apart, where the Master always prayed.

Upon the wall, in an honourable place, hung a wonderful, intricately-written prayer, from the pen of the famous Mishkín Qalam; it is conspicuously signed 'Mishkín Qalam, who am Baha'i'.

Other treasures were shown to us: six pen-written sacred books, presented to the mosque by 'Abbás Effendi. Some others, marvellously illustrated with pen drawings (from India). Also many precious volumes, containing some thousands of the Ḥadíths (traditional utterances of Muḥammad).

Standing about were numbers of Muslim religious students, charming-looking youths, who courteously greeted us.

Here was the large court-yard where the poor congregated every Friday to receive alms, and make their various appeals to their 'Beloved Father of the Poor', 'Abbás Effendi.

Everybody said 'Oh, what a loss to the world. He was Comforter, Protector, and Benefactor to all!'

'Abdu'l-Bahá lived forty years of His sanctified life in this fortress town . . .[75]

During their visit to 'Akká, Lady Blomfield slept in the room of Bahá'u'lláh's wife Ásíyih Khánum in the House of 'Abbúd. She remarked that she was aware all through the night of its benign atmosphere. On her second evening in the city she sat on the balcony of the house outside Bahá'u'lláh's room. As she peered out across the bay to Mount Carmel shimmering in the distance, she described to her daughter the privations suffered by the Holy Family in those years of incarceration.

> In this house were four rooms only! For the pilgrims and for the family! (The men pilgrims who were single, and the families, were accommodated at the Khán.)
>
> One room, the best, was always kept sacred to Bahá'u'lláh. The family, Ásíyih Khánum, the Most Exalted Leaf, their daughter, and the Master surrounded their Beloved with all the devoted care that was possible.
>
> In one of the rooms thirteen persons, pilgrims and the ladies, sometimes slept. A shelf was there, on which an agile pilgrim would repose, and on one occasion rolled off!
>
> This plan was for those days before the marriage of 'Abbás Effendi – when the door was opened through to a room of the larger house. This is next to the smaller house where 'Abbás Effendi brought His bride, and where all His children were born . . .
>
> This is the house where the Kitáb-i-Aqdas, the Most Holy Book, and many Tablets of sublime beauty were written. It was also this house which was one day surrounded with soldiers sent to arrest Bahá'u'lláh and the Master.[76]

Sitárih also paid a visit to the House of 'Abdu'lláh Páshá, where the first groups of pilgrims from the West encountered 'Abdu'l-Bahá and where all the Master's grandchildren were born. At the time of her visit the house was being used as a military hospital. One of the sisters in charge spoke English and told Lady Blomfield, 'Yes, 'Abbás Effendi was a good friend to all. He came to see me, and gave fifty pounds to this hospital. He was a kind friend to my uncle and to me.'[77]

Bahíyyih Khánum and Munírih Khánum joined Lady Blomfield in 'Akká on the second day, having motored over from Haifa along with Shoghi Effendi's sister Rúhangíz and her father Mírzá Hádí. Áqá Ḥusayn, a cook who had been with Bahá'u'lláh in Baghdad, escorted Sitárih and eight other ladies to the prison, to give them reliable facts from his own memory about all the places of the captivity.

'How could I convey the impression of this visit?' wrote Lady Blomfield.

> The Saint Sister, daughter of Bahá'u'lláh, and the Holy Mother, wife of 'Abdu'l-Bahá, as they stood looking at the little, bare rooms, where their

(and our) Beloved Ones were imprisoned! One imagined in what an intimate, poignantly heart-rending flood of memories they walked, as they gazed with grief-filled eyes upon this barrack building, the home for many years of those Two – destined to be the Great Educators of the world, West as well as East, that world which is also wet with tears!

There was the little room on the ground-floor, where Bahá'u'lláh stayed for a time, when He, with His family, arrived in 'Akká. This room is being carefully preserved untouched.

Close by is the vault-like room where the rest of the family and the seventy 'Faithful Ones' who accompanied them, were shut in for those first appalling days. All fell sick with typhoid but two, 'Abbás Effendi and one man, who, therefore, was able to help Him. The Master nursed them, cooked for them, and Himself divided out the portions – seeing to it that none were neglected nor forgotten.

The Greatest Holy Leaf, her eyes charged with memories, was with us while we listened. She had been there in that terrible time, and was sick of that same fever, from the effects of which she has occasionally suffered all through her life.[78]

Another excursion that Lady Blomfield took with 'Abdu'l-Bahá's daughter Rúḥá was to Abú-Sinán, the Druze village in the hills where the Bahá'í community had retreated at the invitation of its leader during the precarious years of the Great War.

'Our car seemed to be taking flying leaps over rocks, then we climbed winding, almost perpendicular roads,' wrote Lady Blomfield. 'Nothing but a Ford car, with a perfect driver, knowing every inch of the way, which was our Khusraw, could safely have accomplished the tests of that motor drive.'[79]

The Shaykh of the place, with some of his sons and nephews, came out to welcome the ladies as they arrived. They were led into the courtyard where the wife of the Shaykh, her daughters, daughter-in-law and their children greeted them.

We mounted many, many steps on the outside of the house and arrived at a very large, beautifully-proportioned room. Under the large windows, round two sides of this reception chamber, were fixed divans.

As we arrived, the younger ladies brought soft, square cushions covered in wonderful brocade of apple-green and gold; these they placed on the divans for the comfort of their honoured guests.

They were full of joy to see Rúḥá <u>Kh</u>ánum, who had not paid them a visit since the passing of her adored Father. Her sorrow overflowed her heart afresh, as these dear Druze ladies wept with her, and she looked round the room, where the Master had so often taught and comforted His people during the dread and fear-laden days of the war.

This was their refuge till some of that ghastly time was overpast, and the Master knew that it would be safe to return to their homes at Haifa, bringing their children, now restored to health.

The view from these windows is glorious, and the whole atmosphere of the place full of calm and rest. No marvel that the dear ones were happy in that haven, in the presence of their Beloved One, and cared for by these devoted, lovely creatures.

Across one end of this room were book-cases filled with beautifully bound books.

How I longed to know what they contained! Sacred writings naturally; but their religion is secret, none but the initiated are ever permitted to either enter their houses of worship, or to read their holy books.[80]

Sitárih was captivated by the Druze women, finding them 'amazingly lovely, with slight, graceful figures, regular features, wonderful eyes with long lashes, deep ivory coloured skins'.

I have never seen so many beautiful women together without one plain face among them. For even the grandmother and great-grandmother were beautiful! The dress is certainly most becoming; there is the white amice, very soft muslin – embroidered, and edged with fine lace. Then an ivory-coloured, fine, supple silk, embroidered with coloured flowers, only showing in front, where the zombaz, a long coat, floated back as they walked with their free, graceful step; this zombaz is sometimes black or dark blue velvet; the head is covered with a large, flowing, white soft veil; this is bound firmly round the head with a band, it might be dark blue, embroidered with gold, forming a sort of coronet; it is tied at the back of the head, the ends falling below the knees, over the snowy veil, nearly reaching the ground. They never show their hair, and it is a mark of great respect to draw their veil over the mouth.

An enchanting baby, one year old, was brought in; even her hair was not to be seen. She wore a quaint little silk bonnet with white frills round the lovely baby face, and a curtain covered the neck. I wanted to see

Baddúrah's head, but the beautiful grandmother, Sit 'Afífíh, only pushed the bonnet a wee bit back, and I did not like to insist by asking again.[81]

As soon as the ladies arrived, sweet iced water was offered to them in pretty glasses. After a while tea came, with delicious Arabian pastry, cakes, sweets, and nuts, followed by very sweet coffee. The Druze pressed Rúḥá Khánum and the other visitors to stay for at least a few days. 'Their hospitality is spontaneous kindness itself,' remarked Sitárih.[82]

When the Druze women found that the ladies were really unable to accept their invitation, they were taken to the *diván*, another comfortable and large reception room. Here they were presented by Rúḥá to Shaykh Sáliḥ, 'a courtly, charming, and fascinating man, ninety years old, who wept bitterly as he welcomed us, for he had a great reverence and love for 'Abdu'l-Bahá'.[83]

When at last the party rose to depart, all of the Druze friends came out into the courtyard, the ladies standing apart.

'I shall always remember that visit to Abú-Sinán,' wrote Sitárih, 'the refuge of the Haifa friends and their children, during the terror-days of the war.'[84]

Six eventful months had been passed by Lady Blomfield in the shelter of 'Abdu'l-Bahá's household, months where she had been touched and gratified to witness the manner in which Shoghi Effendi – despite having his heart broken by the passing of his grandfather – had arisen to take on the mantle of the Guardianship.

'We all felt in him the Manifestation of the untrammelled Spirit of our Beloved Master,' Sitárih wrote to Yúḥanná Dávúd.

His lowliness, too, was very touching. Never would he allow any remark, likening his actions in any way to what the Master would have done! . . .

Now that the Master has returned to the shelter of heaven, it behoves us to show a firm loyalty, and a steadfast unity, which no enemy will have power to injure or to lessen. I think that we all feel that the work for which our Beloved suffered so terribly, should now be carried on all the more earnestly, that we are not called upon for such sacrifices . . . What an enormous amount there accumulates for us to do for the Cause. I look forward to great progress in London![85]

CHAPTER TEN

PREPARING THE GROUND

. . . what I specially want is some few more ladies of her type,
real Bahá'ís whose words and deeds symbolize the
spirit and teachings of the Cause.[1]
Words attributed to Shoghi Effendi

At the time of 'Abdu'l-Bahá's passing a handful of local Bahá'í assemblies were scattered throughout America and Persia. For the young Guardian of the Faith, the priority in the first years of his ministry was to evolve the network of local and national institutions to provide the necessary foundation for the establishment of the Universal House of Justice. Before she left the Holy Land for England, Ethel Rosenberg was instructed by Shoghi Effendi to collate the names of the believers and arrange for the election of a Spiritual Assembly to reach beyond London's boundaries and which would, within a year, evolve into the first National Spiritual Assembly of the British Isles.

As was to be expected with such a new development for a group of individuals unused to formal organization, the process did not go altogether smoothly. After the Assembly was established, it found itself criticized by some of the believers who claimed they had never received voting papers or been informed of the election, an inevitable consequence of there being no formal registration and an incomplete membership roll. Allaying the ill feelings of these friends who felt overlooked was among the many challenges that faced the Assembly as it set about its work.

Although such processes were as new to her as to the rest of the believers, Lady Blomfield felt particularly strongly that the Bahá'ís around Great Britain should fully appreciate the significance of these new institutions and the importance of participating in the electoral process. Not surprisingly, she was among those elected to the London Spiritual Assembly, along with Ethel Rosenberg, Mrs Thornburgh-Cropper, Claudia Coles,

Yúḥanná Dávúd, Mother George, Eric Hammond, George Palgrave Simpson, Helen Grand and a Miss Fry. In addition, Shoghi Effendi recommended that Edward Hall attend meetings, representing the Bahá'ís of Manchester, as well as Dr Esslemont, from Bournemouth.

'I do hope that the appointment of this new Council will mark the beginning of a new and more prosperous era for the Bahai Movement in this country,' wrote Esslemont.[2]

One person conspicuous by his absence in the nascent Bahá'í administration was Wellesley Tudor Pole. On returning from the consultations in Haifa, he more or less distanced himself completely from the Bahá'í community, claiming that after discussion with Shoghi Effendi, he had reached the decision that he would be more effective as a non-member, which would give him added credibility should he be needed to defend the Faith in diplomatic circles. Tudor Pole went on to pursue his esoteric interests and gained fame as a Christian mystic in his own right, particularly associated with the Glastonbury movement, of which Alice Buckton – another early believer who also disappeared from Bahá'í circles – was also a prominent figure. Perhaps Tudor Pole could not see the reason for the organization of the Bahá'í Movement. He had always advocated an open fellowship of races and religions rather than any formalization of codes and practices. Despite his preferences, at the end of his life in 1968 Tudor Pole wrote of his conviction that 'the Baha'i movement has an important part to play in the religious regeneration of the world, and especially the Eastern world'.[3]

The first meeting of the newly-elected Spiritual Assembly of London was held at Mrs Thornburgh-Cropper's home on 17 June 1922. Among the many items under discussion in its first year were the community's meagre financial resources, its public meetings and its publishing ventures. A weekly Wednesday meeting for enquirers was continuing at Lindsay Hall but was poorly attended, despite it being advertised. One decision that the Assembly took to try to improve the situation was to begin the meeting promptly at eight o'clock rather than allowing a quarter of an hour's grace for latecomers. Another question that arose was whether it was appropriate to sing hymns at such meetings. Some of the believers felt strongly that hymns should not be part of the programme. Others, such as the American Claudia Coles, pointed out that at gatherings in the United States during the visit of the Master where there had been hymns, He had expressed His approval of the practice. Lady Blomfield was able to share a letter of the Master to Louise Waite, the composer of many early Bahá'í songs, in which He praised her compositions and encouraged her to continue writing hymns. The Assembly finally concluded that only Bahá'í or strictly non-denominational hymns should be used at the public meetings.

Concerning the publications that were under way, Sitárih was able to lend her assistance to Mírzá Yúḥanná Dávúd, who was translating some of Bahá'u'lláh's Tablets into English. Ethel Rosenberg was also keen that *The Passing of 'Abdu'l-Bahá*, written by Lady Blomfield with Shoghi Effendi, should be republished. Before it took any formal action, the Assembly authorized Rosenberg to write to the United States to find out if the believers there were thinking of reprinting it. The second edition was eventually published in England with revisions made by Sitárih and approved by the Guardian.

An international project supported financially by the Assembly in its early months was that of the interior decoration of a pilgrim house for western believers in Haifa. The initial American sponsors of the building, Harry and Ruth Randall, appealed to the Assembly to furnish one room at a cost of 30 pounds. A new fund was opened and Lady Blomfield and Mrs Thornburgh-Cropper set the ball rolling by generously donating five pounds each.

Cherishing the firsthand accounts of the history of the Faith that had been related to her by the members of the Holy Family, Lady Blomfield was determined also to devote her energies to the book that Shoghi Effendi had encouraged her to write. For a period of two months she left London for Nice in France and transcribed some three hundred pages of notes based on her conversations with the Greatest Holy Leaf, the Holy Mother and other members of the Master's household. On her return, she noticed that each time she shared some of the stories at Bahá'í meetings, it had a profound effect on the believers. In a letter to Shoghi Effendi, she attributed this impact to 'the direct sincerity and simplicity of those dear ones'[4] from whose lips she had taken down the description of the various episodes. Her intention, she told the Guardian, was to 'hand on . . . the impression, the pre-occupation of the spirit which so enfolded me as I listened'.[5]

'Trusting book progressing favourably,' Shoghi Effendi cabled Sitárih. 'Accept my whole-hearted collaboration.'[6]

By 2 May 1923 Lady Blomfield had sent the first of a number of instalments of her proposed book to the Guardian and asked him whether he had any suggestions for an appropriate title. She also asked him if he could select some prayers and writings that could be inserted into the manuscript. She felt hesitant to make this request of the Guardian, 'knowing how the "government is upon your shoulders" as well as upon your heart'.[7] She told him that she was praying that 'strength and guidance' equal to his task would be bestowed upon him and promised to do her best, 'being reinforced by the power of our Master'.[8]

Reinvigorated after his prolonged absence in Switzerland, Shoghi Effendi penned a first letter to his 'spiritual brethren and sisters in Great Britain'[9] in which he informed them of

> The thought, so often comforting and sustaining, that in the counsels of my British co-workers of that land, I shall find spontaneous and undiminished support as well as wise and experienced assistance, is surely one of those forces which will hearten me in the midst of my future labours for the Cause.
>
> That in every one of you our departed Master reposed His future and truest hopes for an able and convincing presentation of the Cause to the outside world, is abundantly revealed in His spoken and written words to you, as well as in His general references to the spirit of sincerity, of tenacity and devotion that animates His friends of that land.
>
> The fierce tests that have raged over that island in the past; the calm and determination with which they have been so bravely faced and surmounted; the seeds of loving fellowship that the Beloved in person has more than once scattered in its soil; the rise, as its result, of a few but indeed capable, reliable, devoted and experienced followers and admirers of the Cause; the splendid and in many instances unique opportunities that are yours – these indeed are cherished thoughts for a land that illumines its past and should cheer its future.
>
> I need hardly tell you how grateful and gratified I felt when I heard the news of the actual formation of a National Council whose main object is to guide, co-ordinate and harmonize the various activities of the friends, and when I learned of its satisfactory composition, its harmonious procedure and the splendid work it is achieving.
>
> My earnest prayer is that the blessing of the Almighty may rest upon all its deliberations, that it may be divinely guided, inspired in its work, may smooth speedily and definitely all differences that may arise, may

promote the all-important work of Teaching, may widen the sphere of its correspondence and exchange of news with the distant parts of the Bahá'í world, may secure through its publications a dignified and proper presentation of the Cause to the enlightened public, and may in every other respect prove itself capable of distinct and worthy achievements.

With abiding affection and renewed vigour I shall now await the joyful tidings of the progress of the Cause and the extension of your activities, and will spare no effort in sharing with the faithful, here and in other lands, the welcome news of the progressive march of the Cause and the unceasing labours of our British friends for the Cause of Bahá'u'lláh.[10]

Lady Blomfield was pleased to see Shoghi Effendi taking up his task with renewed vigour, and the Holy Family was grateful to Sitárih for the many services she had rendered the young Guardian.

'We never forget all the kindnesses you have done to Shoghi Effendi when he was in England,' wrote his aunt Rúḥá, 'and all you did for him all the way from England to Haifa. How you help us all in these sad days after the ascension of the Beloved. You really were great comfort to us at that times when we were terribly suffering from the departure of our dear One. Be sure we all appreciate it very much.'[11]

In April 1923 the Bahá'ís in London elected their Local Spiritual Assembly and later, along with the Bahá'ís in Bournemouth and Manchester, who had also formed their Assemblies, voted for the first National Spiritual Assembly. In the London election, 66 of the 80 believers returned their ballot papers. Sitárih received 55 votes, the highest number for any individual. She was also elected to the first National Spiritual Assembly along with Eric Hammond, Mrs Thornburgh-Cropper, Ethel Rosenberg, George Palgrave Simpson and Mother George from London, Edward Hall and Jacob Joseph from Manchester and Dr Esslemont from Bournemouth.

'You, surely, have laid a firm foundation for the future development of the Cause in those regions,' Shoghi Effendi wrote to the Assembly, 'and my hope is that the National Assembly of Great Britain may, by full, frequent, and anxious consultation, protect the Cause, maintain and promote harmony amongst the friends, and initiate and execute ways and means for the diffusion of its spirit and the promotion of its principles.'[12]

Lady Blomfield was eager to free herself from a number of burdens at home so that she could serve the Guardian with even greater vigour. With this in mind, she moved into a new apartment at 28 Cheyne Walk on the Chelsea Embankment of the River Thames. Her daughter Mary with her husband Basil Hall also took a flat in the same building, which was a convenience and a blessing they all appreciated. With her domestic affairs settled, Sitárih set off again for Switzerland in the summer of 1923, to Mont Pèlerin where, more than a decade before with her daughters and Beatrice Platt, she had collated their copious notes of the Master's talks in Paris. It was time for her to commit herself more fully to the work of the Save the Children Fund and to renew her acquaintance with the international community gathered around the League of Nations in Geneva.

In early August, the Fund's founder, Eglantyne Jebb, joined Sitárih at the Hôtel des Alpes where they discussed plans for the future. Jebb had been contemplating ways by which the worldwide Bahá'í community and the Save the Children Fund could work together. Sitárih had also sent Jebb's sister Dorothy Buxton a handwritten selection of quotations from the Bahá'í writings.

'Thank you ever so much for the extracts and for your great kindness in writing them out for me,' she wrote to Lady Blomfield. 'I love to have them – and all the more in your handwriting! I shall read them very often in my early morning mediation to which I always give ¾ hour.'[13]

'This society is persistently constant to its first aims, that of helping children of need – of whatever Country or Religion they may be – entirely is it free from Racial, Political or Creed prejudice,' Lady Blomfield wrote to Victoria Bedikian, an American believer who was dedicating herself to the care of orphans in her own home. 'This is, of course, what we Bahá'ís desire.'[14]

Mrs Bedikian, known internationally to the Bahá'ís as 'Auntie Victoria', corresponded with children in many countries and established 'Gardens of Fellowship' for the young, giving each garden the name of a flower. She also inspired the editing and publication of a magazine called *Children of the Kingdom*, in which were articles about the various Gardens all over the world. Lady Blomfield and Mrs Bedikian shared an interest in the establishment of a school in the Holy Land.

'Now, would it not be very suitable that a perfect model of a school should be at Haifa?' wrote Lady Blomfield.

Where teachers could be trained in Universal conceptions, and so be a linking up of the east and of the west – in sympathy, in ideals, and in methods – it would be a fitting place for our first big venture of that kind, would it not?

Of course, you know so much about the practical working of the school idea, because of your own splendid gathering together of the little ones – and your suggestions would be of inestimable value.[15]

The needs of the children of Haifa – particularly those from Baháʼí families – were also on the mind of ʻAbduʼl-Baháʼs daughter Rúḥá.

ʻI have been thinking out a plan myself to help some of the Baháʼí children to obtain just a simple education,ʼ she wrote to Lady Blomfield, ʻfor it just breaks oneʼs heart to see these children without any hope of being able to read or write a letter and I wish something could be done for them. Many of the Baháʼís here cannot afford to pay even the small fees [that] are necessary to pay and I wonder if some of the friends would give a little assistance in this matter even if it would be only a few dollars each year, we might be able to select a few of the bright deserving children and give the chance to learn enough to help them obtain a position and earn their own living.ʼ[16]

The plan to establish a school in Haifa did not materialize.

ʻWe cannot as yet see the way clear to establish the Bahai school on Mount Carmel,ʼ Rúḥá told Lady Blomfield, ʻand I thought of this plan which might give at once the chance to some children who would lose it by waiting until the school can be established, for the cost at present is too great.ʼ[17]

Sitárih personally contributed money towards the education of two Baháʼí boys, Badih Irany and his younger brother, whose family was struggling financially. She sent money for their schooling in ʻAkká and for clothing. The boysʼ mother and one of their other two siblings then became ill with malaria so the Holy Family brought the whole family to Haifa. They sent the older boy to carpentry lessons and a younger son and daughter to a school in Haifa.

ʻThe boy is doing very well at the carpentry and his brother is progressing at his new school in Haifa. The whole family is happy and grateful for your kindness to them,ʼ Rúḥá wrote to Sitárih.[18]

Lady Blomfield was also considering establishing a summer school in Switzerland the following year that would bring together teachers from all over the world to discuss ways of furthering the principle of universal education, 'for moulding the Civilization of the future,' she told Bedikian. 'If we are to be privileged to do this glorious work, the Celestial potency will guide and strengthen us!'[19]

Plans were underway to organize a meeting in Geneva in early September to put the proposal in front of some prominent thinkers on education who were already interested in the Bahá'í message.

'We expect to have Mr and Mrs Dreyfus, Professor Stanwood Cobb and Miss Eglantyne Jebb as speakers. Should there be anything ready to publish about our deliberations I will send it to you, in any case I will write something of an account of our proceeding to you. When the leaflet of our plan for the Summer School of next August is ready, I will send some to you. I wish several of the Bahai friends would attend.'[20]

Sitárih spent her days in Geneva meeting numerous officials of the League of Nations who were taking an interest in the Bahá'í message. There were additionally meetings with professors whom she considered 'Bahá'í-minded' to discuss the Cause, presentations to Theosophists and Esperantists, and a talk to an assembly of Christian Socialists. There was also, living nearby, the world-renowned psychiatrist, entomologist and social reformer August Forel, who had embraced the Bahá'í teachings two years previously at the age of 73, amending his will to read, 'I have become a Bahá'í. May this religion live and prosper for the good of mankind; this is my most ardent wish.'[21] Despite his advanced age, Forel was actively planning Bahá'í meetings with a Persian student, 'Abdu'l- Ḥusayn Iṣfahání, in Lausanne.

On Monday 20 August 1923 Sitárih joined an American believer – the progressive educationalist Stanwood Cobb, along with his wife Ida – on a visit to Dr Forel at his home known as La Fourmillière, the 'Ant's Nest', in the Swiss vine-growing area of Yvorne. Forel's wife spent the entire morning preparing food and the guests enjoyed a visit lasting the whole afternoon, joining a party of 15 for supper.

By now in her mid-60s and possibly contemplating how much time and energy she had left to her, Lady Blomfield saw her collaboration with the Save the Children Fund as something tangible that she could offer the world.

'We shall pass on to further work in the Divine Garden, but the children are the World's future, for the happiness of which we are striving,' Sitárih wrote to Victoria Bedikian from Geneva on 23 October 1923.

Miss Eglantyne Jebb, the heroic lady who began the 'Save the Children Fund', which is the greatest effort the world has ever seen, to succour and help those pitiful little sufferers of the great world war, for which grown-up people, immersed in the seas of materialism, and having transferred their worship from the Lord of Compassion to that of the Golden Calf, are responsible, joins with us in the prayer, 'May the Celestial potency so strengthen and guide us in the training of as many children as possible, that the next generation will abhor the crimes of aggression, hatred, bigotry and self-seeking, which lead to the disgrace of "brother slaying brother".'[22]

Plans for a closer collaboration between the Bahá'í community and the Save the Children Fund were put on hold while Jebb had to deal with her ailing mother and the winding up of the Fund's Russian famine relief programme. By the time the worst of the Russian famine was over, it was evident that there was still an ongoing need for Save the Children. Jebb's interests, perhaps assisted by the insights that Lady Blomfield had shared with her from 'Abdu'l-Bahá, lay in promoting a range of constructive child welfare programmes including housing and education as well as health and nutrition. Wherever possible, Jebb believed, aid should be delivered in partnership with local child welfare organizations, strengthening the existing provision to avoid creating dependency, a philosophy pursued by the Fund to this day.

The Save the Children Fund, wrote Lady Blomfield to *Star of the West*, had 'saved multitudes from starvation, Christians, Muslims and Jews, and started thousands on the path of self-support. Today it is the only hope of many children, fatherless and motherless, who wait day after day in the bitter cold to receive their daily ration.'[23] Sitárih shared with Bahá'í readers a recent appeal from the Fund's new President, the Duke of Atholl, suggesting that five dollars could feed 20 children for a week. It was clearly her hope that her fellow believers around the world would support the meritorious work that 'Abdu'l-Bahá had so praised and guided.[24]

Ever creative in dreaming up new projects to promote the teachings, Sitárih contemplated producing a book for children to teach them the major principles of the Bahá'í Faith in simple language. She discussed the subject with a professor in Geneva who was anxious to see it done and translated into Esperanto for use in schools throughout the world.

'I am longing to see its accomplishment,' wrote Lady Blomfield to Mrs

Bedikian, '– so, dear friend, send me anything you feel would be suitable to include.'[25] She also asked May Maxwell in Canada if she knew of any materials: 'It will be a wonderful thing to introduce the Bahá'í Code of Ethics into Schools, where all religious instruction is banned, because of antagonistic dogmas being taught along with the eternal truths, thereby often nullifying the true teaching by contradictions.'[26]

Efforts were also made in Geneva to establish a Bahá'í lending library to ensure literature reached the hands of the many enquirers and interested people Lady Blomfield encountered around the League of Nations. An invaluable addition to the literature that the Bahá'í community now had available was Dr Esslemont's ground-breaking work *Bahá'u'lláh and the New Era*. Shoghi Effendi told Esslemont that he thought it 'the finest presentation that has so far been given of the Cause, and I am confident that it will arouse immense interest'.[27] *Star of the West* wrote, 'It is so complete in its presentation, so condensed, so profound, so original and organized in thought, so simple in style, yet scientific in its analysis that one reads its pages in pure joy.'[28] A review in *The Times* was less enthusiastic: 'Religion is one, no doubt; yet there is variety in religious experience. No sooner do men agree than they agree to differ. Meanwhile, Mr Esslemont sets out the present state of Bahaism methodically, with ample detail and extract from the sacred writings. He is too much the convert to be critical.'[29]

Every afternoon during her stay on Mont Pèlerin, Sitárih gathered friends at the Hôtel des Alpes and read to them from the book she was compiling on the history of the Faith as related by the Holy Family. These episodes, wrote one who heard them, 'she has recorded with such vividness that as she reads them to us we seem to live in the days of the Báb, to glory and to suffer with him and his martyred friends.'[30]

Ethel Rosenberg reported to *Star of the West* that Lady Blomfield was speaking at 'various societies and meetings in favour of our beloved Cause . . . She has prepared a book giving a most interesting account of some of the early events of the Cause, as related to her by the Greatest Holy Leaf and the ladies of the household. It is hoped that it will be printed before long. The news of her successful work in Switzerland fills our hearts with joy . . .'[31]

Sitárih returned to London towards the end of 1923 and was present for the second meeting of the National Spiritual Assembly of the Bahá'ís of the British Isles. She had been in Geneva when the Assembly's first meeting took place on 13 October, during which many elements of how the institution would function were worked out and the Assembly began to ascertain how the Cause was progressing across the country.

There were also the monthly meetings of the Local Spiritual Assembly of London to attend. At its meeting on Saturday 2 February 1924, held at Lady Blomfield's Cheyne Walk apartment, the members discussed their ongoing concerns about the lack of appreciation among the believers about the importance of taking part in Bahá'í elections. Sitárih supported the suggestion that at some of the forthcoming meetings, especially the Naw-Rúz gathering, a clear explanation should be given of what a Spiritual Assembly is, its functions and the necessary qualifications of its members. Much to the pleasure of her colleagues, Lady Blomfield informed the Assembly that, before heading off on her next set of travels, she intended to visit the Manchester, Bournemouth and Brighton believers.

The following month, meeting again at Sitárih's flat, the Assembly's consultation included discussion of those whose names appeared on the voting list but who had not been seen at meetings for some years. Letters had been sent to them asking if they wished to remain on the roll. Only one woman had responded requesting that her name be removed. The question before the Assembly was whether those who had not troubled to reply should be omitted from the list. Lady Blomfield and Elizabeth Herrick both felt strongly that the names should remain and the other members voted in favour of the suggestion.

Undoubtedly, the outstanding event that was to occupy a large proportion of the National Assembly's consultation during the earliest months of its existence was a large conference, 'Living Religions within the British Empire', proposed to run concurrently with the British Empire Exhibition at Wembley. The conference was planned for the autumn of 1924 under the auspices of the University of London School of Oriental Studies and the Sociological Society. Its purpose was to promote the various faiths that then prevailed in the eastern and western dominions of the British Commonwealth. The National Assembly was pleased to find out that one of the members of the conference's organizing committee – possibly the Orientalist Sir E. Denison Ross, Professor of Persian at London University – personally knew Shoghi Effendi and hoped to see him during a forthcoming visit to Syria. The Guardian believed that the conference offered a great opportunity for a wide proclamation of the Bahá'í teachings and carefully began to select representatives from India and America to represent the

Cause at the gathering. He also generously allocated funds to the National Assembly to provide for the expenses of the Baháʼí representatives.

Critical to the impact which the Baháʼí community would make on the conference would be the high standard and accuracy of its delegation's presentation. The Guardian called upon the American national Baháʼí body to commission a comprehensive article from a special committee to be presented at the gathering. It was hoped that Shoghi Effendi himself might be able to attend the conference and present the paper. In a letter of 11 June 1924, received by George Simpson, the Guardian's secretary wrote that he had informed the conference organizers that Shoghi Effendi sincerely hoped to deliver the address in person. The National Assembly was delighted at the prospect and also decided to invite the American Baháʼí lawyer Mountfort Mills to attend. The Guardian, however, once again overburdened by his heavy workload, was forced to withdraw from the Holy Land for much needed spiritual and physical recuperation. Mills delivered the paper, which had been revised by the British National Assembly. The Guardian had authorized the Assembly to undertake corrections in case his absence made it impossible for him to make them himself. Having studied the document, the Assembly came to the conclusion that it would be desirable to elucidate more fully the practical applications of the Baháʼí teachings and to this end a short supplementary paper was prepared and presented by Shoghi Effendi's cousin Ruhi Afnan on the 'Baháʼí Influence on Life'.

On 23 September 1924, the Guardian cabled the National Assembly,

MAY WEMBLEY (*sic* CONFERENCE) FULFIL YOUR FONDEST HOPES PRAY CONVEY AUTHORITIES MY SINCERE REGRET AT INABILITY TO BE PRESENT I WISH THEM FULL SUCCESS IN THEIR NOBLE ENDEAVOURS. SHOGHI[32]

In fact, unforeseen circumstances caused the event to be moved from Wembley to the Imperial Institute in South Kensington. It took place between 22 September and 3 October.

From the moment of the conference's opening address, 'a rare spirit of friendliness and interest characterized each session', *Star of the West* reported, 'placing the individuals in the audience *en rapport* not only with each other, but with the committee and the speakers, and as the Conference wore on toward the end the audience became as a large family, freed from all formality and reserve, and lending the most cordial support and attention to the speakers.'[33]

The Baháʼí presentations, the veteran American travel teacher Nellie French wrote in *Star of the West*, were received with a 'silence at once reverent and profound, and the hearts of the friends present beat high with gladness while they yearned so deeply for the illumination of those listeners as well as for all mankind'.[34]

Mountfort Mills's presentation concluded with these words:

> None can claim that he is a follower of Baháʼuʼlláh until, in spirit, he is a follower of every Messenger who has brightened earth with the 'glad tidings' of the victory of God. None can claim that he is a follower of Baháʼuʼlláh who conceives any portion or aspect of life as non-religious, non-contributive to the eternal ascent of the soul. None can claim that he is a follower of Baháʼuʼlláh whilst secret intolerance separates him from any fellowman. Above all, none can claim that he is a follower of Baháʼuʼlláh whose heart remains barren, fearful or indifferent in this present age – the day which is witness to the overthrow of the foundations of materialism, and the kindling of human hearts with the spirit of universal knowledge and love.[35]

The conference was generally considered by those who arranged it to be a great success. The large attendance was 'most gratifying'[36] and in excess of anything they had been led to expect, especially taking into account that not a penny had been spent on advertising. The gathering also attracted the attention of Prime Minister Ramsay MacDonald, who said in a message,

> Many religions and many creeds live in amity within our Empire, each by their own different way leading our peoples onwards towards some ultimate light. I welcome cordially the objects of the Conference and the knowledge which it spreads amongst us that our peoples, in the aspirations of the Spirit, 'walk not back to back but with an unity in track'.[37]

The Baháʼí community's influence was mainly felt away from the conference platform. A comprehensive selection of literature was displayed at a bookstall and a new catalogue of Baháʼí publications, funded by Mr Asgharzádih, was compiled for delegates. Lady Blomfield made a unique contribution to the proceedings by hosting a well-attended reception for delegates to the conference at Claridges Hotel, for which she was warmly thanked. Shoghi Effendi wrote that her idea of a reception was 'undoubtedly inspired and was admirably executed. It has indeed rejoiced my heart. My love and my gratitude for her wise, patient and fruitful efforts.'[38]

Lady Blomfield noted how many of those attending received the Bahá'í message with joy.

'This seems to have been blessed by confirmations,' she wrote to one Bahá'í friend,[39] and reported later, 'It was wonderful to see such a representative Assembly – Buddhists, Moslems, Parsees, Brahma Somaj – a few Christians and our Bahá'í friends. The photograph of this party is a human document of great interest.'[40] The picture of the reception shows Sitárih sitting stage centre, amidst a wide variety of creeds and nationalities, the guests resplendent in a dazzling range of exotic robes and headdresses.

Another significant outcome of the conference was the introduction of the Bahá'í Faith to a young British environmentalist named Richard St Barbe Baker. He had been serving as Assistant Conservator of Forests in Kenya since 1920 and delivered a paper at the conference on the African tribal religious beliefs that he had encountered. At the conclusion of his talk Claudia Coles rushed up to him and said, 'You are a Bahá'í.' Many of the believers gathered around him to thank him for his presentation, and a few days later Claudia presented him with his first Bahá'í literature. Subsequently, St Barbe – as he liked to be known – founded the internationally renowned organization 'Men of the Trees', now known as the International Tree Foundation, with Shoghi Effendi as its first life member. While St Barbe did not formally enrol as a Bahá'í until 1935, he frequently acknowledged the influence of the teachings on his life and work in the period immediately following the conference in London.

For Lady Blomfield, many seeds were planted during the 'Living Religions' Conference that would occupy her mind in the years immediately ahead. During it, a member of the Religion and Ethics Committee of the League of Nations Union asked for her cooperation. The Committee had been inaugurated with some 30 members five years previously under the chairmanship of the Bishop of Kensington. They were finding, however, that their best efforts were either being persistently obstructed or ignored by the rest of the Union, whose interests were mainly political and economic and who did not like religion.

'It says much for the faith of this Committee, that it held on and did not give up in despair,' commented Sitárih.[41]

With this representative Lady Blomfield worked out new aims and objectives for the committee: 'To enrol the spiritual forces of the World on the side of Justice, Truth and Peace, by entering into the fullest Co-operation with all men and women of Goodwill . . . and the spirit of God (or Good) within us.' The formulation was eventually incorporated, with considerable effort, into the official papers of the committee.

To interest as many people as possible in the proposal 'to bring true religion into politics, not politics into religion', Sitárih arranged two meetings, the first on 19 March 1925.[42] Two months later, on 5 May, a larger and even more representative gathering was held which she described as 'wonderful'.[43] The Bishop of Kensington, John Primatt Maud, 'spoke marvellously. Every word might have been the Master's! And this from a Bishop of our Church!!! He is really a true "Waiting Servant".'[44] Others, including Eglantyne Jebb and representatives of the Muslim, Hindu and Parsee communities, were also present, 'all agreeing in the Universal Spiritual aim!' enthused Lady Blomfield. 'All in the Spirit of the Master – I am sure He was present – though not as yet knowing the Source of the Inspiration.'[45]

Soon afterwards the National Spiritual Assembly of the Bahá'ís received an invitation to become a Corporate Member of the League of Nations Union. A Mr Wren from the Union attended the National Spiritual Assembly meeting on 4 July to explain the workings of the Committee. In the ensuing discussion, while all the Assembly members were in favour of individuals joining the Union, it was felt that there was a risk of the Assembly becoming involved in political matters if it were to join as a corporate body. Mr Wren reassured the Assembly on this point and there was a unanimous vote to join the Union under the auspices of the Religious and Ethics Committee, provided that by so doing it was understood that the Assembly would take no part in any political measures or activities.

The following months were filled for Sitárih with numerous activities in London. There were the consultations of the Local Spiritual Assembly to attend, the meetings of the National Spiritual Assembly, public meetings to support, community activities to take part in, and numerous presentations to give. On 21 January 1925 she was invited by the Eastern and Western Culture Society to give an address on her favourite subject, 'The World Teacher Abdu'l-Baha'. 'Her characteristic fervour aroused keen interest, denoted by the intelligent questions and interesting general discussion which followed her address,' reported the *Bahá'í News Letter*.[46]

Sitárih also received an invitation to make a visit to the Green Acre

Bahá'í School in Eliot, Maine, USA, established in 1894 as a residential school for the study of art, philosophy and religion. After 1900, when its founder Sarah Farmer became, probably, the 'first American Bahá'í to come from the upper class and liberal religious environment of New England',[47] Green Acre's programmes had become increasingly Bahá'í-oriented, presenting the community with a credible forum to present the teachings to America's East coast elite.

'I hoped that conditions of various kinds would so shape themselves that the visit to Greenacre would become a practical possibility,' Lady Blomfield wrote to 'Abdu'l-Bahá's devoted follower May Maxwell, in Montreal. 'Alas! This is not so . . .'[48]

A further invitation to visit the Maxwells also had to be declined. Lady Blomfield conveyed to May Maxwell 'more thanks than a pen is able to convey for your sweet kindness to me, in inviting me to your home, where I should meet so many fellow-citizens of the City of Baha: of course we all meet spiritually in the fragrance of that Garden! . . .'[49]

'Also various obligations at Geneva seem to be calling insistently!' she continued. 'This work is in connection with the very First (in all the World) International Congress of the interests of Children – in August. It is being held under the auspices of the 'Save the Children Fund' which has already achieved so marvellous a success in gathering the 'Declaration of Geneva' endorsed by the League of Nations – thus becoming the "Children's Charter".'[50]

Seven hundred delegates would attend the Congress in Geneva, including representatives of 38 governments and 54 nations. As discussions unfolded, Eglantyne Jebb felt confirmed in her belief that the Congress highlighted the need to universalize the values of Save the Children even further. Her declaration would later evolve into the United Nations Convention on the Rights of the Child, ratified by all but two of the world's nations, making it the most universally accepted human rights instrument in history.

Lady Blomfield had sometimes felt very alone in her work in Geneva and was pleased to learn that the Guardian was keen to establish a Bahá'í office in the city.

'Ever since I first gave the Message there in 1912, in 1914 and in 1920-21-22-23,' she wrote, 'I have been praying that some Bahá'ís would come to my help there.'[51]

In February of 1925 an American Bahá'í, Mrs Jean Stannard, had visited

Shoghi Effendi in Haifa, seeking guidance on where she should move, having spent some years living in the East. She suggested to the Guardian that Lausanne might be a receptive place to promote the teachings. He responded, however, that the most important place to serve was Geneva. By June, Mrs Stannard was in Switzerland, establishing an International Baháʾí Bureau to represent all national centres of the Baháʾí community. She rented a suite of rooms including a large communal area that could seat 60, with doors opening into her office that could accommodate another 40. She also was able to gain admission into a federation of international associations led by the Secretary of the Quakers group in Geneva. Shoghi Effendi was extremely pleased with Jean Stannard's efforts and constantly wrote letters of encouragement, urging her to firmly establish the Bureau and enlarge the scope of its work.[52]

Around the time of Mrs Stannard's arrival, the American journalist and renowned Baháʾí teacher Martha Root also moved to Geneva to assist with the work and to seek contact with Esperantists, as did another American, Katherine Nourse, with her two children. Martha sub-rented another office on the other side of the hall to give the Bureau a small income and also to provide her with a room where she could write and receive her own contacts. For two consecutive years she encouraged delegates from the Esperanto Congresses to come to the Bureau Rooms where they learned about the enthusiasm the Baháʾís had for learning their language. Among those who attended such meetings was Lidia Zamenhof, the daughter of Esperanto's founder, who became interested and later a believer in the Baháʾí Cause.

Shoghi Effendi's cousin Ruhi Afnan wrote a long letter to Sitárih on 24 October 1925 enthusing that 'Geneva seems to have been a very interesting place this year, with the League present and the activities of the friends so hopeful and far reaching.'

> Shoghi Effendi attaches much importance to the centre that is being formed there. The League has made it a rallying point of many idealists and broadminded thinkers. The Baháʾís, therefore, can do much work there in drawing the attention of these people to the importance of the Cause and its Teachings . . .[53]

Through Ruhi Afnan, the Guardian conveyed some highly important guidance to Lady Blomfield to assist her in her efforts in Geneva.

'I spoke to Shoghi Effendi about your activities,' wrote Afnan.

He said 'write her that all these are excellent, but what I specially want is some few more ladies of her type, real Baháʼis whose words and deeds symbolize the spirit and teachings of the Cause'. It is undoubtedly very helpful that we should associate ourselves with these progressive and humanitarian institutions, for by helping them forward we prepare the ground and make the people ready for the acceptance of the Teachings, but we should keep in mind that in preparing the ground our real aim is to sow some seeds and obtain some fruits. To keep exclusive and work only among the friends will surely not take us far. Before long we would see ourselves in a groove, sectarian and ignorant of what is going on in the world outside. Our spirit will die and the Cause will not take a great step forward. By mixing with the people and helping them in their organizations we will appreciate increasingly the importance of the Movement, broaden our views, come to know more progressive persons and work among them. But we should take all these as the means of teaching the Cause.

The Cause has, however, many admirers and its spirit is rather widely spread. What we really need is an increase in the number of those confirmed believers who will share in the responsibilities of the Cause. If London had a few more ladies like you their work would not have been so hampered by your absence. They could spare you and carry the burden themselves.

In short Shoghi Effendi's point is that while undertaking such humanitarian activities you should bear in mind that the real aim is not necessarily that that movement should progress, but that through it the land will be tilled and prepared for the progress of the Cause, that you will that way come in contact with broad-minded people who would accept the Cause and enter the Baháʼi fold. I personally hope that you have obtained some hearing from those semi idealistic politicians and succeeded in teaching them that the aims of the League will not be fully and easily realized without bringing some religious and spiritual force to back it up. Religion is a great power in moulding the actions of man. If properly directed it can become the greatest social bond and perform miracles in stabilizing this troubled world.[54]

Illness laid Lady Blomfield low at the end of July 1925 and she retreated to the southern coastal resort of Hove, close to Brighton, to recover in the sea air.

'Oh I do wish I were going to travel with you,' she wrote to Ella Cooper, named by Shoghi Effendi a Disciple of 'Abdu'l-Bahá, who was passing through London on her way to Geneva, 'but I fear I may not be well enough to travel for at least 10 days or a fortnight as I am trying to recover from an attack of bronchitis made worse by neglecting a cold, and overfatigue. However I am beginning at least to "pick up". Yesterday I went out for a short walk.'[55]

Finally arriving in Geneva, Lady Blomfield discovered that the International Bahá'í Bureau was operating almost entirely in French. She also, perhaps mistakenly, felt that maybe she was not wanted there, or that somehow the Bureau was set up to supersede her own efforts in the city. Shoghi Effendi reassured her in an urgent cable sent from his own retreat in Switzerland:

DEAR LADEE'S PIONEER WORK IN GENEVA GRAVEN UPON MY HEART. DEPLORE MISUNDERSTANDING. SINCERELY TRUSTING IN YOUR SUS-TAINED HIGHLY VALUED COLLABORATION.[56]

In a later, more detailed letter to her, the Guardian wrote,

I specially request you dear Sitárih Khánum to lend your invaluable support to the Bureau which has been established in Geneva and the firm foundations of which you have so diligently laid in the past . . . I would particularly urge you to utilize it as often as you can as an instrument for a direct reference to the Cause and Bahá'u'lláh.[57]

Sitárih did, as a result of this, visit the Bureau from time to time 'to show unity and to greet the friends'[58] and was invited by them to give talks along with Martha Root and Mrs Stannard.

'The Bahá'í community, though working valiantly,' wrote Lady Blomfield's daughter, Mary, 'were not making much headway . . . but they were present at the Centre when anyone wished to enquire about the Cause.'

'The problem my mother had to face was this,' wrote Mary. 'How could the attention of people working in the League be attracted? How could those who were not already interested be brought in? How could the influence of the Cause be widened in the city where it was so much needed? Divine guidance showed my mother the way . . .'[59]

A plan was hatching in Lady Blomfield's ever-creative mind to further build bonds of unity between the followers of different religions and indirectly bring the spirit of Bahá'u'lláh's revelation to people's lives – 'absolutely Bahäi work,' she told May Maxwell, 'though all who join will not at first accept a label, which they will only gradually comprehend'.[60]

Sitárih's initial idea was to

> . . . organize a League (of Religions), under the name of a Union of Righteousness. To be founded on the principles of Right, as agreed by all Religions; differences of doctrines, Creeds and beliefs to be entirely and absolutely excluded; it is to acknowledge and teach the fundamental principles of Righteousness and Brotherhood and Peace to all the Nations and Peoples who join . . .
>
> This would be an immense Spiritual Force of Support for the League of Nations: it would welcome and gather the spirit of God (good) from all religious peoples and bring to Humanity a wider and more exalted understanding of God.[61]

Sitárih planned to ask as many as possible of the most influential whether they would help and support a 'World-wide Movement in this Union of Righteousness, as a spiritual and permanent support for the League of Nations'.[62]

'My mother feared the League's failure because it had not been built upon a spiritual foundation,' wrote Mary Basil Hall.

> It was her intention to promote a spiritual impetus for world peace by presenting Bahá'í principles in a way which would command attention without alienating sympathy by too obvious propaganda for what would be considered by the uninitiated, a new religion. Any kind of religious discussion or practice was banned officially in connection with the work of the League, for reasons which can be well understood. National differences were hard enough to overcome, but if religious controversy had been added, confusion would have become worse confounded. My mother understood this well, but the fact remained that God was shut out of the Council and Assembly more definitely than in the British Houses of Parliament, where at least the members began their sessions with a prayer.[63]

Lady Blomfield informed Shoghi Effendi through his cousin Ruhi Afnan of her plan and received word back that he approved and encouraged the idea. She drafted a pamphlet and sent the wording to the Guardian for his approval.

'Many whom I have met in London and Geneva have promised their cooperation,' she told Shoghi Effendi. 'As I talk with these people, and explain the plan, often they understand the Bahá'í Message, and I find this a wonderful opportunity for spreading the Cause – beside that this work is, in itself, a true Bahá'í effort, with its broad Horizon.'[64]

Sitárih later wondered about calling the organization 'Servants of the Most Great Peace'.

'I do feel that is a great missionary plan unhampered by a 'Label' – which at first, frightens people off . . .' she wrote.[65]

Shoghi Effendi preferred the word 'promoter' instead of servant and sent guidance to her through his secretary on how the movement should progress:

> He approves fully the programme you set out in the leaflet and hopes that you will advance the cause of peace that way. The spirit underlying it is surely Bahá'í and therefore is bound to obtain cordial reception from many open-minded seekers. It is just as you say, there are some persons who are ready to accept social teachings and work for them if they do not bear a special religious stamp, nor have the taint of some creed. This movement of yours, therefore, serves the purpose admirably and can appeal to such tastes.[66]

There was one point, however, which Shoghi Effendi particularly wanted Sitárih to bear in mind,

> . . . namely that all these are means followed in the pursuit of another still nobler aim, which is the progress of the Cause. Such movements help the cause of peace, but real peace cannot be established until and unless the whole Bahá'í programme is adopted. While working for this new movement, therefore, you should remember that the real aim in view is to teach them the Cause and make them active supporters of the only lasting movement . . .[67]

'My dearest Ladee!' wrote Shoghi Effendi, in a postscript in his own handwriting.

It was a real joy, the more so because it was unexpected, to receive a letter direct from you. If I have not been corresponding with you of late it has been not because of indifference and forgetfulness on my part, but simply due to the fact that I am assured that you are continually, devotedly and effectively engaged in spreading the Cause no matter how often you receive messages of encouragement from Haifa or else-where . . .[68]

Touchingly, the Guardian – who usually ended his letters to the western Bahá'ís with 'Your true brother, Shoghi' signs off this postscript, 'I pray that you may be successful and achieve your heart's desire. Your loving son, Shoghi.'[69]

Eventually, Sitárih decided to call her movement, simply, 'For the World's Supreme Peace'. Her introductory leaflet, published in both English and French and headed THE CALL FOR THE WORLD'S SUPREME PEACE, read:

Convinced that Universal Peace will be achieved only when Mankind has discarded Prejudice, racial, patriotic and religious, in recognizing the Essential Brotherhood of the Human Race – certain servants of Humanity, desiring to translate the Ideal of Concord into Action, have initiated a Movement, with the object of drawing into co-operation all Religious Bodies, Learned Societies, Ethical Groups, and Philanthropic Organizations, both of the Eastern and Western Peoples.

In this Movement, questions of diverse creeds and doctrines, involving intolerance and discord, will be entirely excluded, so that the Spirit of Inter-Religious and Inter-Racial respect and friendship may be promoted.

It is intended that Conferences shall be called, from time to time, to further the purpose and extend the influence of the Movement, until a Universal Congress shall be possible, which will truly represent the Religious, Moral and Spiritual life of all men and women of Goodwill on Earth.

Realizing that the only Power which is able to quicken and unite the Spiritual energies of Mankind is the

ONE CREATIVE SPIRIT at the CORE OF ALL RELIGIONS,

the initiators of this Movement feel the urgent Necessity of drawing

INVINCIBLE STRENGTH from that LIFE-GIVING SOURCE,
for the upholding and sustaining of the
Highest Ideals that inspire the League of Nations

This Movement, therefore, by gathering into conscious Unity of Action the Essence of the best and noblest soul-life of Man, could supply to Arbitration and Conciliation that Dynamic Power, which would support the CAUSE OF WORLD PEACE until it becomes a Recognized Aim of the World's Religions and its Governments.

When at length welcomed and brought into practical activity, the POWER of the INFINITE SPIRIT of ONENESS, pervading the Universe, will become available for the Good of the Whole World.

On the reverse side of the leaflet, was written:

Those who receive this leaflet are asked for no material benefits, such as donations etc, but only that they should:

Read the words with close attention,
Give to them their earnest consideration,
Meditate upon them,

And, if they then feel with us that
PEACE between the RELIGIONS of the WORLD is as desirable as PEACE between its NATIONS, and that the Latter in great measure depends on the Former,

Then, to these men and women of Goodwill (in every Race and Kindred) an APPEAL is made that they, recognizing their Spiritual Responsibility, will concentrate the whole Force of their Influence, the Power of their Constructive Thought, and of their Spoken Word, in furtherance of the Practical expression of the Spirit of the Movement, described in the leaflet.

A detachable slip was printed at the bottom of the page with the instruction that it be sent to Lady Blomfield, the Hon. Secretary 'For the World's Supreme Peace'.

The slip read, 'The Ideals expressed in the leaflet, "For the World's Supreme Peace", have my (our) entire sympathy.' There followed a space for names and addresses to be added.'[70]

Lady Blomfield's movement seemed to generate quite a considerable following.

'Under its auspices she gathered together weekly at her hotel, as many as a hundred people at a time,' wrote Mary, 'to hear speakers of high intention and thought from all over the world. Pioneers of non-sectarian philanthropic movements would explain their work. These meetings were attended by people of many races and creeds. The subject of each address would illustrate one principle of the Bahá'í teaching, which my mother would explain from the chair. Occasionally a meeting would be addressed by a Bahá'í teacher of international repute.'[71]

The United Kingdom Bahá'í Archive holds a case stuffed full of returned forms, filled out by those who wished to support the ideals of the leaflet. Among them is one signed by Shoghi Effendi himself. During a return visit to London, Sitárih and Mrs Thornburgh-Cropper organized two gatherings at Caxton Hall, on 7 and 14 October 1926, to promote the movement 'For the World's Supreme Peace'.

In the early days of the Guardianship, Shoghi Effendi had informed the Bahá'ís of Great Britain that it would not be possible for him, in view of his 'manifold and pressing duties, and owing to the extraordinary extension of the Movement in recent times, to correspond with the friends individually and express to them in writing what I always feel in the depth of my heart of brotherly affection and abiding gratitude for their love and sympathy for me'.[72] Despite the relative sparseness of personal communication with the Guardian, compared to that which she had known with the Master, Lady Blomfield conscientiously strove to follow his guidance and, on a personal level, cherished an abiding motherly love for him. The outstanding British believer David Hofman who knew Sitárih in the 1930s recounted that each time Shoghi Effendi was mentioned, she would say affectionately in her deep, lilting Irish accent, 'Ah, the dear boy.'[73]

Sitárih was saddened to learn that Shoghi Effendi's burden had increased further in April 1926 when news reached him of the brutal murder of a number of Bahá'ís in Jahrum in the south of Persia. The instigator of the persecution was Ismá'íl Khán, a chief of the Qashqá'i tribe.

'Once again the woeful tale of unabated persecution . . . has reached our ears, and filled us with a gloom which all the joys and ennobling memories of Riḍván have failed to dispel,' wrote Shoghi Effendi on 22 April 1926.[74]

In other parts of Persia, the Baháʼís were being denied their basic civic rights, including the use of the public baths and essential services. All association and dealing with them was denounced as a violation of the precepts and principles of Islam. The news of such developments came as a great shock to the Guardian.

'Just imagine dear Lady,' wrote Rúḥá to Sitárih, 'the condition of Shoghi Effendi after this dreadful news. One's heart really breaks to see such a young man with such a big responsibility upon his shoulders with so few really sincere and self-sacrificing helpers.'[75]

Sitárih valued her friendships with the members of the Holy Family and often yearned to return to Haifa. She contemplated paying a visit during 1926 but felt that the other demands on her time in Geneva and London should take precedence.

'We regret you could not come this year to visit us,' wrote Rúḥá, 'but as you say our personal desires must be sacrificed for the one supreme desire of our hearts that is to spread this great Message amongst the people of the world which will be the means of bringing the most great Peace.'[76]

'. . . I hope next autumn you will be able to come and give us the pleasure of meeting you again,' wrote Rúḥá. 'My aunt the Greatest Holy Leaf and mother wish very much to meet you before they pass away from this world, because they both think their end is very near.'[77]

Shoghi Effendi had asked Rúḥá to be a member of a social service and infant welfare committee in Haifa, wishing to demonstrate the willingness of the Baháʼí community to cooperate with other denominations. The committee started a welfare centre for infants and Rúḥá was seeking suggestions and assistance, as she herself felt very inexperienced in such matters. Rúḥá's nephew Ruhí had met Eglantyne Jebb and had written to her, as did the wife of the Governor of Haifa.

'I wonder if she received the letters,' Rúḥá wrote to Lady Blomfield. 'Could you do anything in the matter for me by getting her interested in our work. We are all new in this work and would be glad to have help and cooperation from one who is experienced in these matters.'[78]

Rúḥá's daughter Maryam was staying in London when she began to suffer pains in the back of her head, which was disrupting her ability to study.

'Last night I received a letter from Mehrangiz [Shoghi Effendi's sister] saying that Maryam is not well and is getting very thin . . .' Rúḥá told

Sitárih. 'I am really sorry Lady to give you all these troubles. But what else can I do. Surely you will do the best for Maryam as you are just as a mother to her. I really need not to be worried about her.'[79]

Another member of Shoghi Effendi's family, his cousin Suhayl, sought Lady Blomfield's help when he called upon her to assist him in applying for a place at Balliol College, Oxford where the Guardian had himself studied. Suhayl arrived in England but despite Sitárih's best efforts, his desire to study at Balliol did not come to pass and he gave up on the idea.

'My decision, which I will probably stick to, does not deny in any way my deep and lasting appreciation for all your help and kindnesses,' he told Sitárih, 'a motherly affection that I shall cherish throughout my years. Indeed in spite of my disappointment I feel gratified to think that all during my stay in England I received such undeserved kindness and consideration on your part.'[80]

'To call myself your son is much too ambitious,' Suhayl wrote on another occasion, 'but you have certainly been a very kind mother to me.'[81]

'I realize what a beautiful work you are doing,' Rúhá wrote in May 1926, 'and hope that you may be able to convince these souls with whom you come in contact of the great Revelation for this day which will be the means of uniting all religions and creeds and of dispelling racial prejudice and establish universal peace and brotherhood throughout the world.'[82]

The arrival of Martha Root in Britain early in June 1926 began a five-month period of intense activity. The indefatigable teacher travelled the country extensively, giving talks and lectures, meeting the Bahá'ís, generating press interest in a further outbreak of the persecution of the believers in Persia, and organizing the Bahá'í contributions at the eight-day, 18th Universal Esperanto Congress in Edinburgh, held between 31 July and 7 August 1926.

Sitárih accompanied Martha to the Scottish capital and delighted in the great gathering of every religious, political and humanitarian movement represented there.

'What could be more thrilling of a liberal education than to come to Edinburgh to this Universal Esperanto Congress!' wrote Martha,

> The very trip itself was extraordinary. As Esperantists journeyed through various lands en route, they were met at railway stations and ship docks by friends in 'Esperantujo' (the Land of Esperanto). Each one felt himself at home and one family for his brothers and sisters

speaking his dear language showed him the best of the sights in their city, and they showed him love.[83]

The Bahá'ís were granted two sessions at the congress, both held in the Free Church of Scotland where the Master had spoken in 1913. At the first, Martha spoke and answered questions on 'The Positive Power of Universal Religion' in which she clearly set forth the Bahá'í teachings. Then Friedrich Gerstner from Hamburg, editor of the Bahá'í Esperanto magazine *La Nova Tago*, gave a short slide presentation about Haifa and 'Akká and the progress of the Bahá'í Cause in different lands. For the second programme, Martha chaired a talk given by Professor Ernest A. Rogers from California. A nine year old girl, Molly Brown, who would as an adult marry the Hand of the Cause of God Hasan M. Balyuzi, recited words of Bahá'u'lláh.

Lady Blomfield ably assisted Martha with the organization of the gatherings and personally took special pleasure in arranging the flowers for the meetings.

'The decorations were unique,' wrote Martha, 'and so artistic they will be long remembered by all the Congressists.'[84]

Dr Forel sent a cable from Switzerland which read, 'Long live the universal religion of Bahá'u'lláh! Long live the universal auxiliary language, Esperanto!'[85]

After Edinburgh, Martha took off again on a teaching tour, including an invitation to take the Sunday morning service at the Spiritualist church in London where Sir Arthur Conan Doyle, creator of Sherlock Holmes, was president. George Townshend from Ireland, along with Mountfort Mills – as well as Sitárih's devoted friend Hippolyte Dreyfus-Barney – joined Martha on one visit to Professor R. A. Nicholson, who had taken over the post of Professor of Oriental Languages at Cambridge University after Edward G. Browne's death. A talk was also arranged, most probably by Lady Blomfield, for Martha, joined by Laura Dreyfus-Barney, at the Religious and Ethics Committee of the League of Nations. Sitárih then joined Martha for a weekend in Manchester, where this unparalleled promoter of the Bahá'í teachings had been actively teaching for eight days. They held a meeting in the Victoria Hotel, Martha addressed two hundred boys and girls at a Unitarian Sunday school and both spoke in the Reverend H. H. Biggs's Unitarian Church in Altrincham. After the service more than a hundred people remained for nearly two hours to ask questions. (The following year Reverend Biggs was elected to the National Spiritual

Assembly of the Bahá'ís of the British Isles, prompting Shoghi Effendi to question 'his unreserved acceptance of the Faith in its entirety'.[86]) A young girl, Pauline Freitag, later Senior – who had recently joined the Bahá'í Faith in Manchester and who met both Martha and Lady Blomfield on their journey to the city – recalled some seven decades later that their American visitor was 'right bossy' and that Sitárih 'always wore big hats'.[87]

Wishing to give Martha a gift that would be of use to her on her travels, Lady Blomfield presented her with a leather suitcase containing an entire portable kitchen set up to enable her to prepare her own food. Martha continued to use the case for at least the next decade.

Sir Arthur Conan Doyle encountered the Bahá'í Faith again the following year when on 3 October three organizations that promoted interreligious understanding – the Fellowship of Faiths, the Union of East and West, and the League of Neighbours – hosted an 'Appreciation of Christianity' at the City Temple, where 'Abdu'l-Bahá had given His first ever public address 16 years earlier. The meeting featured 'Ten Minute Addresses by Eminent Speakers' on what Christianity means to their various traditions: Sir Arthur Conan Doyle spoke on the spiritualist approach to Christianity, Annie Besant presented the Theosophist perspective, and appreciative words by 'Abdu'l-Bahá about Jesus Christ were read by the celebrated actress Sybil Thorndike, who was a committed pacifist and had some connections with prominent Theosophists.

Early in 1927 the relationship between Christianity and the Bahá'í teachings also came to the fore in a substantial article penned by Lady Blomfield for *Star of the West*, now increasingly being referred to as *The Bahá'í Magazine*. The article provides an insight into how Sitárih saw the Bahá'í Faith in relation to the religion of Christ, whom she continued to revere.

'The Bahá'í Teaching has the universality of the Lord Christ's commands,' she wrote.

> Bahá'u'lláh did not counsel us, any of us, to change our religion, but to obey the Law of God found at the core of each religion, in order that our religion might change us; a very different proposition!
>
> No person touched by the spirit of Christianity can fail, after due consideration, to recognize that the Bahá'í revelation is truly the perfection of Christianity.
>
> For to be a real Christian in Spirit and in Truth is to be a Bahá'í – a follower of the Light – and to be a true Bahá'í is to be a Christian: for

he puts into practice the laws of Christianity, translating the beautiful words into action.

The precepts of Bahá'u'lláh make the same appeal to the institution as Christianity makes to the individual: forasmuch as a Golden Brotherhood cannot be formed out of leaden individuals – the work perforce had to begin with individuals. We cannot have a brotherhood without brothers.[88]

As the 1920s progressed towards their conclusion, the London Spiritual Assembly and the National Spiritual Assembly of the Bahá'ís of the British Isles struggled to move forward in their efforts to establish the Faith's administrative roots and formalize its activities, guided and assisted by its three most experienced members – Lady Blomfield, Ethel Rosenberg and Mary Virginia Thornburgh-Cropper, all of whom had learned lessons at the Master's own table. On 28 November 1926 the London Assembly addressed a letter to the believers commemorating the fifth anniversary of the Master's passing, which concludes:

With Bahá'í love, renewed faith, and deeper reverence may we attain to severance from all save God, then, free from the subtle serpent of the mind, the ego, we shall be of those who move forward to service free from self-deception, because we are severed from all save God. That which we seek in truth, we shall sow in truth. 'God causes things to grow.' 'Abdu'l-Bahá is the witness of this!'[89]

During her visits back to London, Lady Blomfield continued to make contacts and spread the word about the Bahá'í Cause and her movement 'For the World's Supreme Peace'. In addition, she happily hosted meetings in her home, including the Naw-Rúz feast on 21 March 1927. On 7 May the newly-elected London Spiritual Assembly met at the home of Mrs Thornburgh Cropper at 37 Evelyn Mansions, Carlisle Place. Lady Blomfield was joined by Claudia Coles, Mother George, Elizabeth Herrick, George Simpson, Isobel Slade and Mrs Thornburgh-Cropper. Only Ethel Rosenberg and Mr Asgharzádih were absent, the former being in Haifa assisting Shoghi Effendi with some secretarial duties. Lady Blomfield and Ethel Rosenberg were jointly elected vice chair of the London Assembly.

Despite their best efforts, however, the Bahá'ís throughout the British Isles were struggling to find ways to attract enough people to join their community. Even Shoghi Effendi, in a letter written on his behalf, commented, 'It is strange that the English Bahá'ís have really contributed a great deal to the Cause, and in the form of books and publications given us works of real and permanent value – perhaps proportionately more than America, and yet it is such a Herculean affair to bring in new fellow-workers. Perhaps just that difficulty is a sign of their merit – staunch and unflinching adherence once they believe in something.'[90]

Despite the apparent difficulty of confirming people in the Bahá'í Faith, for Lady Blomfield finding and befriending souls who were attuned to the spirit of the age and who were eager to hear about the message never seemed to present problems. In February 1927, for example, she had met Edgar Homan, who was Secretary of the Christian Mystical Lodge of the Theosophical Society and with whom she shared a mutual acquaintance in the Sufi leader Inayat Khan, who had recently passed away. The aim of the Lodge was to 'interpret Christianity in terms of Theosophy and Theosophy in terms of Christianity'. Lady Blomfield presented Homan with a copy of *Paris Talks* for the Lodge's library of esoteric, mystical and psychology books. He, in turn, was intrigued by their conversation about the Bahá'í teachings and invited her to come and speak to his society which was based at 3 Queensborough Terrace, just north of Kensington Gardens. On 25 April Sitárih gave a public lecture at 5:30 in the evening on the Bahá'í Movement. Other talks in the season covered such themes as 'Sane occultism', 'The different layers of consciousness' and 'The psychology of ritual'. At the end of 1927 she received an invitation to recommend a Persian in England or France to attend an International Congress of Social Service in Paris the following year. She wrote to Haifa seeking the Guardian's advice and enclosing two brochures about her movement.

Similarly, in Geneva an international community was growing which was more than willing to support and converse about Lady Blomfield's long-cherished ideals. During her sojourns in the city she continued to organize afternoon meetings every Monday at the Hôtel Beau-Séjour to which she invited those who had signed their forms as well as people from the League of Nations's international circles. Often Sitárih asked well-known personalities from the peace and social welfare movements to speak at the meetings, as a means of attracting an audience and then, as refreshments were offered, she as the chair of the gathering would indirectly bring up some of the teachings and generate questions and answers. In these meetings, wrote her daughter Mary, Lady Blomfield 'attempted to inculcate the principles of the Bahá'í Faith in a way which showed her discrimination and wisdom perhaps more markedly than in any other work she had done for the Cause'.[91]

'"Who is this Persian Prophet you quote so much?" individuals would ask, in the quiet conversations my mother had with them after the meetings,' wrote Mary. 'She would tell them, and thus, the seed was sown.'[92]

Every person who attended one of Lady Blomfield's meetings would write his or her name and address in a book which Sitárih kept for further contact. She would spend hours writing to them about the teachings of Bahá'u'lláh and answering the questions which came in return.

At one meeting, on 6 August 1928, a Dutch zoologist, Professor Bernelot-Moens, spoke on the oneness of humanity from an anthropological perspective. The following week Lady Blomfield addressed the audience about the need to transmute the burning fires of religion and race into the calm light of appreciating friendship. Sir Deva Prasad Sawadhikari talked on one occasion about the 'Cultural and Social Life of India'. At yet another, Dr P. Natarajan, a disciple of the Hindu sage and social reformer Sri Narayana Guru, shared news of his movement's work with orphans and children in Kerala.

On 27 August 1928 Lady Blomfield's gathering coincided with the signing of the Kellogg-Briand pact, a multinational treaty that prohibited the use of war as 'an instrument of national policy' except in matters of self-defence. The meeting's chairman, the Dutch consul Van Notten, called for a two minute silence to give gratitude to God that so many nations had officially outlawed war. The gathering was made up of many races – American, British, Chinese, German, French, Canadian, Spanish, Mexican, Hungarian, Russian, Italian, Mongolian, Tibetan, Ethiopian, Dutch, Swiss – and all reverently observed the silence.

The meetings of 'For the World's Supreme Peace' had continued throughout the summer of 1928 with a wide variety of interesting talks and presentations and Lady Blomfield cementing her friendships with many prominent personalities. Among them was her Irish compatriot Margaret Cousins, a keen advocate for women's suffrage who had been imprisoned in Holloway for her activities. In 1913 Cousins had emigrated to India with her husband and become the country's first woman magistrate. She spoke of her work with Indian women.

The Swedish Countess Louise Lind-af-Hageby, a pioneering animal rights campaigner, spiritualist and women's activist, was another close friend of Lady Blomfield. Sitárih had known her for many decades when one of her old 'companions of the mind', Alfred P. Sinnett, had introduced the Countess to her as a 'Divine Being', a spiritual descendant of St Francis of Assisi. The Countess, with her friend the Duchess of Hamilton, were also working ardently in Geneva, and Lady Blomfield did all she could to help them.

Lady Blomfield also developed an enduring friendship with Gertrude Eaton, who fearlessly worked for the amelioration of the lot of the world's prisoners. Eaton had travelled throughout Europe visiting prisons and exposing to the League of Nations and to the wider world the abuses of those systems. She was happy to speak at her friend's meetings. Madame Eugénie Simon, the President of the 'Ligue de Bonté', spoke in French of the work of her organization in the training of the coming generation.

At each and every meeting Lady Blomfield promoted the ideals that were closest to her heart. One person whom Lady Blomfield met wrote to her after their encounter, 'I believe you are working along right lines: for if the world is ever to escape from the nightmare and horrors of war it must be through the unity of organized religions.'[93]

Despite the great opportunities that Geneva presented, the Bahá'í Bureau was struggling to continue its activities. In October 1927 Lady Blomfield joined a meeting of eight others to consult on the work of the Bureau and whether the resources were available to sustain it. After discussing the situation, the group wrote a letter to the Guardian – who was keen to see the Bureau's work progress – proposing some ideas and asking his advice. In response, he offered a monthly sum of £6, half of which was to be placed towards the expenses of the Bureau and the other half to contribute towards the Bureau's newsletter *Messager Bahá'í*. But, the Guardian specified, others would have to put up the remaining funds needed. After further discussion, for some reason, the majority of the group did not feel disposed to offer the sum and recommended that the Bureau be closed. Conscious of the Guardian's wishes, Julia Culver took on the financial responsibility alone and the office stayed open but with reduced activity. In May 1928 Culver was in need of assistance and suggested to the Guardian that Mrs Emogene Hoagg from Oakland, California, join her in Geneva. The Guardian consented and Mrs Hoagg arrived in June 1928. That same month, the former Bureau was closed and temporary rooms were taken for the summer months. Martha Root returned and a new energy was infused into the life of the Bureau. Lectures were given and social and spiritual gatherings were held. Finally, new quarters were found at 20 bis, rue Général Dufour, in a quiet but artistic quarter of the city close to the university and the opera house.

'The Bureau has been slowly gathering strength and forming a spiritual centre as well as installing gradually an international Bureau library, to which a few friends and Assemblies of different countries have generously contributed books in their native languages,' wrote Hoagg.[94] The International Bahá'í Bureau went on to achieve recognition by the League of Nations and was asked by its Publishing Bureau for a short historical account to appear in its publication. The Bureau also joined the Fédération des Mouvements Internationaux and was legally registered as an international working unit, governed by a local committee under the direct supervision of Shoghi Effendi.

Lady Blomfield's extended absences from British shores, combined with the precarious physical health of her two devoted co-workers Ethel Rosenberg and Mrs Thornburgh-Cropper, led to an interesting discussion at an extraordinary meeting held jointly between the London Assembly and the National Spiritual Assembly on 17 March 1928. Elizabeth Herrick proposed:

> That subject to the approval of the Guardian and their own willingness, our devoted and valued friends of the Bahá'í Cause Mrs Thornburgh-Cropper, Miss Ethel J. Rosenberg and Lady Blomfield – herein named in their chronological order of their service to the Bahá'í Cause – who have from the commencement of the Bahá'í organization been almost invariably elected to serve on the National and London Spiritual Assemblies and who nevertheless find it either impossible or extremely difficult to attend Assembly meetings regularly, and in order that their valued services may be retained as much as possible, as well as in the common interest of the Cause be recommended by the joint Assemblies and the Guardian for appointment as permanent honorary members of both Assemblies, entitled to attend the meetings for the purpose of assisting in consultations and discussions provided always that the 9 elected members of each Assembly alone have the right to vote.[95]

While appreciating the sentiments behind Miss Herrick's motion, the

Assemblies were almost unanimous in rejecting it, saying it could lead to the creation of a spiritual hierarchy, which was against the teachings. The Assemblies also resolved not to bother the Guardian with the matter.

One of Lady Blomfield's greatest strengths was her writing and she relished the opportunity to pen articles about the Bahá'í cause whenever an opportunity presented itself. An approach from the editors of *The Sufi Quarterly*, a 'Philosophical Review' of the Sufi Publishing Association of Geneva, resulted in an article entitled 'The Bahá'ís'. Covering 19 pages of the journal, it appeared in the March 1928 edition.

'*The Sufi Quarterly* is fortunate in having secured an unusually comprehensive account of the inspiration and ideals upon which Baha'ism is built up,' wrote the editor Ronald A. L. Mumtaz Armstrong, 'from one whose long connection with the Baha'i Movement has peculiarly fitted her to present the whole subject in a proper light.'

> Lady Blomfield, as the hostess of the last Baha'i leader, Sir 'Abdu'l-Bahá 'Abbas, during his visits to London, and through her personal acquaintance with his principal friends and followers, has had exceptional opportunities for studying Baha'ism at first hand. Her article will be read with interest, not only by the Baha'is themselves, to whom some aspects of this fresh presentation of their story may ne new, but also by all who have at heart the spiritual welfare of our discordant and material modern world.
>
> In common with the Sufis, though without the inner cult, the Baha'i Movement works to bring nations and the followers of different religions into closer touch, and teaches the highest spiritual ideals. The founder of the Sufi Movement in the West, the late Pir-O-Murshid Inayat Khan, was a warm admirer of 'Abdu'l-Bahá. He would often recall with pleasure a meeting with the Baha'i leader in Paris when the two discussed Eastern music and their respective experiences in Western lands. Perhaps the difference in their methods may best be seen from a part of their conversation then recorded. 'You are preaching the brotherhood of nations?' asked 'Abdu'l-Bahá. And Inayat Khan replied: 'I am not preaching brotherhood, but sowing the seed of Touheed, the unity of God, that from the plant of Sufism fruits and flowers of brotherhood may spring up.'[96]

The editor had left off the true conclusion of the conversation. In her handwriting on her own copy of *The Sufi Quarterly*, Lady Blomfield scribbled, 'I say not unto you "preach the brotherhood of man" – but go forth, be Brothers to all Mankind! Of every Religion, of every Race, of every Nation on Earth!'[97]

Sitárih's purpose in writing the article was, in her own words, 'to give a brief sketch of the Baha'i Movement, in the course of which it is hoped to suggest something of that spirit of love and self-sacrifice by which it is animated.'

To this end also will be brought together a few of the impressions, as far as possible in their own words, made upon certain personalities of the Western world, whether by their coming into personal touch with Bahá'u'lláh himself, or through investigations in Persia. To these may be added the remark of the revered Master of Balliol College, Oxford – Dr Benjamin Jowett – to a fellow professor, that he was deeply interested in the Baha'i Movement. 'This', he said, 'is the greatest Light that has come into the world since Jesus Christ . . . Never let it out of your sight. It is too great and too near for this generation to comprehend. The future alone can reveal its import.'[98]

Among the other 'personalities' whose tributes to the Bahá'í Cause Sitárih chose to include in her article were Professor E. Denison Ross, E.G. Browne of Cambridge, and Lord Curzon of Kedleston.

Particularly touching in Sitárih's article is her description of 'Abdu'l-Bahá, which not only demonstrates the deep affection she continued to cherish for the Master but also the considerable descriptive writing skills at her command:

Those who have had the privilege of knowing 'Abdu'l-Baha in the Prison Fortress of Akka, during his days of captivity, and those who came into personal touch with him in London and Paris, were alike impressed with the great moral beauty of his character, and the indescribable spiritual dignity of his demeanour.

Always did he speak with authority, and not as the mere expounder, albeit a certain gentle courtesy was most conspicuous and seemed to surround him with an atmosphere of loving-kindness, the benign influence of which was felt by all who came into his presence. Whether it were a great minister of State or an ecclesiastical dignitary, a busy toiler for his daily bread, or a sorrow-burthened Princess, a famous artist or a learned barrister, a celebrated physician or a Christian Scientist, a woman suffragist or an Oxford Professor, a poor seamstress or a renowned writer, an inquiring journalist or an able man of science, none was either too great or too insignificant to receive of the bountiful warmth of his sympathetic consideration. He was marvellously energetic, and his presence brought a delightful, vivid gladness.[99]

The article in *The Sufi Quarterly* was well received by readers. Claudia Coles wrote to Lady Blomfield,

I have just finished your inspired article in the Sufi Review for March 1928, and am writing straight off, to tell you how I rejoice in all that you have written, and the way it has been written, and all that you purposed in the writing. Blessed be!

It made me so happy! In my heart I felt the Divine Guidance, and the meaning of this clarion call across the world.

I wish it could be put into a little booklet for us all to have to use every where. I feel such a happiness that this is written and can be made available for use.

How marvellously you have gotten over the Crux of the Baha'i Message . . .

A thousand blessings to you, and warm gratitude and rejoicing in my heart for the faith and the wisdom and the ability and love of the Cause that is a part of the beating of the Divine Artery in the five continents.[100]

While the believers in London and elsewhere in the world struggled to put into practice the guidance Shoghi Effendi was providing for the proper establishment and functioning of institutions, there were a small number who were determined to return the Bahá'í Movement to its former character as an informal fellowship of religions. The believers in London were puzzled on receiving a pamphlet by an American believer, Ruth White, who rejected the organization of the Cause by going so far as to question the authenticity of the Master's Will. White was vehemently opposed to any form of Bahá'í administration and, believing that she was guided by higher powers, declared that the Will was a forgery – a notion which even the most unfaithful members of the Master's family had never ventured to suggest.

At the fortieth meeting of the London Spiritual Assembly, held on 2 February 1929, Ethel Rosenberg was asked to give an account of the reading of the Master's Will as she and Lady Blomfield had witnessed it themselves with their own eyes in the Holy Land, seven years previously. The Assembly was convinced by Ethel's account of the events and decided that no action be taken regarding the pamphlet. Later, Ruth White arrived in London to gain support for her campaign and claimed to have met nearly all the believers in the city. She also claimed to have witnessed great disunity among the members of the National Spiritual Assembly, stating that Lady Blomfield had told her that there was practically no longer a Bahá'í Cause in England and that she had 'come to the conclusion that the Bahá'í Cause cannot be organized'.[101] Were these claims to be believed, they would undoubtedly have added to White's convictions. However, as with every attempt to undermine the authority of the Central Figures of the Faith, White's campaign came to nothing. She eventually, in old age, left the Faith and diverted her interests and allegiance to an Indian guru.

The year 1929 saw Lady Blomfield's own seventieth birthday and the thirtieth anniversary of the passing of Sir Arthur Blomfield. For more than two decades, Sitárih had worked tirelessly for the Cause of Bahá'u'lláh and had never once hesitated in her conviction that the vision of the future of humanity which 'Abdu'l-Bahá had conveyed was emerging, albeit in fits and starts and with enormous struggles and setbacks. In London, the National Spiritual Assembly was hopeful that investing in a suitable Centre would allow meetings to be hosted as and when the believers pleased without the difficulty of renting halls. Suitable premises were found at Walmar House in Upper Regent Street, and the Centre was dedicated on 19 September 1929. Shoghi Effendi was invited to attend the opening but was unable to do so. The Greatest Holy Leaf cabled his response:

GUARDIAN WIRES DEEPLY REGRETS INABILITY PARTICIPATE PERSONALLY DEDICATION GATHERING OVERJOYED BRIGHT PROSPECTS LOVING GOOD WISHES, SHOGHI. BAHÁ'íYYIH.[102]

The Guardian's hopes for the progress of the British community were encouraged by the acquisition of the Centre. On 29 November 1929, a message written on his behalf states that he was 'much hopeful of your new centre in Regent Street . . . and he trusts that it will mark a turning point in the history of the Cause in England – from happy tea-parties at individual homes, into a group of less personal but eager, active and thoughtful workers co-operating in a common service. It is a basis upon which healthy progress is possible . . .'[103]

But the Guardian warned the believers that they should not think that with a permanent centre their events would be automatically more successful.

'We should however, bear in mind that no matter how important the hall may be – the talks given and the unity manifested are of far greater significance.'[104]

In April 1930 the British Bahá'ís gathered for the first annual National Convention to be held at Walmar House. Lady Blomfield was not re-elected to the National Spiritual Assembly. In November Ethel Rosenberg passed away in her sleep at the age of 72. Times – and the British Bahá'í community – were changing.

Sitárih continued to take every opportunity to spread the message of love and unity that she learned from 'Abdu'l-Bahá and to convey the Bahá'í teachings through her movement 'For the Supreme Peace'. Other organizations, such as the Geneva-based International Bureau of Education, called on her to support their efforts by becoming a life member and recruiting subscribers among her friends.

On 1 March 1930 Lady Blomfield was surprised to receive an unexpected cable from Shoghi Effendi:

GREATEST HOLY LEAF AND MYSELF APART FROM OUR LONGING MEET YOU FEEL EXTREME DESIRABILITY YOUR PRESENCE IN HAIFA BEFORE MARCH TWENTY-FIRST IN VIEW OF IMPENDING FAR-REACHING DEVELOPMENTS. STRONGLY FEEL YOU ARE ONLY PERSON SUITED TO OCCASION. WIRING EXPLANATION IN PERSIAN TO ASGHARZADEH. STRICTLY CONFIDENTIAL. KINDLY WIRE. LOVE.[105]

Uncertain of the 'far-reaching developments' which lay in wait, Sitárih prepared to travel once more to the Holy Land and the loving embrace of the Guardian and his blessed great-aunt.

CHAPTER ELEVEN

AMBROSIA AND BREAD

. . . and in the words used there should lie hid the property of milk,
so that the children of the world may be nurtured therewith,
and attain maturity.[1]
Bahá'u'lláh

The telegram that Lady Blomfield received from Shoghi Effendi was tantalizingly cryptic – 'IMPENDING FAR-REACHING DEVELOPMENTS', 'ONLY PERSON SUITED TO OCCASION'.[2] There must have been something of great importance about to transpire in the Holy Land for Sitárih's presence to be requested so urgently and amid such confidentiality.

Any curiosity which Lady Blomfield initially felt about the invitation did not last long. In a separate telegram sent in Persian, arriving on the same day and addressed to Ḍiyá'u'lláh Asg͟harzádih, Shoghi Effendi instructed, 'TELL BLOMFIELD MARIE IS MEANT'.[3] Sitárih was being summoned to be present in Haifa because Queen Marie of Romania anticipated making a historic visit to the Shrines of the Bahá'í Faith – a Cause in support of which she had already made numerous public pronouncements.

Born on 29 October 1875, Queen Marie was the daughter of Queen Victoria's second son, Alfred, Duke of Edinburgh. On her mother's side, her grandfather was Tsar Alexander II of Russia. Both of these monarchs – Victoria and Alexander – had been exalted, first by significant and encouraging messages from Bahá'u'lláh and then a second time by the ready embrace of His teachings by their granddaughter during a period of deep, personal difficulty in her life.

Marie, who reigned for 13 years until 1927 when her husband King Ferdinand died, had been introduced to the Bahá'í teachings by the intrepid travelling teacher Martha Root, who had sent the Queen a copy of Esslemont's book *Bahá'u'lláh and the New Era*. Marie requested a meeting with Martha, which transpired on 30 January 1926 at the Controceni Palace in

Bucharest. Soon after their first encounter, the Queen began to pen a series of unprecedented open pronouncements that were widely syndicated in the newspapers of the United States and Canada. These columns included comments such as,

> A woman brought me the other day a Book. I spell it with a capital letter because it is a glorious Book of love and goodness, strength and beauty ... I commend it to you all. If ever the name of Bahá'u'lláh or 'Abdu'l-Bahá comes to your attention, do not put their writings from you. Search out their Books, and let their glorious, peace-bringing, love-creating words and lessons sink into your hearts as they have into mine.[4]

In response to a letter from Shoghi Effendi expressing his appreciation, the Queen told the Guardian,

> Indeed a great light came to me with the message of Bahá'u'lláh and Abdu'l-Bahá [*sic*]. It came as all great messages come at an hour of dire grief and inner conflict and distress, so the seed sank deeply ...
>
> We pass the message from mouth to mouth and all those we give it to see a light suddenly lighting before them and much that was obscure and perplexing becomes simple, luminous and full of hope as never before.[5]

The sympathy the Queen held and readily proclaimed for the Bahá'í message was hailed by Shoghi Effendi as a 'notable triumph which the unbending energy and indomitable spirit of our beloved Martha has achieved for our sacred Cause.'[6] With the testimonials of the Queen widely circulating, Shoghi Effendi anticipated a transformation in the attitudes of many 'to a Faith the tenets of which have often been misunderstood and sorely neglected. It will serve as a fresh stimulus to the enlightened and cultured to investigate with an open mind the verities of its message, the source of its life-giving principles.'[7]

Martha Root was unsurpassed as a promoter of the Bahá'í Faith. Shoghi Effendi's widow, Rúḥíyyih Rabbaní, wrote of her:

> She believed that in showing this gem and offering it to anyone, king or peasant, she was conferring the greatest bounty upon him he could

ever receive. It was this proud conviction that enabled her, a woman of no wealth or social prestige, plain, dowdily dressed and neither a great scholar nor an outstanding intellectual, to meet more kings, queens, princes and princesses, presidents and men of distinction, fame and prominence and tell them about the Bahá'í Faith than any other Bahá'í in the history of this Cause has ever done.[8]

Shoghi Effendi deeply trusted Lady Blomfield also and hoped that, being a personage of such grace, social status and efficacy as a promoter of the Bahá'í teachings, she would consider literally following in Martha Root's footsteps. In an earlier communication penned on the Guardian's behalf by his cousin and secretary Ruhi Afnan, it was suggested that Sitárih might follow up many of the contacts being made in Europe by Martha Root, among them numerous prominent people. After a report of Martha's activities was received in the Holy Land in March 1926, Ruhi Afnan was asked to write to Sitárih, recounting that,

> Among other interesting things she mentions her interview with Queen Mary [sic] of Rumania who has shown great interest in the Cause and promised to read Dr Esslemont's book. She seems to be so impressed with the teachings as to introduce Miss Root to some of her friends, among them the wife of the Manager of the Grand Opera in Vienna. These two cases show clearly what nice contacts Miss Root has succeeded to make in those regions.
>
> Shoghi Effendi thinks that it would be a great pity if her work should be left, and that the interests aroused be neglected. He would therefore desire, in case your plans fit and you find yourself free, that you should write to Miss Root and ask her whether it would be advisable for you to follow her and pay a visit to those persons whom she has already met and interested. Shoghi Effendi thought you to be the person for such an undertaking but it all depends upon your own desire. He wishes you to take the matter as a mere suggestion and then consult Miss Root before taking any steps . . .
>
> One of the handicaps of the Cause at present is that it is either over-looked or misunderstood by the members of the higher classes of society . . . Miss Root seems to have obtained an entré into this class and if she is followed by a person capable for such a work, great results will undoubtedly ensue.[9]

It does not seem that Lady Blomfield felt able to take up formally Shoghi Effendi's suggestion but certainly she pursued her own contacts with members of the higher classes and by February 1930, when Queen Marie and her daughter Princess Ileana set off on a tour of the Middle East, the Guardian was in no doubt about who he wanted to be present to join him and the Greatest Holy Leaf in greeting the royal party on their visit to the Bahá'í Holy Places.

The royal tour was scheduled to last until April and included stays in Alexandria, Cairo, Jerusalem, Haifa and 'Akká. Queen Marie was certainly keen to carry out her forthcoming pilgrimage to the Shrines of the twin Manifestations of the Bahá'í Faith: 'What an emotion it will be to go to Haifa and Acca,' she wrote to a friend.[10]

On 3 March 1930 Martha Root cabled Marie about her projected journey: 'LOVE. FAITHFUL PRAYERS. HOPE YOU BOTH CAN GO HAIFA.'[11]

In the days leading up to the proposed visit, however, rumours began to circulate in the press, reporting Queen Marie's 'conversion' to 'Bahaism'. Various newspapers covered the story. Britain's *Sunday Express*, for example, reported:

Marie, the Queen Dowager of Romania, and grandmother of the boy King Michael, who is now on her way to Jerusalem, is understood to have recently become a convert to Bahaism. The Queen's new religion has more than 3,000,000 adherents of all creeds, and they describe their faith as a 'union of all other religions'. They declare that their ultimate aim is to bring about the spiritual unification of mankind. Bahaism was founded in Persia in 1844 by a young reformer who announced himself as the Bab (The Gate). An attempt on the life of the Shah two years after the Bab's execution, made by a fanatical follower of the faith, opened an era of martyrdom in Persia. Between 10,000 and 20,000 men and women members of the movement were killed with barbarous cruelty. Many of the martyrs were sawn in two, while others were blown from guns, strangled, or chopped in pieces. A remarkable feature of Bahaism has been the passion for martyrdom of its adherents. Persecutions have continued up to a few years ago, and in 1920 one Hadji Arab was publicly hanged for his faith by the authorities of Sultanabad, Persia. Wealthy Persians who embraced the faith were stripped of their possessions and flung into dungeons. The movement was established in London in 1911, and many converts were gained. Bahaism is also strong in the United States.[12]

As Lady Blomfield returned to Haifa to sit at the side of her much admired friend Bahíyyih <u>Kh</u>ánum in the blessed home of the Master, expectations were high for a truly momentous occasion. But when the Queen's interest in the Baháʼí teachings became more public, her itinerary came under increasing scrutiny by her advisers. Days of waiting followed with little sign of the royal party on the horizon. Shoghi Effendi cabled Queen Marie in Egypt:

> FAMILY OF ABDULBAHA JOIN ME IN RENEWING THE EXPRESSION OF OUR LOVING AND HEARTFELT INVITATION TO YOUR GRACIOUS MAJESTY AND HER ROYAL HIGHNESS PRINCESS ILEANA TO VISIT HIS HOME IN HAIFA. YOUR MAJESTY'S ACCEPTANCE TO VISIT BAHAULLAHS SHRINE AND PRISON-CITY OF AKKA WILL APART FROM ITS HISTORIC SIGNIFICANCE BE A SOURCE OF IMMEASURABLE STRENGTH, JOY AND HOPE TO THE SILENT SUFFERERS OF THE FAITH THROUGHOUT THE EAST. OUR FONDEST LOVE, PRAYERS AND BEST WISHES FOR YOUR MAJESTY'S HAPPINESS AND WELFARE.[13]

Receiving no acknowledgement from the Queen, Shoghi Effendi began to wonder if the numerous newspaper articles about her 'conversion' may have diluted her wish to visit the Shrines of the Báb and Baháʼuʼlláh. It transpired, in fact, that her desire to make the pilgrimage was undiminished; but it was her advisers who feared more the fallout from so public an allegiance of faith.

'Of all things my sympathy for the Baháʼís is also being brought up as a political complication,' the Queen confided to her diary on 8 March.

> This has been taken up from the English side. Who would ever have imagined such a thing? They consider it political propaganda! It is really sometimes a curse to be a Queen. And one meets with almost no comprehension. The world wishes to rule everything on hard-cut lines, there is to be no enthusiasm, no deeper thought, no privacy, no poetry, no ideas only dry reason and selfish calculation. How discouraging it is. I would never have thought that even this would be made a question of . . .[14]

A further cable to Marie from Shoghi Effendi on 26 March, stating, 'DEEPLY REGRET UNAUTHORIZED PUBLICITY GIVEN BY THE PRESS',[15] resulted in a curt response from Romania's minister in Cairo: 'HER MAJESTY REGRETS THAT, NOT PASSING THROUGH PALESTINE, SHE WILL NOT BE ABLE TO VISIT YOU.'[16]

The interference in Queen Marie's itinerary came as a disappointment to the Guardian, to his great-aunt and to Lady Blomfield who, having been a protagonist in so many remarkable episodes in the heroic and formative ages of the Bahá'í Faith, had travelled such a long distance to play her part in what promised to have been another. Rúḥíyyih Rabbaní wrote,

> I remember Shoghi Effendi a number of times describing to me how the Greatest Holy Leaf had waited, hour after hour, in the Master's home to receive the Queen and her daughter – for Her Majesty had actually sailed for Haifa, and this news encouraged Shoghi Effendi to believe she was going to carry out the pilgrimage she had planned; time passed and no news came, even after the boat had docked.[17]

'I so much wish to know the real situation,' Shoghi Effendi wrote to Martha Root,

> . . . whether any malicious propaganda has not dampened her enthusiasm, or whether she is unable to communicate with us. Reporters who called on me, representing the United Press of America, telegraphed to their newspapers just the opposite I told them. They perverted the truth. I wish we could make sure that she would at least know the real situation! But how can we ensure that our letters to her Majesty will henceforth reach her. I feel that you should write to her, explain the whole situation, assure her of my great disappointment. I hope your letter will reach her . . . I cherish the hope that these unfortunate developments will serve only to intensify the faith and love of the Queen, and will reinforce her determination to arise and spread the Cause . . .[18]

Despite the disappointment of those days, Shoghi Effendi's first thought was to assure Martha that she herself should not feel distressed or sad.

'The seeds you have so lovingly, so devotedly, and so assiduously sown will surely germinate,' the Guardian wrote. "'Abdu'l-Bahá is guiding you and will bless your heroic efforts. Persevere, and never lose heart.'[19]

As a gift for Queen Marie, Shoghi Effendi had commissioned a copy of Bahá'u'lláh's Tablet to her grandmother, Queen Victoria, in fine Persian calligraphy and had it illuminated in Tehran. When Marie did not arrive, the Guardian entrusted it to Lady Blomfield with the instruction that – someday, somehow – she should attempt to deliver it into the hands of this first ever royal follower of Bahá'u'lláh.

As the days of waiting for the special visitors succeeded one another, Lady Blomfield determined not to waste the precious hours she had available to her. She continued to note down and collate the stories of the early history of the Faith from the Greatest Holy Leaf and other believers who were residing in, or passing through, Haifa at the time. Perhaps even more than on her previous visit, at a time when 'Abdu'l-Bahá had so recently departed, Sitárih sensed an atmosphere in the household that was very reminiscent of the days spent in His presence. And in Shoghi Effendi's industry she saw the spirit of his illustrious grandfather at work.

Observing the Guardian striding across the hall of the Western Pilgrim House with newly typewritten pages clasped in his hands, Sitárih learned that he was busy with two major pieces of translation – Bahá'u'lláh's outstanding doctrinal work, the Kitáb-i-Íqán, as well as a narrative history of the early days of the Faith by a contemporary follower of the Báb and Bahá'u'lláh known as Nabíl. This book, which appeared in 1932 as *The Dawn-Breakers*, was more than a work of translation, however. Rather, the Guardian effectively recreated Nabíl's narrative in English, combining its original text with other accounts and supporting documents. Over eight months Shoghi Effendi produced some six hundred pages of text with an additional two hundred pages of notes.

'I have been so absorbed in this work that I have been forced to delay my correspondence,' he wrote to Martha Root. 'I am now so tired and exhausted that I can hardly write . . . I am so overcome with fatigue caused by the long and severe strain of the work I have undertaken that I must stop and lie down.'[20]

Nine years previously in London, Shoghi Effendi – then a young Oxford scholar – had expressed his hope that Lady Blomfield might assist him in his work. With her now present in Haifa as he immersed himself in the Íqán and *Nabíl's Narrative*, he called upon Sitárih to review his translations for grammar, accuracy and style. Lady Blomfield was honoured not only to be able to assist the Guardian in his work but to have an early glimpse of two books which would become essential texts for every Bahá'í around the world.

'The Bahá'ís of the West emerged from the experience of reading this history of the life and times of the Báb transfigured,' wrote Rúḥíyyih Rabbaní of *The Dawn-Breakers*, 'it was as if some of the precious blood of those early martyrs had been spattered upon them. They caught a glimpse of the tradition behind them, they saw that this was a Faith for which one carried one's life in one's hand, they understood what Shoghi Effendi was talking about and what he expected from them when he called them the spiritual descendants of the Dawn-Breakers.'[21]

After Sitárih's return from the Holy Land, Shoghi Effendi continued to send her his translation of the Íqán. Further pages were forwarded to George Townshend, another collaborator whose opinions on literary style the Guardian valued highly. In one letter, returning some pages of the Íqán with her suggestions, Lady Blomfield described the translation as 'wonderful'. Hoping that the Guardian would find her comments to be of some use, she wrote, 'Meanwhile I wait for Nabil's. How I miss that glorious Narrative – part of which I had the privilege of seeing – I shall love having some of it again with me, like old times!'[22]

Leaving Haifa was always going to be poignant for Lady Blomfield but perhaps this time she knew that her farewell to Bahíyyih Khánum would be the last time they would see each other on this earthly plane. Described by Shoghi Effendi as 'liege lady' and 'archetype of the people of Bahá',[23] the Greatest Holy Leaf was by now in delicate health. Following Lady Blomfield's departure, Bahíyyih Khánum endured a prolonged spell confined to bed after contracting a cold. She would live only two years more, passing away in the early hours of 15 July 1932. Lady Blomfield had spent many enlightening hours relishing Bahíyyih Khánum's company and, encountering her again in the twilight of her life, Sitárih no doubt longed to complete her book as a befitting tribute to this last survivor of the Faith's heroic age.

Lady Blomfield returned, not to London however but to Geneva.

'I have been to the Bahá'í bureau,' she reported to Shoghi Effendi. 'Talked to them of Haifa, gave the Messages from you and the dear family, which they were rejoiced to receive. I have seen Mrs Hoagg several times – today I go again to the bureau – Mrs Marcus [Isobel] Slade is here for two days, we shall confer on London Bahá'í matters – where all is going well.'[24]

Receiving Sitárih's suggestions for corrections to his ongoing translation of the Kitáb-i-Íqán, Shoghi Effendi incorporated them into his manuscript.

'You know how appreciative he is for this help and therefore I need not express it,' wrote the Guardian's secretary.[25]

Much to Lady Blomfield's satisfaction, Shoghi Effendi also sent a new section of *Nabíl's Narrative*.

'He hopes you will give to it as much of your time as you can spare . . . I am sure you will find the task very interesting, because the history as it develops is becoming more and more absorbing . . .' wrote the Guardian's secretary.[26]

In a postscript in his own handwriting, Shoghi Effendi wrote,

My deepest thanks for your suggestions in connection with the Íqán which I deeply appreciate. I am sending to your address today a further instalment of Nabíl which I trust you will find interesting. I am soon leaving for my summer rest which I need badly, though I am hoping to devote most of my time to the translation of the narrative. I hope to send you some more as soon as I receive the instalment which I am mailing today.[27]

Shoghi Effendi also gave Sitárih permission to extract from the narrative whatever she desired for use in her own book.

In her Geneva hotel Lady Blomfield became absorbed in the stirring account of the life of the Báb and His heroic followers. She would study Shoghi Effendi's translated typescripts once they arrived, then note down her comments and send them back to the Guardian, who always expressed his deep appreciation of her assistance.

By the end of August, just before the new session of the League of Nations got underway, the Guardian's secretary wrote, 'Shoghi Effendi wishes me to drop you these few lines, extend to you his loving greetings and enclose another hundred pages of Nabíl's history. I hope you have time to go over these pages now that the season of Geneva is beginning.'[28]

By 30 September 1930 Sitárih had received the final instalment of *Nabíl's Narrative*.

'It brings the story to the banishment of Bahá'u'lláh from Persia, a most logical place to stop,' wrote his secretary. 'Shoghi Effendi hopes that you have received the previous pages. He has not yet had time to go over the suggestions you have sent him but he is delighted to see that they are numerous . . .'[29]

'My dear Sitarih Khanum,' added the Guardian. 'I am indeed most thankful to you for your painstaking efforts in going over the manuscript and of giving me your valuable suggestions. I trust that you will not be finding it too tedious and exacting a work. I have been working very hard on it, and I trust that it will help advance the interests of the Cause in the West. Again thanking you from the bottom of my heart, Yours affectionately, Shoghi.'[30]

Lady Blomfield found *Nabíl's Narrative* extraordinarily interesting but heart-rendingly sad, bewailing to the Guardian the 'blindness and stupidity of men, who are meant to be human!' Sitárih observed with concern that Shoghi Effendi had been working very hard on the translation instead of resting, but appreciated that 'the task is thrilling' and he was 'carried forward on wings!'[31]

Receiving the final collection of Lady Blomfield's comments, along with the detailed remarks offered by George Townshend, Shoghi Effendi revisited the whole manuscript. But Sitárih's role in the creation of *Nabíl's Narrative* did not end there. The Guardian, remarkably, asked her whether she thought the manuscript was good enough to be published.

'I wish to thank you from the bottom of my heart for the pains you have taken in going so thoroughly over the manuscript which I am afraid you have found in parts tedious and wearisome,' wrote Shoghi Effendi. 'Would you advise its publication? I trust that you are feeling well, and that opportunities to sow the seed and disseminate the knowledge of the Cause are easily forthcoming. I feel rather tired after my strenuous work this summer, and I am now again plunged into an ocean of work on my return to Haifa. Wishing you all success, and assuring you of my prayers at the holy Shrines . . .'[32]

Lady Blomfield was in no doubt that the book should be published.

'I am very sensible of the great privilege which is mine, of being in touch, however humbly, with the descriptions of these marvellous scenes of heroism – these heroines as well as heroes, Sacred Apostles of the Holy Cause!' she replied to the Guardian.

> . . . the people of the world ought to have the opportunity of reading these accounts of the persecutions, torturing and martyrdom of those devoted 'Waiting Servants' of God, whose dauntless courage has preserved for the world that Message in its grandeur, which, but for them, would have been destroyed by the opposing forces of evil. I lack words

to express what to my mind, is the importance of the effect this moving story will have on all who read its Valiant Episodes![33]

Sitárih sent the Guardian detailed comments about the publication, stressing the importance of its being 'in good print'[34] and making suggestions concerning the binding. In reply, Shoghi Effendi's secretary told Lady Blomfield that the Guardian's 'hope in undertaking this task was to present to the western friends the bare facts of the early days of the Movement, so that the same spirit that animated its early servants may again inspire the friends and arouse them to further exertions and sacrifices'.[35]

'My dear Ladee,' added the Guardian.

> I wish to thank you most deeply for the painstaking efforts entailed in going so carefully over the entire manuscript. I greatly value your suggestions and will gladly incorporate them in the final copy. I have been revising it very drastically of late . . . I have been working ten hours a day since I returned home and hope to send it for publication by the end of next month. Again thanking you from all my heart, and with my best wishes to Parvene Khanum, Your true brother, Shoghi. I have added about two hundred pages of notes, all of which I trust will not weary the reader. Shoghi[36]

Nabíl's Narrative once published was widely acclaimed by the Bahá'ís, as expected, but also by those acquaintances of Shoghi Effendi to whom he sent copies. Alfred W. Martin of the Ethical Culture Society described it as a 'magnificent and monumental work', 'a classic and a standard for all time to come'. 'I marvel beyond measure at your ability to prepare such a work for the press over and above all the activities which your regular professional position devolves upon you,' Dr Martin wrote to Shoghi Effendi.[37]

Bayard Dodge, one of the Guardian's professors at the American University in Beirut, wrote to his former student,

> The quality of the English and the delightful ease of reading the translation are extraordinary, as usually a translation is difficult to read. You have been splendid in making the book so neutral and in adding the footnotes, which make the work more a matter of scientific history than anything like propaganda. The force of the book is very great, because the translation is so scientific and the original authorship so

spontaneous, that the whole work must seem genuine, even to the most cynical critic.[38]

During the months she spent in Geneva, aside from reviewing Shoghi Effendi's translations of the Kitáb-i-Íqán and what became known – at George Townshend's suggestion – as *The Dawn-Breakers*, Sitárih continued to contribute as much as she could to the life of the numerous humanitarian organizations gathered in the city. She became particularly involved in the case of refugees from war zones, the 'Heimatlos', who were being cared for by an organization of the League of Nations set up by the Norwegian explorer and diplomat Fridtjof Nansen, who later received the Nobel Peace Prize for this work. The 'Nansen passports', were the first internationally recognized refugee travel documents, issued by the League of Nations to stateless people. By 1942 the passports were honoured by governments in 52 countries.

'I have been working in the Cause of the "Heimatlos", the State-less poor souls, wandering in despair over the face of the earth – calling the attention of "League of Nations" people to their sufferings,' Lady Blomfield told the Guardian. 'The Cause of the Prisons' Reform is proceeding satisfactorily, and the "Native Children of Palestine" will, I expect, be helped by the "Save the Children Fund".'[39]

There were also more meetings of Lady Blomfield's movement 'For the Supreme Peace' and she herself offered a number of presentations to Quaker and Esperanto meetings and at the International Bahá'í Bureau, including one on the life of Ṭáhírih, no doubt informed by the new knowledge she had gained on the famed Persian poetess from her reading of *The Dawn-Breakers*.

Sitárih returned to London at the end of 1930 and transferred her residence for the final time to a large house in the north London suburb of Hampstead, at 8 Burgess Hill, with her daughter Mary and Mary's husband Basil Hall. There over the coming decade, many joyful 'At Home' and holy day meetings would be hosted, their reputation spreading beyond the English capital. The British Bahá'í community as a whole cherished Lady Blomfield's presence amongst them and numerous were the guests from all over the country, indeed the world, who would call in to meet the woman whose life's experience was interwoven with some of the most important moments of their Faith's history. Among the visitors was the American

Bahá'í teacher Mary Hanford Ford, whose lectures in London, as well as further afield in York and Liverpool, had attracted many seekers.

On a sadder note, Sitárih was grieved when one of her most active and capable Bahá'í friends, Claudia Coles, passed away on the anniversary of the Declaration of the Báb, 23 May 1931. Claudia's funeral took place four days later at her home in Warwick Gardens which, according to one report, became that day like a garden of flowers.[40] Lady Blomfield travelled with other mourners including Mary Hanford Ford and Beatrice Irwin to the burial at a country cemetery in the small village of Bledlow Ridge, Buckinghamshire, close to the cottage where Claudia's daughter lived.

The death of both Ethel Rosenberg and Claudia Coles within a six month period was a blow to the British community. On 24 July 1931, Shoghi Effendi's secretary wrote to them:

> Although this year has been on the whole very disastrous because of the terrible loss which the English friends have suffered by the passing of Miss Rosenberg and Mrs Claudia Coles, yet the Guardian hopes that the believers far from being discouraged will be enabled to unite their efforts and to carry on a successful campaign of teaching. He wishes the friends to follow the example of our two distinguished Bahá'í sisters who have recently passed away and to never cease to deliver the Holy Message by every means at their disposal.[41]

In spite of her own increasing problems with health, including painful bouts of neuritis, Lady Blomfield continued to take every opportunity to reach out to like-minded souls and support the countless good causes that captured her lively mind. On Tuesday 9 June, for example, she gave an 'At Home' meeting to further the objects of 'Ben Shemen', a Jewish children's village founded in the spring of 1927 by the doctor and educationalist Dr Siegfried Lehmann, as a refuge and educational centre for orphans and homeless Jewish children, particularly those from Eastern Europe. A film was shown and Sitárih spoke in support of the ideology underlying the village. Bertha Good from the organization shared how the village was completely controlled by the children themselves. The success of the village was due entirely to the initiative of the youngsters, she said, whose suggestions and schemes were often put into practice.

On another occasion, Sitárih addressed the Annual Congress of the International New Thought Alliance, based at 94 Lancaster Gate in

London. On 21 July 1931 she took part in a programme under the banner, 'New thought in religion, science, education, medicine, art, societies and movements'. Sitárih spoke on 'The Revealer of the Bahá'í Message, the Forerunner, the Establisher', alongside a Sufi speaker and a Dr W.A. Griggs on 'The effect of radiation on psychonomy, health and happiness'.

Sitárih's literary pursuits were also continuing as she finally settled down to bring her notes of conversations with the Greatest Holy Leaf and other members of the Holy Family into some semblance of order. In the spring of 1931 Nellie French, an American believer who was chairman of the *Bahá'í World* editorial committee from 1930 until 1946, called on Lady Blomfield and spent several hours with her going over her precious memoirs. French commissioned an article from Sitárih recounting 'Abdu'l-Bahá's visit to London.

'We know how eager you are to make the next volume of the *Bahá'í World* a really beautiful and brilliant collection of interesting material and valuable historical data,' French later wrote to Sitárih, reminding her of the 1 November deadline for the manuscript, 'and we hope that nothing will prevent you from achieving the greatest success in your endeavours and thus demonstrating to our revered Guardian, Shoghi Effendi, our earnest and heartfelt desire to serve him and to comply with his definite instructions.'[42]

Lady Blomfield set to work on the article, with Mary assisting her in recalling people and incidents, and by typing the manuscript for her mother. They met the deadline early and on 23 October 1931, sent her manuscript to Nellie French.

'Of course it is inadequate,' wrote Sitárih. 'Such an event would call for the pen of an Angel Chronicler! It is written with love for Him – that is the only good that can be said for the writer.'[43]

'Just 20 years ago the Glorious Beloved Messenger came to us in London!' Sitárih wrote, and suggested that perhaps a title such as 'Remembering 'Abdu'l-Bahá in London' might be a good one for the article.[44] She also offered to write a similar article of the Paris visits of the Master – an offer that was taken up by the *Bahá'í World* editorial committee and published in volume 6, 1934–1936.

'Today your wonderful narrative arrived,' wrote Nellie French on 7 November.

I cannot tell you how grateful I am that you have done this, and given to the world this priceless record so full of your own spiritual

consciousness and so fragrant with the love of the Covenant which
abides so sacredly in your heart! I really find myself at a loss to know
how to sufficiently express my appreciation.

Of course you know that all things are submitted to the Guardian without even a pen stroke of change in any respect. He makes his
choice and arranges the copy for the *Bahá'í World*. I am telling you this
so that if anyone should ask, you will know that no editing is done
anywhere except in Haifa.[45]

Having spent months bringing her notes together into what would become
an enduring contribution to the burgeoning literature of the Bahá'í Faith,
Lady Blomfield must have been deeply saddened to learn of the passing
of Bahíyyih Khánum on 15 July 1932. During a recent visit of Shoghi
Effendi's sister Mehrangíz to London, Sitárih had passed on a gift to take
back to the Greatest Holy Leaf.

'Unfortunately I did not reach her in time,' Mehrangíz wrote to Sitárih.

I arrived just two days after the funeral . . . The news of Khanum's
departure has been a great blow. I was looking forward to the happy
hours to sit by her side and have some nice chats with her after this
long period of absence from home. It is indeed a great loss for the
family specially for Shoghi Effendi. We shall miss her immensely. The
only consolation that we have is that our beloved Khanum being so
weak physically has through her passing obtained some relief from her
earthly trouble and sufferings.[46]

'I have put the present that you sent for her upon her bed in her room.
It will remain there as your last earthly token to her. As [for] the one to
Grandmother, I gave it to her. She thanks you very much. She is feeling
terribly depressed by Khanum's passing,' wrote Mehrangíz, concluding her
letter, 'Mother sends you her best love; she always remembers the happy
days that you have spent with us at Haifa. She hopes that you will renew
them soon and spend a spring with us in Palestine.'[47]

'Abdu'l-Bahá's daughter Rúhá told Lady Blomfield that the Greatest Holy Leaf was 'everything to us especially after the ascension of our
Beloved father. You can hardly imagine how much we miss her, and how
empty the house looks without her. She was so beautiful till the end, and
so happy to see all the grandchildren around her . . . Poor mother is feeling

so lonely without her, for so many years they were together and now she is missing the two dear souls she has lost.'[48]

Lady Blomfield was not alone in her literary endeavours. Her daughter Mary, too, was writing, having taken it upon herself to give flesh to the pageant play *The Drama of the Kingdom*, the scenario of which had been suggested by 'Abdu'l-Bahá to their neighbour at Cadogan Gardens, Gabrielle Enthoven, some 17 years earlier. Sitárih encouraged and assisted Mary, and Shoghi Effendi expressed a deep interest in, and offered suggestions to, the enterprise.

Seated in the home of Ms Enthoven, the Master had, without any notes and speaking without pause, revealed His vision of a performance portraying the archetypal happenings that occur with the advent of a new Messenger from God. There are those, 'Abdu'l-Bahá told Ms Enthoven, who, having heard of the Coming of the Promised One,

> . . . frown and shrug their shoulders, returning to their work, scoffing and disbelieving. The second type are those who hear the music, strain their ears to catch the meaning of the Message, and their eyes to discern the Mystery.
>
> The blind receive their sight, the deaf their hearing, and those who were dead arise and walk, still wrapped in the garments of death.
>
> Then there are those who will not believe until they have had signs revealed to them, who crave for proof, saying: 'But we want to see the earthquake. If the Promised One is indeed come, the sun should not give his light, the moon should be darkened, and the stars should fall. We await our Promised One till these signs be fulfilled. We expect to see him descend from heaven in clouds of great glory.'[49]

'Abdu'l-Bahá then visualized a great pageant of the world appearing on the stage. 'Grand nobles and kings, high priests and dignitaries of the Churches, jewelled and gorgeously dressed. They look with scorn on those who believe, saying: "Why should we leave our ancient religions?" They look like devils of malice and oppression,' said the Master.[50] Then in a banquet hall, those who believe are depicted singing, dancing and rejoicing, unimpressed by those possessing worldly wealth and knowledge as they too arrive at the festival. The formerly blind see, the deaf hear again, and crowns descend from above and come to rest on each head. In the final scene, those who believe are tested with their very lives. As one by one, they fall to the executioner, lights shine up and out from their lifeless forms.

By January 1933 Lady Blomfield was able to express to Shoghi Effendi her happiness and excitement that Mary's version of *The Drama of the Kingdom* was ready. It was published in a small paperback book by The Weardale Press. The Liberal politician and philanthropist Lord Weardale was president of Save the Children in Britain and the press had previously published numerous important documents and reports for the fund.

Sitárih hoped that the publication would make a great impact on readers and reviewers alike, although she was realistic enough to expect that there would be a range of reactions. She asked the Guardian whether he would like to have copies – and how many – sent to newspapers in Palestine, Egypt and Persia for the purpose of review. She also enquired how many copies the Guardian himself would like to have and whether he would like copies sent to individual Bahá'í friends in Persia. Additionally, she enquired about the wisdom of sending copies or notices about the book to non-Bahá'í friends and acquaintances in Palestine.

'Would the proclamation be too sudden,' she asked Shoghi Effendi, 'or, would it be wiser to let it arrive by degrees?'[51]

Sitárih's anticipation of a diversity of opinions about *The Drama of the Kingdom* was accurate if not a little optimistic. The press reviews, while generally polite about the sentiments expressed in the play, were generally less than enthusiastic.

'Mrs Hall's "Drama" presents the most admirable programme – the rule of love, the brotherhood of religions, the abolition of war, etc.,' wrote the reviewer for *Literary Guide*, 'but is a little vague as to how it is to be brought about. Perhaps it is significant that in the last scene all the adherents of the new faith are shot at the instigation of the wicked priests of the old one.'[52]

The *Gateway* newspaper in Aberdeen wrote that the play gave 'an Oriental answer to what is really the tragic drama, not merely of the kingdom, but of the world.'

The answer is the Buddhist one of Renunciation, which is all right as far as it goes. Personal success, not the diffusion of general social well-being, is the Western touchstone of achievement. Production, distribution, work hours, wages, prices, need organizing, and if a message from the East could persuade the ambitious to turn their ambition in this direction such a message would be welcome. The West produces no Gandhi of sufficient appeal. But 66 pages, crown octavo, in a paper cover, at half-a-crown, does not suggest Renunciation – except to those who are expected to pay it.[53]

The *Edinburgh Evening News* on 6 February was somewhat more positive, 'The message it conveys is one of peace, co-operation, and universalism, and it will be appreciated by all who have at heart the promotion of human welfare by spiritual means.'[54] And the *Literary Guide* described it as 'a colourful representation of the principles of the Bahai Faith'.[55]

But the practicalities of staging *The Drama of the Kingdom* were all the critic for *The Drama* journal could think of: 'Much of it is beautiful, some of it is vague, all of it presents more difficulties to producer and cast than, possibly, the authoress realizes.'[56]

At least the *Bahá'í News* was enthusiastic: 'A new avenue of approach to the Cause is opened by this notable work,' it wrote.[57]

Despite the lukewarm reception, Lady Blomfield remained eager to share *The Drama of the Kingdom* with her many friends and contacts. One, a Sikh – Bahadur Singh Rajah – wrote to her from Chicago thanking her for 'the beautiful Bahai play "The Kingdom", which I received on my arrival here. You will be interested to know that on the day prior to the receipt of this book some of my friends here took me to Wilmette about 20 miles from Chicago to visit the wonderful Bahai Temple. I thought it a rather strange coincidence to get this book from you soon after my visit to this central place of worship to the Bahai World.'[58]

The Bahá'í community in Britain was in a period of transition in the early 1930s. While she continued to serve on the London Spiritual Assembly, only a handful of believers who had joined Sitárih and Mary in welcoming the Master to London two decades earlier remained. The others had either passed away or, like Tudor Pole and Alice Buckton, preferred to align themselves with other esoteric spiritual practices when the Bahá'í Faith became more formally organized under the guidance of the Master's chosen successor, Shoghi Effendi. Even Sitárih's younger daughter, Rose Ellinor, had drifted away from the community, writing to Lutfu'lláh Hakím, towards the end of her life, 'I am afraid, dear Lotfullah, I am not a practising Bahá'í. I am a black sheep, but I revered and loved the Master, and I love God.'[59]

From the end of 1930 until 1934 very little communication seemed to

London
Bahá'í
Community,
1931

Conference on "Living Religions..."

Conference on 'Some Living Religions within the Empire', 22 September – 3 October 1924, held at the Imperial Institute, South Kensington, London

Lady Blomfield
with Masíh
Ágáh, Jamshid
Munajjim and
Abbas Dehkan
in the Western
Pilgrim House,
Haifa, 1930

Lady Blomfield on the balcony of the Western Pilgrim House at 4 Haparsim Street, Haifa

Lady Blomfield and friends, late 1930s

Back row (*left to right*): Habib Bakeroff [Khamsi], Elsie Cranmer, Richard St Barbe Baker, ?, Mark Tobey, ?, ?, ?; middle row (*left right*): Mollie Brown, Elsie Gibbs, Miss Niven (?), Lady Blomfield, Helen Bishop (?), Constance Langdon-Davies, ? Lady Hornell; front row (*left to right*): Claudia Coles (?), Hasan M. Balyuzi, Rosalind Vance (?)

Lady Blomfield with George Townshend and members of his
family. The visit took place in 1935 when Townshend was staying in London,
undertaking a locum tenens for the vicar of a West Kensington church. Townshend
and his family moved into the vicarage for six weeks, a period during which they
visited Lady Blomfield, who took them to her former home in Cadogan Gardens and
showed them the room that 'Abdu'l-Bahá had occupied.

Lady Blomfield and friends
at Sowberry Court

The new headstone at the grave of Lady Blomfield,
Hampstead Municipal Cemetery, London

occur between the British National Assembly and the Guardian. Minutes from the period are scanty, reflecting perhaps five or six brief meetings each year, and those that do exist contain very few references to Shoghi Effendi. A handful of people joined the Baháʾí community from time to time, but souls whose vision of the mission of the Baháʾí Cause transcended the mentality of a separate religious congregation were rare to find. Wednesday night public meetings at the Baháʾí Centre, now at 19 Grosvenor Place, were held, where the presentations were generally made by invitees from other organizations, such as Esperantists, in an attempt to attract like-minded souls into conversations about the Baháʾí principles.

Rather, the community's brightest hope for the future rested with the younger generation of believers, some of whom arrived from Iran to pursue their studies. Foremost amongst them was Hasan M. Balyuzi, a cousin of Shoghi Effendi, who left his homeland to read history at the London School of Economics and became a driving force in the establishment of a London Baháʾí Youth Group. Among other things, at the suggestion of the Guardian, Balyuzi undertook a fortnightly study class of *The Dawn-Breakers* with the group. Within a year of his arrival he was elected to the National Spiritual Assembly of the Baháʾís of the British Isles and brought his spirit, energy and knowledge – and devotion to the Guardian – to the evolving Baháʾí administration. The renowned American painter Mark Tobey was also resident in Britain, teaching art at Dartington College in Devon, and was also elected to the National Spiritual Assembly.

On 22 April 1933, for the Festival of Riḍván, Lady Blomfield hosted a gathering. At it the Youth Group – including Balyuzi, who was a keen amateur actor – performed a play called *We are Still Nine*, written by a young Persian student at the American University of Beirut named Abu'l-Qásim Faizi, who later became – in Shoghi Effendi's words – the 'spiritual conqueror of Arabia' and, along with Balyuzi, a Hand of the Cause of God. The Youth Group also organized an evening party the following week which more than 180 guests attended. The programme included another dramatic piece, entitled *Disinherited*, the story of a young Muslim man disinherited by his father when he falls in love with an Armenian Christian girl. The evening concluded with two and a half hours of dancing.

While a community life was evolving which perhaps for the first time brought younger and senior believers together, also exciting for the Baháʾís was some high-level recognition in political circles. Sir Herbert Samuel, the leader of the Liberal Party in Westminster and formerly the first

High Commissioner for Palestine, had met 'Abdu'l-Bahá and was deeply impressed by His dignity, grace and charm. In a national magazine, the Bahá'ís were excited to read Samuel's opinion that it was 'possible indeed to pick out points of fundamental agreement among all creeds. That is the essential purpose of the Baha'i Religion, the foundation and growth of which is one of the most striking movements that have proceeded from the East in recent generations.'[60]

Lady Blomfield remained certain that the spirit of God was at work in the world. Eager to point out that a Divine Plan was being carried out, she would draw people's attention in her talks to the fact that there were at least three societies working in London for interreligious under-standing, including the Society for the Study of Religions, in which she was most active. She continued to see the League of Nations, despite its weakened state, as the beginnings of a world governing council. Mostly though, she understood – and profoundly for her time – that the evolving Bahá'í administration was creating a pattern for a new World Order, 'to be established in detail universally when the governments and peoples of the world have become aware of their own destiny'.[61] Whenever she was able, she accepted invitations to speak about the Cause or Bahá'í-related themes to organizations that shared her ideals. In December 1933 she introduced a panel of speakers on the theme of peace at the Women's International Film Association. Her introductory remarks demonstrate her fearless proc-lamation of Bahá'í teachings to an audience:

Peace. How shall I speak of Peace?

Peace is an End! Poets and Seers all down the Ages have dreamed of it! Prophets have prophesied its coming.

Martyrs have died for it! Peace is the culminating, the Reward of steadfast, mighty striving!

How shall our striving be directed? A social reformer, who has been described as the Greatest Statesman in the world of modern Days, has given a plan: Face the Truth! Clear away illusions!

This is a century of Deeds, not of words only! The world has been lulled into sleep by words, especially by words! There is much Talk of Justice, but dark deeds of injustice and cruelty mock us on all sides! The glorious ideals must be translated into actions.

Prejudice must be abolished whether between classes, nations, Reli-gions or Races.

'Ye are all the leaves and fruits of one tree, the waves of one ocean.' 'The world is one Home, live ye in unity!' 'Let not a man glory in this that he loves his own country, let him rather glory in this that he loves his kind.'

Letters were sent out by this Reformer to the Sovereigns of the world. Queen, Emperors, Sultan, Shah, Czar and President, calling upon them, as Guardians of their people, to govern them with justice and wisdom to secure Peace at home. And to call together a Great International Arbitration Council of all the nations of the world. Before this council every matter which might lead to War must be brought, and peacefully decided, so that never again should mankind be disgraced by 'brother slaying brother'. 'These ruinous wars shall cease, and the Most Great Peace shall come.'

As we cannot have the great universal Brotherhood without Brothers, so there cannot be Brothers without some method of establishing understanding. Now, such work as that of our speaker, is one of the greatest means of promoting comprehension and appreciation in the minds of the various nations of the world, and therefore, of bringing nearer the 'Great Day of Peace'. In this Day when the very existence of Civilization is threatened, when the hearts of many are failing them for fear, when political and economy plans are being discussed at numerous meetings in many lands, we are met together to consider a *spiritual* plan for attaining that most important matter in the world, 'Universal Peace'.

This Spiritual Plan is contained in the utterances of Bahá'u'lláh. The solution of the problems, which cause War, will be set before us by the speakers. This solution, the Bahá'í Message, has been described as 'too great for small minds'. But I submit that minds are not small in this age. The Radiant Century. Minds have grown capable of great conceptions, they are able to concentrate on Agreements, which are so much more important than Differences.

Agreements are constructive.

Differences are destructive.

In this Day there exists a great idea which is vital, a vast Agreement – it is in the minds and hearts of myriads of men and women in every Religion, race, and nation – it is the 'Need for Peace.'

Throughout the world there is growing and increasing a response to the 'Need for Peace' a steadfast determination to achieve it!

The Spirit of the Age is manifesting in many signs. In the women's petition to the Disarmament Conference, representing 45 millions of women, in 56 countries, there is this significant phrase: 'A great vision has become clear to the eyes of this generation. The vision of the forces of humanity working together toward one single aim, towards a new world order based on mutual understanding and international good will.'

Many years ago Abdul-Bahá said, 'Mankind will be quickened. There is a new cycle of human consciousness in this Radiant century, the world will be seen as one Home. The Blessed Day of Universal Brotherhood will dawn.'

Bahá'u'lláh said: - 'These ruinous wars will cease, and the Most Great Peace will come, for it is written upon a mighty Tablet by the Strong Pen of God.'[62]

As the Bahá'í community continued to grow in ever increasing numbers of centres around the world, Lady Blomfield found herself in demand from Bahá'ís both at home and abroad to share her memories and experiences. The active Bahá'í teacher Albert Vail – a former Unitarian minister from Champaign, Illinois – wrote to Sitárih asking her to share the notes taken from her conversations with the Holy Family as he planned publications of his own to reach the intelligentsia and young people.

' . . . I want to get ready a life of the Báb and His angel-heroes,' wrote Vail,

> . . . of Bahá'u'lláh and His Apostles, of 'Abdu'l-Bahá, our Lord, so that it may prove to men of science and art, to teachers and ministers the greatness and glory and practicability of the Revelation of Bahá'u'lláh. I am also planning a continuation to 'Heroic Lives' for young people with a great deal of Bahá'í material as the Master asked me to do. And for both these works your notes are gloriously fitted. I could insert whole sections, most of them with the words each time that they are Lady Blomfield's notes from her book . . . I could use almost all your narrative if you think best. My thought is to put in western dress the life of these glorious beings so that western thinkers can comprehend their glory.[63]

Lady Blomfield was not at all precious about her notes, believing the stories she had collected were available for all to share in. She answered Albert Vail's request, specifying that he should use the materials in a way that would glorify the Cause of Bahá'u'lláh.

'The precious notes have come,' wrote Vail. 'They are like ambrosia and bread from the heaven of those who are the divine life. How marvellously your narrator and the translator and your faithful recording have made the heroes of the age live before us! The sweetness and joy of their spirit is wonderful beyond all describing.'[64]

Another believer who greatly appreciated the inspiration that Sitárih generously shared was her fellow Irish countryman George Townshend. Townshend had been ordained as a priest in the Episcopal Church of America before returning to his homeland in 1916 to take up employment with the Church of Ireland. Although a devout Bahá'í at the time his association with Lady Blomfield began, Townshend had spent many years in County Galway, where he was incumbent of Ahascragh and Archdeacon of Clonfert. His recognition of the Manifestation of God for this age while professionally serving the church was the cause of a profound inner turmoil for him which only subsided when he finally renounced his orders in 1947.

Townshend was deeply lonely in his position – both as a churchman who believed that Christ had already returned and in his geographical isolation from the nearest Bahá'ís. He yearned to discuss the Faith with others and to participate in activities. In August 1934, in London on business to meet the publisher of his book *The Promise of All Ages*, he stayed one night with Lady Blomfield in Hampstead and deeply appreciated her company. They had much to talk about in addition to their common heritage. They were both passionate lovers of the Bahá'í teachings who enjoyed immersing themselves in spiritual thought and study. They both read voraciously and assisted Shoghi Effendi as he rendered the sacred scriptures of the Bahá'í Faith into English.

'How I long to associate and work with my real companions!' Townshend wrote to Shoghi Effendi.[65]

The following year, Townshend returned to London when he undertook a *locum tenens* for the vicar of a West Kensington church. He and his family moved into the vicarage for six weeks, a period during which Townshend took his children Brian and Una to visit Sitárih, who found a way to return to her former home in Cadogan Gardens and show them the room that 'Abdu'l-Bahá had occupied.

In the autumn of 1934 Lady Blomfield was able to fulfil a request that had been given to her by the Guardian four years earlier. Queen Marie of Romania was in London basking in favourable reviews for her newly published autobiography, *The Story of My Life*. Between events publicizing the book and parties with old friends, like the famous Astor family, Marie took time to visit the royal family at Balmoral in Scotland. King George V and his wife Queen Mary enjoyed Marie's company but she was most delighted to meet the present Queen Elizabeth, at that time a girl of just eight years.

'Little Elizabeth,' she wrote in her diary, 'is just as adorable as she was always said to be. A quite perfect child, friendly, polite, unselfconscious, amiable & intelligent and into the bargain pretty.'[66]

Queen Marie returned to London in early October for two more weeks of pleasure for herself and took up residence at Claridges Hotel, where the Bahá'ís of London had sent a floral arrangement as a gift which greatly pleased the Queen. The visit, however, was cut short when word reached her that her son-in-law, King Alexander of Yugoslavia, had been assassinated in Marseille, along with the French Foreign Minister, by a Macedonian terrorist. Marie's eleven year old grandson Peter, who was at school in Surrey, was now the King of Yugoslavia.

Just five days before the news reverberated around the world, Lady Blomfield was able to inform Shoghi Effendi that she had been able to present to Queen Marie the precious, illuminated Tablet of Bahá'u'lláh to Queen Victoria that the Guardian had prepared as gift for Marie's thwarted visit to the Holy Land in 1930.

'She accepted it with graciousness, and expressed herself as appreciating the beauty of the gift, and the honour conferred by its presentation. She asked me to convey that message to you,' Sitárih wrote to the Guardian.

> Wishing to know why it came into my hands to present, I told her that I was in that country a few years ago, when you (and all of us) were hoping to see her – and our disappointment when that hope was not realized.
>
> She also and her daughter were disappointed, as they did wish to meet you and to visit the Shrines. How often personages are hedged round by conditions over which they have no control, and misunderstanding which it is wise not to provoke!
>
> I wish I could depict the charm, the beauty, and the serenity of

this wonderful Lady, whose perception of the Great Significance of the Glorious 'wholeness' of the Bahá'í Message is so marvellous.[67]

Shoghi Effendi 'learned with profound satisfaction and joy of your interview with Queen Marie of Rumania, as well as of the floral gift which the London friends have made to her on the occasion of her last visit to that centre,' the Guardian's secretary replied.

It was, indeed, very thoughtful of them to avail themselves of this wonderful opportunity for conveying to her their unbounded appreciation of the great historic services she has been able to render the Faith through her publications.

Shoghi Effendi was also deeply gratified to learn that you have been able to present to the Queen the illuminated Tablet of Bahá'u'lláh. You must have surely been guided and inspired in taking such an action, which must have surely deeply impressed the Queen. The Guardian feels, indeed, very happy and grateful to you for having had the faith, courage and confidence to approach that Lady, and to renew to her the sincere and profound interest and appreciation with which the entire community of the believers throughout the world view her noble efforts for the propagation of the Message.[68]

Sitárih learned from the Guardian's letter that Queen Marie had also recently written another beautiful appreciation of the Bahá'í teachings for the upcoming *Bahá'í World* volume, of which Shoghi Effendi sent a reproduction to Lady Blomfield: 'The Bahá'í teaching brings peace to the soul and hope to the heart. To those in search of assurance the words of the Father are as a fountain in the desert after long wandering.'[69]

'I wish to add a few words in person to reaffirm my deep sense of indebtedness to you,' wrote the Guardian. 'The volume will be published before the end of this year. I will gladly send you a copy as a token of my great and abiding attachment to you and gratitude for your manifold kindnesses and services to the Cause of God. Wishing you good health and happiness from all my heart . . .'[70]

The beginning of 1935 appears to have found Lady Blomfield in uncustomary low spirits. Most of the Bahá'í meetings were being held in the evenings and she was not in good enough health to face going out in the cold night air. She was also feeling disappointed that the book of Mary's play, *The Drama of the Kingdom*, was not selling well, especially among the American Bahá'ís. She was grateful at least, she said, that the Master's instructions concerning the play had been carried out and believed its value would be recognized in the future were the pronouncements of 'Abdu'l-Bahá to become better appreciated. Conscious of the sadness that Sitárih was feeling at the lack of interest in the publication, Shoghi Effendi directed the National Spiritual Assembly of the Bahá'ís of the United States of America and Canada to order as many copies as they could and to encourage the Bahá'ís in their country to do the same.

'This, he feels, would be of great encouragement to Lady Blomfield . . .' wrote the Guardian's secretary to the Assembly, 'who, in view of her manifold services to the Cause in England, as evidenced by the important contacts she has lately made with many distinguished people in London and elsewhere, should be accounted as one of the leading and most prominent servants of the Cause, and as such worthy of every praise and assistance.'[71]

'I am urging the American National Assembly to order as many copies as they possibly can of "The Drama of the Kingdom",' Shoghi Effendi assured Sitárih, adding, 'I am praying from the depths of my heart for your success, your happiness, and the removal of every obstacle that stands in your path. Your past services are engraved upon my heart, and I supplicate the Beloved Master to assist you in your endeavours for the extension and consolidation of your historic work in the service of His Cause.'[72]

During her weeks spent indoors, reluctant to venture out into the cold English winter, Lady Blomfield found solace in George Townshend's book *The Promise of All Ages*. Townshend wrote the book under the pseudonym Christophil, since the church offices he held prevented him from teaching anything but the doctrine of the Church of Ireland. By publishing an apologetic work about the Bahá'í Faith, Townshend was breaking the agreements he had with the church and had no legal protection against dismissal from his post. His intention was to resign his orders in due course when his writing earned him enough money to subsist. Ever eager to promote the Bahá'í Cause to people of influence, whatever her personal circumstances, Sitárih sent copies of Townshend's book to Lord Lamington; Sir Amin Jung Bahadur, an Indian diplomat; Sir Jagadish Chandra Bose, the eminent scientist; and to Queen Marie – news of the latter particularly delighting Shoghi Effendi.

Lady Blomfield's love for, and devotion to, the Guardian remained strong. She continued to write to him from time to time for guidance and answers to questions that had long worried her. As efforts were being made in England to abolish capital punishment, her mind turned once again to the subject and whether it was forbidden under Bahá'í law. Shoghi Effendi's secretary replied 'according to the explicit text of the "Aqdas", capital punishment is permitted, but also an alternative has been definitely provided whereby the rigours of such a condemnation can be seriously mitigated. Bahá'u'lláh has given us a choice, and has, therefore, left us free to use our own discretion within certain limitations imposed by His law.'[73]

Given the Bahá'í principle of the equality of men and women, Sitárih was also eager to understand the use of such terms as 'Son of Spirit' and 'Son of Existence' in the Bahá'í writings, particularly in Bahá'u'lláh's Hidden Words.

'The word "son" used in this connection is a kind of collective noun meaning mankind and has, therefore, no connotation of any sex discrimination between man and woman whatever,' the Guardian's secretary advised her.[74]

George Townshend returned to London in July 1936 for a significant – but under-subscribed – event organized by the World Fellowship of Faiths, a society which was established to encourage friendship and the sharing of knowledge among followers of the diverse religions. The organization was founded by the explorer and spiritual writer Sir Francis Younghusband, who was keen that Shoghi Effendi himself might be able to attend the event which was being titled 'The World Congress of Faiths'.

'He wrote me a most courteous reply to my invitation,' reported Younghusband in his book *A Venture of Faith*, 'regretting that his duties prevented him from being present in person but promising to have an address prepared and read on his behalf.'[75]

The event held from 3 to 16 July on the stage of the Great Hall of the University of London – festooned with potted shrubs provided by the forester, and Bahá'í, Richard St Barbe Baker – featured an array of internationally renowned speakers, although public interest was negligible and only a hundred people or so entered through its doors. For two weeks, talks, discussions and meditation sessions were provided. While individual clergymen attended, the Church of England remained deeply suspicious of the event and its aims. The Roman Catholics stayed away altogether.

Shortly before Christmas 1935 the Guardian unhesitatingly chose

George Townshend to write the paper to be read at the Congress – a task that Townshend found exceedingly challenging.

'I had for 5 or 6 weeks a very anxious rush of work for at the busiest season of the year,' he wrote to Lady Blomfield, 'Shoghi wrote asking me for an article for the World Congress to be completed before the end of January. Essays for such occasions need some thinking over and a lot of shaping so from Dec. 20th until ten days ago, I was a busy person, and I am afraid preoccupied. However the paper is now in the hands of the Congress people and I hope to read it myself in London in July. The article is not propaganda but an appreciation of the Nine Points 'Abdu'l-Bahá set forth as a universal Reform Plan in 1911 in London; and I appear as a student of comparative religion and a well wisher to mankind.'[76]

Townshend was forever anticipating that his public espousal of the Bahá'í teachings would result in him losing his job.

'My position in the Church will quickly become untenable, of course,' he wrote to Shoghi Effendi about the possibility of delivering the paper at the Congress, 'but you will understand this will cause me no spiritual sorrow.'[77]

'I expect I'll succeed in reading the paper but what will happen afterwards I can't imagine,' Townshend wrote to Sitárih.[78]

The Bahá'í session at the Congress was presided over by Sir Herbert Samuel who, in his introductory remarks, gave a brief account of the origin of the Faith and reminisced about his meetings with 'Abdu'l-Bahá and Shoghi Effendi during his term of office as High Commissioner of Palestine. He told the audience that if a choice had to be made from among the many religious communities of the world the one which was closest in its aims to the Congress, the Bahá'í community should be chosen.

'For the Bahá'í Faith exists for almost the sole purpose of contributing to the fellowship and unity of mankind,' Younghusband reported Samuel as saying. 'Other communities might consider how far a particular element of their respective faiths could be regarded as similar to those of other communities. But the Bahá'í Faith aimed at combining into one synthesis all those elements in the various faiths which are held in common.'[79]

Following Townshend's reading of the paper he had penned at the request of the Guardian, a variety of Christians, Hindus and Buddhists responded, all eager to promote their own agendas. An evangelical Christian who was supposed to lead the discussion confessed that he had nothing to argue with and took the time to offer his conviction that the churches themselves were a barrier to world fellowship.

'. . . only through this awakening, only through this rebirth can we know God,' contributed a Bahá'í in the audience, a friend of Lady Blomfield's from Geneva, named Gita Orlova. 'To deny one's Prophet is to deny all the Prophets. If you are from Islám, and you say: "I do not believe in Jesus," you do not believe in Muḥammad . . . As Bahá'u'lláh says, 'The lamps are many. The Light is one . . . Speed ye from your sepulchres.'[80]

Townshend's expectation that his reading of the paper would fill the newspapers with headlines such as 'Irish Archdeacon supports new religion' were unfounded. To his amazement and disappointment, nothing he did ever seemed to raise an eyebrow. Besides, the newspapers of the day were preoccupied with the scandalous affair of King Edward VIII with an American divorcee, Wallis Simpson.

A young Englishman recently arrived home from Canada where he had become a Bahá'í became a devoted admirer of Lady Blomfield at this time. David Hofman, an actor, writer and radio announcer, had declared his faith in Bahá'u'lláh at the home of May Maxwell in Montreal. Almost as soon as he returned to British shores Hofman was elected to the National Spiritual Assembly and became the first manager of the Bahá'í Publishing Trust.

In 1963 Hofman was among the first nine members to be elected to the Universal House of Justice and served 25 years on the supreme governing council of the Bahá'í Faith.

Exactly six decades after the days spent with Lady Blomfield, David Hofman warmly recalled his meetings with Sitárih Khánum, as he liked to call her. He remembered her as a 'very friendly, poetic soul', and very short in stature. She was 'about four foot nothing,' he laughed, 'yet still very dignified and regal. The young Bahá'ís called her the Little Empress as it was her custom to wear rather flowing clothes and elaborate hats and scarves.'

'She always spoke about 'Abdu'l-Bahá in a rather low, aristocratic voice,' Hofman remembered. 'If you wanted to know anything about 'Abdu'l-Bahá, you went to Lady Blomfield. She was marvellous like that. She had such a presence and she was so much respected that whenever she was there you only paid attention to Lady Blomfield in the room – so she never had any problem of calling for attention!'

Hofman enjoyed his visits to the Hampstead home that Lady Blomfield shared with her daughter and son-in-law. On one occasion he asked Sitárih to assist him with a job reference. He was acting professionally at the time when one day he saw an advertisement in the *Daily Telegraph* for a television announcer. Television was in its very earliest days. The first regularly scheduled programmes from the BBC began broadcasting from Alexandra Palace in the north of London in November 1936, to just a few hundred viewers in the area.

Hofman applied for the announcer's job and promptly forgot about it, only to be called some weeks afterwards to an interview. Some eight hundred hopeful applicants had been reduced down to six and, finally, Hofman was offered the post on condition that he provide three good referees. He immediately asked Lady Blomfield if she would oblige.

She replied, 'Of course, dear boy,' he recalled.

A few years later, Hofman became friendly with an employee of the BBC's personnel department who told him, 'Your references were impeccable!' His friend said that before they had even approached her, Lady Blomfield had telephoned the studios and told them, 'You must employ him. He's an excellent young man!'

David Hofman also liked to bring his friends to meet Sitárih at home.

'It wasn't a huge palace by any means and not as luxurious as Cadogan Gardens would have been but it was a comfortable, nice house,' he remembered.

> There was a little front garden, then you went up some steps to the front door. There was a reception room on the right, then you went through to a larger reception room, then the garden at the back was downstairs. There was a basement that had french windows going out into the garden and that's where she entertained people and welcomed the friends occasionally.
>
> I was in a play once. We were playing in Golders Green, only ten minutes' walk from her house. So I rang her up and said I was playing there for the week and I'd been talking about the Cause to my colleagues. I asked whether she would give them a tea party between the matinee and the evening performance on the Saturday. She said, 'Of course, dear boy, of course!' So we went over, about seven of us and she laid on a very nice tea, we walked in and out of the french windows and then she gathered us together and gave us a talk about 'Abdu'l-Bahá . . . They thought she was a funny old lady.

Asked about Sitárih's love for the church, David Hofman replied, 'She was a devout Christian. She believed in many of the Christian doctrines, like the Trinity. I remember discussing that one time and she would say "But there is a Trinity dear boy! It's not as some people think, but there is a Trinity."[81]

For well over a decade, since the passing of the Master, Lady Blomfield had been collecting and transcribing her notes of the history of the Bahá'í Faith, as recounted by members of the Holy Family, with the intention of publishing them in book form. With David Hofman's arrival in Britain – and the encouragement of Hasan Balyuzi and Gita Orlova, in addition to her daughter Mary – Sitárih now had supportive souls around her who were eager to assist her to see the task through to completion. As a member of the National Spiritual Assembly, Hofman was instrumental in setting up and managing the Bahá'í Publishing Trust – established to produce basic Bahá'í literature and provide George Townshend with an income from his writing when he finally left the church. Hofman also founded George Ronald Publisher in 1943 in order to offer a wider range of literature on Bahá'í subjects as well as other titles.

Whenever Sitárih shared the stories from her notes, they always generated much interest and emotion.

'When the friends went to her house when she was writing *The Chosen Highway*,' Hofman recalled, 'she would try to dramatize some of the periods when 'Abdu'l-Bahá was under extreme pressure. For instance, she'd speak in her low voice of how the covenant-breakers would go to the authorities and say, "'Abdu'l-Bahá has gone to Ha-ee-fa" – she spoke like that!'[82]

But for one reason or another, Sitárih's book seemed to undergo a slow gestation. Stories, extended passages, even whole chapters that eventually found their way into her book, *The Chosen Highway*, emerged in other well-received articles and talks she prepared, including another essay for *Bahá'í World*, volume 6, chronicling the Master's sojourn in Paris. Less positive was Albert Vail who, returning Lady Blomfield's notes to her, expressed his concern that they would not find much resonance with a western audience.

'As I read and re-read these glorious pages of your "Notes" from those holy lives, or your narrators,' wrote Vail, 'I realize they are, in most part, food for a few heroic self-sacrificing Bahá'ís.'

The reading public in the Western World is not ready for so terrible a tale of sacrifice and suffering, and sorrow as begins, for instance, with the Greatest Holy Leaf's narrative of the exile journey from Tihran to Baghdad. It almost breaks our hearts to read it. The public will not be attracted but repelled. I notice that when He presented the Cause in the West, our divine exemplar 'Abdu'l-Bahá, never dwelt on martyr-dom and suffering. The Orient being ahead of us spiritually loves it and glories in its sacrifices for the Kingdom. It is dear to the angels but not to the comfort-loving European and American . . .

And then, I wonder, will people understand Bahá'u'lláh's going away and leaving His family in Baghdad to the caprice of Subh-i-Azal unless the whole relation between the Light of the World and the Centre of self-seeking is analysed? Doesn't it really need re-writing here and expla-nation, or editing and omitting? The sweetness and glory of the later pages is simply marvellous when the question of spiritual life is all and all. And your description of the women of the household on pp. 107–109 is wonderful and the stories about the Báb perfectly lovely.[83]

Largely dismissing Vail's concerns, Sitárih – greatly assisted by Gita Orlova – pushed ahead and completed the first sections of the book which detailed the life and mission of the Báb, and the story of Bahá'u'lláh, as recounted through the spoken chronicles of His daughter the Greatest Holy Leaf, His daughter-in-law Munírih Khánum, His granddaughter Túbá Khánum, and three early believers – Mírzá Asadu'lláh Káshání, Sakínih Sultán Khánum and Siyyid 'Alí Yazdí. Lady Blomfield then turned her attention to the latter sections of the narrative, largely in her own words, concerning 'Abdu'l-Bahá's visits to London and Paris, the years of the Great War and the period when she and Major Tudor Pole had played their part in alert-ing the British forces to the danger faced by the Master and His family as the Turkish departed Palestine.

In addition to the major work she was carrying out, Lady Blomfield devoted time during 1936 to preparing a fifth edition of *Paris Talks* as well as revis-ing a small eight-page pamphlet titled *Some Utterances of Bahá'u'lláh*. *Paris Talks* was given a supplementary historical note and introduction, penned by Helen Pilkington Bishop, an American believer who had served at the International Bahá'í Bureau in Geneva and was now travelling around Great Britain ardently spreading the teachings. Also assisting Lady Blom-field in the project was a journalist and member of PEN International, Edward Fuller, who lived in Pinner in northwest London. Fuller worked hard on the design and layout of the edition and by mid-July was sending Sitárih rough galley proofs and quotations for prices of publication. He also expressed concern for Lady Blomfield's health.

'I am so grieved to know that neuritis is troubling you – such a crippling complaint,' he wrote to Sitárih, 'especially for one who finds so much writing to do as you do. I do hope you will be quite better soon.'[84]

Just as she had always done in the past, Sitárih sent the latest edition of *Paris Talks* to Shoghi Effendi and keenly distributed it amongst her friends and contacts, particularly as the Christmas season approached. The Guardian was very pleased to receive his copy of the book and asked Lady Blomfield to send a further 20 copies which he wished to deposit in various libraries in Haifa and 'Akká.

One of Lady Blomfield's acquaintances, a Mrs Dudley, was also profoundly grateful for the gift which revived memories in her of 'Abdu'l-Bahá's stay in London.

'How penetratingly truthful are his words, searching the heart,' she wrote to Sitárih.

> When I think of him, I most often see him in his long green robe walking with firm stride in the sunshine of your drawing room at Cadogan Gardens, or bestowing pink roses on guests, who protesting at his largess, departed with the flowers in felicity. And always there is the recollection of the illimitable light of his eyes – the great strength and authority of his every gesture, the invisible glory of his presence. His was a royalty of both worlds.[85]

'Thank you ever so much for this new copy of *Paris Talks*,' wrote Sister Grace Challis, an active believer from Bournemouth. 'I like it so much. The additions are a great improvement, so helpful. I find these talks of 'Abdu'l-Bahá a help always, one never wearies of reading them, trying to absorb the beautiful message they convey.'[86]

On receiving his copy, member of the National Spiritual Assembly and devoted Bahá'í teacher Alfred Sugar – who was largely responsible for the spread of the Faith around Lancashire and over the Pennine hills to Bradford and Leeds – wrote to Sitárih: 'I shall read the "Paris Talks" again with renewed pleasure and advantage. We shall read from it at our Nineteen Day Feast to be held on the 31st.'[87]

'We all look forward to your book on the Greatest Holy Leaf,' added

Mr Sugar, 'this will be a unique and exceptionally valuable contribution to the literature of our Faith; an exposition of a life so heroic and so sweet as to remain an example for all ages. I still retain the sacred joy with which I heard you read extracts from your MS in your home, some months ago.'[88]

Gita Orlova was the best of supporters and assistants to Sitárih during this time. A Californian by birth, she was an actress who had appeared in London in productions of Shakespeare alongside such legendary actors as Sir Herbert Beerbohm Tree and Sir George Alexander. Before the Great War she had formed her own theatre company and toured Europe. In Russia she met and married a nobleman. She stayed in Russia for the duration of the conflict, then served as a nurse during the Russian Revolution, in the converted grand ballroom of the Tzar. She continued to act and appear in early films, and even penned a drama of her own, *The Unbarred Highway*, inspired by the Seven Valleys of Bahá'u'lláh. In November 1936, writing from Stockholm, Gita promised Lady Blomfield that she would 'really be ringing your door bell soon, and hearing again your dear voice, and then we will continue with the magnificent work you are preparing to live down thru the history of the first magic though terrible days of this revelation. You are always in my thought, and I have longed for you here a hundred times. Together we could have swept the whole town like a flame of spirit. My dear love to you, beautiful and wonderful one.'[89]

As work progressed on the second section of her book, Lady Blomfield was conscientious about ensuring that she reported accurately the events to which she had been party in the preceding decades. She turned to an old friend, Wellesley Tudor Pole – who had also been present during those momentous years – to assist her by giving his version of the story of how 'Abdu'l-Bahá had been protected in the dying days of the First World War. After she telephoned him on 12 December 1936, Tudor Pole wrote to her, 'It will be a difficult task to turn up my files of eighteen years ago in regard to the historic incidents referred to by telephone on Saturday connected with the Palestine campaign,' Tudor Pole wrote to Sitárih. 'Have you any particulars by you as a guide in regard to actual dates? I think some account has already appeared in the Bahá'í journals and no doubt these could be looked up . . .'[90]

In response, Lady Blomfield wrote to Shoghi Effendi and asked him to provide her with a number of dates. He, in return, advised her that, since there was no truly accurate history of the Bahá'í Faith then available, it would be preferable that she use as few dates as possible, and only those about which she was quite certain. Sitárih also asked if the Guardian would be willing to write a Foreword for her book. Again, he declined, saying that since he had refused all similar requests made to him by Bahá'í writers, he could not make any exception to the general rule which would disappoint many of those believers.

'Do be assured that I have considered with the utmost care and deliberation your request,' Shoghi Effendi wrote to her, 'and I grieve to find myself in a situation that makes it impossible for me to accede to it. I deeply regret it, and would have been so glad to collaborate with you in your work . . . Please do not be disappointed. The work you have already achieved is historic, and what you will, with the Beloved Master's guidance, accomplish in the future will, I feel sure, ennoble the record of your past services to the Cause of God. You are often in my thoughts and prayers.'[91]

After receiving Lady Blomfield's version of events, Tudor Pole contributed a four-page account of his recollections, which Sitárih included in full in her book.

'It is interesting to remember that even during the darkest periods of the Great War,' Tudor Pole's remarks concluded,

> . . . 'Abdu'l-Bahá's faith in a British triumph never wavered. Indeed, there is no doubt that He possessed foreknowledge not only of the principal events connected with the war itself, but also predicted correctly happenings belonging to the war's aftermath in regard to Palestine in particular and the world in general. He was providentially spared for some years longer to continue sowing the seeds of a spiritual understanding of the significance of universal peace and brotherhood, which seeds will undoubtedly bear a rich harvest of fruit during years that still lie ahead of us.[92]

Shoghi Effendi was 'particularly rejoiced' to learn of Sitárih's progress on her book, which he hoped would 'serve to create widespread interest in the Teachings, and will also help in stimulating the friends to greater service in His path'.[93]

'It is most kind of Madame Orlova to have offered you her help,' wrote the Guardian's secretary, 'which is indeed highly valuable, in arranging the manuscript. The Guardian has just wired to her, urging her to extend her stay in England, so that you, as well as the friends, may continue receiving the benefit of her assistance and co-operation in your teaching efforts.'[94]

As she neared her ninth decade, old age and its accompanying infirmities rarely seemed to dim Lady Blomfield's optimism. Hasan Balyuzi celebrated the 'contagion of her enthusiasm and the brilliance of her talk and description, her close association with the Master and His family, her unique privileges in the service of the Cause, the intense light of her faith . . .'[95]

On her part, Sitárih reciprocated his admiration for her, reporting to Shoghi Effendi her pleasure at Balyuzi's presence in London. As new premises were being refurbished for use as a Bahá'í Centre, she was also happy to welcome the believers to her home for four consecutive Wednesday night public meetings. The following year, 1937, would see Lady Blomfield become something of an institution in her own right – as a well-loved fixture at the newly-born Bahá'í summer schools.

CHAPTER TWELVE

THE PERFUME OF HYACINTHS

I pray that the Beloved may reward you a thousandfold
for your incessant and meritorious labours.[1]
Shoghi Effendi

Three decades after her first encounter in Paris with the message of Bahá'u'lláh – years that had been filled with unremitting labour on her part to promote His teachings – it was a comfort for Lady Blomfield to witness the resurgence of activities in the British Bahá'í community. It was evident to her, as it was to all her fellow believers, that the spirit of progress had everything to do with the energetic services being rendered by Hasan Balyuzi and David Hofman, as well as the travel teaching efforts of Helen Bishop. The year 1936 had witnessed the inauguration of an official Bahá'í summer school and the first issue of the *Bahá'í Journal*, both of which contributed greatly to building the identity of a national Bahá'í community. At the end of the year the National Spiritual Assembly convened a meeting for the first time in Manchester, in a gesture of unity-building which soon evolved into an annual National Teaching Conference held in the north of England. Early in 1937 the Bahá'í Publishing Trust was born, prompting the Guardian to express his pleasure to Hofman:

> Your splendid collaboration with the English believers is, as I am gradually and increasingly realizing it, infusing a new life and a fresh determination into individuals and assemblies which will prove of the utmost benefit to our beloved Cause. Persevere with your remarkable efforts and historic achievements.[2]

In addition to contributing as far as she was able to developments within the Bahá'í community, Lady Blomfield had always kept a close eye on international affairs and loved to observe how the spirit of Bahá'u'lláh's

Revelation was being taken up at all levels of society. She must have been particularly gratified to note the increasingly harmonious relationship between Great Britain and her homeland, Ireland. The Irish Free State had been established in 1922 and lasted five years before the people voted in a referendum to replace the 1922 constitution, establishing the Republic of Ireland with its own president.

For most of the 1930s, Britain was a nation at peace with itself and its neighbours. But in 1937, a sudden change of mood occurred, not because of any domestic disunity but as a result of the external impact of developments overseas. After the wholesale carnage of the Great War, the country had gradually run down its defences during the 1920s, based on the widespread expectation that there would be no more major wars, at least not in the coming decade. Even after the rise to power of Adolf Hitler in Germany and his march into the Rhineland in breach of the Versailles settlement, the overriding public mood in Britain was passive. Nor was there much enthusiasm for upholding the authority of the League of Nations when diplomatic incidents broke out from time to time. In Spain, when the left-wing, democratically-elected Republican government was invaded by General Franco's right-wing Nationalist force, the British government stuck rigidly to its policy of non-intervention, even if this meant the eventual fall of Spain's democracy.

But continental Europe was becoming increasingly turbulent, forcing the government to consider overhauling its national defences, especially in the air, as the expectation was that any future war would largely be fought in the skies. Jews fleeing Hitler's Germany carried stories of the true ambitions of his regime to British awareness. The writers such as W. H. Auden and George Orwell brought home the reality of the Spanish Civil War, along with the accounts of scores of British volunteers who took up arms with the International Brigade, prompted by a new commitment to internationalism.

'How one wishes that the cruel war in Spain would end,' Lady Blomfield's old friend the Reverend Daniel Cooper Hunt wrote to her from his home in Boscombe, Hampshire. 'So many innocent and non-combatants being killed. Why cannot all live in harmony and peace and help each other instead of killing each other?'[3]

Lady Blomfield was ever conscious of 'Abdu'l-Bahá's desire to see wars cease, and East and West united. On 25 March 1937, as a symbol of that often-expressed wish, Shoghi Effendi married Mary Maxwell, the daughter of May and William Sutherland Maxwell of Montreal. Their union, Mary later wrote, drew the 'Occident and the Orient closer to each other'.[4]

Sitárih was thrilled by the news and wrote to the Guardian, 'The joy of knowing that you are so happily married is an ever-present solace to me, whenever I think of your wonderful, your glorious work for the Cause of God; of your life spent for the suffering human race, and your wife's privilege of, in some sense, shedding a fragrance on your path.'[5]

With unwavering faith, Sitárih persevered in promoting the teachings of Bahá'u'lláh, through frequent public talks, her membership of committees and organizations that shared her ideals, and the regular mailing out of literature – including her revised edition of *Paris Talks* – to friends, acquaintances and people of prominence. A regular and much-appreciated occasion was her 'At Home' meeting, to which she always invited an impressive array of distinguished names. On 8 February 1937, for example, the guest list included Viscount Samuel of Carmel; Sir Ronald Storrs; the Conservative MP for Hampstead, George Balfour; the Duchess of Hamilton; Edwina Mountbatten; the Bishop of London, Arthur Winnington-Ingram; Lady Henschel, author of several books on equestrianism and the widow of the conductor Sir George Henschel; her friend the prisoners' rights activist Gertrude Eaton; and the poet Herbert Asquith, son of the former Liberal Prime Minister. Also invited were numerous family members including the wife of her step-son Charles; her step-daughter and her husband; and the architect Sir Reginald Blomfield and his wife.

The enduring enthusiasm that Sitárih's eldest daughter, Mary, had for both the Bahá'í Cause and the dramatic arts found a unique outlet when she and Gita Orlova founded the Bahá'í Theatre Group, which brought together up to 50 young Bahá'ís and their friends, under Orlova's tutelage, to perform in plays and pageants that either promoted the values and teachings of the Faith or simply strengthened intercultural fellowship between the players. On its playbills, the Theatre Group proclaimed its aspiration to 'portray world problems in the light of the principles taught by Bahá'u'lláh . . . to present the drama of other nations, thus promoting inter-racial fellowship, and, by symbolism, satire, or realism, to expose the dangers now threatening spiritual and intellectual civilization. Only original plays will be produced, or translations as yet unseen in this country.'[6]

The Theatre Group staged, among other things, an acted version of Mary's *The Drama of the Kingdom* and a production of Shakespeare's *As*

You Like It, in which Hasan Balyuzi played the melancholic Jaques and the costumes were provided by a new Bahá'í, Kathleen Hyett. Several decades later, Kathleen would dedicate herself to service at the Bahá'í World Centre in Haifa and, in old age, marry David Hofman, after the passing of his first wife Marion. Gita Orlova wrote that it was 'beautiful to see what a method of teaching this Theatre Group idea becomes, not only for the actual members, but for their family and friends. Everyone is impressed by the Bahá'í cooperation, lack of prejudice, and spirit of "the play's the thing".'[7]

On 24 April 1937 the Bahá'í Theatre Group was called upon to perform at the Consecration Ceremony of the Inter-Religious Fellowship on whose Council and Executive Committee Lady Blomfield sat, representing the Bahá'í community. Also serving on the Council was Richard St Barbe Baker and Sitárih's longtime friend, the animal rights campaigner Louise Lind-af-Hageby, a devoted member of the London Spiritualist Alliance. At the Ceremony, chaired by St Barbe Baker, the Theatre Group presented a pageant drama inspired by Bahá'u'lláh's Seven Valleys. Among the various active young believers of the day who appeared in the production were Marguerite Welby, who played the Spirit of Search; Habib Bakeroff and Hasan Balyuzi, who represented Mankind in the valleys of love and contentment respectively; Louis Rosenfield, a Bahá'í of Jewish origin, who played the Spirit of Astonishment; and Molly Brown, later Balyuzi's wife, who played the Spirit of Annihilation. On this occasion the costumes were made by Dorothy Cansdale, another member of the Bahá'í Youth Group, who later made an outstanding contribution to the evolving British Bahá'í community with her husband John Ferraby.

This vibrant group of Bahá'í youth from London had also had a profound impact on the first summer school, begun in 1936 as an initiative of the National Spiritual Assembly. Shoghi Effendi had been deeply impressed to learn of the success of this first event and conveyed his sincere thanks to the youth for their 'remarkable share in making the school such an outstanding success this year. This has been certainly a bold undertaking, considering the limited number and resources of the believers in England. But the results obtained are highly encouraging and augur well for the future of this first English Bahá'í Summer School.'[8]

The Guardian urged all the British believers

. . . to persevere in their efforts for raising the standard, both intellectual and spiritual, of their Summer School and to heighten its prestige
in the eyes of the friends, and of the general non-Bahá'í public outside.
The institution of the Summer School constitutes a vital and insepara-
ble part of any teaching campaign, and as such ought to be given the
full importance it deserves in the teaching plans and activities of the
believers. It should be organized in such a way as to attract the attention of the non-believers to the Cause and thus become an effective
medium for teaching. Also it should afford the believers themselves
an opportunity to deepen their knowledge of the Teachings, through
lectures and discussions and by means of close and intense community
life.[9]

With the Guardian's clear mandate in mind, plans were already well developed by February 1937 for the second summer school to be held that
August. Despite the fact that a venue had not yet been confirmed, Lady
Blomfield was pleased to be asked to open the school, in a session chaired
by the artist Mark Tobey.

A venue was eventually secured in the form of the Friendship Holidays Association Centre, now known as Cromford Court in Matlock,
Derbyshire, close to the city of Sheffield and on the southeastern edge of
the Peak District. The venue was a magnificent country house, standing
amidst 40 acres of formal gardens and woodland with scenic views across
the uplands. Participants paid eight shillings a day and were able to avail
themselves of the facilities for tennis, boating and swimming as well as
taking part in evening dances offered by the Centre.

The three-week long summer school programme included presentations by Richard St Barbe Baker, David Hofman, and a member of
the National Spiritual Assembly of Germany, Adelbert Mühlschlegel.
Non-compulsory prayer sessions were held each morning before breakfast and attendees could opt to attend an intensive study programme on
Bahá'u'lláh's Kitáb-i-Íqán. St Barbe Baker also offered two illustrated lectures, titled 'Some adventures of a forester in Equatorial Africa' and 'The
Rebirth of Palestine'.

On Sunday 1 August, Lady Blomfield travelled up to Matlock to open
the second English Bahá'í summer school. Her theme was 'The World of
Man and the Divine Revelation'.

'The plan for the Bahá'í Summer School includes many principles which may be described as commands from Bahá'u'lláh,' Sitárih began her talk.

> They are Rays of the Sun of Truth and prescriptions, given forth by a Powerful Physician, for the Healing of the sick body of the world. The disruptive influences, afflicting the institutions of the present day, are signs of a sickness, which needs a mighty and compelling Remedy. Various aspects of this vast subject of the Bahá'í Message will be dealt with from day to day as the programme unfolds itself . . . Having been told that we were created by God the Most Glorious, that His love gave us our being, we are here, at the Summer School, to learn what is required of us . . . We have a vast field to investigate: from the breathing into the first man of the Divine soul-ray: through the childhood of the Human Race, unto this Day!

Lady Blomfield's talk traced the evolution of life on the planet until the arrival of humanity as a responsible being 'created to know God and to worship Him'. She introduced the concept of the Manifestations of God as the spiritual Educators of humanity:

> This Manifestation of God in a Human Temple takes place at the dawning of each new Dispensation. We know some of their names: Krishna, Buddha, Moses, Jesus the Christ, Muhammad. Each sent to various races and nations, in appointed epochs of time. According to their spiritual evolution and conditions. A different personality they each have, but the same spirit. In this 'Glorious King of Days', in which we have the privilege of taking part, the followers of these Great Religions are commanded to cast away the prejudices, which have separated them, together with the intolerance and hatred engendered by their differences, and to come together, in a bond of unity, to work as friends for the establishing of that Kingdom for which the Prophets came into the world, suffered and died! . . .
>
> So Bahá'u'lláh calls us to the honour and joy of His service. Because of this Revelation, we may work for spiritual progress with a real, practical knowledge of the nature of man as an individual, and of the high destiny to which he is called. A banquet is set before us. On this table is spread, in the presence of the world – spiritual and material – many beautiful fruits: justice, love, truth, mercy, compassion, beauty, comfort

in grief, solution for all the problems of the modern world, the cessation of war and of tyranny.[10]

Lady Blomfield was, as always, received with tremendous warmth and appreciation. Later the following week she went to speak to some of the other guests holidaying at Cromford Court, a few of whom were moved to seek out the Bahá'ís and enquire further about the Faith.

The summer school of 1937 was deemed a great success. It showed 'once again, the immense services which this institution can render to the Faith', the *Bahá'í Journal* reported in October.

> Of outstanding value is the fact that believers from all over the country are able to meet, live a community life together, and share common experiences as well as study the Teachings together. The organic character of the Bahá'í community is demonstrated and strengthened by Summer School.[11]

While at the summer school Lady Blomfield struck up a friendship with a General Hill and his wife, Phyllis, from Salisbury, who had been invited to the event by Richard St Barbe Baker. Afterwards, Phyllis Hill and her mother were keen to know more about the Bahá'í teachings and attended two gatherings with Sitárih. Phyllis had experienced some sort of religious vision that she could not quite comprehend and so she invited Sitárih and Helen Bishop to Salisbury for a weekend. There the Hills gathered 40 of their friends to learn more about the Cause of Bahá'u'lláh. The visit was another marvellous opportunity for Lady Blomfield to teach the Bahá'í Faith, and her audience was deeply appreciative.

'I feel I must write and thank you from us all for the inspiration you gave us this weekend,' Phyllis Hill wrote afterwards to Sitárih.

> We were very deeply impressed. The teaching of Baha'u'llah seems to fill a great want in this modern world and I feel much more settled in my mind about it since getting the interpretation of my vision. Before I felt it might be either a warning against false prophets or an indication that this was a revelation to be followed, now I feel much more confident that it is the latter so am feeling my way carefully along. You were indeed lucky to have had the wonderful privilege of knowing Abdul-Baha.[12]

Lady Blomfield's charm and genuine affection for people meant that her efforts to teach the Bahá'í Faith rarely seemed to meet with any kind of negative criticism or reaction. Sometimes, though, caution seemed to characterize some of the responses she received. One of her acquaintances, M. F. Wren, told her that he did not think the English would ever join the Bahá'ís actively in large numbers.

'I need not give you my reasons for thinking this and to do so would take more space than I can find in a letter,' he wrote to her.

> But I do think the part the English can and may play in the Baha'i Cause will be most important, as things seem to be working out in the world today. If you are inclined to feel disappointed at any apparent lack of progress may I suggest that consolidation is more important at the moment? Of course I speak only as an observer. You know much more from within the movement . . . I hope the day is not far distant when members of all religions will work together and co-operate 'with the Spirit' for world advancement. That day is not yet, but there are signs even today that it will dawn before long. When it comes, I am sure the Baha'is in all parts of the world will be called upon to play a great part.[13]

However varied the response of her hearers, Sitárih persevered and took every opportunity to speak more about the Cause. On 26 January 1938 she was invited to make some remarks at the new year's luncheon of the London Free Church Federation.

'This is an inter-religious fellowship to promote the spiritual unity of mankind and a reverent attitude towards other faiths whilst remaining loyal to one's own,' said the invitation.[14] The event was held at the City Temple, where 27 years earlier the Master had given His first ever public address to an enthralled congregation. How must Sitárih have felt, knowing that the theme of the luncheon taking place at the same venue was 'World Peace through Spiritual Understanding', a subject that the Master had devoted His entire life to promoting.

Another invitation came from the Salvation Army International Headquarters, asking Lady Blomfield to share a platform with the Prime Minister's wife, Anne Chamberlain, at a meeting at the Hyde Park Hotel about Women's Social Work. The invitation came from Major Lena M. Dennett, whom Lady Blomfield had met and evidently spoken to about the Bahá'í teachings in October 1937.

'The movement is undoubtedly a good one because it makes for the fostering of very real understanding and sympathy between those of various nationalities and religions,' Major Dennett wrote to Sitárih. 'Personally, I think that it would do us all good to lower the barriers which have been built up between us by our creeds and doctrines during the process of time and to worship in simplicity, realizing that the spiritual life is the only thing that really matters.'[15]

On another occasion Sitárih encountered an old friend, a member of the Society for the Study of Comparative Religions to whom she had been endeavouring to teach the Bahá'í Faith for 13 years. He asked her, 'Can you imagine why our Society is so wanting in vitality?'

Lady Blomfield replied frankly: 'The society concerns itself with the past, ignoring the great 'Manifestation' of the present. The Bahá'í Faith is not just a survey of former Religions, the fine philosophies are there also, but it is a way of life – not dry bones but a living Spirit . . . How can a society be vital when it ignores the vitalizing spirit?'[16]

Sitárih informed the Guardian about her friend. 'He is a splendid man, of a rare and noble soul. Pray for him, dear Shoghi, he is worth it.'[17]

As a result of their encounter, the gentleman asked if Lady Blomfield would be willing to speak to the Society. 'It is very probably a way of attracting people of capacity, and a privilege to be invited to make the attempt. Please counsel and pray for me!' she asked the Guardian.[18]

Shoghi Effendi was gratified to hear about the fresh vitality animating the Bahá'ís in London and praised Lady Blomfield for the support she was extending to the teaching work, particularly in her attempts to attract the attention of thoughtful and intelligent people.

'In this connection he wishes me to express the hope that the public address you have requested to deliver on the Cause by the "Society for the Study of Comparative Religions" will be a great success, and that as a result genuine interest will be awakened in the Teachings,' wrote the Guardian's secretary to Sitárih.

He will specially pray that your efforts in this connection may be blessed and yield the maximum results. He wishes me also to assure you that he will remember in his prayers the member of the above-mentioned society whom you have been trying to confirm in the Faith. May Bahá'u'lláh awaken his soul to the truth of His Message and inspire him to actively join the Cause.[19]

'I was truly delighted to hear from you,' added Shoghi Effendi as a foot-note, 'and to know of your steadfastness and increasing success in the service of this noble Faith. You are often in my thoughts and prayers, and I supplicate our Beloved to shower upon you and your dear daughter His imperishable blessings.'[20]

Lady Blomfield's presentation to the Society for the Study of Comparative Religions went ahead on 14 February 1938 at 33 John Street, off Gray's Inn Road. It was one of a series of ten weekly talks that also took in various other religious communities including the Church of Jesus Christ of Lat-ter-day Saints, the Society of Friends, Christian Science and traditional Polynesian religions. Presiding on the night of Sitárih's presentation was Sir E. Denison Ross, recently retired from his post as Professor of Persian at the University of London, where each year he had delivered lectures on the Báb and Bahá'u'lláh. Sitárih considered his presence at the lecture an added grace. She found him to be extremely cordial, especially as he said many appreciative things about Shoghi Effendi and complimented the Guardian's scholarly and beautiful facility with the English language.

Sitárih had been asked to give an account of the history of the Bahá'í Cause, followed by some personal memories of the Master. She began her talk, however, by reading from a letter to the editor she had seen published in *The Times* on 7 August 1937. The letter described how

> . . . the disunity of aim and conflict of interest that now disturb all human life and relationships throughout the world, whether social, national or international . . . is surely today the greatest menace of modern civilization. On one point all thoughtful people must be united. No effective unifying or harmonizing principle has yet been discovered in any system of social or political philosophy, or method of political organization, or science of national, or international statecraft. Quite plainly human ingenuity and human intelligence have failed to find a remedy for the world conditions. It cannot be God's plan or purpose that no remedy should be found. He surely has one . . . What nations imperatively require is a development of the sense of personal responsibility to bring men and women and all administrations and governments to a spirit of loyalty to God. This alone can unite a chaotic world.[21]

Lady Blomfield looked at those gathered and loudly proclaimed, 'The message to this audience and to all the world is this: "The remedy is found!" In this "Great Day of God", the "King of Days", three Holy Ones have been sent to us, bearing the remedy!'[22]

She then proceeded to tell her audience the story of the Báb in wonderful detail, drawing on her own notes and the priceless account of *Nabíl's Narrative*.

'In Western academic circles,' she said, 'the story of the Bábí movement is better known than that of the Bahá'í Faith. The truth is not yet grasped that the first was the seed, and the second the promised bloom.'[23]

As she proceeded to inform her audience of the life of Bahá'u'lláh, Sitárih mentioned that she had heard from His 'beautiful daughter' many stories which she did not have time to share.

'Other events of intense interest were described to me by the wife of 'Abdu'l-Bahá, by His daughters and by other friends who were first hand witnesses of those soul stirring days.'

Detailing some of the necessary features of the new world that Bahá'u'lláh had envisaged, Lady Blomfield quoted extensively from the message He had penned to Queen Victoria.

'It is significant of the completeness of the Revelation of the New Dispensation that the text of His book provides for every emergency confronting human beings in this age,' she said.

'This truth must continue to grow in the consciousness of humanity and be impelled forward until it achieves its destined ascendancy. For man's politics are feeble, God's politics are mighty.'[24]

One month later, Lady Blomfield reported to the Guardian that, 'People were delighted, some of the audience gathered round me, telling me how much they were impressed.'[25] She wondered if it would be wise to invite Sir E. Denison Ross to write the Foreword to her book and asked if Shoghi Effendi thought it a good idea. He did and hoped that the contact she had made with the esteemed professor would serve to deepen further his appreciation of the real significance of the Bahá'í Faith.

'It is always such a deep pleasure to receive direct word from you, and to know you are carrying on with such devotion, zeal and determination your beneficent and manifold activities,' the Guardian told her. 'The success that has attended your latest effort to spread the knowledge of the Cause is highly gratifying. I feel grateful and cheered.'[26]

Despite his multifarious duties and global responsibilities, Shoghi Effendi eagerly encouraged Lady Blomfield to complete her book. He read the first part thoroughly after she sent it to him, made suggestions for improvements and also corrected her Persian spellings. The Guardian even went so far as to send her other notes, asking her to give them some form and add them to the book. She did all that he requested of her and continued with the final section of the book, which included inviting testimonials from those distinguished personages who had encountered the Master: her old friend Mrs Thornburgh-Cropper, Viscount Samuel of Carmel, Lord Lamington, and Sir Ronald Storrs, the former Governor of Jerusalem.

'Their replies are very interesting,' Lady Blomfield told Shoghi Effendi.[27]

Despite the distance of almost two decades, Sir Ronald Storrs's remarks reflected his abiding admiration for 'Abdu'l-Bahá.

'When he came to Jerusalem he visited my house and I never failed to visit him whenever I went to Haifa,' wrote Sir Ronald. 'His conversation was indeed a remarkable planing, like that of an ancient prophet, far above the perplexities and pettiness of Palestine politics, and elevating all problems into first principles.'[28]

Lord Lamington was equally generous when he wrote his praise of the Master: 'There was never a more striking instance of one who desired that mankind should live in peace and goodwill and have love for others by the recognition of their inherent divine qualities.'[29]

Sitárih was anticipating that the book would be ready for publication by the spring of 1938 and was hopeful of its success as many people to whom she read extracts asked her when it would be published. Others, for example a woman from Budapest who visited Lady Blomfield in London, provided her with additional stories to consider including in the narrative. This particular woman's husband was Leópold Stark, the secretary of the Theosophical Society in Budapest.

'She and her husband . . . were of those who made the arrangement for His Visit, and were with Him all through that wonderful time,' Sitárih told Shoghi Effendi. 'This lady is collecting accounts of various episodes which took place in those days. They may be a useful addition to the book.'[30]

A situation then occurred, however, which resulted in a setback that deeply aggrieved Sitárih.

'A Bahá'í friend, with better intentions than ability,' she told the Guardian, 'asked to be allowed to rearrange the manuscript in a more suitable form for publishing. Unfortunately the rearrangement was done without my collaboration, without consulting me, or indeed letting me see what was done!! It was then sent to the publishers (also without my knowledge) who declined it, as being badly put together!'[31]

Thankfully, the damage was not lasting. One of the reviewers for the publisher in question contacted Lady Blomfield about the matter. When she showed him some of her original manuscript, he was impressed and interested to know more about the Bahá'í Cause.

'Although the MS was mutilated,' Sitárih told the Guardian, 'he saw that it would be possible to re-plan the additions, so bringing out its great interest, both for Bahá'í friends, and to introduce the cause to others.'

'It is sad to think that this would have been done last summer, but for the unfortunate circumstance which I have explained,' she mourned. 'I am longing to work upon this task of Love for the Cause, and for the Beloved Master's activities. People are waiting with keen interest to know of the things that took place in His memorable visits.'[32]

Shoghi Effendi's secretary informed Sitárih that the Guardian trusted the book would come out during the course of 1938 and that it would 'help in furthering the teaching work throughout England. He wishes me to assure you of his full approval of the new title you have suggested for your book.'[33]

For the book's title, *The Chosen Highway*, Lady Blomfield had been inspired by the words in a letter of 'Abdu'l-Bahá.

'Look at Me!' the Master had written.

Thou dost not know a thousandth part of the difficulties and seemingly unsurmountable passes that rise daily before my eyes. I do not heed them; I am walking in my chosen highway; I know the destination. Hundreds of storms and tempests may rage furiously around my head; hundreds of Titanics may sink to the bottom of the sea, the mad waves may rise to the roof of heaven; all these will not change my purpose, will not disturb me in the least; I will not look either to the right or to the left. I am looking ahead, far far. Peering through the impenetrable darkness of the night, the howling winds, the raging storms, I see the glorious Light beckoning me forward, forward. The balmy weather is coming, and the voyager shall land safely.[34]

The Faith of Bahá'u'lláh had taken root in the British Isles in the final years of the 19th century when Mary Virginia Thornburgh-Cropper, a

Californian by birth, had accepted His teachings and joined the first group of western pilgrims to meet 'Abdu'l-Bahá in 'Akká. Forty years later, on 15 March 1938, 'Minnie' – as she was affectionately known – passed away, depriving Lady Blomfield of one of her oldest and most trusted companions in the Cause. It was Mrs Thornburgh-Cropper who had put her car at the Master's disposal during His visits to London.

'I can see her tall, graceful figure with her serene angel face shining beneath a crown of silver hair,' wrote Mary Basil Hall, 'her blue eyes, and the soft blend of blues and purples in her dress, gracious to all, and ready to be of constant service to our exalted Guest.'[35]

'Her departure must have surely been deeply felt by the believers, and especially by the older ones who knew her well and intimately . . .' the Guardian's secretary wrote to Lady Blomfield. 'Shoghi Effendi will specially pray at the Holy Shrines for the soul of our departed sister that in the Realms Above it may progress and attain the highest state of spirituality and peace.'[36]

Lady Blomfield lamented the passing of her friend, telling the Guardian that she would 'miss her lovely presence, always radiating Love!'[37]

Shoghi Effendi promised Sitárih, 'I will continue to pray for you, as well as for the soul of our dear, distinguished and departed Bahá'í sister and co-worker, whose passing I truly deplore. Wishing you from the depths of my heart happiness, good health and success.'[38]

Lady Blomfield was filled with admiration at the way the Guardian administered the affairs of the Cause. She was also enamoured with his translations and other writings.

'I am more rejoiced than I can express with *Gleanings* and with your pamphlets, other glorious translations,' she told him on one occasion.[39] On another, 'I write seldom, as I do not wish to add to your burden of letters, but I know that you are aware of my heartfelt devotion to the Guardian of the Faith, and love of the glorious Translations.'[40]

Mrs Thornburgh-Cropper's death was followed shortly by the news that 'Abdu'l-Bahá's widow Munírih Khánum had also passed away, on 30 April 1938. Just three months later Queen Marie of Romania died aged 62 at Peles Castle, in the Carpathian mountains.

'I am now feeling that many more of my loved ones are in the direct "Shelter of Heaven" than still in this mortal world,' Sitárih wrote to Shoghi Effendi.[41]

Of the numerous Christian denominations with which Lady Blomfield had contact, she had always held the work and values of the Salvation Army in great respect. Founded as the East London Christian Mission in 1865, the vision of its founders William and Catherine Booth was to bring the Christian message to the poor, destitute and hungry by meeting both their physical and spiritual needs. With the advancement of education and the relief of poverty among the Salvation Army's charitable objectives, Sitárih had little hesitation when she was invited to open its Annual Sale of Work on 11 May 1938. Her poetic welcome speech is filled with encouragement for the work of the Army as well as quotations from, and allusions to, the sacred texts of the Bahá'í Faith:

> We are met together to show our appreciation of the great work of the Salvation Army. The rescue of those who, without the sympathetic aid of this devoted company, would sink lower and lower into the slough of despond; to lift up myriads of our brothers and sisters 'out of the mire and clay, and set their feet upon a rock'. What a dream!!
>
> This colossal enterprise did not appal the founder of the Salvation Army, whose noble presence, as he stood facing a crowded audience in the Albert Hall inviting them to arise and co-operate with him, must remain a lasting memory to all who saw and heard General Booth on that eventful day. His was a call to translate noble ideals into actions . . .
>
> This work is spreading out and will expand, so magnificent is the courage and faith of these soldiers of life – until not in one town, or one country only, but in every country of the world where men, women and children, the pitiful apathetic people, sleeping a sleep like unto death in its misery, shall be awakened unto a more excellent way and shall realize that they too are children of the Most High God, and inheritors of that kingdom for which we have been praying for nigh 2000 years, where 'His will shall be done in earth as it is in heaven'.
>
> We remember that this prayer of the Lord Christ is also a prophecy which will be fulfilled for His word never returns void . . .
>
> The magnitude of the field of endeavour is astounding, the whole earth is being embraced in the work which is a preparation for the 'coming of the Kingdom'. Masses of unhappy people are being taught the recuperative power of a spiritual springtime, are being awakened to the reality of that light, which lighteth every man who cometh unto the world . . .

As we meditate upon the vast scheme of the Salvation Army, we recognize the presence of the New Cycle of human consciousness, which, in this Radiant Century, is showing itself in an increased understanding of those Powerful Words of our Lord Christ, 'Greater Works shall ye do.' With this awakening of the Pioneer Soul, which we revere as General Booth, it was no longer a vague 'Am I my brother's keeper?' but the Trumpet Blast in answer, 'I am, I am My Brother's keeper. Every human being is my brother and my sister.'

Thus with the authority of true religion, started the Salvation Army on its way. Consisting of soldiers of light, allied to the supreme concourse. Therefore undaunted, unafraid, conscious that the Glorious King of Kings had created Man to know Him and to adore Him.

He had laid upon Man His Image, and revealed to Him His Beauty. Is it not a radiant Cause that we are offered the privilege of supporting? All who wear the Crown of Humanity are invited to assist in this light-bearing work.

And every article made, sold or bought is important in its helpfulness to some poor soul in need. And so I am happy to declare this sale open – to help forward, as far as we are able, the beautiful work of the Salvation Army.[42]

As the worldwide Bahá'í community evolved, Shoghi Effendi was keen to ensure that the institutions of the Administrative Order conceived by Bahá'u'lláh were raised up on solid, legal foundations. By incorporating the Spiritual Assemblies, the Bahá'í institutions could, for example, own property. The Guardian called upon the National Spiritual Assembly of the British Isles to make 'strenuous efforts' to incorporate itself.[43] The Guardian urged David Hofman to approach Lady Blomfield, Major Tudor Pole and Lord Lamington to assist in this task.

'Any help you can extend at the present time to the British National Assembly, who are striving to obtain recognition from the authorities, will be deeply appreciated,' Shoghi Effendi wrote to Sitárih.[44]

Lady Blomfield sent Shoghi Effendi the final chapters of *The Chosen Highway*, concerning the Master, and told the Guardian that she had been asked to open the next Bahá'í summer school with an address on the Báb, and a few days later, an account of 'Abdu'l-Bahá.

'May I be given wisdom and strength for that great privilege!' she wrote.[45]

Shoghi Effendi felt certain that Sitárih's presentations at the summer school would 'create a profound impression upon all the attendants, and stir the friends afresh with the desire to serve and labour for the promotion of our beloved Cause throughout England'.[46]

'As a long-standing and distinguished member of the English Bahá'í Community,' wrote the Guardian's secretary, 'it is surely a great privilege that you should address your new and young fellow-believers, who certainly have much to learn and benefit from your rich and varied experiences of many years in the Cause . . .'[47]

As always, Shoghi Effendi took the time to add a personal note to the letters which his secretary wrote to Lady Blomfield.

'Your letters are always a joy to read,' he told her. 'They greatly stimulate and hearten me in my arduous task, which is growing daily in range and complexity. I heartily welcome the evidences of your increasing participation in the administrative activities of the Faith, and I pray that the Beloved may reward you a thousandfold for your incessant and meritorious labours.'[48]

As Sitárih put the finishing touches to her manuscript of *The Chosen Highway* and filled up spiral-bound books with her pencilled notes for lectures to be given at the coming summer school, Mary was meantime busily writing and staging more dramatic works. Her three act play *The Rector of Hallowdene* was performed in May 1938 by the Bahá'í Theatre Group. On this occasion, acting amongst the usual cast of eager Bahá'í amateurs and their friends was a professional film actor named MacArthur Gordon, who was contracted to Vulcan Pictures. He had been seen in *Melody of My Heart, Such is Life*, and in 1938, *Scruffy*. Another play of Mary's, *The Love of Ming-Y*, was performed the following year in Hornsey Town Hall and for one night at the Phoenix Theatre in London's West End.

The third Bahá'í summer school was held from 30 July to 20 August 1938, at Cudham Hall, a mid-19th century manor house set amidst woods, hills and valleys near Sevenoaks in north Kent, somewhat closer to London than the previous year's excursion to Matlock. As was becoming a tradition, Lady Blomfield opened the school with an address, titled 'The Báb – the Point of a New Creation'. On Thursday 4 August she returned to her favourite subject, ''Abdu'l-Bahá – the Exemplar of the Bahá'í Faith'. Among the other speakers who delivered lectures during the three week period were Hasan Balyuzi, David Hofman and Alfred Sugar from Manchester.

The evenings were programmed with educational talks and social activities. David Hofman recalled delaying Mary's husband, Captain Basil Hall, when the two of them went for an afternoon swim ahead of the Captain's scheduled evening talk on 'Peace Duties of the Navy'. As they drove up to the main building, Hofman noted Mary standing in the doorway, angrily tapping her foot.

Basil Hall was a distinguished retired naval captain who had married Mary, who was his second wife, in 1920. His presentation was to be followed by a fancy dress ball for which Basil had prepared a special costume. Hasan Balyuzi introduced the Captain before his talk, at which point Basil emerged dressed, remembered Hofman, 'in cocked hat, silk breeches, silver buckles on his shoes, sword and everything. He stood up there and bellowed, "Function of the Navy is WAR!" Then he gave us a wonderful talk on what the Navy did in peacetime, about geographical exploration, relief of suffering and everything else.'[49]

Other speakers during the summer school programme included Richard St Barbe Baker lecturing on 'The Soul of Africa', and Ninette de Valois, the legendary choreographer and director of the Vic-Wells ballet. Molly Brown – later Balyuzi – was one of the principal dancers at Sadler's Wells in London and had invited her director to come and address the Bahá'í summer school on the subject of ballet.

The memory of Lady Blomfield at the English summer schools lingered long in the minds of those who were privileged to spend time with her.

'She it was who told us of the Master, who showed us what it meant to follow the True Exemplar,' wrote the *Bahá'í Journal* after her passing. 'A bulwark in need, a friend in trouble, a companion in happiness, may her spirit be ever with us and assist us to manifest those qualities of kindliness, consideration and graciousness of which she was the embodiment.'[50]

By October 1938 Lady Blomfield was slowly completing her book but still did not have anyone to write a Foreword. Sir E. Denison Ross had declined the invitation and she wondered whether she might ask 'Abdu'l-Bahá's daughters – Rúḥá and Túbá – to pen some words for the opening pages since they knew 'the whole matter so well', including the conditions in which Sitárih was privileged to collect her notes. She wanted, though, that the English be all their own.

'I am anxious to keep the atmosphere, as far as possible, of the events of such enthralling interest, as related to me,' she wrote to the Guardian.[51]

There remained certain parts of the book that she felt required further work – maybe there should be the addition of the story of Ṭáhirih and quotations from *Gleanings from the Writings of Baháʼuʼlláh* and other of His own words that related to the events of His life? Should the book include an account of the Guardianship to date?

She concluded her letter to Shoghi Effendi, ʼWith my heartʼs love and thanks for your comforting Messages. Ever affectionately, in His Service, Sara Sitárih Blomfield.ʼ⁵² It was to be the last letter she would ever write to the Guardian.

Shoghi Effendi had no objection to her approaching ʼAbduʼl-Baháʼs daughters to pen the Foreword, nor did he mind the use of suitable passages from Baháʼuʼlláhʼs own writings.

ʼI rejoice to learn of these ceaseless evidences of your vigorous determination to promote in every way possible the manifold interests of our beloved Faith,ʼ the Guardian tenderly told her. ʼThe Beloved, Whom you serve with such diligence, fidelity and loving devotion, extols and rejoices at your accomplishments and noble exertions. I will continue to pray for their extension, success and fruition.ʼ⁵³

As Lady Blomfield awaited Shoghi Effendiʼs comments about her manuscript, the Guardian was completely absorbed in composing a major letter to the American Baháʼís, which was published under the title *The Advent of Divine Justice*. In it he clearly anticipated the coming war that would encircle the entire planet for the ensuing six years.

ʼWho knows but that these few remaining, fast-fleeting years, may not be pregnant with events of unimaginable magnitude, with ordeals more severe than any that humanity has as yet experienced, with conflicts more devastating than any which have preceded them.ʼ⁵⁴

The Guardian deeply appreciated the efforts Lady Blomfield was making to write her precious reminiscences and apologized for the delay in returning her manuscript to her.

ʼYour account is most interesting and indeed excellent in presentation and of real historical value to all students of the Cause,ʼ his secretary wrote. ʼThe Guardian is confident that when published these reminiscences will be eagerly read and widely appreciated by all the believers. He has particularly liked the sections regarding the Masterʼs visit to Paris and London, and thinks they are among the most striking and impressive passages in the whole book . . .ʼ⁵⁵

The Chosen Highway, as it finally appeared, is not entirely as Lady Blomfield intended it. In a letter to Lord Lamington, dated 14 March 1939, she described that the book she was writing would provide a continuous account from the years before the appearance of the Báb until the passing of 'Abdu'l-Bahá.

> To this story is added some narrative of the progress of the Faith down to the present day, including the immense work of the Guardian, Shoghi Effendi, in administering the affairs of the Cause in forty countries, embracing eight hundred Assemblies, the members of which are quietly proceeding to awaken mankind to the necessity of a spiritual outlook on the problems of this great day.[56]

Although her desire to write the story of the Bahá'í Faith in later times was not fulfilled, she completed the manuscript to her satisfaction and enjoyed many visits from David Hofman, who was to publish the book for the Bahá'í Publishing Trust.

'It was my privilege, not only to know Lady Blomfield, but to discuss with her, in company with Mr Balyuzi, the publication of *The Chosen Highway*... As a representative of the Bahá'í Publishing Trust, she authorized me to publish the book and to attend to the final arrangement of the manuscript,' wrote Hofman in the Editor's Note at the beginning of the book.[57]

'The editing and preparing for press was greatly simplified by the amount of work which Sitárih Khánum herself had done, and by the many discussions I had had with her,' wrote Hofman.[58] Privately, he laughed at the creative differences he had on occasion with Lady Blomfield over the publication.

'I was saying something about the book,' he recalled in 1996, 'and she didn't agree with me on something or other, and I insisted, and she stood up – all of her four foot – and looked at me and said, "Dear friend!" You didn't argue with Lady Blomfield you know!'[59]

Sitárih requested that the cover be in Irish blue, 'and this in itself will bring her to mind ...' wrote Hofman.[60]

With no Preface forthcoming from the Master's daughters, Lady Blomfield turned to Hasan Balyuzi to pen a few words of introduction.

'*The Chosen Highway* offers every seeker a real feast of knowledge,' wrote Balyuzi.

It cannot but eternally merit the esteem of the historian.

But the true greatness of this work does not lie in its compendium of narrative and chronicle. It is the spiritual purport of *The Chosen Highway*, the pattern of love, justice, charity, and sacrifice that it weaves and depicts, the chord of harmony that it strikes, which place it in prominent relief. To a world shaken to its depths, it brings the assurance that evil can never achieve the final, the abiding victory.'[61]

Lady Blomfield was now 80 years old, her health and strength were declining and the book – although she did not live long enough to see it published – had finally been completed. Numerous were the friends who stayed in correspondence with her and mourned her absence from their gatherings.

'There is such a long time we have not seen you either in Paris or Geneva,' wrote one, Elisabeth Hesse,

> . . . but I have not forgotten at all the precious blessing it has been to come in contact with you and the inspiration it has meant to hear you in those far gone days in the small islet on the shores of the Lake! How splendid to realize you have never stopped to work so beautifully for Bahá'u'lláh ever since . . . I do hope some way will open that I can meet you again, dear Lady Blomfield . . .[62]

Another friend, Kitty Schopflocher, told Sitárih, 'You are the only lady of culture and refinement that I have met who gives forth that true spirit of love and enthusiasm as is usually found in our more humble brothers and sisters less highly placed.'[63]

When she was physically able, Sitárih endeavoured to support her good causes. She served on the Council of the Save the Children Fund in Britain and was, for a while, its vice president. Early in 1939 she offered to give up her seat to make way for someone younger but her colleagues pressed her to stay on. She also sat on the Advisory Council to St Mary's, a co-educational school at 16 Wedderburn Road, Belsize Park, along with the former Chief Secretary to the British High Commissioner in Palestine, Sir Wyndham Deedes, and her friend, the prison reformer Gertrude Eaton. The aims of St Mary's included enabling each child to discover and develop his own gifts and to make the best of these for himself and others.

'Such a healthy growth can only be attained by training the emotions as well as the intellect, the character as well as the physique,' said the school's brochure,[64] expressing ideals that Lady Blomfield warmly supported.

There was also an invitation to be a patron of The Religious Book Club, established by the famous Foyles bookshop in London's Charing Cross Road. Some six thousand people subscribed to the club, which offered a non-sectarian selection of books and received the patronage of bishops and clergy of the Anglican church, as well as leading ministers of the Free Churches. 'I believe that your support would be of real value in the work of the Club,' Sitárih was told in her invitation letter.[65]

Lady Blomfield's final appearance within the national Bahá'í community was at the 1939 summer school, held at High Leigh in Hoddesdon, Hertfordshire from 23 July to 12 August. There she had the pleasure of meeting George Townshend once again as well as making the acquaintance of Chief Jomo Kenyatta, a guest at the school who had just published his book *Facing Mount Kenya* and who would go on to be the first president of the independent Kenya. The celebrated potter Bernard Leach was also present, along with his lifelong friend, the South African painter Reginald Turvey.

Townshend, still struggling with the conflict of serving the Church of Ireland while believing that Christ had returned, was thrilled to be among the Bahá'ís once more and even played a few spirited games of tennis for a man of 63. But he mourned the fact that the followers of Bahá'u'lláh were so few.

'Accustomed to living in a lonely countryside,' he wrote, 'I appreciated this companionship all the more and I hope to goodness I'll soon find a means of getting out of this and living among Bahá'ís in future.

> Converts will have to be made in tens of thousands to do any real good. Amazing that a Prophet should have come nearly a century ago, should have turned history upside down, and scarce a hundred Britishers should know anything about it.[66]

Anyone who had lived and served, as Lady Blomfield had, through the 'War to end all Wars' must have been deeply saddened when conflict in Europe broke out once more. China and Japan were already locked into their bloody war when Nazi Germany invaded Poland. Britain and France declared war on Germany two days later, on 3 September 1939. Sitárih appears to have spent much time sitting by the radio listening to events as they unfolded and briefly noting the news on her pad along with other thoughts.

'Churchill speaks,' she wrote. 'Hungary no friend with Russia. Russia overwhelming Balkans. 1000 killed in Warsaw. Going to Church today. Mary. Early assistance indispensable. Freud died today 83. Last 25 hours the worst yet. Morale unfailing. Early assistance necessary. Churches and hospitals full of wounded. French government appeased Mussolini. Ukraine renounced. Ship sunk Atlantic. Last night air raids.'[67]

But the outbreak of hostilities seems not to have deterred the British Bahá'í community. Rather it appears to have stimulated the believers to greater teaching efforts. Newly established groups in Torquay and Bradford were showing particular enthusiasm.

'I wish to reaffirm clearly and emphatically', wrote Shoghi Effendi on 20 November 1939,

> . . . my deep sense of gratification and gratitude for the recent and truly remarkable evidences of the devotion, courage and perseverance of the English Bahá'í community in the face of the perils that now confront it. Its members have abundantly demonstrated their profound attachment to their Cause, their unshakeable resolution to uphold its truth and defend its interests, and their unfailing solicitude for whatever may promote and safeguard its institutions. However great and sinister the forces with which they may have to battle in future, I feel confident that they will befittingly uphold the torch of Divine Guidance that has been entrusted to their hands and will discharge their responsibilities with still greater tenacity, fidelity, vigour and devotion.[68]

Wartime conditions demanded that the National Spiritual Assembly had to become increasingly rigorous about membership of the Bahá'í community. David Hofman recalled being visited by police officers who told him that, because of the high percentage of overseas nationals in the community, every Bahá'í in the country would now need to be registered and provided with a formal certificate stating that the bearer was recognized as a member of the Bahá'í community of the British Isles. The believers were required to send two passport-sized photographs to the National Assembly along with their personal details. Always reluctant to have her picture taken, Lady Blomfield sent pictures taken some 40 years earlier, bearing little resemblance to the octogenarian who was now required to carry the credential card that bestowed upon her the membership number 52. Hofman himself took the number 13 as others were too superstitious to want it.

The credential card spelt out the terms and conditions of membership in the Bahá'í community. It was a far cry from the days of the Master when any number of souls could drift in and out of contact with the Bahá'í Movement and pursue their own other spiritual and social interests at the same time. Evidently realizing that her earthly days were numbered, Lady Blomfield must have often reflected on the two priceless occasions when she was able to house the Master in her own apartment. A question which was commonly asked of her was 'Where are those people who crowded to 97 Cadogan Gardens, during the two visits of 'Abdu'l-Bahá, and how have they answered His call?'[69]

Lady Blomfield recalled the words of the Master when He searched for those who would be of assistance to His Cause. 'I have come with a torch in my hand, seeking out those who will arise and help me to bring about the Most Great Peace.'

'Who shall say,' Sitárih reflected,

> . . . how much or how little of the Message given by the Servant of God was understood by those persons, well-known and unknown, gentle and simple, who sought His presence in those days?
>
> States of consciousness and powers of vision being so varied, one visitor would come to hear and to see 'some new thing' out of curiosity, hoping to witness a magic happening, an astounding phenomenon.
>
> Of another kind was a man, who being on his way to Japan, heard that 'Abdu'l-Bahá was in England. He broke his journey at Constantinople, and hastened to London for the joy of spending one evening in His presence!
>
> Still another type of mentality was that of a popular preacher. Often voicing his hope and desire that a Great Messenger would again come to the world, he answered an invitation to visit the Master by sending regrets as he was 'engaged to attend a garden party'.
>
> It is not ours to know how many were conscious of the vital breath of that atmosphere of 'Love and Wisdom and Power', which was always around the Master, more penetrating and significant than even His words, although they were spoken with authority.

Of those who came into touch with that pervading influence, some were awed and transformed. Their very souls seemed wrapt by an unforgettable experience. The power of this atmosphere was overwhelming, but could neither be described nor defined.

Some of the Western visitors felt this hitherto unknown or unaccustomed atmosphere of the Spirit with moving gratitude and awe. To the Eastern guests this wonder was as the air they breathed. They accepted the Power with the reverence of the Oriental soul, trained to recognize the influence of holiness manifest in Him, Who had suffered long years in the Path of God, Who had, at length succeeded in bringing the Message into the open air of the world.

Minds and motives must needs be varied because their quality depends upon the stage of advancement of each in spiritual evolution. Such an awakened consciousness alone determines the capacity to recognize Spiritual Truth.

The appeal of the Word of God to the spirit of man being so intimately sacred, it is not our province to judge any other human being in this matter.

'The earth is full of the signs of God; may your eyes be illumined by perceiving them,' said 'Abdu'l-Bahá.

For our comfort and encouragement we are able to perceive these signs as stars of hope and fulfilment on every hand, whilst they are developing on the crowded stage of the world since 'Abdu'l-Bahá's coming to the West with His warnings and His injunctions.

'The Great Woe' (the World War) proves the truth that when spiritual civilization is neglected and material civilization alone is cultivated, the whole edifice collapses into ruin, there being no firm foundation.

'And great is the fall thereof.'

That terrific catastrophe shows that too few were the helpers who arose in answer to the Master's Call.[70]

For the last few weeks of her life Lady Blomfield was unwell and was moved into a nursing home. On her final day, when she seemed to be recovering, she refused all food, which, Mary believed, was the only remedy that would have preserved her mother. Mary felt that Sitárih must have known that the time had come for her to enter the radiant Kingdom to which she so truly belonged.

Sara Louisa, Lady Blomfield – named Sitárih <u>Kh</u>ánum by 'Abdu'l-Bahá, her beloved Master – passed away peacefully on the final day of the year 1939. This brightest of stars had traversed the night sky and gone out.

On that day, Mary visited Sitárih twice in the home, although she was not with her mother when she passed away. The staff told Mary that Lady Blomfield's passing was peaceful.

'A beautiful death,' they said.[71]

Writing about her mother's final moments Mary reflected that

. . . in the overwhelming sorrow of parting from a wonderful person-ality and a deeply loved mother, it is hard to rejoice in the gladness that is hers, but that must be the predominant note in this account of her beautiful life by one who knew and loved her so well. For I can remember, from the earliest days, her valiant spirit meeting sadness and difficulties with radiant acquiescence and invincible faith. It was as if she knew what rare privilege awaited her, since she it was who wel-comed 'Abdu'l-Bahá to her home when he came to England. She was one of those 'Waiting Servants' who, down the ages, have recognized and acclaimed the Messengers of God in their Day.[72]

Earlier on the day of Lady Blomfield's death, David Hofman had been sharing a car with a number of other Bahá'ís travelling to Manchester for the annual National Teaching Conference. Knowing of Sitárih's illness, he had bought for her a small hyacinth in a pot. As petrol rationing had been imposed since the beginning of the war, Hofman asked the driver of the car whether there would be enough petrol to divert via Hampstead so he could present Sitárih with her gift. There was not.

That night in his hotel room in Manchester, and unaware of her passing, Hofman dreamt of Lady Blomfield – a dream which, more than 50 years later, he vividly recalled as being 'suffused by the perfume of hyacinths'.[73]

The following day word reached the believers gathered in Manchester of her passing. The sad news was duly sent on to the Guardian with whom Lady Blomfield had enjoyed such a rare and unique relationship; she had acted, on the Master's request, as a mother to him. In response, Shoghi Effendi cabled:

PROFOUNDLY GRIEVE PASSING DEARLY BELOVED OUTSTANDING CO-WORKER SITÁRIH <u>KH</u>ÁNUM MEMORY HER GLORIOUS SERVICES

IMPERISHABLE ADVISE ENGLISH COMMUNITY HOLD BEFITTING MEMO-
RIAL GATHERINGS ASSURE RELATIVES MY HEARTFELT SYMPATHY LOVING
FERVENT PRAYERS.[74]

'It is indeed hard', Hasan Balyuzi wrote in his preface to *The Chosen Highway*, 'to believe that Sitárih Khánum is no longer with us in her earthly temple.'[75]

Lady Blomfield was buried at the Hampstead Municipal Cemetery in a Church of England service. During the funeral, the chaplain said that this friend to whom 'Jesus was the inspiration of her life' had 'left behind her an example of hardworking beneficence to the end of her days, a wonderful kindliness of spirit and breadth of sympathy'.[76] The versatility of her sympathies was expressed at the funeral by the presence of representatives of the Save the Children Fund but also the Hampstead Auxiliary Fire Service – to whom she had offered accommodation for the care of children found straying during air raids – the Animals Defence and Anti-Vivisection Society, and of course the Bahá'í community. Two members of the National Spiritual Assembly read Bahá'í prayers and selections from the Hidden Words after the Church of England service, as a number of friends gathered around the grave.

'In the first shock of her parting,' the *Bahá'í Journal* reported, 'we could only think of the actual fact. Now we begin to realize something of the tremendous loss which we have sustained. Summer School, the Riḍván Feast, the Presence of 'Abdu'l-Bahá in England, were all associated in our minds with her.'[77]

Tributes came as well from many of the other organizations to which Lady Blomfield had selflessly devoted her time and energy. The Save the Children Fund devoted more than a full page of its newsletter *The World's Children* to an obituary titled 'Lady Blomfield – Apostle of World Unity', mourning her passing which 'deprived the Save the Children Fund of a devoted and inspiring friend':

The widow of Sir Arthur Blomfield, the Victorian architect who predeceased her by more than forty years, she gave herself to a variety of humanitarian causes with an ardour which persisted to the last days of a long life. With a personal courage which had led her to give active service to the movement for the enfranchisement of women in its least popular days, and invincible faith in the inherent good in all men which made her oblivious of all the sundering distinctions of race and creed and 'colour', she found deep spiritual affinity with the teaching of Baha'u'llah, the Persian mystic. She remained a loyal member of the Church of England in which she was nurtured . . . but what came to be known as the Baha'i movement had in her one of its most faithful disciples . . . Lady Blomfield will always be remembered, not only for her uncompromising devotion to the causes which she espoused, but – on the more personal side of life – for a singularly beautiful deep voice in which she loved to declaim passages from her favourite prophet and from Holy Writ, and for a warm maternal sympathy which took under its wing all sorts and conditions of men.[78]

Sifting through her mother's belongings, Mary was amazed to find a vast amount of jottings – thoughts, dreams, prayers, accounts of visions, 'the effulgence of her beautiful soul, like the song of a bird, irrepressible, ecstatic . . . I was amazed to find how much she had written,' noted Mary, 'not as professional writers express their thoughts in a more or less orderly sequence of filed manuscripts, but on odd pieces of note paper, in engagement books, or diaries, as if she had to write but did not imagine anyone would consider what she had written worth publication.'[79]

Another discovery made by Mary was a poem, the only one, so far as she could tell, that Sitárih had written:

'Ah! Who can understand that which I dream?
And the unheard desires, which without end,
Like tumultuous waves, tumble deliriously,
Terrible, and at the same time sweet as honey
In my soul, immense as the sky!
A dream which came to my soul, heavens high
Vastness reflecting,
Brought desires like waves lashed by the wind
In wild delirium breaking.
Terrible monstrous now, now soft as the zephyrs breathing.
My soul has penetrated far beyond the Choir
Through clouds of opal to the blue dwelling of Causes!
She saw there the Ineffable, and of all these things
She has made an idol, and has set it in my heart.[80]

Faintly written on an old piece of paper, Mary also discovered a prayer which she felt encapsulated the crowning theme of Lady Blomfield's beautiful and saintly life: 'O God! My Beloved!,' Sitárih had pencilled

> All my affairs are in Thy hands. Be Thou the Mover of my actions, the Lode Star of my soul, the Voice that crieth in my inmost being, the object of my heart's adoration! I praise Thee that Thou has enabled me to turn my face unto Thee, that Thou hast set my soul ablaze with remembrance of Thee![81]

'In faith I know she is rejoicing in the presence of the Master and the friends she loved so dearly,' insisted Mary.

> I know that she is radiant in the Kingdom of God. I know that her devoted service to the Cause, which was never for one moment separated in her heart from the Cause of the Eternal Christ, has gained her a high place in the Celestial Garden, and I know that her love is still shining on the friends and dear ones she has left on earth.[82]

AFTERWARDS

Shortly before she passed away Lady Blomfield placed her manuscript for *The Chosen Highway* into the hands of David Hofman and asked Hasan Balyuzi to write the Foreword. In addition to the 'Irish blue' cover specifically requested by Sitárih, Hofman took the liberty of adding to the book a photograph of her 'beautiful and saintly face'.[1] *The Chosen Highway* was prepared for publication early in 1940, within a few weeks of Lady Blomfield's passing.

Shoghi Effendi was pleased to learn that Sitárih's great labour of love had finally come to fruition.

'The Guardian has noted with satisfaction that the arrangements for the publication of "The Chosen Highway" are complete,' wrote his secretary on 27 March 1940, 'and hopes that by the time you receive this letter it will be well on the way to printing.'[2]

Lady Blomfield's book, wrote Balyuzi, would 'forever remain the greatest monument to the achievements of its author. Those who have met Sitárih <u>Kh</u>ánum in person will cherish this book in the tenderness of her remembrance. To others who know of her work, it will convey a vivid portrait of her gifts of the spirit. And to generations unborn it will hand a message rich in enlightenment.'[3]

Announcing the publication of *The Chosen Highway*, the *Bahá'í Journal* wrote that Lady Blomfield's 'association with the Master, with the Holy Family, and the part she played in influencing the British government to protect Their lives in 1918 are indicated in her book and will be recorded elsewhere. These things of themselves assure her the admiration of posterity, and her book its everlasting gratitude.'[4]

The 1940 British edition of *The Chosen Highway* was followed the same year by an American imprint. Numerous further editions appeared in the United States until 1975. In 2007 George Ronald printed the book for the first time. In the Publisher's Note, May Hofman wrote, 'It gives us great pleasure to republish [Lady Blomfield's] book, photographed from the original edition published in 1940 for the British Bahá'í Publishing Trust by George Ronald's founder, David Hofman.'[5]

The Chosen Highway is indeed Sitárih Khánum's enduring legacy, a volume that is to this day cherished by Bahá'ís all over the world.

Following Lady Blomfield's passing the Spiritual Assembly of the Bahá'ís of London – at its meeting on Sunday 6 January 1940 – discussed the arrangement of a memorial meeting, as requested by the Guardian. The Assembly decided to ask Sitárih's daughter, Mary, if she would like to host the gathering in her Hampstead home, which had been the venue for so many feasts and holy day celebrations given by Lady Blomfield throughout the final decade of her life. Mary, herself in poor health, declined the suggestion and the meeting went ahead at the Bahá'í Centre in London on Friday 9 February, 40 days after Sitárih's passing. The Assembly invited the Bahá'ís and some of the close friends of the community who had often attended her 'At Home' meetings. Plans were also made for a later memorial meeting to which a larger number of guests could be invited.

In response to an offer from David Hofman, Shoghi Effendi commissioned an obituary article on Lady Blomfield to be included in volume 8 of *The Bahá'í World*. At the same time the Guardian requested that a brief account of Mrs Thornburgh-Cropper's Bahá'í life also be composed for the volume.

'The passing away of these two long-standing believers has indeed robbed the Cause in England of two of its most distinguished members,' Shoghi Effendi's secretary wrote, 'and the English Bahá'í Community is certainly the poorer now that it has been deprived of their ready and invaluable support.

> The departure of Sitárih Khánum in particular is to be deeply mourned, not only by the members of the Faith throughout England, but by so many of her fellow-believers abroad, and the Guardian himself feels most keenly the loss of so precious and faithful a co-worker, who, in the early days following 'Abdu'l-Bahá's ascension, had proved of such invaluable assistance to him in the discharge of his heavy duties and responsibilities . . .[6]

The four-page 'In Memoriam' article for Sitárih, composed by Mary, was published on page 651 of *Bahá'í World*, bound together for posterity with tributes to so many illustrious early adherents of the Bahá'í Faith who passed away around the same time, among them May Maxwell, Martha Root and Queen Marie of Romania.

In her will Lady Blomfield appointed her step-daughter Adele Dorothy Maud as one of the trustees and executors of her estate along with Mary Basil Hall and Alfred Ravenscroft Kennedy, the son of Lady Blomfield's friend, the late Lord Justice Kennedy. Sitárih left all of her property, including jewellery, books, pictures and china to Mary, who already owned the house in Hampstead where her mother had spent her final years. To her own sister, Cecilia Gilmore, Lady Blomfield left £250 and to Adele £350. Mary and Ellinor received £150 each and their former governess Beatrice Platt was bequeathed £50. Sitárih's son Frank is conspicuously absent from her will.

Of Lady Blomfield's three children, only Mary remained an active supporter of the Bahá'í community throughout her adult life. Before the passing of her husband, Mary was very much occupied with Captain Basil Hall's interests while continuing, as her mother had, to work for many causes.

'As daughter and wife, she was always ready to subordinate her own interests to furthering those of others,' remarked Mary's old friend, Isobel Slade. 'Her warm and enthusiastic nature was ready to support all humanitarian causes and to spend itself in loving service to those who depended on her. Her uncompromising fairness and honesty pervaded her whole outlook on life, yet she always saw the good in others.'[7]

'All the time she was ready to give a helping hand to whomsoever it was, no matter how tired she was,' Isobel Slade wrote. 'She was ready to sacrifice her own leisure and comfort to make others happy.'[8]

Mary's most active contribution to the Bahá'í community was made during her fifties, when she served for five years on the National Spiritual Assembly of the Bahá'ís of the British Isles and for a short period on the National Teaching Committee, of which she was the chairperson. In 1943 she and her younger sister Ellinor decided that all royalties they received for their book, *Paris Talks*, should be given over to the Bahá'í community. Shoghi Effendi advised the National Spiritual Assembly to accept the money into its own national fund.

With Mary's own failing health restricting her active service to the community, she returned to preparing dramatic scripts which, she believed, would be a valuable means of introducing the Bahá'í teachings to the public. From time to time the Bahá'ís attempted to stage one or other of Mary's plays at events with varying success. In 1948 Mary was distressed by the poor standard of the performance of one of them at a summer school, which resulted in members of the audience walking out.

'It's not quite what I contemplate for the use of dramatic scripts,' Mary wrote, before sending her works to Shoghi Effendi with a suggestion of how they might be used to attract audiences to hear about the Bahá'í message.[9]

Of the few surviving believers who also recalled the golden days when the Master had sojourned among them, Mary stayed in contact with Luṭfu'lláh Ḥakím, who returned to the British Isles in 1948 at the Guardian's suggestion. Living in Edinburgh for two years, Ḥakím was able to renew connections with people he had met in 1913 when he had accompanied 'Abdu'l-Bahá to the city. In 1949 Ḥakím contemplated the idea of gathering Lady Blomfield's various talks into a collection for publication. At his request, Mary endeavoured to search out the notebooks from earlier years but the proposed volume seems never to have materialized.

As they reached middle age, both the Blomfield sisters suffered from increasingly poor health. One Christmas, Mary wrote to Ḥakím, 'How I wish I could come and visit you, but I have my sister here seriously ill and cannot leave – even to go to the shops. This will be a very quiet and rather sad Christmas for us.'[10]

Mary passed away, aged 62, on Friday 28 April 1950.

'She was a faithful servant of God all her life,' wrote her sister Ellinor.[11]

During her final illness, Mary had continued to take a keen interest in the progress of the Six Year Plan in which the British Bahá'í community was engaged. Isobel Slade reported that Mary had remained thankful and patient 'and her lovely sense of humour was unfailing to the end'.

'PARVINE GLORIED IN SUCCESS PLAN PASSED TO ABHÁ KINGDOM MORNING 28TH',[12] cabled the National Spiritual Assembly to the Guardian.

Shoghi Effendi responded, 'GRIEVE PASSING DEAR DISTINGUISHED PROMOTER FAITH HER SERVICES UNFORGETTABLE PRAYING PROGRESS SOUL ABHÁ KINGDOM.'[13]

In an echo of events ten years earlier when Lady Blomfield had passed away, the British Bahá'í community received word of Mary's death as it gathered at its National Convention for the election of the National

Spiritual Assembly. To their shock, they learned that Mary's remains were about to be cremated, a procedure that is not permitted to Bahá'ís. While the entire gathering was asked to pray that the matter might be resolved, David Hofman rushed out from the meeting to try to make an urgent telephone call to Ellinor to see if a burial could be arranged instead. He was too late.

'I fear the Bahá'ís are very angry with me for having our beloved Mary's body cremated,' Ellinor wrote to Luṭfu'lláh Ḥakím a week after her sister's passing.

> I cannot help feeling that you, my friend of so long standing, will understand. I have been in very bad health for a long time, and the end was so sudden, and I had prayed so fervently to God, the Father of us all, to make a miracle and to cure her, and I believed He had answered my prayer, as she rallied in a miraculous way when she first came home from hospital – but she suddenly faded away in a few days almost. I was not even with her at the end. She died with a smile of utmost joy on her lips, looking out of the window and up at the sky . . . as if speaking to someone she was infinitely glad to see again. I wanted to have her with me and to nurse her myself and asked if I might but I was not strong enough, or perhaps God thought I was not good enough, so He sent an angel in the form of a maid, belonging to my half-sister Mrs Maud with whom Mary had made her home. The end came so suddenly and was such a severe shock to us – Mrs Maud being nearly 80 years of age – that she arranged for the cremation on the strongest recommendation of the doctor who said, indeed that it was imperative, almost, owing to the nature of the malady. They rang me up to ask my consent at the last moment, and I gave it, so any blame is mine. I was quite prostrated with the shock.[14]

Ellinor had Mary's ashes gathered in an urn and buried in their mother's grave.

Mary and Captain Basil Hall had no children. The house in Hampstead was bequeathed to the National Spiritual Assembly of the Bahá'ís of the British Isles but Mary asked that her sister Ellinor be allowed to remain in the house until she and her husband passed away. Lady Blomfield's step-daughter, Adele, continued to live upstairs. Mary left the balance of her estate to Ellinor.

After suffering for many years from heart problems, Ellinor died, also aged 62, four years later. Having no children of her own, Ellinor left the majority of her possessions to her brother Frank, who was living in Aylesbury. In her will, Ellinor asked to be cremated, with 'no flowers and no mourners'.[15]

The house at 8 Burgess Hill was sold by the National Spiritual Assembly and the capital was put towards the purchase of 27 Rutland Gate in London's Knightsbridge district – a tall, elegant Victorian terraced building that remains the national Bahá'í centre for the United Kingdom. In Mary Basil Hall's honour and as an acknowledgement of her generous gift, the main meeting room on the first floor of the property became known as the 'Parvine Room', after the Persian name given to her by 'Abdu'l-Bahá.

Mary also donated to the national Bahá'í archives a number of original writings of the Master and other items that belonged to Lady Blomfield. Among the treasures were two copies of *Paris Talks* which had been signed by the Master, a samovar which He had given to her, some signed photographs, and a magnificent large oil painting of Lady Blomfield, painted while she was still a young woman. A chair that the Master had often used during His stay at 97 Cadogan Gardens continues to take pride of place in the council chamber of the National Spiritual Assembly.

Frank Blomfield outlived both his sisters, dying at the age of 71 at Newhaven Downs Hospital in Sussex on 23 June 1960. There being no remaining members of his immediate family, he left a sum of £600 to Nancy Bradburne, the daughter of one of his half-brothers.

Lady Blomfield's sister, Cecilia Gilmore, lived in New York until her passing in 1954. She had one daughter, Ruth, who was born in 1906 and passed away, also without having any offspring, in 1973.

Lady Blomfield had been buried at the Hampstead Municipal Cemetery, off Fortune Green Road, not far from the home she shared with Mary. With no descendants or close family members to tend to her final resting place – which also contained the ashes of her daughter – the grave fell into considerable disrepair. When in the early years of the 21st century, Michele Wilburn – a dedicated member of the Bahá'í community of the London Borough of Camden – went to search for it, the dilapidated grave was only identifiable once dense clods of earth and grass were tugged away to reveal Lady Blomfield's name. An approach was made to the cemetery authorities to see if the Bahá'ís could put up a new headstone. To comply with the law, advertisements were placed to determine if any surviving members of the family had any objection to the restoration taking place. There was, as expected, no response and the work proceeded at the instigation of the National Spiritual Assembly. Since 2003 a new polished granite gravestone has marked the grave of Lady Blomfield. The inscription on the headstone reads, in gold letters:

SITÁRIH <u>KH</u>ÁNUM
Sara Louisa, Lady Blomfield
1859–1939
'Abdu'l-Bahá's devoted maidservant
Her Glorious Services Imperishable

And her daughter
MARY ESTHER HALL

On the slab covering the grave there is a golden nine-pointed star, beneath which is written,

O GOD MY BELOVED!

'I long to visit the graves of the friends of God, could this be possible,' 'Abdu'l-Bahá wrote. 'These are the servants of the Blessed Beauty; in His path they were afflicted; they met with toil and sorrow; they sustained injuries and suffered harm. Upon them be the glory of God, the All-Glorious. Upon them be salutation and praise. Upon them be God's tender mercy and forgiveness.'[16]

THE PASSING OF 'ABDU'L-BAHÁ

by Shoghi Effendi and Lady Blomfield

Dear Friends,

It is well known that the loved ones of 'Abdu'l-Bahá, in every part of the world, are anxiously waiting to receive some details of the closing events of his unique and wonderful life. For this reason the present account is being written.

We have now come to realize that the Master knew the day and hour when, his mission on earth being finished, he would return to the shelter of heaven. He was, however, careful that his family should not have any premonition of the coming sorrow. It seemed as though their eyes were veiled by him, with his ever-loving consideration for his dear ones, that they should not see the significance of certain dreams and other signs of the culminating event. This they now realize was his thought for them, in order that their strength might be preserved to face the great ordeal when it should arrive, that they should not be devitalized by anguish of mind in its anticipation.

Out of the many signs of the approach of the hour when he could say of his work on earth: 'It is finished', the following two dreams seem remarkable. Less than eight weeks before his passing the Master related this to his family:

I seemed to be standing within a great Mosque, in the inmost shrine, facing the Quiblih (that Point of Adoration where-unto the worshippers turn, as in a Christian church to the East) in the place of the Imám himself. I became aware that a large number of people were flocking into the Mosque; more and yet more crowded in, taking their places in rows behind me, until there was a vast multitude. As I stood I raised loudly the 'Call to Prayer'. Suddenly the thought came to me to go forth from the Mosque.

When I found myself outside I said within myself, 'For what reason came I forth, not having led the prayer? But it matters not; now that I have uttered the Call to Prayer, the vast multitude will of themselves chant the prayer.'

When the Master had passed away, his family pondered over this dream and interpreted it thus:

He had called that same vast multitude – all peoples, all religions, all races, all nations and all kingdoms – to Unity and Peace, to universal Love and Brotherhood; and having called them, he returned to God the Beloved, at whose command he had raised the Majestic Call, had given the Divine Message. This same multitude – the peoples, religions, races, nations and kingdoms – would continue the WORK to which 'Abdu'l-Bahá had called them, and would of themselves press forward to its accomplishment.

A few weeks after the preceding dream the Master came in from the solitary room in the garden, which he had occupied of late, and said: 'I dreamed a dream and behold the Blessed Beauty, (Bahá'u'lláh) came and said unto me, "Destroy this room!"'

The family, who had been wishing that he would come and sleep in the house, not being happy that he should be alone at night, exclaimed, 'Yes Master, we think your dream means that you should leave that room and come into the house.' When he heard this from us, he smiled meaningly as though not agreeing with our interpretation. Afterwards we understood that by the 'room' was meant the temple of his body.

A month before his last hour, Doctor Sulaymán Rafat Bey, a Turkish friend, who was a guest in the house, received a telegram telling him of the sudden death of his brother. 'Abdu'l-Bahá speaking words of comfort to him, whispered, 'Sorrow not, for he is only transferred from this plane to a higher one; I too shall soon be transferred, for my days are numbered.' Then patting him gently on the shoulder, he looked him in the face and said, 'And it will be in the days that are shortly to come.'

In the same week he revealed a Tablet to America, in which is the following prayer:

Yá Bahá'u'l-Abhá! (O Thou the Glory of Glories) I have renounced the world and the people thereof, and am heartbroken and sorely afflicted because of the unfaithful. In the cage of this world, I flutter even as a frightened bird, and yearn every day to take my flight unto Thy Kingdom.

Yá Bahá'u'l-Abhá! Make me to drink of the cup of sacrifice and set me free. Relieve me from these woes and trials, from these afflictions and troubles. Thou art He that aideth, that succoureth, that protecteth, that stretcheth forth the hand of help . . .

On the last Friday morning of his stay on earth (November 25th) he said to his daughters: 'The wedding of Khusraw must take place today. If you are too much occupied, I myself will make the necessary preparations, for it must take place this day.' (Khusraw is one of the favoured and trusted servants of the Master's Household.)

'Abdu'l-Bahá attended the noonday prayer at the Mosque. When he came out he found the poor waiting for the alms, which it was his custom to give every Friday. This day, as usual, he stood, in spite of very great fatigue, whilst he gave a coin to every one with his own hands.

After lunch he dictated some Tablets, his last ones, to Rúhí Effendi. When he had rested he walked in the garden. He seemed to be in a deep reverie.

His good and faithful servant, Ismá'íl-Áqá, relates the following:

Some time, about twenty days before my Master passed away I was near the garden when I heard him summon an old believer saying: 'Come with me that we may admire together the beauty of the garden. Behold, what the spirit of devotion is able to achieve! This flourishing place was, a few years ago, but a heap of stones, and now it is verdant with foliage and flowers. My desire is that after I am gone the loved ones may all arise to serve the Divine Cause and, please God, so it shall be. Ere long men will arise who shall bring life to the world.' . . .

A few days after this he said: 'I am so fatigued! The hour is come when I must leave everything and take my flight. I am too weary to walk.' Then he said: 'It was during the closing days of the Blessed Beauty, when I was engaged in gathering together his papers, which were strewn over the sofa in his writing chamber at Bahjí that he turned to me and said, "It is of no use to gather them, I must leave them and flee away."

'I also have finished my work, I can do nothing more, therefore must I leave it and take my departure.'

Three days before his ascension whilst seated in the garden, he called me and said, 'I am sick with fatigue. Bring two of your oranges for me that I may eat them for your sake.' This I did, and he having eaten them turned to me, saying 'Have you any of your sweet lemons?' He bade me fetch a few . . . Whilst I was plucking them, he came over to the tree, saying, 'Nay, but I must gather them with my own hands.'

Having eaten of the fruit he turned to me and asked 'Do you desire anything more?' Then with a pathetic gesture of his hands, he touchingly, emphatically and deliberately said: 'Now it is finished, it is finished!'

These significant words penetrated my very soul. I felt each time he uttered them as if a knife were struck into my heart. I understood his meaning but never dreamed his end was so nigh.

It was Ismá'íl-Áqá who had been the Master's gardener for well nigh thirty years who, in the first week after his bereavement, driven by hopeless grief, quietly disposed of all his belongings, made his will, went to the Master's sister and craved her pardon for any misdeeds he had committed. He then delivered the key of the garden to a trusted servant of the Household and, taking with him means whereby to end his life at his beloved Master's Tomb, walked up the Mountain to that sacred place, three times circled round it and would have succeeded in taking his life had it not been for the opportune arrival of a friend, who reached him in time to prevent the accomplishment of his tragic intention . . .

Later in the evening of Friday he blessed the bride and bride-groom who had just been married. He spoke impressively to them. 'Khusraw,' he said, 'you have spent your childhood and youth in the service of this house; it is my hope that you will grow old under the same roof, ever and always serving God.'

During the evening he attended the usual meeting of the friends in his own audience chamber.

In the morning of Saturday, November 26th, he arose early, came to the tea room and had some tea. He asked for the fur-lined coat which had belonged to Bahá'u'lláh. He often put on this coat when he was cold or did not feel well, he so loved it. He then withdrew to his room, lay down on his bed and said, 'Cover me up. I am very cold. Last night I did not sleep well, I felt cold. This is serious, it is the beginning.'

After more blankets had been put on, he asked for the fur coat he had taken off to be placed over him. That day he was rather feverish. In the evening his temperature rose still higher, but during the night the fever left him. After midnight he asked for some tea.

On Sunday morning (November 27th) he said: 'I am quite well and will get up as usual and have tea with you in the tea room.' After he had dressed he was persuaded to remain on the sofa in his room.

In the afternoon he sent all the friends up to the Tomb of the Báb, where on the occasion of the anniversary of the declaration of the Covenant a feast was being held, offered by a Parsi pilgrim who had lately arrived from India.

At four in the afternoon, being on the sofa in his room he said: 'Ask my sister and all the family to come and have tea with me.'

After tea the Mufti of Haifa and the head of the Municipality, with another visitor, were received by him. They remained about an hour. He spoke to them about Bahá'u'lláh, related to them his second dream, showed them extraordinary kindness and even more than his usual courtesy. He then bade them farewell, walking with them to the outer door in spite of their pleading that he should remain resting on his sofa. He then received a visit from the head of the police, an Englishman, who, too, had his share of the Master's gracious kindness. To him he gave some silk hand-woven Persian handkerchiefs, which he very greatly appreciated.

His four sons-in-law and Rúhí Effendi came to him after returning from the gathering on the mountain. They said to him: 'The giver of the feast was unhappy because you were not there.' He said unto them:

But I was there, though my body was absent, my spirit was there in your midst. I was present with the friends at the Tomb. The friends must not attach any importance to the absence of my body.

In spirit I am, and shall always be, with the friends, even though I be far away.

The same evening he asked after the health of every member of the Household, of the pilgrims and of the friends in Haifa. 'Very good, very good,' he said when told that none were ill. This was his very last utterance concerning his friends.

At eight in the evening he retired to bed after taking a little nourishment, saying: 'I am quite well.'

He told all the family to go to bed and rest. Two of his daughters however stayed with him. That night the Master had gone to sleep very calmly, quite free from fever. He awoke about 1:15 a.m., got up and walked across to a table where he drank some water. He took off an outer night garment, saying: 'I am too warm.' He went back to bed and when his daughter Rúhá Khánum, later on, approached, she found him lying peacefully and, as he looked into her face, he asked her to lift up the net curtains, saying: 'I have difficulty in breathing, give me more air.' Some rose water was brought of which he drank, sitting up in bed to do so, without any help. He again lay down, and as some food was offered him, he remarked in a clear and distinct voice: 'You wish me to take some food, and I am going?' He gave them a beautiful look. His face was so calm, his expression so serene, they thought him asleep.

He had gone from the gaze of his loved ones!

The eyes that had always looked out with loving-kindness upon humanity, whether friends or foes, were now closed. The hands that had ever been stretched forth to give alms to the poor and the needy, the halt and the maimed, the blind, the orphan and the widow, had now finished their labour. The feet that, with untiring zeal, had gone upon the ceaseless errands of the Lord of Compassion were now at rest. The lips that had so eloquently championed the cause of the suffering sons of men, were now hushed in silence. The heart that had so powerfully throbbed with wondrous love for the children of God was now stilled. His glorious spirit had passed from the life of earth, from the persecutions of the enemies of righteousness, from the storm and stress of well nigh eighty years of indefatigable toil for the good of others.

His long martyrdom was ended!

Whilst yet the gloom of their bereavement was hanging darkly over the disconsolate ladies of the Household, a granddaughter of the Master had a wondrous dream of him: he was speaking with his beloved sister, the Greatest Holy Leaf, in the very room where, in the early hours of the day, it was the custom of the ladies to assemble in his presence, chanting the morning prayers, and to take their morning tea. He turned to her and said: 'Wherefore are ye all perturbed, why lament and be sorrowful? With you all I am well pleased. For a long time have I desired to join my Father, the Blessed Beauty. I was ever beseeching Him to take me to His Rose-garden above, and now that my prayer is granted, how happy, how joyous, how rested I am. Therefore grieve not.'

He then counselled them in many ways, exhorting them to follow at all times the commandments of Bahá'u'lláh.

Early on Monday morning November 28th the news of this sudden calamity had spread over the city, causing an unprecedented stir and tumult, and filling all hearts with unutterable grief.

The next morning, Tuesday November 29th, the funeral took place; a funeral the like of which Haifa, nay Palestine itself, had surely never seen; so deep was the feeling that brought so many thousands of mourners together, representative of so many religions, races and tongues.

The High Commissioner of Palestine, Sir Herbert Samuel, the Governor of Jerusalem, the Governor of Phoenicia, the Chief Officials of the Government, the Consuls of the various countries resident in Haifa, the heads of the various religious communities, the notables of Palestine, Jews, Christians, Moslems, Druses, Egyptians, Greeks, Turks, Kurds, and a host of his American, European and native friends, men, women and children, both of high and low degree, all, about ten thousand in number, mourning the loss of their Beloved One.

This impressive, triumphal procession was headed by a guard of honour, consisting of the City Constabulary Force, followed by the Boy Scouts of the Moslem and Christian communities holding aloft their banners, a company of Moslem choristers chanting their verses from the Qur'án, the chiefs of the Moslem community headed by the Mufti, a number of Christian priests, Latin, Greek and Anglican, all preceding the sacred coffin, upraised on the shoulders of his loved ones. Immediately behind it came the members of his family, next to them walked the British High Commissioner, the Governor of Jerusalem, and the Governor of Phoenicia. After them came the Consuls and the notables of the land, followed by the vast multitude of those who reverenced and loved him.

On this day there was no cloud in the sky, nor any sound in all the town and surrounding country through which they went, save only the soft, slow, rhythmic chanting of Islám in the Call to Prayer, or the convulsed sobbing moan of those helpless ones, bewailing the loss of their one friend, who had protected them in all their difficulties and sorrows, whose generous bounty had saved them and their little ones from starvation through the terrible years of the 'Great Woe'.

'O God, my God!' the people wailed with one accord, 'Our father has left us, our father has left us!'

O the wonder of that great throng! Peoples of every religion and race and colour, united in heart through the Manifestation of Servitude in the life-long work of 'Abdu'l-Bahá!

As they slowly wended their way up Mount Carmel, the Vineyard of God, the casket appeared in the distance to be borne aloft by invisible hands, so high above the heads of the people was it carried. After two hours' walking they reached the garden of the Tomb of the Báb. Tenderly was the sacred coffin placed upon a plain table covered with a fair white linen cloth. As the vast concourse pressed round the Tabernacle of his body, waiting to be laid in its resting place, within the vault, next to that of the Báb, representatives of the various denominations, Moslems, Christians and Jews, all hearts being ablaze with fervent love of 'Abdu'l-Bahá, some on the impulse of the moment, others prepared, raised their voices in eulogy and regret, paying their last homage of farewell to their loved one. So united were they in their acclamation of him, as the wise educator and reconciler of the human race in this perplexed and sorrowful age, that there seemed to be nothing left for the Bahá'ís to say.

The following are extracts from some of the speeches delivered on that memorable occasion.

The Moslem voicing the sentiments of his co-religionists spoke as follows:

O concourse of Arabians and Persians! Whom are ye bewailing? Is it he who but yesterday was great in his life and is today in his death greater still? Shed no tears for the one that hath departed to the world of Eternity, but weep over the passing of Virtue and Wisdom, of Knowledge and Generosity. Lament for yourselves, for yours is the loss, whilst he, your lost one, is but a revered Wayfarer, stepping from your mortal world into the everlasting Home. Weep one hour for the sake of him who, for well nigh eighty years, hath wept for you! Look to your right, look to your left, look East and look West and behold, what glory and greatness have vanished! What a pillar of peace hath crumbled! What eloquent lips are hushed! Alas! In the tribulation there is no heart but aches with anguish, no eye but is filled with tears. Woe unto the poor, for lo! goodness hath departed from them; woe unto the orphans, for their loving father is no more with them! Could the life of Sir 'Abdu'l-Bahá 'Abbás have been redeemed by the sacrifices of many a precious soul, they of a certainty would gladly have offered up their lives for his life. But Fate hath otherwise ordained. Every destiny is pre-determined and none can change the Divine Decree. What am I to set forth the achievements of this leader of mankind? They are too glorious to be praised, too many to recount. Suffice it to say that he has left in every heart the most profound impression, on every tongue most wondrous praise. And he that leaveth a memory so lovely, so imperishable, he, indeed, is not dead. Be solaced then, O ye people of Bahá! Endure and be patient; for no man, be he of the East or of the West, can ever comfort you, nay he himself is even in greater need of consolation.

The Christian then came forward and thus spoke:

I weep for the world, in that my Lord hath died; others there are who, like unto me, weep the death of their Lord . . . O bitter is the anguish caused by this heart-rending calamity! It is not only our country's loss but a world affliction . . . He hath lived for well-nigh eighty years the life of the Messengers and Apostles of God. He hath educated the souls of men, hath been benevolent unto them, hath led them to the Way of Truth. Thus he raised his people to the pinnacle of glory, and great shall be his reward from God, the reward of the righteous! Hear me O people! 'Abbás is not dead, neither hath the light of Bahá been extinguished! Nay, nay! this light shall shine with everlasting splendour. The Lamp of Bahá, 'Abbás, hath lived a goodly life, hath manifested in himself the true life of the Spirit. And now he is gathered to glory, a pure angel, richly robed in benevolent deeds, noble in his precious virtues. Fellow Christians! Truly ye are bearing the mortal remains of this ever lamented one to his last resting place, yet know of a certainty that your 'Abbás will live forever in spirit amongst you, through his deeds, his words, his virtues and all the essence of his life. We say farewell to the material body of our 'Abbás, and his material body vanisheth from our gaze, but his reality, our spiritual 'Abbás, will never leave our minds, our thoughts, our hearts, our tongues.

O great revered Sleeper! Thou hast been good to us, thou hast guided us, thou hast taught us, thou hast lived amongst us greatly, with the full meaning of greatness, thou hast made us proud of thy deeds and of thy words. Thou hast raised the Orient to the summit of glory, hast shown loving kindness to the people, trained them in righteousness, and hast striven to the end, till thou hast won the crown of glory. Rest thou happily under the shadow of the mercy of the Lord thy God, and He verily, shall well reward thee.

Yet another Moslem, the Mufti of Haifa, spoke as follows:

I do not wish to exaggerate in my eulogy of this great one, for his ready and helping hand in the service of mankind and the beautiful and wondrous story of his life, spent in doing that which is right and good, none can deny, save him whose heart is blinded . . .

O thou revered voyager! Thou hast lived greatly and hast died greatly! This great funeral procession is but a glorious proof of thy greatness in thy life and in thy death. But O thou whom we have lost! Thou leader of men, generous and benevolent! To whom shall the poor now look? Who shall care for the hungry and the desolate, the widow and the orphan?

May the Lord inspire all thy household and thy kindred with patience in this grievous calamity, and immerse thee in the ocean of His grace and mercy! He verily, is the prayer-hearing, prayer-answering God.

The Jew when his turn came, paid his tribute in these words:

Dans un siècle de positivisme exagéré et de matérialisme effréné, il est étonnant et rare de trouver un philosophe de grande envergure tel que le regretté 'Abdu'l-Bahá 'Abbás parler à notre coeur, à nos sentiments et surtout chercher à éduquer notre âme en nous inculquant les principes les plus beaux, reconnus comme étant la base de toute religion et de toute morale pure. Par ses écrits, par sa parole, par ses entretiens familiers comme par ses colloques célèbres avec les plus cultivés et les fervents adeptes des théories sectaires, il a su persuader, il a pu toujours convaincre. Les exemples vivants sont d'un autre pouvoir. Sa vie privée et publique était un exemple de dévouement et d'oubli de soi pour le bonheur des autres . . .

Sa philosophie est simple, direz vous, mais elle est grande par cette même simplicité, étant conforme au caractère humain qui perd de sa beauté lorsqu'il se trouve faussé par les préjugés et les superstitions . . . 'Abbás est mort à Caiffa, en Palestine, la Terre Sacrée qui a produit les prophètes. Devenue stérile et abandonnée depuis tant de siècles elle ressucite de nouveau et commence à reprendre son rang, et sa renommée primitive. Nous ne sommes pas les seuls à pleurer ce prophète, nous ne sommes pas les seuls à le glorifier. En Europe, en Amérique, que dis-je, dans tout pays habité par des hommes conscients de leur mission dans ce bas monde assoiffé de justice sociale, de fraternité, on le pleurera aussi. Il est mort après avoir souffert du despotisme, du fanatisme et de l'intolérance. Acre, la Bastille turque, lui a servi de prison pendant des dizaines d'années. Bagdad la capitale Abbasside a été aussi sa prison et celle de son père. La Perse, ancien berceau de la Philosophie douce et divine, a chassé ses enfants qui ont conçu leurs idées chez elle. Ne voit-on pas là une volonté divine et une préférence marquée pour la Terre Promise qui était et sera le berceau de toutes les idées généreuses et nobles? Celui qui laisse après lui un passé aussi glorieux n'est pas mort. Celui qui a écrit d'aussi beaux principes a agrandi sa famille parmi tous ses lecteurs et a passé à la postérité, couronné par l'immortalité.[1]

The nine speakers having delivered their funeral orations, then came the moment when the casket which held the pearl of loving servitude passed slowly and triumphantly into its simple, hallowed resting place.

O the infinite pathos! that the beloved feet should no longer tread this earth! That the presence which inspired such devotion and reverence should be withdrawn! Of the many and diverse journals that throughout the East and West have given in their columns accounts of this momentous event, the following stand as foremost among them:

Le Temps, the leading French paper, in its issue of December 19th, 1921, under the title '*Un Conciliateur*' (a peace maker), portrays graphically the life of 'Abdu'l-Bahá, the following being some of its extracts:

Un prophète vient de mourir en Palestine. Il se nommait Abdoul Baha, et il était fils de Bahaou'llah, qui créa le bahaisme, religion 'unifiée' qui n'est autre que le babisme qu'avait observé le Comte de Gobineau. Le Bab, Messie du Babisme, se proposait modestement de régénérer la Perse, ce qui lui couta la vie, en 1850. Bahaou'llah et son fils Abdoul Baha, 'l'esclave de son père,' n'ambitionnaient pas moins que la régéneration du monde. Paris a connu Abdoul Baha. Ce vieillard magnifique et débonnaire répandit parmi nous la parole sainte il y a quelque dix ans. Il était vêtu d'une simple robe vert olive et coiffé d'un turban blanc . . . Sa parole était douce et berceuse, comme une litanie. On l'écoutait avec un plaisir recueilli, encore qu'on ne le comprit point; car il parlait en persan . . . Le bahaisme, c'est en somme la religion de la charité et de la simplicité. C'est en même temps, amalgamés, le judaisme, le christianisme, le protestantisme, et la libre pensée. Abdoul Baha se réclamait de Zoroastre, de Moise, de Mahomet et de Jésus. Peut-être jugerez vous que cette unification est à la fois trop nombreuse et confuse. C'est qu'on ne comprend rien aux choses sacrées si l'on n'est inspiré par la foi . . . Sous le turban blanc ses yeux reflétaient l'intelligence et la bonté. Il était paternel, affectueux et simple. Son pouvoir, semblait-il, lui venait de ce qu'il savait aimer les hommes et savait se faire aimer d'eux. Appelé à témoigner de l'excellence de cette religion naïve et pure, nous pûmes honnêtement confesser notre foi par cette formule: Que les religions sont belles quand elles no sont pas encore.[2]

The *Morning Post*, two days after his passing, among other highly favourable comments, concluded its report of the Movement in the following words:

The venerated Baha'u'llah died in 1892 and the mantle of his religious insight fell on his son Abdul' Baha, when, after forty years of prison life, Turkish constitutional changes permitted him to visit England, France and America. His persistent messages as to the divine origin and unity of mankind were as impressive as the Messenger himself. He possessed singular courtesy. At his table Buddhist and Mohammedan, Hindu and Zoroastrian, Jew and Christian, sat in amity. 'Creatures,' he said, 'were created through love; let them live in peace and amity.'

The *New York World* of December 1, 1921 published the following:

Never before Abdu'l Baha did the leader of an Oriental religious movement visit the United States . . . As recently as June of this year a special correspondent of *The World* who visited this seer thus described him: 'Having once looked upon Abdu'l Baha, his personality is indelibly impressed upon the mind: the majestic venerable figure clad in the flowing *aba*, his head crowned with a turban white as his head and hair; the piercing deep set eyes whose glances shake the heart; the smile that pours its sweetness over all.'

Even in the twilight of his life Abdu'l Baha took the liveliest interest in world affairs. When General Allenby swept up the coast from Egypt he went for counsel first to Abdu'l Baha. When Zionists arrived in their Promised Land they sought Abdu'l Baha for advice. For Palestine he had the brightest hopes. Abdu'l Baha believed that Bolshevism would prove an admonition to the irreligious world.

He taught the equality of man and woman, saying: 'The world of humanity has two wings, man and woman. If one wing is weak, then the bird cannot fly' . . .

The Times of India in its issue of January 1922 opens one of its editorial articles as follows:

> In more normal times than the present the death of 'Abdu'l Baha, which was sorrowfully referred to at the Bahai Conference in Bombay, would have stifled the feelings of many who, without belonging to the Bahai brotherhood, sympathize with its tenets and admire the life-work of those who founded it. As it is we have learned almost by chance of this great religious leader's death, but that fact need not prevent our turning aside from politics and the turmoil of current events to consider what this man did and what he aimed at.

Sketching then in brief an account of the History of the Movement it concludes as follows:

> It is not for us now to judge whether the purity, the mysticism and the exalted ideas of Bahaism will continue unchanged after the loss of the great leader, or to speculate on whether Bahaism will some day become a force in the world as great or greater than Christianity or Islam, but we would pay a tribute to the memory of a man who wielded a vast influence for good, and who, if he was destined to see many of his ideas seemingly shattered in the world war, remained true to his convictions and to his belief in the possibility of a reign of peace and love, and who, far more effectively than Tolstoi, showed the West that religion is a vital force that can never be disregarded.

Out of the vast number of telegrams and cables of condolence that have poured in, these may be mentioned:

> His Britannic Majesty's Secretary of State for the Colonies, Mr Winston Churchill, telegraphing to His Excellency the High Commissioner for Palestine, desires him to convey to the Bahai Community, on behalf of His Majesty's Government, their sympathy and condolence on the death of Sir 'Abdu'l Baha 'Abbas K.B.E.

On behalf of the Executive Board of the Bahá'í American Convention, this message of condolence has been received:

He doeth whatsoever He willeth. Hearts weep at most great tribulation. American friends send through Unity Board radiant love, boundless sympathy, devotion. Standing steadfast, conscious of his unceasing presence and nearness.

Viscount Allenby, the High Commissioner for Egypt, has wired the following message, through the intermediary of His Excellency the High Commissioner for Palestine dated November 29th, 1921:

Please convey to the relatives of the late Sir 'Abdu'l Baha 'Abbas Effendi and to the Bahai community my sincere sympathy in the loss of their revered leader.

The loved ones in Germany assure the Greatest Holy Leaf of their fidelity in these terms:

All believers deeply moved by irrevocable loss of our Master's precious life. We pray for heavenly protection of Holy Cause and promise faithfulness and obedience to Centre of Covenant.

An official message forwarded by the Council of Ministers in Baghdad, and dated December 8th, 1921, reads as follows:

His Highness Sayed Abdurrahman, the Prime Minister, desires to extend his sympathy to the family of His Holiness 'Abdu'l Baha in their bereavement.

The Commander in Chief of the Egyptian Expeditionary Force sent through His Excellency the High Commissioner for Palestine these words of sympathy:

General Congreve begs that you will convey his deepest sympathy to the family of the late Sir 'Abbas al-Bahai.

The Theosophical Society in London communicated as follows with one of the followers of the Faith in Haifa:

For the Holy Family Theosophical Society send affectionate thoughts.

One of the foremost figures in the little and hallowed town of Nazareth wired the following:

> With the profoundest sorrow and regret we condole with you on the occasion of the setting of the Day-Star of the East. We are of God, and to Him we shall return.

The thousands of Bahá'ís in Teheran, the capital of Persia, remembering their Western brethren and sisters in London assure them of their steadfast faith in these words: 'Light of Covenant transferred from eye to heart. Day of teaching, of union, of self sacrifice.'

And lastly, one of the distinguished figures in the academic life of the University of Oxford, a renowned professor and an accomplished scholar, whose knowledge of the Cause stands foremost among that of his colleagues, in the message of condolence written on behalf of himself and wife, expresses himself as follows:

> The passing beyond the veil into fuller life must be specially wonderful and blessed for one, who has always fixed his thoughts on high and striven to lead an exalted life here below.

On the seventh day after the passing of the Master, corn was distributed in his name to about a thousand poor of Haifa, irrespective of race or religion, to whom he had always been a friend and a protector. Their grief at losing the 'Father of the Poor' was extremely pathetic. In the first seven days also from fifty to a hundred poor were daily fed at the Master's house, in the very place where it had been his custom to give alms to them.

On the fortieth day there was a memorial feast, given to over six hundred of the people of Haifa, Acre and the surrounding parts of Palestine and Syria, people of various religions, races and colours. More than a hundred of the poor were also fed on this day. The Governor of Phoenicia, many other officials and some Europeans were present.

The feast was entirely arranged by the members of the Master's household. The long tables were decorated with trailing branches of Bougainvillaeas. Its lovely purple blooms mingled with the white narcissus, and with the large dishes of golden oranges out of the beloved Master's garden made a picture of loveliness in those spacious lofty rooms, whose only other decoration was the gorgeous yet subdued colouring of rare

Persian rugs. No useless trivial ornaments marred the extreme dignity of simplicity.

The guests received, each and all, the same welcome. There were no 'chief places'. Here, as always in the Master's home, there was no respecting of persons.

After the luncheon the guests came into the large central hall, this also bare of ornament, save only for the portrait of Him they had assembled to honour and some antique Persian tapestries hung upon one wall. Before this was placed a platform from which the speeches were made to the rapt and silent throng, whose very hearts were listening.

The Governor of Phoenicia, in the course of his address, spoke the following:

> . . . Most of us here have, I think, a clear picture of Sir 'Abdu'l-Bahá 'Abbás, of his dignified figure walking thoughtfully in our streets, of his courteous and gracious manner, of his kindness, of his love for little children and flowers, of his generosity and care for the poor and suffering. So gentle was he, and so simple that, in his presence, one almost forgot that he was also a great teacher and that his writings and his conversations have been a solace and an inspiration to hundreds and thousands of people in the East and in the West . . .

Others who followed spoke in appreciation of the work and life of 'Abdu'l-Bahá. The following are only a few extracts from their addresses:

> A voice calling aloud from Teheran, echoed from 'Iraq, sounding in Turkish lands, swaying the Holy Land which hearkened to its melody, and wherein it rose, developed and deepened, till at last its reverberations resounded throughout Egypt, stretched across the seas to the West and thence to the New World.
>
> A voice summoning mankind to love, to unity and to peace; a voice the source whereof, had it been anything but purity of motive, could in no wise have succeeded in sending its waves with the swiftness of lightning throughout the world.
>
> Hail to 'Abbás, the pride and glory of the East, in an age that has witnessed the rise of knowledge and the fall of prejudice; he who has attained the glorious summit of greatness; he whom the Standards of triumph have hastened to welcome: he whose star arose in Persia,

shedding its light upon the minds of men, the signs of which have multiplied in the heaven of glory till it set in full radiance on this our horizon; he whose principles have humbled the peoples and kindreds of the world even as Bahá himself had done before him . . .

I believe, and firmly believe, that he whose loss we now lament, having lived eighty years in this world below counselling the people's of the world with his tongue, guiding them by his pen, setting before them a goodly example by his glorious deeds, has now chosen to lead and guide them by his silence.

Let us then in our thoughts and meditations pay our tribute to him. And though the other day at his door I made you weep, yet now it is my duty to appeal and ask you to forget your sorrow and refrain from lamentation and cease from shedding tears. Truly, Sir 'Abbás departed from us in body, but he ever lives with us in his abiding spirit, in his wondrous deeds. Though he has passed away, yet he has left for us a glorious heritage in the wisdom of his counsels, the rectitude of his teachings, the benevolence of his deeds, the example of his precious life, the sublimity of his effort, the power of his will, his patience and fortitude, his steadfastness to the end.

And now finally let us turn to the writings of 'Abdu'l-Bahá, to his words of farewell, his counsels, his prayers, his appeal and his prediction. His detailed and powerfully written Will and Testament reveals the following words of general counsel to all his friends:

O ye beloved of the Lord! In this sacred Dispensation, conflict and contention are in no wise permitted. Every aggressor deprives himself of God's grace. It is incumbent upon everyone to show the utmost love, rectitude of conduct, straightforwardness and sincere kindliness unto all the peoples and kindreds of the world, be they friends or strangers. So intense must be the spirit of love and loving-kindness that the stranger may find himself a friend, the enemy a true brother, no difference whatsoever existing between them.

For universality is of God and all limitations are earthly.

Thus man must strive that this reality may manifest virtues and perfections, the light whereof may shine upon everyone. The light of the sun shineth upon all the world and the merciful showers of Divine

Providence fall upon all peoples. The vivifying breeze reviveth every living creature, and all beings endued with life obtain their share and portion at His heavenly board. In like manner the affections and loving-kindness of the servants of the One True God must be bountifully and universally extended to all mankind. Regarding this, restrictions and limitations are in no wise permitted.

Wherefore, O my loving friends! Consort with all the peoples, kindreds and religions of the world with the utmost truthfulness, uprightness, faithfulness, kindliness, good-will and friendliness; that all the world of being may be filled with the holy ecstasy of the grace of Bahá; that ignorance, enmity, hate and rancour may vanish from the world, and the darkness of estrangement amidst the peoples and kindreds of the world may give way to the Light of Unity. Should other peoples and nations be unfaithful to you, show your fidelity unto them; should they be unjust towards you, show justice towards them; should they keep aloof from you, attract them to yourselves; should they show their enmity, be friendly towards them; should they poison your lives, sweeten their souls; should they inflict a wound upon you, be a salve to their sores. Such are the attributes of the sincere! Such are the attributes of the truthful!

O ye beloved of the Lord! Strive with all your heart to shield the Cause of God from the onslaught of the insincere, for such souls as these cause the straight to become crooked and all benevolent efforts to produce contrary results.

Regarding the afflictions and trials that have befallen him in this world and his desire for martyrdom, 'Abdu'l-Bahá reveals the following:

O God, my God! Thou seest this wronged servant of Thine, held fast in the talons of ferocious lions, of ravening wolves, blood-thirsty beasts. Graciously assist me, through my love for Thee, that I may drink deep of the chalice that brimmeth over with faithfulness to Thee and is filled with Thy bountiful Grace; so that, fallen upon the dust, I may sink prostrate and senseless whilst my vesture is dyed crimson with my blood. This is my wish, my heart's desire, my hope, my pride, my glory. Grant, O Lord, my God and my Refuge, that in my last hour, my end may, even as musk, shed its fragrance of glory! I call Thee to witness that no day passeth but that I quaff my fill from this cup, so grievous are the misdeeds wrought by them that have broken the Covenant, kindled discord, showed their malice, stirred sedition in the land and dishonoured Thee amidst Thy servants. Lord, shield Thou from these Covenant-breakers the mighty stronghold of Thy Faith, and protect Thy secret Sanctuary from the onslaught of the ungodly.

Thou art in truth, the Mighty, the Powerful, the Gracious, the Strong!

Lord! Thou seest all things weeping over me, and my kindred rejoicing in my woes. By thy glory, O my God! even amongst my enemies, some have lamented my troubles and my distress, and of the envious ones a number have shed tears because of my cares, my exile and my afflictions. They did this because they found naught in me but affection and care, and witnessed naught but kindliness and mercy. As they saw me swept into the flood of tribulation and adversity, and exposed even as a target to the arrows of fate, their hearts were moved with compassion, tears came to their eyes and they testified, declaring: 'The Lord is our witness; naught have we seen in him but faithfulness, generosity and extreme compassion.' The Covenant-breakers, foreboders of evil, waxed fiercer in their rancour, rejoiced as I fell a victim to the most grievous ordeal, bestirred themselves against me, and made merry over the heart-rending happenings around me.

Lord! My cup of woe runneth over, and from all sides blows are fiercely raging upon me. The darts of affliction have compassed me round and the arrows of distress have rained upon me. Thus tribulation overwhelmed me, and my strength, because of the onslaught of the foeman, became weakness within me, whilst I stood alone and forsaken in the midst of my woes. Lord, have mercy upon me, lift me up unto Thyself and make me to drink from the chalice of martyrdom, for the wide world with all its vastness can no longer contain me. Thou art verily the Merciful, the Compassionate, the Gracious, the All-Bountiful.

He prays for the protection of his friends:

O Lord, my God! Assist Thy loved ones to be firm in Thy Faith, to walk in Thy ways, to be steadfast in Thy Cause. Give them Thy grace to withstand the onslaught of self and passion, to follow the light of Divine

Guidance. Thou art the Powerful, the Gracious, the Self-Subsisting, the Bestower, the Compassionate, the Almighty, the All-Bountiful!

For his enemies this is his prayer:

I call upon Thee, O Lord, my God! with my tongue and with all my heart, not to requite them for their cruelty and their wrong deeds, their craft and their mischief, for they are foolish and ignoble, and know not what they do. They discern not good from evil, neither do they distinguish right from wrong, nor justice from injustice. They follow their own desires and walk in the footsteps of the most imperfect and foolish amongst them. O my Lord! have mercy upon them, shield them from all afflictions in these troubled times, and grant that all trials and hardships may be the lot of this, Thy servant, that has fallen into this darksome pit. Single me out for every woe and make me a sacrifice for all Thy loved ones! O Lord, Most High! May my soul, my life, my being, my spirit, my all, be offered up for them! O God, my God, lowly, suppliant and fallen upon my face, I beseech Thee, with all the ardour of my invocation, to pardon whomsoever hath hurt me, to forgive him that hath conspired against me and offended me, and to wash away the misdeeds of them that hath wrought injustice upon me. Vouchsafe unto them Thy goodly gifts; give them joy, relieve them from sorrow, grant them peace and prosperity; give them Thy bliss and pour upon them Thy bounty. Thou art the Powerful, the Gracious, the Help in peril, the Self-Subsisting.

Touching the importance of teaching the Cause of God, these are his words:

O ye that stand fast in the Covenant! When the hour cometh that this wronged and broken-winged bird will have taken its flight unto the Celestial Concourse, when it will have hastened to the Realm of the Unseen and its mortal frame will have been either lost or hidden neath the dust, it is incumbent upon the Afnán that are steadfast in the Covenant of God and have branched from the Tree of Holiness; the Hands (pillars) of the Cause of God (the glory of the Lord rest upon them), and all the friends and loved ones, one and all, to bestir themselves and arise with heart and soul and in one accord to diffuse the sweet savours of God, to teach His Cause and to promote His Faith. It behoveth them not to rest for a moment, neither to seek repose. They must disperse themselves in every land, pass by every clime and travel throughout all regions. Bestirred, without rest and steadfast to the end, they must raise in every land the triumphant cry, 'Yá Bahá'u'l-Abhá' (O Thou the Glory of Glories), must achieve renown in the world wherever they go, must burn brightly even as a torch in every meeting, and must kindle the flame of divine love in every assembly; that the Light of Truth may rise resplendent in the midmost heart of the world, that throughout the East and throughout the West a vast concourse may gather under the shadow of the Word of God, that the sweet savours of holiness may be diffused, that faces may radiantly shine, that hearts may be filled with the Divine Spirit and souls may heavenly life attain.

The disciples of Christ forgot themselves and all earthly things, forsook all their cares and belongings, purged themselves of self and passion, and with absolute detachment, scattered far and wide, calling the peoples of the world to the Divine Guidance, till at last they made the world another world, illumined the surface of the earth, and even to their last hour, proved self-sacrificing in the pathway of that Beloved One of God. Finally in various lands they suffered glorious martyrdom. Let them that are men of action follow in their footsteps.

Whosoever and whatsoever meeting becometh a hindrance to the diffusion of the Light of Faith, let the loved ones give them counsel and say: 'Of all the gifts of God the greatest is the gift of teaching. It draweth unto us the grace of God and is our first obligation. Of such a gift why do we deprive ourselves? Nay, our lives, our goods, our comfort, our rest we offer them all in sacrifice for the Abhá Beauty, and teach the Cause of God. Caution and prudence however, must be observed even as recorded in the Book. The veil must in no wise be suddenly rent asunder.'

As to the foundation of the faith of the people of Bahá:

This is the foundation of the faith of the people of Bahá, may my life be offered up for them; His Holiness the Exalted One, the Báb, is the Manifestation of the Unity and Oneness of God and the forerunner of the Ancient Beauty; the Abhá Beauty, (may my life be a sacrifice for His steadfast friends), is the Supreme Manifestation of God and the Day Spring of His Most Divine Essence. All others are servants unto

Him and do His bidding. Unto the Most Holy Book every one must turn, and all that is not expressly recorded therein must be referred to the Universal House of Justice. That which this body, whether unanimously, or by a majority, doth carry, that is verily the truth and the purpose of God Himself. Whoso doth deviate therefrom is verily of them that love discord, hath shown forth malice and turned away from the Lord of the Covenant.

Regarding the loyalty of the people of Bahá to sovereign authority and the laws of the country he reveals:

O ye beloved of the Lord! It is incumbent upon you to be submissive to all Monarchs that are just, and show your fidelity to every righteous King. Serve ye the Sovereigns of the world with utmost truthfulness and loyalty. Show obedience unto them and be their well-wishers. Without their leave and permission do not meddle with political affairs, for disloyalty to the just Sovereign is disloyalty to God Himself. This is my counsel and the commandment of God unto you. Well is it with them that act accordingly.

He concludes one of the sections of his Testament with this prayer:

O God, my God! I call Thee, Thy Prophets and Thy Messengers, Thy Saints and Thy Holy Ones, to witness that I have declared conclusively Thy proofs unto Thy loved ones, and set forth clearly all things unto them, that they may watch over Thy Faith, guard Thy straight Path and protect Thy resplendent Law. Thou art verily, the All-Knowing, the All-Wise!

And now, turning from his Will and Testament to his epistles and Tablets, we read the following, a word of caution, which he reveals in his last general Tablet to his loved ones all over the world:

O ye beloved ones! Guard the Cause of God. Let not sweetness of tongue beguile you; nay rather, consider the motive of every soul and ponder over the thought he cherisheth. Be ye then straightway mindful and on your guard. Avoid them and be not aggressive, and turn away from censure and slander. Leave him in the hand of God.

A clear and unmistakable prediction which he made regarding the glorious unfolding of the Cause in the not distant future is forcibly revealed in a letter he wrote whilst under the threat of the Committee of Investigation during the darkest days of his incarceration in Acre:

> Now in the world of being the hand of divine power hath firmly laid the foundations of this all-highest bounty and this wondrous gift. Whatsoever is latent in the innermost of this holy cycle shall gradually appear and be made manifest, for now is but the beginning of its growth and the day-spring of the revelation of its signs. Ere the close of this century and of this age, it shall be made clear and evident how wondrous was that spring-tide and how heavenly was that gift!

A similar and even more definite utterance, prophesying the rise of the Movement, he makes in a Tablet revealed after the Great War to a Kurdish friend, resident in Egypt. These are his very words:

> Now concerning the verse in Daniel, the interpretation whereof thou didst ask, namely, 'Blessed is he who cometh unto the thousand three hundred and thirty five days.' These days must be reckoned as solar and not lunar years. For according to this calculation a century will have elapsed from the dawn of the Sun of Truth, then will the teachings of God be firmly established upon the earth, and the Divine Light shall flood the world from the East even unto the West. Then, on this day, will the faithful rejoice!

Confirming and explaining further the hidden meaning of the above mentioned verse he reveals the following in one of his earlier Tablets:

> O servant of God! The afore-mentioned thousand three hundred and thirty-five years must be reckoned from the day of the flight (Hegira) of His Holiness Muhammad, the Apostle of God, salutations and blessings rest upon Him, at the close of which time the signs of the rise, the glory, the exaltation, the spread of the Word of God throughout the East and the West shall appear.

In one of his last Tablets, counselling the company of the friends of God, he breathes this fresh, encouraging spirit:

Regard not the person of 'Abdu'l-Bahá, for he will eventually take his leave of you all; nay, fix your gaze upon the Word of God. Should it rise and be exalted, rejoice, be glad and thankful even if 'Abdu'l-Bahá be under a drawn sword, be confined or be cast into bonds. For that which is of transcending importance is the Holy Temple of the Cause of God, and not the mortal frame of 'Abdu'l-Bahá. The loved ones of God must arise with such steadfastness, that should in one moment hundreds of souls, even as 'Abdu'l-Bahá himself, be made a target for the darts of woe, nothing whatsoever shall affect or lessen their firm resolve, their intention, their ardour, their enkindlement, their service to the Cause of God . . . This, O ye beloved of the Lord, is my counsel and my exhortation unto you. Well is it with him whom the Lord aideth to do even as bidden in this pure and sanctified Tablet.

The circular letter published on the occasion of the Master's departure from this world by the Spiritual Assembly of Teheran, contains extracts of a Tablet revealed fourteen years ago by the pen of the Centre of the Covenant, some of which are the following:

O ye my faithful loved ones! Should at any time afflicting events come to pass in the Holy Land, never feel disturbed and agitated; fear not, neither grieve. For whatsoever thing happeneth will cause the Word of God to be exalted and His divine fragrances to be diffused. Make firm your steps and with utmost steadfastness arise to serve His Cause . . . The Spirit of God and His glory rest upon him that is firm and steadfast in the Covenant!

Among his utterances regarding his passing away from this world, he assures us as follows:

Remember whether or not I be on earth, my presence will be with you always.

Again in a Tablet addressed to one of the friends in the United States of America, he depicts the future glory of the Sacred Tree of God whereof he is the Most Great Branch:

Fear not if this Branch be severed from this material world and cast aside its leaves; nay, the leaves thereof shall flourish, for this Branch will grow after it is cut off from this world below, it shall reach the loftiest pinnacles of glory, and it shall bear such fruits as will perfume the world with their fragrance.

His very last Tablet, graciously revealed for his loved ones in Stuttgart, conveys his reflections upon this transient world, and his counsels to his loved ones that dwell therein:

O ye beloved of the Lord! In this mortal world, nothing whatsoever endureth. The peoples of the earth dwell therein and spend a number of days uselessly, ultimately descending neath the dust, repairing to the home of eternal silence, leaving behind them no achievement, no blessing, no result, no fruit. All the days of their life are thus brought to naught. Whereas the children of the Kingdom sow seeds in the fertile soil of Truth, that will eventually spring up and bring forth many a harvest and shall forever bestow upon mankind its increase and bountiful grace. They shall obtain eternal life, attain unto the imperishable bounty, and shine even as radiant stars in the firmament of the Divine Kingdom. The Glory of Glories rest upon you!

And now, what appeal more direct, more moving, with which to close this sad yet stirring account of his last days, than these his most touching, most inspiring words?

Friends! The time is coming when I shall be no longer with you. I have done all that could be done. I have served the Cause of Bahá'u'lláh to the utmost of my ability. I have laboured night and day, all the years of my life. O how I long to see the loved ones taking upon themselves the responsibilities of the Cause! Now is the time to proclaim the Kingdom of Bahá! Now is the hour of love and union! This is the day of the spiritual harmony of the loved ones of God! All the resources of my physical strength I have exhausted, and the spirit of my life is the welcome tidings of the unity of the people of Bahá. I am straining my ears toward the East and toward the West, toward the North and toward the South that haply I may hear the songs of love and fellowship chanted in the meetings of the faithful. My days are numbered, and, but for this, there is no joy left unto me. O how I yearn to see the friends united even as a string of gleaming pearls, as the brilliant Pleiades, as the rays of the sun, as the gazelles of one meadow!

The mystic Nightingale is warbling for them all; will they not listen? The Bird of Paradise is singing; will they not heed? The Angel of Abhá is calling to them; will they not hearken? The Herald of the Covenant is pleading; will they not obey?

Ah me, I am waiting, waiting, to hear the joyful tidings that the believers are the very embodiment of sincerity and truthfulness, the incarnation of love and amity, the living symbols of unity and concord. Will they not gladden my heart? Will they not satisfy my yearning? Will they not manifest my wish? Will they not fulfil my heart's desire? Will they not give ear to my call?

I am waiting, I am patiently waiting.

***

Prayer revealed by 'Abdu'l-Bahá and now recited by his loved ones at his hallowed shrine.

'Abdu'l-Bahá says:

Whoso reciteth this prayer with lowliness and fervour will bring gladness and joy to the heart of this servant; it will be even as meeting him face to face.

He is the All-glorious!

O God, my God! Lowly and tearful, I raise my suppliant hands to Thee and cover my face in the dust of that Threshold of Thine, exalted above the knowledge of the learned, and the praise of all that glorify Thee. Graciously look upon Thy servant, humble and lowly at Thy door, with the glances of the eye of Thy mercy, and immerse him in the Ocean of Thine eternal grace.

Lord! He is a poor and lowly servant of Thine, enthralled and imploring Thee, captive in Thy hand, praying fervently to Thee, trusting in Thee, in tears before Thy face, calling to Thee and beseeching Thee, saying:

O Lord, my God! Give me Thy grace to serve Thy loved ones,

strengthen me in my servitude to Thee, illumine my brow with the light of adoration in Thy court of holiness, and of prayer to Thy Kingdom of grandeur. Help me to be selfless at the heavenly entrance of Thy gate, and aid me to be detached from all things within Thy holy precincts. Lord! Give me to drink from the chalice of selflessness; with its robe clothe me, and in its ocean immerse me. Make me as dust in the pathway of Thy loved ones, and grant that I may offer up my soul for the earth ennobled by the footsteps of Thy chosen ones in Thy Path, O Lord of Glory in the Highest!

With this prayer doth Thy servant call Thee, at dawn-tide and in the night-season. Fulfil his heart's desire, O Lord! Illumine his heart, gladden his bosom, kindle his light, that he may serve Thy Cause and Thy servants.

Thou art the Bestower, the Pitiful, the Most Bountiful, the Gracious, the Merciful, the Compassionate!

Sitárih Khánum (Lady Blomfield)
Shoghi
Haifa, Palestine,
January 1922

APPENDIX TWO

THE BAHÁ'ÍS

From *Sufi Quarterly* by
SITÁRIH KHÁNUM (Lady Blomfield)

The purpose of this article is to give a brief sketch of the Bahá'í Movement, in the course of which it is hoped to suggest something of the atmosphere of that spirit of love and self-sacrifice by which it is animated.

To this end also will be brought together a few of the impressions, as far as possible in their own words, made upon certain personalities of the Western world, whether by their coming into personal touch with Bahá'u'lláh himself, or through investigations in Persia. To these may be added the remark of the revered Master of Balliol College, Oxford – Dr Benjamin Jowett – to a fellow-professor, that he was deeply interested in the Bahá'í Movement. 'This', he said, 'is the greatest Light that has come into the world since Jesus Christ . . . Never let it out of your sight. It is too great and too near for this generation to comprehend. The future alone can reveal its import.'

The Báb

Let us glance for a moment at the earlier scenes of this drama, of which the prologue stretches far back into the centuries that are past.

In Shiraz, a city of Persia, was born in AD 1819 a child who was named 'Alí Muhammad. As he grew from childhood he became more and more 'renowned for his piety and virtue, his courtesy of manner, and the beauty of his person'. He spent his youth in the study of the Holy Writings, and became remarkable for his knowledge of their spiritual significance.

In the year 1844, this young man declared his mission calling men to repentance. Soon after, he proclaimed himself the Forerunner of the 'Great Prophet' who had been expected for centuries. He assumed the title of the Báb, signifying Gate or Door (of Heaven and of Wisdom). 'What he intended by the term Báb, was this, that he was the channel of grace from some great Person still behind the veil of glory, who was the possessor of countless and boundless perfections, by whose will he moved, and to the bond of whose love he clung. The Báb was ever repeating and meditating on the qualities and attributes of that absent-yet-present, regarded-and-regarding Person of his. Thus he makes a mention of Him, whereof this is the purport: 'Though the ocean of woe rageth on every side, and the bolts of fate follow in quick succession, and the darkness of griefs and affliction invade soul and body, yet is my heart brightened by the remembrance of Thy countenance and my soul is as a rose-garden from the perfume of Thy nature.'

He (the Báb) invited men to the work of 'preparing His way' by freeing themselves from spiritual bondage. In many Tablets, and in the Book of Bayán (literally, Revelation) – as well as in his spoken word – the Báb exhorted his countrymen to return to the original purity of Religion, so that they might be ready to receive the 'Great One: Him whom God should make manifest'. Many enthusiastic hearers answered his call. The good news spread with wondrous swiftness. The Báb was hailed by a great number 'as the Dawn which should break upon a dark and perplexed world'. The alarm of those mainly responsible for that darkness and per-plexity was awakened, they feared the loss of their power, prestige, and pecuniary benefits. Instigated by these persons, the Báb was arrested, taken from prison to prison, and, after many mock trials, finally shot at Tabriz in 1850.

After the execution of the 'beautiful youth, with the shining face, who walked in a serene, sedate manner', the authorities determined to stamp out the movement. Then burst forth a violent storm of persecution, in which tens of thousands of the Báb's followers were massacred. All classes were included; nobles and peasants, learned and unlearned, men, women, and children were martyred. Firm and steadfast in their faith, they suffered confiscation of their property and exile; they endured the most horrible mutilations; 'they were tortured, not accepting deliverance'; they were faithful unto death, even the most violent and cruel that could be devised.

None was ever known to recant: 'out of weakness they were made strong'. 'My life is of no importance,' said a child of twelve years old, 'but to insult the Holy One is impossible' – and the torturers carried out their ghastly threats. Verily 'the Tree of Life was watered by the red blood of martyrs', for the remnant of those who were saved, steadfast as the martyred, and ready, if need be, to suffer the same fate, awaited the coming of 'Him Whom God should make manifest', whose way had been prepared by the Báb. At what cost of 'cruel mockings and scourgings, bonds and imprisonments, torments and early death', we may read in a narrative of the time, which describes with a direct simplicity the 'Episode of the Báb', of whom the world was not worthy.

Of the Báb Professor Ross, of London University, has written: 'His wonderful life needs no comment. If ever a life spoke for itself, it is the Báb's, with its simplicity, integrity, and unswerving devotion to the Truth that was born in him. He felt the Truth in him, and in the proclamation of that Truth, he moved neither hand nor foot to spare himself, but unflinchingly submitted to all manner of injustice and persecution, and finally to an ignominious death. His influence on his hearers penetrated deeper than their curiosity or their minds, it reached their hearts, and inspired them with a spirit of self-sacrifice, renunciation, and devotion as remarkable and as admirable as his own.'

Bahá'u'lláh (Jamál-i-Mubárak)

Among the first to recognize the inspired source of the new doctrine of the Báb was a young and wealthy man of noble birth, Mírzá Husayn 'Alí Núrí, allied to the royal family of Persia, and whose gentleness and philanthropy had won for him the title of Father of the Poor. Now he is revered by innumerable people as Bahá'u'lláh, signifying 'The Splendour of the Glory of God'.

During the reign of horror, after the death of the Báb, he was arrested, and, in spite of his powerful family influence, thrown into a dungeon, chained to five other disciples. In this state of torment he was kept for several months. He was then deprived of his property and estates, and with his family driven into exile. The hardships and privations suffered on this journey to Baghdád were doubly cruel, as the children were very young, and the snow was on the ground. A number of families of the faithful and persecuted followed him and soon grew to look upon him as their leader. The greatness of his personality began to attract numbers of cultivated and learned men, who, having discovered the whereabouts of the exiled band of Persians, journeyed to hear his teaching. His power and influence alarmed afresh his ever-vigilant enemies, who persuaded those in authority to summon him to Constantinople. Thence he was banished to Adrianople; but the sound of the Voice crying aloud the Message of Regeneration could not be silenced; its influence could not be stayed. Bahá'u'lláh's teaching had a more universal note than that of the Báb. Not only were religious perversions in Persia to be reformed, but the whole world was to be united in one great bond of brotherhood, and peace and goodwill, under a universal code of love and honour – free from superstition, hatred and war. Then came a day when he proclaimed to his eldest son, 'Abbás Effendi, and a few intimate friends, that he was the 'Promised One', 'He whom God should make manifest'.

This was in 1863 – nineteen years after the proclamation of the mission of the Báb, and in accordance with his prophecy. In spite of all opposition, the sacred Message was persistently proclaimed – God, speaking again through His great Manifestation, would lead mankind to recognize the Sun of Truth shining at the core of all religions: for as 'in the realm of Conscience, naught but the Ray of God's Light can command, and on the throne of the heart none but the pervading power of the King of Kings should rule' – therefore all men, developing their spiritual nature, would make such progress in divine virtue, that they should become regenerated through love, and this renewal should gather every nation together under the 'Tent of Unity'.

Letters were sent to the crowned heads of Europe. 'We trust that God will assist the Kings of the earth to illuminate and adorn the earth with the effulgent light of the Sun of Justice' – Bahá'u'lláh wrote; and he charged them to look upon themselves as trustees of God, and guardians, under His Rule, of their people; and he called upon these powerful ones of the world, as servants of the Most High Lord of Mercy, to put an end to the horrors of War.

Again he was exiled – this time to the far off Eastern fortress of 'Akká, in the Holy Land. In this town he remained, persecuted, tormented, until he returned to God in 1892. From the 'most great Prison', he sent out his messages; and in his captivity he wrote laws for the spiritual guidance of the world of the future. 'For, as nothing can prevent the radiance of the sun descending to give life to the gardens of earth, and no man prevent the fall of the rain from heaven, so, no earthly power can prevent the fulfilment of the word of God.'

His long years of tedious banishment and imprisonment, sometimes in chains, sometimes in his own hired house, always surrounded by spies seeking excuses for renewed persecutions – all these tribulations he accepted with joy and a marvellous patient dignity. 'My captivity is not my abasement: it is indeed a glory to me', he said. He left to his eldest son, 'Abbás Effendi, henceforth 'Abdu'l-Bahá (The Servant of the Glory of God), the mission of carrying his message into all the world.

Few persons of the Western world ever succeeded in obtaining the privilege of coming into the presence of Bahá'u'lláh.

Fortunately, Professor Edward Granville Browne of Cambridge, 'after many disappointments and failures, attained the fulfilment of his hopes, in a manner surpassing his most sanguine expectations'.

I propose to quote his description of a memorable visit to Bahjí near 'Akká:

'So here at Bahjí was I installed as a guest, in the very midst of all that Baha'ism accounts most noble and most holy, and here did I spend five most memorable days, during which I enjoyed unparalleled and unhoped-for opportunities of holding intercourse with those who are the very fountain-heads of that mighty and wondrous spirit which works with invisible but ever-increasing force for the transformation and quickening of a people who slumber in a sleep like unto death. It was in truth a strange and moving experience, but one whereof I despair of conveying any save the feeblest impression. I might, indeed, strive to describe in greater detail the faces and forms which surrounded me, the conversations to which I was privileged to listen, the solemn melodious reading of the sacred books, the general sense of harmony and content which pervaded the place, and the fragrant shady gardens whither in the afternoon we sometimes repaired; but all this was as nought in comparison with the spiritual atmosphere with which I was encompassed.

'The spirit which pervades the Bahá'ís is such that it can hardly fail to affect most powerfully all subjected to its influence. It may appal or attract; it cannot be ignored or disregarded. Let those who have not seen, disbelieve me if they will, but, should that spirit once reveal itself to them, they will experience an emotion which they are not likely to forget.

'Of the culminating event of this my journey some few words at least must be said. During the morning of the day after my installation at Bahjí . . . I found myself in a large apartment, along the upper end of which ran a low divan, while on the side opposite the door were placed two or three chairs. Though I dimly suspected whither I was going and whom I was to behold (for no distinct intimation had been given to me), a second or two elapsed ere, with a throb of wonder and awe, I became definitely conscious that the room was not untenanted. In the corner where the divan met the wall sat a wondrous and venerable figure, crowned with a felt head-dress of the kind called *táj* by dervishes (but of unusual height and make), round the base of which was wound a small white turban. The face of him on whom I gazed, I can never forget though I cannot describe it. Those piercing eyes seemed to read one's very soul; power and authority sat on that ample brow; while the deep lines of the forehead and face implied an age which the jet-black hair and beard seemed to belie.

'No need to ask in whose presence I stood, as I bowed myself before one who is the object of a devotion and love which kings might envy and emperors sigh for in vain!

'A mild dignified voice bade me be seated, and then continued. "Praise be to God that thou hast attained! . . . Thou hast come to see a prisoner and an exile . . . We desire but the good of the world and the happiness of the nations; yet they deem us a stirrer up of strife and sedition worthy of bondage and banishment . . . That all nations should become one in faith and all men as brothers; that the bonds of affection and unity between the sons of men should be strengthened; that diversity of religion should cease, and differences of race be annulled – what harm is there in this? . . . Yet so it shall be: these fruitless strifes, these ruinous wars shall pass away, and the Most Great Peace shall come . . . Do not you in Europe need this also? Is not this that which Christ foretold? . . . Yet do we see your kings and rulers lavishing their treasures more freely on means for the destruction of the human race than on that which would conduce to the happiness of mankind . . . These strifes and this bloodshed and discord must cease, and all men be as one kindred and one family . . . Let not a man glory in this that he loves his country: let him rather glory in this, that he loves his kind . . ."

'Such, so far as I can recall them, were the words, which, besides many others, I heard from Bahá'u'lláh.

'Let those who read them consider well with themselves whether such doctrines merit death and bonds, and whether the world is more likely to gain or lose by their diffusion.

'My interview lasted altogether about twenty minutes, and during the latter part of it Bahá'u'lláh read a portion of an epistle (law?) whereof the translation is as follows:

'"He is God, exalted is His state, wisdom and utterance! The True One (glorious is His glory), for the shewing-forth of the gems of ideals from the mine of man, hath, in every age, sent a trusted one. The primary foundation of the faith of God and the religion of God is this, that they should not make diverse sects and various paths the cause and reason of hatred. These principles and laws and firm sure roads appear from one Dawning-place and shine from one Dayspring, and these diversities were out of regard for the requirements of the time, season, ages, and epochs . . . Make firm the girdle of endeavour, that perchance religious strife and conflict may be removed from amongst the people of the world and be annulled.

'"For love of God and His servants engage in this great and mighty matter. Religious hatred and rancour is a world-consuming fire, and the quenching thereof most arduous, unless the hand of Divine Might give men deliverance from this unfruitful calamity. Consider a war which happeneth between two states: both sides have foregone wealth and life: how many villages were beheld as though they were not! This precept is in the position of the light in the lamp of utterance.

'"O people of the world, ye are all the fruit of one tree and the leaves of one branch. Walk with perfect charity, concord, affection, and agreement. I swear by the Sun of Truth, the light of agreement shall brighten and illumine the horizon. The all-knowing Truth hath been and is the witness to this saying. Endeavour to attain to this high supreme station which is the station of protection and preservation of mankind. This is the intent of the King of intentions, and this is the hope of the Lord of hopes."'

The utterances of Bahá'u'lláh are of two classes. In one class he writes or speaks simply as a man who has been charged by God with a message to his fellows, while again sometimes his words have authority of the direct utterance of God Himself. Bahá'u'lláh writes in the Book of Íqán:

'There are two stations for the Suns rising from the Daysprings of Divinity. One is the station of Unity and condition of Oneness. "We make no distinction between any of them" (Qur'an, S. 2). Thus it is said, "Verily, they who swear fealty unto thee, swear fealty unto God . . ."

'In this station, all are sent forth from the presence of that ideal King and Eternal Essence . . .

'The other station is that of distinction, creation and human limitations. In this station for each one a temple is designated, a mission is indicated, a manifestation is decreed, and certain limitations are assigned. Each one is named by a certain name, characterized by certain qualities and appointed to a new Cause and Law.

'In the station of Oneness and rank of Singleness, pure Sublimity, Divinity, Unity and absolute Deity have been and are ascribed to those Essences of Existence, because they are all seated upon the throne of the Manifestation of God' . . . that is, the appearance and the beauty of God is revealed by their beauty.

'But in the second station, which is that of distinction, separation, limitation and temporal condition and indication, they show forth absolute servitude, real need and utter lowliness: as it is said: "Verily, I am the servant of God", and "Verily, I am only a man like you" (Qur'an, S. 41).

'If it be heard from the Perfect Manifestations: "Verily, I am God", it is true and without doubt, for . . . through their Manifestation, Attributes and Names, the Manifestation of God, the Attributes of God and the Name of God appear upon earth . . . Likewise if they say: "We are the servants of God", this also is confirmed and evident, for outwardly they have appeared with the utmost degree of servitude. No one [else] hath the courage to appear in the world with that manner of servitude!

'Thus those Essences of Existence when submerged in the seas of Eternal Holiness and when ascending to the summits of the significances of the Ideal King, utter declarations of Unity and Deity. Were one to consider attentively, he will find that even in this state they witness in themselves the utmost humility and lowliness in the presence of the Absolute Existence and Real Life as though accounting themselves utterly non-existent and deeming mention of themselves in that court as polytheism . . .

'Therefore, whatever they may say and claim, including Divinity, Deity, Prophethood, Messengership, Successorship, Imamat or Servitude, is true and without doubt.'

When Bahá'u'lláh speaks as a man, the station he claims for himself is that of utter humility, of 'annihilation in God'. What distinguishes the 'Manifestation', in his human personality, from other men, is the completeness of his self-abnegation as well as the perfection of his powers. In all circumstances he is able to say, as did the Lord Jesus in the Garden of Gethsemane, 'Nevertheless not my will but Thine be done.'

Thus in his epistle to the Shah of Persia Bahá'u'lláh says: 'I was asleep on my couch: the breaths of my Lord, the Merciful, passed over me and awakened me from my sleep; and commanded me to proclaim betwixt Earth and Heaven. This was not on my part but on His part, and to this bear witness the denizens of the realm of His power and His kingdom, and the dwellers in the cities of His Glory, and Himself, the Truth. I am not impatient of calamities in His way, nor of afflictions for His love and at His good pleasure – God hath made afflictions as a morning shower to His green pasture, and as a wick for His lamp whereby Earth and Heaven are illumined.' And again: 'By God, though weariness should weaken me and hunger should destroy me, though my couch should be made of the hard rock and my associates of the beasts of the desert, I will not blench, but will be patient, as the resolute and determined are patient, in the strength of God, the King of Pre-existence, the Creator of the Nations: and under all circumstances I give thanks unto God.'

In the Hidden Words Bahá'u'lláh speaks from the station of Divinity.

'O SON OF SPIRIT!

'My first counsel is this: Possess a pure, kindly and radiant heart, that thine may be a sovereignty, heavenly, ancient, imperishable and everlasting.'

'O SON OF BEING!

'Love Me, that I may love thee. If thou love Me not, My love can in no wise reach thee. Know this, O servant.'

'O SON OF SPIRIT!

'I have created thee rich; wherefore impoverish thyself? Noble I made thee; why dost thou abase thyself? Out of the essence of knowledge I manifested thee; why seekest thou any one beside Me? Of the clay of Love I moulded thee; why dost thou busy thyself with another? Turn thy sight unto thyself, that thou mayest find Me standing within thee, Powerful, Mighty and Supreme.'

'O SON OF SPIRIT!

'Know verily that he who exhorts men to equity, and himself does injustice, is not of Me, even though he bear My Name.'

'Abdu'l-Bahá

Until 1908, sixteen years after the passing of Bahá'u'lláh, 'Abdu'l-Bahá was himself confined in the fortress of 'Akká, where the system of watchful persecution was continued. Having endured a lifetime of exile and imprisonment, a 'captive for the cause of God', he was liberated, at the age of sixty-four, by the Young Turk Party. Now, at last, after forty long years, borne with the cheerfulness of high faith in his mission to succour the suffering sons of men, he was able to make plans for carrying out the charge laid upon him by Bahá'u'lláh. 'That cry of Regeneration, raised behind prison walls, now echoes abroad in the hearts of men', for 'Abdu'l-Bahá came and proclaimed the Message to the Western world!

'I waited forty years in prison to bring this Message to you; are you pleased to receive such a guest?' he said to those who awaited him in London.

Those who have had the privilege of knowing 'Abdu'l-Bahá in the Prison Fortress of 'Akká, during his days of captivity, and those who came into personal touch with him in London and Paris, were alike impressed with the great moral beauty of his character, and the indescribable spiritual dignity of his demeanour.

Always did he speak with authority, and not as the mere expounder, albeit a certain gentle courtesy was most conspicuous, and seemed to surround him with an atmosphere of loving-kindness, the benign influence of which was felt by all who came into his presence. Whether it were a great minister of State or an ecclesiastical dignitary, a busy toiler for his daily bread, or a sorrow-burthened Princess, a famous artist or a learned barrister, a celebrated physician or a Christian Scientist, a woman suffragist or an Oxford Professor, a poor seamstress or a renowned writer, an inquiring journalist or an able man of science, none was either too great or too insignificant to receive of the bountiful warmth of his sympathetic consideration. He was marvellously energetic, and his presence brought a delightful, vivid gladness. 'When a man turns his face to God, he finds sunshine everywhere; all men are his brethren', he said to us one day. Never was he sad, save of the battle of Benghazi. 'My heart is grieved:' – he looked very sorrowful as he spoke – 'I wonder at the human cruelty which still exists in the world. There is nothing so heart-breaking as an outburst of men's savagery. I charge you all that each one of you concentrate the thoughts of your hearts on Love and Unity; when a thought of war comes, oppose it by a stronger thought of Peace. Do not think the Peace of the world an ideal impossible of attainment; nothing is impossible to the Divine Benevolence of God! Through this Power comes the success of the most colossal undertakings.'

'Abdu'l-Bahá with a serene aloofness counselled a detachment from personality. It is to be borne in mind that he himself claimed no title but

'Abdu'l-Bahá, i.e. the servant of the Splendour of God, so that there can never be any controversy concerning his station. He called to all the friends of God in every region of the earth to arise and help him in the Service of Humanity, in the well-being of the world, and in the spreading of Divine love and kindness! He inspired the Bahá'ís (literally, Friends of God and Followers of the Light) with an amazing enthusiasm for the cause of the Love of God. They hold that there is nothing else in this world worthy of their life's devotion. The service of the brotherhood of man is their inspiration – that all the children of God, our Father, out of every tribe and nation, should be gathered together in a Spiritual Unity, is their aim and high endeavour. To be zealously engaged in the working out of the Supreme Design, under the one Divine Architect of the Universe, is their joyful occupation. To serve as soldiers in the army of Love and Light, ever vanquishing the powers of hatred and darkness on the battlefield of the world is their ambition. 'Abdu'l-Bahá did not suggest our leaving our own beloved form of Truth, but rather that we should strive to enlarge its horizon, free ourselves from the uncharitableness of narrowing prejudices and set our hearts and minds on the Divine work of bringing it into the Grand Unity.

He enjoined upon all an unvarying courtesy and kindness in every relation of life, however fraught with difficulty, reminding us that where soldiers of the world draw their swords, soldiers of God clasp each others' hands; that to be nominally a Christian is easy: to be a real Christian is hard; and that, whilst we must not neglect to 'render unto Caesar the things that are Caesar's', we must diligently 'render unto God the things that are God's'.

The 'Followers of the Light' are at all times charged to be loyal adherents of all just and righteous governments, and to be law-abiding citizens, in whatever country they may dwell. They have no form of membership nor institutions to differentiate them outwardly from other people. The Cause asks only for the hearts of its followers. When the heart is in the work, giving and doing are privileges and not obligations.

Professor Edward Granville Browne thus describes 'Abdu'l-Bahá. 'Soon after this, a sudden stir without announced the arrival of fresh visitors . . . one of whom . . . as I guessed from the first, by the extraordinary deference shewn to him by all present, was none other than Bahá'u'lláh's eldest son, 'Abbas Effendi. Seldom have I seen one whose appearance impressed me more. A tall strongly-built man holding himself straight as an arrow, with white turban and raiment, long black locks reaching almost to the shoulder, broad powerful forehead indicating a strong intellect combined with an unswerving will, eyes keen as a hawk's, and strongly-marked but pleasing features: such was my first impression of 'Abbas Effendi, "the Master" (*Aḱa*) as he *par excellence* is called by the Bahá'ís. Subsequent conversation with him served only to heighten the respect with which his appearance had from the first inspired me. One more eloquent of speech, more ready of argument, more apt of illustration, more intimately acquainted with the sacred books of the Jews, the Christians and the Muhammadans, could, I should think, scarcely be found, even amongst the eloquent, ready, and subtle race to which he belongs. These qualities, combined with a bearing at once majestic and genial, made me cease to wonder at the influence and esteem which he enjoyed even beyond the circle of his father's followers. About the greatness of this man and his power no one who had seen him could entertain a doubt.'

Mr. Horace Holley has also left on record an account, which is well worth reproduction, of his first meeting with 'Abdu'l-Bahá, at Thonon on the Lake of Geneva.

'Prepared in some measure for the meeting by the noble mountain scenery through which we had passed, we approached the hotel feeling ourselves strangely aloof from the tourist world. If I could but look upon 'Abdu'l-Bahá from a distance I considered that I should fulfil a pilgrim's most earnest desire.

'Groups of people were walking quietly about under the trees . . . My wife pressed my arm . . . I looked up quickly . . . and saw a stately old man, robed in a cream-coloured gown, his white hair and beard shining in the sun.

'He displayed a beauty of stature, an inevitable harmony of attitude and dress I had never seen nor thought of in men. Without having ever visualized the "Master", I knew that this was he. I seemed to have turned into some most sensitive sense-organ as if eyes and ears were not enough for this sublime impression. In every part of me I stood aware of 'Abdu'l-Bahá's presence . . . A glory, as it were, from the summits of human nature poured into me and I was conscious of a most intense impulse to admire.

'In 'Abdu'l-Bahá I felt the awful presence of Bahá'u'lláh, and, as my thoughts returned to activity, I realized that I had thus drawn as near as men now may to pure spirit and pure being . . . I had entered the Master's presence and become a servant of a higher will . . . Even my memory of that temporary change of being bears strange authority over me. I know what men can become . . .

'After what seemed a cycle of existence this state passed . . . and I advanced to accept 'Abdu'l-Bahá's hearty welcome . . .

'I yielded to a feeling of reverence which contained more than the solution of intellectual or moral problems. To look upon so wonderful a human being, to respond utterly to the charm of his presence – this brought me continual happiness . . . The tribute which poets have offered our human nature, in its noblest manifestation, came naturally to mind as I watched his gestures and listened to his stately, rhythmic speech . . . Patriarchal, majestic, strong, yet infinitely kind, he appeared like some just king, that very moment descended from his throne to mingle with a devoted people. 'Abdu'l-Bahá, even more impressive walking than seated, led the way . . . Our party included some Orientals. I could not help remarking the bearing of these splendid men . . . All were natives of countries in which Baha'ism has not only been a capital offence in the eyes of the law, but the object of constant popular hatred and persecution; yet not one, by the slightest trace of weariness or bitterness, showed the effect of hardship and wrong upon the soul. Toward 'Abdu'l-Bahá their attitude was beautifully reverent. It was the relationship of disciple to master . . . The dinner was throughout cheerful and animated. 'Abdu'l-Bahá answered questions and made frequent observations on religion in the West. He laughed heartily from time to time – indeed, the idea of asceticism or useless misery of any kind cannot attach itself to this fully-developed personality.'

Finally, it may be of interest to add an extract from a talk recorded by Mírzá Valíyu'lláh Khán Varqá. 'My father', said Valíyu'lláh Khán, 'was much with Bahá'u'lláh. One night Bahá'u'lláh, as he strode back and forth in his room, said to my father:

'"At stated periods souls are sent to Earth by the Mighty God with what we call *the power of the Great Ether*. And those who possess this power can do anything: they have ALL power."

'"Even this walk of mine", said Bahá'u'lláh, "has an effect in the world. Jesus Christ had this power. The people thought Him a poor young man whom they had crucified; but He possessed *the power of the Great Ether*; therefore he could not remain underground. This ethereal power rose and quickened the world. And now look to the Master, for this power is his!"'

'Bahá'u'lláh', added Valíyu'lláh Khán, 'taught my father much about Agha. AGHA (*Master*) you know, is one of the titles of 'Abdu'l-Bahá, and *The Greatest Mystery of God* is another, and *The Greatest Branch* is still another. By all these we call him in Persia.

'*The Blessed Perfection*, Bahá'u'lláh, revealed the station of 'Abdu'l-Bahá to my father. And my father wrote many poems to the Master, though the Master would scold him and say, "You must not write such things to me!" But the heart of my father would not keep quiet. On one occasion he wrote:

> '*O Dawning-Place of the Beauty of God!*
>   *I know Thee!*
> *Though Thou wrap Thyself in ten thousand veils,*
>   *I know Thee!*
> *Though Thou shouldst wear the tatters of a beggar,*
>   *Still would I know Thee!*'

Lord Curzon of Kedleston, in his *Persia* (published in 1892), wrote of the Bahá'í Movement with deep appreciation. 'Beauty', he says, 'and the female sex also lent their consecration to the new creed, and the heroism of the lovely but ill-fated poetess of Kazvin, Zarrín-Táj (*Crown of Gold*), or Kurrat-el-Ain (*Solace of the Eyes*), who, throwing off the veil, carried the missionary torch far and wide, is one of the most affecting episodes in modern history . . . The lowest estimate places the present number of Bahá'ís in Persia at half a million. I am disposed to think, from conversations with persons well-qualified to judge, that the total is nearer one million. They are to be found in every walk of life, from the ministers or nobles of the Court to the scavenger or the groom, not the least arena of their activity being the Mussulman priesthood itself. It will have been noticed that the movement was initiated by Seyids, Hajis, and Mullahs, i.e. persons who, either by descent, from pious inclination, or by profession, were intimately concerned with the Mohammedan creed. If one conclusion more than another has been forced upon our notice by the retrospect in which I have indulged, it is that a sublime and unmurmuring devotion has been inculcated by this new faith, whatever it may be . . . Tales of magnificent heroism illumine the bloodstained pages of Bábí and Bahá'í history. Ignorant and unlettered as many of its votaries are, and have been, they are yet prepared to die for their religion, and the fires of Smithfield did not kindle a nobler courage than has met and defied the more refined torture-mongers of Teheran. Of no small account, then, must be the tenets of a creed that can awaken in its followers so rare and beautiful a spirit of self-sacrifice.'

Mr. Bernard Temple, also, has given some impressions of the Bahá'ís in a lecture before the Royal Society of Arts in London (in May, 1910) . . . 'I believe that events are shaping in Asia which may end in reconstructing the whole fabric of present-day internationalism, and add a chapter to the world's history as dramatic and momentous as any that has been written. The Bahá'í Movement arose in Persia . . . The number of Bahá'ís in the world is now stated to exceed two millions. Not less than one fifth of the population of Persia has embraced Baha'ism. In Turkey, Egypt, North India, and elsewhere Bahá'ís are becoming numerous – even among the Sikhs, the Buddhists, Taoists, Shintoists, and the Persian Jews. Many Parsees have become Bahá'ís, and their teaching has been adopted in Russia, Germany, France, the United States, and England. The number of Bahá'ís in London is appreciable, and smaller circles exist elsewhere . . . In its essential character it is not so much a religion as a religious movement. Therein lies its force, promise, and historical momentousness. There has arisen . . . thanks to the freshness and fineness of Persian thought, a regenerative influence of almost incalculable energy.'

On November 28th, 1921, 'Abdu'l-Bahá passed away at Haifa, and something of the loss felt by his followers may be gathered from a letter written then to his family by a gentleman of Arabia, who extolled the Master in the terms of Eastern enthusiasm:

> If the trees of all the woods, gardens, and forests of the world were made into pens;
> Were the waters of all the rivers, lakes, seas, and oceans of Earth con verted into ink;
> Were all the mountains, hills, and plains rolled out into one mighty scroll;
> And were the whole human race, from the beginning of time, to write and write and write – yet would they fail in setting forth the majesty of Thy service to Humanity.
> Therefore, O 'Abdu'l-Bahá, Servant of the living God, we say
> NOTHING.

By the will of 'Abdu'l-Bahá his grandson, Shoghi Effendi, still at Balliol College, Oxford, when his grandfather passed away, was appointed to the position of 'Guardian of the Cause of God'. His tasks and responsibilities are many and onerous. Bahá'í Assemblies are now formed in almost every country of the world; their correspondence, dealing with the manifold affairs of the Cause, receives his untiring attention; while the translation of the Bahá'í Tablets and Laws is an immense undertaking. Of these, probably not more than a third have been done into Western tongues, but this work, as well as the rest, is felt by the Bahá'ís to be in excellent and worthy hands. May God prosper the Cause!

CHRISTIANITY IN THE BAHÁ'Í MESSAGE

by LADY SITARIH BLOMFIELD[1]

No one has ever loved Christ as I do.
'Abdu'l-Bahá

Should a servant desire to make the words, deeds and actions of other servants, learned or ignorant, the standard for knowing God and His chosen ones, he shall never enter the Rizwan of the knowledge of the Lord of Might.
Bahá'u'lláh

Hundreds of thousands of our Eastern brothers, both Jews and Moslems, have learned, through the teaching of 'Abdu'l-Bahá, that His Holiness Christ is the Spirit, the divine Son of God.

Some young Jewish men came from Persia on a pilgrimage to the Holy Land; after saluting 'Abdu'l-Bahá, and being blessed by Him, they said: 'Now we go to Jerusalem, to pray for pardon, and to weep for the blindness of our forefathers in that they rejected and crucified our Messiah. Our parents also laid this charge upon us: "that we should convey their lamentation, and for them implore forgiveness."'

Again a young Jewish soldier came to 'Abdu'l-Bahá saying: 'I cannot acknowledge their supposed Messiah, whom they call Jesus Christ, but I can understand and accept Bahá'u'lláh as our Messiah.'

'Abdu'l-Bahá said to him: 'You cannot become a disciple of Bahá'u'lláh until you believe that His Holiness Christ is the Spirit, the divine Son of God.'

A doctor, who had been in Alexandria, where he saw 'Abdu'l-Bahá and witnessed His Christ-like life, told me that for the first time he was able to understand what the Lord Christ must have been like. 'Now I am able to believe,' he said.

The Bahá'í Teaching has the universality of the Lord Christ's commands.

Bahá'u'lláh did not counsel us, any of us, to change our religion, but to obey the Law of God found at the core of each religion, in order that our religion might change us; a very different proposition!

No person touched by the spirit of Christianity can fail, after due investigation and consideration, to recognize that the Bahá'í revelation is truly the perfection of Christianity.

For to be a real Christian in Spirit and in Truth is to be a Bahá'í – a follower of the Light – and to be a true Bahá'í is to be a Christian: for he puts into practice the laws of Christianity, translating the beautiful words into action.

The precepts of Bahá'u'lláh make the same appeal to the institution as Christianity makes to the individual: forasmuch as a Golden Brotherhood cannot be formed out of leaden individuals – the work perforce had to begin with individuals. We cannot have a brotherhood without brothers. This teaching does not merely say, 'Teach men to be brothers', but 'Go ye out into all the world, to the East and the West, to the North and to the South, wherever your calling may take you – and be brothers to all men – whether of your own nation, colour or creed, or of any other people or race or religion. Be brothers of help and comfort, of sympathy and understanding, showing loving kindness to all without limit.' It will help us to attain to this vitalizing Truth, i. e. that the perfection in the teaching of Bahá'u'lláh is of the same nature as the teaching of the Lord Christ – brought to the needs of the present day of this world, which is 'wet with tears'.

It will help us to understand this sublime Truth if we consider some of the utterances of 'Abdu'l-Bahá, given in explanation of this connection, and published in the 'Wisdom Talks in Paris and London'.

When you meet a stranger be unto him a friend. If he seems to be lonely, try to help him; give him of your willing service; if he be sad, console him, if poor, succour him, if oppressed, rescue him, if in misery, comfort him. In so doing you will manifest (to the world) that, not in words only, but in deed and in truth you think of all men as your brothers.

What a profit is there in agreeing that universal friendship is good, and talking of the solidarity of the Human Race as a grand ideal? Unless these thoughts are translated into the world of action they are useless.

The wrong in the world continues to exist, because people only talk of their ideals, and do not strive to put them into practice. If actions took the place of (these) words, the world's misery would very soon be changed into comfort.

In the past, as in the present, the Spiritual Sun of Truth has always shone from the horizon of the East. On the Eastern horizon arose the Lord Christ. Bahá'u'lláh lived and taught in the East. Although the Sun of Christ dawned in the East, the Radiance thereof was apparent in the West, where the effulgence of its glory was more clearly seen. The divine light of His teaching shone with a greater force in the Western world, where it has made a more rapid headway than in the land of its birth.

The perfect man is a polished mirror reflecting the Sun of Truth; manifesting the attributes of God. The Lord Christ said: 'He that hath seen me hath seen the Father' – God manifested in man. In the Manifestation of God, the perfectly polished mirror, appear the qualities of the Divine, in a form that man is capable of comprehending.

In the early days the civilization of Christianity was the best and most enlightened in the world.

The Christian Teaching was illumined by the Divine Sun of Truth, therefore its followers were taught to love all men as brothers, to fear nothing, not even death; to love their neighbours as themselves, and to forget their own selfish interests in striving for the greatest good of humanity. The grand aim of the Religion of Christ was to draw the hearts of all men nearer to God's effulgent Truth.

If the followers of the Lord Christ had continued to carry out these principles with steadfast faithfulness, there would have been no need for (this) the renewal of the Christian Message, no necessity for a reawakening of His people! For a great and glorious civilization would now be ruling the world, and the Kingdom of Heaven would have come on earth. But instead of this, what has taken place? Men turned away their faces from following the divinely illuminated precepts of their master, and winter fell upon the hearts of men. For, as the body of man depends for life upon the rays of the Sun, so the celestial virtues cannot grow in the soul without the radiance of the Sun of Truth.

God leaves not His children comfortless, but, when the darkness of winter overshadows them, then again He sends His Messengers with a renewal of the Blessed Spring. The Sun of Truth appears again on the horizon of the world, shining into the eyes of those who sleep, awakening them to behold the glory of a new Dawn.

Then again the Tree of Humanity blossoms anew and brings forth the fruit of righteousness for the healing of the nations.

Because man has stopped his ears to the voice of truth, and shut his eyes to the sacred light, for this reason has the darkness of war and tumult, unrest and misery, desolated the earth.

May every child of God be brought into the radiance of the Sun of Truth, that the darkness (of evil) may be dissipated by the penetrating rays of Its glory, and the winter's hardness and cold be melted away by the merciful warmth of its shining.

The sound of the Song of Christ once echoed over all the lands of the Western world, and entered the hearts of its people . . . It is a long time since the Sun of Truth, mirrored forth by the Lord Christ, has shed its radiance upon the West, for the Face of God has become veiled by the sin and forgetfulness of Man. But now again, praise be unto God, the Holy Spirit speaks anew unto the world! The constellation of love and wisdom and power is once more shining from the Divine Horizons to give joy to all who turn their faces to the Light of God.

Bahá'u'lláh has rent the veil of prejudice and superstition which was stifling the souls of men! May heart and soul be vivified in every man; so will they all rejoice in a 'New Birth'. Then shall humanity put on a new garment in the Light of the Love of God, and it shall be the Dawn of a New Creation. May you all be faithful and loving workers in the Building of the New Spiritual Civilization, the elect of God, in willing, joyful obedience, carrying out His supreme design.

'No worldly power can achieve the Universal Love.'

As the Lord Christ 'came not to destroy the Law but to fulfil the Law,' so Bahá'u'lláh came to usher in that Kingdom, for which Christ Jesus taught us to pray nigh two thousand years ago. Not anti-Christian, but extra-Christian! is this teaching. And again the following words of 'Abdu'l-Bahá to help us to a better understanding.

His enemies placed upon the head of the Lord Christ a crown of thorns, but before it earthly crowns of gold and jewels have bowed down, humbling their majesty, and might, and power, before the meek and lowly Lord.

Christ is ever in the world of existence. He has never disappeared from it . . . Rest assured that Christ is present. The spiritual beauty we see around us in this day is from the breathings of Christ.

The brilliant star of Christ Jesus rose from the Eastern horizon upon the Israelites, brightening the world, until all sects and creeds and nations were taught the beauty of unity. There cannot be any stronger proof than this that He was the Word of God. As Christ brought His message to the people, so Bahá'u'lláh brings the same Message, renewing and reiterating the commands that Deeds may take the place of Words.

Each time God sends a Great One to us, we are given new life, but the truth each manifestation brings is the same, and from the same source. The truth never changes, but man's vision changes. It is dulled and confused by the complication of outward forms. What are forms? The truth is easy to understand, although the outward forms in which it is expressed (often) bewilder the intelligence. As men grow (in spirit) they see the unimportance of man-made forms and sometimes despise them. Therefore many leave the churches, because the latter often emphasize the external only.

'Truth is one, though its manifestations may be very different. The notes in the flute are many, the Musician is One!'

Bahá'u'lláh proclaimed that the truth for this age was the realization of the spiritual brotherhood of man. Accordingly at 'Abdu'l-Bahá's table were gathered men of all nations, classes, creeds, and languages of the world. It is the only place on earth where Christians, Jews, Moslems, Zoroastrians, Hindus, Buddhists met and ate together in perfect harmony and friendly understanding.

'But your caste?'

The Hindu pilgrim replied, 'But there is no caste, in the presence of 'Abdu'l-Bahá.'

Bahá'u'lláh taught the oneness of humanity; that is to say, all the children of men are under the mercy of the Great God. He has placed the crown of humanity on the head of every one of the servants of God. Therefore all nations and peoples must consider themselves brethren.

They are the branches, leaves, blossoms, and fruits of One Tree.

To establish this (Kingdom of God on earth), Bahá'u'lláh underwent great difficulties, hardships, imprisonments and great persecution! But in the prison fortress (of 'Akká) He reared a Spiritual Palace, and from the darkness of His prison He sent out a great Light to the world.

Professor Michael Sadler speaking in this connection said: 'Though we all, in our devotional allegiance, have our own individual loyalties, to all of us 'Abdu'l-Bahá brings a message of Unity, of Sympathy and of Peace. He bids us all be real and true in what we profess to believe; and to treasure above everything the Spirit behind the form. With Him we bow before the Hidden Name; before that which is of every life the Inner Life! He bids us worship in perfect loyalty to our own faith, but with ever stronger yearning after union, brotherhood, and love, so turning ourselves in spirit, and with our whole heart, that we may enter more into the mind of God, which is above class, above race, and beyond time.'

I could, if time permitted, cite many instances of great thinkers and workers for the human race, who see in the teachings of Bahá'u'lláh the great remedy for the evil diseases which afflict the sick body of Humanity, indeed a Dynamic Christianity. Dr. David Starr Jordan, of Leland Stanford University, California, U.S.A., said: 'There is One who is able to unite the East and the West: those two, the spiritual and material civilization; and that one is 'Abdu'l-Bahá, for He walks the Mystic Way with practical feet.' He tells us what is needed now, in this day.

One morning a number of people, members of various sects awaited an audience to argue their various faiths and usefulness of their respective societies. 'Abdu'l-Bahá said: 'I respect all who work for the good of mankind, of whatever religions they call themselves. You should learn to recognize truth from whatever point in the horizon it is shining. People think religion is confined in a temple to be worshipped at an altar. In reality it is an attitude to divinity which is reflected through life.'

The call of Bahá'u'lláh is to the waiting servants of God, the 'ten thousand times ten thousand' who are not in one church only, or in one country, or in one race, or in one class! But who are everywhere in every country, in every religion, in every race, in every class, constituting the spiritual leaven of the whole human family, and who in their various spheres, are working for the good of mankind. The call is especially to those servants to arise in this Great Day of God and serve the oneness of the whole of humanity by being first of all themselves united. When united, said 'Abdu'l-Bahá, those of you who have been ants will now become eagles, those who have been drops of water will, when flowing together, make a mighty river, carrying the waters of life into the desert, barren places of the earth!

BIBLIOGRAPHY

Abdo, L.C.G. *Religion and Relevance: The Bahá'ís in Britain 1899–1930.* Doctoral thesis. University of London School of Oriental and African Studies, 2003.

'Abdu'l-Bahá. *Memorials of the Faithful.* Wilmette, IL: Bahá'í Publishing Trust, 1971.

— *Paris Talks.* London: Bahá'í Publishing Trust, 1995.

— *The Promulgation of Universal Peace.* Wilmette, IL: Bahá'í Publishing Trust, 1982.

— *Selections from the Writings of 'Abdu'l-Bahá.* Haifa: Bahá'í World Centre, 1978.

— *Some Answered Questions.* Wilmette, IL: Bahá'í Publishing Trust, 1981.

— *Tablets of the Divine Plan.* Wilmette, IL: Bahá'í Publishing Trust, 1977.

— *The Will and Testament of 'Abdu'l-Bahá.* Wilmette, IL: Bahá'í Publishing Trust, 1971.

'Abdu'l-Bahá in London. London: Bahá'í Publishing Trust, 1987.

Adamson, Hugh C. and Philip Hainsworth. *Historical Dictionary of the Bahá'í Faith.* Lanham, MD: Scarecrow Press, 1998.

Afnan, Elham. "'Abdu'l-Bahá and Ezra Pound's Circle', in *Journal of Bahá'í Studies*, vol. 6, no. 2, June–September 1994. Ottawa: Association of Bahá'í Studies, 1994.

Afroukhteh, Dr Youness. *Memories of Nine Years in 'Akká.* Oxford: George Ronald, 2003.

The Architect and Contract Reporter. 3 November 1899.

Arnold, Sir Edwin. *The Light of Asia.* London: Kegan Paul, Trench, Trubner & Co. Ltd., 1938.

Bahá'í Journal. October 1937; March 1940.

Bahá'í News. September 1931; Summer 1933.

The Bahá'í World. vols. 1–12, 1925–54. rpt. Wilmette, IL: Bahá'í Publishing Trust, 1980.

Bahá'í World Centre Archives. Various documents, Tablets and letters, details of which can be found in the endnotes.

Bahá'u'lláh. *Gleanings from the Writings of Bahá'u'lláh.* Wilmette, IL: Bahá'í Publishing Trust, 1983.

— *The Hidden Words.* Wilmette, IL: Bahá'í Publishing Trust, 1990.

— *The Kitáb-i-Aqdas*. Haifa: Baháʼí World Centre, 1992.

— *Tablets of Baháʼuʼlláh revealed after the Kitáb-i-Aqdas*. Haifa: Baháʼí World Centre, 1978.

Balyuzi, H. M. *ʼAbduʼl-Bahá: The Centre of the Covenant of Baháʼuʼlláh*. Oxford: George Ronald, 2nd ed. with minor corr. 1987.

— *Baháʼuʼlláh: The King of Glory*. Oxford: George Ronald, 1980.

— *Edward Granville Browne and the Baháʼí Faith*. Oxford: George Ronald, 1970.

Barbour, G.F. *The Life of Alexander Whyte*. London: Hodder and Stoughton, 1925.

Barrett, David V. *Sects, ʼCultsʼ & Alternative Religions*. London: Blandford, 1996.

Basil Hall, Mary. *Drama of the Kingdom: A Pageant Play*. London: Weardale Press, 1933.

— *Sitarih Khanum (Sara, Lady Blomfield), A Brief Account of Her Life and Work by Her Daughter, Mary Basil Hall*. United Kingdom Baháʼí Archives.

Bateman, Charles T. *R.J. Campbell, M.A. Pastor of the City Temple, London*. London: S.W. Partridge, 1903.

Benet, William Rose. *The Readerʼs Encyclopaedia*. London: A & C Black, 1965.

Benham, Patrick. *The Avalonians*. Glastonbury: Gothic Image Publications, 1993.

Benstock, Shari. *Women of the Left Bank*. London: Virago, 1986.

Blomfield, Alfred. *A Memoir of Charles James Blomfield, D.D.* London: John Murray, 1863.

Blomfield, Lady [Sitárih Khánum; Sara Louise]. ʼAn Account of the Visit to Stuttgartʼ. United Kingdom Baháʼí Archives.

— *The Chosen Highway*. Oxford: George Ronald, rpt. 2007.

— *The First Obligation*. London: Caledonian Press, 1921.

— ʼShort Story of Some Work for Unity During the Past Year Sept. 1924–25ʼ.

Blomfield, Sir Reginald. *Byways: Leaves from an Architectʼs Notebook*. London: John Murray, 1929.

— *Memoirs of an Architect*. London: Macmillan and Co., 1932

— *A Suffolk Family: Being an Account of the Family of Blomfield in Suffolk*. London: Chiswick Press, 1916.

Boyles, Ann. ʼThe Language of the Heart: Arts in the Baháʼí World Communityʼ, in *Baháʼí World 1994–5*. Oxford: World Centre Publications, 1996.

Browne, Edward G. ʼIntroductionʼ, *A Travellerʼs Narrative*. Cambridge: Cambridge University Press, 1891.

Buckton, Alice. *Eager Heart*. London: Methuen, 1904.

The Builder. 4 November 1899.

ʼThe Call for the Worldʼs Supreme Peaceʼ. Pamphlet.

Cameron, Glenn and Wendi Momen. *A Basic Bahá'í Chronology*. Oxford: George Ronald, 1996.

Campbell, R.J. *City Temple Sermons*. London: Fleming H. Revell, 1903.

— *The New Theology*. London: Macmillan and Co., 1907.

Carpenter, J. Estlin. *Comparative Religion*. London: Williams and Norgate, 1913.

Century of Light. Haifa: Bahá'í World Centre, 2001.

Cheyne, T.K. *Reconciliation of Races and Religions*. London: Adam & Charles Black, 1914.

Collins, William P. *Bibliography of English-Language Works on the Bábí and Bahá'í Faiths, 1844–1985*. Oxford: George Ronald, 1990.

The Compilation of Compilations. Prepared by the Universal House of Justice 1963–1990. 2 vols. [Mona Vale NSW]: Bahá'í Publications Australia, 1991.

Cutting, Tracy. *Beneath the Silent Tor: The Life and Work of Alice Buckton, 1867–1944*. Wells: St Andrew's Press, 2004.

Daily Express. Sunday, 2 March 1930.

Daily Mirror. Tuesday, 12 November 1918.

Daniel, Clifton (ed.). *The 20th Century Day by Day*. London: Dorling Kindersley, 2000.

Denny, Barbara and Carolyn Starren. *Kensington Past*. London: Historical Publications, 1998.

The Drama, March 1933.

Edinburgh Evening News. Saturday, 6 February 1933.

Edwards, Natasha (ed.). *Paris Time Out Guide*. London: Penguin Books, 1998.

'Eglantyne Jebb – Founder of Save the Children', Save the Children Fund website http://www.savethechildren.net/alliance/about_us/history.html and http://www.leader-values.com/Content/detail.asp?ContentDetailID=794

Elsberry, Terence. *Marie of Romania: The Intimate Life of a 20th Century Queen*. New York: St. Martin's Press, 1972.

Ensor, Sir Robert. *England 1870–1914*. Oxford: Clarendon Press, 1936.

Esslemont, J. E. *Bahá'u'lláh and the New Era*. London: Bahá'í Publishing Trust, 1974.

— Pilgrimage diary. United Kingdom Bahá'í Archives.

Foçillon, Henri. 'An Appreciation of Edwin Scott', in *Paintings by Edwin Scott*. Washington: Smithsonian Institution, 1970.

Foster, R.F. (ed.). *The Oxford History of Ireland*. Oxford: Oxford University Press, 1989.

French, Patrick. *Younghusband: The Last Great Imperial Adventurer*. London: Flamingo, 1995.

Gail, Marzieh. *Bahá'í Glossary*. Wilmette, IL: Bahá'í Publishing Trust, 1976.

Garis, M. R. *Martha Root: Lioness at the Threshold.* Wilmette, IL: Bahá'í Publishing Trust, 1983.

The Gateway, mid-February 1933.

George, Florence. *Notes on the early days of the Bahá'í Faith in London, 1942.* United Kingdom Bahá'í Archives.

Gilchrist, Cherry. *Theosophy: The Wisdom of the Ages.* San Francisco: Harper, 1996.

Guéry, Annaick. *May Bolles-Maxwell.* Paris: Association Bahá'íe de Femme, 1998.

Hall, E. T. *The Beginning of the Bahá'í Cause in Manchester.* Manchester: Bahá'í Assembly, 1925. (Cover title: *The Bahá'í Dawn, Manchester.*)

Hall, Lucy. 'Father's meeting with 'Abdu'l-Bahá'. United Kingdom Bahá'í Archives.

Hammond, Eric. *The Splendour of God.* London: John Murray, 1909.

Hardy, Thomas. *Wessex Poems and Other Verses.* Otley: Woodstock Books, 1994.

Harper, Barron. *Lights of Fortitude: Glimpses into the Lives of the Hands of the Cause of God.* Oxford: George Ronald, 1997.

Harris, Rosemary. *Alice Buckton, 1867–1944.* Glastonbury: Chalice Well Trust, no date.

Hattersley, Roy. *The Edwardians.* London: Little, Brown, 2004.

Hellaby, Madeline. *Sarah Ann Ridgway.* Oxford: George Ronald, 2003.

Herrick, Elizabeth. 'Abdul Baha visits the poor on Christmas Night'. United Kingdom Bahá'í Archives.

— 'Christmas in London with Abdul Baha'. United Kingdom Bahá'í Archives.

— *Unity Triumphant: The Call of the Kingdom.* London: Kegan Paul Trench Trubner and Company, 1923.

Hey, David. *The Oxford Dictionary of Local and Family History.* Oxford: Oxford University Press, 1997.

Hibbert, Christopher. *Queen Victoria: A Personal History.* London: Harper Collins, 2001.

Hitchcock, Henry-Russell. *Architecture: Nineteenth and Twentieth Centuries.* London: Pelican, 1971.

Hofman, David. *George Townshend.* Oxford: George Ronald, 1983.

Hogensen, Kathryn Jewett. *Lighting the Western Sky: The Hearst Pilgrimage and the Establishment of the Bahá'í Faith in the West.* Oxford: George Ronald, 2010.

Hollinger, Richard (ed.). *'Abdu'l-Bahá in America: Agnes Parsons' Diary.* Los Angeles: Kalimát Press, 1996.

Holy Bible. King James Version. London: Collins, 1839.

Houghton, C. C. *A Walk about Broadway.* Shepperton: Ian Allan, 1980.

Howard Gordon, Frances. *Glastonbury: Maker of Myths.* Glastonbury: Gothic Image, 1982.

Hügel, Baron F. von. *Letters to a Niece*. London: Fount, 1995.

ITN Factbook. London: Guild Publishing, 1990.

Jasion, Jan Teofil. *Never Be Afraid to Dare: The Story of 'General Jack'*. Oxford: George Ronald, 2001.

John O'London's Weekly. Saturday, 25 March 1933.

Johnson, Malcolm. *Bustling Intermeddler? The Life and Work of Charles James Blomfield*. Leominster: Gracewing, 2001.

Journal of Proceedings of the Royal Institute of British Architects. 9 April 1891 and 25 June 1891.

Journal of the Royal Institute of British Architects. 25 November 1899.

Keats, John. 'Bright Star', *circa* 1818–19.

Khadem, Riaz. *Shoghi Effendi in Oxford*. Oxford: George Ronald, 1999.

Khursheed, Anjam. *The Seven Candles of Unity*. London: Bahá'í Publishing Trust, 1991.

Kling, Jean L. *Alice Pike Barney: Her Life and Art*. Washington: National Museum of American Art, 1994.

'Lady Blomfield – Apostle of World Unity', in *The World's Children*, March 1940.

Lee, Sidney. *The Concise Dictionary of National Biography*. Oxford: Oxford University Press, 1903.

Literary Guide, July 1933.

Loftus Hare, William. *Religions of the Empire*. London: Duckworth, 1925.

Ma'ani, Baharieh Rouhani. *Leaves of the Twin Divine Trees*. Oxford: George Ronald, 2008.

MacDonald, Lyn. *The Roses of No Man's Land*. London: Michael Joseph, 1980.

Marcus, Della L. *Her Immortal Crown: Queen Marie of Romania and the Bahá'í Faith*. Oxford: George Ronald, 2000.

Martin, Douglas. 'The Mission of the Báb: Retrospective, 1844–1994', in *The Bahá'í World 1994–5*. Oxford: World Centre Publications, 1996.

Maud, Constance Elizabeth. *Sparks among the Stubble*. London: Philip Allan & Co., 1924.

Maxwell, May. *An Early Pilgrimage*. Oxford: George Ronald, 1976.

McClelland, Donald R. *Where Shadows Live: Alice Pike Barney and Her Friends*. Washington: Smithsonian Institution, 1978.

McNamara, Brendan (comp.). *Connections: Essays and Notes on Early Links between the Bahá'í Faith and Ireland*. Cork: Tusker Keyes, 2007.

Metelmann, Velda Piff. *Lua Getsinger: Herald of the Covenant*. Oxford: George Ronald, 1997.

Momen, Moojan. *The Bábí and Bahá'í Religions, 1844–1944: Some Contemporary Western Accounts*. Oxford: George Ronald, 1981.

— *Dr. John Ebenezer Esslemont*. London: Bahá'í Publishing Trust, 1975.

— 'Esslemont's Survey of the Bahá'í World, 1919–1920', in Peter Smith (ed.). *Bahá'ís in the West*. Los Angeles: Kalimát Press, 2004.

Momen, Wendi. *A Basic Bahá'í Dictionary*. Oxford: George Ronald, 1989.

Morgan, Kenneth O. *The Sphere Illustrated History of Britain 1789–1983*. London: Sphere, 1985.

Mulley, Clare. *The Woman Who Saved the Children: A Biography of Eglantyne Jebb, Founder of Save the Children*. Oxford: Oneworld, 2009.

Mulvihill, Margaret. *Charlotte Despard*. London: Pandora, 1989.

Nabíl-i-A'zam. *The Dawn-Breakers: Nabíl's Narrative of the Early Days of the Bahá'í Revelation*. Wilmette, IL: Bahá'í Publishing Trust, 1970.

New York Times. Friday, 6 June 1914.

Oxford Times, Saturday, 4 January 1913.

Pakula, Hannah. *Queen of Roumania*. London: Eland, 1984.

Pankhurst, Christabel. *Unshackled*. London: Cresset Women's Voices, 1987.

Pankhurst, Sylvia. *The Suffragette Movement*. London: Virago, 1977.

Parsons, Derek. *Broadway: A Village History*. Pershore: Cornmill Press, 1996.

Phelps, Myron H. *The Master in 'Akká*. Los Angeles: Kalimát Press, 1985.

Philips, Charles, et al. *The 20th Century Year by Year*. London: Marshall Publishing, 2000.

Phillips, Jessie. 'Bahaism'. *The Christian Commonwealth*, 9 August 1911.

Rabbani, Ahang. "Abdu'l-Bahá in Abu-Sinan: September 1914 – May 1915', in *Bahá'í Studies Review*. London: Association for Bahá'í Studies (UK), 2005.

Rabbaní, Rúhíyyih. *The Priceless Pearl*. London: Bahá'í Publishing Trust, 1969.

Randall-Winckler, Bahíyyih, in collaboration with M. R. Garis. *William Henry Randall: Disciple of 'Abdu'l-Bahá*. Oxford: Oneworld, no date [1996].

Remey, Charles Mason. *Through Warring Countries to the Mountain of God*. Washington DC: Charles Mason Remey, 1915.

Richardson, John. *The Annals of London*. London: Cassell & Co, 2000.

Rodriguez, Suzanne. *Wild Heart: Natalie Clifford Barney and the Decadence of Literary Paris*. New York: Ecco, 2003.

Royce, Alan. *Alice Buckton: A Short Account of a Fascinating Life*. Author's copy.

Ruhe, David. S. *Door of Hope*. Oxford: George Ronald, 1983.

Russell, George W. E. *Basil Wilberforce: A Memoir*. London: John Murray, 1917.

Shoghi Effendi. *The Advent of Divine Justice*. Wilmette, IL: Bahá'í Publishing Trust, 1990.

— *Bahá'í Administration*. Wilmette, IL: Bahá'í Publishing Trust, 1995.

— *Citadel of Faith: Messages to America 1947–1957*. Wilmette, IL: Bahá'í Publishing Trust, 1995.

— *God Passes By*. Wilmette, IL: Bahá'í Publishing Trust, rev. ed. 1995.

— *Messages to the Bahá'í World*. Wilmette, IL: Bahá'í Publishing Trust, 1971.

— *The Unfolding Destiny of the British Bahá'í Community: The Messages of the Guardian of the Bahá'í Faith to the Bahá'ís of the British Isles*. London: Bahá'í Publishing Trust, 1981.

— *The World Order of Bahá'u'lláh*. Wilmette, IL: Bahá'í Publishing Trust, 1991.

— and Lady Blomfield. *The Passing of 'Abdu'l-Bahá*. Stuttgart: Heppeler, 1922.

Skrine, Francis H. *Bahaism*. London: Longmans, Green and Co., 1912.

Slack, Kenneth. *The City Temple: A Hundred Years*. London: Elders' Meeting, 1974.

Smith, George. *The Dictionary of National Biography*. Oxford: Oxford University Press, 1965.

Smith, Peter. *The Bábí and Bahá'í Religions: From Messianic Shi'ism to a World Religion*. Cambridge: Cambridge University Press, 1987.

— *A Concise Encyclopedia of the Bahá'í Faith*. Oxford: Oneworld, 2000.

Smith, Phillip R. 'The Development and Influence of the Bahá'í Administrative Order in Great Britain, 1914–1950', in Richard Hollinger (ed.). *Community Histories*. Studies in the Bábí and Bahá'í Religions, vol. 6. Los Angeles: Kalimát Press, 1992.

— 'What was a Bahá'í? Concerns of British Bahá'ís, 1900–1920', in Moojan Momen (ed.). *Studies in the Bábí and Bahá'í Religions: Studies in Honor of the Late Hasan M. Balyuzi*. Los Angeles: Kalimát Press, 1988.

Star of the West. rpt. Oxford: George Ronald, 1984.

Star of the West Sifter.

Stashower, Daniel. *Teller of Tales: The Life of Arthur Conan Doyle*. London: Penguin Books, 2000.

Stockman, Robert H. *The Bahá'í Faith in America, Early Expansion, 1900–1912*, vol. 2. Oxford: George Ronald, 1995.

Street, Arthur E. 'Sir Arthur Blomfield ARA', in *Journal of the Royal Institute of British Architects*, 25 November 1899.

The Sufi Quarterly, vol. III, no. 4.

Taherzadeh, Adib. *The Child of the Covenant*. Oxford: George Ronald, 2000.

— *The Covenant of Bahá'u'lláh*. Oxford: George Ronald, 1992.

Tamadun ul Molk. *Report of an Address on the Bahai Movement*. East Sheen: The Bahai Press, 1910.

Taylor, A. J. P. *English History 1914–1945*. Oxford: Clarendon Press, 1965.

Thomson, David. *England in the Nineteenth Century*. Harmondsworth, Middx.: Penguin Books, 1955.

Tibballs, Geoff. *The Titanic.* London: Carlton Books, 1997.

The Times. Thursday, 21 April 1887; Saturday, 23 April 1887; Wednesday, 1 November 1899; Wednesday, 30 November 1921; Tuesday, 27 November 1923.

Tomalin, Claire. *Thomas Hardy: The Time-Torn Man.* London: Penguin Viking, 2006.

Tudor Pole, Wellesley. *The Silent Road.* London: Neville Spearman, 1965.

— *Writing on the Ground.* London: Neville Spearman, 1968.

Tudor Pole, Wellesley and Rosamond Lehmann. *A Man Seen Afar.* Saffron Walden: C. W. Daniel, 1983.

— and Elizabeth Gaythorpe. *My Dear Alexias: Letters from Wellesley Tudor Pole to Rosamond Lehmann.* Saffron Walden: C. W. Daniel, 1979.

United Kingdom Bahá'í Archives. Various documents and letters, details of which can be found in the endnotes.

Vader, John Paul. *For the Good of Mankind: August Forel and the Bahá'í Faith.* Oxford: George Ronald, 1984.

Villiers, Oliver G. *Wellesley Tudor Pole: Appreciation and Valuation.* Canterbury: Oliver Villiers, 1977.

Vries, Jelle de. *The Babi Question You Mentioned.* Herent: Peeters, 2002.

Ward, Allan L. *239 Days: 'Abdu'l-Bahá's Journey in America.* Wilmette, IL: Bahá'í Publishing Trust, 1979.

Washington, Peter. *Madame Blavatsky's Baboon: A History of the Mystics, Mediums, and Misfits Who Brought Spiritualism to America.* London: Secker, 1993.

The Watchtower, vol. 28, 1 March 1907.

Weinberg, Robert. *Ethel Jenner Rosenberg: The Life and Times of England's Outstanding Bahá'í Pioneer Worker.* Oxford: George Ronald, 1995.

White, Ruth. *The Bahá'í Religion and Its Enemy the Bahai Organization.* Rutland, VT: Tuttle, 1929.

Whitehead, O. Z. *Some Bahá'ís to Remember.* Oxford: George Ronald, 1983.

— *Some Early Bahá'ís of the West.* Oxford: George Ronald, 1976.

Wilson, A. N. *The Victorians.* London: Hutchinson, 2002.

Wilson, Simon. *British Art from Holbein to the Present Day.* London: Tate Gallery, 1979.

Wolfson, Robert and John Laver. *Years of Change: Europe 1890–1945.* London: Hodder and Stoughton, 1978.

'Writers and Writing, Extracts from the Bahá'í Writings on the Subject of'. *Bahá'í Studies Review*, vol. 10, 2001–2002. London: Association of Bahá'í Studies – English Speaking Europe, 2002.

Younghusband, Sir Francis. *A Venture of Faith.* London: Michael Joseph, 1937.

NOTES AND REFERENCES

Preface and Introduction

1. *Century of Light*, p. 66.
2. ibid.
3. Basil Hall, *Sitarih Khanum*, p. 1.
4. 'Bright Star', love sonnet by John Keats, *circa* 1818–19.

Chapter One: Becoming Lady Blomfield

1. Bahá'u'lláh, *Hidden Words*, Arabic no. 53.
2. *The Times*, Thursday, 21 April 1887.
3. ibid.
4. Denny and Starren, *Kensington Past*, p. 9.
5. Basil Hall, *Sitarih Khanum*, p. 2.
6. Blomfield (Reginald), *Suffolk Family*, p. 11.
7. Quoted in ibid. p. 13.
8. Blomfield (Reginald), *Byways*, p. 264.
9. Blomfield (Alfred), *Memoir*, p. 50.
10. Blomfield (Reginald), *Suffolk Family*, p. 15.
11. Hibbert, *Queen Victoria*, p. 19.
12. Blomfield (Alfred), *Memoir*, p. 225.
13. Blomfield (Reginald), *Suffolk Family*, p. 15.
14. Blomfield (Alfred), *Memoir*, p. 201.
15. Johnson, *Bustling Intermeddler*, p. 157.
16. Blomfield (Alfred), *Memoir*, p. 205.
17. Smith, *Concise Dictionary*, p. 1272.
18. Street, 'Sir Arthur Blomfield', in *Journal of the Royal Institute of British Architects*, 25 November 1899, p. 36.
19. Blomfield (Reginald), *Memoirs of an Architect*, p. 35.
20. ibid. p. 36.
21. Tomalin, *Thomas Hardy*, p. 69.
22. Hardy, *Wessex Poems*, no.48.
23. Blomfield (Reginald), *Memoirs of an Architect*, p. 35.
24. *The Builder*, 4 November 1899, p. 407.
25. Blomfield (Reginald), in *The Architect and Contract Reporter*, 3 November 1899, p. 277.
26. Quoted in Blomfield (Reginald), *Memoirs of an Architect*, p. 35.

27. Street, 'Sir Arthur Blomfield', in *Journal of the Royal Institute of British Architects*, 25 November 1899, p. 36.
28. *The Times*, Saturday, 23 April 1887.
29. Basil Hall, *Sitarih Khanum*, p. 2.
30. Street, 'Sir Arthur Blomfield', in *Journal of the Royal Institute of British Architects*, 25 November 1899, p. 36.
31. Macvicar Anderson, quoted in ibid. 25 June 1891, p. 362.
32. Blomfield (Arthur), quoted in ibid. pp. 363–5.
33. ibid.
34. *The Architect and Contract Reporter*, 3 November 1899, p. 277.
35. *The Times*, Wednesday 1 November 1899, p. 7.
36. Street, 'Sir Arthur Blomfield', in *Journal of the Royal Institute of British Architects*, 25 November 1899, p. 36.
37. ibid.
38. *The Builder*, 4 November 1899, p. 407.

Chapter Two: The Search for Truth

1. 'Abdu'l-Bahá, *Promulgation*, p. 274.
2. Basil Hall, *Sitarih Khanum*, p. 1.
3. Houghton, *A Walk about Broadway*, p. 5.
4. Basil Hall, *Sitarih Khanum*, p. 6.
5. Poem in the handwriting of Lady Blomfield. United Kingdom Bahá'í Archives.
6. Warren Smith, quoted in Abdo, *Religion and Relevance*, p. 16.
7. Russell, *Wilberforce*, p. 113.
8. Benham, *Avalonians*, p. 68.
9. Basil Hall, *Sitarih Khanum*, p. 22.

Chapter Three: The Highway Chosen

1. Bahá'u'lláh, *Hidden Words*, Persian no. 7.
2. Benstock, *Women of the Left Bank*, p. 13.
3. Charles Mason Remey, quoted in Jasion, *Never Be Afraid to Dare*, p. 20.
4. Marion Jack, quoted in ibid. p. 19.
5. Edward G. Browne, quoted in Balyuzi, *King of Glory*, p. 372.
6. ibid. pp. 379–80.
7. Blomfield, *Chosen Highway*, p. 1.
8. ibid.
9. ibid.
10. ibid.
11. ibid.
12. May Maxwell, quoted in Balyuzi, *'Abdu'l-Bahá*, pp. 80–1.
13. Blomfield, *Chosen Highway*, p. 2.
14. ibid. pp. 2–3.
15. Charlotte Despard, quoted in Mulvihill, *Charlotte Despard*, p. 68.
16. Basil Hall, *Sitarih Khanum*, p. 16.
17. Hammond, *Splendour of God*, p. 8.
18. ibid. pp. 11, 14.
19. Blomfield, *Chosen Highway*, p. 149.

20. *Bahai News* [*Star of the West*], vol. 1, no. 6, p. 12.
21. ibid. p. 13.
22. Ensor, *England 1870–1914*, p. 421.
23. *Bahai News* [*Star of the West*], vol. 1, no. 8, p. 3.
24. Blomfield, *Chosen Highway*, p. 149.
25. *Bahai News* [*Star of the West*], vol. 1, no. 18, p. 5.
26. ibid. p. 1.
27. ibid. pp. 3–4.
28. ibid. p. 6.
29. Blomfield, *Chosen Highway*, p. 2.
30. ibid. p. 149.
31. *Star of the West*, vol. 2, nos. 7 and 8, p. 14.
32. 'Abdu'l-Bahá, *Selections*, no. 219, pp. 274–5.
33. Phillips, 'Bahaism', in *The Christian Commonwealth*, 9 August 1911, p. 779.
34. ibid.
35. Momen, *Bábí and Bahá'í Religions*, p. 324.
36. Wellesley Tudor Pole, in *Star of the West*, vol. 2, no. 9, p. 3.
37. Blomfield, *Chosen Highway*, p. 149.
38. ibid. p. 146.

Chapter Four: The Master's Hostess

1. *'Abdu'l-Bahá in London*, p. 53.
2. Blomfield, *Chosen Highway*, pp. 149–50.
3. ibid. p. 150.
4. Shoghi Effendi, *God Passes By*, pp. 279–80.
5. *Century of Light*, p. 20.
6. *'Abdu'l-Bahá in London*, p. 53.
7. Blomfield, *Chosen Highway*, p. 150.
8. ibid.
9. Basil Hall, *Sitarih Khanum*, pp. 8–11.
10. Blomfield, *Chosen Highway*, p. 151.
11. *Star of the West*, vol. 2, no. 11, p. 2.
12. ibid. p. 6.
13. ibid. pp. 6–7.
14. Blomfield, *Chosen Highway*, pp. 150–1.
15. ibid. p. 151.
16. ibid. p. 153.
17. ibid. p. 156.
18. ibid.
19. ibid. pp. 157–8.
20. Maud, *Sparks*, p. 87.
21. *Star of the West*, vol. 2, no.12, p. 3.
22. Basil Hall, *Sitarih Khanum*, p. 9.
23. *'Abdu'l-Bahá in London*, p. 85.
24. *Star of the West*, vol. 2, no.11, p. 7.
25. ibid. pp. 7–8.
26. *Star of the West*, vol. 2, no. 12, p. 10.
27. *Star of the West*, vol. 2, no. 11, p. 4.

28. 'Abdu'l-Bahá in London, pp. 19–20.
29. Star of the West, vol. 2, no. 11, p. 8.
30. ibid. p. 4.
31. ibid. p. 8.
32. Balyuzi, 'Abdu'l-Bahá, p. 142.
33. ibid. p. 146.
34. ibid.
35. Blomfield, Chosen Highway, pp. 153–4.
36. Star of the West, vol. 2, no. 12, p. 12.
37. Blomfield, Chosen Highway, p. 154.
38. Star of the West, vol. 2, no. 12, p. 12.
39. 'Abdu'l-Bahá in London, pp. 22–4.
40. Basil Hall, Sitarih Khanum, p. 9.
41. Star of the West, vol. 2, no.12, p. 12.
42. Blomfield, Chosen Highway, pp. 152–3.
43. Basil Hall, Sitarih Khanum, pp. 10–11.
44. Blomfield, Chosen Highway, p. 161.
45. Maud, Sparks, p. 88.
46. Blomfield, Chosen Highway, p. 171.
47. ibid. p. 152.
48. ibid. pp. 164–5.
49. Weinberg, Rosenberg, pp. 132, 134.
50. Blomfield, Chosen Highway, p. 169.
51. ibid.
52. Basil Hall, Sitarih Khanum, pp. 13–14.
53. Psalms 43:3.
54. 'Abdu'l-Bahá in London, p. 81.
55. Star of the West, vol. 2, no. 12, p. 7.
56. Anonymous account of 'Abdu'l-Bahá's visit to Bristol, p. 2. United Kingdom Bahá'í Archives.
57. Blomfield, Chosen Highway, pp. 166–7.
58. Anonymous account of 'Abdu'l-Bahá's visit to Bristol, p. 3. United Kingdom Bahá'í Archives.
59. ibid. p. 5.
60. Blomfield, Chosen Highway, p. 167.
61. Basil Hall, Sitarih Khanum, p. 11.
62. Maud, Sparks, pp. 90–1.
63. Basil Hall, Sitarih Khanum, p. 7.
64. Blomfield, Chosen Highway, pp. 169–70.
65. Afnan,' 'Abdu'l-Bahá and Ezra Pound's Circle', in Journal of Bahá'í Studies, vol. 6, no.2, June–September 1994, p. 8.
66. Blomfield, Chosen Highway, pp. 159–61.
67. ibid. pp. 162–3.
68. 'Abdu'l-Bahá in London, p. 34.
69. ibid. pp. 38–9.
70. Blomfield, Chosen Highway, pp. 163–4.
71. ibid. pp. 165–6.
72. Basil Hall, Sitarih Khanum, pp. 8–9.

73. Letter from Edward G. Browne to Lady Blomfield, 1 October 1911. United Kingdom Bahá'í Archives.
74. Blomfield, *Chosen Highway*, pp. 173–4.
75. Tablet of 'Abdu'l-Bahá addressed to Lady Blomfield, October 1911. Bahá'í World Centre Archives. Provisional translation approved for publication by the Universal House of Justice.
76. ibid.

Chapter Five: The Diadem of Most Great Guidance

1. *Star of the West*, vol. 3, no. 19, p. 3.
2. 'Abdu'l-Bahá, *Paris Talks*, p. 26.
3. Blomfield, *Chosen Highway*, p. 179.
4. Basil Hall, *Sitarih Khanum*, p. 14.
5. Blomfield, *Chosen Highway*, pp. 179–80.
6. ibid. p. 186.
7. ibid. p. 180.
8. ibid. p. 181.
9. ibid. p. 183.
10. 'Abdu'l-Bahá, *Paris Talks*, p. 28.
11. ibid. p. 29.
12. Blomfield, *Chosen Highway*, pp. 184–5.
13. ibid. p. 185.
14. Reported in the pilgrimage diary of Dr J. E. Esslemont. United Kingdom Bahá'í Archives.
15. A Message from 'Abdu'l-Bahá to the Early English Bahá'ís. United Kingdom Bahá'í Archives.
16. Blomfield, *Chosen Highway*, p. 187.
17. 'Abdu'l-Bahá, *Paris Talks*, pp. 168–9.
18. 'Abdu'l-Bahá, *Promulgation*, pp. 16–17.
19. 'Abdu'l-Bahá, *Paris Talks*, p. 172.
20. Blomfield, An Account of the Visit to Stuttgart. United Kingdom Bahá'í Archives, p. 2.
21. ibid. p. 3.
22. ibid. p. 4.
23. ibid. p 5.
24. ibid.
25. ibid. p. 6.
26. ibid. p. 7.
27. Reported in 'News Notes', *Star of the West*, vol. 2, no. 17, p. 8.
28. Blomfield, An Account of the Visit to Stuttgart. United Kingdom Bahá'í Archives, p. 10.
29. ibid. p. 11.
30. ibid. pp. 12–13.
31. ibid. p. 14.
32. ibid. pp. 17–19.
33. ibid. p. 23.
34. ibid. p. 24.

35. Letter from Lady Blomfield to 'Abdu'l-Bahá, 11 December 1911. United Kingdom Bahá'í Archives.
36. ibid.
37. ibid.
38. Tablet of 'Abdu'l-Bahá addressed to Lady Blomfield, December 1911. Bahá'í World Centre Archives. Provisional translation approved for publication by the Universal House of Justice.
39. Tablet of 'Abdu'l-Bahá addressed to Lady Blomfield, 4 January 1912. Bahá'í World Centre Archives. Provisional translation approved for publication by the Universal House of Justice.
40. 'Abdu'l-Bahá, *Paris Talks*, p. 5.
41. Letter from Ahmad Sohrab to Lady Blomfield, 31 January 1912. United Kingdom Bahá'í Archives.
42. ibid.
43. From a Tablet of 'Abdu'l-Bahá addressed to Lady Blomfield, 29 March 1912. Bahá'í World Centre Archives. Provisional translation approved for publication by the Universal House of Justice.
44. 'With Abdul-Bahá in London', *Star of the West*, vol. 3, no. 19, p. 3.
45. Tablet of 'Abdu'l-Bahá addressed to Lady Blomfield. Undated. Bahá'í World Centre Archives. Provisional translation approved for publication by the Universal House of Justice.
46. From a Tablet of 'Abdu'l-Bahá addressed to Lady Blomfield, 12 February 1912. Bahá'í World Centre Archives. Provisional translation approved for publication by the Universal House of Justice.
47. ibid.
48. Rolland, quoted in Momen, *Bábí and Bahá'í Religions*, p. 54.
49. From a Tablet of 'Abdu'l-Bahá addressed to Lady Blomfield, 29 March 1912. Bahá'í World Centre Archives. Provisional translation approved for publication by the Universal House of Justice.
50. ibid.
51. Letter from Lady Blomfield to Ahmad Sohrab, 10 March 1912. United Kingdom Bahá'í Archives.
52. ibid.
53. Letter from Ethel Rosenberg to Ahmad Sohrab, 16 March 1912. United Kingdom Bahá'í Archives.
54. ibid.
55. Letter from Lady Blomfield to Ahmad Sohrab, 10 March 1912. United Kingdom Bahá'í Archives.
56. Letter from Ahmad Sohrab to Lady Blomfield, 21 March 1912. United Kingdom Bahá'í Archives.
57. From a Tablet of 'Abdu'l-Bahá addressed to Lady Blomfield, 29 March 1912. Bahá'í World Centre Archives. Provisional translation approved for publication by the Universal House of Justice.
58. Letter from Ahmad Sohrab to Lady Blomfield, 21 March 1912. United Kingdom Bahá'í Archives.
59. From a Tablet of 'Abdu'l-Bahá addressed to Lady Blomfield, 29 March 1912. Bahá'í World Centre Archives. Provisional translation approved for publication by the Universal House of Justice.

60. ibid.
61. Hollinger, *Agnes Parsons' Diary*, p. 12.
62. 'Abdu'l-Bahá, *Promulgation*, pp. 46–8.
63. Letter from Lady Blomfield to Louise Waite, 9 June 1913. United States Bahá'í Archives.
64. Letter from Lady Blomfield to 'Abdu'l Bahá, undated fragment. Bahá'í World Centre Archives.
65. ibid.
66. Letter from Lady Blomfield to 'Abdu'l-Bahá, 6 July 1912. Bahá'í World Centre Archives.
67. ibid.
68. From a Tablet of 'Abdu'l-Bahá addressed to Lady Blomfield, 21 August 1912. Bahá'í World Centre Archives. Provisional translation approved for publication by the Universal House of Justice.
69. From a Tablet of 'Abdu'l-Bahá addressed to Lady Blomfield, 15 July 1912. Bahá'í World Centre Archives. Provisional translation approved for publication by the Universal House of Justice.
70. ibid.
71. From a Tablet of 'Abdu'l-Bahá addressed to Lady Blomfield, 21 August 1912. Bahá'í World Centre Archives. Provisional translation approved for publication by the Universal House of Justice.
72. Letter from the Archbishop of Canterbury to Lady Blomfield, 22 July 1912. United Kingdom Bahá'í Archives.
73. Draft letter from Lady Blomfield to the Archbishop of Canterbury, July 1912. United Kingdom Bahá'í Archives.
74. Letter from Lady Blomfield to 'Abdu'l-Bahá, 30 July 1912. Bahá'í World Centre Archives.
75. Letter from the Archbishop of Canterbury to Lady Blomfield, 30 November 1912. United Kingdom Bahá'í Archives.
76. From a Tablet from 'Abdu'l-Bahá addressed to Lady Blomfield, 21 August 1912. Bahá'í World Centre Archives. Provisional translation approved for publication by the Universal House of Justice.
77. From a Tablet of 'Abdu'l-Bahá addressed to Lady Blomfield, 29 March 1912. Bahá'í World Centre Archives. Provisional translation approved for publication by the Universal House of Justice.
78. From a Tablet from 'Abdu'l-Bahá addressed to Lady Blomfield, 15 July 1912. Bahá'í World Centre Archives. Provisional translation approved for publication by the Universal House of Justice.
79. Letter from Lady Blomfield to 'Abdu'l-Bahá, 30 July 1912. Bahá'í World Centre Archives.
80. From a Tablet of 'Abdu'l-Bahá addressed to Lady Blomfield, 21 August 1912. Bahá'í World Centre Archives. Provisional translation approved for publication by the Universal House of Justice.
81. Letter from T. K. Cheyne to Lady Blomfield, 11 September 1912. United Kingdom Bahá'í Archives.
82. Letter from T. K. Cheyne to Lady Blomfield, 21 October 1912. United Kingdom Bahá'í Archives.
83. ibid.

84. Invitation card. United Kingdom Bahá'í Archives.
85. Card from Estlin Carpenter to Lady Blomfield, 7 November 1912. United Kingdom Bahá'í Archives.
86. Blomfield, *Chosen Highway*, p. 168.
87. From a Tablet from 'Abdu'l-Bahá addressed to Lady Blomfield, 17 September 1912. Bahá'í World Centre Archives. Provisional translation approved for publication by the Universal House of Justice.

Chapter Six: The Brilliant Light

1. From a Tablet from 'Abdu'l-Bahá addressed to Lady Blomfield, 7 March 1913. Bahá'í World Centre Archives. Provisional translation approved for publication by the Universal House of Justice.
2. Shoghi Effendi, *God Passes By*, p. 295.
3. ibid.
4. Sohrab, 'With Abdul-Baha on SS. "Celtic"', *Star of the West*, vol. 3, no. 16, p. 2.
5. ibid.
6. ibid.
7. Fraser, 'Abdul-Baha's Arrival in England', *Star of the West*, vol. 3, no. 17, p. 2.
8. Lucy Hall, 'Father's meeting with 'Abdu'l-Bahá'. United Kingdom Bahá'í Archives.
9. Sohrab, 'With Abdul-Baha on SS. "Celtic"', *Star of the West*, vol. 3, no.16, p. 2.
10. *Star of the West*, vol. 3, no. 17, p. 3.
11. ibid. p. 5.
12. 'With Abdul-Bahá in London', *Star of the West*, vol. 3, no. 19, p. 3.
13. ibid.
14. From a Tablet from 'Abdu'l-Bahá addressed to Lady Blomfield, 29 March 1912. Bahá'í World Centre Archives. Provisional translation approved for publication by the Universal House of Justice.
15. Graham, 'Joan Waring', in McNamara, *Connections*, p. 58.
16. ibid.
17. 'Abdu'l-Bahá, quoted in *Star of the West*, vol. 3, no. 19, p. 4.
18. Basil Hall, *Sitarih Khanum*, p. 15.
19. 'With Abdul-Bahá in London', *Star of the West*, vol. 3, no. 19, p. 5.
20. Blomfield, *Chosen Highway*, pp. 161–2.
21. 'With Abdul-Bahá in London', *Star of the West*, vol. 3, no. 19, p. 4.
22. ibid. p. 5.
23. Balyuzi, *'Abdu'l-Bahá*, p. 347.
24. 'With Abdul-Bahá in London', *Star of the West*, vol. 3, no. 19, p. 5.
25. ibid. p. 6.
26. ibid.
27. 'Abdul-Bahá in London', *Star of the West*, vol. 3, no. 17, p. 5.
28. ibid. pp. 6–7.
29. ibid. p. 9.
30. ibid. pp. 9–10.
31. ibid. p. 10.
32. Blomfield, *Chosen Highway*, p. 154.
33. ibid.
34. 'With Abdul-Bahá in London', *Star of the West*, vol. 3, no. 19, p. 7.
35. Blomfield, *Chosen Highway*, pp. 154–5.

36. Attributed to 'Abdu'l-Bahá in an anonymous report, entitled 'The Master witnesses a mystery play and talks with the actors afterwards'. United Kingdom Bahá'í Archives.
37. ibid.
38. ibid.
39. 'With Abdul-Bahá in London', *Star of the West*, vol. 3, no. 19, p. 7.
40. Attributed to 'Abdu'l-Bahá in a letter of Ahmad Sohrab, 22 December 1912. United Kingdom Bahá'í Archives.
41. ibid.
42. ibid.
43. ibid.
44. Skrine, *Bahaism*, p. 66.
45. Letter from F. H. Skrine to Lady Blomfield, 22 December 1912. United Kingdom Bahá'í Archives.
46. Blomfield, *Chosen Highway*, p. 152.
47. ibid.
48. Letter of Ahmad Sohrab, 22 December 1912. United Kingdom Bahá'í Archives.
49. Letter of Ahmad Sohrab, 23 December 1912. United Kingdom Bahá'í Archives.
50. ibid.
51. Letter of Ahmad Sohrab, 24 December 1912. United Kingdom Bahá'í Archives.
52. Balyuzi, *'Abdu'l-Bahá*, p. 350.
53. Letter of Ahmad Sohrab, 25 December 1912. United Kingdom Bahá'í Archives.
54. Anonymous report, ''Abdu'l-Bahá's Christmas Day in London'. United Kingdom Bahá'í Archives.
55. Letter of Ahmad Sohrab, 25 December 1912. United Kingdom Bahá'í Archives.
56. 'With Abdul-Baha in London', *Star of the West*, vol. 3, no. 19, p. 3.
57. Attributed to 'Abdu'l-Bahá, in Herrick, 'Christmas in London with Abdul Baha'. United Kingdom Bahá'í Archives.
58. ibid.
59. ''Abdul-Baha at the "Salvation Army" Shelter', *Star of the West*, vol. 3, no. 18, p. 8; and Herrick, 'Abdul Baha visits the poor on Christmas Night', United Kingdom Bahá'í Archives.
60. Letter of Ahmad Sohrab, 25 December 1912. United Kingdom Bahá'í Archives.
61. ibid.
62. Attributed to 'Abdu'l-Bahá in an anonymous report entitled ''Abdu'l-Bahá's Christmas Day in London'. United Kingdom Bahá'í Archives.
63. Letter of Ahmad Sohrab, 25 December 1912. United Kingdom Bahá'í Archives.
64. 'Abdu'l-Bahá, *Paris Talks*, pp. 176–7.
65. Herrick, 'Christmas in London with Abdul Baha'. United Kingdom Bahá'í Archives.
66. Letter from T. K. Cheyne to Lady Blomfield, 23 December 1912. United Kingdom Bahá'í Archives.
67. ibid.
68. Blomfield, *Chosen Highway*, p. 168.
69. ibid. pp. 168–9.
70. *Oxford Times*, 4 January 1913.
71. ibid.
72. ibid.

73. Letter from T. K. Cheyne to John Craven. Oxford Baháʾí community website.
74. Cheyne, *Reconciliation of Races and Religions*, p. ix.
75. Carpenter, *Comparative Religion*.
76. Blomfield, *Chosen Highway*, p. 169.
77. Letter of Mirza Ahmad Sohrab, 1 January 1913. United Kingdom Baháʾí Archives.
78. ibid.
79. ibid.
80. ibid.
81. Letter of Mirza Ahmad Sohrab, 2 January 1913. United Kingdom Baháʾí Archives.
82. *Star of the West*, vol. 3, no.18, p. 9.
83. ibid. p. 10.
84. Objects of the Women's Freedom League, as stated on the League's letterhead.
85. Mulvihill, *Charlotte Despard*, pp. 99–100.
86. Letter of Mirza Ahmad Sohrab, 2 January 1913. United Kingdom Baháʾí Archives.
87. Letter from Florence A. Underwood to Lady Blomfield, 4 January 1913. United Kingdom Baháʾí Archives.
88. Letter of Mirza Ahmad Sohrab, 3 January 1913. United Kingdom Baháʾí Archives.
89. Attributed to ʿAbduʾl-Bahá in a letter of Mirza Ahmad Sohrab, 4 January 1913. United Kingdom Baháʾí Archives.
90. ʿAbduʾl-Bahá, *Paris Talks*, pp. 179–81.
91. Letter of Mirza Ahmad Sohrab, 6 January 1913. United Kingdom Baháʾí Archives.
92. ibid.
93. Letter of Mirza Ahmad Sohrab, 10 January 1913. United Kingdom Baháʾí Archives.
94. Attributed to ʿAbduʾl-Bahá, in a letter of Mirza Ahmad Sohrab, 11 January 1913. United Kingdom Baháʾí Archives.
95. Letter of Mirza Ahmad Sohrab, 10 January 1913. United Kingdom Baháʾí Archives.
96. Attributed to ʿAbduʾl-Bahá, in a letter of Mirza Ahmad Sohrab, 11 January 1913. United Kingdom Baháʾí Archives.
97. Blomfield, *Chosen Highway*, p. 172.
98. Letter of Mirza Ahmad Sohrab, 12 January 1913. United Kingdom Baháʾí Archives.
99. ibid.
100. Quoted in ibid.
101. ibid.
102. Blomfield, *Chosen Highway*, p. 168.
103. 'Abdul-Bahá at Clifton, England', *Star of the West*, vol. 4, no. 1, p. 4.
104. ibid. p. 6.
105. Balyuzi, *ʿAbduʾl-Bahá*, p. 370.
106. Blomfield, *Chosen Highway*, pp. 176–7.
107. Basil Hall, *Drama of the Kingdom*, p. 2.
108. Blomfield, *Chosen Highway*, p. 152.
109. Transcript of ʿAbduʾl-Baháʾs address at Woking Mosque. United Kingdom Baháʾí Archives.
110. 'Abdul-Baháʾs Visit to Woking, England', *Baháʾí World*, vol. 3, 1928–1930, p. 279.
111. ibid.
112. Blomfield, *Chosen Highway*, p. 174.

113. ibid.
114. From a Tablet from 'Abdu'l-Bahá addressed to Lady Blomfield, 1 February 1913. Bahá'í World Centre Archives. Provisional translation approved for publication by the Universal House of Justice.
115. ibid.

Chapter Seven: Pure and Goodly Deeds

1. Bahá'u'lláh, cited in Shoghi Effendi, *Advent of Divine Justice*, pp. 24–5.
2. From a Tablet of 'Abdu'l-Bahá addressed to Lady Blomfield, 30 March 1913. Bahá'í World Centre Archives. Provisional translation approved for publication by the Universal House of Justice.
3. ibid.
4. Letter from Luṭfu'lláh Ḥakím to Lady Blomfield. March 1913. United Kingdom Bahá'í Archives.
5. Letter from Rúḥá to Lady Blomfield, 26 July 1913. United Kingdom Bahá'í Archives.
6. Letter from Rúḥá to Lady Blomfield, 2 September 1913. United Kingdom Bahá'í Archives.
7. Letter from Mírzá 'Alí-Akbar to Lady Blomfield, 8 January 1914. United Kingdom Bahá'í Archives.
8. Letter from Mírzá 'Alí-Akbar to Lady Blomfield, 13 May, 1913. United Kingdom Bahá'í Archives.
9. Letter from Lady Blomfield to Maude Holbach, 28 November 1913. United Kingdom Bahá'í Archives.
10. Letter from Luṭfu'lláh Ḥakím to Lady Blomfield, March 1913. United Kingdom Bahá'í Archives.
11. Provisional translation, in the handwriting of Dr Luṭfu'lláh Ḥakím, of a letter from 'Abdu'l-Bahá to T. K. Cheyne dated November 1913 found in the United Kingdom Bahá'í Archives.
12. From a Tablet from 'Abdu'l-Bahá addressed to Lady Blomfield, 21 April 1914(?). Bahá'í World Centre Archives. Provisional translation approved for publication by the Universal House of Justice.
13. Letter from Lady Blomfield to 'Abdu'l-Bahá, 21 March 1913. Bahá'í World Centre Archives.
14. From a Tablet from 'Abdu'l-Bahá addressed to Lady Blomfield, March 1913. Bahá'í World Centre Archives. Provisional translation approved for publication by the Universal House of Justice.
15. Attributed to 'Abdu'l-Bahá in a letter from Luṭfu'lláh Ḥakím to Lady Blomfield, March 1913. United Kingdom Bahá'í Archives.
16. Shoghi Effendi, *God Passes By*, p. 294.
17. From a Tablet from 'Abdu'l-Bahá addressed to Lady Blomfield, 15 September 1913. Bahá'í World Centre Archives. Provisional translation approved for publication by the Universal House of Justice.
18. Remey, *Through Warring Countries*, pp. 30–1.
19. Letter from Lady Blomfield to Maude Holbach, 28 January 1914. United Kingdom Bahá'í Archives.
20. ibid.
21. ibid.

22. ibid.
23. From a Tablet from 'Abdu'l-Bahá addressed to Lady Blomfield, 24 February 1914. Bahá'í World Centre Archives. Provisional translation approved for publication by the Universal House of Justice.
24. ibid.
25. From a Tablet from 'Abdu'l-Bahá addressed to Lady Blomfield, 24 February 1914. Bahá'í World Centre Archives. Provisional translation approved for publication by the Universal House of Justice.
26. From a Tablet from 'Abdu'l-Bahá addressed to Lady Blomfield, 14 October 1914. Bahá'í World Centre Archives. Provisional translation approved for publication by the Universal House of Justice.
27. ibid.
28. See Pankhurst (Christabel), *Unshackled*.
29. 'Queen unruffled by suffrage plea', *New York Times*, 6 June 1914.
30. See Pankhurst (Sylvia), *The Suffragette Movement*.
31. 'Queen unruffled by suffrage plea', *New York Times*, 6 June 1914.
32. *The Milwaukee Journal*, 22 June 1914.
33. 'Queen unruffled by suffrage plea', *New York Times*, 6 June 1914.
34. Letter from Joseph Hannen to Lady Blomfield, 7 September 1914. United States Bahá'í Archives.
35. Letter of Ahmad Sohrab, 23 June 1914. United States Bahá'í Archives.
36. See Pankhurst (Sylvia), *The Suffragette Movement*.
37. Hattersley, *The Edwardians*, p. 221.
38. Pankhurst (Sylvia), in *The Suffragette*, 7 August 1914.
39. Morgan, *Sphere Illustrated History*, p. 116.
40. 'Abdu'l-Bahá, *Promulgation*, p. 376.
41. Attributed to 'Abdu'l-Bahá, in 'The World is at the Threshold of a Most Tragic Struggle', *Star of the West*, vol. 5 no.11, p. 165.
42. *Star of the West*, vol. 5, no. 16, p. 244.
43. From a Tablet from 'Abdu'l-Bahá addressed to Lady Blomfield, 14 October 1914. Bahá'í World Centre Archives. Provisional translation approved for publication by the Universal House of Justice.
44. George, Florence. Notes. United Kingdom Bahá'í Archives.
45. From a Tablet from 'Abdu'l-Bahá addressed to Lady Blomfield, 14 October 1914. Bahá'í World Centre Archives. Provisional translation approved for publication by the Universal House of Justice.
46. MacDonald, *Roses*, p. xi.
47. Basil Hall, *Sitárih Khánum*, p. 17.
48. Letter from Alma Knobloch, 25 September 1914, *Star of the West*, vol. 5, no.13, p. 199.
49. Blomfield, *Chosen Highway*, p. 189.
50. ibid.
51. ibid. p. 190.
52. Letter from Elinore Hiscock, *Star of the West*, vol. 6, no. 6, p. 43.
53. Blomfield, *Chosen Highway*, p. 190.
54. Momen, *Bábí and Bahá'í Religions*, p. 421.
55. ibid. p. 420.
56. ibid. pp. 421–2.

57. ibid. p. 422.
58. ibid.
59. ibid.
60. ibid. pp. 422–3.
61. ibid. p. 423.
62. Quoted in Rabbani, 'Abdu'l-Bahá in Abu-Sinan', *Bahá'í Studies Review*, 2005, pp. 98–9.
63. Letter from Dr Esslemont to Luṭfu'lláh Ḥakím, 23 May 1915. United Kingdom Bahá'í Archives.
64. Letter from Ethel Rosenberg to Helen Goodall, 23 November 1917. United Kingdom Bahá'í Archives.
65. ibid.
66. Letter of Lady Blomfield to Ahmad Sohrab, 25 July 1917. United Kingdom Bahá'í Archives.
67. ibid.
68. Letter from Tudor Pole to Ethel Rosenberg, 22 December 1917. United Kingdom Bahá'í Archives.
69. Momen, *Bábí and Bahá'í Religions*, p. 333.
70. Blomfield, *Chosen Highway*, p. 219.
71. Letter from Lady Blomfield to Ethel Rosenberg, 23 January 1918. United Kingdom Bahá'í Archives.
72. Handwritten note of Lady Blomfield, dated 24 January 1918. United Kingdom Bahá'í Archives.
73. Blomfield, *Chosen Highway*, p. 219.
74. Momen, *Bábí and Bahá'í Religions*, p. 333.
75. Blomfield, *Chosen Highway*, p. 219.
76. Momen, *Bábí and Bahá'í Religions*, p. 334.
77. Letter from Luṭfu'lláh Hakim to Lady Blomfield, 11 February 1918. United Kingdom Bahá'í Archives.
78. Letter from R. Graham to Lord Lamington, 31 January 1918. United Kingdom Bahá'í Archives.
79. Letter from Balfour to Lord Lamington, 30 September 1918. United Kingdom Bahá'í Archives.
80. Letter from Tudor Pole to Ethel Rosenberg, 4 November 1918. United Kingdom Bahá'í Archives.
81. Letter from Shoghi Effendi to Dr Esslemont, 19 November 1918. United Kingdom Bahá'í Archives.
82. *Daily Mirror*, 12 November 1918, p. 2.
83. *Star of the West*, vol. 10, no. 7, p. 137.
84. Tudor Pole's diary, 16 November 1918. United Kingdom Bahá'í Archives; and *Star of the West*, vol. 9, no. 17, p. 186.
85. Letter from Shoghi Effendi to Dr Esslemont, 19 November 1918. United Kingdom Bahá'í Archives.
86. Tudor Pole's diary, 20 November 1918. United Kingdom Bahá'í Archives.
87. ibid.
88. Letter from Tudor Pole to Ethel Rosenberg, 29 November 1918. United Kingdom Bahá'í Archives.
89. Blomfield, *Chosen Highway*, p. 226.

90. *Star of the West*, vol. 9, no. 17, p. 189.
91. Letter to General Allenby, 19 May 1919. United Kingdom Bahá'í Archives.
92. Letter from Ethel Rosenberg to Roy Wilhelm, May Maxwell and Helen Goodall, 28 March 1919. United Kingdom Bahá'í Archives.
93. Letter to Sir Arthur Money, 19 May 1919. United Kingdom Bahá'í Archives.
94. Letter to Balfour, 22 March 1919. United Kingdom Bahá'í Archives.
95. Blomfield, *Chosen Highway*, p. 221.
96. Letter from Tudor Pole to Lady Blomfield, 25 January 1919. United Kingdom Bahá'í Archives.
97. From a Tablet from 'Abdu'l-Bahá addressed to Lady Blomfield, 16 May 1919. Bahá'í World Centre Archives. Provisional translation approved for publication by the Universal House of Justice.
98. From a Tablet from 'Abdu'l-Bahá addressed to Lady Blomfield, 29 July 1919. Bahá'í World Centre Archives. Provisional translation approved for publication by the Universal House of Justice.
99. ibid.
100. Tablet from 'Abdu'l-Bahá to David Buchanan, quoted in Balyuzi, *'Abdu'l-Bahá*, pp. 437–8.
101. 'Abdu'l-Bahá, *Selections*, no. 71, p. 109.
102. Vail, 'Editorial – The Dawn of the Most Great Peace', *Star of the West*, vol. 9, no. 14, p. 157.
103. Letter from J. E. Esslemont, in *Star of the West*, vol. 9, no. 17, p. 197.
104. Shoghi Effendi, *Citadel*, p. 36.
105. Shoghi Effendi, *World Order*, pp. 191–2.
106. 'Abdu'l-Bahá, *Selections*, no. 227, p. 306.
107. Basil Hall, *Sitarih Khanum*, p. 18.
108. ibid.

Chapter Eight: The First Obligation

1. 'Abdu'l-Bahá, Foreword to Blomfield, *First Obligation*, p. 2.
2. Basil Hall, *Sitarih Khanum*, pp. 1–2.
3. From a Tablet from 'Abdu'l-Bahá addressed to Lady Blomfield, 29 July 1919. Bahá'í World Centre Archives. Provisional translation approved for publication by the Universal House of Justice.
4. ibid.
5. Balyuzi, 'Preface' to Blomfield, *Chosen Highway*, p. v.
6. From a Tablet from 'Abdu'l-Bahá addressed to Lady Blomfield, 19 January 1920. Bahá'í World Centre Archives. Provisional translation approved for publication by the Universal House of Justice.
7. ibid.
8. 'Eglantyne Jebb – Founder of Save the Children', Save the Children Fund website http://www.savethechildren.net/alliance/about_us/history.html and http://www.leader-values.com/Content/detail.asp?ContentDetailID=794
9. Blomfield, *First Obligation*, p. 10.
10. ibid. pp. 10–11, 13–14.
11. From a Tablet from 'Abdu'l-Bahá addressed to Lady Blomfield, 11 March 1920. Bahá'í World Centre Archives. Provisional translation approved for publication by the Universal House of Justice.

12. ibid.
13. Letter from Lady Blomfield to 'Abdu'l-Bahá, 30 January 1920.
14. From a Tablet from 'Abdu'l-Bahá addressed to Lady Blomfield, 6 June 1920. Bahá'í World Centre Archives. Provisional translation approved for publication by the Universal House of Justice.
15. From a Tablet from 'Abdu'l-Bahá addressed to Lady Blomfield, October 1920. Bahá'í World Centre Archives. Provisional translation approved for publication by the Universal House of Justice.
16. From a Tablet from 'Abdu'l-Bahá addressed to Lady Blomfield, 6 June 1920. Bahá'í World Centre Archives. Provisional translation approved for publication by the Universal House of Justice.
17. From a Tablet from 'Abdu'l-Bahá addressed to Lady Blomfield, 15 August 1920. Bahá'í World Centre Archives. Provisional translation approved for publication by the Universal House of Justice.
18. From a Tablet from 'Abdu'l-Bahá addressed to Lady Blomfield, October 1920. Bahá'í World Centre Archives. Provisional translation approved for publication by the Universal House of Justice.
19. From a Tablet from 'Abdu'l-Bahá addressed to Lady Blomfield, 6 June 1920. Bahá'í World Centre Archives. Provisional translation approved for publication by the Universal House of Justice.
20. Quoted in Mulley, *The Woman Who Saved the Children*, p. 297.
21. From a Tablet from 'Abdu'l-Bahá addressed to Lady Blomfield, October 1920. Bahá'í World Centre Archives. Provisional translation approved for publication by the Universal House of Justice.
22. Quoted in Mulley, *The Woman Who Saved the Children*, p. 297.
23. ibid. p. 298.
24. Letter from Lady Blomfield to 'Abdu'l-Bahá, 9 June 1921. Bahá'í World Centre Archives.
25. ibid.
26. Blomfield, *First Obligation*, p. 14.
27. Letter from Lady Blomfield to 'Abdu'l-Bahá, 9 June 1921. Bahá'í World Centre Archives.
28. ibid.
29. From a Tablet from 'Abdu'l-Bahá addressed to Lady Blomfield, 23 July 1921. Bahá'í World Centre Archives. Provisional translation approved for publication by the Universal House of Justice.
30. Blomfield, *First Obligation*, p. 2.
31. ibid. p. 4.
32. ibid.
33. ibid. p. 9.
34. ibid. pp. 9–10.
35. ibid. p. 11.
36. ibid. pp. 12–13.
37. ibid. p. 13.
38. ibid. p. 16.
39. Blomfield, *Chosen Highway*, p. 214.
40. ibid.
41. Maud, *Sparks*, pp. 110–11.

42. Blomfield, *Chosen Highway*, pp. 214–15.
43. From a Tablet from 'Abdu'l-Bahá addressed to Lady Blomfield, 11 March 1920. Baháʾí World Centre Archives. Provisional translation approved for publication by the Universal House of Justice.
44. Rabbaní, *Priceless Pearl*, p. 38.
45. Quoted in Khadem, *Shoghi Effendi in Oxford*, pp. 116–17.
46. Letter from Rúḥá to Lady Blomfield, 14 February 1921. United Kingdom Baháʾí Archives.
47. Letter from Corinne True to Lady Blomfield, 9 June 1921. United Kingdom Baháʾí Archives.
48. Letter from Luṭfuʾlláh Ḥakím, 13 April 1921. United Kingdom Baháʾí Archives.
49. Letter from Rúḥá to Lady Blomfield, 14 February 1921. United Kingdom Baháʾí Archives.
50. Letter from Lady Blomfield to 'Abdu'l-Bahá, 9 June 1921. Baháʾí World Centre Archives.

Chapter Nine: Dawn of the Guardianship

1. 'Abdu'l-Bahá, *Will and Testament*, para. 58.
2. Shoghi Effendi, *God Passes By*, p. 309.
3. ibid. p. 311.
4. Rabbaní, *Priceless Pearl*, p. 39.
5. Letter from Dr Esslemont to Luṭfuʾlláh Ḥakím, 8 December 1921. United Kingdom Baháʾí Archives.
6. Provisional translation of a Tablet from 'Abdu'l-Bahá addressed to Lady Blomfield, 11 March 1920. Baháʾí World Centre Archives.
7. *Star of the West*, vol. 12, no.16, pp. 252–3. It does not appear from further accounts that Asgharzádih did in fact take part in the journey back to the Holy Land.
8. ibid. p. 253.
9. *The Times*, Wednesday, 30 November 1921. United Kingdom Baháʾí Archives.
10. Shoghi Effendi and Lady Blomfield, *The Passing of 'Abdu'l-Bahá*, p. 16.
11. Momen, *Bábí and Baháʾí Religions*, p. 348.
12. ibid.
13. Letter from Dr Esslemont to Luṭfuʾlláh Ḥakím, 8 December 1921. United Kingdom Baháʾí Archives.
14. Rabbaní, *Priceless Pearl*, p. 40.
15. ibid. pp. 40–1.
16. 'Abdu'l-Bahá, quoted in *God Passes By*, p. 275.
17. Letter from Lady Blomfield to Mary Basil Hall, 4 January 1922. United Kingdom Baháʾí Archives.
18. ibid.
19. Weinberg, *Ethel Jenner Rosenberg*, p. 184.
20. Letter from Lady Blomfield to Mary Basil Hall, 4 January 1922. United Kingdom Baháʾí Archives.
21. ibid.
22. ibid.
23. Blomfield, *Chosen Highway*, pp. 89–90.
24. Letter from Lady Blomfield to Mary Basil Hall, 4 January 1922. United Kingdom

Bahá'í Archives.

25. Shoghi Effendi and Lady Blomfield, *The Passing of 'Abdu'l-Bahá*, pp. 19–20.

26. Letter from Lady Blomfield to Mary Basil Hall, 5 January 1922. United Kingdom Bahá'í Archives.

27. *Star of the West*, vol. 13, no. 2, pp. 40–1.

28. ibid. pp. 41–2.

29. Rabbaní, *Priceless Pearl*, p. 47.

30. ibid.

31. ibid.

32. Letter from Lady Blomfield to Mary Basil Hall, 5 January 1922. United Kingdom Bahá'í Archives.

33. Letter from Lady Blomfield to Mary Basil Hall, 11 February 1922. United Kingdom Bahá'í Archives.

34. Letter from Lady Blomfield to Mary Basil Hall, 5 January 1922. United Kingdom Bahá'í Archives.

35. Letter from Lady Blomfield to Mary Basil Hall, 11 February 1922. United Kingdom Bahá'í Archives.

36. ibid.

37. ibid.

38. Handwritten account by Lady Blomfield. United Kingdom Bahá'í Archives.

39. Letter from Lady Blomfield to Mary Basil Hall, 25 February 1922. United Kingdom Bahá'í Archives.

40. ibid.

41. ibid.

42. *Star of the West*, vol. 13, no. 4, p. 68.

43. Undated letter from Lady Blomfield to Mary Basil Hall. United Kingdom Bahá'í Archives.

44. ibid.

45. Rabbaní, *Priceless Pearl*, p. 56.

46. Undated letter from Lady Blomfield to Mary Basil Hall. United Kingdom Bahá'í Archives.

47. Letter from Lady Blomfield to Mary Basil Hall, 25 February 1922. United Kingdom Bahá'í Archives.

48. Letter from Lady Blomfield to Mary Basil Hall, 2 April 1922. United Kingdom Bahá'í Archives.

49. Letter from Lady Blomfield to Mary Basil Hall, 24 March 1922. United Kingdom Bahá'í Archives.

50. Shoghi Effendi and Lady Blomfield, *The Passing of 'Abdu'l-Bahá*, p. 3.

51. Randall-Winckler, *William Henry Randall*, p. 202.

52. ibid. pp. 210–11.

53. ibid. p. 211.

54. Letter from Lady Blomfield to Mary Basil Hall, 18 March 1922. United Kingdom Bahá'í Archives.

55. Letter from Lady Blomfield to Mary Basil Hall, 24 March 1922. United Kingdom Bahá'í Archives.

56. Letter from Lady Blomfield to Mary Basil Hall, 27 March 1922. United Kingdom Bahá'í Archives.

57. ibid.

58. Letter from Lady Blomfield to Mary Basil Hall, 30 March 1922. United Kingdom Bahá'í Archives.

59. ibid.

60. Letter from Lady Blomfield to Mary Basil Hall, 2 April 1922. United Kingdom Bahá'í Archives.

61. ibid.

62. ibid.

63. ibid.

64. ibid.

65. ibid.

66. ibid.

67. ibid.

68. ibid.

69. ibid.

70. ibid.

71. Letter from Lady Blomfield to Mary Basil Hall, 24 March 1922. United Kingdom Bahá'í Archives.

72. ibid.

73. *Star of the West*, vol. 13, no. 4, pp. 81–2.

74. Letter from Lady Blomfield to Yúḥanná Dávúd, 21 June 1922. United Kingdom Bahá'í Archives.

75. Blomfield, *Chosen Highway*, pp. 230–1.

76. ibid. pp. 232–3.

77. ibid. p. 233.

78. ibid. pp. 233–4.

79. ibid. p. 198.

80. ibid. pp. 198–9.

81. ibid. pp. 200–1.

82. ibid. p. 201.

83. ibid.

84. ibid.

85. Letter from Lady Blomfield to Yúḥanná Dávúd, 21 June 1922. United Kingdom Bahá'í Archives.

Chapter Ten: Preparing the Ground

1. Words of Shoghi Effendi conveyed in a letter from Ruhi Afnan to Lady Blomfield, 24 October 1925. United Kingdom Bahá'í Archives.

2. Letter from Dr Esslemont to Luṭfu'lláh Ḥakím, 18 June 1922. United Kingdom Bahá'í Archives.

3. Tudor Pole, *Writing on the Ground*, p. 164.

4. Letter from Lady Blomfield to Shoghi Effendi, 1 February 1923. Bahá'í World Centre Archives.

5. ibid.

6. Cable from Shoghi Effendi to Lady Blomfield, 3 January 1923. Bahá'í World Centre Archives.

7. Letter from Lady Blomfield to Shoghi Effendi, 2 May 1923. Bahá'í World Centre Archives.

8. Letter from Lady Blomfield to Shoghi Effendi, 1 February 1923. Bahá'í World Centre Archives.

9. Shoghi Effendi, *Unfolding Destiny*, p. 9.

10. ibid. pp. 10–11.

11. Letter from Rúḥá to Lady Blomfield, 20 March (no year given). United Kingdom Bahá'í Archives.

12. Shoghi Effendi, *Unfolding Destiny*, p. 16.

13. Letter from Dorothy Buxton to Lady Blomfield, 15 February 1924. United Kingdom Bahá'í Archives.

14. Letter from Lady Blomfield to Victoria Bedikian, 15 August 1923. United Kingdom Bahá'í Archives.

15. ibid.

16. Letter from Rúḥá to Lady Blomfield, 16 September (no year given). United Kingdom Bahá'í Archives.

17. Letter from Rúḥá to Lady Blomfield, 26 May 1926. United Kingdom Bahá'í Archives.

18. ibid.

19. Letter from Lady Blomfield to Victoria Bedikian, 15 August 1923. United Kingdom Bahá'í Archives.

20. ibid.

21. Vader, *For the Good of Mankind*, p. 18.

22. Letter from Lady Blomfield to Victoria Bedikian, 21 November 1923. United Kingdom Bahá'í Archives.

23. *Star of the West*, vol. 14, no. 11, p. 342.

24. ibid. pp. 342–3.

25. Letter from Lady Blomfield to Victoria Bedikian, 23 October 1923. United States Bahá'í Archives.

26. Letter from Lady Blomfield to May Maxwell, Whitsuntide 1925. Estate of 'Amatu'l-Bahá Rúḥíyyih Khánum.

27. Momen, *Esslemont*, p. 27.

28. *Star of the West*, vol. 14, no. 8, p. 250.

29. *The Times*, Tuesday, 27 November 1923.

30. *Star of the West*, vol. 14, no. 10, p. 307.

31. *Star of the West*, vol. 14, no. 9, p. 276.

32. Shoghi Effendi, *Unfolding Destiny*, p. 27.

33. *Star of the West*, vol. 15, pp. 264–5.

34. ibid. p. 266.

35. Loftus Hare, *Religions of the Empire*, p. 319.

36. ibid. p. 5.

37. ibid. p. 6.

38. Shoghi Effendi, *Unfolding Destiny*, p. 30.

39. Letter from Lady Blomfield to May Maxwell, Whitsuntide 1925. Estate of 'Amatu'l-Bahá Rúḥíyyih Khánum.

40. Blomfield, 'Short Story of Some Work for Unity during the Past Year', September 1924–5. United Kingdom Bahá'í Archives.

41. ibid.

42. Invitation card to 'Lady Blomfield at Home', Tuesday 5 May 1925. United Kingdom Bahá'í Archives.

43. Letter from Lady Blomfield to May Maxwell, Whitsuntide 1925. Estate of 'Amatu'l-Bahá Rúḥíyyih Khánum.

44. ibid.

45. ibid.

46. *Bahá'í News Letter*, no. 6, July–August 1925. United Kingdom Bahá'í Archives.

47. Stockman, *Bahá'í Faith in America*, vol. 2, p. 142.

48. Letter from Lady Blomfield to May Maxwell, Whitsuntide 1925. Estate of 'Amatu'l-Bahá Rúḥíyyih Khánum.

49. ibid.

50. ibid.

51. ibid.

52. See 'Short History of the International Bahá'í Bureau at Geneva, Switzerland', Bahá'í World vol. 4.

53. Letter from Ruhi Afnan to Lady Blomfield, 24 October 1925. United Kingdom Bahá'í Archives.

54. ibid.

55. Letter from Lady Blomfield to Ella Cooper, 31 July 1925. United States Bahá'í Archives.

56. Cable from Shoghi Effendi to Lady Blomfield, 1 July 1925. Bahá'í World Centre Archives.

57. Letter written on behalf of Shoghi Effendi, 7 February 1926, appended to which is a postscript in his own handwriting. Bahá'í World Centre Archives.

58. Letter from Lady Blomfield to Shoghi Effendi, 23 January 1926. Bahá'í World Centre Archives.

59. Basil Hall, *Sitarih Khanum*, p. 20.

60. Letter from Lady Blomfield to May Maxwell, Whitsuntide 1925. Estate of 'Amatu'l-Bahá Rúḥíyyih Khánum.

61. ibid.

62. Blomfield, 'Short Story of Some Work for Unity During the Past Year Sept. 1924–25'.

63. Basil Hall, *Sitarih Khanum*, p. 20.

64. Letter from Lady Blomfield to Shoghi Effendi, 23 January 1926. Bahá'í World Centre Archives.

65. ibid.

66. Letter written on behalf of Shoghi Effendi, 7 February 1926, appended to which is a postscript in his own handwriting.

67. ibid.

68. ibid.

69. ibid.

70. 'The Call for the World's Supreme Peace', pamphlet. United Kingdom Bahá'í Archives.

71. Basil Hall, *Sitarih Khanum*, p. 21.

72. Shoghi Effendi. *Unfolding Destiny*, p. 13.

73. Conversation between the author and David Hofman, 9 October 1996.

74. Shoghi Effendi, *Unfolding Destiny*, p. 49.

75. Letter from Rúḥá to Lady Blomfield, 6 May 1926. United Kingdom Bahá'í Archives.

76. ibid.

77. ibid.
78. ibid.
79. Letter from Rúḥá to Lady Blomfield, 9 December (no year given). United Kingdom Baháʾí Archives.
80. Letter from Suhayl Afnan to Lady Blomfield. Undated. United Kingdom Baháʾí Archives.
81. Letter from Suhayl Afnan to Lady Blomfield, 30 May 1927. United Kingdom Baháʾí Archives.
82. Letter from Rúḥá to Lady Blomfield, 6 May 1926. United Kingdom Baháʾí Archives.
83. Root, 'The Universal Esperanto Congress at Edinburgh', *Star of the West*, vol. 17.
84. ibid.
85. ibid.
86. Shoghi Effendi, *Unfolding Destiny*, p. 71.
87. Conversation between the author and Pauline Senior *circa* 1996.
88. Blomfield, 'Christianity in the Baháʾí Message', *Star of the West*, vol. 17, p. 354.
89. Circular letter from the London Spiritual Assembly 'to the Friends in El Baha', 28 November 1926. United Kingdom Baháʾí Archives.
90. Shoghi Effendi, *Unfolding Destiny*, p. 73.
91. Basil Hall, *Sitarih Khanum*, p. 18.
92. ibid. p. 21.
93. Letter from E. Everett Reid to Lady Blomfield, 18 May 1929. United Kingdom Archives.
94. *Baháʾí World*, vol. 4, p. 260.
95. Minutes of an extraordinary meeting held jointly by the National Spiritual Assembly and the London Spiritual Assembly, 17 March 1928. United Kingdom Baháʾí Archives.
96. *The Sufi Quarterly*, vol. III, no. 4, p. 206.
97. Note in Lady Blomfield's handwriting on her copy of *The Sufi Quarterly*. United Kingdom Baháʾí Archives.
98. *The Sufi Quarterly*, vol. III, no. 4, p. 206.
99. ibid. p. 218.
100. Letter from Claudia Coles to Lady Blomfield, 6 May 1928. United Kingdom Baháʾí Archives.
101. White, *The Baháʾí Religion*, p. 99.
102. Shoghi Effendi, *Unfolding Destiny*, pp. 86–7.
103. ibid. p. 87.
104. ibid. p. 88.
105. Cable from Shoghi Effendi to Lady Blomfield, 1 March 1930. Baháʾí World Centre Archives.

Chapter Eleven: Ambrosia and Bread

1. From a Tablet of Baháʾuʾlláh to an individual, in 'Writers and Writing', *Compilation*, vol. 2, p. 407.
2. Cable from Shoghi Effendi to Lady Blomfield, 1 March 1930. Baháʾí World Centre Archives.
3. Cable from Shoghi Effendi to Ḍiyáʾuʾlláh Asgharzádih, 1 March 1930. Baháʾí World Centre Archives.

4. Rabbaní, *Priceless Pearl*, p. 109.
5. ibid. p. 108.
6. Shoghi Effendi, *Unfolding Destiny*, p. 56.
7. ibid. p. 60.
8. Rabbaní, *Priceless Pearl*, p. 107.
9. Letter from Ruhi Afnan to Lady Blomfield, 6 March 1926. United Kingdom Bahá'í Archives.
10. Quoted in Marcus, *Her Immortal Crown*, p. 163.
11. ibid. p. 168.
12. *Daily Express*, 2 March 1930.
13. Quoted in Marcus, *Her Immortal Crown*, p. 169.
14. ibid. pp. 168–9.
15. ibid. p. 170.
16. ibid.
17. Rabbaní, *Priceless Pearl*, p. 115.
18. Quoted in Marcus, *Her Immortal Crown*, p. 174.
19. ibid.
20. Rabbaní, *Priceless Pearl*, p. 217.
21. ibid. p. 218.
22. Letter from Lady Blomfield to Shoghi Effendi, 26 June 1930. Bahá'í World Centre Archives.
23. Quoted in Ma'ani, *Leaves of the Twin Divine Trees*, p. 218.
24. Letter from Lady Blomfield to Shoghi Effendi, 26 June 1930. Bahá'í World Centre Archives.
25. Letter written on behalf of Shoghi Effendi to Lady Blomfield with postscript in the Guardian's handwriting, 4 July 1930. Bahá'í World Centre Archives.
26. ibid.
27. ibid.
28. Letter written on behalf of Shoghi Effendi to Lady Blomfield, 28 August 1930. Bahá'í World Centre Archives.
29. Letter written on behalf of Shoghi Effendi to Lady Blomfield with postscript in the Guardian's own handwriting, 20 September 1930. Bahá'í World Centre Archives.
30. ibid.
31. Letter from Lady Blomfield to Shoghi Effendi, 11 October 1930. Bahá'í World Centre Archives.
32. Letter written on behalf of Shoghi Effendi to Lady Blomfield with postscript in his own handwriting, 4 November 1930. Bahá'í World Centre Archives.
33. Letter from Lady Blomfield to Shoghi Effendi, 20 December, 1930. Bahá'í World Centre Archives.
34. ibid.
35. Letter written on behalf of Shoghi Effendi to Lady Blomfield with postscript in his own handwriting, 19 January 1931.
36. ibid.
37. Rabbaní, *Priceless Pearl*, p. 215.
38. ibid. p. 216.
39. Letter from Lady Blomfield to Shoghi Effendi, 11 October 1930. Bahá'í World Centre Archives.

40. *Bahá'í News*, September 1931, p. 6.
41. Memorandum on Ethel Jenner Rosenberg, Research Department of the Bahá'í World Centre, p. 4.
42. Letter from Nellie French to Lady Blomfield, 1 July 1931. United Kingdom Bahá'í Archives.
43. Letter from Lady Blomfield to Nellie French, 23 October 1931. United States Bahá'í Archives.
44. ibid.
45. Letter from Nellie French to Lady Blomfield, 7 November 1931. United Kingdom Bahá'í Archives.
46. Letter from Mehrangíz to Lady Blomfield, 16 September 1932. United Kingdom Bahá'í Archives.
47. ibid.
48. Letter from Rúhá to Lady Blomfield, 17 March 1933. United Kingdom Bahá'í Archives.
49. Balyuzi, *'Abdu'l-Bahá*, p. 498.
50. ibid. p. 499.
51. Letter from Lady Blomfield to Shoghi Effendi, 26 January 1933. Bahá'í World Centre Archives.
52. *Literary Guide*, March 1933.
53. *The Gateway*, mid-February 1933.
54. *Edinburgh Evening News*, 6 February 1933.
55. *Literary Guide*, March 1933.
56. *The Drama*, March 1933.
57. *Bahá'í News*, Summer 1933.
58. Letter from Bahadur Singh Rajah to Lady Blomfield, 30 August 1933. United Kingdom Bahá'í Archives.
59. Letter from Rose Ellinor Maule to Lutfu'lláh Hakím, 4 May 1950. United Kingdom Bahá'í Archives.
60. *John O'London's Weekly*, 25 March 1933.
61. Notes for a talk by Lady Blomfield, 'The Signs of God', given to the Society for the Study of Religions. United Kingdom Bahá'í Archives.
62. Notes for a talk by Lady Blomfield to the Women's International Film Association. United Kingdom Bahá'í Archives.
63. Letter from Albert Vail to Lady Blomfield, 25 March 1934. United Kingdom Bahá'í Archives.
64. Letter from Albert Vail to Lady Blomfield, 8 June 1934. United Kingdom Bahá'í Archives.
65. Hofman, *George Townshend*, p. 121.
66. Pakula, *Queen of Roumania*, p. 400.
67. Letter from Lady Blomfield to Shoghi Effendi, 4 October 1934. Bahá'í World Centre Archives.
68. Letter written on behalf of Shoghi Effendi to Lady Blomfield with postscript in his own handwriting, 31 October 1934. Bahá'í World Centre Archives.
69. *The Bahá'í World*, vol. 5, 1932–1934. p. iv.
70. Letter written on behalf of Shoghi Effendi to Lady Blomfield with postscript in his own handwriting, 31 October 1934. Bahá'í World Centre Archives.
71. Letter written on behalf of Shoghi Effendi to the National Spiritual Assembly of

the United States and Canada, 22 January 1935. Bahá'í World Centre Archives.

72. Letter written on behalf of Shoghi Effendi to Lady Blomfield with postscript in his own handwriting, 19 January 1935. Bahá'í World Centre Archives.

73. ibid.

74. ibid.

75. Younghusband, *Venture of Faith*, p. 50.

76. Letter from George Townshend to Lady Blomfield, 6 February 1936. United Kingdom Bahá'í Archives.

77. Hofman, *George Townshend*, p. 125.

78. Letter from George Townshend to Lady Blomfield, 6 February 1936. United Kingdom Bahá'í Archives.

79. Younghusband, *Venture of Faith*, p. 152.

80. Helen Bishop, 'A Session at the World Congress of Faiths', *Bahá'í World*, vol. 7, p. 644.

81. Conversation between the author and David Hofman, 9 October 1996.

82. ibid.

83. Letter from Albert Vail to Lady Blomfield, 6 November 1936, United Kingdom Bahá'í Archives.

84. Letter from Edward Fuller to Lady Blomfield, 15 July 1936. United Kingdom Bahá'í Archives.

85. Letter from Mrs Dudley to Lady Blomfield, 14 December 1936. United Kingdom Bahá'í Archives.

86. Letter from Grace Challis to Lady Blomfield, 14 January 1937. United Kingdom Bahá'í Archives.

87. Letter from Alfred Sugar to Lady Blomfield, 22 Deccember 1936. United Kingdom Bahá'í Archives.

88. ibid.

89. Letter from Gita Orlova to Lady Blomfield, 5 November 1936. United Kingdom Bahá'í Archives.

90. Letter from Tudor Pole to Lady Blomfield, 14 December 1936. United Kingdom Bahá'í Archives.

91. Letter written on behalf of Shoghi Effendi to Lady Blomfield with postscript in his own handwriting, 24 December 1936. Bahá'í World Centre Archives.

92. Blomfield, *Chosen Highway*, p. 225.

93. Letter written on behalf of Shoghi Effendi to Lady Blomfield with postscript in his own handwriting, 24 December 1936. Bahá'í World Centre Archives.

94. ibid.

95. Balyuzi, in Blomfield, *Chosen Highway*, p. v.

Chapter Twelve: The Perfume of Hyacinths

1. Letter written on behalf of Shoghi Effendi to Lady Blomfield with postscript in his own handwriting, 17 August 1938. Bahá'í World Centre Archives.

2. Shoghi Effendi, *Unfolding Destiny*, p. 112.

3. Letter from Daniel Cooper Hunt to Lady Blomfield, 5 January 1937. United Kingdom Bahá'í Archives.

4. Rabbaní, *Priceless Pearl*, p. 153.

5. Letter from Lady Blomfield to Shoghi Effendi, 29 December 1937. Bahá'í World Centre Archives.

6. Bahá'í Theatre Group playbill for The Rector of Hallowdene, May 1938. United Kingdom Bahá'í Archives.
7. *Bahá'í World*, vol. 7, p. 470.
8. Shoghi Effendi, *Unfolding Destiny*, p. 110.
9. ibid.
10. Handwritten notes for talk by Lady Blomfield given at Summer School, Matlock, 1 August 1937. United Kingdom Bahá'í Archives.
11. *Bahá'í Journal*, October 1937.
12. Letter from Phyllis Hall to Lady Blomfield, 26 October 1937. United Kingdom Bahá'í Archives.
13. Letter from M. F. Wren to Lady Blomfield, 6 October 1937. United Kingdom Bahá'í Archives.
14. Invitation from E. J. K. Bagnall to Lady Blomfiled, January 1938. United Kingdom Bahá'í Archives.
15. Letter from Major Lena M. Dennett to Lady Blomfield, 14 October 1937. United Kingdom Bahá'í Archives.
16. Reported in a letter from Lady Blomfield to Shoghi Effendi, 29 December 1937. United Kingdom Bahá'í Archives.
17. ibid.
18. ibid.
19. Letter written on behalf of Shoghi Effendi to Lady Blomfield with postscript in his own handwriting, 11 January 1938. Bahá'í World Centre Archives.
20. ibid.
21. Handwritten notes of talk by Lady Blomfield to the Society for the Study of Comparative Religions, 14 February 1938. United Kingdom Bahá'í Archives.
22. ibid.
23. ibid.
24. ibid.
25. Letter from Lady Blomfield to Shoghi Effendi, 18 March 1938. United Kingdom Bahá'í Archives.
26. Letter written on behalf of Shoghi Effendi to Lady Blomfield with postscript in his own handwriting, 26 March 1938. Bahá'í World Centre Archives.
27. Letter from Lady Blomfield to Shoghi Effendi, 18 March 1938. United Kingdom Bahá'í Archives.
28. Blomfield, *Chosen Highway*, p. 227.
29. ibid. p. 221.
30. Letter from Lady Blomfield to Shoghi Effendi, 29 December 1937. United Kingdom Bahá'í Archives.
31. ibid.
32. ibid.
33. Letter written on behalf of Shoghi Effendi to Lady Blomfield with postscript in his own handwriting, 11 January 1938. Bahá'í World Centre Archives.
34. 'Abdu'l-Bahá, quoted in Piff Metelmann, *Lua Getsinger*, p. xii.
35. *Bahá'í World*, vol. 8, 1938–1940, p. 649.
36. Letter written on behalf of Shoghi Effendi to Lady Blomfield with postscript in his own handwriting, 26 March 1938. Bahá'í World Centre Archives.
37. Letter from Lady Blomfield to Shoghi Effendi, 18 March 1938. Bahá'í World Centre Archives.

38. Letter written on behalf of Shoghi Effendi to Lady Blomfield with postscript in his own handwriting, 26 March 1938. Bahá'í World Centre Archives.
39. Letter from Lady Blomfield to Shoghi Effendi, 29 December 1937. Bahá'í World Centre Archives.
40. Letter from Lady Blomfield to Shoghi Effendi, 18 March 1938. Bahá'í World Centre Archives.
41. Letter from Lady Blomfield to Shoghi Effendi, 8 July 1938. Bahá'í World Centre Archives.
42. Handwritten notes of talk by Lady Blomfield to Salvation Army, 11 May 1938. United Kingdom Bahá'í Archives.
43. Shoghi Effendi, *Unfolding Destiny*, p. 120.
44. Letter written on behalf of Shoghi Effendi to Lady Blomfield with postscript in his own handwriting, 29 November 1938. Bahá'í World Centre Archives.
45. Letter from Lady Blomfield to Shoghi Effendi, 8 July 1938. Bahá'í World Centre Archives.
46. Letter written on behalf of Shoghi Effendi to Lady Blomfield with postscript in his own handwriting, 17 August 1938. Bahá'í World Centre Archives.
47. ibid.
48. ibid.
49. Conversation between the author and David Hofman, 9 October 1996.
50. *Bahá'í Journal*, March 1940.
51. Letter from Lady Blomfield to Shoghi Effendi, 30 October 1938. Bahá'í World Centre Archives.
52. ibid.
53. Letter written on behalf of Shoghi Effendi to Lady Blomfield with postscript in his own handwriting, 29 November 1938. Bahá'í World Centre Archives.
54. Shoghi Effendi, *Advent of Divine Justice*, p. 72.
55. Letter written on behalf of Shoghi Effendi to Lady Blomfield, 16 March 1939. Bahá'í World Centre Archives.
56. Blomfield, *Chosen Highway*, p. vii.
57. ibid.
58. ibid.
59. Conversation between the author and David Hofman, 9 October 1996.
60. Blomfield, *Chosen Highway*, p. viii.
61. Balyuzi, in ibid. p. vi.
62. Letter from Elizabeth Hesse to Lady Blomfield, 5 January 1939. United Kingdom Bahá'í Archives.
63. Letter from Kitty Schopflocher to Lady Blomfield, 23 January 1939. United Kingdom Bahá'í Archives.
64. Brochure for St Mary's School, p. 2. United Kingdom Bahá'í Archives.
65. Letter from E. M. Grady to Lady Blomfield, 6 May 1939. United Kingdom Bahá'í Archives.
66. Hofman, *George Townshend*, p. 163.
67. Notepad of Lady Blomfield, September 1939. United Kingdom Bahá'í Archives.
68. Shoghi Effendi, *Unfolding Destiny*, p. 133.
69. Blomfield, *Chosen Highway*, pp. 174–5.
70. ibid. pp. 175–6.

71. Basil Hall, *Sitarih Khanum*, p. 24.
72. ibid.
73. Conversation between the author and David Hofman, 9 October 1996.
74. Shoghi Effendi, *Unfolding Destiny*, p. 136.
75. Blomfield, *Chosen Highway*, p. v.
76. See 'Lady Blomfield – Apostle of World Unity', in *The World's Children*, March 1940, p. 39.
77. *Bahá'í Journal*, March 1940.
78. *The World's Children*, March 1940, p. 39.
79. Basil Hall, *Sitarih Khanum*, pp. 21–2.
80. Quoted in ibid. p. 22.
81. ibid p. 24.
82. ibid.

Afterwards

1. Blomfield, *Chosen Highway*, p. viii.
2. Shoghi Effendi, *Unfolding Destiny*, p. 138.
3. Blomfield, *Chosen Highway*, p. v.
4. *Bahá'í Journal*, March 1940.
5. Blomfield, *Chosen Highway*, p. ix.
6. Shoghi Effendi, *Unfolding Destiny*, pp. 136–7.
7. Isobel Slade, Handwritten tribute to Mary Basil Hall. United Kingdom Bahá'í Archives.
8. ibid.
9. Letter from Mary Basil Hall to Luṭfu'lláh Ḥakím, 21 June 1949. United Kingdom Bahá'í Archives.
10. Letter from Mary Basil Hall to Luṭfu'lláh Ḥakím, undated. United Kingdom Bahá'í Archives.
11. Letter from Ellinor Maule to Luṭfu'lláh Ḥakím, 4 May 1950. United Kingdom Bahá'í Archives.
12. Shoghi Effendi, *Unfolding Destiny*, p. 473.
13. ibid. p. 246.
14. Letter from Ellinor Maule to Luṭfu'lláh Ḥakím, 4 May 1950. United Kingdom Bahá'í Archives.
15. Last will and testament of Rose Ellinor Cecilia Maule, 13 April 1954.
16. 'Abdu'l-Bahá, *Memorials of the Faithful*, p. 12.

Appendix One: The Passing of 'Abdu'l-Bahá

1. In a century of exaggerated positivism and unbridled materialism, it is astonishing and rare to find a philosopher of great scope, such as the lamented 'Abdu'l-Bahá 'Abbás, speak to our hearts, to our feelings, and especially seek to educate our soul by inculcating in us the most beautiful principles, which are recognized as being the basis of all religion and of all pure morality. By His Writings, by His spoken Word, by His intimate conversations as well as by His famous dialogues with the most cultivated and the most fervent adepts of sectarian theories, He knew how to persuade; He was always able to win our minds. Living examples have a special power. His private and public life was an example of devotion and of forgetfulness of self for the happiness of others . . .

His philosophy is simple, you will say, but it is great by that very simplicity, since it is in conformity with human character, which loses some of its beauty when it allows itself to be distorted by prejudices and superstitions . . . 'Abbás died in Haifa, Palestine, the Holy Land which produced the prophets. Sterile and abandoned for so many centuries, it is coming back to life and is beginning to recover its rank and its original renown. We are not the only ones to grieve for this prophet; we are not the only ones to testify to His glory. In Europe, in America, yea, in every land inhabited by men conscious of their own mission in this base world, athirst for social justice, for brotherhood, He will be mourned as well. He is dead after suffering from despotism, fanaticism and intolerance. 'Akká, the Turkish Bastille, was His prison for decades. Baghdád, the Abbasid capital, has also been His prison, and that of His Father. Persia, the ancient cradle of gentle and divine philosophy, has driven out her children, who brought forth their ideas within her. May one not see herein a divine will and a marked preference for the Promised Land which was and will be the cradle of all generous and noble ideas? He who leaves after Him so glorious a past is not dead. He who has written such beautiful principles has increased His family among all His readers and has passed to posterity, crowned with immortality.

2. A prophet has died in Palestine. He was called 'Abdu'l-Bahá, and He was the son of Bahá'u'lláh, who created Bahá'ism, a 'unified' religion which is none other than the Bábism which had been observed by Comte de Gobineau. The Báb, the Messiah of Bábism, modestly proposed the regeneration of Persia, which cost Him His life, in 1850. Bahá'u'lláh and His son, 'Abdu'l-Bahá, 'the slave of his father', had no lesser goal than the regeneration of the world. Paris has known 'Abdu'l-Bahá. This magnificent friendly old man sowed among us His holy word some ten years ago. He was dressed in a simple olive green robe and wore a white turban . . . His speech was sweet and soothing, like a litany. One heard Him with a rapt pleasure, even without understanding Him – for He spoke in Persian . . . Bahá'ism is in essence the religion of love and simplicity. It is at the same time an amalgamation of Judaism, Christianity, Protestantism, and free thought. 'Abdu'l-Bahá appealed to the authority of Zoroaster, Moses, Muhammad and Jesus. You may feel that this unification is too numerous and too confused. The fact is that one understands nothing about sacred things if one is not inspired by faith . . . Under the white turban His eyes mirrored intelligence and goodness. He was fatherly, affectionate and simple. His power, it seemed, came to Him from His ability to love men and make Himself loved by them. When we were called upon to testify to the excellence of this simple and pure religion, we were able honestly to confess our faith, in this formula: 'How beautiful religions are when they are not yet [fr = "*encore*"].'

Appendix Three: Christianity in the Bahá'í Message

1. This is a reproduction of an article by Lady Blomfield entitled 'Christianity in the Bahá'í Message', published in *Star of the West*, vol. 17, p. 354.

INDEX

This index is alphabetized word for word; thus 'Ben Shemen' precedes 'Benedict XV'. Hyphens are treated as spaces. The words 'a', 'al', 'an', 'and', 'de', 'd'', 'for', 'in', 'is' 'of', 'on', 'the', 'to' and 'with' in entries are ignored. The Blomfields are alphabeticized according to their first names, regardless of their titles.

447